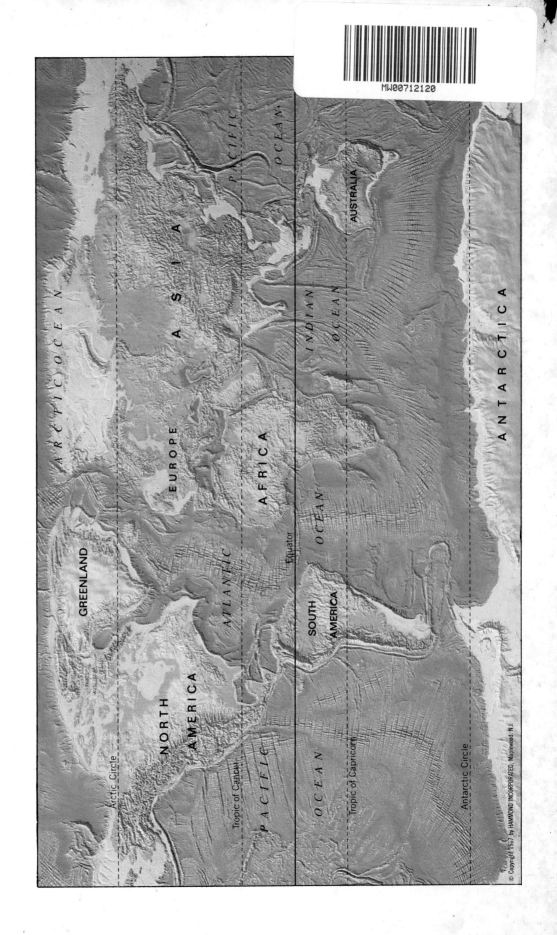

ARCTIC OCEAN

GREENLAND

NORTH AMERICA

EUROPE

ASIA

PACIFIC OCEAN

ATLANTIC

AFRICA

Equator

INDIAN OCEAN

AUSTRALIA

OCEAN

SOUTH AMERICA

PACIFIC

OCEAN

ANTARCTICA

Arctic Circle

Tropic of Cancer

Tropic of Capricorn

Antarctic Circle

EUROPE

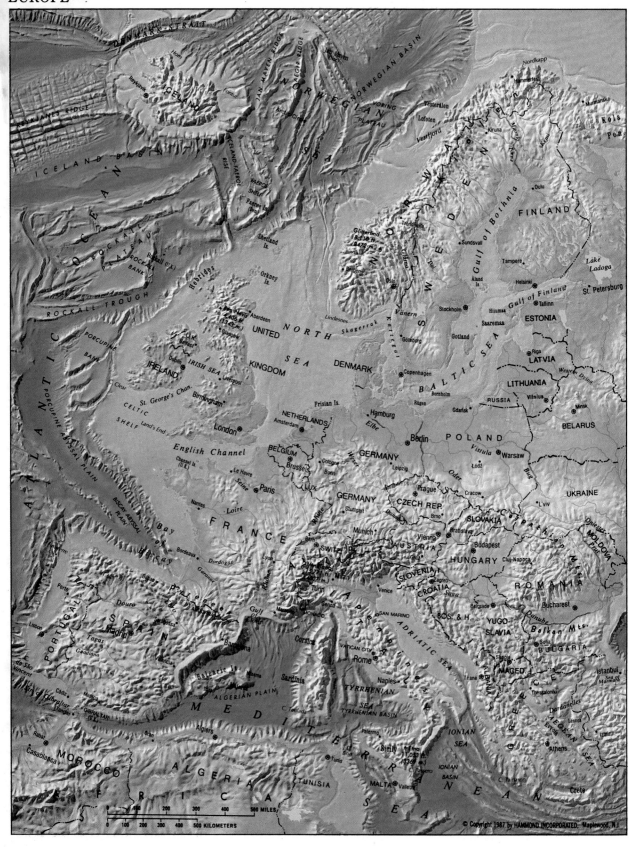

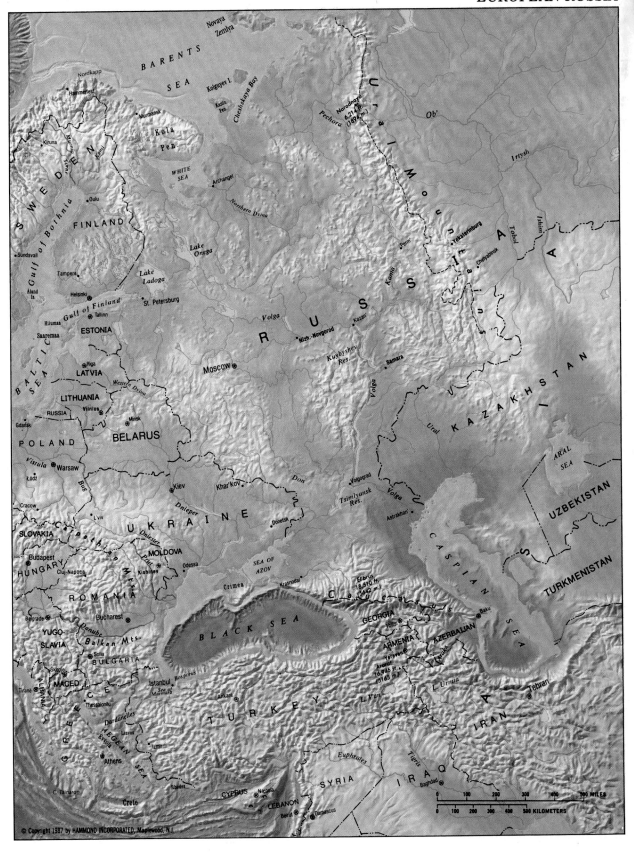

Novaya
Zemlya

BARENTS

SEA

Nordkapp
Hammerfest
Murmansk
Kola
Pen.
Kolguyev I.
Kanin
Pen.
Chëshskaya Bay

Kiruna
Kemi

WHITE
SEA
Archangel

Narodnaya
6,214 ft.
(1894 m.)
Pechora

Ob'

Irtysh

SWEDEN

Sundsvall
Oulu
FINLAND

Northern Dvina

Ural Mountains

Perm

Yekaterinburg

Tobol

Ishim

R

U

S

S

I

A

Tampere

Lake
Onega

Lake
Ladoga

Chelyabinsk

Åland
Is.
Helsinki
Gulf of Finland
St. Petersburg
Tallinn

Volga

Kama

Samara

Hiiumaa
Saaremaa
ESTONIA

Nizh. Novgorod

Kazan'

Gulf of Bothnia

BALTIC SEA

Riga
LATVIA

Moscow

Kuybyshev
Res.

Western Dvina

Samara

Volga

LITHUANIA
Vilnius
Minsk

KAZAKHSTAN

Gdańsk
RUSSIA

ARAL
SEA

POLAND
BELARUS

Ural

Warsaw
Vistula

Kiev
Khar'kov

Don

Volgograd

Volga

UZBEKISTAN

Łódź
Bug

Cracow
L'viv
UKRAINE
Dnieper

Tsimlyansk
Res.

Astrakhan'

Dniester
Donetsk

CASPIAN

SEA

TURKMENISTAN

SLOVAKIA
Carpathian Mts.

MOLDOVA

HUNGARY
Budapest
Cluj-Napoca
Kishinev
Odessa

SEA OF
AZOV

ROMANIA
Crimea

Krasnodar

Elbrus
18,510 ft.
(5642 m.)

Belgrade
Bucharest
YUGO-
SLAVIA
Danube
Balkan Mts.
Sofia

BLACK SEA

GEORGIA
Tbilisi
Baku

Skopje
BULGARIA

ARMENIA
Yerevan
AZERBAIJAN

ALBANIA
MACED.
Tirane
Istanbul
Sea of
Marmara
Bosporus

Ararat
16,946 ft.
(5165 m.)

GREECE
Thessaloniki
Dardanelles
Lesvos

L. Urmia

L. Van

Tehran

C. Taínaron
Euboea
Izmir

Ankara

TURKEY

IRAN

Athens
AEGEAN
SEA

Euphrates

Tigris

Rhodes
Crete
CYPRUS
Nicosia

SYRIA

IRAQ
Baghdad

LEBANON
Beirut
Damascus

0	100	200	300	400	500 MILES
0	100	200	300	400	500 KILOMETERS

AFRICA

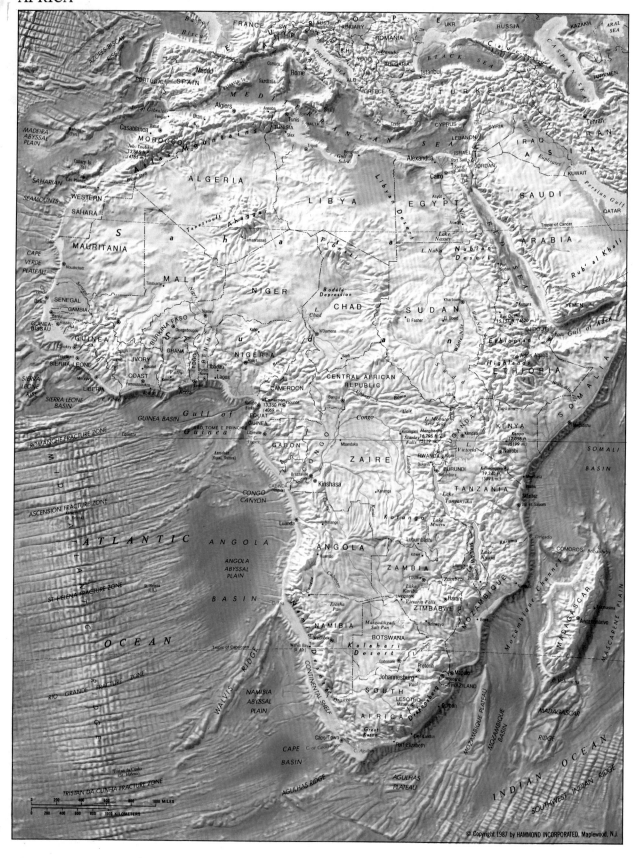

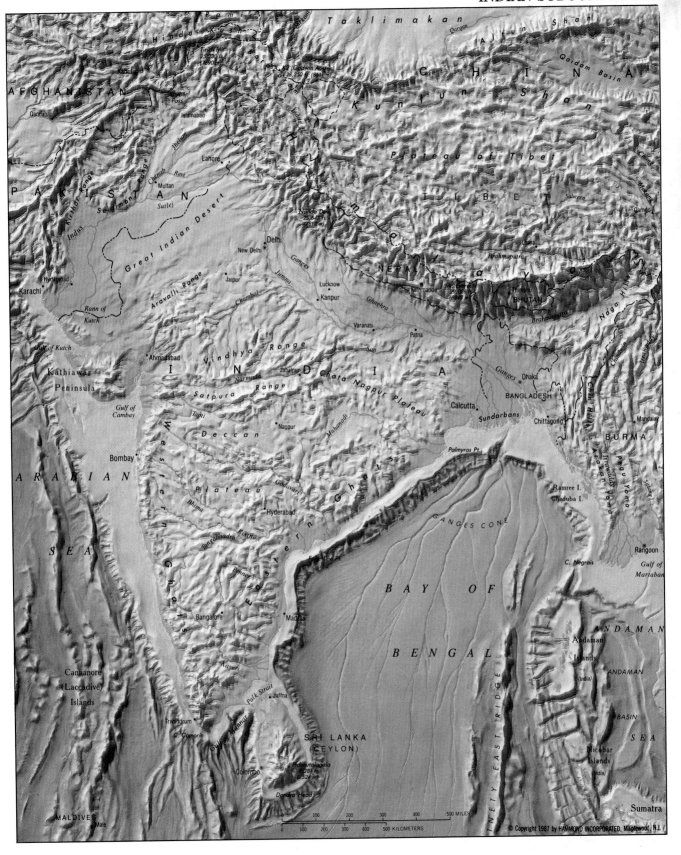

AFGHANISTAN

Qandahar

Kabul

Khyber Pass

Hindu Kush

Tirich Mir 25,230 ft. (7690 m)

Taklimakan

Qarqan

Altun Shan

Qaidam Basin

CHINA

Chang

Mekong

K2 (Godwin Austen) 28,250 ft. (8611 m)

Kunlun Shan

Srinagar

Islamabad

Plateau of Tibet

TIBET

Salween

Tsamdo

P A K I S T A N

Kirthar Range

Sulaiman Range

Indus

Chenab

Ravi

Multan

Sutlej

Jhelum

Lahore

Great Indian Desert

Nanda Devi 25,645 ft. (7817 m)

Himalaya

Lhasa

Brahmaputra

Naga Hills

Hyderabad

Karachi

Rann of Kutch

New Delhi

Delhi

Jaipur

Aravalli Range

Ganges

Jumna

Chambal

Lucknow

Kanpur

Ghaghra

NEPAL

Kathmandu

Mt. Everest 29,028 ft. (8848 m)

Thimbu

BHUTAN

Brahmaputra

Chin Hills

Pegu Yoma

Irrawaddy

Arakan Yoma

Chindwin

Gulf of Kutch

Kathiawar Peninsula

Gulf of Cambay

Ahmadabad

Vindhya Range

Narmada

Satpura Range

Tapti

I N D I A

Jabalpur

Chota Nagpur Plateau

Varanasi

Son

Mahanadi

Patna

Ganges

Sundarbans

Dhaka

BANGLADESH

Calcutta

Chittagong

Mandalay

BURMA

Bombay

Western Ghats

Deccan

Plateau

Bhima

Nagpur

Godavari

Hyderabad

Krishna

Tungabhadra

Palmyras Pt.

Ramree I.

Cheduba I.

Mandalay

Sittang

Rangoon

C. Negrais

Gulf of Martaban

A R A B I A N

S E A

Eastern Ghats

Penner

Bangalore

Kaveri

Madras

False Div. Pt.

GANGES CONE

B A Y   O F

B E N G A L

NINETY EAST RIDGE

A N D A M A N

Andaman Islands

(India)

ANDAMAN

Cannanore (Laccadive) Islands

Palk Strait

Jaffna

Trivandrum

C. Comorin

Gulf of Mannar

SRI LANKA (CEYLON)

Pidurutalagala 8,281 ft. (2524 m)

Colombo

Dondra Head

BASIN

SEA

Nicobar Islands

(India)

Sumatra

MALDIVES

Male

| 100 | 200 | 300 | 400 | 500 MILES |
| 0 | 100 | 200 | 300 | 400 | 500 KILOMETERS |

EAST AND SOUTHEAST ASIA

NORTH AMERICA

RUSSIA

BEAUFORT SEA

CANADA BASIN

GREENLAND (Den.)

ICELAND

Queen Elizabeth Islands

Ellesmere I.

Denmark Strait

ICELAND BASIN

REYKJANES RIDGE

IRMINGER BASIN

Pt. Barrow

BEAUFORT SHELF

Banks I.

Melville I.

Devon I.

Parry Channel

Baffin Bay

Arctic Circle

St. Lawrence I.

Bering Strait

Brooks Range

Anchorage

Victoria I.

Baffin I.

Davis Strait

Nuuk

LABRADOR BASIN

Great Bear L.

Yellowknife

Laurentian

Hudson Bay

Ungava Peninsula

C. Chidley

LABRADOR SEA

Gulf of Alaska

Alexander Arch.

Prince Rupert

Queen Charlotte Is.

Great Slave L.

L. Athabasca

CANADA

Peace

Athabasca

Churchill

Nelson

James Bay

Rupert

Smallwood Res.

Churchill

Newfoundland

Gander

Vancouver I.

Victoria

Vancouver

Columbia

Edmonton

Saskatchewan

Saskatoon

North

South

Calgary

Regina

L. Winnipeg

Albany

Plateau

Gulf of St. Lawrence

Cape Breton I.

GRAND BANKS OF NEWFOUNDLAND

St. John's

C. Race

Seattle

Mt. Rainier

Portland

Missouri

Red

Winnipeg

Thunder Bay

L. Superior

Duluth

Sudbury

St. Lawrence

Québec

St. John

Halifax

PACIFIC

C. Mendocino

San Francisco

Great Basin

Great Salt Lake

Salt Lake City

Mt. Whitney 14,494 ft.

Death Valley

Missouri

North Platte

South Platte

Omaha

Minneapolis

Mississippi

Milwaukee

Chicago

L. Michigan

Detroit

L. Huron

Toronto

L. Erie

Cleveland

Pittsburgh

L. Ontario

Buffalo

Ottawa

Montréal

Boston

C. Cod

GEORGES BANK

New York

Philadelphia

Washington

UNITED STATES

Denver

Pikes Peak 14,110 ft. (4301 m.)

Kansas City

Indianapolis

Cincinnati

Columbus

Ohio

Norfolk

BERMUDA (U.K.)

Bermuda RISE

Los Angeles

San Diego

Colorado

Phoenix

Tucson

Albuquerque

Arkansas

Wichita

Tulsa

St. Louis

Ozark Plateau

Nashville

Memphis

Tennessee

Mt. Mitchell 6,684 ft. (2037 m.)

Charlotte

C. Hatteras

HATTERAS ABYSSAL PLAIN

Appalachian Mts.

CONTINENTAL SHELF

Guadalupe (Mex.)

Gulf of California

Sierra Madre

El Paso

Ciudad Juárez

Chihuahua

Fort Worth

Dallas

Red

Oklahoma City

Birmingham

Atlanta

Jacksonville

MOLOKAI FRACTURE ZONE

California

C. San Lucas

Culiacán

San Antonio

Houston

New Orleans

Florida

Tampa

C. Canaveral

Miami

Pen.

BAHAMAS

NARES ABYSSAL PLAIN

Tropic of Cancer

CLARION FRACTURE ZONE

Is. Revillagigedo (Mex.)

Monterrey

Corpus Christi

Gulf of Mexico

SIGSBEE DEEP

Tampico

Bay of Campeche

CAMPECHE BANK

Mérida

Yucatán

Yucatán Pen.

Havana

CUBA

Santiago de Cuba

HAITI

DOM. REP.

San Juan

PUERTO RICO

Turks and Caicos Is. (U.K.)

West Indies

PUERTO RICO TRENCH

Guadalajara

Mexico City

Popocatépetl 17,887 ft. (5452 m.)

Campeche

Veracruz

BELIZE

CAYMAN TRENCH

JAMAICA

Santo Domingo

Greater Antilles

NETH. ANT.

VENEZ. BASIN

CLIPPERTON FRACTURE ZONE

Clipperton I. (Fr.)

Acapulco

MIDDLE AMERICA TRENCH

MEXICO

GUATEMALA

Guatemala

EL SALVADOR

San Salvador

HONDURAS

Tegucigalpa

NICARAGUA

Managua

NICARAGUA RISE

COLOMBIA BASIN

ARUBA (Neth.)

CARIBBEAN SEA

Curaçao (Neth.)

Bonaire

Windward Is.

Caracas

VENEZUELA

SOUTH

1000 MILES

1000 KILOMETERS

GUATEMALA BASIN

Cocos I. (C.R.)

COSTA RICA

San José

PANAMA

Panamá

Panama Canal

Barranquilla

Magdalena

Orinoco

Bogotá

COLOMBIA

AMERICA

© Copyright 1987 by HAMMOND INCORPORATED, Maplewood, N.J.

SOUTH AMERICA

CIVILIZATIONS OF THE WORLD

CIVILIZATIONS
OF THE WORLD

The Human Adventure

SECOND EDITION

VOLUME B: FROM 1300 TO 1800

Richard L. Greaves
Florida State University

Robert Zaller
Drexel University

Philip V. Cannistraro
Drexel University

Rhoads Murphey
University of Michigan

■ HarperCollins*CollegePublishers*

Executive Editor: Bruce Borland
Director of Development: Betty Slack
Project Editor: Susan Goldfarb
Assistant Art Director: Lucy Krikorian
Text Design: Delgado Design, Inc.
Cover Design: Delgado Design, Inc.
Photo Researcher: Leslie Coopersmith
Production Manager: Willie Lane
Compositor: Waldman Graphics, Inc.
Printer and Binder: R. R. Donnelly & Sons Company
Cover Printer: The Lehigh Press, Inc.

Cover illustration: Codex Nuttall, Mixtec, c. 1450. Laurie Platt Winfrey, Inc.

Title page photo: Alcazar Palace, Toledo. Wim Swaan.

Part-opening art: Part Three: From Gutenberg Bible (Innervisions/Rare Books and Manuscripts Collection, New York Public Library, Astor, Lenox, and Tilden Foundations); Part Four: From preface to *Alzire, ou les Américains*, by Voltaire, Amsterdam, 1736 (Innervisions/Rare Books and Manuscripts Collection, New York Public Library, Astor, Lenox, and Tilden Foundations).

Civilizations of the World: The Human Adventure, Second Edition (Volume B: From 1300 to 1800)

Library of Congress Cataloging-in-Publication Data

Civilizations of the world : the human adventure / Richard L. Greaves
... [et al.]. — 2nd ed.
   p.   cm.
   Includes indexes.
   Contents: v. A. To 1500 — v. B. From 1300 to 1800 — v. C. From 1800
   ISBN 0-06-500678-X (v. A). — ISBN 0-06-500679-8 (v. B) — ISBN 0-06-500680-1 (v. C)
   1. Civilization—History. I. Greaves, Richard L.
CB69.C576   1993c
909—dc20   92-39937
                                                   CIP

93 92 91 90 9 8 7 6 5 4 3 2 1

CONTENTS IN BRIEF

CONTENTS

CHAPTER 24   EUROPE'S CENTURY OF GENIUS   633

CHRONOLOGIES AND GENEALOGIES

M A P S A N D G R A P H S

P R E F A C E

The demise of the Soviet empire and the subsequent restructuring of international relations underscore the premise of this book: Our ability to relate to other cultures and peoples demands some understanding of their history and values, and without this understanding there can be no responsible citizenship, no informed judgment, and no effective commitment to seek peace and dignity for all. Americans do not live in isolation from people in Asia, Africa, Europe, Latin America, and the Middle East. Our ability to understand and respect one another necessitates an awareness of our historical roots.

Civilizations of the World was from its beginning a *world* history—a conscious effort to broaden the Western cultural background of most students by giving substantial coverage to all the major civilizations and by trying to place historical events, customs, and cultures in a global context. The enthusiastic reception of the first edition of *Civilizations of the World: The Human Adventure* has shown the extent to which many of our professional colleagues and their students find this approach meaningful.

BIOGRAPHICAL PORTRAITS

World histories sometimes fail to give students a sense of personal intimacy with the subject. Migratory movements, famines and plagues, trading patterns, and imperial conquests are all important in history, but the individual also matters. Scholars used to write about the past in terms of its "great men" (rarely its women). The great figures still appear in our text, of course, as in any broad historical study. But to give a true sense of the diversity of the human achievement, we have included in most chapters biographical portraits of significant personalities from each epoch and region of the globe, not all famous in their own time but each an important reflection of it. Among them are cultural figures, such as the Greek poet Sappho, the Japanese artist Hokusai, and the German dramatist Bertolt Brecht. Others are religious leaders, such as Guatama Buddha; St. Clare, founder of the Roman Catholic order of Poor Sisters; and the Quaker pamphleteer Margaret Fell. Some were prominent in the political world: the rebel Chinese emperor Hung-wu; the South American liberator Simón Bolívar; India's Indira Gandhi; and David Ben-Gurion, a founding father of Israel. Others, such as England's Mary Wollstonecraft and the Soviet feminist Alexandra Kollontai, were especially concerned with women's rights; some, like Isabella Katz, testified to the endurance of the human spirit. All offer special insights into the times of which they were a part.

URBAN PORTRAITS

Civilization begins with the city, and modern society is increasingly urban. We have therefore provided accounts of how cities around the world have developed. Some of the cities—Italy's Pompeii and Mexico's Teotihuacán, for example—are now in ruins, while others—Shanghai, Baghdad, Moscow—are thriving. Jerusalem, Paris, Tokyo (Edo), and Rome are revisited at different periods to give a sense of how they changed over time. Like the biographical portraits, the urban portraits are fully integrated into the narrative and provide instructors with excellent topics for discussion, essay questions, and unusual lecture themes. Students will find them intriguing subjects for term papers.

WOMEN AND MINORITIES

This text continues to focus particularly on women and minorities. The contributions of women to both Western and non-Western societies—whether as rulers, artists and writers, revolutionaries, workers, or wives and mothers—are systematically considered. The biographical portraits are the most obvious illustrations of the attention given to women, but discussions of their contributions are also interwoven throughout the text's narrative. Special consideration is also given to the role of minorities. Four African or African-American figures are highlighted in the portraits: the dancer and social activist Josephine Baker, the African monarch Mansa Musa, Jomo Kenyatta of modern Kenya, and Dr. Martin Luther King, Jr. As one of the founders of Western civilization and a significant force throughout their history, the Jews are covered more fully in this text than in any comparable work. They are followed from their settlement in ancient Palestine to their persecution and exile under the Romans and from their medieval migrations to their return to Palestine and the founding of modern Israel. By recounting the histories of these groups, we hope to make students aware of their achievements.

SOCIAL AND CULTURAL COVERAGE

Recent scholarship has placed considerable emphasis on social and cultural history. That scholarship is reflected throughout this text, but perhaps most clearly in two chapters that are unique among survey texts. Chapter 7, "The Ancient World Religions," offers a comparative overview of the great religions and philosophies of the ancient world, with a discussion of Islam immediately following, in Chapter 8. Chapter 22, "The Societies of the Early Modern World," provides a broad overview of such key aspects of the world's societies in the sixteenth and seventeenth centuries as marriage, the family, sexual customs, education, poverty, and crime. Moreover, at eight different points throughout the text we pause to consider four significant sociocultural themes: writing and communication, the human image, mapping, and the human experience of death. Here again are special opportunities for distinctive lectures, discussions, essay topics, and research papers.

MAP ATLAS AND FULL-COLOR ART INSERTS

Two types of special color inserts are featured in the book. The first, included in the front matter, is an eight-page full-color atlas showing the physical characteristics of major areas of the globe. This section is intended as a reference that students can use to improve their knowledge of geography. More than 100 maps appear in the text itself.

In addition to the atlas, the combined volume includes eight full-color inserts titled "The Visual Experience," each insert featuring about eight illustrations—of painting, sculpture, architecture, and objets d'art—that are related in a meaningful way to the text's presentation of history. In the split volumes, selected color inserts are included. The text illustrations consist of a separate program of nearly 400 engravings, photographs, and other images chosen for their historical relevance.

PRIMARY SOURCE DOCUMENTS

To enhance the usefulness of this text, we have provided not only a generous complement of maps and illustrations but also a comprehensive selection of primary sources. By studying these documents—usually four or five per chapter—students can sample the kinds of materials with which historians work. More important, they can engage the sources directly and so participate in the process of historical understanding. To emphasize the sense of history as a living discipline, we survey changing historiographic interpretations of the Renaissance, the French Revolution, imperialism, and fascism.

READING LISTS

The discipline of history goes far beyond merely amassing raw data such as names, places, and dates. Historical study demands analysis, synthesis, and a critical sense of the worth of each source. As a guide to students who wish to hone their historical understanding and analytical skills, an up-to-date reading list is provided at the end of each chapter.

MAJOR CHANGES IN THE SECOND EDITION

The most significant change in the second edition involves a substantial increase in the coverage of Africa and the Americas before 1500. Early Africa now has a newly written chapter (Chapter 9) of its own, as do the early Americas (Chapter 10). The latter includes innovative coverage of the Amerindians of North America as well as the Eskimos. The discussion of modern Africa in Chapter 40 has also been substantially rewritten, and recent developments in Asia, Latin America, the Middle East, Europe, and North America are discussed. To take advantage of the latest scholarship, the authors have rewritten the four chapters dealing with western Asia, Egypt, the Greeks, and the Romans (Chapters 1, 4, 5, and 6). A new biographical portrait, featuring Mansa Musa, appears in Chapter 9. The coverage of fascism has been consolidated in Chapter 37, and Chapter 38 now incorporates the origins of the Cold War. Chapter 22, on comparative social history in the early modern period, which students and professors have found highly stimulating, has been likewise revised. Other changes appear throughout the text, reflecting both new scholarship and suggestions from readers.

In revising this book the authors have benefited from the research of many others, all of whom share our belief in the importance of historical study. To the extent that we have succeeded in introducing students to the rich and varied heritage of the past, we owe that success in a very special way to our fellow historians and to the discipline to which we as colleagues have dedicated our careers.

RICHARD L. GREAVES
ROBERT ZALLER
PHILIP V. CANNISTRARO
RHOADS MURPHEY

SUPPLEMENTS

The following supplements are available for use in conjunction with this book.

For Instructors

- *Instructor's Resource Manual* by Richard L. Greaves and Robert Zaller. Prepared by authors of the text, this instructor's manual includes lecture themes, special lecture topics, topics for class discussion and essays, a film list, identification and map items, and term paper topics. Also included is *Mapping the Human Adventure: A Guide to Historical Geography* by Glee Wilson, Kent State University. This special addition provides over 30 reproducible maps and exercises covering the full scope of world history.

- *Discovering World History Through Maps and Views* by Gerald Danzer, University of Illinois, Chicago. Created by the recipient of the AHA's 1990 James Harvey Robinson Award for his work in the development of map transparencies, this set of 100 four-color acetates is a unique instructional tool. It contains an introduction on teaching history through maps and a detailed commentary on each transparency. The collection includes cartographic and pictorial maps, views and photos, urban plans, building diagrams, and works of art.

- *Test Bank* by Edward D. Wynot, Florida State University. Approximately 50 multiple-choice and 10 essay questions per chapter. Multiple-choice items are referenced by text page number and type (factual or interpretive).

- *TestMaster Computerized Testing System.* This flexible, easy-to-master test bank includes all of the test items in the printed *Test Bank*. The TestMaster software allows you to edit existing questions and add your own items. Tests can be printed in several different formats and can include figures such as graphs and tables. Available for IBM and Macintosh computers.

- *Grades.* A grade-keeping and classroom management software program that maintains data for up to 200 students.

For Students

- *Study Guide* by Richard L. Greaves and Robert Zaller. Prepared by authors of the text, each chapter contains a chapter overview; map exercises; study questions; a chronology; and identification, completion, short answer, and document exercises, along with a list of term paper topics.

- *SuperShell Computerized Tutorial.* This interactive program for IBM computers helps students learn major facts and concepts through drill and practice exercises and diagnostic feedback. SuperShell provides immediate correct answers and the text page number on which the material is discussed. Missed questions appear with greater frequency; a running score of the student's performance is maintained on the screen throughout the session.

- *Mapping World History: Student Activities* by Gerald Danzer, University of Illinois, Chicago. A free map workbook featuring exercises designed to teach students to interpret and analyze cartographic materials as historical documents. The instructor is entitled to a free copy of the workbook for each copy of the text purchased from HarperCollins.

- *TimeLink Computer Atlas of World History* by William Hamblin, Brigham Young University. This HyperCard Macintosh program presents three views of the world— Europe/Africa, Asia, and the Americas—on a simulated globe. Students can spin the globe, select a time period, and see a map of the world at that time, including the names of major political units. Special topics such as the conquests of Alexander the Great are shown through animated sequences that depict the dynamic changes in geopolitical history. A comprehensive index and quizzes are also included.

ACKNOWLEDGMENTS

The authors are grateful to Bruce Borland, history editor; Susan Goldfarb, production editor; and Bruce Emmer, copy editor. This book could not have been completed without the invaluable assistance of Judith Dieker Greaves, editorial assistant to the authors. The authors wish additionally to thank the following persons for their assistance and support: Lili Bita Zaller, Philip Rethis, Kimon Rethis, Robert B. Radin, Julia Southard, Robert S. Browning, Sherry E. Greaves, Stephany L. Greaves, and Professors Eric D. Brose, Roger Hackett, Sean Hawkins, Victor Lieberman, Winston Lo, Donald F. Stevens, Thomas Trautmann, and Edward D. Wynot, Jr.

The following scholars read the manuscript in whole or in part and offered numerous helpful suggestions:

Karl Barbir
Siena College

Robert F. Brinson
Santa Fe Community College

Christopher E. Guthrie
Tarleton State University

Craig Harline
University of Idaho

George J. Lankevich
Bronx Community College

Dennis Reinhartz
University of Texas at Arlington

Irvin D. Solomon
Edison Community College

Gerald Sorin
SUNY—New Paltz

Glee E. Wilson
Kent State University

Edward D. Wynot, Jr.
Florida State University

Donald L. Zelman
Tarleton State University

We are also indebted to the reviewers of the first edition:

Dorothy Abrahamse
California State University, Long Beach

Winthrop Lindsay Adams
University of Utah

George M. Addy
Brigham Young University

Jay Pascal Anglin
University of Southern Mississippi

Charmarie J. Blaisdell
Northeastern University

William A. Bultmann
Western Washington University

Thomas Callahan, Jr.
Rider College

Miriam Usher Chrisman
University of Massachusetts, Amherst

Jill N. Claster
New York University

Cynthia Schwenk Clemons
Georgia State University

Allen T. Cronenberg
Auburn University

John Dahmus
Stephen F. Austin State University

Elton L. Daniel
University of Hawaii at Manoa

Leslie Derfler
Florida Atlantic University

Joseph M. Dixon
Weber State College

John Patrick Donnelly
Marquette University

Mark U. Edwards, Jr.
Harvard University

Charles A. Endress
Angelo State University

Stephen Englehart
California State Polytechnic University, Pomona

William Wayne Farvis
University of Tennessee

Jonathan Goldstein
West Georgia College

Edwin N. Gorsuch
Georgia State University

Joseph M. Gowaski
Rider College

Tony Grafton
Princeton University

Coburn V. Graves
Kent State University

Janelle Greenberg
University of Pittsburgh

Udo Heyn
California State University,
   Los Angeles

Clive Holmes
Cornell University

Leonard A. Humphreys
University of the Pacific

Donald G. Jones
University of Central Arkansas

William R. Jones
University of New Hampshire

Thomas Kaiser
University of Arkansas at Little Rock

Thomas L. Kennedy
Washington State University

Frank Kidner
San Francisco State University

Winston L. Kinsey
Appalachian State University

Thomas Kuehn
Clemson University

Richard D. Lewis
Saint Cloud State University

David C. Lukowitz
Hamline University

Thomas J. McPartland
Bellevue Community College

Elizabeth Malloy
Salem State College

John A. Mears
Southern Methodist University

V. Dixon Morris
University of Hawaii at Manoa

Marian Purrier Nelson
University of Nebraska at Omaha

William D. Newell
Laramie County Community College

James Odom
East Tennessee State University

William G. Palmer
Marshall University

William D. Phillips, Jr.
San Diego State University

Paul B. Pixton
Brigham Young University

Ronald R. Rader
University of Georgia

Leland Sather
Weber State College

Kerry E. Spiers
University of Louisville

Paul Stewart
Southern Connecticut State University

Richard G. Stone
Western Kentucky University

Alexander Sydorenko
Arkansas State University

Teddy Uldricks
University of North Carolina at Asheville

Raymond Van Dam
University of Michigan, Ann Arbor

John Weakland
Ball State University

David L. White
Appalachian State University

Richard S. Williams
Washington State University

Glee E. Wilson
Kent State University

John E. Wood
James Madison University

Martin Yanuck
Spelman College

ABOUT THE AUTHORS

Philip V. Cannistraro. A native of New York City, Philip V. Cannistraro, an authority on modern Italian history and culture, received the Ph.D. degree from New York University in 1971. Currently Professor of History at Drexel University, Cannistraro served as head of the Department of History and Politics from 1982 to 1986, and again from 1988 to 1990. He also taught at Florida State University and has been a visiting professor at New York University and St. Mary's College, Rome. He has lectured widely in Italy and in the United States and is American editor of the Italian historical quarterly *Storia Contemporanea.* The recipient of two Fulbright-Hays fellowships, Cannistraro is an active member of the Society for Italian Historical Studies and the American Italian Historical Association. His numerous publications include *La Fabbrica del Consenso: Fascismo e Mass Media* (1975), *Poland and the Coming of the Second World War* (with E. Wynot and T. Kovaleff, 1976), *Italian Fascist Activities in the United States* (1976), *Fascismo, Chiesa e Emigrazione* (with G. Rosoli, 1979), *Historical Dictionary of Fascist Italy* (1981), and *Italian Americans: The Search for a Usable Past* (with R. Juliani, 1989). Cannistraro has coauthored a biography of Margherita Sarfatti due to be published in 1993 and is currently writing a biography of Generoso Pope.

Richard L. Greaves. Born in Glendale, California, Richard L. Greaves, a specialist in Reformation and British social and religious history, earned his Ph.D. degree at the University of London in 1964. After teaching at Michigan State University, he moved in 1972 to Florida State University, where he is now Robert O. Lawton Distinguished Professor of History, Courtesy Professor of Religion, and Co-Director of the Center for British and Irish Studies. A Fellow of the Royal Historical Society, Greaves has received fellowships from the National Endowment for the Humanities, the American Council of Learned Societies, the Andrew Mellon Foundation, the Huntington Library, and the American Philosophical Society. The 22 books he has written or edited include *John Bunyan* (1969), *Theology and Revolution in the Scottish Reformation: Studies in the Thought of John Knox* (1980), *Saints and Rebels: Seven Nonconformists in Stuart England* (1985), *Deliver Us from Evil: The Radical Underground in Britain, 1660–1663* (1986), *Enemies Under His Feet: Radicals and Nonconformists in Britain, 1664–1677* (1989), *Secrets of the Kingdom: British Radicals from the Popish Plot to the Revolution of 1688–1689* (1992), and *John Bunyan and English Nonconformity* (1992). The Conference on British Studies awarded Greaves the Walter D. Love Memorial Prize for *The Puritan Revolution and Educational Thought: Background for Reform* (1969), and his *Society and Religion in Elizabethan England* (1981) was a finalist for the Robert Livingston Schuyler Prize of the American Historical Association. He was president of the American Society of Church History in 1991.

Rhoads Murphey. Born in Philadelphia, Rhoads Murphey, a specialist in Chinese history and in geography, received the Ph.D. degree from Harvard University in 1950. Before joining the faculty of the University of Michigan in 1964, he taught at the University of Washington; he has also been a visiting professor at Taiwan University and Tokyo University. From 1954 to 1956 he was the director of the Conference of Diplomats in Asia. The University of Michigan granted him a Distinguished Service Award in 1974. Currently president of the Association for Asian Studies, Murphey has served as editor of the *Journal of Asian Studies* and *Michigan Papers in Chinese Studies.* The Social Science Research Council, the Ford Foundation, the Guggenheim Foundation, the National Endowment for the Humanities, and the American Council of Learned Societies have awarded him fellowships. A prolific author, Murphey's books include *Shanghai: Key to Modern China* (1953), *An Introduction to Geography* (4th ed., 1978), *A New China Policy* (with others, 1965), *Approaches to Modern Chinese History* (with others, 1967), *The Scope of Geography* (3rd ed., 1982), *The Treaty Ports and China's Modernization* (1970), *China Meets the West: The Treaty Ports* (1975), *The Fading of the Maoist Vision* (1980), and *A History of Asia* (1992). *The Outsiders: Westerners in India and China* (1977) won the Best Book of the Year award from the University of Michigan Press.

Robert Zaller. Robert Zaller was born in New York City and received a Ph.D. degree from Washington University in 1968. An authority on British political history and constitutional thought, he has also written extensively on modern literature, film, and art. He has taught at Queens College, City University of New York; the University of California, Santa Barbara; and the University of Miami. He is currently Professor of History and former head of the Department of History and Politics at Drexel University. He has been a Guggenheim Fellow and is a member of the advisory board of the Yale Center for Parliamentary History and a Fellow of the Royal Historical Society. His book *The Parliament of 1621: A Study in Constitutional Conflict* (1971) received the Phi Alpha Theta prize for the best first book by a member of the society, and he was made a fellow of Tor House in recognition of *The Cliffs of Solitude: A Reading of Robinson Jeffers* (1983), the inaugural volume of the Cambridge Studies in American Literature and Culture series. His other books include *Lives of the Poet* (1974) and *Europe in Transition, 1660–1815* (1984). He has edited *A Casebook on Anaïs Nin* (1974) and *Centennial Essays for Robinson Jeffers* (1991) and has coedited, with Richard L. Greaves, the *Biographical Dictionary of British Radicals in the Seventeenth Century* (3 volumes, 1982–1984). With Richard L. Greaves and Jennifer Tolbert Roberts he is a coauthor of *Civilizations of the West: The Human Adventure* (1992). His recent publications include studies of Samuel Beckett, Philip Guston, Bernardo Bertolucci, and the English civil war.

A Note on the Spelling
of Asian Names and Words

Nearly all Asian languages are written with symbols different from our Western alphabet. Chinese, Japanese, and Korean are written with ideographic characters, plus a phonetic syllabary for Japanese and Korean. Most other Asian languages have their own scripts, symbols, diacritical marks, and alphabets, which differ from ours. There can thus be no single "correct spelling" in Western symbols for Asian words or names, including personal names and place names—only established conventions. Unfortunately, conventions in this respect differ widely and in many cases reflect preferences or forms related to different Western languages. The Western spellings used in this book, including its maps, are to some extent a compromise, in an effort to follow the main English-language conventions but also to make pronunciation for English speakers as easy as possible.

Chinese presents the biggest problem, since there are a great many different conventions in use and since well-known place names, such as Peking or Canton, are commonly spelled as they are here in most Western writings, even though this spelling is inconsistent with all of the romanization systems in current use and does not accurately represent the Chinese sounds. Most American newspapers and some journals now use the romanization system called *pinyin*, approved by the Chinese government, which renders these two city names, with greater phonetic accuracy, as Beijing and Kwangzhou but which presents other problems for most Western readers and which they commonly mispronounce.

The usage in this book follows the most commonly used convention for scholarly publication when romanizing Chinese names, the Wade-Giles system, but gives the pinyin equivalents for modern names (if they differ) in parentheses after the first use of a name. Readers will encounter both spellings, plus others, in other books, papers, and journals, and some familiarity with both conventions is thus necessary.

In general, readers should realize and remember that English spellings of names from other languages (such as Munich for München, Vienna for Wien, and Rome for Roma), especially in Asia, can be only approximations and may differ confusingly from one Western source or map to another.

CIVILIZATIONS OF THE WORLD

Crisis and Recovery in Europe

Famine, pestilence, war, and death—the four horsemen of the Apocalypse—ravaged Europe with unprecedented fury in the fourteenth century. The devastation inflicted by the bubonic and pneumonic plague, recurring famine, and the Hundred Years' War contributed to serious economic decline and a change in people's outlook. The prestige of the papacy suffered too when its headquarters shifted to Avignon, which proved to be the prelude to the most scandalous schism in the history of the western church. Nevertheless, around 1450 Europe began to experience a dramatic revival as population growth resumed, commerce and manufacturing ex-

The fourth horseman of the Apocalypse: "And I saw, and behold, a pale horse, and its rider's name was Death, and Hades followed him: and they were given power over a fourth of the earth, to kill with sword and with famine and with pestilence and by wild beasts of the earth" (Rev. 6:8). To the people of the fourteenth and fifteenth centuries, this prophecy seemed to be coming true in their own age. [Giraudon/Art Resource]

panded, and the states of western Europe and Russia attained greater unity and built strong central governments. In Italy, Germany, Hungary, and Poland, however, territorial princes and cities prevented the growth of centralized states. Europe in the fourteenth and fifteenth centuries moved from an age of adversity to one of recovery and in doing so laid the foundations for the early modern era.

Famine and the Black Death

From the late tenth through the thirteenth centuries the population of Europe grew as farmers expanded the amount of land under cultivation and increased the supply of food. But neither the population growth nor the food supply increased uniformly, and marginal settlements, where the possibility of extreme hunger was always high, arose throughout Europe. Even in the more prosperous agricultural regions, poor distribution facilities often resulted in pockets of famine. By 1300 the population had expanded so rapidly that most Europeans faced grave peril should the fragile agricultural economy be disrupted by unfavorable changes in the weather patterns. The warming trend that characterized the period from the mid-eighth to the mid-twelfth centuries was reversed as Europe entered what climatologists call the Little Ice Age, which lasted approximately two centuries. In the late thirteenth century heavy rains and unexpected freezes began to wreak havoc with the food supply. The threat of famine, which became more pronounced in the 1290s, culminated between 1315 and 1317 in the greatest crop failures of the Middle Ages. Soaring grain prices placed food beyond the reach of many, especially in urban areas, where sometimes as many as one in ten died from starvation or malnutrition. Marginal lands had to be abandoned as the poor sought relief in towns or in more productive regions, thereby increasing the strain on the food supply. As famines continued to recur throughout the fourteenth century, the most serious consequence was the debilitating effect of chronic and severe malnutrition on much of the population. Physically weakened, most Europeans were highly vulnerable to disease, especially tuberculosis.

The bubonic plague is caused by bacteria that live in an animal's blood or a flea's stomach and is thus easily transmitted, particularly by fleas on rats. The first symptom in a human is a small, blackish pustule at the point of the flea bite, followed by the swelling of the lymph nodes in the neck, armpit, or groin. Then come dark spots on the skin caused by internal bleeding. In the final stage the victim, convulsed by severe coughing spells, spits blood, exudes a foul body odor, and experiences severe neurological and psychological disorders. Bubonic plague, however, was not always fatal, especially if the pus was thoroughly drained from the boil; up to half its victims survived. A more virulent form of the plague—the pneumonic variety—was transmitted by coughing and was nearly always fatal. Both forms devastated Europe.

Plague had ravaged the Byzantine Empire in the 540s and eventually extended from central and southern Asia to Arabia, North Africa, and the Iberian peninsula and north as far as Denmark and Ireland. Some 200,000 people may have died in Constantinople alone between the fall of 541 and the spring of 542. When this outbreak finally ended in 544, more than 20 percent of the people of southern Europe had died. Further outbreaks followed for another 200 years, after which Europe was free of most epidemic diseases until the mid-fourteenth century. But the bacterial strains responsible for the plague continued to survive in the Gobi Desert of Mongolia. From there the plague was transmitted both east and west by nomadic tribesmen, perhaps forced to move their flocks to new regions when hot winds began drying up the pastures of central Asia.

The plague reached epidemic proportions in the Gobi Desert in the late 1320s and from there may have spread first to China. The Chinese had already been weakened by famine brought on by drought, earthquakes, and then flooding in the early 1330s. The Black Death followed, reducing the population nearly 30 percent (from 125 million to 90 million) before the end of the century. By 1339 the plague had begun its westward march, carried slowly but widely by migrating central Asian rodents and more rapidly by traders along the caravan routes and shipping lanes.

The impact on Asia and the Middle East was devastating. According to one chronicler, "India was depopulated; Tartary, Mesopotamia, Syria, [and] Armenia were covered with dead bodies; the Kurds fled in vain to the mountains."[1] Constantinople and Alexandria were struck in 1347; both cities suffered heavy losses, the latter witnessing perhaps 1,000 deaths a day in early 1348. It was worse in Cairo, one of the largest cities in the world with its population of 500,000; there some 7,000 probably died each day at the peak of the plague. By 1349 it had spread throughout the Muslim world, killing a third of the people and possibly as many as half of those who lived in towns.

The Black Death was brought to western Europe when a Genoese ship carrying infected rats from the Crimea docked at Messina, Sicily, in October 1347. Within months the plague struck the great ports of Venice and Genoa, then spread throughout the rest of Italy, devastating Florence especially. By the end of 1348 most of France and the southern tip of England had been hit, and a year later the infected areas stretched from Ireland

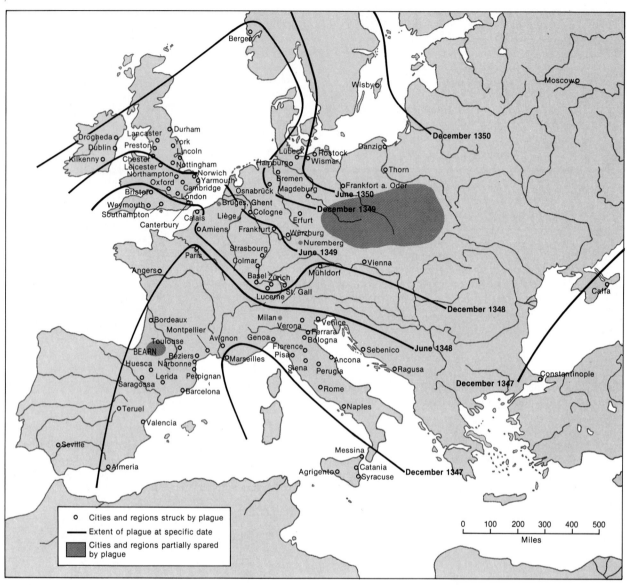

15.1 *Spread of the Plague in Europe*

and Norway to Würzburg and Vienna. The plague moved relentlessly through northern Germany and Scandinavia, finally reaching western Russia in 1351 and 1352. Severe outbreaks again struck Europe in 1362 and 1375. Until the end of the fifteenth century no decade passed without at least one outbreak, and the plague continued to pose a serious threat to Europeans for two centuries after that. Surviving records are inadequate to determine accurate mortality figures, but the Black Death of the late 1340s probably claimed 25 million lives, perhaps a third of Europe's population. No war in history has destroyed so large a percentage of the people.

Europeans had no knowledge of the cause of the plague, though many attributed it to something mysterious in the atmosphere; many Christians were convinced it was divine punishment for their sins. Some fled from the towns to the countryside, where the pestilence was less frequent. Officials of port cities tried in vain to turn away ships carrying signs of the infection, and some towns barred visitors in the hope of keeping the plague at bay. Reaction among the people varied considerably. Convinced of imminent death, some opted for the unbridled pursuit of sensual pleasures, while others turned to ascetic extremes, such as the itinerant flagellants, who ritualistically whipped themselves, wore penitential dress, and bore crucifixes. Others turned to black magic

A procession of flagellants during the Black Death. Note the bare backs and the whips. [Lauros-Giraudon/Art Resource]

and witchcraft, while some shunned anything Asian or blamed the Jews, many of whom were massacred. At Basel the bodies of slain Jews were floated down the Rhine in wine casks; 2,000 were slaughtered in Strasbourg, 600 in Brussels. People who tried to cure the sick relied on bleeding, cauterizing the boils, applying assorted substances to draw off the poison, and administering soothing potions. Many physicians fled, so the clergy often ministered to the sick and thus suffered extensively themselves. Entire Dominican friaries in Tuscany and Languedoc were decimated, and perhaps a third of the German clergy perished.

The social and economic effects of the plague were profound. In several respects the Muslim response to the Black Death differed from that of Christians. Whereas the latter were preoccupied with guilt and fear, Muslims tended to regard the plague, like the *jihad*, or holy war, as an opportunity to achieve martyrdom and thus as a vehicle of divine mercy. "Their wounds had been similar" to those of holy warriors, said one Islamic

tradition, "so they joined the martyrs."[2] Unlike the Christians, the Muslims therefore thought it was wrong to flee from a plague-stricken area, though in part this may also have involved some realization that flight could spread the disease. Theologically, however, Muslims denied that the plague was contagious, inasmuch as it was supposed to be divinely bestowed on a community deserving of special favor. Europeans, in contrast, were firmly convinced that the plague was infectious. The practical result was that Christians feared the Black Death, whereas the Muslims tended to accept it as they accepted such disasters as droughts and floods.

In the Middle East the immediate effect of the plague was a sharp rise in wages for laborers and a decrease in rents and income for the propertied classes. Yet there was no long-term improvement in the living standards of rural workers, particularly in Egypt and Syria, because a large increase in military needs to defend the region meant heavier taxes. Only in the case of urban workers did income rise sufficiently to bring an increase in real wages. In Europe hundreds of villages were severely depopulated or disappeared altogether, reducing the value of land and driving up wages as the labor supply plummeted. As in the Middle East initially, peasants who survived found their services in greater demand and could obtain better terms from their landlords or find more accommodating ones elsewhere, while others moved into the towns as artisans. Falling rents and rising wages prompted landowners to seek legislation fixing wages at low levels and restricting access to urban occupations. A French ordinance of 1351 limited wage increases to no more than a third of the preplague level, while the more ambitious English Statute of Laborers of the same year fixed wages at the pre-1349 rates and prohibited the employment of cheap female workers in place of men. Spanish, Portuguese, and German governments made similar attempts to control wages, but none was very effective. The French and the English also enacted measures to curtail the rising cost of food.

Catastrophe and Rebellion

In Europe the dislocation caused by the plague, coupled with the restrictive measures against the peasants and the artisans, contributed to explosive unrest in the late fourteenth century. In 1358 many peasants in northern France joined in uprisings known as the Jacquerie (*Jacques* was a name nobles used to address a peasant). Already embittered by efforts to limit their wages, the peasants were angered by heavy financial exactions to support French forces in the Hundred Years' War and by marauding bands of mercenaries from whom the nobles offered them no protection. The peasants began their rampage in May, killing, raping, burning, and destroying a number of castles. They had, however, neither strong leaders nor a program of reform. Priests, craftsmen, and lesser merchants joined them before the nobles ruthlessly suppressed the rebellion throughout the summer by means of widespread massacres. In the end, some 20,000 died.

Social revolt erupted in England in 1381, fueled by the peasants' resentment at efforts to restrict their economic advances, long-standing bitterness over aristocratic cruelty toward them, and governmental efforts to impose a poll or head tax to pay for the war against France. Peasants in the south, where the rebellion broke out, were also upset by French raids on their lands. Led by the priest John Ball and the journeyman Wat Tyler, the revolt soon spread throughout much of the country as urban workers joined the peasants. The killing and destruction was stemmed only when the young king, Richard II (1377–1399), met with the rebels and promised reform. Instead the nobles regrouped and carried out a campaign of retribution. Radical rebel demands— the equality of all men before the law, the granting of most church property to the people, and the end of mandatory peasant labor on the lords' demesnes (personal lands)—were not met, though the government ceased collecting the head tax.

The Jacquerie and the Wat Tyler rebellion are but the most famous examples of the revolts that swept parts of Europe in the century after the Black Death first appeared. The peasants of Languedoc rose up in 1382 and 1383, Catalonian peasants were frequently in arms, and peasants and miners rebelled in Sweden in 1434. Much of the unrest erupted in the cities, where artisans de-manded more political power and where the working poor were chained in poverty by repressive guilds. The greatest urban revolt was that of the *ciompi* (cloth workers) in Florence in 1378, but there were uprisings as well in Paris and Rouen in France, at Ghent in Flanders, at Brunswick and Lübeck in the Holy Roman Empire, and at Barcelona and Seville in Spain. No other period in the Middle Ages experienced as much social unrest as the century 1350–1450.

The Hundred Years' War

Between 1337 and 1453 the English and the French engaged in a series of armed conflicts collectively known as the Hundred Years' War, though in fact the two countries spent less than half this period in actual fighting. Each side went to war because it felt the other threatened its security and blocked its rightful ambitions. The war began when King Edward III of England (1327–1377) claimed the French throne as his own. The last three Capetian monarchs, the sons and heirs of Philip IV, had died without leaving a male heir. Although Edward III, Philip's maternal grandson, was the closest male heir, the French nobles supported the claim of Philip of Valois, a cousin of Philip IV's sons. At first Edward accepted the decision and even swore the vassal's oath of fealty to Philip at Amiens for his holdings in Aquitaine. English involvement in France, however, stood

On the left the English rebel Wat Tyler is slain as Richard II watches, while on the right the king calms a mob of angry peasants. [British Museum]

◉ Peasant Rebellion: ◉
A Call for Communalism

The English peasants who rebelled in 1381 were motivated in part by resentment against the landed aristocracy. One of those who encouraged such hostility was the priest John Ball, whose views reflect a basic communalism.

Ah, ye good people, the matters goeth not well to pass in England, nor shall not do till everything be common, and that there be no villains [serfs] nor gentlemen, but that we may be all [made one] together, and that the lords be no greater masters than we be. . . . We be all come from one father and one mother, Adam and Eve: whereby can they say or show that they be greater lords than we be, saying by that they cause us to win and labor for that they dispend? . . . They dwell in fair houses, and we have the pain and travail, rain and wind in the fields; and by that that cometh of our labors they keep and maintain their estates: we be called their bondmen, and . . . [unless] we do readily them service, we be beaten; and we have no sovereign to whom we may complain, nor that will hear us nor do us right. Let us go to the king.

Source: G. C. Macaulay, ed., *The Chronicles of Froissart*, trans. J. Bourchier, Lord Berners (London: Macmillan, 1924), p. 251.

squarely in the way of the ambition of the French sovereigns to extend their authority throughout the country. No less important as a cause of the war was Anglo-French rivalry over Flanders. Its count was Philip's vassal, but Flemish towns depended on English wool for their textile industry. English support for the Flemings when they rebelled against their count threatened French domination in the region, whereas French control jeopardized English trade. Another grievance was France's support for the Scots, which prevented the English from exercising lordship over their northern neighbors.

As the two sides embarked on war, France was seemingly the stronger, with greater wealth and a population three times the size of England's. The French had the advantage of fighting on terrain they knew, but this in turn subjected their peasants to the ravages of war. The French kings, moreover, had to cope with the fact that some of their own subjects—the Burgundians, the Flemish, and the Gascons of Aquitaine—allied with the English at various times during the war. For most of its duration the French monarchs were unable to provide either strong military leadership or sound fiscal policies to finance the fighting. The English, despite the popular support marshaled by Edward III and a string of impressive military victories, were unable to inflict a total defeat on France because they had neither the manpower nor the funds to dominate such a vast land. In the end the English were largely reduced to a policy of intimidation, which failed in the face of renewed French resolve.

England's early victories were the result of the military superiority of its longbowmen, who could lay down a barrage of arrows powerful enough to pierce French armor at a distance of up to 200 yards. The effectiveness of the English archers was demonstrated at Crécy in 1346, at Poitiers a decade later, and at Agincourt in 1415. Although the French also had longbows, they failed to use them effectively. The turning point of the war came in 1429 as the English besieged Orléans. Charles, the sickly dauphin (crown prince), his plight desperate, gambled on an illiterate peasant girl from the village of Domrémy who claimed to have been sent by heavenly messengers. Accompanied by fresh troops dispatched by the dauphin, Joan of Arc, though only 17, inspired the French with a vision of victory. The English in any event were on the verge of withdrawing from Orléans, but Joan's sense of divine mission and the dauphin's decision to accept the royal crown as Charles VII in May 1429 gave the French new life. When the Burgundians captured Joan a year later, the English hoped to discredit her by having her tried and executed as a heretic, but instead they created a martyr. A posthumous trial found her innocent in 1456, and in 1920 she was canonized as a saint. In the years that followed her death in 1431, the French, with the Burgundians at their side after 1435, relentlessly drove the English out of France, leaving them in 1453 with only Calais.

Joan of Arc as she may have looked, shown here holding a banner with the fleur-de-lis, the royal emblem of France. [Giraudon/Art Resource]

The French victory was facilitated by the growth of national feeling and the effective use of gunpowder and heavy artillery. Not only were the new cannons useful in besieging fortifications, but they also demoralized enemy forces and frightened their horses. In the end the war was beneficial to the French monarchy, for during its course the kings acquired both a monopoly on the sale of salt, the *gabelle* or tax on which became a major source of royal income, and the right to impose other taxes, including a direct tax called the *taille*, without the approval of the Estates General. These funds were necessary to support the standing army introduced in the war. In contrast, the English monarchs were able to maintain the war only by repeatedly seeking parliamentary approval for taxation, thereby making Parliament an indispensable part of the government. By the war's end the principle was established that neither taxes nor other forms of legislation could be implemented without parliamentary approval, and Parliament had taken the first steps to hold royal officials accountable to them or risk impeachment. England and France thus began to follow strikingly different paths of monarchical government, the former eventually culminating in constitutional monarchy, the latter in absolute rule.

The social consequences of the war were profound. In both countries the rural economy was hit hard by the loss of men to the recurring campaigns, especially as the population fell sharply because of the Black Death. In addition to the soldiers killed in battle, the English callously murdered thousands of French civilians. The war brought higher taxes, disrupted trade, and contributed to the shortage of manpower on the farms of both countries. The change in the manner of fighting had significant long-term effects. Both the longbow and the use of guns enhanced the value of commoners on the battlefield and thus encouraged the development of larger armies. Those armies in turn required greater and greater financial support from the state in contrast to the smaller feudal forces. The cannons meant major changes in the construction of city walls, which had to be much thicker. At the same time, however, siege trains capable of attacking towns were generally beyond the reach of all but sovereigns and the greater princes; the military changes thus contributed to the evolution of more unified states. Economically, the demand for cannons, guns, and ammunition sparked the growth of the armaments industry and the mining companies that provided it with the necessary raw materials. Thus in the long run the socioeconomic effects of the war were more important than its territorial consequences.

The Spiritual Crisis of the Late Medieval Church

Against a backdrop of widespread misery caused by famine, pestilence, and war, the medieval church was rocked by scandal and division in the late fourteenth and early fifteenth centuries, precisely at a time when strong spiritual leadership was desperately needed. The French king, Philip IV, emboldened by his earlier victory over Pope Boniface VIII, successfully pressured Pope Clement V (1305–1314), himself French, to move the seat of the papacy from Rome to Avignon in 1309. Although an imperial city under papal control, Avignon was not only on the French border but was French in language and culture. The papacy remained at Avignon until 1377, a period usually referred to as the Babylonian Captivity, an allusion to the period in which the ancient Hebrews were held captive in Babylon. Avignon had the advantage of freeing the popes from the turmoil then disrupting Rome and the Papal States, but it also placed the papacy under a greater degree of French influence. Of the 134 cardinals appointed during the Avignon period, 111 were French. The English, the Germans, and many Italians were displeased at the specter of a papacy in the shadow of French power, and Rome was particularly hard hit because its economy had rested so heavily on papal revenues. But perhaps most of the resentment against the Avignon popes stemmed from their efforts to create new sources of income to offset decreased revenue from the Papal States. The collection of annates, usually the first year's income from an ecclesiastical position, or expectatives, a fee for the right to be appointed to a particular ecclesiastical position when it became vacant, created the impression that the popes were more concerned with material than spiritual matters.

Disillusion with the papacy became even more pronounced as a result of the great schism that scandalized the church from 1378 to 1417. In 1377 Pope Gregory XI (1370–1378), persuaded by Catherine of Siena and Bridget of Sweden, moved the papal court back to Rome. When he died a year later, Roman mobs intimidated the cardinals to elect an Italian pope who would keep the papacy in Rome. The cardinals obliged with the reform-minded Urban VI (1378–1389), but five months later a group of mostly French cardinals declared Urban's election void and elected a rival pope, Clement VII, a cousin of the French king, Charles V. Europeans had witnessed schisms before, but nothing like the spectacle that now divided Christendom, largely along political lines. Clement, ruling from Avignon, had the support of France and its allies, Castile, Aragon, Naples, and Scotland, whereas Urban was backed by England, Portugal, Flanders, and the Holy Roman Empire. The Bohemians, Hungarians, Poles, and Scandinavians also supported the Roman pope. As each pope claimed to be the true vicar of Christ and condemned the other, the schism raised serious questions about the validity of priests' authority and the sacraments they administered. In addition to casting disrepute on the leaders of the church, the schism encouraged the spread of heresy and mysticism, with its stress on the inner life of the spirit rather than church matters and liturgy.

When it became apparent that neither the Roman nor the Avignonese pope would yield to his rivals in the interest of unity, reformers called for a church council to end the scandal. Advocates of reform contended that a council of the church exercised authority superior to that of a pope and was ultimately responsible for faith and unity. In its attempt to limit papal power, this Conciliar theory drew on a medieval intellectual tradition that in the past had been very controversial. In 1324, for instance, Marsiglio of Padua, the rector of the University of Paris, had argued in his *Defender of the Peace* that because the people are the ultimate source of authority in church and state, a church council is superior to the pope. Marsiglio went even further, insisting that the church's power was entirely restricted to spiritual matters; hence the pope had no claim to temporal authority. By reducing the church to a community within the state, he challenged its traditional claim to superiority. Although the church condemned Marsiglio's theories in 1327, his ideas provided a useful arsenal for those intent on disputing papal primacy. Among the most important

of these were theologians at the University of Paris, especially Jean Gerson and Pierre d'Ailly, who espoused Conciliar arguments as the means to end the papal schism.

With the support of most monarchs, a group of cardinals representing Rome and Avignon summoned a council to meet at Pisa in 1409. There both popes were deposed and a new one chosen, but because neither pope accepted the council's action, there were now three claimants to Peter's chair. The embarrassing schism was resolved only when a new council met in the German city of Constance beginning in 1414. It took three years and the energetic support of Sigismund, the Holy Roman Emperor, to restore unity through the election of an Italian cardinal as Martin V (1417–1431). One of the three feuding popes resigned, but the others had to be deposed. The church subsequently regarded the Roman popes as the legitimate line. In addition to ending the schism, the Council of Constance issued two decrees supporting Conciliar views, the first of which asserted that a general council of the church derived its authority directly from Christ and thus could compel the obedience of popes "in matters pertaining to the faith, the extinction of the schism, and the form of the church." The second decree called for the next two councils to meet after intervals of five and seven years and subsequent ones every decade. The council also addressed the question of heresy, particularly the problem of John Hus.

The Challenge of Heresy: Wyclif and Hus

Symptomatic of the church's problems in the fourteenth and early fifteenth centuries was the enthusiastic reception in England and Bohemia of ideas that challenged the very core of orthodox teaching. The Oxford professor John Wyclif (c. 1330–1384) not only denied papal claims to temporal power, as Marsiglio of Padua had done, but also demanded that prelates (cardinals, archbishops, and bishops) relinquish their political offices and that the church divest itself of its property. In the tradition of Francis of Assisi, he insisted that the clergy should devote themselves to poverty and piety. On the crucial question of authority, Wyclif insisted that it rested in the Bible alone, which, he argued, should be in the language of the people. In this spirit he began preparing an English version of the Bible. Wyclif also called for the abolition of many traditions, including pilgrimages, the sale of indulgences, the veneration of saints, and the doctrine of transubstantiation—the belief that the substance of the bread and wine miraculously becomes the body and blood of Christ in the Eucharist. Convinced that the true church was composed only of people divinely predestined to believe in God, Wyclif

---

◉ Marsiglio on the Power of the People ◉

In his Defender of the Peace, *Marsiglio of Padua makes a strong case for the people as the fundamental source of authority and the maintenance of peace as the primary task of a government.*

The authority to make laws belongs only to the whole body of the citizens . . . or else it belongs to one or a few men. But it cannot belong to one man alone . . . for through ignorance or malice or both, this one man could make a bad law, looking more to his own private benefit than to that of the community, so that the law would be tyrannical. For the same reason, the authority to make laws cannot belong to a few; for they too could sin . . . in making the law for the benefit of a certain few and not for the common benefit, as can be seen in oligarchies. . . . Since all the citizens must be measured by the law according to due proportion, and no one knowingly harms or wishes injustice to himself, it follows that all or most wish a law conducing to the common benefit of the citizens. . . .

It is hence appropriate . . . that the whole body of citizens entrust to those who are prudent and experienced the investigation, discovery, and examination of the standards, the future laws or statutes. . . . After such standards, the future laws, have been discovered and diligently examined, they must be laid before the assembled whole body of citizens for their approval or disapproval. . . . The laws thus made by the hearing and consent of the entire multitude will be better observed, nor will anyone have any protest to make against them.

Source: Marsilius of Padua, *Defensor pacis*, trans. A. Gewirth (Toronto: University of Toronto Press, 1980), pp. 48, 54–55.

---

daringly argued that salvation was independent of the institutional sacraments, and he denied both papal and clerical power to excommunicate the righteous from the true church. Wyclif's clear distinction between the spiritual church of true believers and the corrupt temporal institution presided over by the popes appealed to Christians disgusted by the events of the 1300s. Wyclif enjoyed powerful support among aristocrats in England, who saw in his teachings the possibility of acquiring the church's wealth. Many of his ideas were condemned, and he was expelled from Oxford. Wyclif's followers, known as Lollards, kept his ideas alive in England well into the sixteenth century despite heavy persecution. Ultimately they helped prepare the ground for the Protestant Reformation.

Wyclif's ideas were carried to Bohemia by Czech students studying at Oxford and by members of the household of Anne of Bohemia, who married King Richard II of England in 1381. The leader of the Bohemian reformers, John Hus (1369–1415), rector of the University of Prague, embraced some of Wyclif's teachings, especially his concept of the true church as a body of saints and the need for sweeping reforms. Hus, whose views struck a responsive chord among Czech nationalists resentful of the domination of foreign ecclesiastics, enjoyed the backing of King Wenceslas, brother of the Emperor Sigismund. When Sigismund offered Hus a guarantee of safe conduct in order to discuss his views at the Council of Constance, Hus accepted, though he had already been excommunicated. The council, which had previously condemned Wyclif's tenets, accused Hus of heresy. He was tried and convicted, turned over to Sigismund's officials, and burned at the stake in 1415; promises made to heretics, Sigismund was assured, were not binding. A year later Hus' disciple, Jerome of Prague, met the same fate. Their militant followers, fired in part by Czech patriotism, mounted a fierce rebellion that lasted from 1421 to 1436. In the end the Bohemians were left with considerable authority over their own church, an example that was not lost on Martin Luther a century later as he pondered the need for reform in the German church.

The Late Medieval Outlook

The crises of the fourteenth and early fifteenth centuries had a striking effect on people's outlook: famine, plague,

◉ A Corrupt Clergy: Wyclif's Indictment ◉

John Wyclif's attack on the moral evils of the clergy struck a responsive chord among many Englishmen.

We should put on the armor of Christ, for Antichrist has turned his clerks [clergymen] to covetous and worldly love, and so blinded the people and darkened the law of Christ, that his servants be thick, and few be on Christ's side. And always they despise that men should know Christ's life, . . . and priests should be ashamed of their lives, and especially these high priests, for they reverse Christ both in word and deed. . . .

O men that be on Christ's half, help ye now against Antichrist! for the perilous time is come that Christ and Paul told [of] before. . . . For three sects fight here, against Christian[s]. . . . The first is the pope and cardinals, by false law that they have made; the second is emperors [and] bishops, who despise Christ's law; the third is these Pharisees [i.e., friars]. . . . All these three, God's enemies, travel in hypocrisy, and in worldly covetousness, and idleness in God's law. Christ help his church from these fiends, for they fight perilously.

Source: J. H. Robinson, ed., *Readings in European History*, vol. 1 (Boston: Ginn, 1904), pp. 497–498.

and war influenced the cult of death and decay; the Hundred Years' War affected the cult of chivalry and the growth of national literature; and the Babylonian Captivity and the papal schism prompted social criticism and the views of nominalists and mystics.

The Cult of Death

The preoccupation with death induced by the massive fatalities resulting from famine and plague manifested itself in various ways. In the minds of the pious, greater attention was given to the Last Judgment, a popular motif in both art and literature. A few church walls still feature murals of the Last Judgment dating from this period. Others found solace in the Pietà, a depiction of Mary holding the dead Christ in her arms—a poignant symbol for grieving parents who shared her sense of personal loss and the hope of resurrection. Painters commonly depicted figures of death, and sculptors placed skeletal figures instead of traditional effigies on tombs. Nothing, however, more graphically reveals the fascination with death than the *danse macabre*, the dance of death that was not only portrayed in art but also acted out as an eerie drama and celebrated in poetry. The *danse macabre* may, in fact, be related to the psychological and neurological disorders that accompanied the plague. A recurring theme in these representations is the equality of all persons in death, a sharp counterpoint to a society preoccupied with social hierarchy. There was no more vivid reminder of this than the Churchyard of the Innocents in Paris, where skulls and bones were heaped by the thousands along the cloister walls.

The Chivalric Ideal

Juxtaposed with this cult of death and decay, with its democratic implications, was another cult, more positive in outlook and restricted in its social appeal—the cult of chivalry. Here was a code for knights and nobles, the last gasp of a way of life and warfare gradually being pushed into the shadows by new methods of fighting, the rising mercantile order, and a gradual shift in importance from ancestry to talent as the key to a successful political career. The late medieval cult of chivalry, with its idealized knights and exalted ladies, was the swan song of the old order. The chivalric code exalted war, but there was nothing particularly glorious when England's peasant archers cut down the cream of the French knighthood at Crécy, Poitiers, and Agincourt. Efficiency, technology, and discipline replaced bravado, loyalty, and dignity on the battlefield, a change that ultimately revolutionized and depersonalized warfare by shifting the burden from the landed elite to the masses. As if to protest the passing of the old order, the aristocracy put greater emphasis on the trappings of chivalry: pageants, tournaments, and glitter. When Francis I of France and Henry VIII of England met in 1520, chivalric trappings were so extravagant that contemporaries described the scene as a "field of cloth of gold." Extravagance and overstatement were indicative of the fact that

This sixteenth-century Flemish illustration depicts the churchyard of the Church of the Innocents in Paris. On its walls was a painting of the Dance of Death, below which skulls and bones were neatly stacked for public viewing. [Giraudon/Art Resource]

chivalry, once primarily a military code of conduct, had been transformed into an elegant charade, a form of escapism.

National Literatures

The Hundred Years' War encouraged the further development of national vernacular literature. There are, of course, earlier examples of medieval literature in native tongues, such as the *Song of Roland*, the *Nibelungenlied*, and the poetry of the troubadours, but the contributions of Dante, Chaucer, and Villon were critical in shaping national languages out of regional dialects. All three writers sharply criticized late medieval society and the church.

Dante Alighieri (1265–1321), who held various civic offices in his native Florence before being forced into exile in 1301 by a rival political faction, spent the last two decades of his life traveling throughout Italy in search of patrons. Embittered by the divisiveness of the Italian states, Dante used these years to write in defense of the vernacular and to compose his epic poem, *The Divine Comedy* (1310–1321), so named because it progresses from a fearsome vision of hell in the first part, the *Inferno*, to a happy ending as the reader is guided through purgatory to paradise. The scenes from hell, peopled with everyone from actual popes and priests to politicians and queens, are used by Dante to condemn such

evils as ecclesiastical corruption, political treachery, and immorality. On other levels the journey is an allegory of the Christian life and a pictorial *summa* of medieval ethical and religious teachings akin in spirit to the scholastic *summae* of Thomas Aquinas.

Disenchantment with contemporary society, especially the church, is also reflected in Geoffrey Chaucer's *Canterbury Tales* (1387–1400). The son of a wine merchant, Chaucer (c. 1340–1400) fought in the Hundred Years' War before serving in various capacities as a royal official. It was probably on a mission to Florence that he learned of Dante's work, which influenced his own writings. Many of his poems, such as *The Legend of Good Women*, deal with the theme of love, while others, such as *The Parliament of Fowls*, may reflect contemporary political events. In the characters, anecdotes, and moral fables of *The Canterbury Tales* he probed English society, making particularly incisive and satirical comments about the foibles and hypocrisy of ecclesiastics. The thrust is similar in a nearly contemporary work titled *The Vision of Piers Plowman*, usually attributed to William Langland (c. 1330–c. 1400). The work's 11 poetic visions reflect the crises of the 1300s, especially as they affected the peasants, and are highly critical of the failings of the church even while reaffirming faith in Christian principles.

The poetry of the Frenchman François Villon (1431–c. 1463) is the voice of the downtrodden and criminal element in a society thrown into turmoil by the

◉ Death and Decay ◉

François Villon's poetry reflects not only his own experiences among the lowly and the criminal in France but also the fifteenth century's fascination with death and decay.

Death makes one shudder and turn pale,
Pinches the nose, distends the veins,
Swells out the throat, the members fail,
Tendons and nerves grow hard with strains.
O female flesh, like silken skeins,
Smooth, tender, precious, in such wise
Must you endure so awful pains?
Aye, or go living to the skies.

The following lines were written while Villon was under sentence of death; he describes the fate that awaits his body.

The rain has washed us through as through a sieve,
And the sun dried us black to caricature;
Magpies and crows have had our eyes to rive
And made of brows and beards their nouriture.
Never we pause, no moment's rest secure,
Now here, now there, as the winds fail or swell,
Always we swing like clapper of a bell.
Pitted as thimble is our bird-pecked skin.
Be not of our ill brotherhood and fell,
But pray to God we be absolved of sin!

Source: The Complete Works of François Villon, trans. J. U. Nicolson (New York: Covici Friede, 1931), pp. 32, 108.

Hundred Years' War. A convicted murderer, thief, and brawler as well as a graduate of the University of Paris, Villon was in and out of jail and was for a time under sentence of death. The themes of his ballads range from the ways of the Parisian underworld and his drinking companions to meditations on the beauty of life as he contemplated the skeletons in the Churchyard of the Innocents. The specter of death stalks much of his work, reflecting the popularity of this theme in the fifteenth century.

Nominalists and Mystics

While the great vernacular writers criticized their social and religious world, William of Ockham (c. 1290–1349), an English Franciscan theologian, mounted a sweeping challenge to the scholastic teaching that prevailed in the universities. Ockham asserted that only individual things, not essences or universals, were real and knowable, a philosophical theory known as nominalism. Knowledge could therefore be attained by direct experience rather than by philosophical speculation. Contrary to the scholastics, he argued that the principal doctrines of Christianity, such as the existence of God and the immortality of the soul, were incapable of rational proof and had to be affirmed on the basis of faith alone. By removing the rational basis for Christian belief, Ockham opened the way to skepticism, a path followed by some of his disciples. Ockham's principles convinced him that the popes could not possess absolute authority, even in matters of faith; hence he contributed to Conciliar theory by insisting on the supremacy of general councils.

The rational and institutional approach to Christianity was also challenged by mystics, who urged the importance of seeking God within oneself. One of the most influential mystics was the Dominican friar Meister Eckhart (c. 1260–1328), a German, who taught that the mystical union of the human and the divine could be achieved in the soul through the purifying work of divine grace. Because the views of both Eckhart and Ockham were sufficiently different from traditional teaching, they had to defend themselves against charges of heresy before the papal court at Avignon, and Eckhart had to recant.

The real strength of late medieval mysticism was among the laity, particularly in Germany and the Netherlands. There the Dutchman Gerhard Groote (1340–1384) founded a movement known as the *devotio moderna* ("modern devotion"), which combined a strong sense of morality with an emphasis on the inner life of the soul rather than liturgy and penitent acts such as fasting and pilgrimages. After his death his followers established the Brethren and the Sisters of the Common Life—lay believers who lived in strictly regulated religious houses and devoted themselves primarily to the education of young boys. Some of the most influential religious leaders of the late fifteenth and sixteenth centuries, including Erasmus of Rotterdam, studied in these schools. The literary classic of this movement, Thomas à Kempis' *Imitation of Christ*, was a devotional handbook that emphasized personal piety and ethical conduct. Its message that "a humble husbandman who serves God is better than a proud philosopher" reflected a widespread desire among the laity to find relief from the material problems of their age through simple piety.

Economic Recovery

Europe recovered from the calamities of the fourteenth and early fifteenth centuries in large measure because of renewed population growth, economic diversification, and technological inventions spurred by the labor shortages resulting from the Black Death. As the population began to return to its former levels in the late fifteenth and sixteenth centuries, there was once again an abundant labor supply as well as improved productivity and greater economic diversification. Merchants increasingly branched out into fields as varied as banking, textile and weapon manufacturing, and the mining of iron ore and silver. The Germans modernized the mines by harnessing horsepower and waterpower to crush ore, operate their rolling mills, pump water from mine shafts, and run the lifts. Blast furnaces were constructed to make cast iron. Dutch fishermen learned to salt, dry, and store their fish while at sea, thus enabling them to stay out longer and increase their catch. The Hundred Years' War, as we have seen, stimulated the armaments industry, and the invention of movable metal type not only led to a new industry in printing but also greatly encouraged the manufacture of paper.

The textile industry experienced some growth in this period. The production of woolens in Flanders and the cities of northern Italy, however, declined in the fifteenth century, primarily because the English monarchs made a concerted effort to build up their native wool industry by imposing low export duties on cloth and high ones on raw wool. Woolen manufacturing also expanded in France, Germany, and Holland, and new textile industries such as silk and cotton began to develop. In Venice some 3,000 persons were involved in the production of silk, 16,000 in the manufacture of cotton. Several thousand were employed in the Venetian arsenal, the greatest shipyard and probably the largest industrial establishment in Europe.

The growth in manufacturing went hand in hand with a dramatic increase in commerce and the rise of great merchants and their organizations. The latter included the seven major guilds in Florence, the six merchant corporations known as the *Corps de Marchands* in Paris, and the 12 Livery Companies in London. Firms in Europe's leading commercial centers established branch offices in other cities, and exchanges or bourses were opened to facilitate financial transactions. Banking houses developed rapidly; Florence had 33 in 1472. There were state banks in such places as Genoa, Venice, Augsburg, Hamburg, and Barcelona. As rulers as well as merchants found themselves in need of loans, the demand for credit grew, thus undermining the hostility of the medieval church to most interest charges. The Genoese pioneered the development of insurance, especially for merchants engaged in seaborne trade. The dominant role of northern Italians in banking was aided by the fact that the most stable coins of this period were Florentine florins and Venetian ducats.

Ships in the Mediterranean trade called at the Italian ports of Pisa and Genoa as well as at Marseilles and Narbonne in France and Barcelona in Aragon, but the heart of this commerce was really Venice. Its 3,300 ships, some of them capable of carrying as much as 250 tons of cargo, plied the waters from the North Sea and Spain to North Africa, Syria, and the Black Sea. In contrast, Genoa, itself a major maritime power, had 2,000 ships. Cloth from Europe was traded in the East for spices, dyes, sugar, silks, and cotton. Shipping in northern Europe was mostly the province of the Hanseatic League, whose members included Lübeck, Danzig, and Hamburg. Their ships ranged from Scandinavia and Russia to England, Flanders, and northern Italy. From the states of the Baltic and the North Sea they obtained fish, timber, naval stores, grain, and furs in exchange for wine, spices, and cloth. Much of the commerce moved through the ports of the Low Countries; in 1435 an average of 100 ships a day docked at Bruges. In the late fifteenth and sixteenth centuries the power of the Hanseatic League began to wane, partly owing to internal problems but mostly because of the growing power of states such as England and Denmark, whose merchants demanded an end to Hansa privileges and a greater role in the carrying trade.

Political Renewal: The Quest for Unity and Authority

Economic revival was accompanied in western Europe and Russia by the development of relatively strong centralized states. The political crises of the era of adversity had increased the need for state governments to raise substantial tax revenue. Such revenue made it feasible to think in terms of a professional army rather than a feudal levy, but this in turn increased the costs of government. So too did the growth of royal bureaucracies, which were essential not only to raise the revenue but also to administer the more unified realms. Greater unity was in general beneficial to the business community; hence the monarchs typically found important allies in the towns. Urban support was translated into tax revenues (though many French towns enjoyed exemptions), an enlarged pool from which government officials could be selected, and political backing in the drive for sovereignty.

The decline of particularism—the dominance of local and regional authorities rather than a central government—was in most respects a blow to the landed aristocracy, but they were appeased by exemptions from most taxes and frequent appointments to political office. The landed elite were also prominently represented in the national assemblies, where they enjoyed power and prestige greater than that bestowed on urban delegates. The achievement of national sovereignty was possible in large measure because the power of the landed aristocracy was not so much crushed as altered: in the new system, many of them became staunch supporters of the crown, not its traditional enemy. In the case of Russia and Spain, the development of a centralized state was carried out as part of a drive to expel hitherto dominant invaders—the Mongols in Russia and the Muslims in Spain.

The Rise of Muscovy

During the period of Mongol domination, Russia was a conglomeration of feudal principalities, but in the fourteenth century the princes of Moscow began to "gather the Russian land" by expanding their borders through marital alliances, inheritance, purchases, and conquests. In this process they were aided by three factors: the strategic location of Moscow near tributaries of the Volga and Oka rivers, Mongol reliance on the Muscovites to collect tribute from other Russians, and the support of the Russian Orthodox church, whose metropolitan archbishop made Moscow the religious capital of the Russians in the fourteenth century. As Mongol power declined late in that century, the Muscovite princes ceased to be agents for the Mongols and took up the mantle of patriotic resistance. Their new role was made abundantly clear when Grand Prince Dimitri defeated the Tatars, as the Russians called the Mongols, in 1380 at Kolikovo, southeast of Moscow. The war of liberation continued well into the fifteenth century, during which time Moscow was besieged numerous times. Even after the Mongols were driven out, their influence pervaded many areas of Russian life, including military organization, criminal law, the system of tax collection, and above all the principle of unqualified obedience to the state. In a very real sense, Russian sovereigns ruled much as the Mongol khans had.

The foundation of a strong Russian state was laid by Ivan III, known as Ivan the Great (1462–1505), who was determined to prevent the recurrence of the factional struggles that had plagued his father's reign. To counterbalance the power of the hereditary boyars, or nobles, Ivan created a class of serving aristocracy by offering them lifetime grants of land in return for their service, a practice somewhat akin to that used earlier in the feudal states of western and central Europe. Ivan also enhanced his status as the result of his marriage to the Italian-educated Zoë, niece of the last Byzantine emperor, Constantine XI (died 1453). Henceforth Ivan began to refer to himself as the successor of the Byzantine emperors, adopting the Byzantine double eagle as the symbol of Russia, introducing Byzantine ceremonies at court, and calling himself Autocrat and Tsar ("Caesar"). At Zoë's urging, Italian architects were commissioned to design the Kremlin, a fortresslike palace befitting the tsar's pretensions to grandeur. Russian scholars contributed to the new image by asserting that Moscow was the third Rome (after Rome and Byzantium, each of which had fallen) and thus the center of Christianity. In the words of one Russian apologist, "The tsar is in nature like to all men, but in authority he is like to the highest God."

Ivan expanded the boundaries of his state, first by conquering the republic of Novgorod, a trading center with access to the Baltic Sea. Seizing approximately 80 percent of the former republic's land, he retained possession of more than half of it and used the rest to expand his serving aristocracy. In the process he exiled thousands of boyars, merchants, and smaller landowners. In 1500 he invaded Lithuania, hoping to conquer Smolensk; although he failed in this objective, by 1503 he had successfully expanded his borders to the west.

Above all, Ivan consciously advanced his claim to be ruler "of all the Russias," a title that even the prince of Lithuania had recognized in 1492. Unlike his predecessors, who limited their claim of ownership to royal estates and their inhabitants, Ivan asserted an unprece-

15.2 The Expansion of Russia

dented right to all Russian lands. It was in this context that Ivan issued a new code of laws—the Sudebnik—for the Russian people in 1497. Ivan can justly be regarded as the founder of the modern Russian state and the architect of an absolute tsardom.

The Spain of Isabella and Ferdinand

The unification of Spain was made possible by the marriage in 1469 of Isabella, the future queen of Castile (1474–1504), and Ferdinand, the future king of Aragon (1479–1516). Of the two kingdoms, Castile was by far more populous and wealthier. It was, moreover, an expanding state as it continued the campaign to reconquer Granada from the Muslims, a goal finally achieved in 1492. That done, Spain could turn its attention to overseas exploration, a pursuit in which the Portuguese had already taken the lead.

The marriage of Isabella and Ferdinand did not effectively unite the two countries, each of which spoke a different language and retained its own laws, taxes, monetary system, military, and customs. The two sov-

The marriage of Ferdinand of Aragon and Isabella of Castile made the unification of Spain possible. [Arxiu MAS, Barcelona]

ereigns left Aragon largely alone, free to keep its provincial assemblies, the Cortes, although royal supervision was exercised through viceroys appointed by the crown. Understandably, the monarchs concentrated on Castile, whose Cortes supported their quest for order and whose new council was the principal agency for the implementation of royal policy. In the work of centralization the sovereigns had the support of the towns, which were liberally represented in the Cortes, and of the hidalgos—knights who did not enjoy the tax-exempt status of the nobles and therefore sought employment from the crown. A number of the hidalgos served as *corregidors*, administering local districts, performing judicial functions, and supervising urban affairs. Although the role of the nobles in the government was somewhat reduced, they still exercised considerable influence through the powerful military brotherhoods established in the twelfth century, the Santiago, Calatrava, and Alcántara. To bring them under greater royal authority, Ferdinand became the head of each of the three great brotherhoods. The Mesta, the organization of large sheep farmers, also had to be controlled, for its pay-

ments were a primary source of royal revenue in the period before Spain began importing large quantities of American bullion.

The deeply devout Isabella and the pragmatic Ferdinand made the Catholic church a key instrument in their centralizing work. Isabella's most important minister, Cardinal Francisco Ximenes (c. 1436–1517), carried out a program of reform centering around the restoration of ecclesiastical discipline, thus reinforcing central authority. In 1482 Pope Sixtus IV granted the sovereigns the *real patronato* ("Royal Patronage"), giving them the right to make the major ecclesiastical appointments in Granada; this was later extended to Spanish America and then to Spain as a whole. Even more striking as a demonstration of royal authority in religion was the campaign of Isabella and Ferdinand to enforce religious orthodoxy. Although the Inquisition had been introduced into Spain by a papal bull in 1478, it soon became an instrument controlled by the crown and run by the queen's confessor, Tomás de Torquemada (died 1498). In 1492, the year Isabella and Ferdinand entered Granada in triumph, the Jews were given the option of being baptized as Christians or losing their property and going into exile; approximately 150,000 left. Ten years later Ximenes persuaded Isabella to expel professing Muslims. Jews and Muslims who converted—*Conversos* and *Moriscos*, respectively—were subject to the terrors of the Inquisition if their sincerity was doubted. Spain achieved religious unity, but at the cost of expelling or alienating productive minorities, curtailing intellectual freedom, and destroying toleration.

England: The Struggle for the Throne

By the time England concluded the Hundred Years' War in 1453, royal authority, already checked by the growth of parliamentary power in the areas of legislation and taxation, had been undermined by bastard feudalism. By this practice a small group of powerful nobles who controlled much of the country's landed property used their wealth to employ private armies through a practice known as livery and maintenance. The retainers in their hire wore distinctive clothing (livery), served primarily for pay rather than for the use of land as in the traditional feudal arrangement, and could expect legal assistance—often involving intimidation or bribery—if they got in trouble while serving their lord. Many of these retainers were recruited from the ranks of soldiers who had fought in the Hundred Years' War. The powerful magnates who hired these private armies exerted enormous influence on the monarchs through the royal Council and commanded strong support from their followers in Parliament. These circumstances made it possible for Henry of Bolingbroke, a grandson of Edward III, to force the abdication of Richard II, another grandson, in 1399. Parliament dutifully confirmed Bolingbroke's assumption of the crown as Henry IV (1399–1413), the first ruler of the house of Lancaster.

The reign of Henry IV's grandson, Henry VI (1422–1461), who became king at the age of 9 months, was conducive to the further growth of the magnates' power during his regency and then during the bouts of insanity that afflicted him as an adult. The result was the outbreak of civil war between the feuding factions, the houses of Lancaster and York. In the sixteenth century this came to be known as the Wars of the Roses when William Shakespeare, in *Henry VI*, assigned the symbol of the Tudor dynasty, a red rose, to the Lancastrians; the Yorkist symbol was a white rose. Henry's queen, Margaret of Anjou, was unwilling to see power pass to Richard, duke of York, great-grandson of Edward III and heir apparent before the birth of Henry's son. Richard's son, Edward IV (1461–1483), finally succeeded in capturing the throne in 1461 and forcing Henry VI to abdicate. The house of Lancaster staged a brief comeback in 1470–1471, though Edward soon regained control,

after which Henry VI mysteriously died in the Tower of London.

The Wars of the Roses were over, giving Edward the opportunity to improve his position by carefully shepherding his finances, establishing firm control over the Council, and expanding royal authority in Wales and northern England. At his death in 1483 his brother Richard, regent for the young Edward V, had the new king and his brother imprisoned. They too died mysteriously, possibly at the instigation of their uncle, who assumed the throne as Richard III (1483–1485). Although Richard suppressed one rebellion provoked by the renewal of factional strife, in 1485 Henry Tudor, who was remotely related to the house of Lancaster, invaded England with French backing and defeated Richard in the battle of Bosworth Field. Once again Parliament willingly recognized the victor's claim to the throne, and Henry's marriage to Edward IV's daughter, Elizabeth of York, helped heal the reopened wounds dividing the English ruling order.

Henry VII (1485–1509) resumed the task of strengthening royal authority that Edward IV had begun, notably by making the crown financially secure and building up a modest surplus in the treasury. Instead of increasing taxes, he made effective use of income from crown lands, judicial fees and fines, and feudal dues such as wardship rights. He also avoided costly foreign adventures, with the exception of a brief and futile invasion of France in 1492 in an attempt to keep Brittany independent. Apart from token forces, Henry had no standing army, but he made good use of unpaid justices of the peace drawn from the ranks of the gentry to maintain order in the counties, thereby reducing the crown's dependence on the nobility. Henry also used his Council, which could sit as a court (called the Star Chamber), to maintain order and impose swift justice; people cited before it had no right to legal counsel and could be compelled to testify against themselves. Like Edward IV, he selected men for the Council because of their loyalty to him rather than their status as magnates. He negotiated two strategic alliances, one of which involved the marriage of his daughter Margaret to James IV of Scotland. From that line came the Stuart dynasty, which governed both countries in the seventeenth century and unified them in the kingdom of Great Britain in 1707. The second alliance involved the marriage of Henry's elder son, Arthur, to Catherine of Aragon, daughter of Ferdinand and Isabella. After Arthur died of tuberculosis, Henry arranged for Catherine's marriage to his younger son, Prince Henry. When in the late 1520s the latter tired of Catherine, who had failed to provide him with a male heir, he set in motion the events that led to England's break with the Catholic church. By the time of his death in 1509, Henry VII had imposed substantial order and unity on England and, in the Statutes of Drogheda (1495), had made the Parliament and laws of Ireland subject to English control as well.

Valois France

Charles VII (1422–1461) laid the foundation for the recovery of the French monarchy in the late fifteenth century, not least by his victory over the English in the Hundred Years' War. Despite the large size of the kingdom, the continued presence of feudal traditions and local privileges, and the existence of a representative assembly, the Estates General, the French kings were at last in a position to unify the country, aided by a new spirit of national feeling. Because of the war Charles had been able to form the first French standing army, supported by the *taille*, a direct tax for which he did not have to seek the approval of the Estates General after 1439. In fact, meetings of the Estates were very rare between 1441 and 1614, after which there were no sessions until 1789. In 1438 Charles had also brought the French church firmly under royal control in a pronouncement called the Pragmatic Sanction of Bourges. It set forth "Gallican liberties" (similar to the *real patronato* later introduced in Spain) such as the right of the French church to choose its own prelates and an end to the payment of annates to Rome.

Once England was defeated, the greatest threat to the French monarchy was the duchy of Burgundy, whose dukes, Philip the Good (1419–1467) and Charles the Bold (1467–1477), entertained thoughts of making their state a powerful middle kingdom between France and the Holy Roman Empire. Their lands included not only the duchy of Burgundy in eastern France but also the Franche-Comté, Flanders, and other areas of the Netherlands. To establish a viable middle kingdom, Charles the Bold attempted to conquer Alsace and Lorraine, thereby linking Burgundy with the Low Countries, the major source of his extensive wealth. The French king, Louis XI (1461–1483), responded to this threat by subsidizing the armies of the Swiss Confederation, who defeated and killed Charles in 1477. In the absence of a male heir, his Burgundian lands were seized by France, though Charles' daughter Mary and her new husband, Maximilian of Habsburg, retained possession of the Low Countries. The royal domains were increased again in 1480 and 1481 when Louis inherited the Angevin lands of Anjou, Maine, and Provence. Only Brittany remained beyond the pale of his authority, but that was remedied in 1491 when his son and heir, Charles VIII (1483–1498), employed military force to compel Anne, duchess of Brittany, to marry him.

Although the crafty Louis XI had shunned war wherever possible in favor of diplomacy and intrigue, Charles VIII recklessly involved France in a disastrous attempt to dominate Italy. The stage had been set when Louis succeeded not only to the Angevin lands in France but also to the Angevin claim to the throne of Naples, now occupied by the Aragonese. Louis had wisely done nothing about the claim, though he had involved himself in

The French king Louis XI was a homely man who enjoyed a game of chess. He significantly expanded the royal domain by acquiring the duchy of Burgundy. [Ronald Sheridan/ Ancient Art and Architecture Collection]

the political affairs of northern Italy. Charles, however, was determined to assert his Neopolitan claim, and in 1494 he invaded Italy, thus precipitating a great power struggle for control of the Italian peninsula that lasted 65 years. By February 1495 he had reached Naples, where he was crowned in May. Although the duke of Milan, Ludovico il Moro (1451–1508), had encouraged the French invasion as a means of weakening his own enemies—Naples, Florence, and the papacy—he soon recognized that a French presence in Italy threatened everyone. He threw his support to the newly formed League of Venice, consisting of the empire, the papacy, and the Venetians, which forced Charles out of Italy.

Charles' successor, Louis XII (1498–1515), was likewise determined to pursue his Italian ambitions. This time the French had papal support, for Pope Alexander VI (1492–1503) was primarily interested in weakening the Venetians, who were competing with him for domination of central Italy. Louis obtained the support of Ferdinand of Aragon by offering to partition Naples with him. Louis' primary goal was the conquest of Milan, which he claimed as his own because his mother had been a member of the Visconti family, which ruled the duchy until 1447. Ludovico was accordingly accused of usurping the ducal title and imprisoned for the rest of his life by the French—perhaps a fitting end for the man who had first encouraged French intervention in Italy.

Once Pope Julius II (1503–1513) had secured the Papal States, he enlisted Spain, Venice, the Swiss Confederation, and the Holy Roman Empire in a Holy League to drive France out of Italy, an end they accomplished in 1513. Under Francis I (1515–1547) the French returned again in 1515, this time sparking a series of wars with the Habsburgs that drained France financially and damaged the prestige of the monarchy. Nevertheless, as in the case of the Hundred Years' War, military needs and financial demands led to the continued expansion and centralization of the royal administration, thus strengthening the king's hold on the realm and laying the foundation for the subsequent development of absolutism in France.

Italy: Papal States and City-States

While Russia and the western European states were developing stronger, more centralized governments in the fifteenth century, in Italy, Germany, Hungary, and Poland regional states and princes consolidated their power, effectively blocking the emergence of nations. The struggle in the High Middle Ages between the papacy and the Hohenstaufen emperors left the Italians without a strong government capable of extending its sway throughout the peninsula. Nor did any state possess a theoretical claim to serve as the nucleus for a unified nation. From Rome the popes governed the Papal States, a band extending across central Italy, but their claims to authority were international in scope. The popes themselves did not acquire their position by hereditary succession but by an elective process that was not limited to Italians. The papacy's temporal authority in Italy was severely reduced during the Avignon period and further damaged during the great schism. Beginning with Martin V, the fifteenth- and early-sixteenth-century popes were therefore preoccupied with reestablishing their temporal power. Popes such as Alexander VI of the Spanish Borgia family and Julius II were less spiritual leaders than temporal princes willing to use any means to extend their power. Alexander relied heavily on his son Cesare, who had few moral principles, while Julius personally led his forces into battle.

In the fourteenth and fifteenth centuries the communal governments of northern Italy experienced substantial internal tensions resulting from economic and social changes. Rapid urban growth, the development of textile industries, and the rise of a sizable proletariat excluded from the hope of prosperity by privilege-conscious guilds created such strife that Milan and Florence turned to men who were virtual despots to preserve order. So too did some of the smaller cities, such as Mantua. Often these despots were *condottieri*, mercenary generals whose hired armies provided them with the force necessary to keep order. In the south the kingdom of Naples and Sicily had problems of a different nature because of foreign domination. In 1282 the Sicilians revolted against their French Angevin rulers and turned for assistance to Aragon. Throughout the fourteenth century the Angevins and the Aragonese contested southern Italy until, in 1435, Alfonso the Magnanimous of Aragon drove the Angevins out of Naples. As we have seen, it was the decision of Charles VIII of France to reassert the Angevin claim that led to the French invasion of Italy in 1494.

The Duchy of Milan

From its strategic position in the heart of the Po valley and at the base of the trade routes leading across the Alps into northern Europe, Milan developed rapidly as an industrial center specializing in textiles and arms. The medieval commune suffered, however, not only from social tensions but also from a struggle for power between Guelph (propapal) and Ghibelline (proimperial) factions. Under the leadership of the Visconti family the Ghibellines triumphed in 1277, effectively ending communal government and establishing despotic rule. The Visconti—dukes of Milan beginning in 1395—employed *condottieri* to extend their control in the Po valley. The last of the Visconti dukes, Filippo Maria, introduced the mulberry plant, laying the foundation for Milan's silk industry.

When Filippo died without a male heir in 1447, the Milanese revived communal government, but their so-called Ambrosian Republic proved unable to govern effectively. Thus in 1450 the *condottiere* Francesco Sforza, Filippo Maria's son-in-law, reestablished ducal rule. Apart from extending Milan's control over Genoa, Francesco attempted to maintain a balance of power in Italy among the five principal states: Milan, Venice, Florence, Naples, and the Papal States. To this end he was an architect of the Italian League (1455), which also included some of the lesser states and was in part designed to prevent French aggression. Thus when Francesco's son Ludovico connived with Charles VIII of France to intervene in Italian affairs, he foolishly undermined his father's policy, thereby contributing not only to the devastating wars that ensued but to the demise of

15.3 *Italy, c. 1494*

the Sforza dynasty as well. After the French were ousted, the family's rule was briefly restored between 1512 and 1535, at which time the Holy Roman Emperor Charles V acquired Milan.

CATERINA SFORZA, THE DESPOT OF FORLÌ

The complex world of fifteenth-century Italian politics is reflected in the career of the sensuous and beautiful Caterina Sforza (c. 1463–1509), daughter of Francesco

Sforza's son, the second duke of Milan. Although she received a humanist education (see Chapter 16), she displayed no interest in classical authors or philosophical issues, but she was intrigued by history as well as riding and dancing. For political reasons Caterina's father arranged her marriage to Pope Sixtus IV's nephew, Girolamo Riario. The pope subsequently gave them control of the towns of Forlì and Imola, northeast of Florence, but Caterina's husband was assassinated by political rivals in 1488. She retained power by ruling in her son's name, thanks to assistance from the armies of Milan and Bologna, and avenged her husband's murder by staging a spectacle of brutality in which the bodies of some of the conspirators were dismembered and scattered in the

Caterina Sforza, countess of Forlì. [Marburg/Art Resource]

piazza of Forlì. That done, she sought to restore unity to her possessions by launching an extensive program of public building in Forlì, including a lavish park.

Although a campaign to extend her territory to the northeast failed because of opposition from Venice, her importance was such that she was courted by all the major Italian states. When the French invaded Italy in 1494, Caterina, fearful of Venice, refused to join the Holy League against France, opting instead for a neutrality that favored the French and their Florentine allies. The assassination of her lover in 1495 prompted her to instigate another bloody vendetta, but it also opened the way for her secret marriage a year or two later to Giovanni de' Medici, second cousin of the Florentine ruler Lorenzo the Magnificent. About this time she underwent a period of spiritual searching in which she wrote to the reformer Girolamo Savonarola, who urged her to seek redemption through pious works and just rule.

Caterina's final period of political crisis began in 1498 when the Venetians raided her lands, but she was saved by military aid from Milan and the outbreak of fighting between the Venetians and the Florentines. While Caterina was occupied with Venice, Pope Alexander VI and

his son, Cesare Borgia, plotted to increase their control over the Papal States, particularly the region that included Caterina's lands. Her main ally, Milan, was preoccupied in 1499 with the threat of a new French invasion, thanks to a pact between France and Venice signed in February. A month later the pope, calling Caterina a "daughter of iniquity," claimed her lands. Negotiations with Niccolò Machiavelli, the Florentine envoy, failed to achieve an effective alliance, nor were the assassins she dispatched to kill Alexander VI successful. Cesare Borgia's army struck in the autumn, forcing Caterina to send her children and treasures to Florence for safety. She retreated to a fortress with her troops, destroying all buildings in the area that might shelter the enemy, cutting down the trees, and flooding the marshes. Italy watched as the papal army relentlessly attacked until she was finally captured—and raped by Cesare—in January 1500. For a year she was imprisoned in a Roman dungeon. Without support from any major Italian state, her efforts to regain her territories failed, forcing her to seek refuge in Florence. Her last years were spent attending to her household, her garden, her horses, and her soul. Contemporaries called her the "Amazon of Forlì," a tribute to her ability to hold her own in a political world governed by the ethics of power.

Florence and the Medici

Bitter social conflict disrupted Florence throughout the fourteenth and early fifteenth centuries. Thanks to its banking houses and its textile industry the city was typically prosperous in this period, though it suffered severely when England's Edward III repudiated his debts and caused major banking houses to fail and again when 50,000 of its 80,000 inhabitants died in the plague. The periodic crises intensified social tensions that were already present. In part the turmoil was caused by an unusual degree of social mobility in Florentine society. The older nobles, the *grandi*, had been effectively excluded from power in 1293 through a constitution called the Ordinances of Justice, the work of the newly rich capitalists who dominated the seven greater guilds. In 1343 they in turn were successfully challenged by the craftsmen of the lesser guilds and their allies, the shopkeepers and small businessmen. The *ciompi* had their turn in 1378, when they revolted and won the right to organize their own guilds and have a say in political affairs. Feuding between the lesser guilds and the *ciompi* enabled the wealthy merchants to regain control in the early 1380s under the leadership of the Albizzi family. When the Albizzi blocked the rise of new capitalists to power but could not win a war against neighboring Lucca, they were exiled in 1434 by partisans of the Medici family.

Cosimo de' Medici (1389–1464) and his successors, who dominated Florentine politics except for brief intervals until 1737, governed as despots by manipulating republican institutions, often from behind the scenes. In addition to working with Francesco Sforza to create a balance of power in Italy and prevent French aggression, Cosimo introduced a graduated income tax and curried favor among the lesser guilds and workers. His grandson, Lorenzo the Magnificent (1449–1492), was the object of an assassination plot by the Pazzi family that killed his brother Giuliano while the two were worshiping in the cathedral at Florence in 1478. The plot had the support of Girolamo Riario, Caterina Sforza's husband, as well as Pope Sixtus IV. The pope resented the Medici's alliance with Venice and Milan, which was intended to block the extension of his authority in the northern Papal States. Although the assassination attempt failed, Lorenzo had to defend Florence against an attack by papal and Neapolitan forces. His son Piero was less able, and as a result of territorial concessions made to the French in 1494, he was ousted by the Florentines. Republican government was restored and for four years a spirit of religious frenzy prevailed under the sway of the fiery Dominican Girolamo Savonarola (see Chapter 16). The republic's alliance with France isolated Florence from other Italian states, but in 1512 Pope Julius II persuaded the Florentines to join the Holy League against Louis XII and allow the Medici to return.

Bust of Lorenzo de' Medici by Verrocchio. [National Gallery of Art, Washington, Samuel H. Kress Collection]

VENICE: THE REPUBLIC OF ST. MARK

In sharp contrast to the Florentines and the Milanese, the Venetians enjoyed a remarkable degree of social and political stability, in large measure because the merchant oligarchy that governed the republic was a closed group limited to families listed in the Golden Book. This register of more than 200 names included only families represented in the Great Council prior to 1297. Venice had neither a landed nobility nor a large industrial proletariat to challenge the dominance of its wealthy merchants, and the republic, because of its relative isolation, had not become embroiled in the Guelph-Ghibelline feud that left cities such as Florence with a tradition of bitter factionalism. There was never a successful revolution in Venice.

The Venetian government was a tight-knit affair. The 240 or so merchant oligarchs who sat in the Great Council elected the Senate, the principal legislative body, as well as the ceremonial head of state, called a *doge*, and other government officials. The most powerful body in the state was the annually elected Council of Ten, which met in secret, focused on security, and in an emergency could assume the powers of all other government officials. To the Venetians' credit, the merchant oligarchy disdained despotic rule, thereby maintaining the support of those excluded from the political process.

In the fourteenth and fifteenth centuries the Venetians engaged in a program of expansion that made them a commercial empire. This involved a bitter contest with Genoa for control of trade in the eastern Mediterranean, a struggle that ended with Genoa's defeat in 1380. In the meantime, the Venetians embarked in 1329 on a campaign to acquire territory in northern Italy to assure both an adequate food supply and access to the Alpine trade routes. Conquering such neighboring states as Padua and Verona brought the Venetians face to face with Milan and the Papal States, both of which were also expanding, as well as with the Habsburgs and the Hungarians, who were unsettled by Venetian expansion around the head of the Adriatic. The struggle on the mainland diverted crucial resources from the eastern Mediterranean, where Turkish expansion in the late fifteenth century gravely threatened Venetian interests. More dangerous than the lengthy war with the Turks (1463–1479) was the threat posed to Venice by the League of Cambrai, formed in 1508 and 1509 by Pope Julius II to strip Venice of its territorial acquisitions. Members of the league included Emperor Maximilian, Louis XII, and Ferdinand of Aragon. Although the league

⊕ The Glories of Venice ⊕

The civic pride of the Venetians is manifest in the 1423 deathbed oration of the doge Tommaso Mocenigo, which was delivered to a group of senators.

This our city now sends out in the way of business to different parts of the world ten millions of ducats' worth yearly by ships and galleys, and the profit is not less than two million ducats a year. . . . Every year there go to sea forty-five galleys with eleven thousand sailors, and there are three thousand ship's carpenters and three thousand caulkers. . . . There are one thousand noblemen whose income is from seven hundred to four thousand ducats. If you go on in this manner you will increase from good to better, and you will be the masters of wealth and Christendom; everyone will fear you. But beware . . . of waging unjust war. . . . Everyone knows that the war with the Turks has made you brave and experienced of the sea; you have six generals to fight any great army, and for each of these you have . . . enough [men] to man one hundred galleys; and in these years you have shown distinctly that the world considers you the leaders of Christianity. You have many men experienced in embassies and in the government of cities, who are accomplished orators. You have many doctors of divers sciences, and especially many lawyers, wherefore numerous foreigners come here for judgment of their differences, and abide by your verdicts. You mint coins, every year a million ducats of gold and two hundred thousand of silver. . . . Therefore, be wise in governing such a State.

Source: P. Lauritzen, *Venice: A Thousand Years of Culture and Civilization* (London: Weidenfeld & Nicolson, 1978), p. 87.

---

seized some of Venice's Italian lands, a reprieve came when the pope, increasingly fearful of French ambitions, negotiated peace preparatory to forming the Holy League against France. Venice was still an important state, but Turkish expansion coupled with the discovery of new trade routes to Asia eroded its role as a Mediterranean power.

At the peak of its influence in the fifteenth and early sixteenth centuries, Venice was a city of striking contrasts. The fabulous wealth of the merchant oligarchy was reflected in the palatial houses that lined the Grand Canal, none more glittering than the Ca' d'Oro (1421–1440), with its polychrome marble and gilded paint. Living space in the city was at a premium, hence not even the wealthiest patricians could acquire spacious lots. Away from the Grand Canal there was no special residential district for the merchant oligarchy, whose homes were scattered throughout the city. Venice had its poor, but generally there was employment for them, particularly in the shipbuilding, textile, and fishing industries. Food prices were regulated, and grain was periodically distributed without charge to the needy, but there was considerable reluctance to provide regular relief until 1528, when the city was inundated with refugees because of famine and war. The Venetians traded

in slaves, and some blacks were kept in Venice as household servants, though the slave trade declined as the Turks pushed the Venetians out of the Mediterranean. The Venetians were mostly tolerant of the foreign minorities who settled in the city, but that attitude did not fully extend to the Jews. In the late fourteenth century the Jews of Venice were required to wear yellow badges, and beginning in 1423 they could not own real estate. Finally, in 1516 the Jews were forced to live in a special district known as the ghetto. It was, however, unthinkable to exclude them from the republic, as they had been from Spain, for the community required their medical expertise and their ability to provide funds, particularly in time of war. Venice was more tolerant of the Jews than were other Italian states.

The Holy Roman Empire

The destruction of imperial power in the thirteenth century during the struggle between the Holy Roman Empire and the papacy left Germany badly divided. When the princes ended the Great Interregnum (1254–1273) by placing Rudolf of Habsburg (1273–1291) on the imperial throne, they were not interested in creating a strong centralized government that would diminish their own influence. Although the Habsburgs dreamed of creating a strong dynastic state, their own dominions were limited to Austria, giving them little control over the princes and towns in other regions. The virtual independence of the more powerful princes was confirmed in 1356 when Emperor Charles IV issued the Golden Bull, affirming that the empire was an elective monarchy. Henceforth new emperors were chosen by four hereditary princes, each of whom was virtually sovereign—the count palatine of the Rhine, the duke of Saxony, the margrave of Brandenburg, and the king of Bohemia—and three ecclesiastical princes—the archbishops of Cologne, Mainz, and Trier. In the century and a half that followed, lesser princes emulated the seven electors by establishing a strong degree of authority within their own states, a process that involved them in a struggle with the knights and administrative officials who wanted virtual independence for their fiefs. In Germany the territorial princes triumphed over both the emperor and the knights. Their power was reflected in the Imperial Diet, a representative assembly whose three estates comprised the electoral princes, the lesser princes, and the imperial free cities. Similar assemblies existed in the principalities. The Swiss took advantage of weak imperial authority to organize a confederation of cantons, or districts—13 by the early 1500s—that were essentially independent.

Although Habsburg power within the empire was weak, Maximilian negotiated a series of strategic marriage alliances that vastly increased the family's power. His own marriage to Charles the Bold's daughter, Mary of Burgundy, had led to the acquisition of the Low Countries, and the marriage of his son Philip to Ferdinand and Isabella's daughter Joanna made it possible for Maximilian's grandson Charles to inherit Spain and its possessions. Emperor Charles V (1519–1556) thus ruled the Habsburg lands in Germany, the Low Countries, Spain, Spanish territories in the New World, and the Aragonese kingdom of Naples and Sicily; no larger dominion had existed in Europe since the time of Charlemagne.

Spanish possessions in Italy brought Charles V into a bitter confrontation with the French king, Francis I, who was no less determined to press his own Italian claims. Although Charles was also concerned with the threat of advancing Turkish armies on the Danube, in 1525 he crushed the French at Pavia, near Milan, capturing Francis and forcing him to relinquish both his Italian claims and the duchy of Burgundy. Francis quickly reneged and allied with the Turks, who defeated the Hungarian army at Mohács in 1526. When the major Italian states (except Naples) allied with France in the League of Cognac, the imperial armies again invaded,

THE INHERITANCE OF CHARLES V

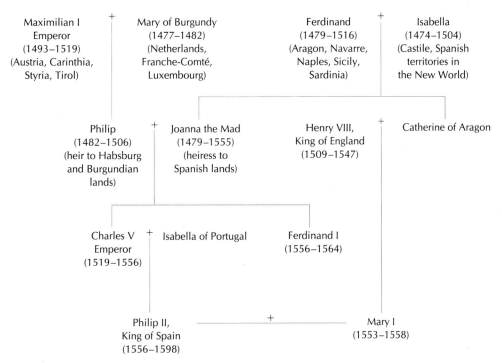

Maximilian I Emperor (1493–1519) (Austria, Carinthia, Styria, Tirol) + Mary of Burgundy (1477–1482) (Netherlands, Franche-Comté, Luxembourg)

Ferdinand (1479–1516) (Aragon, Navarre, Naples, Sicily, Sardinia) + Isabella (1474–1504) (Castile, Spanish territories in the New World)

Philip (1482–1506) (heir to Habsburg and Burgundian lands) + Joanna the Mad (1479–1555) (heiress to Spanish lands)

Henry VIII, King of England (1509–1547) + Catherine of Aragon

Charles V Emperor (1519–1556) + Isabella of Portugal

Ferdinand I (1556–1564)

Philip II, King of Spain (1556–1598) + Mary I (1553–1558)

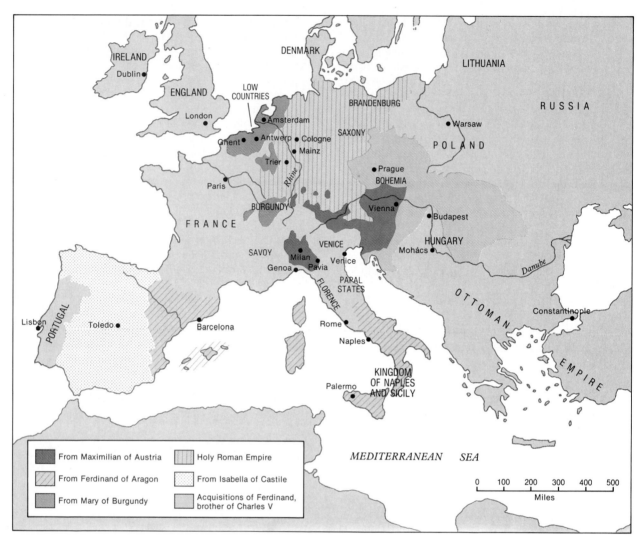

15.4 *The Empire of Charles V*

this time sacking Rome in 1527 when their pay was late, an event that was widely regarded as the major atrocity of the sixteenth century. Louise of Savoy and Margaret of Austria negotiated a peace, the terms of which restored Burgundy to France. A year later, however, Pope Clement VII recognized Habsburg domination in Italy by crowning Charles both emperor and king of Italy, the last time the two crowns were bestowed on the same person. Although Francis renewed the war against Charles twice more (1536–1538, 1542–1544), not even an alliance with the Turks and German Protestant princes was sufficient to achieve a decisive military victory. When the Habsburg-Valois wars finally ended in 1559, Milan and Naples remained under Habsburg control. The Habsburgs, however, had failed to establish a unified state in Germany.

Eastern Europe

Although the Hungarians had developed a reasonably strong state in the 1200s, during the following century they were weakened by a dynastic struggle involving Bavarian, Bohemian, and Angevin claimants; the Angevins triumphed with the support of the papacy. There were further problems due to the frequent absences of King Sigismund (1387–1437) from the country, partly because of his campaigns against the Turks and partly because of his responsibilities as Holy Roman Emperor (1433–1437). In 1458 the nobles gave the crown to Matthias Corvinus (1458–1490), son of the great military leader János Hunyadi, who had successfully repulsed the Turks. Matthias increased royal authority through administrative and judicial reforms, higher taxes, and the creation of a standing army. Abroad he used Hungary's new power to conquer Bohemia, Moravia, and Austria. Following his death, however, a disputed succession enabled Maximilian to regain Austria and to bring Hungary into the imperial orbit by two dynastic marriages involving his grandchildren, Mary and Ferdinand. The nobles subsequently took advantage of weak rulers to disband the standing army. As in Germany, the real struggle in Hungary then took place between the magnates and the lesser nobility. Although the latter won their claim to equality in the eyes of the law, in practice the magnates were dominant.

Poland was an immense state—the largest in Europe after its union with Lithuania in the late 1300s—but it too failed to establish a strong central government. The position of the nobles was enhanced when King John Albert (1492–1501), in need of funds, allowed a national diet composed only of nobles to impose taxes on the towns and peasants. His successor accepted a statute requiring the diet's approval of all new legislation, further eroding royal authority. Although Sigismund II (1548–1572) allied with the lesser nobles in order to curtail the power of the magnates, his death without an heir enabled the nobles to assert their right to elect a successor. Henceforth Poland was in fact as well as in theory an elective monarchy in which real power rested in the hands of the nobility.

Politically, the fifteenth and early sixteenth centuries were a major watershed in European history. The failure of the Italians, Germans, Hungarians, and Poles to establish strong centralized states left them vulnerable to their neighbors and a perpetual source of temptation to expansionist-minded states. In contrast, the newly unified states of western Europe found themselves in an excellent position to take advantage of the economic possibilities opened up by *the great voyages of discovery. It took the combined economic and military resources of these states to prosper in the expanding global trade. Nevertheless, although the Italian states failed to unify, their impressive economic growth, historical tradition, and sense of civic independence enabled them to provide intellectual and cultural leadership for Europe in the Renaissance.*

Notes

1. R. S. Gottfried, *The Black Death: Natural and Human Disaster in Medieval Europe* (New York: Free Press, 1983), p. 36.
2. M. W. Dols, *The Black Death in the Middle East* (Princeton, N.J.: Princeton University Press, 1977), p. 113.

Suggestions for Further Reading

Allmand, C. *The Hundred Years' War: England and France at War, c. 1300–c. 1450.* Cambridge: Cambridge University Press, 1988.

Barraclough, G. *The Origins of Modern Germany.* New York: Norton, 1984.

Becker, M. B. *Florence in Transition,* 2 vols. Baltimore: Johns Hopkins University Press, 1967–1968.

Contamine, P. *War in the Middle Ages,* trans. M. Jones. New York: Blackwell, 1984.

Crummey, R. O. *The Formation of Muscovy, 1304–1613.* New York: Longman, 1987.

Dollinger, P. *The German Hansa,* trans. D. S. Ault and S. H. Steinberg. Stanford, Calif.: Stanford University Press, 1970.

Dols, M. W. *The Black Death in the Middle East.* Princeton, N.J.: Princeton University Press, 1977.

Gillingham, J. *The Wars of the Roses: Peace and Conflict in Fifteenth-Century England.* London: Weidenfeld & Nicolson, 1981.

Goodman, A. *A History of England from Edward II to James I.* New York: Longman, 1977.

Gottfried, R. S. *The Black Death: Natural and Human Disaster in Medieval Europe.* New York: Free Press, 1983.

Guenee, B. *States and Rulers in Later Medieval Europe,* trans. J. Vale. Oxford: Blackwell, 1985.

Hale, J. R. *Florence and the Medici: The Pattern of Control.* London: Thames & Hudson, 1977.

Hay, D. *Europe in the Fourteenth and Fifteenth Centuries,* 2nd ed. New York: Longman, 1989.

Holmes, G. *Europe: Hierarchy and Revolt, 1320–1450.* New York: Harper & Row, 1975.

Hook, J. *Lorenzo de' Medici.* London: Hamilton, 1984.

Huizinga, J. *The Waning of the Middle Ages*. Garden City, N.Y.: Doubleday, 1954.

Kenny, A. J. P. *Wyclif*. New York: Oxford University Press, 1985.

Lane, F. C. *Venice: A Maritime Republic*. Baltimore: Johns Hopkins University Press, 1973.

Larner, J. *Italy in the Age of Dante and Petrarch, 1216–1380*. New York: Longman, 1980.

Leff, G. *The Dissolution of the Medieval Outlook: An Essay on Intellectual and Spiritual Change in the Fifteenth Century*. New York: New York University Press, 1976.

McNeill, W. H. *Plagues and Peoples*. Garden City, N.Y.: Anchor/Doubleday, 1976.

Mollat, M., and Wolff, P. *The Popular Revolutions of the Late Middle Ages*, trans. A. L. Lytton-Sells. London: Allen & Unwin, 1973.

Post, R. R. *The Modern Devotion*. Leiden: Brill, 1968.

Renouard, Y. *The Avignon Papacy, 1305–1403*, trans. D. Bethell. London: Faber & Faber, 1970.

Swanson, R. N. *Church and Society in Late Medieval Europe*. Oxford: Blackwell, 1989.

Tierney, B. *Foundations of the Conciliar Theory*. Cambridge: Cambridge University Press, 1955.

Vale, M. *The Angevin Legacy and the Hundred Years' War, 1250–1340*. Oxford: Blackwell, 1990.

Waley, D. *The Italian City-Republics*, 3rd ed. New York: Longman, 1988.

———. *Later Medieval Europe from Saint Louis to Luther*, 2nd ed. New York: Longman, 1985.

Wood, C. T. *Joan of Arc and Richard III: Sex, Saints, and Government in the Middle Ages*. New York: Oxford University Press, 1988.

CHAPTER 16

New Horizons: The European Renaissance

The social, political, and economic developments of the Renaissance era described in Chapter 15 were most apparent in the changes they wrought on the culture of the Middle Ages: a fresh approach to the heritage of "pagan" antiquity and a new attempt to blend its values with those of Christianity; the rise of court- and city-sponsored scholars known as humanists, whose espousal of ancient values was linked to the secularization of political power; and a new style in the arts that reflected these changes. At the heart of the cultural renaissance was a shift in the way some people viewed themselves, based on a fresh evaluation of the legacy of classical antiquity. Yet the new intellectual and artistic expression of the Renaissance remained deeply rooted in the past and coexisted with a centuries-old medieval vision. Construction of the largest Gothic cathedral in Italy was still under way in Milan in the mid-1490s when

Petrarch is usually recognized as the first of the Renaissance humanists. [Marburg/Art Resource]

Leonardo da Vinci, working nearby, painted the Last Supper. By then the new developments in thought, education, and the arts we call the Renaissance had been developing for a century and a half. Interpreting the Renaissance has always posed a special but intriguing challenge to students of history, particularly in light of the fact that no comparable phenomenon occurred in the advanced Asian societies, which enjoyed cultural continuity.

The Urban Setting of the Renaissance

The Renaissance originated in fourteenth- and fifteenth-century Italy, which, unlike the rest of Europe, had an essentially urban culture. In Italian towns, where wealth was crucial in establishing one's social status, the emergent capitalists increasingly sought to patronize persons of intellectual and aesthetic talent, partly as a demonstration of piety, partly as an indication of cultural refinement, and partly as a manifestation of civic pride. When these conditions combined in Florence with a special sense of civic and historical awareness, particularly of the value of humanistic ideals as a unifying element in the face of external dangers from rival city-states, the stage was set for the Renaissance.

It is easy to understand why the Renaissance, inspired by the classical world, should have begun in Italy, with its abundance of classical monuments; but at first glance it is somewhat more difficult to explain why it developed first in Florence. Unlike Rome, Florence had few classical remains, nor did it possess the advantages of a port and a maritime economy like Genoa and Venice, which might bring it into contact with new currents of thought. The Venetians enjoyed not only a lucrative trade with the eastern Mediterranean but also close cultural ties with the Greeks. Even Milan was better situated because of its strategic position for trans-Alpine trade.

Florence's principal advantage was its location astride the trade route between Rome and the north, a route familiar to the many pilgrims who flocked to the Holy City. Because of its location, Florence was coveted by the expansionist Visconti rulers in Milan, and Florentine efforts to preserve the independence of their city fostered civic pride and a stronger awareness of their historical heritage. In turn, their interest in Greek and Roman politics reinforced their fascination with classical ethics, literature, and education. Writers and artists tested themselves against Roman models, hoping to find in a glorious past the inspiration to meet the challenges of the present. The humanists, moreover, saw themselves as living in a postmedieval world, reuniting themselves with the ancient world. In so doing, they created the notion of the thousand-year Middle Ages.

❧ FLORENCE: A PANORAMA

The thirteenth century had been one of economic growth for Florence, especially in the fields of finance and textiles. Florentines established themselves as the preeminent bankers of Europe as well as tax collectors for the papacy. Using wool imported from England and Spain, they manufactured high-quality cloth for the markets of western Europe and the eastern Mediterranean. Two major catastrophes in the fourteenth century—the bankruptcies caused when King Edward III of England repudiated his debts and the devastation of the plague—failed to destroy the city's determination to prosper. Its economy was organized around 21 guilds, of which the most important were the wool manufacturers, the wool finishers, the silk manufacturers, and the bankers.

The political, social, and economic life of the city was dominated by the patricians, whose wealth enabled them to purchase land and contract marriages with the landed aristocracy, thus expanding the city's sway over the countryside. As we saw in Chapter 15, the traditional aristocracy had been ousted from its domination of the city by the great guilds in 1293, but in the late fourteenth century the guilds were in turn challenged by an alliance of artisans, shopkeepers, and owners of small businesses. Throughout this period of turmoil the patricians and guilds patronized humanists and artists, in part to encourage civic unity. When the conservative patricians feuded among themselves in the 1430s, a faction led by Cosimo de' Medici triumphed, leaving the Medici family in control of Florence for the rest of the Renaissance era, except for the brief republican periods in 1494–1512 and 1527–1530. Even during these periods the Medici continued to support scholars and artists.

Florence underwent striking changes during the Renaissance period. Located on the banks of the Arno River—torrential in the winter, a trickle in the summer—the city was surrounded by fertile fields and picturesque hills. Beyond them to the north lay the Apennines, while Pisa and the sea lay down the Arno to the west. The city had the appearance of a walled forest, particularly after the last of its three walls was erected between 1284 and 1328. Nearly 40 feet high and 6 feet thick, the outer wall had 73 towers and was surrounded by a moat. By the mid-1200s there were over 275 other towers and tall buildings within the city, partly because of the need for space but mostly because towers were symbols of aristocratic power as well as refuges during the vendettas that plagued Italian society. Some towers were as high

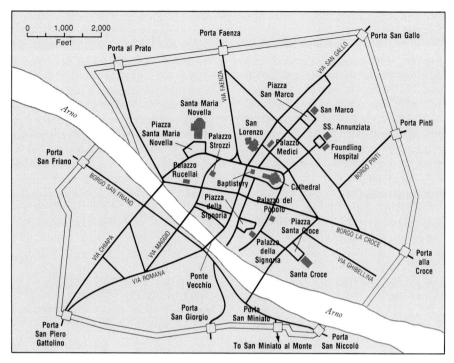

16.1 *The Florence of the Medici*

as 230 feet, roughly the equivalent of a modern 20-story building. On the eve of the Renaissance the towers were reduced in size when the patricians, who dominated the urban economy, triumphed over their landed aristocratic rivals. From the late thirteenth century the more substantial homes were built for merchants with different needs and tastes. The great fire of 1304, the result of feuding between rival Guelph factions, destroyed some 1,700 houses and resulted in a major rebuilding effort. After the bubonic plague killed 50,000 of the city's 80,000 inhabitants in the mid-1300s, recovery was slow, and by 1500 Florence had only grown to between 50,000 and 70,000 inhabitants, or roughly half the size of Venice and Milan.[1]

Well into the Renaissance period Florence's main buildings made it visually a Gothic city. The great cathedral, begun in 1296, was Tuscan Gothic, apart from the innovative dome added in the fifteenth century, which heralded the beginning of Renaissance architecture. The cathedral manifested civic pride and reflected Florence's rivalry with Pisa and Siena, each of which was also building a cathedral. The Florentines were determined to exceed the greatest classical monuments:

The Florentine Republic, soaring ever above the conception of the most competent judges, desires that an edifice should be constructed so magnificent in its height and in its beauty that it shall surpass anything of the kind pro-

duced in the time of their greatest power by the Greeks and Romans.[2]

Two of Florence's most beautiful churches, Santa Croce and Santa Maria Novella, were rebuilt in the Gothic style by the Franciscans and Dominicans, respectively, in the 1200s. The two major palaces, the Palazzo del Pòpolo and the Palazzo della Signoria, are also Gothic and fortresslike in appearance. Erected in 1255, the former (now called the Bargello) was the residence of the captain of the people, who commanded armed societies representing the people's interests during periods when they exercised political dominance over the nobility. The Palazzo del Pòpolo was also a meeting place for the city's councils. The Palazzo della Signoria (commonly known as the Palazzo Vecchio, or "old palace") was begun in 1299 to house the guild representatives who governed the city. The palaces and chapels constructed during the Renaissance contrast sharply with the Gothic structures, symbolizing a new outlook and a changing set of values.

The Patronage of Arts and Letters

Support for humanists and artists in the Renaissance came principally from guilds and religious brotherhoods, the state, and wealthy families and oligarchs.

Clergymen and merchants of more modest means also provided some backing, but their support appears to have had no significant impact on the development of the new scholarship and artistic styles. Persons with newly acquired wealth patronized artists and scholars as a means of demonstrating their status and enhancing their reputation. This meant commissions for painters to depict religious themes that incorporated portraits of the donors, for architects to design funeral chapels, and for sculptors to create impressive tombs.

As guild and civic patronage declined in the early fifteenth century due to an economic recession, families and individuals increasingly supported artists, writers, and scholars, thus increasing the scope for innovative themes and styles, particularly ones that reflected the values and interests of the patrons. All of this helped improve the artists' own social and economic status. In the medieval period they were commonly regarded as mere artisans, but by the early sixteenth century some artists had become well-to-do. The best known were much in demand, and a highly sophisticated appreciation had developed of their individual styles and talents. Some became famous and acquired a wide following, thus inaugurating the modern Western cult of the artist. Giorgio Vasari recorded anecdotes about them and facts about their careers in his book of biographical sketches, *The Lives of the Painters*. Florence, with its status-conscious patricians, its deep-rooted civic pride, its historical interest in classical Rome, and its willingness to embrace new concepts and styles, became the first setting for the Renaissance.

Before long, Rome and Milan also became important centers of patronage. Because the economy of Rome relied for the most part on the papacy, it had suffered a period of decline when the popes and their vast bureaucracy resided at Avignon. Without major manufacturing and removed from the principal trade routes, Rome stagnated economically, its population declined, and its government proved unable to control the lawless. The early-fifteenth-century popes thus had their hands full trying to restore order, though prosperity returned with the papal administration. Pope Nicholas V (1447–1455), himself a humanist, used church funds to beautify the city. Papal patronage brought Renaissance painters such as Fra Angelico (1387–1455) to Rome from Tuscany, sponsored the philologist Lorenzo Valla (1405–1457), and established a major library of classical authors. With Pope Sixtus IV (1471–1484) and his nephew, Pope Julius II (1503–1513), providing patronage to the greatest artists of their age, Rome supplanted Florence as the heart of the Renaissance during Julius' pontificate.

The Renaissance spread to Venice under strikingly different circumstances. The Venetian merchant oligarchy, primarily concerned with affairs of the republic and lucrative foreign trade, was still heavily influenced by Byzantine taste in the fourteenth and early fifteenth centuries. Because merchants returning from the Middle East brought art objects for St. Mark's Cathedral, the styles of the eastern Mediterranean were familiar. Byzantine mosaics adorned the interior of St. Mark's as well as the churches of neighboring Ravenna. Nevertheless, Renaissance ideals began to make headway as Florentine artists worked in nearby Padua, which the Venetians dominated politically, and as humanists won the support of the Venetian Senate for their printing press. Two technical developments—the introduction of oil-based paints from the Flemings about 1475 and the use of canvas—were important to the development of Renaissance painting. The new canvases were far more adaptable to the humid Venetian climate than the traditional wood or plaster and thus could readily be used to decorate religious and civic buildings. The Senate, churches, and charitable societies patronized painters such as Giovanni Bellini (c. 1430–1516) and his family. In Venice the Renaissance adapted to the merchant oligarchy's luxurious tastes and fondness for pageantry, thereby setting a rather different course from the Renaissance in Florence and Rome.

The Humanists

The bond that knit humanists together was a commitment to study classical literary texts for their own sake rather than as handmaidens to Christian theology. The goal of such study, basic to the Renaissance, was nothing less than the revitalization of political, social, and religious institutions through the infusion of classical values. Humanists were engaged not in sponsoring a rebirth of the classics but in reorienting their approach toward them. An awareness of the thought and art of classical antiquity had never been completely lost in the medieval period and in fact had grown substantially since the late eleventh century. The reorientation that began in the 1300s entailed a shift in emphasis from the study of theology and metaphysics to the study of grammar, rhetoric, poetry, ethics, and history.

The humanists generally espoused two basic ideals: reverence for the full scope of "pagan" as well as Christian antiquity and belief in the distinctiveness of the individual, though the civic humanists of the early fifteenth century tended to subordinate the individual to the city-state. In contrast to the medieval tendency to seek virtue through solitude, the humanists sought virtue in the public sphere. Although Italian humanists focused almost exclusively on secular things, and some even assumed a personal attitude of religious skepticism, most remained traditional Catholics. Their interest in pagan literature gave way to a concern for early biblical and patristic literature, especially north of the Alps, where they were determined to blend humanistic and Christian concerns. Many Italian humanists deemphasized ritual and sacrament. Instead they stressed such temporal concerns as the performance of civic duties, the fulfillment of which brought a civic renown that pushed the medieval quest for spiritual immortality into the shadows.

The Age of Petrarch

The earliest humanists addressed the needs of the social groups that emerged triumphant in the political struggles within the Italian city-states in the fourteenth century. As these groups consolidated their hold on power, they were ready to embrace a new psychological consciousness oriented largely toward worldly ends rather than the otherworldly ideals that had dominated the medieval outlook. The humanists provided the flattering self-image the patricians sought by praising the worth of the individual, the dignity of political affairs, secular accomplishments, and even the pursuit of personal glory. The success of the humanists was directly related to the existence of a responsive audience of the social and po-

litical elite, an audience warmly receptive to the humanist use of eloquence to validate the lifestyle and public role of the patriciate.

The most prominent of the early Renaissance humanists, Petrarch (Francesco Petrarca, 1304–1374), son of a political exile from Florence, gave up the study of law to devote himself to a public literary career, a vocation that he virtually invented. Fascinated by classical antiquity, he wrote biographies of famous Romans and composed *Africa*, a Latin epic in the style of the *Aeneid* to honor the Roman general Scipio Africanus. He even penned letters to his classical heroes—Horace, Livy, Virgil, and especially Cicero—and published them as *Letters to the Ancient Dead*. His best-known work is a charming collection of love sonnets in Italian to Laura, a married woman in Avignon. For more than 20 years he idealized her, always from a distance, until she died in the plague in 1348. Although much of Petrarch's work was secular, he made some efforts to harmonize classical and Christian teachings. Cicero's Stoic concepts, he thought, were compatible with the Gospel, and he used a series of dialogues with St. Augustine to explore his own feelings of sin and guilt. Contemptuous of both scholastics and the uneducated, committed to the criti-

◉ Petrarch on Petrarch ◉

As an elderly man, Petrarch pondered his life and the values of a humanist. Like many humanists, he developed a strong interest in religion in his later years.

I have always possessed an extreme contempt for wealth; not that riches are not desirable in themselves, but because I hate the anxiety and care which are invariably associated with them. . . . Nothing displeases me more than display, for not only is it bad in itself and opposed to humility, but it is troublesome and distracting. . . .

The greatest kings of this age have loved and courted me. They may know why; I certainly do not. With some of them I was on such terms that they seemed in a certain sense my guests rather than I theirs. . . . I fled, however, from many of those to whom I was greatly attached; and such was my innate longing for liberty that I studiously avoided those whose very name seemed incompatible with the freedom that I loved.

I possessed a well-balanced rather than a keen intellect—one prone to all kinds of good and wholesome study, but especially inclined to moral philosophy and the art of poetry. The latter, indeed, I neglected as time went on, and took delight in sacred literature. Finding in that a hidden sweetness which I had once esteemed but lightly, I came to regard the works of the poets as only amenities.

Among the many subjects that interested me, I dwelt especially upon antiquity, for our own age has always repelled me, so that, had it not been for the love of those dear to me, I should have preferred to have been born in any other period than our own.

Source: F. A. Ogg, ed., *A Source Book of Mediaeval History* (New York: American Book Company, 1907), pp. 471–472.

cal study of manuscripts, and concerned about his reputation with posterity, Petrarch was an exemplar for later humanists.

Petrarch's divergence from an essentially medieval outlook is evident when he is compared with the greatest figure of the previous generation, Dante Alighieri (1265–1321). Exiled from Florence with Petrarch's father, Dante foreshadowed one aspect of the Renaissance by using vernacular Italian for his masterpiece, *The Divine Comedy*. Petrarch subsequently expressed the ideal of a unified Italian motherland in the poem *Italia mia* ("My Italy"). But Dante's *Divine Comedy* more closely reflects the spirit of Thomas Aquinas' *Summa Theologica* than the ideals of the humanists. Its three-line stanzas symbolizing the Trinity, its treatment of the present life as a preparation for eternity, and its traditional interpretation of sins and virtues are evocations of the medieval world. The subordinate role of classical knowledge in Dante's scheme is apparent when Virgil, after guiding Dante through hell and purgatory, is replaced for the journey through paradise by Beatrice, a symbol of revelation. Beatrice also figures prominently in Dante's *Vita nuova* ("New Life"), his spiritual autobiography. Unlike Petrarch's love for Laura, which is intensely personal and secular, Dante's lifelong passion for Beatrice is symbolic of Christ's love for his church. The two types of love reflect the difference between the medieval and Renaissance outlooks.

Petrarch's friend and student, Giovanni Boccaccio (1313–1375), is remembered for his *Decameron,* a collection of 100 short stories related by ten young people who fled the plague that ravaged Florence in 1348. The racy tales were mostly borrowed from classical, medieval, and Eastern sources. Unlike Geoffrey Chaucer, who used some of the same material in *The Canterbury Tales*, Boccaccio gave his work a more secular flavor by omitting the usual moral commentary. Boccaccio's most substantive work, an encyclopedia of classical mythology titled *Genealogy of the Gods*, maintains the medieval fascination with allegory but is humanistic in its praise of poetry and its assertion that learning remakes the natu-

ral person into the civil person. Like other humanists, Boccaccio was convinced that he was part of a new age, for Petrarch, he said, had "cleansed the fount of Helicon," the abode of the mythical classical muses, "swampy with mud and rushes, restoring its waters to their former purity."[3]

Civic Humanists

The second stage of humanism, which lasted from approximately 1375 to 1460, was staunchly committed to the proposition that humanistic scholarship must be brought to bear on public affairs. Cicero, one of the humanists' heroes, had after all been an active statesman in the Roman republic. Civic humanists held community service in high regard as a justification for the positions and privileges of the patriciate. Learning thus became a tool to benefit society as well as a means to assert political influence. Taking note of their predecessors' interest in rhetoric, the civic humanists extolled it as the basis for a new standard of nobility to which patricians were urged to aspire. Rhetoric, which entailed not only eloquence but also the application of knowledge to specific problems, could reputedly preserve society and mold good citizens by making law and morality effective. Eloquence became a way of life, as relevant to princes and ruling elites as to poets and teachers, not least because it made possible a strong degree of self-confidence.

The civic humanists espoused a belief in political liberty for a broadly defined elite and in civic patriotism, which in Florence involved a concerted attempt to preserve the city's freedom from Milanese aggression. In the late fourteenth and early fifteenth centuries Florence had three chancellors who were civic humanists: Coluccio Salutati, Leonardo Bruni, and Poggio Bracciolini. During his 31-year chancellorship, Salutati, a disciple of Petrarch, boasted that Florence was the "mother of freedom," a theme echoed by Bruni and Poggio. Bruni's *History of Florence* was written in the conviction that history involves the use of examples to teach philosophy and

HIGHLIGHTS OF THE ITALIAN RENAISSANCE

	Philosophical influences	Letters	Arts
Early Humanists (1325–1375)		• Petrarch • Boccaccio	• Giotto
Civic Humanists (1375–1460)		• Bruni • Vergerio • Christine de Pisan	• Masaccio • Ghiberti • Donatello
Neoplatonists, Machiavelli, Guicciardini (1460–1576)		• Ficino • Pico • Castiglione • Vittoria Colonna	• Botticelli • Leonardo da Vinci • Raphael • Michelangelo • Titian

that "the careful study of the past enlarges our foresight in contemporary affairs." The political liberty extolled by the civic humanists was never fully realized in Renaissance Florence, however, and such liberty as did exist was sharply reduced after Cosimo de' Medici began to dominate city politics in 1434. Faced with the realities of the Medici oligarchy, which effectively undermined constitutional government, the humanists accepted Medici patronage and generally retreated from the political arena to their scholarship and contemplation.

The Florentine Academy and the Neoplatonists

The decline of the civic humanists and the flowering of Neoplatonism in late-fifteenth-century Florence marked the beginning of humanism's third stage. Instead of a primary concern with the problems and duties of civil life and a preoccupation with such works as Aristotle's *Ethics* and Plutarch's *Lives*, interest shifted to Plato and the ideal of the contemplative life. The seeds of this transformation had been planted in the 1390s when the Greek scholar Manuel Chrysoloras taught Greek in the city; among his pupils was the civic humanist Bruni. Bruni subsequently translated Plato and other classical and Christian authors. Greek studies received a further impetus in 1439 when hundreds of Greeks came to Ferrara and Florence to attend an ecumenical council. At the urging of one of them, Cosimo de' Medici eventually endowed an academy near Florence in 1462. The academy provided the setting for philosophical discussions presided over by Marsilio Ficino (1433–1499). The atmosphere was semireligious: the disciples sang hymns praising Plato, burned a lamp before his bust, and adopted as their motto "Salvation in Plato." Ficino himself prepared editions of the works of Plato and Plotinus.

Renaissance Neoplatonism was a fascinating, eclectic mixture of ideas from classical thought, Christian dogma, and astrology. Ficino and his followers stressed the uniqueness of humankind, including personal worth and dignity as well as the power to transform oneself spiritually by choosing the good. Above all, each person was free, though one's sphere of action was circumscribed by the stars. Those who chose to pursue the higher things of life aspired to the release of their souls from the perishable world of matter. The Neoplatonic ideal was otherworldly; the Neoplatonic experience, emotional. Neoplatonism's moving force was love, and its direction was the rational life. To know God was the ultimate goal, attainable only by separating from the material world. The Neoplatonists were deeply sensitive to beauty, which they intimately associated with truth and goodness, all of which were earthly manifestations of Platonic forms. The Neoplatonic love of symbolic allegory, Christian mysticism, and beauty made the philos-

ophy attractive to such Renaissance artists as Botticelli, Raphael, and Michelangelo.

Through their eclectic, mystical philosophy, the Florentine Neoplatonists effectively moved beyond the range of traditional humanists. The latter's shift of emphasis from metaphysics to ethics was reversed by the Neoplatonists, but without returning to the traditional and orthodox philosophical views of the medieval scholastics. The Neoplatonists also broke with the civic humanists by turning their backs on public affairs and the campaign for political freedom—perhaps a prudent choice in the treacherous political atmosphere of Medici Florence. Nevertheless, something of the original humanist ideal remained in their respect for human dignity and the freedom to choose one's destiny. This ideal was expressed most eloquently in the *Oration on the Dignity of Man* by Ficino's disciple, Pico della Mirandola (1463–1494). Drawing on his vast reading in Jewish, Christian, and Arabic works, the erudite Pico accorded humans a special rank in the universal chain of being where they could ponder the plan of the universe and marvel at its beauty. Although Renaissance Neoplatonism was quietist in its avoidance of political activism, it was nevertheless radical in its rejection of church hierarchy in favor of an emphasis on individual enlightenment.

Education and Scholarship

The central goal of a humanist education was to develop the virtuous individual, one who would live a moral, disciplined life not only for personal enrichment but also for the benefit of society. This education, however, was intended for the socially elite, not commoners. A number of humanists urged major changes in the educational curriculum, particularly at the secondary level, in order to accomplish this end. An education focusing on the humanities was deemed to have the greatest practical relevance for daily living because it addressed the whole person. The humanist ideal in education was neatly summarized by Pietro Paolo Vergerio (1370–1444), a student of Chrysoloras and a friend of Bruni:

> We call those studies *liberal* which are worthy of a free man; those studies by which we attain and practice virtue and wisdom; that education which calls forth, trains, and develops those highest gifts of body and of mind which ennoble men, and which are rightly judged to rank next in dignity to virtue only. . . . Amongst these [studies] I accord the first place to history, on grounds both of its attractiveness and of its utility.[4]

For the humanists virtue entailed not only the fundamental principles of morality but also an ethical ideal that encompassed both self-determination and an awareness of personal worth. Vergerio and his colleagues drew extensively on classical authors such as Quintilian in developing this concept of a humanist education.

One of the leading Renaissance educators, Vergerio's friend Vittorino da Feltre (died 1446), established a model secondary school at Mantua called the Happy House. Scholarships enabled the children of the poor to attend, and unlike many other schools girls were welcome. The curriculum included the humanities, religion, mathematics, drawing, and physical education—riding, fencing, swimming, and martial skills. Appropriate attention was given to proper diet and dress, so that education was concerned with the whole of life.

The ideas of the humanist educators are reflected in the Renaissance's most influential handbook of manners, *The Book of the Courtier* (1527) by Baldassare Castiglione (1478–1529). Deliberately limited in scope as a guide for aristocrats in the service of their prince, the book depicts the ideal courtier as someone knowledgeable in Greek, Latin, and the vernacular. His accomplishments would also range from music and poetry to dancing and sports. In sharp contrast to the image of a courtier as a hard-drinking, arrogant swordsman, Castiglione's courtier is a well-mannered, cultivated, and versatile gentleman, as much at home in the salon and the concert chamber as in the halls of power. The courtier, moreover, must be an educator—not of young people but of the prince, who must be taught the ways of virtue, especially temperance. Many of the same qualities are to be found in the aristocratic lady who, said Castiglione, should be adorned with "admirable accomplishments." Nevertheless, she was to shun "manly" sports such as riding and tennis as well as musical instruments that required ungainly physical effort, such as trumpets, fifes, and drums. While Castiglione idealized women as objects of courtly love, in practice he expected them to maintain an appropriate degree of subservience to men. *The Book of the Courtier* was immensely influential throughout Europe and was still widely consulted as a guide to aristocratic bearing in the eighteenth century. It marked a turning point in the refinement of manners that left a permanent mark on the European upper classes.

Another fundamental concern of the humanists was the search for accurate texts from classical Greece and Rome. This quest encouraged the humanists to ransack archives to find as many early manuscripts as possible. To produce good texts they had to develop critical tools, especially philology (the study of the origins of language), paleography (the study of ancient manuscripts), and textual criticism. Lorenzo Valla used the principles of textual criticism to demonstrate that the eighth-

---

◉ Aristocratic Women ◉

Baldassare Castiglione's Book of the Courtier *reflects the humanist interest in shaping the aristocratic woman to please the men. Note here how the courtier is expected to teach her as well as to revel in her beauty.*

Many faculties of the mind are as necessary to woman as to man; likewise gentle birth, to avoid affectation, to be naturally graceful in all her doings, to be mannerly, clever, prudent, not arrogant, not envious, not slanderous, not vain, not quarrelsome, not silly, to know how to win and keep the favor of her mistress and of all others, to practice well and gracefully the exercises that befit women. . . . Beauty is more necessary to her than to the courtier, for in truth that woman lacks much who lacks beauty. Then, too, she ought to be more circumspect and take greater care not to give occasion for evil being said of her. . . .

Let him obey, please and honor his lady with all reverence, and hold her dearer than himself, and prefer her convenience and pleasures to his own, and love in her not less the beauty of mind than of body. Therefore let him take care not to leave her to fall into any kind of error, but by admonition and good advice let him always seek to lead her on to modesty, to temperance, to true chastity. . . .

In such fashion will our courtier be most acceptable to his lady, and she will always show herself obedient, sweet and affable to him, and as desirous of pleasing him as of being loved by him.

Source: B. Castiglione, *The Book of the Courtier,* trans. L. E. Opdycke (New York: Scribner, 1901), passim.

century Donation of Constantine was a forgery. Some experts already suspected that this document, by which Emperor Constantine (died 337) allegedly endowed the papacy with vast lands, was fraudulent, but Valla laid any doubt to rest by demonstrating that it contained language and references unknown in Constantine's day. His exposure of the Donation was a triumphant exhibition of the powers of humanist scholarship in challenging tradition and the political authority that rested on it.

Valla also used his command of classical languages to prove that there were errors in the official version of the Bible, the Latin Vulgate. Because of his belief in the supremacy of faith over reason, however, his loyalty to the church was not shaken. Thanks to the patronage of Pope Nicholas V (1447–1455), himself a humanist, he was even appointed apostolic secretary. Valla's application of philological and historical techniques to the Donation and the Vulgate provided the foundation for major advances in textual criticism in the sixteenth century, particularly in the field of biblical scholarship, as reflected in the work of Desiderius Erasmus.

Humanists Outside Italy

The ideals of the Italian humanists were carried beyond the Alps in the late fifteenth century by students, scholars, and merchants. The rapid development of the printing industry, particularly in the Rhineland cities, also facilitated the spread of humanist scholarship. The great pioneers were the German Peter Luder (c. 1415–1474), a hard-drinking poet whose insistence on the importance of classics in the curriculum helped make the University of Heidelberg a leading center of humanist thought, and the Dutchman Rudolf Agricola (c. 1443–1485). After spending ten years in Italy, where he was deeply influenced by Petrarch's writings, Agricola gathered a group of humanist disciples at Heidelberg. His goal was to surpass the Italians in classical learning, wresting from "haughty Italy the reputation for classical expression which it has nearly monopolized . . . and aim to it ourselves." His wide-ranging interests extended from philosophy and Greek to mining, a subject on which he wrote a treatise.

In England, too, the humanists carried their message to the universities. Both William Grocyn (c. 1466–1519), who lectured at Oxford, and Thomas Linacre (c. 1460–1524), who taught at Cambridge and was interested in classical medicine, had studied in Florence. Among Grocyn's friends were three of the greatest humanists of the sixteenth century, his pupil Thomas More, John Colet, and Erasmus (all discussed in Chapter 17). The English were also acquainted with humanist ideals through the presence of Italian scholars at the royal court. Other Italian humanists took their views to the courts of Spain, Hungary, and Poland, where the University of Cracow achieved eminence as a center of humanist studies.

Humanist ideas had already begun to penetrate France before its armies invaded Italy in 1494, but the military adventure heightened interest in Italian scholarship and the arts. Early French humanists such as Guillaume Budé (1468–1540) and Lefèvre d'Étaples (1455–1536) knew Greek and had varied interests. In addition to writing about Byzantine law and ancient coinage, Budé persuaded King Francis I to found a library at Fontainebleau, the origin of the famous Bibliothèque Nationale in Paris. Lefèvre, who had studied at Florence and Padua, was noted for philological and biblical studies, particularly his *Commentary on the Epistles of St. Paul*. His emphasis on grace, faith, and predestination may have influenced the Protestant reformer John Calvin, though Lefèvre never left the Catholic church.

The literary accomplishments of the French humanists are exemplified by Marguerite d'Angoulême (1492–1549), sister of Francis I, and François Rabelais (c. 1495–1553), successively a Franciscan friar, a Benedictine monk, and a secular priest and medical doctor. Marguerite's prolific writing ranged from poetry to religious treatises, but her most famous work was the *Heptaméron*, a collection of 70 short, racy stories akin to Boccaccio's *Decameron*. Rabelais' *Gargantua* and *Pantagruel*, tales about giants enamored of life and drinking, offer a satirical portrait of sixteenth-century society peppered with humanist insights about the human condition. Gargantua's advice to his son Pantagruel is a fitting summary of the humanists' exhortation to their disciples: "I urge you to spend your youth making the most of your studies and developing your moral sense."

Women and Renaissance Culture

More than 30 women humanists of the Renaissance have been identified, though few wrote major works. This was probably due more to social barriers than to a lack of creative talent. Women almost never attended a university. They thus had no opportunity to enter the learned professions, although there was a female doctor of medicine at Salerno, Italy, in 1422. Women humanists typically acquired their education from their fathers or from private tutors, which effectively eliminated all but those of princely, aristocratic, or patrician status. During the early Renaissance their intellectual careers were confined to their late teens and early twenties if they opted to marry, for marital obligations and spousal pressure made intellectual commitments extremely difficult. The advent of printing, however, provided literate women with the opportunity to pursue a variety of studies, including medicine, religion, and the classics—a devel-

After Christine de Pisan's husband died when she was only 25, she supported herself and her three children as a writer. Among her patrons were Philip the Bold, duke of Burgundy, and Queen Isabella of Bavaria. [Bavarian State Library, Munich]

opment often reflected in paintings of the Annunciation showing Mary reading a book. The usual alternative to marriage—entry into the religious life—was tantamount to rejecting the world in favor of a book-lined cell. For intellectually gifted young women the choice was difficult, more so because men typically regarded learned women as intellectual oddities, male minds in female bodies. An educated woman was often thought to have exchanged female concerns, such as needles and wool, for male ones, such as pens and books.

Although male humanists praised women in general, they usually preferred that learned women remain safely unwed and likened them to Amazon queens and armed warriors or viragos. In the courtly love tradition of the Middle Ages men were supposed to please the ladies, whereas in the Renaissance women were molded to satisfy the gentlemen. As the Renaissance ideal of learning spread, girls and young women of the upper estates received better educations than their medieval counterparts, but the classical material they studied reinforced notions of male superiority. Their education was to enable them not to enter the learned professions but to act as ladies of the court, patronesses of the arts, and dec-

orative presences who added gracefulness to their households.

The contributions of learned Renaissance women were varied. Many wrote Latin letters, orations, treatises, and poems. Alessandra Scala of Florence had a command of Greek equaled by few Western scholars. The ranks of humanist poets embraced such women as Christine de Pisan (c. 1364–c. 1431), a French writer of Italian descent whose works included a biography of King Charles V of France, and Lucrezia Tornabuoni, mother of Lorenzo the Magnificent and author of religious hymns. As the Renaissance extended north of the Alps, more young women received a humanist education and took up their pens to write literary, religious, and historical works. The range of topics available to women was, however, restricted by social custom since most secular subjects were thought to be the province of men. Even in the religious realm women were expected to confine themselves to hymns and poems, devotional works, and translations. "Great things by reason of my sex I may not do," admitted the English translator Anne Locke. Thus humanist education tantalized bright young women even as society thwarted their ambitions by tightly hedging in their possibilities for intellectual expression. No wonder Christine de Pisan lamented that she had not been "born into this world as a member of the masculine sex." She found consolation in her prolific writings, for these enabled her to reflect that "now I am truly a man."

❦
VITTORIA COLONNA, POET AND PHILOSOPHER

One of the most gifted Renaissance women, Vittoria Colonna belonged to a powerful Roman family with vast holdings in the Papal States and southern Italy. Among her relatives were a pope and 30 cardinals. Born in 1492 at Marino, near Rome, she was the daughter of Fabrizio Colonna, grand constable of the kingdom of Naples. Although her marriage at the age of 19 to the marchese of Pescara, a Spaniard, had been arranged for political reasons 15 years earlier, she nevertheless fell in love with him. Often absent on military service, the marchese died in 1525, leaving her childless. In his memory Vittoria wrote sonnets idealizing him as a saint despite the fact that he had been faithless to her, contemptuous of Italians, and treasonous in his political dealings. Imbued with Neoplatonic concepts, Vittoria envisioned a reunion with him in a better, spiritual life. Her love sonnets, written in the tradition of Petrarch, won her acclaim in humanist circles, particularly from the great literary stylist Pietro Bembo and from Castiglione, who gave her a manuscript of his *Courtier* to critique.

◉ The Case for Educating Young Ladies ◉

One of the most gifted women writers of the Renaissance, Christine de Pisan argued on behalf of offering girls the same educational opportunities as boys.

If it were customary to send little girls to school and to teach them the same subjects as are taught to boys, they would learn just as fully and would understand the subtleties of all arts and sciences. Indeed it may be they would understand them better . . . for just as women's bodies are more soft than men's, so too their understanding is more sharp. . . . If they understand less it is because they do not go out and see so many different places and things but stay home and mind their own work. For there is nothing which teaches a reasonable creature so much as the experience of many different things.

[Rectitude personified next speaks to Christine.] Your father, who was a natural philosopher, was not of the opinion that women grow worse by becoming educated. On the contrary, as you know he took great pleasure from seeing your interest in learning. Your mother, however, who held the usual feminine ideas on the matter, wanted you to spend your time spinning, like other women, and prevented you from making more progress and going deeper into science and learning in your childhood. But as the proverb says, what nature gives may not be taken away. So you gathered what little drops of learning you could and consider them a great treasure and are right to do so.

Source: J. O'Faolain and L. Martines, eds., *Not in God's Image* (New York: Harper Torchbooks, 1973), pp. 181–182.

Vittoria's religious sonnets reflect both her ascetic piety and her Neoplatonism, which together sought to liberate the spirit by subduing the flesh. In Neoplatonic imagery she expressed her hope to "mount with wings" in order to reach true light and love. Hers was an intensely personal experience: "I write," she said, "only to free myself from my inner pain." Her sonnets manifest a keen interest in church reform, a concern she shared with a number of her friends, including Cardinal Contarini, a chief architect of the Catholic Reformation. Although one of her closest friends, Bernardino Ochino, ultimately defected to the Protestants, she remained loyal to the Catholic church.

Vittoria found a kindred spirit in Michelangelo, whom she met shortly after he had begun painting the Sistine Chapel ceiling in 1508. He was Vittoria's "most singular friend" and she his "love," capable of causing "a withered tree to burgeon and to bloom." Their intimacy, in which Michelangelo found spiritual solace and artistic inspiration, was not sexual. They corresponded extensively and exchanged sonnets, the tone of which is reminiscent of Petrarch's sonnets to Laura, but in an unmistakably Christian context. Michelangelo wrote madrigals and painted at least three works for her and probably a portrait as well. He must have been sympathetic to her ascetic convictions, which were so pronounced after her husband's death. She fasted and wore hair shirts until Cardinal Reginald Pole, a key figure in the Catholic Reformation, persuaded her to adopt a more moderate course. She spent much of the period between 1541 and her death in 1547 in monasteries, a reminder that many Renaissance humanists saw their religious and humanist principles as fully compatible.

Machiavelli and the Culture of Power

The evolution of the humanist movement is nowhere more apparent than in its attitude toward history. Initially the humanists were preoccupied with the recovery of classical Roman texts that they could use as a standard against which to measure their own society. They then broadened their horizon to the study of classical history with a view to using its lessons as a guide to human affairs and the improvement of political and social institutions. Lorenzo Valla's use of textual criticism exemplifies the humanists' refinement of scholarly techniques. Finally, in the sixteenth century, disillusioned by their inability to reshape the present by the application of historical ideals, humanist historians relinquished their belief in the ability of simple virtue to triumph over external forces. Those who thought in theological terms explained such forces as the will of God directing human history. Instead of examining the past with a view to improving the present, most historians and their readers increasingly used the historical record to justify their religious beliefs or the political ambitions of their respective states.

The disillusionment characteristic of the sixteenth-century humanist historians was a product of earlier conditions, particularly in northern and central Italy. The failure of republican government in Florence and the French invasion of 1494 virtually demolished the hopes of the earlier humanists. Power replaced virtue as the cardinal principle in the conduct of human affairs, particularly in the thought of Niccolò Machiavelli (1469–1527). He was in his twenties when the French invaded Italy, prompting the ruler of Florence, Piero de' Medici, to try to save the city by territorial concessions. For this the Florentines overthrew Piero, revived their republican government, and rallied to the reforming message of the impassioned Dominican friar Girolamo Savonarola (1452–1498). For four years the Florentines were caught up in a frenzy of revivalism directed against materialism, immorality, corruption, and godlessness. Bonfires claimed everything from sumptuous clothing and stylish wigs to books and works of art. By 1498 the zeal had ebbed, and Savonarola, having infuriated the immoral Alexander VI by his candid criticism, was burned as a heretic on trumped-up charges. The Council of Ten, which assumed the direction of Florentine affairs, made Machiavelli its secretary and one of its diplomats. Fascinated by the practice of statecraft, the young official traversed Italy conducting the business of his republic. His career was abruptly terminated in 1512 when the Medici returned to Florence and ousted the republican government. Machiavelli himself was tortured and sent into exile.

In his enforced idleness he reflected on the political problems of Italy and its history in his principal works, *The Prince* and the *Discourses on Livy*. Machiavelli brought to his writing not only a knowledge of Roman history and the works of such humanist historians as Bruni and Poggio but also considerable firsthand experience of the realities of contemporary politics and diplomacy. *The Prince* (1513), dedicated to Lorenzo de' Medici, grandson of Lorenzo the Magnificent, has sometimes been interpreted as if it were a satire on the politics of despotism. On the contrary, it reflects the sober realism of a middle-aged diplomat and a theoretical brilliance that has earned Machiavelli a reputation as the founder of modern political science. *The Prince* has rightly been called "the greatest of all theoretical explorations of the politics of innovation";[5] its primary theme deals with the "new prince"—the political innovator who

has just seized power—and his dealings with his subjects, some of whom have been ousted from power, while others expect rewards he cannot bestow.

The Medici now dominated not only Machiavelli's beloved Florence but even Rome, where Leo X (1513–1521), Lorenzo the Magnificent's son, had just become pope. Machiavelli intended to prod the Medici into embracing an ethic of power shorn of religious or ethical limitations as the only effective means to achieve a stable, secure Italy free of "barbarian" intervention. His was a creed of action, not reflection, of pragmatism rather than idealism. He praised Roman republicanism because it had been a successful tool of power and praised republican government in general if it embodied *virtù*, or inner strength. As he pondered the meaning of history, he concluded that it was shaped by a recurring cycle of events; instead of evolution and progress, there was mere repetition.

Although Machiavelli did not regard historical study as a quest for virtue, he reflected humanist influence in a variety of other ways; for him, as for Bruni, history is a storehouse of examples and should be studied to ascertain both the causes and the cures of current problems. Because history repeated itself, present ills could be treated by imitating solutions that were successful in the past. Everything in the present and the future had a counterpart in antiquity, the happiest time in history. Machiavelli's concept of the imitation of antiquity is an extreme application of the humanist tendency to venerate the classical world. One can find similar parallels in Confucian thought. In formulating his principles of statecraft, Machiavelli ransacked classical history to find material for his argument and also drew on his own practical experience in politics. Between them he found justification for the political principles that make *The Prince* famous: Be deceitful and cunning in dealing with rivals; do as people actually do rather than as they ought to do; regard the state—the prince—as supreme, recognizing that the end justifies the means; always place military security first; avoid neutrality, especially in dealing with other states; instill fear in one's subjects as the best means to compel obedience; undertake great enterprises to divert attention from internal problems. Such was the culture of power, and in espousing it Machiavelli broke with the traditional model of the good ruler, whether Confucian, Aristotelian or Judeo-Christian.

Machiavelli's Florentine contemporary, Francesco Guicciardini (1483–1540), surpassed him as a historian, particularly in his determination to discover the reasons for human behavior and explore the way institutions work. His first *History of Florence*, written during the republican era, characterized Lorenzo the Magnificent as a tyrant, but two decades later he found Lorenzo's Florence preferable to the now discredited republic. His attitude changed even more in his last work, a *History of Italy*, in which Lorenzo was glorified, reflecting Guic-

◉ Machiavelli's Advice ◉
to a Renaissance Prince

The advice Machiavelli tendered in The Prince *reveals a degree of cynicism based on his experience in Renaissance politics.*

How praiseworthy a prince is who keeps his promises and lives with sincerity and not with trickery, everybody realizes. Nevertheless, experience in our time shows that those princes have done great things who have valued their promises little, and who have understood how to addle the brains of men with trickery; and in the end they have vanquished those who have stood upon their honesty. . . .

For a prince, then, it is necessary . . . to appear merciful, trustworthy, humane, blameless, religious—and to be so—yet to be in such measure prepared in mind that if you need to be not so, you can and do change to the contrary. . . . A prince, and above all a prince who is new, cannot practice all those things for which men are considered good, being often forced, in order to keep his position, to act contrary to truth, contrary to charity, contrary to humanity, contrary to religion. Therefore he must have a mind ready to turn in any direction as Fortune's winds and the variability of affairs require. . . .

Hate is incurred as much by means of good deeds as of bad. Therefore . . . if a prince wishes to keep his position, he is often forced to be not good, because when that group—whether the masses, the soldiers, or the rich—which you decide you need to sustain yourself, is corrupt, you have to adapt yourself to its nature in order to please it. Then good works are your enemies.

Source: N. Machiavelli, *The Chief Works and Others*, trans. A. Gilbert, vol. 1 (Durham, N.C.: Duke University Press, 1965), pp. 64, 66, 72.

ciardini's disillusionment with the inability of the Italian states to unify against foreign aggression. The optimism of the early humanists—their faith in the ability to shape states and their leaders—was abandoned in the face of hostile external forces and the assumption of power by men with the trappings of Renaissance culture but without the ideals of humanistic virtue. Although Guicciardini was the better historian, Machiavelli had a much greater historical impact because of the popularity—and notoriety—of *The Prince*, with its calculated disregard of traditional morality and its pithy, provocative appeal to political "realism."

The Printing Revolution

Machiavelli's *Prince* was too scandalous to be published during his lifetime, but other works of Renaissance scholarship were printed despite some humanist opposition to putting learned works in the hands of commoners. Movable metal type, developed in Germany in the fifteenth century, was vastly superior to the technique of block printing. The Chinese and Koreans, of course, had already invented movable type, but it had less appeal to them because their scripts consisted of thousands of different characters. Metal type was more durable as well as more flexible than wooden blocks because individual letters could be reused in new combinations. By 1300 linen paper, which had been introduced from East Asia through the Islamic world, was in common use, thus setting the stage for the new presses. Johann Gutenberg of Mainz, one of the pioneers of the new technology, published his first known work, an indulgence proclamation by Pope Nicholas V, in 1454. The first of his magnificent Bibles appeared two years later. The new press spread rapidly throughout western and central Europe; by 1500 there were 73 in Italy, 50 in Germany, 39 in France, 24 in Spain, and smaller numbers in other countries.

The fact that Italy had more presses than any other country was largely due to the impact of the Renaissance, despite humanist misgivings about putting learned works in the hands of the masses. The finest press was that of the humanist Aldus Manutius in Venice. His Aldine Press published at least 30 first editions of Greek classics, a tremendous benefit to Renaissance

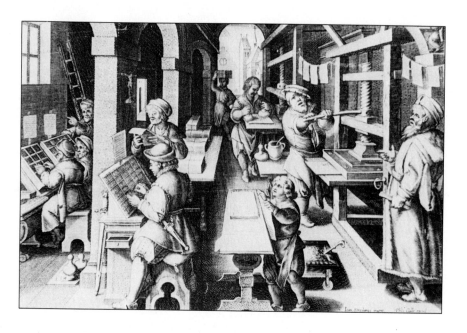

In this sixteenth-century print shop, the men at the left are setting type, their colleague at the center rear is inking a plate of type, the man at the right is printing a sheet on the press, and the youth in the foreground is setting the wet sheets out to dry. [Bettmann Archive]

scholarship. Aldus also founded an academy of his own in Venice that was especially devoted to encouraging humanist authors and editors. The nucleus of the academy consisted of Greek exiles whose knowledge of classical Greek civilization thus found its way into print and henceforth became available to scholars throughout the West. The influential northern humanist Erasmus of Rotterdam (c. 1466–1536) perfected his Greek during a stay with Aldus.

The changes brought about by the printing press reached virtually every aspect of life. As the price of books fell and their number increased, there was a greater incentive to acquire and improve reading skills. The expansion of the literate population in turn offered new opportunities to writers and eventually freed some from the need to find and please wealthy patrons. Religious topics, works on astrology, and popular tales were prominent on the early book lists, as were editions of the Bible, especially once vernacular versions became common in the sixteenth century. The press proved a boon to scholarship by making more accurate editions possible, by standardizing maps and images as well as texts, and by encouraging cross-cultural interchange. Ideas spread with greater rapidity, and there was more inducement to develop new theories. Codifying and cataloging became commonplace, and the use of running titles at the top of each page, regular page numbering, and indexing helped order the thoughts of readers. Printing also increased the likelihood of a document's preservation. Through printing, collections of laws and ordinances became available to a wider public, with beneficial effects for the practice of law as well as for public discourse about political affairs. By the sixteenth cen-

tury, however, both church and state found it necessary to step up their censorship. The advent of printing made propaganda possible, and in the seventeenth century newspapers began replacing the pulpit as the primary source of news in urban areas. Printing also increased the reputation—or infamy—of authors and eventually made it possible for some writers, such as the English dramatist Aphra Behn (c. 1640–1689), to earn a living by their pens alone. Gutenberg and his colleagues thus set in motion one of the most sweeping revolutions in history.

The Fine Arts

The Renaissance ushered in significant changes in artistic style and taste, reflecting the absorption of humanist ideals. The most prominent hallmarks of Renaissance painting and sculpture—fascination with classical themes, expressions of individualism, a more self-confident embracing of secular themes—reflected humanist concerns. Technical advances in painting were also possible after oil-based paints were brought to Italy from Flanders in the late fifteenth century. Painters had previously worked in fresco, which involved the application of pigment to wet plaster, and tempera, which entailed mixing pigments with a sizing, such as eggs. Oils enabled the painter to achieve a detail, clarity, and permanence of color not possible with fresco or tempera. Renaissance artists also achieved the ability to give the illusion of dimensionality by using gradations between light and dark to model their figures and by applying mathematical principles to create the visual illusion of objects receding into space.

The Renaissance in the fine arts was greatly facilitated by an expansion of patronage, especially by lay people. Not only did this lead to an increased demand for paintings and statues, but the expanded circle of patrons—towns, guilds, religious brotherhoods, patricians, aristocrats, and church leaders—broadened traditional tastes and themes, thus leading to a new richness and diversity in art. The dictates of patrons also popularized the intermingling of sacred and secular, instances of which are apparent earlier in the stained glass and statuary of the Gothic cathedrals. Some patrons wanted their portraits included alongside those of the Virgin and saints, as testimony to their piety as well as their wealth, though again there are instances of this in the Middle Ages. The blending of secular and sacred is also seen in the rather free interchanging of style and organization between classical and religious themes: Venus is represented as a secularized Mary, Mary as a spiritualized Venus. The inquisitive mind of the humanists combined with the sundry tastes of patrons to encourage a greater range of artistic expression.

Early Renaissance Painting

In the Middle Ages, painting was the least developed of the principal fine arts. Giotto (c. 1266–1337), a Florentine, revitalized it and provided the bridge between the medieval era and the early Renaissance. Boccaccio overstated the case when he praised Giotto for reviving painting after it had "been in the grave" for centuries, but Giotto's contributions were rightly recognized when he was made head of the cathedral workshop in Florence, an honor previously accorded only to architects and sculptors. In a series of frescoes on the walls of a chapel in Padua depicting the life of Christ, Giotto's narrative power, evocation of human emotion, and use of spatial depth turned the chapel walls into a stage on which the central events of the Christian faith were acted out. His work was seen as the harbinger of a new era; in the words of Giorgio Vasari, he ushered in the "good modern manner." Although none of Giotto's immediate disciples equaled their master, his frescoes on the walls of Florentine chapels became textbooks for later generations of Renaissance painters, including Masaccio and Michelangelo.

The frescoes of the Florentine artist Masaccio (1401–1428) revolutionized painting. His treatment of the nude figures of Adam and Eve being expelled from the Garden of Eden displays a naturalism and psychological penetration very different in spirit from Giotto's paintings. Both here and in a masterly fresco of the Trinity, the Virgin, and St. John, Masaccio links the Christian

In Masaccio's *Holy Trinity* (1428), God the Father holds the cross while the Holy Spirit descends in the form of a dove. Mary is to the left of the cross, St. John is to the right, and below them are the kneeling donors. Masaccio's use of linear perspective gives the fresco a striking sense of depth. [Alinari/Art Resource]

and the classical by setting his scenes against a Roman arch. These two paintings demonstrate a dramatic advance in the ability to render a sense of depth, and the expulsion scene in particular is notable for its use of shading, a technique known as *chiaroscuro*, which enhanced the pictorial effect by conveying the reflection of light from three-dimensional surfaces. Masaccio's discoveries encouraged his contemporaries and successors to continue experimenting, and Michelangelo himself was among those who sketched Masaccio's work in order to learn his techniques.

The impact of Neoplatonism on Renaissance painting is manifest in the works of the Florentine Sandro Botticelli (1444–1510), a tanner's son. Through his Medici patrons he came into contact with Marsilio Ficino and the Florentine Academy. His famous paintings of Venus—emerging from the sea on a giant shell, celebrating the arrival of spring in the company of Mercury and Cupid, or reclining with Mars as mythological lovers—reflect the Neoplatonic notion of Venus as the source of divine love. But Botticelli, the poet of lyrical beauty, sometimes had to paint more mundane subjects at the behest of his Medici patrons. After they crushed the revolt of the Pazzi in 1478 they commissioned him to depict the execution of the rebels as a warning to others; the painting was destroyed after the Medici were forced into exile.

Later Renaissance Painting: A New Phase

The early Renaissance achievements in rendering the human figure, three-dimensionality, chiaroscuro, and individualized portraiture became the foundation of the mature period of Renaissance painting that began in the late 1400s and lasted approximately a century. The late Renaissance is distinguished as an era in which the great artists combined creative talents with intense individuality, thereby producing a highly personal style. At the end of the fifteenth century there was a noticeable rise in the status of leading artists, the result of which was greater freedom from the dictates of patrons. Information about the artists was disseminated more widely, and the great ones were increasingly thought of in terms of genius and referred to as "divine." Leonardo da Vinci, said Vasari, manifested *grazia divina*—divine grace. Interest in and respect for the artist's personality grew, and two artists—the sculptor Benvenuto Cellini and the painter Albrecht Dürer—even wrote autobiographies, expressing the Renaissance fascination with the individual. It became increasingly common too for artists to paint their own portraits, and Dürer even depicted himself nude. The elite who could afford art valued the artist's development of a distinctively personal style, especially in the case of artists who acquired international reputations. When Titian left Venice in 1547 to paint Holy Roman Emperor Charles V at Augsburg, he was besieged with requests from people who wanted to own one of his works. In the late Renaissance more people collected art, thus encouraging the notion that a cultured person should own a few paintings or bronze statues.

Leonardo da Vinci

Although no single painting or date marked a sharp cleavage between the early and late Renaissance, Leonardo da Vinci's *Virgin of the Rocks*, done in the early 1480s, can claim to be the first late Renaissance painting. By this point in his career Leonardo (1452–1519) had already developed a keen interest in nature. In the *Virgin of the Rocks* (see "The Visual Experience: Art of the Renaissance"), for instance, he chose a semidark grotto with an abundance of plant life and a pool for his setting. Although the natural details are faithfully rendered, the total effect is one of mystery and poetic vision—of a psychological world. Coming as it did against a tradition of artistic development dedicated to rendering nature faithfully, the *Virgin of the Rocks* is an intensely personal statement by the artist, as is his famous portrait of the Mona Lisa (*La Gioconda*), with its dreamlike background expressive of the personality of the subject.

About the time he was working on the *Virgin of the Rocks*, Leonardo left Florence and his native Tuscany for Milan, where he acquired the duke's patronage. There he painted his masterpiece, *The Last Supper*, on the wall of a church refectory, unfortunately using an experimental paint that has decayed over the years. The key to this masterful study in human psychology lies in Leonardo's philosophy of art: "A good painter has two chief objects to paint—man and the intention of his soul. The former is easy, the latter hard, for it must be expressed by gestures and the movement of the limbs."[6] For Leonardo, gestures reveal the inner drama as the disciples react to Christ's stunning statement that one of them will betray him. Space is mathematically ordered through the use of recurring rectangles, especially on the walls and ceiling, and the placement of the disciples in groups of three, united by their gestures. The serene Christ, his arms outstretched and his head framed against a window of symbolic light, is in the shape of a pyramid, Leonardo's favorite organizing device, while Judas, his profile rendered in symbolic darkness, has not been separated from the rest of the disciples as had been usual in earlier paintings of the same theme, such as Giotto's famous fresco. The innovation is deliberate; the psychological insight, unsurpassed.

Leonardo's genius as a painter was only one of his many interests. He is the supreme example of the Renaissance ideal—a virtuoso whose intellectual curiosity led him into a host of fields. His notebooks contain ideas and sketches for military inventions, many of which were not realized for centuries, including submarines, turbines, and prototypes of a tank and a helicopter. His studies of human anatomy were based on the dissection of more than 30 corpses. After examining fossils discovered in the mountains, he concluded that the biblical account of creation was inaccurate. An accomplished ri-

⊚ Leonardo on Art and Nature ⊚

The Renaissance determination to return to the sources, whether in nature or in classical antiquity, is evident in Leonardo da Vinci's insistence that a painter must study the natural world rather than merely imitate the works of his predecessors.

The painter will produce pictures of small merit if he takes for his standard the pictures of others, but if he will study from natural objects he will bear good fruit. As was seen in the painters after the Romans who always imitated each other and so their art constantly declined from age to age. After these came Giotto, the Florentine, who—not content with imitating the works of Cimabue, his master—being born in the mountains and in a solitude inhabited only by goats and such beasts, and being guided by nature to his art, began by drawing on the rocks the movements of the goats of which he was keeper. And thus he began to draw all the animals which were to be found in the country, and in such wise that after much study he excelled not only all the masters of his time but all those of many bygone ages. Afterwards this art declined again, because every one imitated the pictures that were already done; thus it went on . . . [until] Masaccio showed by his perfect works how those who take for their standard any one but nature—the mistress of all masters—weary themselves in vain.

Source: E. G. Holt, ed., *Literary Sources of Art History* (Princeton, N.J.: Princeton University Press, 1947), pp. 178–179.

der and a lover of horses, he sketched dozens of them preparatory to designing a gargantuan (but unfinished) equestrian statue for the Sforza family. Town planning, architecture, botany, music, and optics were among his wide-ranging interests. Above all he was supremely self-confident; after he listed his talents in military engineering for the duke of Milan, he added: "I can do in painting whatever may be done, as well as any other, be he who he may."[7]

Raphael, Michelangelo, and the Roman Renaissance

After Julius II became pope in 1503, the center of the Renaissance shifted from Florence to Rome. Julius used his patronage to make the city the artistic and intellectual capital of the West. Raphael Sanzio (1483–1520), a native of Umbria in central Italy, studied various works of Leonardo and Michelangelo in Florence before going to Rome. Commissioned by Julius to paint frescoes in several rooms of the Vatican Palace, Raphael reflected the synthesis of the classical and the Christian in the Renaissance by juxtaposing two magnificent scenes, one linking the earthly and heavenly churches by the sacrifice of the mass, the other an assembly of classical philosophers and scientists grouped around Plato and

Aristotle. The faces in the latter work include those of Leonardo and Michelangelo as well as his own, a characteristic late Renaissance touch. Raphael is also renowned for a series of gentle Madonnas that carefully blend naturalism with idealized beauty.

Michelangelo Buonarroti (1475–1564), another native son of Tuscany, was already in Rome to paint the ceiling of the Sistine Chapel when Raphael arrived in 1508. Deeply influenced by Neoplatonism, the temperamental Michelangelo created a massive work (128 by 44 feet) fusing Hebrew and classical themes. Christianity is only implicitly present in the sense that the pagan sibyls and the Hebrew prophets were thought to point to the advent of the Messiah. The work abounds in symbolism: the Neoplatonic contrast between light and darkness, spirit and matter; the recurring triads, basic to the numeric symbolism of Neoplatonism; the relationship of earthly knowledge (pagan sibyls) and divine revelation (Hebrew prophets); and the tree imagery in the central panels, which is both biblical, as in the tree of good and evil, and an allusion to Julius II's family name, Della Rovere ("of the oak tree"). Michelangelo's painting *The Last Judgment* on the east wall of the chapel was added much later, between 1532 and 1541, and reveals the somber, deeply religious mood that characterized the final period of the artist's life, as well as his fascination with Dante.

In the central panel of this portion of Michelangelo's Sistine Chapel ceiling (1508–1512), God gives the spark of life (a Neoplatonic concept) to Adam. [Marburg/Art Resource]

Titian and the Venetian Renaissance

In their basic conviction that art must transcend nature, Michelangelo and Titian (c. 1487–1576) were in full accord, yet their paintings are strikingly different. In contrast to Michelangelo's preoccupation with statuesque figures and Neoplatonic symbolism, Titian epitomizes Venice's fascination with light and color, reflecting the play of light on its waterways and palatial buildings. An immensely prolific and successful artist, Titian was appointed painter to the republic of Venice, and he enjoyed the patronage of numerous sovereigns and aristocrats, among them Emperor Charles V. Titian's themes range from devout Christian subjects to sensuous reclining nudes, from classical mythology to contemporary portraits. His is an elegant art, befitting the clients for whom

he painted. Only in his late paintings, such as his depiction of Christ being crowned with thorns, does he forsake vibrant colors and rich textures in favor of subdued tones and gloomy light. Like Michelangelo, Titian spent his last years engaged in deep religious introspection. At the personal level, both men manifested the Renaissance origins of the religious reform movements that swept Europe in the sixteenth century.

Sculpture: From Virtuosity to Introspection

In sculpture as in painting, Renaissance artists strove to achieve greater naturalism, individualization, and, in sculptural reliefs, a keen sense of depth. Sculptors such as Lorenzo Ghiberti (1378–1455) and Donatello

(1386–1466) influenced contemporary painters as they pioneered these developments. Ghiberti's crowning achievement, the bronze doors of the baptistery in Florence, were intended to imitate nature in the classical Greek style. As Michelangelo later did on the Sistine Chapel ceiling, Ghiberti used only scenes from the Old Testament in his ten panels, flanked with portrait busts

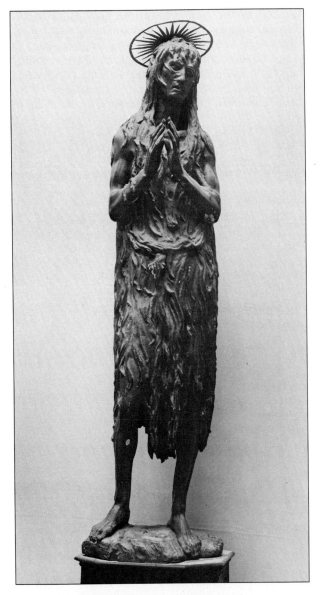

The vivid realism of Donatello's wood statue of the aged penitent Mary Magdalene (1454–1455) is roughly comparable to the realism of Japanese sculptors in the Kamakura period (thirteenth and fourteenth centuries). [Alinari/Art Resource]

of pagan sibyls and Hebrew prophets as the heralds of Christ's coming. He succeeded brilliantly in fulfilling his commission from city officials and the guild of merchants to produce a work with "the greatest perfection, the most ornamentation, and the greatest richness."[8]

Ghiberti's pupil, the Florentine Donatello, exhibited a bold, revolutionary style that is evident in his bronze statue of David, the first freestanding nude sculpture since antiquity. Wearing only a shepherd's hat and military leggings, David, with his idealized face and physique, is the antithesis of Donatello's melancholy, emaciated figure of Mary Magdalene. In his portrayal of her as a time-ravaged penitent, there is no hint of the usual Renaissance preoccupation with beauty, for Donatello's outlook has become more introspective, his concern with matters of the spirit more predominant. In the works of Donatello, Leonardo, and Michelangelo a steady progression can be seen from an early concern with innovation and virtuosity to a later preoccupation with inward states and spiritual experience.

Michelangelo's first love was sculpting, an art he approached through his Neoplatonic convictions in the belief that his task was to liberate the living figure encased in a block of marble. Like Donatello, Michelangelo in his early years produced statues of sublime beauty, as if he were perfecting rather than duplicating nature. Instead of pursuing mathematically ordered perfection in the manner of Leonardo, he relied on inspiration to determine ideal proportions. His success is apparent in two majestic works completed in his twenties: the Pietà, in which Mary's youthful face is as supremely beautiful as Raphael's Madonnas, and a towering statue of David, resolutely awaiting Goliath, the heroic physique in every sense an idealized rendition of male anatomy. To Vasari—as to the Florentine government which commissioned the work—Michelangelo's David was a political symbol indicating that Florence "should be boldly defended and righteously governed, following David's example." Michelangelo's last works stand in vivid contrast to these idealized, confident statues. The Pietàs of his final years are unfinished, two of them partially smashed by his own hand. One Pietà includes the figure of Nicodemus, the Pharisee who had asked Jesus how a person could "be born when he is old"; Nicodemus was in fact a self-portrait of Michelangelo, whose own searching in these years was for the assurance of spiritual rebirth. The late Pietàs were a plea for his own redemption, the culmination of the Renaissance quest for individual fulfillment at the deepest, most personal level.

Women Artists

Although relatively little is known about women artists in this period, some achieved both acceptance and a degree of fame. Michelangelo, for instance, took a special interest in the painter Sofonisba Anguissola (c. 1535–1625) of Cremona, whose five sisters also painted. Vasari visited their household and described the works of each woman. For nearly two decades Anguissola, who specialized in individual and group portraits, painted at the court of King Philip II of Spain. The English monarch Henry VIII patronized a number of women painters, paying one of them—Levina Teerling (c. 1515–1576), a manuscript illuminator—even more for her work than he paid the famous portraitist Hans Holbein. Royal patronage was also bestowed on Catharina van Hemessen (1528–c. 1587) of the Netherlands, who enjoyed the support of Queen Mary of Hungary and painted some intriguingly introspective portraits. In the area of sculpture the leading woman artist was probably Properzia Rossi (c. 1490–1530) of Bologna, whose work is reminiscent of the sculptural reliefs of Ghiberti. That women artists were active and relatively prosperous during the Renaissance is unmistakable, although it is difficult to reconstruct their contributions because so many of their works were subsequently lost or destroyed.

Architecture and Classical Inspiration

Inspired by the architectural principles and motifs of classical antiquity, Renaissance architects rejected the Gothic style in favor of one that recalled the arches, columns, capitals, and ordered simplicity of Greco-Roman buildings. The artist who pioneered Renaissance architecture, the Florentine Filippo Brunelleschi (1377–1446), solved the greatest architectural puzzle of the fif-

The Cathedral of Santa Maria del Fiore dominates the skyline of Florence. Begun in the Tuscan Gothic style, the church, with its gleaming marble exterior, is crowned by Brunelleschi's dome, a triumph of Renaissance architecture. The companile (bell tower) was designed by Giotto. [Wim Swann]

teenth century—the design and construction of a suitable dome for the cathedral in Florence—by meticulously studying ancient Roman buildings, particularly the Pantheon. His solution was to build an inner dome to support the massive outer dome, thus avoiding the supports that had become unsightly to the tastes of his time, to use a drum below the dome to contain its outward thrust, and to place a lantern atop the dome to stabilize the entire structure. The result was not only technologically innovative but also aesthetically pleasing, as anyone who views Florence from the surrounding hills can attest. Brunelleschi's other designs, including a chapel for the Pazzi family and the Foundling Hospital in Florence, are even more distinctly Renaissance in spirit, with their graceful arches and their concern with classical order.

When Michelangelo set about to design the dome for St. Peter's Basilica in Rome, he studied Brunelleschi's dome. Other architects had already worked on St. Peter's, including Donato Bramante and Raphael, and Michelangelo's main contribution was the soaring dome. It was intended to crown a church in the shape of a Greek cross, with four equal arms, but in the early seventeenth century the western arm was extended into a long, traditional nave, upsetting the careful balance that Bramante and Michelangelo had envisioned. Michelangelo regarded his work on St. Peter's as both a divine commission and an offering of his talents to God: "It was God who laid this charge upon me. . . . I undertook it for the love of God, in whom is all my hope."9

Like Brunelleschi, Andrea Palladio (c. 1518–1580), the leading architect of the Venetian Renaissance, made a special trip to Rome to study classical buildings. Convinced that the numeric ratios basic to musical harmony were found throughout the universe and were thus derived from God, Palladio designed his buildings to embody mathematical symmetry. His specialty was the rural villa, of which his best-known example is the Villa Rotunda near his native Vicenza, not far from Venice. The building, mathematically perfect, is cubic, with an interior cylinder, a saucer-shaped dome, and four matching Ionic porches reminiscent of Greek temple façades. Numerous eighteenth-century architects were influenced by Palladio, particularly in Italy, England, and North America. Renaissance architecture provided the inspiration for some of the most famous buildings in the new American republic, including the Capitol, which reflects the influence of Michelangelo's dome, and Thomas Jefferson's house at Monticello in Virginia, which is indebted to Palladio.

Northern Art

North of the Alps the transition from Gothic to Renaissance came in the fifteenth century. Pioneering Flemish

Jan van Eyck's heavily symbolic painting *The Arnolfini Wedding* (1434) is typical of late medieval–early Renaissance Flemish art. [National Gallery, London]

artists took advantage of the discovery of oil paints to develop an artistic style that was primarily concerned with capturing realism by depicting intricate details; surface appearances mattered more than form, anatomy, or motion. The fascination with detail is evident in the work of Jan van Eyck (c. 1390–1441). In his portrait of the Medici banker Giovanni Arnolfini and his bride, his ties to the medieval world are still apparent in the painting's traditional symbolism: the dog represents fidelity, the single burning candle the all-seeing Christ; the statue on the bedpost is St. Margaret, patron saint of childbirth, and the shoes have been removed to symbolize the holy ground of the sacrament of matrimony. Although the work is suffused with religious meaning, in the last resort the painting is about the union of two individuals and the status they enjoy—concerns common to Italian Renaissance painters of this period.

While these artists concentrated on external appearances, the Dutch painter Hieronymus Bosch (c. 1450–1516) created symbolic scenes so imaginative that spe-

Compare Pieter Brueghel's
Wedding Dance (1566), a
rustic scene full of robust
peasants, with the bourgeois
couple painted by van Eyck.
Brueghel's paintings do not
exhibit the usual Flemish
concern with sharp detail.
[Detroit Institute of Arts]

cialists are still attempting to decipher his meaning. The
world of his *Garden of Earthly Delights* is peopled with
emaciated nudes, unnatural beasts, flying creatures, bit-
ing toads, burning ruins, couples making love, and exotic instruments of torture. At first sight the work appears medieval in its inspiration, but in fact Bosch was
daringly individualistic in allowing his imagination to engage in flights of fantasy with unmistakable sensual and
sexual overtones. The intent, however, was clearly to
warn viewers of the consequences of erotic pleasure as
their eyes moved from the Garden of Eden on the left,
through the depiction of sensual joys in the center panel,
to the fires of hell on the right. Artistic creativity
triumphed over the bonds of tradition, but without sac-
rificing the customary moral message.

Renaissance art culminated in the work of the Flemish painter Pieter Brueghel the Elder (c. 1525–1569),
whose circle of friends apparently included some humanists. Although he visited Italy, he was never very
impressed by classical art but instead was influenced by
Bosch and other painters of the Netherlands. He was
intrigued by peasant life and by landscapes, particularly
the Alpine scenery he saw on his Italian trip. His delightful peasant scenes celebrate folk customs such as
dances and wedding feasts, often with a touch of humor.
There was a serious side to Brueghel, who used his
works to condemn religious bigotry and Spanish bar-
barity in the Netherlands. The inscriptions on his copper
engravings were so outspoken, in fact, that he had his
wife destroy them as he neared death. Brueghel's almost
total lack of interest in classical models and his contin-

ued use of traditional symbolism and moralizing underscore the fact that northern Renaissance artists retained
far more of the medieval heritage than their counterparts in Italy.

Perspectives on the Renaissance

"Out of the thick Gothic night our eyes are opened to
the glorious torch of the sun," wrote the French writer
François Rabelais, reflecting the Renaissance belief in
the birth of a new age of cultural brilliance following a
millennium of darkness and ignorance. Petrarch contrasted the "ancient" world, the period before the Roman
emperors adopted Christianity, with the "modern" era,
which he described as a time of barbarism and darkness.
Thus was born the unfortunate notion of the Dark Ages.
To one fifteenth-century Florentine businessman the
compendious writings of the medieval scholastics darkened learning by their "subtleties and confusion." It was
thus a natural step to describe the new epoch as a
rinàscita—a rebirth or renaissance, a term adopted by
Vasari to describe the renaissance of the arts. Vasari was
on solid ground when he cited the dramatic changes that
had occurred in the fourteenth and fifteenth centuries
in painting, sculpture, and architecture. The notion of
the Renaissance was expanded by later historians to in-

clude not only developments in philosophy and literature but virtually every aspect of civilization from statecraft to the economy.

A tendency to exalt the Renaissance developed in the eighteenth century, as reflected in the French philosopher Voltaire's willingness to depict Italy as the successor to the glories of classical Greece. The corollary of this was the denigration of the Middle Ages, which appeared to Voltaire as a dark age of irrationality and superstition. The romantics who followed, however, evaluated the Middle Ages more positively, taking their inspiration from its religious culture and finding their historical roots in medieval states rather than the classical heritage. But the Renaissance was once again thrust to the fore in a remarkably influential book by the Swiss historian Jacob Burckhardt (1818–1897), *The Civilization of the Renaissance in Italy*. First published in 1860, Burckhardt's book develops the Renaissance as an age dominated by the revival of classical antiquity, the development of a pronounced individualism (the awareness and expression of personality), and a fresh discovery of the world of nature and humankind. This was possible, he argued, only because of the genius of the Italians, "the first modern people of Europe who gave themselves boldly to speculations on freedom and necessity." Thus, according to Burckhardt, the Renaissance as a distinctive epoch in the history of civilization was born in the political turbulence that engulfed Italy in the fourteenth and fifteenth centuries. By the time that Burckhardt had finished his wide-ranging exploration of this age, he had provided a synthesis in which the Renaissance amounted to nothing less than a major turning point in European history.

Burckhardt's emphasis on the glories of the Renaissance was taken a step further by the English literary critic John Addington Symonds, whose seven-volume study, *The Renaissance in Italy* (1875–1886), sharply distinguished between the Middle Ages, which he likened to the shores of the Dead Sea, and the Renaissance. The history of the latter he exalted as "the history of the attainment of self-conscious freedom." The Renaissance, he contended, was the seedbed of the essential qualities that distinguish the modern from the ancient and medieval worlds, especially the emancipation of reason from its medieval bondage.

The sharp break drawn by Burckhardt and Symonds between the Middle Ages and the Renaissance was challenged by medieval specialists, whose research demolished the stereotype of the Middle Ages as a time of ignorance and "semibarbarism." Claiming to find the roots of the Renaissance in the twelfth century, some medievalists asserted that the Renaissance should be considered the last phase of the Middle Ages, not the beginning of the modern world. In 1927 the American historian Charles Homer Haskins published *The Renaissance of the Twelfth Century*. Pointing to such phenomena as the revival of the Latin classics and Roman law, the recovery of Greek science and philosophy, and the beginnings of the European universities—a revival of learning in the fullest sense—Haskins argued that the more famous Italian Renaissance was in reality the culmination of a movement that had begun in the late eleventh century and continued without a major break into the early modern period. We err, he argued, if we attempt to draw too sharp a distinction between successive periods of history. Haskins' attack on the Burckhardt-Symonds school did not deprecate the achievements of the Renaissance. Some medievalists did, however, pointing out that in many respects, such as its emphasis on magic and the occult, the Renaissance was actually less "rational" than the Middle Ages, and its science less advanced than in the thirteenth and fourteenth centuries. Even the term *Renaissance*, one medievalist contended, is detrimental to historical understanding because it has discouraged the study of the Middle Ages and obscured the truth that modern life owes far more to the medieval era than to classical Greece and Rome.

After World War II, Wallace Ferguson asserted a compromise interpretation according to which the Renaissance was an age of transition between the medieval and modern eras. Basic to this argument is the conviction that the changes that occurred in the Renaissance were profound, encompassing a transformation of institutions, outlook, culture, and economies. Although some critics objected that all periods involve transition, advocates of this view insisted that, taken together, the changes produced a distinctive cultural period that is neither medieval nor modern, though elements of both can be found in it.

The debate continues today. Much of the discussion has concentrated on the nature of Renaissance humanism, which has been variously defined as an educational system focusing on Greek and Roman classics, a cult of rhetoric and oratory, a philosophical method of rational inquiry, a philosophy of human dignity and individualism, or scholarly endeavor devoted to establishing new criteria of political liberty and civic responsibility.

In the face of so many interpretations, historians have come to realize that humanists were in reality a diverse group of individuals whose concerns were far from identical. The simplest definition of humanism treats it as the *studia humanitatis*, the study of grammar, rhetoric, poetry, history, and ethics in classical texts as distinct from the scholastic emphasis on logic and metaphysics. By this interpretation, humanism is an academic movement rather than a philosophy or a pattern of life based on the quest to imitate classical antiquity. Scholars generally recognize the medieval interest in the classics but distinguish the scholastics' selective approach—picking and choosing things that supported the Christian world view—from the humanist attempt to use all of antiquity as a means of challenging medieval assumptions and reconciling the full legacy of Western culture with its religion.

Another group of historians traces the origins of humanism to the political conditions in Italy and the need to develop a predominantly secular interpretation of government in order to throw off the bondage of the church. One exponent of this view contends that the evolutionary process of Renaissance humanism "began with the secularization of government itself and inevitably went on to engulf society at large."[10] Political conditions, particularly in Florence, provide the basis for a different interpretation: that the leaders of the city-states encouraged the emphasis on the glories of classical antiquity to assert their own political identity and to unite the people behind their rule. Humanistic ideals in this view were welcomed because they healed rifts between competing social groups and unified the community in the face of threats from other city-states. Whereas Burckhardt and Symonds highlighted the individual, a number of recent studies stress the civic nature of humanism and the importance of social groups such as the patriciate.

Although initially the intellectual and artistic developments in the Renaissance were the province of the socially elite, in the long run many commoners enjoyed them as well. Statues and paintings were displayed in churches, civic buildings, and town squares, and such architectural gems as the Florence Cathedral and St. Peter's Basilica were of course open to the public. Michelangelo's statue of David was placed in front of the Palazzo della Signoria, and statues by Donatello were publicly displayed in Florence and Padua. As printing spread, books became less expensive, making it possible for the literary achievements of the Renaissance to reach a wider audience than anyone could have anticipated in 1400. Because husbands or wives could read to families, and masters to apprentices, the high levels of illiteracy were less a barrier to the dissemination of literature than might be imagined. As humanist ideas were accepted into the curriculum and new schools were founded, Renaissance teachings reached a wider and wider audience. Despite the unwillingness of many humanists to support a liberal education for the masses, the Renaissance was the first step in an educational revolution that swept Europe beginning in the sixteenth century. The Renaissance concern with accurate texts, the keen interest in the classical world (the birthplace of Christianity), and the spread of the printed word also contributed to the Protestant Reformation in the same century. So did the humanist interest in reviving Christianity and integrating it with the culture of antiquity.

Notes

1. L. Martines, *Power and Imagination: City-States in Renaissance Italy* (New York: Knopf, 1979), p. 168.
2. P. G. Ruggiers, *Florence in the Age of Dante* (Norman: University of Oklahoma Press, 1964), p. 43.
3. J. B. Ross and M. M. McLaughlin, eds., *The Portable Renaissance Reader* (New York: Viking, 1968), pp. 124–125.
4. W. H. Woodward, *Vittorino da Feltre and Other Humanist Educators: Essays and Versions* (Cambridge: Cambridge University Press, 1912), pp. 102, 106.
5. J. G. A. Pocock, *The Machiavellian Moment* (Princeton, N.J.: Princeton University Press, 1975), p. 154.
6. A. Blunt, *Artistic Theory in Italy, 1450–1600* (London: Oxford University Press, 1964), p. 34.
7. E. G. Holt, ed., *Literary Sources of Art History* (Princeton, N.J.: Princeton University Press, 1947), p. 170.
8. Ibid., p. 90.
9. Ibid., p. 197.
10. W. Ullmann, *Medieval Foundations of Renaissance Humanism* (London: Elek, 1977), p. 9.

Suggestions for Further Reading

Antal, F. *Florentine Painting and Its Social Background.* New York: Harper & Row, 1975.

Baron, H. *The Crisis of the Early Italian Renaissance: Civic Humanism and Republican Liberty in the Age of Classicism and Tyranny,* rev. ed. Princeton, N.J.: Princeton University Press, 1966.

Baxandall, M. *Painting and Experience in Fifteenth-Century Italy.* New York: Oxford University Press, 1988.

Brucker, G. A. *Renaissance Florence,* rev. ed. Berkeley: University of California Press, 1983.

Chabod, F. *Machiavelli and the Renaissance*, trans. D. Moore. London: Bowes & Bowes, 1958.

Clark, K. *Leonardo da Vinci: An Account of His Development as an Artist*. Baltimore: Penguin Books, 1967.

De Grazia, S. *Machiavelli in Hell*. Princeton, N.J.: Princeton University Press, 1990.

Eisenstein, E. L. *The Printing Press as an Agent of Change: Communications and Cultural Transformations in Early Modern Europe*, 2 vols. Cambridge: Cambridge University Press, 1979.

Ferguson, W. K. *The Renaissance in Historical Thought: Five Centuries of Interpretation*. Boston: Houghton Mifflin, 1948.

Gilbert, F. *Machiavelli and Guicciardini: Politics and History in Sixteenth-Century Florence*. Princeton, N.J.: Princeton University Press, 1965.

Goldthwaite, R. A. *The Building of Renaissance Florence*. Baltimore: Johns Hopkins University Press, 1980.

Hale, J. R. *Renaissance Europe: Individual and Society, 1480–1520*. Berkeley: University of California Press, 1978.

Herlihy, D. *Medieval and Renaissance Pistoia*. New Haven, Conn.: Yale University Press, 1967.

Holmes, G. *Florence, Rome and the Origins of the Renaissance*. Oxford: Clarendon Press, 1986.

———. *The Florentine Enlightenment, 1400–1450*. New York: Pegasus, 1969.

Hook, J. *Lorenzo de' Medici: A Historical Biography*. London: Hamilton, 1984.

King, M. L. *Venetian Humanism in an Age of Patrician Dominance*. Princeton, N.J.: Princeton University Press, 1986.

Klapisch-Zuber, C. *Women, Family, and Ritual in Renaissance Italy*. Chicago: University of Chicago Press, 1985.

Kristeller, P. O. *Renaissance Thought: The Classic, Scholastic, and Humanistic Strains*. New York: Harper & Row, 1961.

———. *Renaissance Thought and Its Sources*. New York: Columbia University Press, 1979.

Labalme, P. H., ed. *Beyond Their Sex: Learned Women of the European Past*. New York: New York University Press, 1980.

Levey, M. *Early Renaissance*. Baltimore: Penguin Books, 1967.

———. *High Renaissance*. Baltimore: Penguin Books, 1975.

Maclean, I. *The Renaissance Notion of Woman*. Cambridge: Cambridge University Press, 1980.

Martines, L. *Power and Imagination: City-States in Renaissance Italy*. New York: Knopf, 1979.

———. *The Social World of the Florentine Humanists, 1390–1460*. Princeton, N.J.: Princeton University Press, 1963.

Muir, E. *Civic Ritual in Renaissance Venice*. Princeton, N.J.: Princeton University Press, 1980.

Murray, P., and Murray, L. *The Art of the Renaissance*. London: Thames & Hudson, 1978.

Niccoli, O. *Prophecy and People in Renaissance Italy*, trans. L. G. Cochrane. Princeton, N.J.: Princeton University Press, 1990.

Partner, P. *Renaissance Rome, 1500–1559: A Portrait of a Society*. Berkeley: University of California Press, 1977.

Ralph, P. L. *The Renaissance in Perspective*. New York: St. Martin's Press, 1973.

Ross, J. B., and McLaughlin, M. M., eds. *The Portable Renaissance Reader*. New York: Viking, 1953.

Ruggiers, P. G. *Florence in the Age of Dante*. Norman: University of Oklahoma Press, 1964.

Stephens, J. *The Italian Renaissance: The Origins of Intellectual and Artistic Change Before the Reformation*. New York: Longman, 1990.

Stinger, C. S. *The Renaissance in Rome*. Bloomington: Indiana University Press, 1985.

Ullmann, W. *Medieval Foundations of Renaissance Humanism*. London: Elek, 1977.

Weinstein, D. *Savonarola and Florence: Prophecy and Patriotism in the Renaissance*. Princeton, N.J.: Princeton University Press, 1970.

The Human Image (I)

Across the ages and around the globe, from the pre-historic cave dwellers of Europe and the rock painters of Africa to our own century of abstract painting and sculpture, every culture has represented the human figure in its art. Successive generations of artists in each civilization have used a rich variety of styles and techniques, but their efforts reveal the common concerns that underlie the human experience.

The meaning of a statue or a painting can be understood fully only in its historical context, for works of art have different functions, depending on the religions, the philosophies, and the values of the culture that produces them. Yet the focus of most artistic traditions has been on the human figure. How one culture has portrayed human beings in its art tells much about the society in which the artist worked. Thus while experts often debate the exact meaning or purpose of a particular work of art, broad cultural patterns can easily be discerned by comparing the artistic treatment accorded the human figure. In a very real sense, art serves as a language by which civilizations communicate their concerns and aspirations as they explore the meaning of existence.

The earliest known representations of the human figure were carved perhaps 30,000 years ago in central Europe. The exaggerated breasts and roundness of the body in these female figures suggest that they served as fertility images; they typically have no facial features. The remains of an ivory statue of the so-called Brno Man in present-day Czechoslovakia dates from approximately the same period but reveals much more attention to the head, which has deep-set eyes and short hair. The Brno Man seems to have been part of a burial ritual.

The unknown sculptors who executed these early Paleolithic (Old Stone Age) works rendered the human figure with a naturalism that was not true of the cave art painted 15,000 years later. The powerful realism that makes the cave paintings of France and Spain famous was devoted almost exclusively to the depiction of animals, and human figures were rarely painted or carved on the walls. When humans were represented, they often appear as abstract forms such as boxes with sticks for arms and legs.

The Addaura finds of Sicily are a rare exception. These caves contain human figures dating from 10,000 to 8000 B.C. incised in outline into the rock face. The nature of the scene is unknown, but the images are exceptionally supple and expressive. Indeed, no earlier wall art renders the human figure with such grace, and, judging from surviving evidence, several thousand

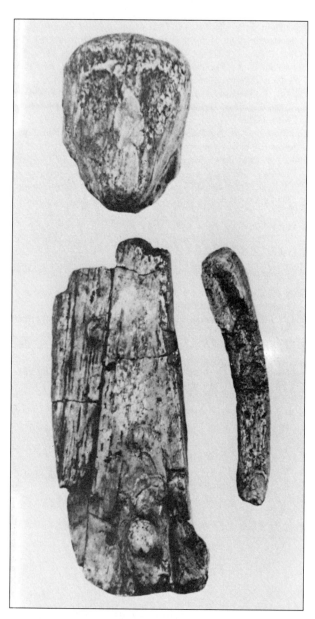

Man from Brno, Czechoslovakia. [Moravian Museum, Brno]

years passed before such skill in representing humans occurred again.

The shift from hunting and gathering to a farming culture that ushered in the Neolithic (New Stone) Age around 8000 B.C. saw the first permanent village com-

Ritual Dance, rock engraving, c. 10,000 B.C., cave of Addaura, Monte Pellegrino, Palermo, Italy. [H. W. Janson]

munities created in western Asia. Humans began to view themselves and their world differently, and a much more sophisticated skill in depicting the human figure emerged. At Jericho, just north of the Dead Sea, archaeologists have uncovered sculptured heads dated to 7000 B.C., made by refashioning human skulls with colored plaster and seashell eyes. These heads, which appear to have been placed above graves, were modeled with great skill, and some had painted features. They may represent the first attempts at individual portraiture.

When compared across many cultures and long stretches of time, all these representations of the human figure suggest the varieties of ritual and belief common to early civilizations. Indeed, clay statues of fertility goddesses made in Anatolia around 6000 B.C. bear a remarkable resemblance to figures from Romania produced 1,000 years later, and both appear quite similar to the Venus of Willendorf, carved 20,000 years earlier.

One of the most extraordinary representations of the human form in Neolithic art is a male figure, also from Romania (c. 4000 B.C.). Modeled from dark clay, the

Man from Cernavoda, Romania. [EastFoto/ Sovfoto]

features and limbs of the small statue are reduced to a stark, bold design that conveys a forceful sense of monumentality in miniature form. The man is seated on a stool and holds his head between his hands, a Neolithic "thinker" captured by the artist in the universal pose of contemplation 6,000 years before the French sculptor Auguste Rodin created his famous version of the same subject.

Ancient Egypt, which enjoyed political unity for more than 2,000 years, produced a remarkably consistent artistic culture obsessed with continuity and permanence. Statues of the pharaohs show the basic Egyptian approach to rendering the human figure: the anatomy and drapery are realistic, but the features are highly idealized, conveying not an individual portrait but the notion of divine power. Less formal portraits of ordinary people, however, are exceptionally lifelike, showing the facial features of a real person.

Egyptian artists adhered to strict rules for representing the human body. They generally rendered the body according to exact proportional ratios between its parts. The poses of the figures are often almost anatomically impossible, with shoulders facing the front while heads and legs face to the right. Despite this stylization, Egyptian artists were capable of achieving great naturalism, as in the relief of Akhenaton, Nefertiti, and three of their children.

The civilization of the Indus valley in the same period (c. 3000–1500 B.C.) stands in sharp contrast to Egyptian culture. Its cities developed no large-scale public art such as the pyramids or the monumental statues of the pharaohs, and the works that survive are small and delicate. A male torso found at Harappa, carved in limestone sometime between 3000 and 2000 B.C., suggests a civilization with markedly different values. The highly skilled sculptor has captured the texture of youthful flesh, softly and sensuously depicted in the swelling body. Contrasted to the rigidity of Egyptian statues, this torso appears to be a living, moving body. Nowhere else was the human figure represented at such an early date with such sensitivity.

In the ancient Aegean the human figure ultimately achieved what is probably its most famous representation. The painting and sculpture of Crete from around 1500 B.C. show influence from Egypt, yet very few human figures were depicted in explicitly religious or political postures in Minoan art. The major exceptions are the strange snake-goddess statues, which must have been worshiped by an unknown cult.

In depicting the human figure, Greeks soon became engrossed in the search for order and ideal beauty, which they saw as complementary aspects of life. Nowhere is this better illustrated than in the freestanding statues of nude young men known as *kouroi* ("youths") produced in Archaic Greece. The pose is stiff, with head held high, eyes focused straight ahead, broad shoulders, narrow waists, arms held down at the side with clenched fists, and one leg striding. The purity, simplicity, and balance of the anatomical form, almost abstract in its conception, must surely have been a deliberate effort to equate natural beauty with divine order through the representation of the human form—for the Greeks made no distinction between the physical features of humans and those of gods.

The principal subject and the greatest achievement of classical Greek art was its treatment of the nude body, which it presented with increasingly greater freedom and suppleness. Indeed, Greek artistic triumphs, such as Praxiteles' *Hermes with Dionysus* or the later *Venus de Milo* and the winged *Victory of Samothrace*, have so conditioned us to equate beauty with the human form that Western art has been concerned with the depiction of human beings ever since.

Because their art sought to achieve a sense of the ideal, the early Greeks left little in the way of actual portraiture, which was introduced into Western art during the later Hellenistic period. The Romans excelled at portraying not only the physical likenesses of real people but their character and psychology as well. Roman art generally lacked the universal sensuousness and idealized beauty of the Greeks and was more concerned with a straightforward rendering of civic and political values. Much Roman sculpture and statuary in the imperial period was devoted to representing the emperor, a practice begun by Augustus, who was keenly aware of its propaganda value. Roman imperial art was never as monumental as Egyptian art had been, but it contrasted strongly with that of the Greeks, who regarded statues of their rulers as vulgar and stamped their likenesses only on coins. But not all Roman art was official, and there was a particularly keen interest in portraiture. In relief sculpture and in portrait busts, Roman depictions of the human form are marked by a direct rendering of individual features and characteristics.

The image of the Buddha, which was to dominate much of Asian art, was first depicted in human form at the time when the Romans were producing portraits of their civic leaders. Because doctrine held that the Buddha—the "enlightened one"—eventually achieved transcendence of the senses and of self, he had been depicted for centuries only by means of abstract symbols. But a new school of Buddhist thought that emerged in the first century A.D. conceived of the Buddha as an eternal god and provided him with a host of divinities, known as bodhisattvas, to assist him. The need for icons as visual aids to this new creed became apparent. Competition with Hinduism, which practiced the worship of personalized deities, also led to the adoption of a human image for the Buddha.

Head of the Buddha from Gandhara, third century A.D. [Victoria and Albert Museum, London]

Among the earliest images of the Buddha were third-century statues produced in the border region comprising much of modern day Afghanistan and Pakistan, where Greek and Roman cultural influences were strong. The features of these Buddhas suggest a sensual spirituality that would be a trademark of Indian art. A more purely Indian classical style emerged in the fifth century under the Guptas, where statues that have no equivalent in the West portray the Buddha as more a divine essence than a real person. As Buddhist influences spread eastward into China, Southeast Asia, and Japan, images of the Buddha were fashioned according to local artistic conventions and styles.

Aside from Buddhist influences, early Chinese art generally avoided depictions of the human figure. Taoist philosophy stressed that humans were not dominant in nature but merely a part of it, so secular

Chinese art preferred landscapes and animals to portraits. The excavation of imperial tombs from the Chin dynasty (221–207 B.C.) unearthed a stunning collection of more than 500 life-size clay warriors. From the Han dynasty on, emperors were painted in lifelike portraits, as were famous sages, such as Confucius and Lao-tze. Portraits of courtiers and court ladies were also important, although often as part of large scenes of court life and the palace world.

In the millennium from the fifth to the fifteenth centuries, the human figure predominated almost everywhere in art, largely to serve religious or political purposes. The major exception was Islamic art, where Arab tradition and Muslim doctrine generally proscribed the representation of living things. The Koran, however, specifically prohibited only statuary, and some Islamic painting did portray human figures. After about 800, Muslim theologians launched a campaign against representation, arguing that an artist who made images of living things usurped the divine creative act. The human figure disappeared thereafter in large-scale art for public display, although it survived in miniatures, manuscript illuminations, and private art, in large part as a result of the influence of non-Muslim artists.

In the medieval West and in Byzantium two religious images—Christ and the Virgin Mary—dominated painting and sculpture. Although these images varied greatly in artistic style and emphasis from century to century and from one region to another, they served to convey basic precepts of Christian belief. In the early-sixth-century mosaics of the Byzantine city of Ravenna, Christ still appears as the beardless and youthful miracle worker of early Christian art, but he was later transformed into the bearded, lean-faced image that became familiar throughout the Christian world.

A similar transformation occurred in representations of the Virgin Mary as the Madonna, the mother of Christ. Byzantine icons conformed to strict formal rules of design that were repeated over and over. They reveal a stiffness of treatment and an almost abstract quality that is related to mosaic art. The northern Gothic imagination transformed the serenity of the icon into a highly expressionistic *Pietà* whose agonized faces and grotesque wounds evoke the horror of Christ's grief-stricken mother. During the Renaissance, Italian painters produced serene and often sensual Madonnas that depict a mother and child with only muted reference to Christian symbolism.

Indian artists of the same period, intent on rendering an inner spirituality, ignored the Western obsession with the lifelike, giving their work instead a peculiar tension between spirituality and sensual beauty. A seventh century wall painting of a bodhisattva presents an exquisite vision of harmony, the personification of compassion and tenderness, that is in marked contrast to Western paintings of the Virgin Mary or of Christ

Miracle of the Loaves and Fishes, mosaic, c. 504. [Alinari/Art Resource]

Pietà, German, early fourteenth century. [Marburg/Art Resource]

and torsos. Large-scale figure sculpture came to Japan with the introduction of Buddhism, as can be seen in the enormous Buddha and bodhisattva statues from the eighth century.

Unique artistic cultures also developed in Africa and Central America. Near the village of Nok, in northern Nigeria, the discovery of terra-cotta sculpture testifies to a thriving civilization as early as 400 B.C. Besides representations of animals, startling human figures and large heads were produced. The heads are highly stylized, generally cylindrical or conical, but each one has expressive features that clearly suggest individual personalities. These clay works were no doubt modeled after wood carvings, for many suggest the carved masks so familiar in African art.

Although Nok culture disappeared after the third century A.D., it seems to have exercised an important and lasting influence on the later cultures of West Africa. Terra-cotta and brass heads were found at Ife, in southwestern Nigeria, dating probably from the twelfth century. Human features are brilliantly rendered in these masterpieces. These and similar heads are no

Bodhisattva of Mercy, Chinese, eleventh or twelfth century. [Nelson-Atkins Museum of Art, Kansas City, Missouri]

from the same period. Similarly, Chinese statues of bodhisattvas from the T'ang dynasty reveal the beauty of the figure in the traditional Indian pose. Even in Hindu religious sculpture, so filled with symbolic images, Indian artists remained faithful to the sensuous quality of their artistic traditions. A bronze statue from around 1000 A.D. shows the graceful four-armed figure of Siva Nataraja dancing within a flaming halo, creating a magnificent three-dimensional effect.

In Sung China, the major representation of a human figure, after the Buddha, was Kuan-yin, the bodhisattva of mercy, who is generally shown as a sexless deity in either male or female form. But a glazed pottery statue from the same period demonstrates that the Chinese were equally capable of the most straightforward representation.

No native deities were depicted in Japanese art before the Buddha, and the only earlier human likenesses were terra-cotta figures from the fourth to the sixth centuries consisting of human heads atop tubelike limbs

Head of a Nigerian queen, twelfth or thirteenth century. [Museum of Antiquities, Ife, Nigeria]

Wrestler, c. 400 B.C. [Doug Bryant/DDB Stock Photo]

The Toltec god Chacmool, c. 1200, found at Chichén Itzá. [Andrew Rakoczy/Art Resource]

doubt idealized forms rather than portraits. Such sculptural traditions apparently evolved in West Africa without outside influences; indeed, European artists produced no works of equal subtlety during this period.

In marked contrast to the refinement of African sculpture stand the early carvings of Central America. Although the Olmecs of Mexico were capable of sophisticated works, such as a stone wrestler that dates from around 400 B.C., or small jade figures of infants, nonetheless their culture seems to be more aptly characterized by the colossal monolithic heads made during the same period.

Later cultures in the region, such as the Toltecs, also created striking stone sculptures and carved reliefs that often appear intimidating. Thus the god Chacmool is

THE VISUAL EXPERIENCE
Art of the Renaissance

Giotto's *Lamentation*, a fresco painted for the Scrovegni Chapel in Padua, is one of the most eloquent depictions of grief in early Renaissance art. [Scala/Art Resource]

The Neoplatonic concern with beauty is apparent in this celebration of spring, *Primavera* by Sandro Botticelli. The Venus figure in the center represents spring; Mercury and the three Graces are to the left; at the right, a nymph being chased by the wind god Zephyr is transposed into the goddess Flora (in the flowered dress) while Cupid hovers above. [Scala/Art Resource]

Leonardo da Vinci's *Virgin of the Rocks* masterfully combines the artist's intense interest in natural phenomena and human anatomy with traditional religious devotion. [Giraudon/Art Resource]

Raphael's *Madonna with the Goldfinch* uses the pyramidal composition he learned from Leonardo's *Virgin of the Rocks*, but whereas Leonardo depicted Mary against a mysterious landscape, Raphael's is a model of clarity. The painting reflects Raphael's fusion of pagan beauty and Christian piety. [Scala/Art Resource]

Michelangelo's depiction on the Sistine Chapel ceiling of the first sin and Adam and Eve's expulsion from Eden underscores the Neoplatonic contrast between the physical (evil) and the spiritual (good). [Scala/Art Resource]

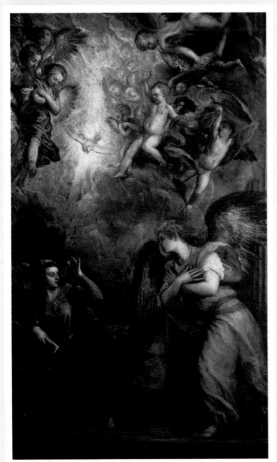

This dramatic painting of the Annunciation by Titian shows the archangel Gabriel announcing to Mary that she will give birth to the Messiah. [Scala/Art Resource]

Sofonisba Anguissola painted her three sisters playing chess in 1555. She provided a role model for other Italian women who sought careers in art. Approximately fifty of her works, most of them portraits, have survived. [Jerzy Nowakowski; National Museum, Poznan, Poland]

Hieronymus Bosch's depiction of hell is the right panel of his *Garden of Earthly Delights*. Bosch was a narrative painter whose visions provoked the imagination. These scenes suggest the dangers of sensualism, such as an undue fondness for music or sexual pleasure. [Scala/Art Resource]

frequently rendered as a reclining human figure in severely foreshortened geometric shape, whose expression suggests a hostile and forbidding countenance.

Since the first Paleolithic carvers had worked their primitive sculptures tens of thousands of years earlier, the human figure had been depicted in a great variety of styles, but for broadly similar purposes. It served as a religious icon or political symbol, as a way of representing ideal beauty or activity, or as a means of commenting on the human condition. Although every generation has addressed these themes anew, the art of the modern world has remained constant to their expression.

Suggestions for Further Reading

Breckenridge, J. D. *Likeness: A Conceptual History of Ancient Portraiture.* Evanston, Ill.: Northwestern University Press, 1968.

Clark, K. *The Nude: A Study in Ideal Form.* Princeton, N.J.: Princeton University Press, 1956.

De Dilva, A., and Von Simson, O. *Man Through His Art,* Vol. 6: *The Human Face.* New York: Graphic Society, 1968.

Garland, M. *The Changing Face of Beauty.* New York: Barrows, 1957.

Kubler, G. *The Art and Architecture of Ancient America.* Harmondsworth, England: Penguin Books, 1962.

Lee, S. *A History of Far Eastern Art.* New York: Abrams, 1974.

Leroi-Gourhan, A. *Treasures of Prehistoric Art.* New York: Abrams, 1967.

Man: Glory, Jest, and Riddle: A Survey of the Human Form Through the Ages. San Francisco: M. H. de Young Memorial Museum, California Palace of the Legion of Honor, and San Francisco Museum of Art, 1965.

Mayor, A. H. *Artists and Anatomy.* New York: Artist's Limited Edition, 1984.

Mode, H. *The Woman in Indian Art.* New York: McGraw-Hill, 1970.

Relouge, I. E., ed. *Masterpieces of Figure Painting.* New York: Viking, 1959.

Richter, G. *The Portraits of the Greeks,* rev. R. R. R. Smith. Oxford: Phaidon, 1984.

Rowland, B. *The Art and Architecture of India.* Baltimore: Penguin Books, 1967.

Schultz, B. *Art and Anatomy in Renaissance Italy.* Ann Arbor, Mich.: UMI Research Press, 1985.

Segal, M. *Painted Ladies: Models of the Great Artists.* New York: Stein & Day, 1972.

Smart, A. *The Renaissance and Mannerism in Italy.* New York: Harcourt Brace Jovanovich, 1971.

Walker, J. *Portraits: 5,000 Years.* New York: Abrams, 1983.

Wentinck, C. *The Human Figure in Art from Prehistoric Times to the Present Day,* trans. E. Cooper. Wynnewood, Pa.: Livingston Publishing, 1970.

Willett, F. *African Art: An Introduction.* New York: Praeger, 1971.

PART·THREE

The Early Modern World

The early modern world began with crisis and renewal in three of its major civilizations—those of western Europe, the Islamic regions, and China—and catastrophe for a fourth, the Aztec and Inca cultures of the Western Hemisphere.

In Europe, recovery from the demographic disaster of the Black Death had just been achieved when the Catholic church, the dominant social institution of Europe for 1,000 years, was challenged and riven by a movement of protest and reform— hence the name it took, the Protestant Reformation—which touched off a century and a quarter of internecine warfare, both within and between states, and left a permanently divided Christianity in western Europe.

Despite the scars left by the Reformation, Europe began a remarkable career of expansion and conquest in the early modern period that was to make it the dominant world civilization by the nineteenth century. Following their discovery of the Western Hemisphere—named by Europeans "the Americas"— Spanish and Portuguese adventurers rapidly conquered the Aztec and Inca empires, whose populations were soon decimated by exploitation and epidemic. Within Europe itself, a population increasingly urban and (after the development of movable type) literate had begun to come under the sway of centralized state bureaucracies and a new economic regime, capitalism, based on mobile labor, expanded commerce, and production for profit. The sixteenth and seventeenth centuries also saw a reconceptualization of the physical world, the scientific revolution, that was to transform human understanding of and relation to the natural environment.

Europe itself faced challenge from the east, where a new Islamic empire, that of the Ottoman Turks, extinguished the 1,000-year Christian empire of Byzantium, occupied much of southeastern Europe as well as the Middle East, and twice stood before the gates of Vienna. More loosely governed than the states of Europe, but also less politically divided, the Ottomans presided over a brilliant cultural and religious revival and showed again the remarkable capacity of Islam to achieve rapid unification and expansion. The Mughal dynasty in India and the Safavids in Iran produced a new age of prosperity and cultural splendor in south-central Asia.

While Europe and the Islamic world were both expanding, a new Chinese dynasty, the Ming, threw off the Mongol yoke of the early fourteenth century and inaugurated a golden age in the world's most populous and prosperous state. After probing westward by sea as far as Africa, the Ming turned inward. Commercialization and urbanization grew, and the arts flourished. A brisk and lucrative foreign trade nonetheless continued, mainly with Southeast Asia but also with the West through Muslim and Venetian intermediaries. By the sixteenth century, Jesuit missionaries had reached China, as had the first Western trading ships, which began to clash in the waters of Japan and Southeast Asia. ■

The Reformation

The forces unleashed in the Reformation struck deeply at the roots of Western values and shattered the fragile unity of medieval Christendom. Sparked by reformers who raised profound questions concerning conscience and authority, the new movements were successful because of favorable political and social conditions in the sixteenth century that supported alternative Christian views. The crisis of conscience that marked the dismantling of medieval Christendom was a poignant one for reformers on all sides of the struggle. In a society where belief and conduct had always been regulated by authority from above, the rival claims of Christian leaders initiated a period of militant zeal and frightening upheaval. Since neither camp proved able to impose its views on its opponents, the West was henceforth divided by competing ecclesiastical institutions, antagonistic creeds, and conflicting claims to religious authority.

Archbishop Thomas Cranmer was burned at the stake in Oxford on March 21, 1556, after reaffirming his Protestant faith. [Ronald Sheridan/Ancient Art and Architecture Collection]

Fear, doubt, and outright hostility led to persecutions and witch-hunting, but the Reformation was also an age in which the goals of religious renewal were embodied in high ideals and noble visions.

The Late Medieval Church

The medieval church derived considerable strength from its ability to renew itself from within. The Gregorian reform of the eleventh century, subsequent monastic reforms, and the founding of the mendicant orders in the thirteenth century all gave vitality to the church. In the early fifteenth century, reformers successfully ended the Papal Schism at the Council of Constance, but further reform attempts generally failed. The major reason was lack of effective papal leadership. Fifteenth-century popes were occupied not only with their roles as Italian princes and as patrons of the arts but also with the challenge to their power posed by the reformers. Renaissance popes proved unwilling to address the deep-rooted problems that reform movements, particularly that of John Hus in Bohemia, sought to redress. Although the better popes were capable administrators and notable patrons of the arts, none instituted major ecclesiastical reforms, and Pius II (1458–1464) even prohibited appeals to church councils.

Lay Piety

Demands for reform were made by persons intent on preserving the unity or spiritual supremacy of the church, not on destroying it; theology was not an issue for them, save in the cases of heretical groups such as the Hussites in Bohemia or the Lollards in England. Particularly in German-speaking lands, popular piety remained strong and was probably increasing. Visitors from Italy were impressed by the people's devotion, much of which was rooted in traditional family piety. The development of the printing press dramatically increased the circulation of religious material, though Bibles were still fairly expensive on the eve of the Reformation. Some 10,000 different sermons, mostly in Latin, were in print by 1500, and popular manuals for religious devotion encouraged spiritual training in the home.

The growth of piety was also reflected by the fact that more churches were constructed in German lands in the fifteenth century than in any preceding period. Religious clubs or organizations for laypersons were founded at a striking pace in the fourteenth and fifteenth centuries. Typical of these were the Brethren of the Common Life, established in the Netherlands in the fourteenth century, and the Brotherhood of the Eleven Thousand Vir-

Hans Holbein the Younger's rendering of the Dance of Death reflects the fifteenth- and early-sixteenth-century preoccupation with dying, which was in part responsible for the piety and religious concern of this period. In this panel a child is snatched by death. [Giraudon/Art Resource]

gins, founded at Cracow and Cologne a century later. While some brotherhoods, such as the Common Life, were involved in education, most were associations to foster piety through communal praying and singing. In large measure, then, the Reformation was possible because the heightened sense of religious awareness among the people, often expressed outside the institutional church, was not matched by reform of the chronic problems.

Institutional Decay

Two of the most critical problems of the church involved the quality and training of the clergy and ecclesiastical finances. Although the moral standards and educational preparation of the ministry did not substantially decline in the fifteenth century, many people, particularly north of the Alps, were growing impatient with priests who were sometimes flagrantly immoral or semiliterate, particularly as the educational level of many laypersons began to rise. The problem was compounded by the moral laxity of many of the church's leaders, including Pope Alexander VI (1492–1503) and numerous cardinals and prelates. In an age acutely conscious of mortality, there was a demand for spiritual shepherds capable of relieving fears and providing religious guidance. Sensitivity to such needs was often lacking among the higher clergy—notably the archbishops and bishops—who were normally younger sons from aristocratic families pursuing ecclesiastical careers for wealth and political power and had little contact with commoners.

At the level of the parish priesthood, minimal incomes made it difficult to recruit educated men, although some able individuals fostered the growth of popular piety. As a result, most parish priests were drawn from the lowest ranks of society. In the absence of seminaries, the parish priests received on-the-job training from neighboring colleagues and were ill-prepared to instruct parishioners in the complex teaching of the church. The church's future welfare required the recruitment of dedicated priests, an educational program to train them, their effective supervision by bishops, adequate salaries, and the expulsion of unfit men from the priesthood.

The problem of attracting able men at the parish level was directly related to defects in the church's economic structure and officialdom. Although the church was an immensely wealthy institution with vast landholdings, its riches were unequally distributed. In contrast to the opulent lifestyles enjoyed by the archbishops and bishops, most parish priests barely eked out a living; some administrators in the church improved their positions by holding multiple benefices (church livings), a practice that normally detracted from religious duties. Others never visited their parishes but hired poorly paid vicars to perform their duties. Beneficed priests were also in the awkward position of obtaining income from their parishioners by collecting tithes (usually paid in goods, such as wheat) and fees (for baptisms, marriages, and burials). Because tithes were mandatory, they often caused disputes and resentment, particularly among the poor or those dissatisfied with the absenteeism and the low moral and educational levels of the priests. In Germany and Switzerland, peasants and artisans in the fifteenth and sixteenth centuries often condemned these abuses. In addition to the abolition of serfdom and a decrease in rents, they demanded religious reforms, including a reduction of church lands and clerical wealth. In the resulting uprisings, flags depicting a peasant's shoe beside Christ on a white cross symbolically united religious and social protest.

Christian Humanists and the Quest for Reform

The need for institutional reform in the church was a dominant theme of the Christian humanists of northern Europe. To the principles of the Italian humanists they fused the teachings of primitive Christianity in the hope that they might achieve a return to the purity of the early church and its simple but deep-rooted faith. Many northern humanists placed special emphasis on the study of biblical languages and the publication of accurate scriptural texts. Likewise, the humanist attack on corruption and meaningless ceremony in the church prepared the way for Protestant demands for reform and a justification for the break with Rome. Yet the older generations of northern humanists generally remained loyal to Catholicism. In England, Sir Thomas More chose death over renunciation of the church when the latter was demanded of him by King Henry VIII. However, many in the younger generation, such as John Calvin and William Tyndale, found their humanist principles compatible with Protestantism. Indeed, humanists and Protestants each looked to the past as the basis for their proposed reforms—humanists to the classical world, Protestants to the early church—and both shared a deep interest in history.

The Challenge of Hebrew Scholarship: Reuchlin and Hutten

One of the leading biblical scholars among the Christian humanists was Johann Reuchlin (1455–1522), a German authority on Hebrew language and thought. He ran afoul of a converted Jew named Johann Pfefferkorn, who had Emperor Maximilian's authorization to examine Jewish materials in order to identify ones that attacked Christianity. With the support of Dominican scholastics in Cologne, Pfefferkorn attempted to suppress all Jewish literature on the basis of its hostility to Christianity, but Reuchlin objected because Jewish texts had religious and cultural value. When Maximilian condemned his attacks on Pfefferkorn in 1512, Reuchlin retaliated by branding his enemies "pigs" and "children of the devil." Pfefferkorn had the backing of several leading theological faculties, but Reuchlin was defended by a number of German humanists, particularly Ulrich von Hutten and Crotus Rubeanus. These two men wrote the satirical *Letters of Obscure Men* (1515), which purportedly came from the pens of Pfefferkorn's friends and made them appear ridiculous. Hutten, who had once condemned Pope Julius II as the "pest of the world," regarded the papacy as the source of Christendom's troubles. A German patriot, he applauded when Martin Luther attacked the pope's authority to issue indulgences in 1517.

Erasmus, Prince of the Humanists

The greatest Greek scholar among the northern humanists was Desiderius Erasmus of Rotterdam (c. 1466–1536), a pupil of the Brethren of the Common Life and later a student at the University of Paris. Much of his scholarly career was spent in Basel, though he was widely traveled and visited England several times. One of the great triumphs of Renaissance scholarship was his edition of the New Testament in Greek, first published in 1516. In its preface, he made an eloquent plea for Bibles in the vernacular: "I would that even the lowliest women read the Gospels and Pauline Epistles.... Would that ... the farmer sing some portion of them at the plough."[1] Erasmus thus anticipated one of the major accomplishments of the Protestant Reformation, the bringing of the Bible to the common people.

Erasmus' religious beliefs are summarized in his idea of a "philosophy of Christ," by which he meant a disciplined life of love and service for God and other people. In contrast to the complexities of the scholastics, Erasmus stressed the simple teachings of Jesus; the heart of religion was faith and love in action, not ritualistic observance. In his great classic, the *Praise of Folly*, he mercilessly satirized such Catholic practices as pilgrimages, the veneration of relics, the sale of indulgences, and the mechanical use of the rosary. Erasmus condemned war as a denial of Christian love and insisted that peace was essential for the spread of education and scholarship. He even condemned war against the Turks on the ground that any victories they might win against Europeans were divinely ordained as a means to chastise Christians. Nowhere is his repudiation of the philosophy of might more evident than in his *Education of a Christian Prince* (1516), written for Charles of Habsburg, the future Emperor Charles V. Erasmus' ideal ruler—devoted to peace, guided by honesty and right religion, concerned for the welfare of his people—was diametrically opposed to Machiavelli's prince. Erasmus was the epitome of a Christian idealist: "We may shortly behold," he wrote in 1517, "the rise of a new kind of golden age. So great is the heaven-sent change we see in the minds of princes, who bend all their powers to the pursuit of peace."[2]

The Humanists in England

John Colet and Sir Thomas More, both friends of Erasmus, were the leading Christian humanists in England. Colet (c. 1466-1519) founded St. Paul's School for boys

Hans Holbein painted Erasmus of Rotterdam, the influential Christian humanist whose stinging criticism of abuses in the Catholic church helped set the stage for the Protestant Reformation. Erasmus himself, however, remained a Catholic. [Metropolitan Museum of Art, New York]

in London, with a curriculum devoted to the critical study of Latin and Greek as well as religion. Colet's scriptural expositions were noted for their attention to historical context and literal meaning, and some of his sermons fearlessly denounced corruption in the church.

More (1478–1535), an able diplomat and later Lord Chancellor for Henry VIII, depicted the model society of a Renaissance humanist in *Utopia* (1516), a shrewd work of social criticism coupled with autobiographical reflections. His book envisioned a communal society in which "life and work [are] common to all," education is universal and compulsory, and crime is largely nonexistent because there would be no extremes of wealth and poverty. Utopia ("nowhere" in Greek) was a tolerant society in which one enjoyed the freedom to believe as one wished, so long as one did not coerce others or use religion to promote sedition. There is tragic irony in the fact that More, who was beheaded for refusing to accept

---

◉ A Bible for the People ◉

In The Paraclesis, *Erasmus argued for the importance of having the Bible translated into the language of the people. This was directly related to his belief in the essential simplicity of the Christian message.*

I greatly dissent from those men who would not have the Scripture of Christ translated into all tongues that it might be read diligently by private and secular men and women, as though Christ had taught such dark and insensible things that they could only be understood by a few divines, or else as though the pith and substance of the Christian religion consisted chiefly in this, that it be not known. Peradventure it is most expedient that the counsels of kings should be kept secret, but Christ would have his counsels and mysteries spread abroad as much as possible. I desire that all women should read the Gospel and Paul's epistles, and I would to God they were translated into the tongues of all men, so that they might not only be read and known by the Scots and Irishmen, but also by the Turks and Saracens. Truly it is one degree to good living, yea the first . . . to have a little sight into the Scripture, though it be but a gross knowledge . . . and that some should err and be deceived. I would to God the plowman would sing a text of the Scripture at his plow, and the weaver at his loom. . . . I would that all the communication of the Christian should be of the Scripture, for in a manner we ourselves are such as our daily speech is.

Source: Erasmus, *An Exhortation to the Diligent Study of Scripture* (London, 1529), pp. 8–9 (edited to conform with modern usage).

Henry VIII's headship over the English church, dreamed of a day when a ruler would recognize that it was "arrogant folly for anyone to enforce conformity with his own beliefs by means of threats or violence."[3] Yet More himself had supported the persecution of heretics in his capacity as Henry's chancellor. In the end, More, like Erasmus, found Protestant theology unacceptable, but his call for reform helped pave the way for the Reformation.

Luther and the German Reformation

The event that triggered the Protestant Reformation—or Revolt, as Roman Catholics often call it—was associated with the church's financial policy as well as popular piety. Late in 1514, Pope Leo X revived a campaign originally launched by Julius II to rebuild St. Peter's Basilica in Rome, the money for which was to be raised partly through the sale of indulgences. An indulgence cancelled or reduced the temporal punishment for sin. Retribution and forgiveness for one's sins were the central

focus of the sacrament of penance, which included confession and the performance of prescribed penalties. Catholic theology advanced the belief that few people lived such exemplary lives that the remission was complete. Most Christians therefore had to be purified in purgatory after they died before they could enter heaven. Beginning in 1476, the papacy claimed the power to reduce the time that souls spent in purgatory by transferring to them the surplus good deeds of Christ and his saints (stored in the "treasury of merit"). This it would do for anyone who purchased indulgences, usually in return for monetary gifts to the church. As early as the thirteenth century, the papacy had sold indulgences as a source of income, though reformers at the Council of Constance in 1415 protested this practice. It continued, partly because so many shared in the profits and partly because many common folk sincerely believed that their money could speed their loved ones or themselves through purgatory.

In the spring of 1517, the papacy completed preparations for the sale of indulgences in northern Germany. However, a university professor in the Saxon town of Wittenberg, Martin Luther (1483–1546), raised serious questions about indulgences and soon challenged the authority of the papacy itself. No issue was more central to the Reformation than this question of authority.

Luther: The Early Years and the Attack on Indulgences

Luther's father, an ambitious miner who became part owner of a mine, provided a good education for his son, including a year's study with the Brethren of the Common Life. As Luther prepared to study law after graduating from the University of Erfurt, he was deeply troubled by religious doubts. Terrified by a lightning storm, he promised St. Anne, the patron of miners, that he would become a monk in return for his safety, and shortly thereafter he became an Augustinian friar. Although the rigors of the monastic routine brought no relief from his deep-seated fears of divine wrath, he remained in the order.

A trip to Rome on Augustinian business in 1510 confirmed Luther's feeling that the church was too worldly and needed reform. As he prepared lectures on the Bible at the University of Wittenberg, to whose faculty he had been assigned, he became convinced that no amount of human effort could save a person from the awesome judgment of God; salvation (or justification) could come only through the divine gifts of grace and faith. Luther vividly likened the human condition to that of a worm trapped in the ordure of the bowels, unable to escape unless God plucked the soul from the filth. From this conviction of salvation by faith alone, Luther gained the spiritual strength to become a religious leader, although personal fears continued to plague him. More than 15 years later he confessed that he was still terrified when he heard God called "just." It was this unusual sensitivity to human unworthiness and the need for divinely bestowed faith that made him rebel at the commercialism of the indulgence hawkers, particularly Johann Tetzel, who dramatically evoked the appeal of relatives suffering in purgatory: "Pity us, pity us. We are in dire torment from which you can redeem us for a pittance."[4]

Although Luther had criticized indulgences in 1516, it was not until the people of Wittenberg purchased them from Tetzel the following autumn that his views attracted serious attention. Intended at first only for academic debate, the 95 theses that Luther issued on October 31, 1517, challenged belief in papal authority to release souls from purgatory. Finding no scriptural authority for indulgences, Luther insisted that believers received full forgiveness for their sins through faith and repentance, not letters of indulgence. Within weeks, the theses were translated from Latin into German, printed, and distributed throughout Germany, creating a sensation. Summoned to Rome for examination on charges of heresy, Luther instead received a hearing in Augsburg, thanks to the intervention of his prince, Frederick of Saxony. As one of the seven electors of the Holy Roman Empire empowered to select a successor when the aged Maximilian died, Frederick was a man Pope Leo X dared not

alienate. For political reasons, then, no effective action was taken to suppress Luther, who gained vital time to work out the implications of his views on authority and salvation by faith.

Toward a New Theology

In a debate at Leipzig with the papal spokesman Johann Eck in 1519, Luther moved closer to an open break with the church by rejecting the authority of the pope and the infallibility of church councils and by referring with approval to John Hus, the Bohemian heretic. Further reflection led Luther to write three reform manifestos in 1520. Their publication broadcast his views widely and was enormously effective in winning support for them. The first of the treatises was the *Address to the Christian Nobility of the German Nation*, an appeal to the emperor, the German princes and knights, and the imperial cities to cast off papal bondage. In a work with pronounced nationalistic overtones, Luther repudiated three fundamental papal claims: superior jurisdiction over temporal powers, the sole authority to interpret Scripture, and the exclusive right to summon a general council of the church.

In his second treatise, *On the Babylonian Captivity of the Church*, Luther rejected four of the sacraments for which he found no biblical basis, retaining only baptism, the Lord's supper, and penance (which he later dropped). Here too he set forth his concept of the priesthood of all believers, repudiating the traditional Catholic distinction between the clergy and the laity: "We are all equally priests . . . we have the same power in respect to the Word and the sacraments."[5] He conceded that to preach required the church's approval, thereby preserving a sense of order. Finally, in *The Liberty of the Christian Man*, Luther explained his doctrine of salvation by faith alone, insisting that good deeds were necessary fruits of this faith. On these principles Protestantism was founded.

Before the last two of these treatises appeared, Pope Leo issued a bull, *Exsurge domine*, commanding Luther to retract his assertions or be excommunicated. Luther and his supporters responded to this challenge by publicly burning copies of the bull and the canon law. Luther finally received a formal hearing in April 1521, three months after his excommunication, when he appeared before the imperial Diet at Worms. The decision to leave the safety of Saxony was an act of courage, despite a guarantee of safe conduct from the new emperor, Charles V. As Luther knew, a similar promise had not saved Hus from the flames a century earlier. Expecting to debate his views before the Diet, Luther was stunned when ordered to retract his statements without an opportunity to defend himself. To the emperor and the nobles Luther responded the following day: "I am neither

⊛ Luther on Justification by Faith ⊛

One of Luther's strongest statements of the doctrine of justification by faith alone appears in his commentary on Paul's epistle to the Galatians. First published in 1535, the commentary was based on lectures delivered at the University of Wittenberg four years earlier.

We imagine as it were two worlds, the one heavenly and the other earthly. In these we place these two kinds of righteousness, being separate the one far from the other. The righteousness of the law is earthly and hath to do with earthly things, and by it we do good works. But as the earth bringeth not forth fruit except first it be watered and made fruitful from above . . . even so by the righteousness of the law, in doing many things we do nothing, and in fulfilling of the law we fulfil it not, except first, without any merit or work of ours, we be made righteous by the Christian righteousness, which nothing appertaineth to the righteousness of the law, or to the earthly and active righteousness. But this righteousness is heavenly and passive: which we have not of ourselves, but receive it from heaven: which we work not, but apprehend it by faith; whereby we mount up above all laws and works. Wherefore like as we have borne (as St. Paul saith) the image of the earthly Adam, so let us bear the image of the heavenly (1 Cor. 15:49), which is the new man in a new world, where is no law, no sin, no sting of conscience, no death, but perfect joy, righteousness, grace, peace, life, salvation, and glory.

Why, do we then nothing? Do we work nothing for the obtaining of this righteousness? I answer: Nothing at all.

Source: Martin Luther, *A Commentary on St. Paul's Epistle to the Galatians,* ed. P. S. Watson (Westwood, N.J.: Revell, 1953), p. 25.

---

able nor willing to revoke anything, since to act against one's conscience is neither safe nor honest."[6] The break with Rome was now complete, for Luther had rejected the fundamental Catholic doctrine of the combined authority of Scripture and tradition. Neither pope nor church councils could be the final court of appeal, as authority resided in the Bible and the conscience of the believer, duly enlightened by the Holy Spirit through Scripture. The emphasis on individual conscience became one of the most important elements in the Protestant tradition.

Although the emperor was unmoved by Luther's stand, he honored the safe conduct. Taking no chances, Frederick hid Luther in his castle at Wartburg, where Luther, disguised as "Sir George," translated Erasmus' Greek New Testament into German. Excommunicated by the church and outlawed by the empire, he could not return to Wittenberg for nearly a year. He remained there until his death in 1546, secure only because of political and religious rivalries within the empire and Charles' preoccupation with military campaigns against the French and the Turks.

Religion and Social Reform

Luther's program of reform had major religious and social consequences. Refusing to recognize the Roman church as the true church of Christ, he set out to establish an institution that conformed to his view of the New Testament. He and his supporters rejected prayers to the saints, the veneration of relics, indulgences, and pilgrimages because they regarded them as superstitious and unscriptural. The monasteries in Lutheran territories were dissolved, resulting in a major redistribution of wealth that ultimately improved the social position of the wealthier urban citizens as well as the princes and the aristocracy. Mandatory celibacy for the clergy was also ended. Regarded by Catholics as a superior state, celibacy now was given no more importance than marriage, which gained a new dignity. Luther himself married a former nun, Katherine von Bora, who bore him six children. The effects of these changes on women were mixed, for although wives were no longer regarded as inferior to celibate women, the closing of nunneries

The propaganda war between Protestants and Catholics made effective use of the printing press, as in the case of Hans Holbein's woodcut depicting Luther as the "German Hercules." Having vanquished such Catholic teachers as Thomas Aquinas and William of Ockham, Luther uses his cudgel to thrash the Cologne inquisitor who attacked Reuchlin, the Hebrew scholar. [Zentralbibliothek, Zurich]

deprived women of a vocational option. Fathers, however, could no longer place their daughters in convents to avoid providing dowries for them.

In most respects Luther's view of women was traditional, predicated on their subordination to men and a belief in the inferiority of their abilities. They should, he said, "remain at home, sit still, keep house, and bear and bring up children." But even though he regarded wives as subject to their husbands, he viewed them as partners in marriage. Because Luther made the family the focal point of society and church, wives had a new dignity. Thus Luther accepted women's spiritual equality with men, but he refused to allow them a formal role in the preaching or teaching ministry of the church or in politics. Nevertheless, some women became active in the spread of Lutheranism. Argula von Grumbach, who came from an aristocratic Bavarian family and had a humanist education, distributed Lutheran books, conducted religious services in her home, and corresponded with Luther. Elizabeth of Braunschweig converted people in Hanover and Göttingen to Lutheranism and furthered the Protestant cause in letters to political leaders. But Argula's and Elizabeth's roles in the Lutheran movement owed more to their aristocratic status than to Luther's encouragement of female activity.

In Lutheran churches the sermon was accorded a prominent place, services were conducted in the vernacular, and congregational participation was increased, especially through the singing of hymns. The more active role of the laity and the significance attached to the sermon led to greater attention to education. Luther wanted a primary school in every parish and a secondary school in every sizable town, with provision for the education of girls as well as boys. With his colleague Philip Melanchthon, he urged civil authorities to establish and support schools, drawing especially on the wealth obtained by the closing of monasteries and other Catholic institutions. Because of the importance of the Bible, which Luther insisted must be in the vernacular, Protestantism became a major incentive to the growth of literacy.

At first, the religious confusion of the opening years of the Reformation brought a reduction in the number of students, especially at the universities; enrollment at the University of Vienna fell from 661 students in 1519 to 12 in 1532. An alarmed Erasmus complained that "wherever Lutheranism prevails, there learning disappears." But Luther and his colleagues successfully pressed civic officials and territorial princes to establish new schools. The Lutherans had several outstanding educational reformers, including Johannes Bugenhagen, who organized school systems in Germany and Denmark that included separate institutions for girls. The most influential Lutheran educator was Johannes Sturm, whose secondary school (called a "gymnasium") at Strasbourg became the pattern for similar schools throughout Europe. Divided into ten grades, the curriculum included Latin, Greek, religion, and logic. Lutherans also founded new universities in Germany, including those at Marburg and Jena. Luther's own university at Wittenberg attracted 16,000 students between 1520 and 1560, of whom a third were foreigners.

The Growth of the Lutheran Movement

Luther's views spread rapidly, aided by the printing press, the reformer's own eloquence, the zeal of numer-

◎ A Lutheran Woman Speaks Out ◎

*Argula von Grumbach, one of Luther's most prominent female disciples,
was undaunted by the traditional domination of males in theological
matters. In 1523 she wrote a stinging letter rebuking the faculty of the
University of Ingolstadt for condemning a young Lutheran teacher.*

Where do you read in the Bible that Christ, the apostles, and the prophets imprisoned,
banished, burned, or murdered anyone? You tell us that we must obey the magistrates.
Correct. But neither the pope, nor the Kaiser, nor the princes have any authority over the
Word of God. You need not think you can pull God, the prophets and the apostles out of
heaven with papal decretals drawn from Aristotle, who was not a Christian at all. I am not
unacquainted with the word of Paul that women should be silent in church (1 Tim. 1:2)
but, when no man will or can speak, I am driven by the word of the Lord when he said,
"He who confesses me on earth, him will I confess and he who denies me, him will I
deny" (Matt. 10; Luke 9). . . . I would be willing to come and dispute with you in German
and you won't need to use Luther's translation of the Bible. . . . I send you not a woman's
ranting, but the Word of God.

Source: R. H. Bainton, *Women of the Reformation in Germany and Italy* (Minneapolis: Augsburg, 1971),
pp. 97–98, 100.

ous German merchants, especially in the Hanseatic
towns, and the prospects for material gain by people who
coveted Catholic lands and wealth. Various German
princes as well as cities such as Hamburg and Magde-

**Medallion depicting Argula von Grumbach,
one of Luther's leading female supporters.
[Government Coin Collection, Munich]**

burg requested that Luther's friends and pupils fill their
pulpits and lecterns. The work of reform went forward
by winning the support of established leaders, not by
revolution. For this reason, Luther himself strenuously
opposed any attempt to alter the political order.

In the German cities the reform typically followed a
threefold course, beginning with the preaching of Protestant tenets, followed by the growth of popular support
and finally by the backing of the magistrates. While the
reformers recognized that the last step was critical, the
magistrates were cautious, not wanting to introduce religious change until they were assured that it would not
destroy traditional social ties. The magistrates were also
pressured by Charles V to remain Catholic. When some
finally decided to support Protestantism, they did so
with deliberation, stretching out the work of reform over
a period of years: 11 in Constance, 13 in Nuremberg,
21 in Osnabrück. Wary of creating new popes, the magistrates were frequently unwilling to grant the preachers
all the changes they sought. In Strasbourg, for instance,
Martin Bucer's attempt to transfer control of the city's
religious and moral life to the church was rejected. Some
magistrates inaugurated the religious change with debates rigged so that the Protestants prevailed, as happened at Nuremberg and Constance. Because of their
concentration, urban populations were especially open
to the influence of popular preaching and the Protestant
works that flowed from the press, the results of which
were evident in the demonstrations of voting support
often accorded the Protestants in the early 1530s.

Luther himself corresponded with Hussite leaders in Bohemia, and his doctrines were preached as far afield as Hungary, Prussia, and the Netherlands. Beyond the German states, however, only the Scandinavian lands adopted Lutheranism, which suited the political needs of the kings of Denmark and Sweden as they worked to unify their countries. Adopting Lutheranism made it possible for them to confiscate ecclesiastical lands and assert greater authority over the clergy. As a province of Denmark, Norway too became Lutheran, and Protestant teachings spread as well into Finland. Within Germany, Luther's views provoked bitter divisions that ultimately led to social upheaval and civil war.

Initially the German peasants regarded Luther as a leader who would help them attain not only their religious goals but social reform as well. The success of Luther's movement was tied, however, to the support of princes, nobles, and wealthy burghers, without whose backing he would have been subjected to the power of the empire and the church. Thus despite his sympathy for many peasant demands—which included reduced rents, the abolition of serfdom, and an end to unlawful punishment—he preached patience when peasants rebelled in southern and central Germany in the summer of 1524. He refused to support their call for the termination of serfdom on the grounds that such action not only violated biblical respect for property but "would make all men equal, and turn the spiritual kingdom of Christ into a worldly external kingdom." As the Peasants' Revolt became increasingly violent the following year, Luther reacted against the killing, arson, desecration of churches, and destruction of property. In May 1525 he published his pamphlet *Against the Rapacious and Murdering Peasants*, urging the nobility in God's name to "cut, stab, and strangle" the rebels. The peasants were crushed with dreadful severity: some 300 were beheaded in front of the town hall at Frankenhausen, and altogether the Peasants' Revolt claimed between 70,000 and 100,000 lives.

Although Luther's support for the nobles tied his movement to the conservative social order, Catholics seized on the revolt to accuse Lutheranism of fomenting social rebellion. In 1525 and 1526 both sides organized defensive leagues, but Charles V, who remained steadfastly Catholic, was prevented from crushing the Protestants by hostilities with the French, with whom he fought four major wars over northern Italy and Naples between 1521 and 1559. He was preoccupied too by the advancing Turkish forces of Suleiman the Magnificent (1520–1566), which soundly defeated the Hungarians at Mohács in 1526 and advanced to the very gates of Vienna before retreating.

Political and military pressures forced Charles to allow the German princes a degree of religious toleration at the Diet of Speyer the same year. When he revoked this freedom in 1529, the Lutheran princes and urban delegates protested, giving birth to the term *Protestant*. In response to Charles' demand at the 1530 Diet of Augsburg that Lutherans return to the Catholic fold, the Protestant princes organized the Schmalkaldic League to defend themselves. Although the emperor defeated the league in 1547, his armies were in turn vanquished five years later, forcing him to return to a policy of limited religious toleration. Finally, in 1555 both sides agreed in the Peace of Augsburg that each prince had the right to determine whether the people of his territory would be Catholic or Lutheran. Only in some of the German cities where toleration was already practiced did the people themselves retain the right to choose their own faith. Northern Germany became mostly Lutheran, as did Württemberg and most of the cities of the south, though much of southern Germany remained loyal to Catholicism.

The Reformed Tradition

While Lutheranism developed in the German states, a different variety of Protestantism emerged in Switzerland. There, under the leadership of Ulrich Zwingli in Zurich and later John Calvin in Geneva, the Reformed tradition distinguished itself from Lutheranism by simpler forms of worship, emphasis on the weekly sermon rather than the celebration of the Lord's supper (undertaken only four times a year rather than weekly), greater stress on moral discipline, and a denial of Christ's physical presence in the Lord's supper. In Switzerland, a loose confederation of 13 independent states (cantons) and allied areas, there was widespread disenchantment with conditions in the church, stemming mostly from the impact of the Christian humanists and the reforming spirit kindled by the Councils of Constance (1414–1418) and Basel (1431–1449). Although the cantons were overwhelmingly Catholic, feelings against abuses in the church ran so strongly that in 1520 the Swiss diet ordered the execution of anyone selling church offices. Along with the desire for reform, there were mounting protests in the cantons against the recruitment of Swiss men for foreign military service.

Ulrich Zwingli and the Swiss Reformation

The son of a peasant and village magistrate, Ulrich Zwingli (1484–1531), the founder of the Reformed tradition, was educated by humanists at Bern, Vienna, and Basel. Intellectually he was a disciple of Erasmus. After serving as a chaplain to Swiss mercenaries, he was moved by their heavy losses to condemn such employment. As a priest in the Great Minster at Zurich, Zwingli became an outspoken critic of indulgences. While comforting the sick during an outbreak of the plague in 1519, his own illness deepened his religious convictions and ultimately spurred his interest in reform. In 1522 he condemned fasting during Lent as unscriptural and reformed the liturgy. Finding no biblical evidence for clerical celibacy, he denounced it and married a poor widow. "I know of no greater scandal," he wrote caustically, "than that priests are not allowed to take lawful wives but may keep mistresses if they pay a fine."[7] In a series of public debates, he called for a return of the church to its original simplicity and for the peaceful removal of all images, relics, and altars. Because he allowed only psalm singing in church, the minster organ was chopped into pieces. For Zwingli, nothing was acceptable in religion unless it was revealed in Scripture.

From Zurich the reform movement spread by 1529 to Bern and Basel, as well as beyond the confederation to the German cities of Strasbourg and Constance. Civil war between Catholics and Protestants briefly erupted in 1529, after which Zwingli met with Luther to forge a Protestant union. At Marburg, however, the two leaders strongly disagreed on the nature of the Lord's supper. Zwingli, believing that Christ was present only spiritually in the sacrament, rejected Luther's insistence on a "real" (physical and spiritual) presence. The failure at Marburg was followed by renewed civil war in Switzerland when, despite Zwingli's protests, the Protestant cantons blockaded the Catholic districts in 1531, forcing them to fight or starve. Zwingli died in the battle of Kappel that year, and his body was quartered and burned because he was considered to have been a heretic. Leadership of the reform movement in Zurich was taken up by his son-in-law, Heinrich Bullinger. Following the war, the right of each canton to decide its own religion was recognized.

John Calvin

The Reformed tradition founded by Zwingli became a major international force under the guidance of John Calvin (1509–1564), the son of a French attorney and secretary to the bishop of Noyon. After a broad education in theology, law, classical languages, and humanistic studies at the Universities of Paris, Orléans, and Bourges, Calvin joined Catholic humanists in Orléans and Paris interested in religious reform in the late 1520s. Shortly after his conversion to Protestantism, he was briefly imprisoned in 1534 and then forced into hiding.

When the French government stepped up the persecution of Protestants that autumn, Calvin fled to Basel, where he met Bullinger and other reformers. There he wrote the classic of Reformation Protestantism, the *Institutes of the Christian Religion* (1536). In it he provided a thorough introduction to a Protestant view of the

Christian faith, concentrating on the nature and work of God, the redemption of sinners, and the role of the church and sacraments in the Christian life. On a trip to Strasbourg later that year, he stopped in Geneva, which had just ended Catholic worship under the leadership of Guillaume Farel. Needing assistance, Farel pressured Calvin to stay, threatening him with God's wrath until he became "terrified and shook." Together they imposed a public confession of faith on citizens to distinguish the devout from the unfaithful, called for educational reform, and punished immorality. These measures, coupled with changes in worship and the abolition of holy days, provoked such strong resentment that the two men were exiled in 1538.

Settling in Strasbourg, Calvin became the pastor of a congregation of French exiles, lectured at Johannes Sturm's gymnasium, and revised his *Institutes*. Influenced by the teachings of Paul and Augustine, Calvin proclaimed that because human nature was totally corrupt, belief in God was impossible without the irresistible gift of faith. Only those chosen by God before creation—the elect—received this gift; all others—the reprobate—were left to their sins and condemned to eternal damnation. In his mind, the doctrine of predestination revealed not only God's justice and majesty but also his mercy in providing salvation for the elect despite their unworthiness. Too much inquiry into this doctrine was discouraged:

> **Let them remember that when they inquire into predestination they are penetrating the sacred precinct of divine wisdom. If anyone with carefree assurance breaks into this place, he will not succeed in satisfying his curiosity and he will enter a labyrinth from which he can find no exit.**[8]

Like Luther and Zwingli, Calvin accepted the authority of Scripture alone, which he regarded as "a declaration of the word of God," and refused to consider the teachings of the early church fathers and church councils as equally binding. He insisted, however, that only those enlightened by the Holy Spirit could properly understand the Bible. With other Protestants, Calvin recognized only two sacraments, baptism and the Lord's supper; his concept of the latter was closer to Zwingli's idea of a spiritual presence than to Luther's view. Influenced by the Strasbourg reformer Martin Bucer, Calvin developed a "democratic" plan for church government that called for the election of ministers by the congregation and the joint participation of ministers and popularly elected lay elders in running the church. Calvin's stress on the disciplined moral life and a godly society made his movement a potent force.

One of the most important themes in Calvin's thought was his treatment of vocation as a Christian duty, a concept he shared with other Protestants. He gave all legitimate professions a sense of Christian purpose, so that

◎ Eternally Chosen, Eternally Damned ◎

Calvin's Institutes of the Christian Religion, *perhaps the finest theological work of the Protestant Reformation, put great emphasis on the sovereignty of God. The most famous manifestation of this was Calvin's insistence that God determined the eternal destiny of each person before the creation of the world.*

We shall never be clearly convinced as we ought to be, that our salvation flows from the fountain of God's free mercy, till we are acquainted with his eternal election, which illustrates the grace of God by this comparison, that he adopts not all promiscuously to the hope of salvation, but gives to some what he refuses to others. Ignorance of this principle evidently detracts from the Divine glory, and diminishes real humility. . . .

Predestination we call the eternal decree of God, by which he has determined in himself, what he would have to become of every individual of mankind. For they are not all created with a similar destiny; but eternal life is foreordained for some, and eternal damnation for others. . . .

We affirm that this counsel, as far as concerns the elect, is founded on his gratuitous mercy, totally irrespective of human merit; but that to those whom he devotes to condemnation, the gate of life is closed by a just and irreprehensible, but incomprehensible, judgment. . . .

The will of God is the highest rule of justice; so that what he wills must be considered just, for this very reason, because he wills it. When it is inquired, therefore, why the Lord did so, the answer must be, Because he would. But if you go further, and ask why he so determined, you are in search of something greater and higher than the will of God, which can never be found.

Source: John Calvin, *Institutes of the Christian Religion,* trans. J. Allen (Philadelphia: Presbyterian Board of Christian Education, 1928), vol. 2, pp. 140–165 passim.

one's job became a principal means of serving God. To work was to worship. This outlook brought new dignity to occupations as diverse as business, the crafts, and agriculture. The artisan no less than the minister, Calvin insisted, was divinely called to his vocation.

Calvin's view of wealth was equally significant for economic development. In his judgment, God intended that money be used to better the human condition, and thus, within limits, usury (or interest) had a positive function. Like Luther, Calvin was conscious of the plight of debtors, but if charging interest was consistent with the good of the community, usury was acceptable. Interest rates, however, could never be excessive. Luther, by contrast, prohibited all usury as unscriptural with the exception of loans by which the borrower prospered. For Calvin the governing economic principle was always the mutual responsibility of citizens for the common welfare. Although he never sanctioned the unlimited acquisition of wealth or equated riches with godliness, his emphasis on work and discipline in the context of Christian vocation as well as his limited acceptance of usury were compatible with the growth of a capitalistic economy.

❦ GENEVA IN THE AGE OF CALVIN

After the election of men favorable to his cause, Calvin returned to Geneva in 1541. The city was the largest in its region, with a population of approximately 10,000. Under Calvin, Geneva became the international center of Reformed Protestantism and attracted more than 5,000 religious refugees from France, Italy, England, and Scotland, many of whom were artisans and merchants who contributed to the city's prosperity. Among the newcomers were many booksellers and printers, who helped make Geneva one of Europe's foremost publication centers. Throughout most of the 1500s, books were the city's primary export and were only supplanted late in the century by the export of silk, an industry introduced by Italians. Because Geneva had little industry of its own apart from printing, the economy was based on commerce. Its artisans produced mostly for the local market rather than the export trade.

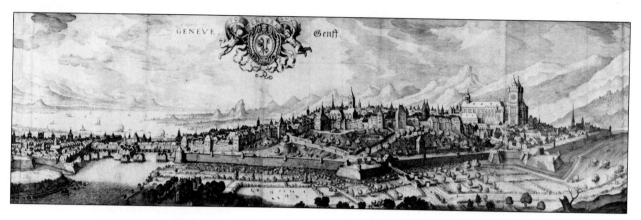

Geneva in the late sixteenth century, its skyline dominated by St. Peter's Cathedral. [British Library]

Genevans prized their independence, which they achieved on the eve of Calvin's arrival by rebelling from Savoy. The heart of Genevan government was its three councils: the 25-member Little Council served as an executive body, the Council of Two Hundred determined municipal policy, and the Council of Sixty conducted foreign relations. Under Calvin's leadership, these institutions protected the Protestant church, safeguarded property, and imposed moral standards on private behavior. Although Calvin himself never held political office, his advice was sought on such matters as foreign policy, taxes, and military defense.

The councils approved his ecclesiastical ordinances, establishing four offices in the church: pastors, teachers, elders, and deacons (who were responsible for poor relief and assisting the sick). Each of the 12 elders was assigned a district in Geneva and required to oversee its families. Through the Consistory, composed of the ministers and elders, Calvin imposed strict discipline on the people for such offenses as absence from church, sexual immorality, swearing, drunkenness, bawdy songs, card playing, and even criticizing Calvin himself. More serious offenses were turned over to the city government. Between 1542 and 1546 fully 76 persons were banished and 58 executed for heresy, adultery, blasphemy, and witchcraft. In the quest to make Geneva an example of godliness, the Consistory even questioned children about the conduct of their parents. Discipline and obedience were crucial.

As the years passed, Calvin, like Luther, grew even more intolerant of opposition and demanded that his critics be punished. The intolerance of the two leaders, like that of most of their fellow reformers, grew out of their belief in the need for a unified Christendom and was the practical result of the need to define the churches they had created. In 1552 Calvin persuaded the city councils to declare that his *Institutes* contained the "pure doctrine" and should not be questioned. The extent to which

Calvin's supporters would go in defending his theology became apparent the next year when the Spanish physician and lay theologian Michael Servetus (1511–1553) visited Geneva, thoroughly scandalizing the citizens by his views. The author of works attacking the doctrine of the Trinity, the baptism of infants, and original sin, he was already a man whom the Catholics regarded as a heretic. After a trial in which he clashed with Calvin personally, Servetus was burned at the stake. Calvin's treatment of him was praised by Catholic and Protestant leaders alike. From 1555 until his death in 1564, Calvin ruled Geneva with little opposition.

Geneva made a determined effort in this period to deal with the needy. Before Calvin's arrival, the small medieval hospitals were reorganized into the Hospital of the Holy Spirit, which cared for the elderly, the sick, the indigent, and widows and orphans. Outside the city walls was a smaller hospital for victims of the plague. Responsibility for the main hospital was vested in the deacons, who obtained funding from the city government as well as from private charity. Support for the hospital was sometimes the largest item in the city budget. In addition to providing free care for the needy in the hospital, every medical doctor was required, beginning in 1569, to treat the poor without charge.

Calvin supervised a sweeping reform of the school system that replaced the old secondary schools with a gymnasium patterned after Johannes Sturm's in Strasbourg. A new academy, established to train superior students for leadership in church and state, developed into the modern University of Geneva. Beginning in 1536, all children had to attend primary school, but girls were barred from the secondary level. No reformer was more aware than Calvin of the value of education to instruct young people in religious beliefs.

Like Luther, Calvin accepted the traditional notion of female inferiority and the subject position of women in marriage. He too recognized their spiritual equality but refused to allow women a ministerial role in the church. In the secular sphere, when a woman inherited a crown, Calvin interpreted the event as a divine reproach to men. Apart from their responsibilities in the home, women were assigned the task of educating the young. In practice, however, Calvinist women of aristocratic background were prominent in the movement. Jeanne d'Albret, mother of King Henry IV of France, was a leader of the Huguenots (as the French Calvinists were called), while Madeleine Mailly, Comtesse de Roye, worked on behalf of the Huguenot cause with both the French government and German Protestant princes. Yet in Geneva, Calvin neither allowed women to serve as deaconesses nor favored their participation in city government, although his own wife was virtually his partner in the work of religious reform.

Under Calvin, Geneva was the focal point of an expanding network of reformers who carried his message as far afield as France, the Netherlands, England, Scotland, and even Hungary. With its strict morality and religious fervor, Geneva was the nerve center of a militant, determined Protestantism.

The Radical Reformation

Although both the Lutheran and Reformed traditions appealed to Scripture as their authority and worked to restore the church to its original simplicity, as early as the mid-1520s radical critics expressed dissatisfaction with the extent and pace of reform. In their judgment, Luther and Zwingli had compromised their principles in order to win the support of the powerful. Most of the radical critics became known as Anabaptists ("Rebaptizers"), a group that quickly became an abomination to the propertied classes and the major religious groups.

The Anabaptists

In 1523 Conrad Grebel (1498–1526), a follower of Zwingli and a member of a prominent patrician family in Zurich, became impatient with the slowness of reform. The following year he attacked Zwingli's view of baptism, insisting that the rite must be confined to believing adults as a mark of their spiritual rebirth. After a public debate in January 1525, the Zurich town council ruled in favor of Zwingli, but Grebel and his followers—the Swiss Brethren—refused to conform. For their defiance, they faced banishment or execution by drowning, a cruel parody of their baptismal practices and a poignant reminder of how intolerant some Protestants could be toward others. The Brethren rejected the traditional concept of a state church in favor of congregations composed of believers alone. Accepting the Lord's supper as a simple meal to commemorate Christ's death, they celebrated it in private homes. Of more concern to the landed classes, the Brethren insisted that pastors must be chosen by individual congregations and supported by voluntary gifts, not tithes. Because so many tithes were now paid directly to laymen rather than to the clergy, the Anabaptist call for voluntary tithing was viewed by both clergy and laity as an attack on property rights. Equally radical was the Brethren's insistence on separating from the evil world, which entailed a refusal to participate in civil government or military service, both of which involved the taking of life. They also declined to pay taxes for military purposes and rejected oaths, which traditionalists regarded as basic to the maintenance of law and order. In the eyes of the authorities, the Anabaptists were dangerous social revolutionaries, while religious leaders not only detested their theological views but also feared that the separation of church and state that the Anabaptists advocated would lead to the secularization of society.

The Kingdom of Münster and Its Consequences

Initially the Anabaptists were not identified with any social group, but in the aftermath of the Peasants' Revolt in Germany they attracted large numbers of peasants and artisans. In 1534 the Anabaptists seized control of the German city of Münster, where they expelled or persecuted all who disagreed with them. Under the leadership of a charismatic Dutch tailor, John of Leiden, they founded a theocratic kingdom, based on the laws of the Old Testament. Polygamy was practiced, and John himself took 16 wives. Initially, an unmarried woman had to accept any marriage proposal, though female opposition finally became so intense that women were given the right to decline offers. A woman, however, could have only one husband and faced capital punishment for adultery. In Münster all property was held in common. Within the city walls there was wild anticipation that King John would soon rule the world in preparation for the second coming of Christ, but the rest of Europe was appalled. The armies of the Catholic bishop of Münster and the Protestant Philip of Hesse, acting together, recaptured the city in 1535, executed the Anabaptist leaders, and publicly displayed their bodies as a warning to others. The Münster fiasco intensified the persecution of Anabaptists throughout the Holy Roman Empire, which in 1529 had revived an old Byzantine law making rebaptism a capital offense. By the early 1600s, several thousand Anabaptists had been executed.

Persecution encouraged the migration of Anabaptists to other areas, particularly the Netherlands, Poland, Bohemia, and Moravia. Shunning the excesses of Münster, these groups distinguished themselves by their quiet piety and strict morality. The most prominent of these sects was the Mennonites, founded by Menno Simons (1496–1561), whose followers eventually spread as far as Russia and North America.

Spiritualists and Rationalists

During the heady days of the early Reformation, a handful of radicals claimed to be prophets bearing special revelations from God. One of the most prominent was the revolutionary Thomas Müntzer (died 1525), who accepted only the authority of the Holy Spirit and endorsed the use of violence to advance the Gospel. Offering to raise 30 squads to slaughter the ungodly, Müntzer urged the elector Frederick to establish a new kingdom for the faithful. Exiled from Saxony, he preached social revolution in southern Germany and helped incite the Peasants' Revolt, during which he was executed. Spiritualists from Zwickau near the Bohemian border favored the slaughter of all the ungodly in Europe, whether at their own hands or by the Turks. In contrast to such men, Sebastian Franck (c. 1499–c. 1542) was an intellectual who rejected Lutherans and Anabaptists alike for their dogmatism. Repudiating the authority of the Bible, he argued for a religion based entirely on the inner life of the Spirit and free from all dogma and sacraments.

Whereas the Spiritualists were essentially mystics, another group of Protestant radicals advocated a religion that was predominantly rational and ethical. Distinguishing themselves by their rejection of the Trinity, they criticized predestination and original sin and favored religious toleration. In addition to Servetus, the leading rationalists included Lelio Sozzini (1525–1562) and his nephew Faustus (1539–1604), whose followers, the Socinians, were found primarily in Poland and England. There they helped prepare the foundation for seventeenth-century Deism, the ancestor of modern Unitarianism. One of the greatest literary works of the radical Reformation was Sebastian Castellio's *Concerning Heretics and Whether They Should Be Punished by the Sword of the Magistrate.* Castellio (1515–1563) condemned Calvin for supporting Servetus' execution and offered a ringing defense of religious toleration. To burn a heretic, he asserted, "is not to defend a doctrine, but to kill a man."[9] The legacy of the religious radicals was the concept of religious freedom, an idea slow to win acceptance because of the conviction that religious diversity led to the breakdown of the social and political order.

The English Reformation

In contrast to the reform movements instigated by Luther, Zwingli, and Calvin, the Reformation in England was fundamentally an act of state rather than the work of a religious leader. The relative ease with which the break with Rome was accomplished owed much to widespread dissatisfaction with the Catholic church and to the work of early reform movements. Popular hostility toward the clergy had grown because of their tithes and fees, and many people were disillusioned by priestly ignorance and immorality. Animosity was particularly strong among the Lollards, the underground group whose radical views, inherited from John Wyclif in the fourteenth century, were spread by itinerant cloth workers. Many Lollards embraced Lutheran ideas in the 1520s, and their literature was published by Protestants to demonstrate that their own pleas for reform were firmly rooted in the English past. Lutheran cells were formed at Oxford and Cambridge, and from them Protestant theology began to infiltrate the clergy. In London a covert group of merchants known as the Christian Brethren spread the Protestant message, which they had learned as traders on the Continent. With their support, William Tyndale (c. 1492–1536) translated the New Testament and the Pentateuch into English, with marginal notes that stridently attacked the papacy and the Catholic priesthood. Many early Protestant leaders in England had been educated as humanists and were deeply influenced by Erasmus. Well before the Reformation, English humanists such as John Colet had made strong pleas for reform, unwittingly helping prepare the way for the break with Rome.

The King's "Great Matter"

The state's decision to reject papal authority was not made primarily for religious reasons. The strong-willed King Henry VIII (1509–1547), the second of the Tudor rulers, had been married since 1509 to Catherine of Aragon, by whom he had one surviving child, Princess Mary. The prospect of leaving the new dynasty in a woman's hands raised fears of another dynastic struggle like the fifteenth-century Wars of the Roses. The fact that Henry had become infatuated with Anne Boleyn, a lady of the court, contributed to his decision to seek a new wife and produce a male heir. But to marry Anne required a church-approved annulment of his marriage to Catherine. The latter's position was strengthened by the fact that the army of her nephew, Emperor Charles V, controlled Rome in 1527 and temporarily held the pope prisoner. Unable to act freely, Clement VII delayed the annulment hearings. Exasperated, Henry summoned Parliament in 1529 to bring pressure on the pope, correctly anticipating that it would demand reforms. But the pope remained unresponsive.

Henry cowed the English clergy by threatening to punish them for enforcing papal authority in the church courts. Giving in, they recognized the king as head of

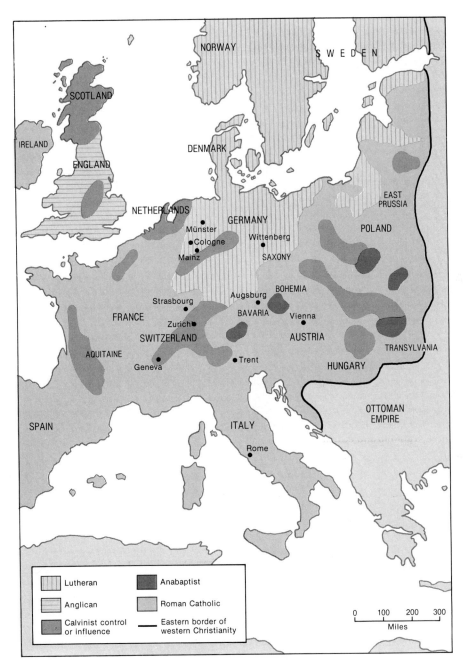

17.1 The Division of Christendom, c. 1550

the English church "as far as the law of Christ allowed." Under the leadership of Henry's new adviser, Thomas Cromwell (1485–1540), a friend of the English Lutherans, Parliament renewed its complaints against religious abuses. When Henry learned in January 1533 that Anne was pregnant, he secretly married her without waiting to resolve the status of his marriage to Catherine. In March, Parliament passed the Act in Restraint of

Appeals, drafted largely by Cromwell, which prohibited legal appeals to Rome without royal permission. Asserting that "this realm of England is an empire," the act affirmed the country's legal independence of all foreign authority. Two months later the new archbishop of Canterbury, the Protestant Thomas Cranmer (1489–1556), moved the Convocation of the Clergy to declare Henry's marriage to Catherine null and void, and on June 1 Anne

Henry VIII of England. [National Portrait Gallery, London]

Boleyn was crowned queen of England. Three months later she gave birth to Princess Elizabeth.

Royal Supremacy

Most of the changes during Henry's reign involved the seizure of papal authority by the crown rather than theological issues as on the Continent. Church funds previously paid to Rome now went to the English government. The king received the right to make appointments to all major church offices, as well as the final authority for all ecclesiastical legislation. In the 1534 Act of Supremacy, Parliament recognized the king as "the only supreme head in earth of the Church of England." To deny him this title was treason. An act of succession recognized the children of Henry and Anne as heirs to the throne. For refusing to accept the succession and the royal supremacy in the church, Sir Thomas More and Bishop John Fisher, Catherine's outspoken supporter, were executed in 1535. Catherine remained loyal to the Catholic faith until her death in 1536—an event celebrated by Henry and Anne, both brightly clad in yel-

low, with a banquet and a joust. Four months later Anne was executed on trumped-up charges of adultery and incest with her brother. In reality, Henry could forgive neither her arrogance nor her failure to bear him a son.

Although Henry generally remained loyal to Catholic dogma, Protestants welcomed certain changes in the Church of England. An officially approved translation of the Bible in English by Miles Coverdale was published in 1535, and the following year Cromwell ordered that every church have a copy of the Bible in English and Latin. Between 1536 and 1540 the monasteries were dissolved and their properties confiscated by the crown. Some of the land was sold, enabling the lesser aristocracy (or gentry) in particular to expand their holdings. Because the monasteries had been centers of education and hospitality, the social effects of their dissolution were profound. Although some theological concessions were temporarily made to Protestants for political reasons, the king's conservative religious ideals were reflected in the Six Articles of 1539. Except for papal supremacy, they supported Catholic teachings on the sacraments, the celibacy of priests, and vows of chastity. The religious position of the Church of England in this period is best described as Henrician Catholicism, or Catholicism without monastic institutions or obedience to Rome.

The Edwardian Reformation

After Henry's death in 1547, the Church of England became increasingly Protestant. Henry was succeeded by his 9-year-old son, Edward VI (1547–1553), whose mother, Jane Seymour, Henry's third queen, had died after childbirth. Real power rested at first in the hands of the king's uncle, Edward Seymour, duke of Somerset. Under his direction Parliament repealed the Six Articles and dissolved the chantries, which were endowments to support priests who said masses for the dead. In 1549 Parliament passed an act of uniformity requiring all ministers to use the *Book of Common Prayer*, an English liturgy prepared by Archbishop Cranmer. When Somerset failed to suppress rioting peasants in 1549, he was overthrown by John Dudley, soon to be duke of Northumberland. Under his leadership the English church became even more firmly Protestant. A second act of uniformity required clergy and laity alike to use the revised *Book of Common Prayer*, which simplified the worship service and required ministers to wear only a plain black robe and a white vestment. Communion tables replaced stone altars, and confession was made by the congregation as a whole rather than individually to priests. Royal approval was also given to the Forty-two Articles, a Protestant confession of faith.

The Edwardian Reformation, however, was secure only as long as the king lived, for the heir apparent, Prin-

THE REFORMATION

Protestants	Catholics	Cultural highlights
	Oratory of Divine Love (1494)	
		More's *Utopia* (1516)
		Erasmus' Greek New Testament (1516)
Luther's Ninety-five Theses (1517)		
Founding of the Anabaptists (1523–1524)		Grünewald (c. 1460–1528)
	Capuchins (1528)	Dürer (1471–1528)
	Barnabites (1530)	
	Somaschi (1532)	Michelangelo's *Last Judgment* (1532–1541)
Act of Supremacy, England (1534)		
Kingdom of Münster (1534–1535)	Ursulines (1535)	
Calvin returns to Geneva (1541)	Society of Jesus (1540)	Holbein (1497–1543)
First *Book of Common Prayer* (1549)	Council of Trent (1545–1563)	
Peace of Augsburg (1555)	Marian reaction in England (1553–1558)	
Scottish Reformation (1560)		
Elizabethan settlement (1559–1563)		Palestrina (c. 1525–1594)

cess Mary, was a determined Catholic. As Edward lay dying of tuberculosis in 1553, Northumberland tried desperately to save himself by preventing Mary from becoming queen. He persuaded Edward to name as his heir Lady Jane Grey, Northumberland's daughter-in-law and a great-granddaughter of Henry VII. But when Edward died in July, the English people overwhelmingly supported Mary as the rightful ruler. As Northumberland was brought into London following his capture, "all the streets [were] full of people, which cursed him, and called him traitor without measure."[10] A month later he died on the scaffold as the new queen prepared to introduce the Counter-Reformation, already under way on the Continent.

The Catholic Revival: A Church Militant

The spirit of reform prevailed within the Catholic church as well as outside it, partly stimulated by the shock of the Protestant secession. The demands for change were matched by a determination to maintain the ideals of the medieval church. Conciliarism, the major source for reform in the late medieval period, had lost much of its force by the early 1500s. The Fifth Lateran Council (1512–1517), meeting in Rome, adopted no significant reforms. Efforts to improve the church, however, were under way in various states, including France, where Cardinal Georges d'Amboise (died 1510) imposed more effective discipline on the monasteries. In Spain, Queen Isabella's confessor, Cardinal Francisco Ximenes (c. 1436–1517), the archbishop of Toledo, improved ed-

ucation for the clergy, placed tighter controls on errant priests and monks, and encouraged humanist learning at the new University of Alcala.

A characteristic feature of Catholic revival was the founding of new organizations, beginning with the Oratory of Divine Love, established in Italy in 1494. Composed of clergy and laity, its members emphasized piety and charitable work for the poor and the sick. The Capuchins (1528), inspired by Francis of Assisi's ideal of poverty, devoted themselves to helping the common people. Other new orders, such as the Barnabites (1530) and the Somaschi (1532), focused on the problems of poverty and disease. The Somaschi, who founded hospitals and orphanages, also took an interest in the plight of prostitutes. The role of women in the Catholic revival is reflected in the Congregation of the Holy Angels (an auxiliary of the Barnabites), the Capucines (the female counterpart of the Capuchins), and the Ursulines, who specialized in educating young women.

ANGELA MERICI AND THE URSULINES

The new sense of spiritual dedication that was reviving the Catholic church is exemplified in the life of Angela Merici, the daughter of a minor country gentleman. Born in 1474 in the republic of Venice, she was orphaned at age 10. As a young woman she was deeply influenced by the piety of local nuns and recluses as well as by the devotional activities of the Oratory of Divine Love. She took part as a layperson in the work of the Franciscans but did not take formal vows. Merici devoted herself to charitable work, helping the sick and the poor as well as teaching girls. While praying in the fields in 1506, she had a vision in which she was promised that "before your death, you will found a society of virgins." Ten years later she established a school for girls, primarily to teach the catechism.

At Brescia in 1531, Merici, now partially blind, recruited a dozen young women as teachers, and in 1535, when the group had grown to 28, she founded the Company of St. Ursula (Ursulines). Like the Franciscans, she rejected the concept of a cloistered order in favor of social activism, insisting that her religious sisters live and work among the people. Because of the novelty of this idea, the pope did not approve her order until 1565, after her death. Although no formal vows were required, Merici's rule demanded poverty, chastity, and obedience. Each sister was allowed to live in her own home and work with her family and neighbors. Until her death in 1540, she served as superior general of the Ursulines. Her *Testament and Souvenirs* expresses her ideals, especially gentleness and concern for others. Her movement had more than doubled in size by 1536 and became the greatest teaching order for women.

Ignatius of Loyola and the Jesuit Order

The most influential of the new orders, the Society of Jesus, was founded by Ignatius of Loyola (1491–1556), the son of a Basque nobleman. A French cannonball shattered his right leg as he fought in Charles V's army at Pamplona in 1521. Profoundly influenced during his recovery by biographies of Francis and Dominic, he dedicated his life to serving the Virgin Mary. After a period of meditation in monasteries and study at the Universities of Alcala and Paris, Ignatius and a small band of disciples vowed to go to the Holy Land to convert Muslims. Finding the way to Palestine blocked by fighting between the Venetians and the Turks, they preached instead to the Italians. Ignatius' constitution for a new order, which reflected the trend toward centralized government in this period, was approved by Pope Paul III in 1540. Governed by a general directly responsible to the pope, the order was highly structured in order to supervise its active, mobile apostles. Although the traditional monastic vows were required, Jesuits were exempt from the typical duties of monks, such as reciting the church offices. The society's purpose was to advance and defend the Catholic faith.

The Jesuits concentrated on four activities. To persuade secular rulers to suppress Protestantism, they served as confessors and propagandists in Catholic courts. To keep the masses loyal to the Catholic faith, the Jesuits stressed confession, achieving some popularity because of their principle that there is "no sin without specific intent" to commit it. The society was partic-

Ignatius of Loyola, founder of the Society of Jesus. This is an engraved copy of a portrait originally painted in 1584 by Alonzo Sanchez Coello under the direction of a former associate of Ignatius'. [SEF/Art Resource]

ularly successful in its efforts to improve education, especially at the secondary level, where strict discipline and obedience to the church were emphasized. After surveying the educational facilities of the church and finding the secondary schools wanting, the Jesuits launched a program to build new schools (or "colleges"). By 1640 there were approximately 520 of these secondary schools in Europe, teaching some 150,000 boys. Up to half of the students were the children of peasants and artisans, who paid no tuition. The curriculum was based on the *Ratio studiorum* ("plan of studies"), which sought to combine the best of humanist teaching with traditional Catholic beliefs, and to instill in students a strong sense of obedience to the church. Instruction was in Latin and occasionally Greek but not the vernacular. Classical texts were edited to remove "pagan" elements, and explanatory notes interpreted everything from the Catholic perspective. To motivate learning, competition was encouraged: student against student, class against class, school against school. Jesuit schools were highly successful in providing church and state with educated officials and in helping check the expansion of Protestantism.

Finally, the Jesuits, determined to carry their message throughout the world, dispatched missions to Asia,

Africa, and North and South America as well as to such European states as England and Poland. Their leading missionary, Francis Xavier (1506–1552), who preached in India, Ceylon, the Moluccas, and Japan, died half frozen and starved as he prepared to enter China. By 1557 the Jesuits had missions in the Congo, Morocco, and Ethiopia, and they also worked in Florida (1566) and Virginia (1570) as well as Brazil, Peru, and Mexico. Late in the century the Jesuit Matteo Ricci established the nucleus of a Christian church in China at Peking (see Chapter 18), and another Jesuit, Benedict de Goes, disguised as an Armenian merchant, crossed the Khyber Pass and traveled through Afghanistan and Turkistan to China. Between 1581 and 1712 no fewer than 376 Jesuits sailed for China, although a third of them died en route. The most influential Jesuit missionary to India, Roberto de Nobili (1577–1656), who was knowledgeable in Sanskrit and the Vedas, permitted his converts to retain some of their cultural traditions, such as the celebration of Hindu feasts, as long as they embraced the fundamental principles of Christianity. At times he even wore the clothing of a Brahman ascetic. This willingness to tolerate non-Western cultures coupled with their knowledge of Western science and technology helped make the Jesuits very effective missionaries.

The religious experience of Ignatius provided the basis for his *Spiritual Exercises*, a handbook to develop self-mastery and spiritual discipline. The *Exercises* call for a period of intense self-examination and meditation, at the culmination of which the disciple experiences a sense of unity with God through the surrender of mind and will. In contrast to Protestantism, which stressed the importance of the individual conscience, Ignatius emphasized the church's authority: "To be right in everything, we ought always to hold that the white which I see, is black, if the Hierarchical Church so decides it."[11] This unqualified devotion and obedience to the church was at the heart of the Catholic revival.

The Council of Trent and the Inquisition

Catholic reformers were anxious for the papacy to convene a general council to deal with the Protestant challenge and make needed changes, but the popes, fearing a loss of their power and preoccupied with political concerns, were slow to act. Pope Paul III, a humanist who appointed a number of reformers to the College of Cardinals and even offered a cardinal's hat to Erasmus, finally yielded to pressure from Charles V and summoned a council. Convened in 1545 at Trent in northern Italy,

◉ Obedience: The View of Ignatius ◉

One of the dominant features of Ignatius of Loyola's thought was his emphasis on discipline and order. In this 1553 letter to Jesuits in Portugal, he returns to the theme of obedience that was fundamental to his Spiritual Exercises.

We may the more readily allow other religious orders to surpass us in the matter of fasting, watching, and other austerities in their manner of living, which all of them devoutly practice. . . . But in the purity and perfection of obedience and the surrender of our will and judgment, it is my warmest wish, beloved brethren, to see those who serve God in this Society signalize themselves. . . .

   Make it a practice to recognize Christ our Lord in any superior you may have, and with all devotion, reverence and obey the Divine Majesty in him. This will seem the less surprising if you take note that St. Paul bids us obey our civil and pagan superiors as we would Christ, from whom flows all legitimate authority. . . .

   He who wishes to make an absolutely complete offering of himself must in addition to his will include his understanding, which is the . . . highest degree of obedience. The result will be that he not only identifies his will with that of the superior, but even his thought, and submits his own judgment to the superior's judgment, to the extent that a devout will can bend the understanding.

Source: Ignatius of Loyola, *St. Ignatius' Own Story: As Told to Luis González de Cámara, with a Sampling of His Letters,* trans. W. J. Young (Chicago: Regnery, 1956), pp. 111–115 passim.

The Council of Trent in session, 1562–1563. The cardinals and papal legates sit prominently on the left, flanked by archbishops on their right. [British Museum]

it met intermittently until 1563 and was dominated by conservative Italians loyal to the papacy, although in the early stages there was also some sympathy for the Protestants. Neither the laity nor the lower clergy were allowed to vote at its sessions.

In matters of theology, the council firmly reasserted all the doctrines challenged by the Protestants. On the crucial issue of authority, it reaffirmed the importance of both Scripture and tradition, "with an equal pious devotion and reverence" to each. It recognized the Latin Vulgate as the official version of the Bible, with the church having the sole right to determine its "true sense and interpretation." The doctrine of salvation by faith and good works was asserted. All seven sacraments

were acknowledged, and the wine in the Eucharist was reserved for the clergy alone. The council reaffirmed the central Catholic doctrine of transubstantiation—the belief that the substance of the bread and wine miraculously become the body and blood of Christ in the Eucharist—thereby rejecting the Lutheran doctrine that the bread and wine coexist with Christ's body and blood and the Reformed emphasis on the spiritual presence alone of Christ in the Lord's supper. It insisted on celibacy for the clergy, reaffirmed the invocation of saints and the veneration of relics, and refused to abolish indulgences and the doctrine of purgatory, despite their role in igniting the Protestant revolt. The theological interpretation of the Thomists, the disciples of Thomas

Aquinas, prevailed, and the council therefore marked the triumph of the tradition-minded scholastics over the reforming Catholic humanists in the church.

In addition to settling the church's theology, the council reformed church discipline. Henceforth, every bishop, unless he had a papal dispensation, was required to live in his diocese and supervise his clergy. To improve the education of priests, a seminary was to be established in every diocese. Selling ecclesiastical offices and appointing relatives to church positions were condemned. Such reforms brought a new spirit of determination to the church in its struggle with Protestantism.

As Catholicism regained the offensive, the church launched the Roman Inquisition in 1542 at the urging of Loyola and Giampietro Cardinal Caraffa (1476–1559). As head of the Inquisition, Caraffa directed a commission of six cardinals empowered under Roman law to use torture, accept hearsay evidence, and keep the accused ignorant of the charges against them. The Inquisition was especially effective in stamping out Protestantism in Italy, but it also stifled intellectual life and even closed down the University of Modena in 1546. One of the Inquisition's most notable victims was the Dominican monk Giordano Bruno, who was burned at the stake in Rome in 1600 for unorthodox views about God and for teaching that the universe is infinite and contains innumerable suns and planets like our own (see Chapter 24). The Sacred Congregation of the Holy Office, which oversaw the Inquisition, also imposed its *Index of Prohibited Books*. Among the works it banned were Erasmus' writings, vernacular translations of the Bible, Boccaccio's *Decameron*, and *The Prince* by Niccolò Machiavelli. To Protestants, the *Index* and the Inquisition were further proof that Catholicism was the church of the Antichrist, as Luther had argued.

The Counter-Reformation in England

Mary Tudor's accession to the English throne in 1553 provided the Catholics with a golden opportunity to recover an entire state that had been lost to Protestantism. Following the advice of her cousin Charles V to proceed slowly, she began by having Parliament repeal the religious legislation of Edward VI's reign. This action, coupled with the announcement of her impending marriage to Charles V's son, Philip of Spain, provoked a Protestant rebellion led by Sir Thomas Wyatt. After the revolt was crushed, Parliament repealed the antipapal legislation of Henry VIII, and in November 1554 England was officially reconciled to the Catholic church. Most of the lands previously confiscated from the church were not, however, returned. Prodded by the zealous queen, Parliament also revived a fifteenth-century law allowing the

church to condemn and the state to burn heretics. Nearly 300 Protestants died in the flames, most of them laborers and more than 50 of them women. The most famous victim, former Archbishop Cranmer, had been coerced into retracting his Protestant beliefs, but as the fire was lit his courage returned: holding the hand that had signed the retraction in the flames, he reaffirmed his Protestantism. Accounts of the martyrs hardened Protestant commitments. The words of the martyred Hugh Latimer were prophetic: "We shall this day light such a candle, by God's grace, in England, as I trust shall never be put out."[12]

Faced with persecution, some 800 Protestants fled to the Continent, where most settled in such Reformed cities as Geneva, Zurich, Strasbourg, and Frankfurt. In exile, John Foxe collected material for his *Acts and Monuments*, an immensely popular history of Christian martyrs from the early church to his own day. Other exiles prepared a new edition of the Bible in English—the Geneva version (1560)—complete with marginal notes attacking Catholicism and advocating Calvinism. Until it was finally supplanted by the Authorized (King James) version in the next century, the Geneva Bible was probably the most influential book in England. Three other exiles—John Ponet, John Knox, and Christopher Goodman—made lasting contributions to political theory by advocating the revolutionary idea that common people have the right to overthrow tyrannical and idolatrous rulers, a theory also espoused by the Jesuits against Protestant sovereigns. Knox, however, reflected traditional thinking in *The First Blast of the Trumpet Against the Monstrous Regiment of Women*, which argued that women normally have no right to govern.

The Counter-Reformation failed in England largely because of the intense revulsion the burnings caused and also because Mary had no Catholic heir. The unpopularity of Mary's marriage to Philip, symbol of Catholic orthodoxy and Spanish imperialism, also contributed to the failure. If Mary had been able to give birth to the heir she desperately wanted, Catholicism might have regained its dominance in England, but the accession in 1558 of Elizabeth I, Mary's half sister and the daughter of Anne Boleyn, destroyed the English Counter-Reformation. The foundation of the Elizabethan religious settlement was an act of supremacy that made Elizabeth supreme governor of the church and an act of uniformity that required the use of the *Book of Common Prayer*. In 1563 the queen issued the Thirty-nine Articles, a revised version of Edward VI's doctrinal statement. England thus moved firmly into the Protestant orbit, followed by Scotland under the leadership of John Knox in 1560. Throughout Catholic Europe, however, Catholicism was successfully reinvigorated by its new orders—especially the Society of Jesus—and by the reforms of the Council of Trent.

The Reformation and the Jews

The repressive side of the Catholic Reformation had an immediate and negative impact on European Jews. They were less affected by the Protestant Reformation, in part because they had been evicted from Geneva in 1490, well before Calvin's era, as many had been from German cities. In the earliest stages of the Reformation, Luther expected the Jews to convert to his movement, but when they failed to do so, he became increasingly hostile toward them. Finally he insisted that the German princes deport them to Palestine or at least force them to return to agricultural occupations and prohibit them from practicing usury. Luther even demanded that Jewish books be confiscated and synagogues burned. In the course of the Catholic Reformation the plight of the Jews similarly worsened as the hitherto tolerant papal position was reversed. Beginning in 1553, the Talmud was publicly burned in Italy, and two years later Caraffa, now Pope Paul IV, issued a bull ordering that the Jews be segregated in their own quarter (the "ghetto"), which was to be enclosed with high walls and, at night, locked gates. Jews were banned from the professions, prohibited from employing Christian servants, refused the right to own real estate, and forced to wear yellow hats as a badge. Although the Jews were not expelled from the Papal States, they could live only in cities such as Rome and Avignon under close supervision. The ghetto concept gradually spread until it became a hallmark of European Jewish life.

As the persecution of the Jews intensified in Reformation Europe, substantial numbers migrated to Poland, where rulers such as Sigismund I (1506–1548) tolerated minorities. The number of Jews in Poland rose from 50,000 in 1500 to 500,000 in 1650. In some of the bigger towns, such as Cracow and Lublin, large ghettos developed. Polish Jews generally enjoyed far greater choice of occupation than Jews in western Europe, and they were permitted substantial self-government in matters involving Jewish law.

The Witch-Hunt

In striking contrast to the idealism that characterized much of the Protestant movement and the Catholic revival, the Reformation helped spread a terrifying new wave of cruelty and popular hysteria. The age of spiritual renewal paradoxically contributed to the most extensive period of witchcraft persecutions in Western history, sparked in large measure by the breakdown of religious

An attack on the Jews of Frankfurt in 1614 illustrates the virulence of recurrent anti-Semitism in Europe. [Marburg/Art Resource]

unity. Belief in witches originated in ancient times, and the medieval church had organized those ideas into a systematic demonology. Witchcraft persecutions began in the context of the thirteenth-century crusades against the Albigensians and were revived by the papacy in 1484. Within two years a handbook, the *Malleus Maleficarum* ("The Hammer of the Wicked"), appeared with instructions for the discovery and interrogation of witches. Twenty-nine editions were published by 1669, testifying to the continuing interest in witchcraft.

Reformers and Witches

At the heart of the witch-hunt was an unquestioned acceptance of the reality of the Devil and the pervasive effects of his influence in the world. Luther, for instance, claimed to have had repeated confrontations with Satan, many of which he described in anal terms. On one occasion he threatened to defecate in his pants and hang them around the Devil's neck to drive him away. In Protestant propaganda the pope became the personification of the Devil. Determined to win and hold the people's allegiance, the reformers intensified the belief in the widespread presence of satanic influence by repeatedly linking Catholicism with Satan. To Luther, monasticism was the Devil's "sweet latrine," and monks were attacked on the grounds that they had made a pact with Satan to obtain supernatural powers. For this reason, Luther believed that witches must be burned. In Geneva, Calvin appealed to the Bible (Exod. 22:18) as a divine sanction for the execution of witches. As Protestant preachers took their gospel of justification by faith into new areas of Europe, they carried with them demands for the persecution of witches. Lutherans introduced the witch-hunt to Denmark, northern Germany, and Bavaria, and Calvinists carried it to Scotland and Transylvania.

Catholic persecution of witches had begun, as we have seen, even before the Reformation. Protestant attempts to associate the papacy with Satan were countered by Catholic charges that Luther and his colleagues were tools of the Devil. Catholics also drew on late medieval demonology to justify their accusations of witchcraft. The persecution of witches increased as the intensity of religious hostility provoked by Catholics and Protestants grew. Persecution was especially vicious in areas, such as the Rhineland and Bavaria, that were re-

conquered from the Protestants. Chief among the Jesuits in this work was Peter Canisius (1521–1597), whose activities ranged from popular evangelism and the founding of Jesuit colleges to demands for the trial of witches. Witch burnings also followed in the wake of the Catholic recapture of Poland and Flanders, but in areas where Catholic uniformity was not effectively challenged, such as Italy and Spain, reported incidents of witchcraft were apparently fewer. Burning witches—like burning heretics—became a means of purging society of evil, of purifying the community while the reformers cleansed the church.

Choosing the Victims

Although men as well as women could be accused as witches, most victims were female, probably because of the medieval notion that as the "weaker sex" they were more susceptible to the Devil's enticements. In England women were apparently accused more often than men because they were more likely to resist economic and social change. Of the 291 persons accused of witchcraft

---

◉ Women and Witchcraft ◉

The popular handbook on witchcraft Malleus Maleficarum *attempted to explain why so many women were accused of being witches. These deprecatory views of female inferiority and frailty were widespread in this period.*

As for the first question, why a greater number of witches is found in the fragile feminine sex than among men; it is indeed a fact that it were idle to contradict, since it is accredited by actual experience. . . .

For some learned men propound this reason; that there are three things in nature, the Tongue, an Ecclesiastic, and a Woman, which know no moderation in goodness or vice; and when they exceed the bounds of their condition they reach the greatest heights and the lowest depths of goodness and vice. . . .

Others again have propounded other reasons why there are more superstitious women found than men. And the first is, that they are more credulous; and since the chief aim of the devil is to corrupt faith, therefore he rather attacks them. . . .

The second reason is, that women are naturally more impressionable, and more ready to receive the influence of a disembodied spirit; and that when they use this quality well they are very good, but when they use it ill they are very evil.

The third reason is that they have slippery tongues, and are unable to conceal from their fellow-women those things which by evil arts they know; and, since they are weak, they find an easy and secret manner of vindicating themselves by witchcraft. . . .

To conclude. All witchcraft comes from carnal lust, which is in women insatiable.

Source: M. Summers, trans., *Malleus Maleficarum* (London: Rodker, 1928), pp. 41–44, 47.

in the English county of Essex in the period 1560 to 1680, fully 268 were women. Although many of the victims were stereotypical older widows or spinsters, younger women were often persecuted on the Continent, and there are cases of men and children suffering as well. To extract confessions, torture was often used (except in England), which led to more accusations and executions. Convicted witches were normally burned on the Continent and hanged in England. During the course of the witch-hunt, from the mid-sixteenth to the mid-seventeenth century, the number of victims probably reached 30,000. Only as religious passions waned, social upheaval receded, and a new spirit of rationalism took hold in the mid-1600s did the hunt die down.

Although the witchcraft trials were in large measure due to the breakdown of religious unity, religion alone cannot account for the full force of the persecutions. The social and economic changes that occurred in the West beginning in the fifteenth century created enormous tension, adding to the uncertainties and hostility resulting from the religious upheavals. A growing population, increasing poverty, devastating crop failures, and a rising crime rate made many people fearful and insecure. They continued to find scapegoats for their problems in social nonconformists—witches, Jews, and homosexuals, all of whom were persecuted. The link between them was sometimes explicit: Jews, for instance, were often accused of witchcraft. The witch-hunt was a result of credulity and uncertainty produced by widespread socioeconomic changes and group jealousies as well as passionate religious rivalries.

The Cultural Impact of the Reformation

Protestantism had a significant impact on the arts in the areas it dominated, whereas the effects of the Catholic revival on culture were not generally visible until the late sixteenth century. Because Protestantism, especially the Reformed tradition, adopted a negative attitude toward the use of images and the veneration of saints, artists in Protestant regions found virtually no demand for religious statues and little interest in paintings for churches. They adapted by catering to the growing secular market for paintings and providing artwork for the burgeoning publishing industry. Similarly, although architects initially were not needed by Protestant leaders, who took over their churches from the Catholics, they found an outlet for their talents by designing palatial residences for princes and nobles. Henry VIII's palace at Hampton Court and Francis I's château at Chambord, both of

which reflected the growth of the centralized state, provided further impetus for such building. The Protestant rejection of the mass and the general simplification of the church service created a demand for suitable music, particularly hymns and psalm settings. The artistic impact of the Reformation on the Catholic church was more delayed, but its influence was strongly felt in the revival of the church after the Council of Trent and in the seventeenth-century movement known as the baroque (see Chapter 24).

Grünewald, Dürer, and Holbein

The dilemma that the Reformation posed for the artist is illustrated by the career of Matthias Grünewald (c. 1460–1528), a German who became court painter for the archbishop of Mainz. A man of many talents in the Renaissance tradition, he supervised the rebuilding of the archbishop's castle. His major work, an altarpiece for the monastic church at Isenheim in Alsace, was finished on the eve of the Reformation. The massive altarpiece, with its flanking panels closed, depicts the anguish of Christ on the cross, his body discolored, his feet blackened, and his flesh lacerated. With the panels opened, however, the inner pane reveals the triumphant resurrected Christ bathed in the glow of an eerie red light. Other altar paintings followed for Catholic patrons. Yet Grünewald himself became a Lutheran, and in 1525 he participated in the Peasants' Revolt. The archbishop of Mainz dismissed him for his beliefs in 1526, and he spent his last years in Protestant Saxony. Only his skills as an artist and his willingness to paint traditional altarpieces had enabled him to obtain Catholic patronage despite his Lutheran sympathies.

Born in the German city of Nuremberg, Albrecht Dürer (1471–1528) became the greatest artist of the German Renaissance. Twice he went to Italy, bringing back to Germany an understanding of Renaissance ideals and techniques. He was one of the first non-Italian artists to acquire an international reputation and the first northern artist to provide a rich account of his life through self-portraits, personal correspondence, and a diary. In addition to his paintings, he produced superb woodcuts and engravings; his illustrations for books and his sale of prints to ordinary folk helped make him a wealthy man. His woodcut *The Four Horsemen of the Apocalypse*, done near the turn of the century, reflects the popular apocalyptic spirit of northern Europe.

A Christian humanist in the early 1500s, Dürer captured the spirit of his friend Erasmus' *Handbook of a Christian Knight* in his engraving *Knight, Death, and the Devil*. His own spiritual doubts were resolved when he embraced Lutheranism: "If God helps me to meet Mar-

Albrecht Dürer's engraving *Knight, Death, and the Devil* (1513) reflects the confidence of humanists in the ability of the Christian faith to triumph over the enemies of humankind. [Museum of Fine Arts, Boston]

tin Luther," he wrote in 1520, "I shall carefully draw his portrait and engrave it on copper as a lasting remembrance of this Christian who helped me out of great distress."[13] After his conversion, his style became more austere. His engraving of the Last Supper and his painting of four apostles (John, Peter, Paul, and Mark) reveal the simple style of his Protestant years. Quotations from Luther's German New Testament appear on the twin frames of *The Four Apostles*. Like Grünewald, Dürer continued to accept commissions from Catholic patrons after his conversion, although he hoped to establish a distinctively Protestant tradition of monumental art.

The son of an Augsburg painter, Hans Holbein the Younger (1497–1543) achieved prominence as the greatest portrait painter of the sixteenth century. Like Dürer, he was a friend of Erasmus (whose portrait is one of Holbein's masterpieces) as well as a book illustrator. Holbein settled in Basel, but when the Protestant reform created a hostile atmosphere for artists there, Erasmus recommended him to Sir Thomas More in England. Henry VIII commissioned some of his most famous portraits, including those of the king himself and of three of his six wives, Anne Boleyn, Jane Seymour, and Anne of Cleves. Among Holbein's most fascinating works are 41 woodcuts depicting the late medieval "dance of death" and a series of drawings satirizing abuses in the Catholic church. Holbein died of the plague in 1543, but his influence on English portraiture continued for decades.

Music and the Reformation

Although Protestant reformers repudiated the ornate polyphonic masses of the late medieval period, they retained music in the worship service. To Luther, music was "an endowment and a gift of God" that made people cheerful and chased away the Devil. Luther himself composed at least eight hymns, including the still popular "A Mighty Fortress Is Our God," and wrote sacred texts for German folk tunes. A Lutheran hymnal appeared in 1524. Although Zwingli's radical liturgical reform led to the destruction of church organs in Zurich, the year after his death a new organ was built in the minster and congregational singing was introduced. In Geneva, Calvin approved of psalm singing, and the practice quickly spread throughout the Reformed churches. One of the main objections to traditional religious music was the difficulty of understanding the words, which prompted English reformers in the 1560s to condemn most choral music. To most people, however, the simplification of religious music was a matter of regret:

> What shall we now do at church, since all the saints are taken away, since all the goodly sights we were wont to have, are gone, since we cannot hear the . . . chanting, and playing upon the organs, that we could before?[14]

The Catholics too were concerned that elaborate musical compositions were obscuring the sacred texts. The Council of Trent enacted regulations designed to encourage simplicity as well as to ban the use of secular themes in religious works. Polyphony, however, was not prohibited, so long as the words of the mass could be clearly understood. After the council, the Roman Curia urged an end to the use of lay singers as well as all instruments except the organ in religious services, but compliance was never complete. The challenge to blend simplicity with musical beauty was brilliantly met in the masses and motets, or sacred compositions, of the Italian composer Giovanni Palestrina (c. 1525–1594), whose works, often sung by unaccompanied choirs, manifest a sense of monumental grandeur. His work reflected the achievements of the Renaissance composers and remained the model for Catholic devotional writers down to the nineteenth century.

The changes in art and music that occurred in the first half of the sixteenth century reflect the effects of the religious convulsions that shook Europe. Henceforth the West was permanently divided in its religious beliefs and institutions. Yet out of that diversity eventually came the demands for freedom of religion and thought that are now fundamental to the concept of liberty. In other ways, too, the Reformation made significant contributions to the quality of Western life. Better education and improved care for the needy and the helpless were direct fruits of Protestant and Catholic idealism. But there was a dark side to the Reformation era, manifested in the religious wars to which the bellicose attitudes of Protestant and Catholic alike led. For more than a century the hostilities rooted in rival religious convictions parodied the love that was at the core of Christian teaching. This aspect of the Reformation was also reflected in brutal religious persecutions and in witchcraft trials and burnings. The Reformation era dramatically pitted the authority of religious institutions against the claims of individual conscience. Unresolved in the sixteenth century, this clash remained a source of tension well into modern times. The fervency of the religious debate had global implications as well, particularly as Catholic missionaries carried their message to Asia, Africa, and the Americas.

Notes

1. Desiderius Erasmus, "The Paraclesis," in *Christian Humanism and the Reformation: Selected Writings*, ed. J. C. Olin (New York: Harper & Row, 1965), p. 97.
2. *The Correspondence of Erasmus*, trans. R. A. B. Mynors and D. F. S. Thompson, vol. 4 (Toronto: University of Toronto Press, 1977), p. 261.
3. Sir Thomas More, *Utopia*, trans. and ed. R. M. Adams (New York: Norton, 1975), p. 80.
4. R. H. Bainton, *Here I Stand: A Life of Martin Luther* (New York: Abingdon-Cokesbury, 1950), p. 78.
5. Martin Luther, "The Babylonian Captivity of the Church," in *Three Treatises* (Philadelphia: Muhlenberg Press, 1960), p. 248.
6. V. H. H. Green, *Luther and the Reformation* (New York: Capricorn Books, 1964), p. 98.
7. G. R. Potter, *Huldrych Zwingli* (London: Arnold, 1978), p. 24.
8. John Calvin, *Institutes of the Christian Religion*, ed. J. T. McNeill, trans. F. L. Battles, vol. 2. (Philadelphia: Westminster Press, 1960), pp. 922–923.
9. Sebastian Castellio, "Contra libellum Calvini," in *Concerning Heretics*, ed. R. H. Bainton (New York: Columbia University Press, 1935), p. 271.
10. C. Wriothesley, *A Chronicle of England During the Reigns of the Tudors, from A.D. 1485 to 1559*, vol. 2, ed. W. D. Hamilton (London: Camden Society, 1877), p. 91.
11. *The Spiritual Exercises of St. Ignatius*, trans. E. Mullan, ed. D. L. Fleming (St. Louis: Institute of Jesuit Sources, 1978), p. 234.
12. D. M. Loades, *The Oxford Martyrs* (London: Batsford, 1970), p. 220.
13. W. Strauss, ed., *The Complete Drawings of Albrecht Dürer*, vol. 4 (New York: Abaris Books, 1974), p. 1905.
14. R. L. Greaves, *Society and Religion in Elizabethan England* (Minneapolis: University of Minnesota Press, 1981), p. 458.

Suggestions for Further Reading

Bainton, R. H. *Erasmus of Christendom*. New York: Scribner, 1969.
———. *Women of the Reformation in Germany and Italy*. Minneapolis: Augsburg, 1971.
Benesch, O. *The Art of the Renaissance in Northern Europe: Its Relation to the Contemporary Spiritual and Intellectual Movements*, rev. ed. London: Phaidon, 1965.
Bossy, J. *Christianity in the West, 1400–1700*. New York: Oxford University Press, 1985.
Bouwsma, W. J. *John Calvin: A Sixteenth-Century Portrait*. New York: Oxford University Press, 1987.
Caraman, P. *Ignatius Loyola: A Biography of the Founder of the Jesuits*. San Francisco: Harper, 1990.
Cohn, N. *The Pursuit of the Millennium*, rev. ed. New York: Oxford University Press, 1970.
Dickens, A. G. *The English Reformation*. London: Batsford, 1964.
Edwards, M. *Luther's Last Battles*. Ithaca, N.Y.: Cornell University Press, 1983.
Erikson, E. H. *Young Man Luther: A Study in Psychoanalysis and History*. New York: Norton, 1962.
Evennett, H. O. *The Spirit of the Counter-Reformation*. Notre Dame, Ind.: Notre Dame University Press, 1970.
Gäler, U. *Huldrych Zwingli: His Life and Work*, trans. R. Gritsch. Philadelphia: Fortress Press, 1986.
Ginzburg, C. *The Night Battles: Witchcraft and Agrarian Cults in the Sixteenth and Seventeenth Centuries*, trans. J. Tedeschi and A. Tedeschi. London: Routledge & Kegan Paul, 1983.
Grimm, H. *The Reformation Era, 1500–1650*, 2nd ed. New York: Macmillan, 1965.
Hsia, R. P. *Social Discipline in the Reformation*. London: Routledge & Kegan Paul, 1990.
Jensen, D. *Reformation Europe: Age of Reform and Revolution*. Lexington, Mass.: Heath, 1981.
Kingdon, R. M., ed. *Transition and Revolution: Problems and Issues of European Renaissance and Reformation History*. Minneapolis: Burgess, 1974.

Levack, B. P. *The Witch-Hunt in Early Modern Europe.* New York: Longman, 1987.

Loades, D. *Mary Tudor.* Oxford: Blackwell, 1989.

Martz, L. L. *Thomas More: The Search for the Inner Man.* New Haven, Conn.: Yale University Press, 1990.

McGrath, A. E. *The Intellectual Origins of the European Reformation.* Oxford: Blackwell, 1987.

Monter, E. W. *Calvin's Geneva.* New York: Wiley, 1967.

———. "Women in the Age of Reformation." *Becoming Visible: Women in European History,* ed. R. Bridenthal and C. Koonz. Boston: Houghton Mifflin, 1987.

Oberman, H. *Luther: Between God and the Devil,* trans. E. Walliser-Schwarzbart. New Haven, Conn.: Yale University Press, 1989.

———. *The Roots of Anti-Semitism in the Age of Renaissance and Reformation,* trans. J. I. Porter. Philadelphia: Fortress Press, 1984.

O'Connell, M. R. *The Counter-Reformation, 1559–1610.* New York: Harper & Row, 1974.

Ozment, S. E. *The Age of Reform (1250–1550): An Intellectual and Religious History of Late Medieval and Reformation Europe.* New Haven, Conn.: Yale University Press, 1980.

———. *The Reformation in the Cities: The Appeal of Protestantism to Sixteenth-Century Germany and Switzerland.* New Haven, Conn.: Yale University Press, 1975.

Potter, G. R. *Huldrych Zwingli.* London: Arnold, 1978.

Russell, P. A. *Lay Theology in the Reformation: Popular Pamphleteers in Southwest Germany, 1521–1525.* Cambridge: Cambridge University Press, 1986.

Scarisbrick, J. J. *The Reformation and the English People.* Oxford: Blackwell, 1984.

Skinner, Q. *The Foundations of Modern Political Thought,* Vol. 2: *The Age of Reformation.* Cambridge: Cambridge University Press, 1978.

Spitz, L. *The Religious Renaissance of the German Humanists.* Cambridge, Mass.: Harvard University Press, 1963.

Sprunger, K. "God's Powerful Army of the Weak: Anabaptist Women of the Radical Reformation." *Triumph over Silence: Women in Protestant History,* ed. R. L. Greaves. Westport, Conn.: Greenwood Press, 1985.

Strauss, G. *Luther's House of Learning: The Indoctrination of the Young in the German Reformation.* Baltimore: Johns Hopkins University Press, 1978.

Warnicke, R. M. *The Rise and Fall of Anne Boleyn: Family Politics at the Court of Henry VIII.* Cambridge: Cambridge University Press, 1989.

Williams, G. H. *The Radical Reformation.* Philadelphia: Westminster Press, 1962.

The Age of European Discovery

The century and a half from 1450 to 1600 was one of the most extraordinary periods in Western history. The religious convulsions that shattered Christian unity and helped spur a global missionary effort occurred in the context of daring voyages of exploration and the beginnings of extensive trade that laid the foundation for a world economy. By 1450 the West, which had long lagged behind the more culturally and technologically sophisticated Indians and East Asians, developed the technological innovations, forms of commercial organization, and spiritual and materialistic ideals that enabled it to dominate much of the world by the nineteenth century. Mastery of the high seas was the key to global expansion, and the financial support and incentives for

The greatest of the merchant-capitalists was Jakob Fugger of Augsburg, shown here with his chief accountant in 1519. The signs on the walls identify Fugger branches in such cities as Lisbon, Cracow, Rome, and Innsbruck. [Herzog Anton Ulrich Museum, Brunswick, Germany]

this endeavor were made possible by the development of merchant capitalism and the increasing centralization of European states. The shift in trade routes from the Mediterranean to the Atlantic paved the way for Spain and Portugal, and later England, France, and the Netherlands, to become major powers.

Europe on the Eve of Exploration

By the mid-fifteenth century Europe was on the road to recovery after the demographic catastrophe caused by the Black Death. One of the most crucial elements in the revival was a new and rapid growth in population. Demographers are still analyzing evidence, but the broad outlines of this growth are now well established. Between 1460 and 1620 the population of Europe nearly doubled, to approximately 100 million people. In some places, particularly the cities of western Europe, the rise was even sharper. Antwerp grew from 20,000 in 1440 to 100,000 in 1560, and Rome doubled its population, also to 100,000, between 1526 and 1600. This demographic growth increased the pressure on land and food as demand outstripped supply, thus spurring inflation while preventing many Europeans from rising above the subsistence level. Demographic recovery also meant the end of the period of improved conditions for the peasantry brought on by the Black Death in the mid-1300s. Simultaneously, however, the rising population provided not only an abundant labor supply but also economic incentives for agricultural improvements, commercial expansion, and overseas exploration and settlement. Population growth thus provided much of the impetus for economic expansion.

Land Tenures and Agricultural Development

The devastation of the population by the Black Death and, in France, the Hundred Years' War (1337–1453) resulted in a shortage of peasant labor and a decrease in the amount of land under cultivation. For many peasants in western Europe the resulting demand for their services made it possible to escape the bonds of serfdom, trading the security of the old system for freedom and its attendant risks. Those who rented lands might profit by their industry, but they were also subject to potentially ruinous increases in rent. Whether the landlord or the tenant prospered was normally determined by the terms on which the land was held, as well as by tax obligations. Long-term leases, which some English

peasants enjoyed, were usually beneficial to the holders. Tenants in parts of France and western Germany whose tenure could be inherited might likewise prosper, for they were free to farm the land and sell the produce as they saw fit in return for a fixed payment to their landlords. In parts of Italy and France, short-term leases, which required the peasants to pay a fixed share of their crops to landlords, were common and helped the latter keep pace with rising food costs. Peasants without secure tenure, however, faced a troubled future in which the value of their services was as uncertain as their ability to continue working the land. Such tenants were at the mercy of landlords, who had to choose between opportunities for economic advancement and traditional obligations for their tenants' welfare.

Landed aristocrats whose tenants could inherit tenure or had long-term leases suffered a loss in real income as prices rose faster than rents. The lesser aristocracy often reacted by supporting wars and overseas conquest because of the prospect of new lands and financial gain. When the reconquest of the Iberian peninsula from the Moors was completed in 1492, the interest of the Spanish hidalgos, or lesser nobles, shifted to the New World. Other aristocrats, especially in France and England, shored up their finances by forming strategic alliances—typically by marriage—with rising merchant families, who shared their wealth in return for social prestige. Although some of the old nobility bitterly resented this infusion of new blood into their ranks, those who formed such alliances brought the landed elite into a closer relationship with the emerging world of overseas exploration and capitalistic investment.

Landlords whose tenants did not enjoy secure tenure had a wider range of options. This was especially the case in Spain, Portugal, southern Italy, parts of England, eastern Germany, and Poland. Some lords were content simply to raise rents at will—"rack-renters," they were called by bitter peasants and social critics. The more enterprising, however, took advantage of their power to embark on new economic ventures. In some instances this meant enclosing their lands, evicting their tenants, and converting from tillage to the pasturing of sheep. More often it meant an end to the old open-field system of farming, in which land was divided into strips and production was largely for the local market, in favor of larger, more productive farms that produced commercially for the wider marketplace. These new farms required the employment of agricultural hands, usually for subsistence wages, in place of peasants with a degree of personal attachment to the land. In many places agriculture thus became a commercial endeavor. This pattern was not equally distributed. It occurred often in England but rarely in Spain, where most hidalgos thought anything pertaining to business was beneath their dignity as warriors. In eastern Germany, Poland, and Russia landlords took advantage of western Europe's inability to feed itself by enclosing their lands in order to produce large quantities of grain for export. Unlike the English, they did not evict their peasants but forced them into gradual serfdom. The extent of western Europe's inability to feed itself in the face of rising population is amply demonstrated by the fact that approximately 6 million tons of grain had to be imported from the Baltic region between the mid-1500s and the mid-1600s.

The changes in the period from 1450 to 1600 caused substantial agrarian unrest in the English Midlands and eastern Europe, where large-scale commercial agriculture became commonplace, and throughout western Europe, where most peasants worked small plots and often worried about the security of their holdings. The Peasants' Revolt in 1524–1525, which Martin Luther denounced, was but one manifestation of this discontent. Commercial farming, however, was essential if the expanding population, particularly in the towns, was to be fed from the mid-sixteenth century on.

Commercial Innovation and Expansion

The economic depression that gripped Europe in the fourteenth and early fifteenth centuries had been beneficial to the towns in certain respects. Despite urban riots, declining production caused by the drop in population, and war, the price of manufactured goods and wages for skilled workers generally rose while the cost of grain declined, thus increasing overall urban prosperity.

Merchants adapted to the new conditions by developing stronger organizations, diversifying their activities, and improving business procedures. Temporary partnerships, neither efficient nor conducive to expansion, were replaced by permanent companies, often formed around prominent families such as the Medici in Florence or the Fuggers in Augsburg. These firms were vulnerable during recessions when borrowers defaulted on their loans. Businessmen who survived learned to break up their firms into several independent partnerships. The importance of diversification was also recognized, as merchants engaged in a combination of commerce, banking, manufacturing, and sometimes overseas trade. Diversification encouraged the development of new industries: linens in Cambrai, iron in Liège, and weapons in Milan, among others. Economic growth was enhanced by more widespread use of double-entry bookkeeping, which uses parallel columns to balance credits and debits, and bills of exchange, which facilitate the transfer of large sums of money without risking the shipment of currency or bullion. These developments helped provide the capital accumulation that made exploration and the growth of overseas trade possible.

No family better illustrates the success of the new merchants than the Fuggers of Augsburg. By the time Jakob Fugger became a merchant in 1478, the family had been conducting business in the city for a century, mostly trading in the spices and silks that came through Venice. Jakob Fugger branched out into banking and mining, acquiring virtual control of the silver mines in the Tirol through his loans to the Habsburg emperors Maximilian I and Charles V. His company also dominated the copper supply in Europe by its acquisition of Hungarian mines and the construction of processing plants. To help repay his loans, Charles V gave the Fuggers a lease for the revenues of the Spanish orders of knighthood, which included the mercury monopoly in Spain. As bankers for the papacy, the firm handled the sale of the indulgences that Luther attacked in 1517. At his death in 1525, Jakob Fugger was the richest merchant-banker in Europe. By 1545 the Fugger firm had become the largest in Europe, a distinction that had belonged to the Medici in Florence a century earlier. The Fugger fortune, however, was more than five times as large as that of the Medici in 1440. Fugger trading posts extended in 1525 from the Mediterranean to the Baltic and from Cracow to Lisbon.

In the fifteenth century the western end of the trade in eastern spices and silks was still dominated by the Venetians. Goods from eastern Asia and the Moluccas (the Spice Islands) were taken to Malacca on the Malay peninsula, where they were transferred to Arab or Indian ships for transport to the Malabar coast of western India. From there the cargoes were taken either by way of the Persian Gulf and the Euphrates River to Beirut and Aleppo, Syria, or through the Red Sea and overland to Alexandria, Egypt. From Aleppo, Beirut, and Alexandria the Venetians dominated the trade as it passed into Europe.

The heart of this commerce was spices, a crucial item for the preparation of meat in an age that lacked refrigeration and for the general enhancement of foods that were otherwise monotonously dull or tainted. Fresh meat was commonly available only in the fall; during the rest of the year, most people who had beef ate the salted variety, which spices made more palatable. Spices were also used for medicines, perfumes, and incense in religious ceremonies. As population increased, the demand for spices intensified. Most of them came from southern and eastern Asia: pepper from India, the East Indies, and West Africa; cloves from the Moluccas; nutmeg and mace from the East Indies; cinnamon from Ceylon; and ginger from China and the Malabar coast. In addition to spices, there was also commerce in cotton cloth from India; silk, porcelain, and rhubarb (used medicinally) from China; and precious stones from India, Tibet, and Ceylon. Despite the enormous expense of conducting

◉ Fugger Money: The Price of Power ◉

*Merchants who loaned money to princes often ran a considerable risk,
but in addition to interest on loans they might acquire valuable favors
or monopolies. When, in April 1523, Jakob Fugger had to press Emperor
Charles V to repay his debts, the Habsburg ruler was reminded that he
owed his crown at least in part to Fugger money.*

Your Imperial Majesty doubtless knows how I and my kinsmen have ever hitherto been disposed to serve the House of Austria in all loyalty to the furtherance of its well-being and prosperity; wherefore, in order to be pleasing to your Majesty's grandsire, the late Emperor Maximilian, and to gain for your Majesty the Roman crown, we have held ourselves bounden to engage ourselves towards divers princes who placed their trust and reliance upon myself and perchance on no man besides. We have, moreover, advanced to your Majesty's agents for the same end a great sum of money, of which we ourselves have had to raise a large part from our friends. It is well known that your Imperial Majesty could not have gained the Roman crown save with mine aid, and I can prove the same by the writings of your Majesty's agents given by their own hands. In this matter I have not studied mine own profit. For had I left the House of Austria and had been minded to further France, I had obtained much money and property, such as was then offered to me. How grave a disadvantage had in this case accrued to your Majesty and the House of Austria, your Majesty's royal mind well knoweth.

Source: R. Ehrenberg, *Capital and Finance in the Age of the Renaissance: A Study of the Fuggers and Their Connections,* trans. H. M. Lucas (New York: Harcourt, Brace, n.d.), p. 80.

---

this trade, including heavy tolls and the risk of lost cargoes, the profits were substantial. There was, then, ample incentive to discover new routes to the East, particularly since so much of the spice trade had fallen into the hands of the Muslims and was monopolized in the Mediterranean by the Venetians.

The Search for New Trade Routes

The voyages of exploration that began in the late fifteenth century were impelled by crusading zeal against the Muslims and the quest for profit. However, they would not have been possible without various technological developments that were no less significant than the later inventions that led to the Industrial Revolution. Europeans already possessed some knowledge of Asia, thanks largely to the thirteenth-century travels of Franciscan missionaries and merchant-explorers such as Marco Polo. But only the sea afforded an opportunity to establish direct commercial links with the sources of spices, cotton, linen, and other goods. Direct sea contact

required improvements in ships, weapons, and navigational tools.

Technology and Seafaring

Oars powered the galleys that plied the Mediterranean, giving them independence from the wind but requiring too much human labor to make arduous overseas voyages feasible. The galleys of Venice and Genoa could range the coast of the eastern Atlantic from Morocco to Flanders by the thirteenth century, but they were unsuited for exploration on the high seas and lacked the cargo space to make long voyages practicable. By 1400 the maritime states of Europe had developed large, broad-beamed ships powered primarily by square-rigged sails. Because such ponderous vessels generally had to sail with the wind, their maneuverability was severely restricted. By studying Arab ships that were capable of sailing the Indian Ocean and by borrowing multiple masts and sternpost rudders from the Chinese, the Portuguese developed a new vessel, a two- or three-masted caravel that combined square-rigged and lateen sails. Although the caravels were relatively small, the use of square-rigged sails, multiple masts, and stern-post

This model of a four-masted caravel illustrates the triangular lateen sails. Caravels were not large vessels. [National Maritime Museum, Greenwich, England]

rudders instead of awkward steering oars eventually made it possible to build ships large enough to make long voyages profitable and gave them greater speed when running with the wind, while the lateen sail (a smaller triangular sail somewhat like those on modern sailboats) permitted greater maneuverability and the capacity to sail at an angle to the wind instead of only with it. The masts were subsequently combined on larger vessels, including warships, and this became the norm in Europe. Most of the ships the Portuguese used to explore the West African coast were caravels, but beginning in the 1490s larger ships were also used.

The ability of the new vessels to sail the high seas rather than merely hug the shoreline created immediate navigational problems, but these were surmountable with instruments already at hand. The compass, originally Chinese but in use in the West by the thirteenth century, enabled a navigator to steer a course; the astrolabe facilitated the determination of latitude by measuring the approximate height of the sun and stars. However, the accuracy of the astrolabe and its successor, the quadrant, was adversely affected by the rolling of the ship. Portuguese navigators commonly hugged the coasts of Africa, landing every few days to use their instruments on shore.

Navigation was also aided by the increased sophistication of maritime charts known as *portolani*, prepared primarily from firsthand observations of sailors rather than by academic geographers. In the 1400s the work of geographers was dominated by Ptolemy's *Geography*, a book that dated from the second century A.D. Among its major errors were the invention of a southern continent that linked Africa and China, miscalculations concerning the size of the earth, and the notion that the Southern Hemisphere could not be navigated because of its excessive heat. The *portolani* mapped coastlines, including those of rivers and harbors. When the Portuguese explored the West African coast, they prepared similar charts, thereby adding to the fund of useful geographic knowledge.

In addition to developing better ships and navigational devices, Europeans acquired naval mastery by adapting artillery to their vessels and by gradually improving naval gunnery and the equally critical ability to maneuver their still small ships for maximum military advantage. This gave them a considerable advantage over Arab galleys and the often larger Chinese junks. Galleys relied on the traditional tactics of ramming or sailing alongside and boarding, while the cannon—developed first in twelfth-century China—though often heavier on Indian and Chinese ships than those on European vessels, were fixed and could not be effectively aimed. The Venetians pioneered the Western use of naval artillery in the fourteenth century, but the Portuguese were the first westerners to recognize the value of directing fire against an enemy's ships rather than the soldiers they carried. The capabilities of the new armaments were demonstrated when Vasco da Gama bombarded the Indian port of Calicut in 1502 and when the Portuguese destroyed an Indian fleet near Diu in western India in 1509, thereby asserting their right to sail the Indian Ocean.

The Motives for Portuguese Expansion

Portuguese expansion was originally viewed in terms of a new crusade against the Muslims. In this regard the Portuguese hoped to establish an alliance with the legendary and mythical Prester (Elder) John, reputedly an enormously wealthy ruler whom some Europeans identified with the emperor of Ethiopia, others with the emperor of China. With his help they hoped to establish a new front in the centuries-old war against the "infidel." Their second goal, however, was to bypass Islamic middlemen by going directly to Guinea in West Africa for gold and pepper. Given the scarcity of bullion in Europe, the Portuguese hoped to increase their power by monopolizing the gold trade with the Ashanti and Fanti peoples of the Gold Coast. Initially, then, the voyages did not stem from a desire to discover new lands or a search for a direct route to the spices and wealth of eastern and southern Asia. On the contrary, Portugal's first move—the successful capture in 1415 of the Muslim city of Ceuta in northern Morocco—launched a program of African expansion. The Portuguese thus initiated the European attempt to expand Western military, commercial, and religious sway to regions far away from the Holy Land.

After 1415 Prince Henry the Navigator (1394–1460), younger son of King John I of Portugal, began dispatching frequent expeditions to explore the western coast of Africa. The knowledge his mariners gained was examined by the scientists and cartographers he patronized at Sagres on Cape St. Vincent in southwestern Portugal. As a result of these voyages, in the 1460s and 1470s Portugal established relations with the rulers of West Africa and constructed forts and trading stations. By 1500 the Portuguese had replaced the Muslims as the dominant commercial power in this region, and gold was now imported directly to Lisbon and Antwerp. In the fifteenth century the Portuguese also developed plantations on their islands in the eastern Atlantic, including São Tomé on the Gulf of Guinea, where they forced black slaves to grow sugarcane for export to Europe. Portuguese traders sent more than 1,000 slaves a year to Lisbon in the late 1400s, and by 1530 the traffic in slaves was more valuable than the shipments of gold. From the Africans the Portuguese also obtained ivory, ebony, and pepper in return for copper dishes and cheap fabrics and jewelry.

Voyages of Exploration

Inspired by the work of Prince Henry, the Portuguese extended their vision to the East, particularly with the support of the prince's grandnephew, King John II (1481–1495), himself a geographer. In 1487 the voyages of exploration along the West African coast culminated when Bartholomeu Dias successfully sailed around the African cape, which was soon named "Good Hope." It was another decade, however, before Vasco da Gama had a fleet of four ships ready to strike out for India. Indian (and earlier Chinese) ships had long been trading across the Indian Ocean; hence da Gama was able to hire an Indian pilot in East Africa to guide him to India. Da Gama arrived at Calicut on the Malabar coast in May 1498 after a voyage of 10½ months from Lisbon. Neither the Hindu rulers nor the Arab merchants were particularly pleased to see the Portuguese, who represented a threat to their domination of the spice trade. For their part the Portuguese were unimpressed by the Indians: although "well disposed and apparently of mild temper," at first sight they seemed "covetous and ignorant." The women, however, were described, from a clearly racist perspective, as generally "ugly and of small stature."[1] Portuguese fleets, spurred on by the 3,000 percent profit realized by da Gama's voyage, sailed again in 1500 and 1502. The 1500 voyage was notable because Pedro Cabral, blown off course in a storm, sailed far enough westward to reach Brazil. Da Gama's bombardment of

Calicut on the 1502 voyage was a clear signal that European presence in the East could not be established without the threat of military power.

Although Prince Henry had been interested in exploring the Atlantic, the Portuguese missed the opportunity to sponsor the voyages that led to the European discovery of the Americas. As early as 1484 the Genoese sailor Christopher Columbus (1451–1506) tried unsuccessfully to persuade John II to support a westward expedition, the ultimate goal of which was to find a sea route to the Indies. Not until 1492 did Columbus find backing when the Spanish rulers Ferdinand and Isabella, concerned about recent Portuguese discoveries of the eastern sea route to Asia, gave him their support after the conquest of Granada. With a fleet of three ships, Columbus reached what were probably the Bahamas in October 1492 but mistakenly identified them as "the islands which are set down in the maps at the end of the Orient." Searching for Japan, which he estimated to be

This recently discovered portrait of Christopher Columbus, attributed to the Spanish artist Pedro Berruguete, a contemporary, is believed to be the most accurate depiction of the explorer.
[Grazia Neri Agency]

◉ The Amerindians: Columbus' View ◉

In February 1493 Columbus wrote a fascinating letter recording what he and his crew saw when they arrived in the New World. To Columbus, of course, these were Asian islands that he thought would yield substantial quantities of gold, spices, cotton, and mastic (a resin). Most of the letter is devoted to a description of the "well-formed" Indians and their reaction to Columbus' men.

In thirty-three days, I passed from the Canary Islands to the Indies. . . . There I found very many islands filled with people innumerable, and of them all I have taken possession for their highnesses, by proclamation made and with the royal standard unfurled, and no opposition was offered to me. . . .

Many times it has happened that I have sent ashore two or three men to some town to have speech, and countless people have come out to them, and as soon as they have seen my men approaching they have fled, even a father not waiting for his son. And this, not because ill has been done to anyone; on the contrary, at every point where I have been and have been able to have speech, I have given to them of all that I had, such as cloth and many other things, without receiving anything for it; but so they are, incurably timid. It is true that, after they have been reassured and have lost their fear, they are so guileless and so generous with all they possess, that no one would believe it who has not seen it. . . .

I took by force some of them, in order that they might learn and give me information of that which there is in those parts, and so it was that they soon understood us, and we them, either by speech or signs, and they have been very serviceable. I still take them with me, and they are always assured that I come from Heaven. . . . The others went running from house to house and to the neighboring towns, with loud cries of, "Come! Come to see the people from Heaven!"

Source: C. Jane, trans. and ed., *Select Documents Illustrating the Four Voyages of Columbus,* vol. 1 (London: Hakluyt Society, 1930), pp. 2, 8, 10.

only 2,400 miles west of Europe, he discovered Cuba and Hispaniola. From the latter he acquired a small quantity of gold and some jewelry by bartering with the natives, whom he called "Indians" (people of the Indies). Although he made three subsequent voyages, Columbus was convinced until his death in 1506 that he had discovered a sea route to eastern Asia. He carried some 1,500 settlers on his second voyage, but not until his third trip (1498) did the first Spanish women migrate to the New World.

For his exploits Columbus wanted to be honored as "the Admiral of the Ocean Sea," yet increasingly in his later years he also thought of himself as one who was divinely ordained to help Spain liberate the Holy Land. Reflecting the late medieval belief that the end of the world was imminent, he was convinced that God had made him "the messenger of the new heaven and the new earth of which he spoke in the Apocalypse of St. John . . . and he showed me the spot where to find it."[2]

When the Portuguese learned of Columbus' initial voyage, John II, unwilling to believe that the explorer had landed in eastern Asia, laid claim to the new territory on the grounds of their proximity to the Azores. Ferdinand and Isabella thereupon appealed to the pope, the Spaniard Alexander VI, who awarded the new discoveries to Spain. The pope also drew a line of demarcation approximately 300 miles west of the Azores and the Cape Verde Islands, giving Spain the rights of exploration to territory west of the line. In the Treaty of Tordesillas (1494), John II persuaded the Spanish to move the line some 800 miles farther west. Although no one apparently realized it at the time, Brazil fell into the Portuguese sphere of influence because of the change.

The significance of what Columbus had found became apparent only as other explorers made new findings. Sailing for England in 1497 and 1498, the Venetian John Cabot discovered the region of Cape Breton and Labrador, where he found an abundance of fish but no

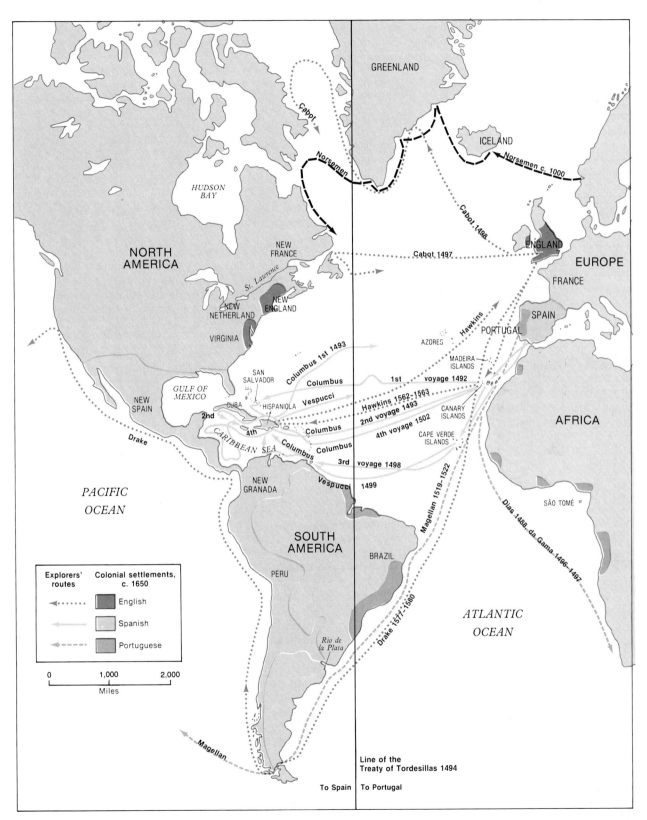

18.1 *Voyages of Exploration to the Americas*

spices. Undeterred, Cabot was convinced that he had almost reached Japan, where he mistakenly thought "all the spices of the world have their origin, as well as the jewels."[3] It was not Cabot or Columbus who persuaded Europeans to accept the discovery of a new continent but the Florentine Amerigo Vespucci (1454–1512), a geographer who participated in Spanish and Portuguese voyages that extended from Cape Hatteras in modern North Carolina to the Rio de la Plata, the modern border between Argentina and Uruguay. His published letters popularized the idea of the New World, which came to be called America in his honor.

Accepting the presence of new continents did not dissuade European rulers from their belief in the viability of a western sea route to Asia by which the Portuguese monopoly of the spice trade could be broken. The key, they reasoned, was the discovery of a western passage. The Spaniard Vasco Núñez de Balboa's accidental sighting of the Pacific Ocean in 1513 as he was searching for gold on the isthmus of Panama stimulated interest. Ultimately, the Portuguese mariner Ferdinand Magellan (1480–1521) found a westward route in 1519 by taking a small Spanish fleet through the foggy and dangerous straits near the southern tip of South America that now bear his name. From there he sailed across the Pacific to the Philippines, where he and 40 of his men were killed. Magellan's navigator, Juan Sebastián del Cano, made his way with the two remaining caravels to the Moluccas, where he took on a load of cloves. Rather than risk the Straits of Magellan a second time, del Cano and a skeleton crew of 18 returned to Spain by way of the Indian Ocean and the Cape of Good Hope. The other ship was captured by the Portuguese as it attempted to sail back across the Pacific to Mexico. In this fashion Magellan's crew accomplished the first circumnavigation of the globe. It took three years to complete and imposed terrible hardships on the crews, who suffered from scurvy and were forced to eat rats, sawdust, and hides on the long passage across the Pacific.

For a time Spanish hopes to dominate the Moluccas quickened, but it soon became apparent that the Spaniards were no match for the Portuguese in the East. In 1529 Emperor Charles V, preoccupied by his wars with the French, sold Spain's rights in the Moluccas to Portugal. By that time Spain already had more than it could manage in America, although it retained the Philippines and began a 300-year link between Manila and its New World empire centered in Mexico. The Manila galleon, as it was called, carried yearly shipments of Mexican and Peruvian silver from Acapulco to Manila and Chinese silk, lacquer, and porcelain back to both New and Old Spain. Manila grew as an entrepôt, or intermediary center, for trade with China, and New World silver flowed into the Chinese market with major consequences for the Ming and Ch'ing dynasty economy and its growing commercialization. New World crops, especially potatoes and maize, also entered China via Manila and helped make possible subsequent major increases in population.

Westerners in Asia and Africa

Portuguese and later Dutch settlements in Africa were incidental to the drive into Asia but served as way stations and provisioning bases along the sea route. Although the Portuguese extended the slave trade from West Africa to Brazil and sought a few other African goods, including gold, they did not penetrate inland and their coastal bases were few and scattered. Access to the interior was made more difficult by mangrove swamps, rain forests, or steep cliffs as well as by hostile African states, and the few Portuguese settlements were confined to tiny footholds on the coast or offshore islands. Their primary objective was indicated by the names they gave to their two main African bases. Algoa Bay ("to Goa," now Port Elizabeth in South Africa) and Delagoa Bay ("from Goa," now Maputo in Mozambique). Both names were derived from Goa, the administrative center of Portugal's Asian enterprise established in 1510 on the west coast of India and for which the African bases were to serve as provisioning stops.

The Portuguese and Africa

The gold, and later the slaves, that the Portuguese obtained from scattered parts of the coasts of West and East Africa were important sources of profit, but the Portuguese established permanent African bases only in Angola on the southwest coast and at Algoa and Delagoa. In addition, they seized and occupied Madeira, the Azores, the Cape Verde Islands, and a few other offshore bases. Their presence greatly increased the slave trade, already thriving in Africa, by opening additional markets, especially in the New World. The Portuguese impact on several African societies went far beyond their relatively small power and numbers. They tried repeatedly to extend their power inland and on some occasions sacked and burned African towns or cities and pillaged overland trade routes. Although they could occasionally raid the interior, the Portuguese lacked the means for establishing control there, and their chief objective remained the Indies.

Cape Verde, where the city of Dakar now stands, was reached only after traversing the long, waterless desert coast of the northwest. Farther south, the kingdoms of Ghana and Benin offered trade at coastal ports, although the main commodities, gold and slaves, came from far-

Situated on the Tagus River, Lisbon became one of Europe's busiest ports in the sixteenth century because of Portugal's trade with Africa and Asia. By the end of the century, however, much of this trade had shifted to Antwerp. [Granger Collection]

ther inland. Much of the interior of West Africa was controlled by the empire of Mali, centered at Timbuktu on the upper Niger River. Gold and slaves moved from Timbuktu north across the great desert by camel caravans to the Mediterranean. The arrival of the Portuguese at the coast marked a shift of trade routes toward West African ports, from which European and New World markets could be reached more easily and cheaply. Timbuktu and the Mali empire slowly declined as the coastal centers of trade grew more rapidly in the centuries following the start of European expansion.

Persisting southward in their long search for a sea route to the Indies, the Portuguese found the dense rain forests of the Congo region impossible to penetrate. Inland navigation on the great river was blocked by falls and rapids, where the Congo tumbles off the steep escarpment that rises only a few miles from the coast around nearly the whole of Africa. The same problem hampered access from the east coast. Along the Congo coast, ivory and slaves were available to traders, but the coastal cultures were less highly developed than many of those inland, of which the Portuguese learned little except that they were the source of most of the trade goods. The coasts of Angola and Southwest Africa were part of the great southern desert and thus somewhat easier to penetrate, but also less rewarding. Having come this far south along the coast, however, the Portuguese badly needed a base for supply and refitting; they finally established one at Luanda in Angola by 1530. Once Bartholomeu Dias had made it around the Cape of Good Hope in 1488 and was followed a decade later by Vasco da Gama, the road to the Indies lay open and the bases in Mozambique on the east coast were more useful. The Portuguese traded and raided northward along the East African coast and for a time even tried to control Mombasa in what is now Kenya. Somali resis-

tance, as well as competition and opposition from the long-established Arab traders in coastal East Africa, soon ejected the Portuguese except as traders. The Europeans were resented for their arrogance and aggressiveness. Their efforts to move inland from Mozambique and to open the area to Jesuit missionaries were ultimately repelled by the African kingdom of Vakaranga, although the Europeans continued to buy slaves and other goods on the coast.

Traders in Asia

For over two centuries after Europeans made contact with Asia by sea they remained insignificant on the Asian scene, a handful of people the natives dismissed as barbarians. At sea and along the Asian coasts they had the upper hand, but their power on land extended little beyond the range of their naval guns. The Portuguese and later the Dutch built a strong position in the spice trade, but in Asian commerce as a whole, even its seaborne component, their role was minor. They bought spices and a few other goods in preexisting markets at established ports, such as Calicut, where they had already been collected by Asian traders, and then hauled them to Europe. The Portuguese never and the Dutch only much later had an involvement in production, and both continued to compete as traders with numerous Chinese, Indian, Southeast Asian, and Arab entrepreneurs, who did the bulk of the assembly. Only in the transporting of Asian goods to Europe did they have a monopoly, and there the Portuguese in time faced intense competition from the Dutch and the English (see Chapter 19). As if to emphasize their role as ocean carriers with their improved ships for long voyages, the Portuguese developed a highly profitable trade between

China and Japan, carrying Chinese silks and porcelains (and some Southeast Asian spices) from the Canton area to Nagasaki in southwestern Japan and bringing back Japanese silver and copper for China. They, and later the English, also found profit in hauling Southeast Asian and Chinese goods to India and exchanging them for Indian cottons, which had an even larger and more eager market in Europe.

Recognizing their weakness on land or in trade competition with Asian and Arab merchants, Europeans built on their strength at sea by occupying and fortifying coastal footholds at key points along the sea routes. Ideally these were in areas on the fringes of the great Asian empires or where the local power was weak or could be persuaded to grant privileges in return for favors. The latter often included Western naval help against pirates, rebels, or small rival states. The Portuguese seized Goa on the Indian west coast in 1510 and soon made it into their major Asian base. The small area around the city was not then part of any powerful Indian state. The Portuguese saw they had little hope of controlling the larger ports farther south, such as Calicut, although they did establish some smaller bases elsewhere on the Malabar coast in the west. From Goa, however, their ships could patrol the entire coast and essentially control Indian Ocean trade. Goa was a logical choice as the administrative center of the extensive Portuguese trade network farther east, and it prospered so much on the profits of that trade that it became known as "Golden Goa."

A commercial empire stretching another 6,000 miles east by sea, through all of Southeast Asia (except the Philippines) and on to China and Japan, required other bases too. The most obvious control points over the sea lanes eastward from India were Colombo in Ceylon (now Sri Lanka) and Malacca in Malaya. The Palk Strait between India and Ceylon was too shallow for shipping, and the route around Sumatra and through the Sunda Strait between Sumatra and Java was longer and plagued by reefs and currents, with no safe harbors along the Sumatran west coast. Traffic to and from East Asia was therefore funneled through the Straits of Malacca. The Portuguese seized the town of Malacca, commanding the straits, in 1511, but Malaya at that period was thinly settled and relatively unproductive. Malacca's role was primarily strategic, although it did some entrepôt business to and from Southeast Asia. Colombo, which the Portuguese also fortified after establishing themselves there about 1515, was able to draw on the nearby production of cinnamon, which the Ceylonese made from the bark of a rain forest tree, and thus played a commercial role as well.

For trade with China and Japan, the Portuguese somewhat later established their chief base at Macao, at the seaward edge of the Canton delta. There they could be a little freer of the restrictions imposed on foreign merchants at Canton by the Ming government and be tolerated by the Chinese authorities, enough to permit modest fortifications and a small permanent settlement. From the Chinese point of view, these unruly and barbaric foreigners were in any case better shunted off to such a remote neck of land and closed off by a wall (which still stands) where they could not make trouble and where they could govern themselves according to their own customs. In the sixteenth century the Ming were still close to the height of their power and effectively excluded all foreigners except for tribute missions and a handful of traders at the fringes. There was no comparable Portuguese territorial base in Indonesia, where in any case no large state existed at this time. The Portuguese dominated the spice trade and excluded rival Europeans by intimidation of local sultans, alliances or treaties with others, and a scattered string of forts as far east as Ternate and Amboina in the Moluccas.

The shape and nature of the Portuguese commercial empire is clearly defined by its emphasis on strategically located ports, most of them already long in existence, and on domination of the sea lanes. The Portuguese controlled no territory beyond the immediate area of the few ports named, and traded in the hundreds of other ports in competition with Asian and Arab traders. Even so, their effort was overextended, and by the latter part of the sixteenth century they could no longer maintain what control they had earlier established. Their home base was tiny as well as poor; it could not provide either manpower or funds to sustain the effort required to maintain their overseas stations against competition. As the century ended, they were rapidly being ousted by the Dutch in Southeast Asia and were soon to be eliminated as serious competitors in the rest of the Asian trade by the other rising European power, the English. Many Portuguese stayed on, picking up crumbs of trade and also operating as pirates. As in Africa, they had from early days married local women, and from the seventeenth century virtually all of them in Asia were Eurasians, though commonly carrying Portuguese names and retaining the Catholic faith to which they had been converted. To this day names such as Fernando or de Souza are common in coastal South India, Sri Lanka, Malacca, and Macao. As the power of the Portuguese faded, their bases were no longer a threat, which is why Portugal retained formal sovereignty over Goa until it was forcibly reclaimed by India in 1961. The fiction of Portuguese control is maintained even today for Macao, an arrangement that suits the Chinese government for the present.

Religious Concerns

From the beginning, the crusade against Islam and the winning of souls for the Catholic church had been Por-

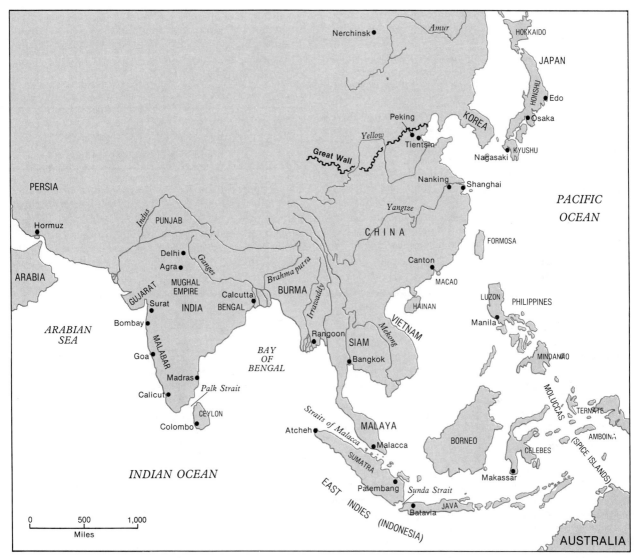

18.2 Asia in the Age of Early European Expansion

tuguese goals equal to trade in importance. When Vasco da Gama arrived in Calicut in 1498 and was asked what he sought, he is said to have replied, "Christians and spices." His ships carried missionary priests, and their effort played a major role in the 1500s. In 1511, after Affonso de Albuquerque (1453–1515), chief architect of the Portuguese commercial empire in Asia, had been named viceroy of the Indies in 1508, he wrote of his plan to capture Malacca:

The first aim is the great service which we shall perform to our Lord in casting the Moors out of this country and quenching the fire of the sect of Mohammed. . . . And the other is the service we shall render to the king . . . in taking this city, because it is the source of all the spiceries

and drugs which the Moors carry every year. . . . For I hold it certain that if we take this trade of Malacca away from them, Cairo and Mecca will be entirely ruined, and Venice will receive no spiceries unless her merchants go and buy them in Portugal.[4]

When Albuquerque took Malacca, he massacred all the Muslims but tried to make allies or friends of the few other inhabitants. In insular Southeast Asia, by now predominantly Muslim, these were not attitudes or policies calculated to ingratiate the Portuguese. Their cruel practice of conversion by torture, their pitiless extortion, and their slaughter of "heathen" Hindus and Buddhists as well as their ancient Muslim foes earned them hatred. The Portuguese record during their century of power in

Asia is at least as horrendous as that of the Spanish in the New World, and their decline was regretted by no one.

The Chinese remained aloof from these Western maritime and commercial rivalries and kept their distance at Canton, where European traders were not even permitted to enter the city but did their business outside the walls during the six-month trading season and then were obliged to depart until the next year. Successive Portuguese, Dutch, and English efforts to break these restrictions by trading elsewhere on the China coast were repelled, as Europeans did not have the means to challenge the Dragon Throne. (Dutch and English involvement in Asia are discussed in Chapter 19). The sixteenth-century missionary effort to penetrate China was more successful, at least for a time. For the Jesuits, as for all later missionary groups, China was the chief goal, if only because of its immense population, its so-

phisticated culture, and the knowledge that it lacked an indigenous religion of salvation. Successive Jesuit efforts to enter the country failed after Francis Xavier died off the south China coast in 1552, still cherishing the dream of converting China's millions.

❦
MATTEO RICCI: MISSIONARY TO THE MING COURT

The pioneer of the Jesuit effort in China was Matteo Ricci. He was born at Ancona in 1552, where he soon demonstrated his scholastic ability and magnetic personality. At the age of 16 he went to Rome to study law and at 19 entered the Society of Jesus, where he distinguished himself in mathematics and geography. In 1577

◉ A European View of China ◉

Asians did not think much of Europeans, especially in this period, when they could easily be seen as crude ruffians. An Italian traveler to early-seventeenth-century India, Niccolò Manucci, recorded Indian views that agreed closely with those of the Chinese, Japanese, and other Asians. They believed that Europeans "have no polite manners, that they are ignorant, wanting in ordered life, and very dirty." The Europeans, however, were far more positive about Asia, which they had come so far to seek, in terms of both its wealth and its civilization. Here is a sampling of a Jesuit's account of China in 1590.

There are such a number of artificers ingeniously framing sundry devices out of gold, silver, and other metals . . . and other matters convenient for man's use, that the streets of cities being replenished with their shops and fine workmanship are very wonderful to behold. . . . Their industry does no less appear in founding of guns. . . . To these may be added the art of printing . . . and with marvelous facility they daily publish huge multitudes of books. . . . You may add two more, that is to say navigation and discipline of war, both of which have been in ancient times most diligently practiced. . . . The people of China do above all things profess the art of literature, and learning it most diligently, they employ themselves a long time and the better part of their age therein. . . . Graduates of the second degree are elected in each province, and a certain number . . . ascend to the highest pitch of dignity. . . . Out of this order the chief magistrates are chosen. . . . Magistrates bear office for the space of three years, yet for the governing of each province men of another province are selected . . . [so that] judges may give sentence with a far more entire and incorrupt mind than if they were among their own kinsfolk and allies. . . . Over and besides all these there is an annual magistrate [the imperial censor] . . . whose duty it is to make inquisition of all crimes, and especially the crimes of magistrates. . . . Hence it is that all magistrates . . . are kept within the limits of their callings.

Source: N. Manucci, "An Excellent Treatise of the Kingdome of China," in *The Principal Navigations,* vol. 2, ed. R. Hakluyt (London, 1600), pp. 88–97 passim. The manuscript was written in Macao and captured by the English on its way to Lisbon.

he determined to pursue his career in the East and arrived in Goa the following year. After finishing his religious training, he taught in the college there until 1582, when he was called to Macao to prepare himself for the challenge of China. There he began diligent study of written and spoken Chinese and in 1583 became the first Jesuit to enter China, although at first only as a "guest" in Kwangtung province near Canton. There he continued his study of the Confucian classics and in 1589 built a church in the Chinese architectural style. By this time he had discovered that priests of any kind were associated with the now despised Buddhists, and he therefore adopted the dress as well as the manner and education of a Confucian scholar.

Ricci was a compelling person, tall and vigorous with flashing blue eyes, a curly beard (which assured the Chinese of his sagacity), and a resonant voice. What impressed them most, however, was his remarkable learning, combining as it did most of contemporary Western achievements, including cartography, and a thorough mastery of the classical Chinese corpus. He also had a phenomenal memory and made use of a variety of mnemonic devices to assist it. This was a tremendous help to a scholar, especially for learning Chinese characters. Ricci was accordingly much sought after by Chinese who wanted to succeed in the imperial examinations or wanted their sons to do so. This enhanced his acceptability, as did his success in dissociating himself from the Portuguese traders at Macao. In 1595 he and his missionary colleagues were permitted to move north to the Yangtze valley and in 1601 to establish their permanent base at Peking.

The reigning emperor, Ming Wan-li, had become incompetent and concerned only with pleasures; the court was corrupt and full of scheming factions. Ricci finally caught the emperor's fancy by presenting him with two clocks and a clavichord, a precursor of the piano. When asked to demonstrate it, Ricci composed some "edifying" madrigals for his majesty to sing. Later he was given a special imperial stipend and was accepted at court as an outstanding and useful scholar. As the first missionary to China and one who fully understood how Chinese society worked, Ricci concentrated on the well-placed. To avoid alienating them and to make Christianity more understandable and appealing, he represented it as a system of ethics similar to and compatible with Confucianism, leaving out such potentially upsetting parts as the crucifixion, the virgin birth, and the equality of all persons. He also avoided discussion of Christian theology. This abbreviated version of the faith got the Jesuits in trouble with Rome later on, but it made excellent sense if the aim was to interest the Chinese. Ricci avoided preaching or overt efforts at conversion, and when he died in 1610, he was buried at Peking in a special plot granted by the emperor. He and his colleagues won few converts, but they saw their role as preparing

Matteo Ricci with a Chinese convert to Christianity, Li Paulus, who translated European works on astronomy from Latin into Chinese. [New York Public Library]

the ground for a later assault by easing the Chinese into accepting the less controversial parts of Christianity and by masquerading as Confucian scholars. With his sharp mind, vast erudition, and winning personality, Ricci was an ideal person for such a role, but interest in him as a scholar never led to an equivalent interest in the religion he came to China to plant.

Such success as Ricci and his successors achieved was largely the result of their use of some of the new fruits of the European Renaissance as a lure, especially early clocks, improvements in the calendar, maps of the world, astronomy, and glass prisms. Such things intrigued the Chinese and ingratiated the Jesuits at court as learned men. By now they had necessarily learned not only the Chinese language but also the full deportment of the Confucian scholar as the vital credential for acceptance. They also understood that in this hierarchical society, the key to missionary success was to convert the people at the top, especially the emperor, and that preaching to the masses would only earn them a reputation as troublemakers. Aided by their Confucian guise as men of learning, they made some converts among gentry and court officials, but though they interested successive emperors, they never converted many Chinese. Western technology was more appealing than Western religion; this has remained true into our own times. In the end, the Jesuit effort was undermined by the pope, who refused to permit their softening of Catholic doctrine or the acceptance of some Confucian rites in order to avoid offending potential converts. The controversy simmered for years, but the ground had been cut out from under the Jesuits, and they were ultimately expelled in the early eighteenth century. Meanwhile, their accounts of China became an important source of Western knowledge.

The Russian Advance in Asia

Russian expansion across Siberia was slow but involved permanent Russian occupation and domination of this vast territory and its technologically less developed peoples, whose numbers were also small. By 1637 the Russians had reached the Pacific coast north of what is now Vladivostok, but they were behind the western Europeans in making direct contact with China. Early Russian explorers followed the major Siberian rivers, but these flow northward into the Arctic. Gradually a network of fortified garrisons and trading posts spread eastward. When the Amur River was reached, it was eagerly used as an easier route leading to more productive areas and to the sea. Russian presence in the Amur valley came to Chinese attention when northern Manchurian tribes, tributary vassals of the Ch'ing dynasty, appealed for help. Mongol groups were also trading with the Russians, which further alarmed the Chinese. Two successive Russian embassies to Peking, in 1654 and 1676, requesting trade privileges, refused to perform the required prostrations before the emperor and were sent away. By the 1680s the Ch'ing, now having consolidated their power within China, began to establish new routes and military colonies in the Amur region and put naval ships on the river itself. The Russians were quickly chased out, and a large Ch'ing army besieged the one remaining Russian fortress. The Russians now agreed to negotiate and sent an ambassador to their major post at Nerchinsk, on an upper Amur tributary but still within Siberia.

The treaty concluded there in 1689 confirmed the Amur region as Chinese and obliged the Russians to destroy their remaining fortress but accepted limited Russian trade rights by camel caravan to Peking, in part because the Chinese court wanted to maintain the supply of fine Russian furs from Siberia. A later treaty in 1727 excluded Russia from Mongolia and further delimited the boundary between Russia and China, leaving the Russians only Siberia. The Ch'ing emperor K'ang Hsi would not deal directly with "barbarians," still less go to them, so he sent as his representatives two Jesuits from the court, whom he deemed appropriate agents for the management of such affairs. Nevertheless, the Treaty of Nerchinsk treated both sides as essentially equal sovereign states. It was the only such treaty China agreed to with a Western state until the nineteenth century, when China was forced to abandon the pretense of political superiority and accept inferior status. Until 1842 the various "sea barbarians" could be treated as savages, though Russia as a rival and adjacent land power had to be dealt with differently. Fear of Russia and its ambitions remained a fixture in the Chinese mind and was later intensified by Russian expansion into Manchuria.

The Catholic missionary drive in Asia met with the greatest success under the Spanish in the Philippines, where there was no sophisticated indigenous religious tradition to oppose it. The Japanese too, as a small, remote, and, in their own view, less developed people, were far more open than the Chinese or the Indians to new ideas, even of foreign origin. Where Chinese, and often Indians, with their cultural pride and self-confidence, tended to dismiss anything foreign as undesirable, the Japanese remained curious and sought opportunities to learn, as they had done from T'ang China. The sixteenth century, sometimes called "Japan's Christian century," saw significant numbers of Christian converts as well as a flourishing trade with Europeans, centered in Nagasaki but also at Osaka, Edo (Tokyo), and other ports. After missionary work in Goa and the East Indies, Francis Xavier spent two years (1549–1551) in Japan preaching, teaching, and disputing with Buddhist monks. But Christians were soon branded troublemakers. Rival Catholic religious orders contended with one another, often violently, as did the Portuguese, Spanish, Dutch, and English. Their ships and arms were often used in domestic Japanese factional fighting and intrigue, and Christianity was also seen as corrupting the Confucian loyalty of the Japanese and making converts potential subversives. Christianity was suppressed by 1640; thousands of converts were crucified, and all foreigners were expelled. The Japanese were forbidden to go abroad, and contact with the world beyond China was limited to one Dutch ship a year, allowed to trade only on an island in Nagasaki harbor.

The first burst of Western activity in Asia thus ended with only minor success. It was the Europeans who sought out the East, because Europe, poor and backward by comparison with the riches of Asia, was eager for contact. Columbus carried with him on his first voyage a copy of Marco Polo's journal, with its account of the immense wealth of Cathay; the riches of India and Southeast Asia were even better known via Arab traders. The discovery of the New World was thus an accidental incident on the road to Asia. In terms of power, the Europeans were no match for the great Asian empires or even for lesser states, and they had nothing desirable to offer in trade with the more sophisticated economies of the East. This was to inhibit European contacts for several more centuries. The Europeans had to be content with a few tiny and insecure footholds on the coast, where they competed with Asian and Arab merchants. Sometimes, at the whim of the Asian states, they were thrown out and had their goods confiscated.

Only at sea were the Europeans powerful—hence in part the Dutch success in controlling most of the trade of insular Southeast Asia—and there they tended to cancel one another out as rivals. Their chief commercial advantage was in the carrying trade, where their ships made them competitive but where they served mainly Asian markets. Soon after the Portuguese arrival, Asian shipbuilders on the Indian west coast began to adopt a Western-looking rig in the hope of scaring off pirates, sometimes adding dummy gun ports for the same purpose. Although Portuguese power subsequently faded in the face of Dutch and English competition, often forcing the Portuguese into piracy, the Asians continued to acknowledge Western superiority at sea. As the first British consul at Shanghai was to remark over three centuries later in 1843: "By our ships our power can be seen, and if necessary, felt."[5] This was to remain the principal basis of Western success in Asia throughout the centuries from 1498 to the end of colonialism in the ashes of the Second World War. In the early period, however, Asians saw Westerners as clever with ships but ignorant, dirty, contentious, drunken, uncivilized, and treacherous. To Asia's later cost, they were largely ignored. That seemed reasonable enough in the splendid and confident context of Mughal India, Ming and Ch'ing China, and Tokugawa Japan, and it remained so for another two or three centuries, until these Asian orders declined while Europe began to ride the wave of new industrial and technological power.

The European Conquest of the Americas

While the Portuguese fashioned a commercial empire in the East, the Spanish imposed a colonial empire on much of Mexico and South and Central America. Faced with uncertain economic prospects at home, the hidalgos who led the assault on the Aztecs and the Inca came in search of gold, but they were also deeply influenced by the crusading ideal and saw this adventure as a means of serving God. The combination of materialistic and spiritual motives was potent enough to provide them with the confidence to take on civilized peoples who vastly outnumbered them. In the end, however, the keys to their success were their technological superiority and the fact that both the Aztecs and the Inca were the over-

lords of a vast Amerindian population, some of whom actually fought on the side of the Spaniards. The Aztecs and Inca were also at a disadvantage because their empires, unlike those in Africa, were highly centralized and thus ill-suited to keep up resistance once their rulers had fallen.

Conquistadors, Aztecs, and Inca

The first of the great triumphs of the Spanish conquistadors began in 1519, the same year that Magellan set out on his historic voyage. Under the command of Hernando Cortés (1485–1547), a former law student who had participated in the conquest of Cuba, a force of some 600 men, 16 horses, and a few cannon landed in Mexico near Veracruz (which Cortés founded). Although the Amerindians resisted him at first, Cortés gradually won them over, aided by his Amerindian mistress and translator, Doña Marina. With the aid of 1,000 Tlaxcala Amerindians, the long-standing enemies of the Aztecs, he advanced on the capital at Tenochtitlán, an impressive city whose population of approximately 90,000 was nearly the equal of Europe's largest cities. Dominated by an enormous temple, pyramids, and the royal palace, the city was built on mud dredged from Lake Texcoco. Impressive for its orderly streets and canals, its open squares bustling with commerce, and its whitewashed public buildings, Tenochtitlán was ruled by the war-chief Montezuma from 1502 to 1520. In a society dominated by war, all able-bodied Aztec men received military training. So many warriors died in battle that the Aztecs had to practice polygamy. Bearing children was therefore highly regarded, and a woman who died in childbirth received the same ceremonial rites as a warrior who perished on the battlefield. The main motive for the warfare was the need to acquire victims with which to appease the sun god, who fed on blood obtained by ripping out the hearts of living people. Women were rarely among the sacrificial victims. In practical terms, human sacrifice functioned as a means to terrorize subject Amerindians, which helps explain their unwillingness to defend the Aztecs against Cortés.

Despite initial threats from the Aztecs, Cortés was allowed to enter the capital peacefully, but in a matter of days he used the pretext of an attack on his garrison at Veracruz to imprison Montezuma. An Indian uprising in which Montezuma was killed forced Cortés to flee in July 1520, but 13 months later he regained Tenochtitlán with the help of the Tlaxcala. The fighting destroyed most of the city, but amid its ruins the Spaniards built Mexico City, complete with a Catholic cathedral and, in 1551, the University of Mexico.

The attack on the Inca was commanded by Francisco Pizarro (c. 1474–1541), a former associate of Balboa.

◉ The Splendors of Tenochtitlán ◉

When Cortés' party entered the Aztec capital of Tenochtitlán, it was cordially received and given a tour of the city. An eyewitness account by a member of the party records the city's splendor and teeming life.

When we arrived at the great market place . . . we were astounded at the number of people and the quantity of merchandise that it contained, and at the good order and control that was maintained, for we had never seen such a thing before. Each kind of merchandise was kept by itself and had its fixed place marked out. Let us begin with the dealers in gold, silver, and precious stones, feathers, mantles, and embroidered goods. Then there were other wares consisting of Indian slaves both men and women; and I say that they bring as many of them to that great market for sale as the Portuguese bring negroes from Guinea. . . .

So we stood looking about us, for that huge and cursed temple stood so high that from it one could see over everything very well, and we saw the three causeways which led into Mexico. . . . We saw the bridges on the three causeways which were built at certain distances apart through which the water of the lake flowed in and out from one side to the other, and we beheld on that great lake a great multitude of canoes, some coming with supplies of food and others returning loaded with cargoes of merchandise; and we saw that from every house of that great city and of all the other cities that were built in the water it was impossible to pass from house to house, except by drawbridges which were made of wood or in canoes; and we saw in those cities Cues (temples) and oratories like towers and fortresses and all gleaming white, and it was a wonderful thing to behold.

Source: B. Díaz del Castillo, *The True History of the Conquest of New Spain,* ed. G. Garcia, trans. A. P. Maudslay, 5 vols. (London: Hakluyt Society, 1908–1933), 2: 70–71, 74–75.

With a force of only 180 men and 27 horses he set out in 1531 to conquer an empire ruled by Atahualpa with his army of 30,000. The overconfident Atahualpa agreed to meet with Pizarro, whom he seriously underestimated. Pizarro took him prisoner, extracted an enormous ransom, and then executed him for allegedly murdering his half brother. In 1533 Pizarro captured the Inca capital at Cuzco in the Peruvian Andes, after which the remaining Inca maintained a tiny but independent state high in the mountains at Machu Picchu. To maintain better communications with other Spanish authorities, Pizarro founded Lima on the coast of Peru in 1535. The University of San Marcos was established there 16 years later under a grant from Emperor Charles V. Conquest of the Inca was facilitated by the dissatisfaction of subordinate Amerindians with Inca domination, as well as by internal dissension among the Inca themselves.

Spanish Rule in the Americas

Virtually from the beginning, the Spanish confronted difficult legal questions concerning the status of the Amerindians. The problem was compounded by religious considerations, for the papal decision in 1493 that recognized Spain's claim to most of the Western Hemisphere also made the Spaniards responsible for the conversion of its inhabitants. As Spanish subjects and, in time, Christians, what legal rights did they possess? The conquerors, vastly outnumbered by their subject population, sought an essentially feudal form of government, with considerable local autonomy for their own colonists, and the right to treat the Amerindians as forced laborers. In sharp contrast, the influential Dominican friar Bartolomé de las Casas contended that as fellow Christians and subjects of the Spanish crown, the Amerindians were entitled to full legal rights and protection. Although the Spanish government was unwilling to provide the colonists much autonomy, it gave selected conquistadors and other Spaniards the right to collect tribute from specified villages and to impose forced labor. Those who exercised this power—the *encomenderos,* or protectors—were required to render military service and pay the salaries of the clergy. Because of abuses, this system was modified in the mid-sixteenth century. The authority to compel labor was transferred to colonial officials, and forced workers were paid according to a

18.3 Colonial Empires in America, c. 1600

fixed rate. Legally, the Amerindians could not be enslaved, but in practice their situation was little different
from slavery.

Administration of the Spanish empire in America was
directed by two viceroys who received their instructions
from the Council of the Indies in Spain. The viceroyalty
of New Spain, with headquarters in Mexico City, embraced Spanish territories in North America, the West
Indies, Venezuela, and the Philippines, and the viceroyalty of Peru, governed from Lima, included the rest of
Spanish South America. Under the viceroys were lesser
provincial governors. Both the viceroys and the lesser
governors shared authority with conciliar courts known
as *audiencias*, which gave them advice and had the

power to overturn their decisions. This system of checks and balances safeguarded royal prerogatives, but it also deprived colonial government of administrative efficiency.

The Economy of Spanish America

Nothing was more important in determining the pattern of Spanish settlement than the sites of gold and silver deposits and the availability of native labor to mine them. On his first voyage, Columbus had found gold in Hispaniola, and more was soon discovered in Cuba and Puerto Rico. At first the gold was obtained from shallow diggings or extracted from streambeds. Such mining, however, was labor-intensive, and as the Amerindian population declined, it became more profitable to graze cattle or raise sugarcane. Many Amerindians soon died because of forced labor or diseases introduced by the Spanish. The conquest of the Aztecs and Inca, whose gold artifacts were seized and melted down, was of enormous economic importance because it led to the discovery of rich silver deposits in the 1540s. The greatest of these was an extraordinary mountain of silver at Potosí, in the Andes, discovered in 1545. By 1570 Potosí had a population of 120,000, nearly the same as Paris. The introduction of the latest technology by German miners—a water-powered stamp mill and a mercury amalgamation process that purified the silver—made the mines so productive that silver became the most im-

portant export to the mother country. By 1570 no less than 97 percent of the bullion shipped to Spain was silver. As the output of European mines declined in the late sixteenth century, the flow of silver from the New World continued to increase, rising in the 1590s to more than 10 million ounces a year. Altogether, according to official accounts, the Spanish treasure fleets transported 180 tons of gold and 16,000 tons of silver to Seville between 1500 and 1650. Much of the wealth, 20 percent of which went to the crown as the "royal fifth," was used to pay for imports, service the royal debt, and finance war.

No less significant, particularly for the future history of the Americas, was the introduction of large estates. Some, the haciendas, were used to rear animals or raise cereal crops, but in tropical regions sugar and tobacco plantations were established, patterned after the sugar plantations of Atlantic islands such as the Azores and the Canaries, which had in turn been influenced by Genoese plantations in Cyprus and Crete. Unlike the haciendas, which used Amerindian workers, the primary laborers on the plantations were African slaves. Although both the plantation system and the trade in African slaves predated the Spanish conquests in the Americas, the success of the conquistadors opened up vast new markets for the sale of blacks. Africans were accustomed to working in tropical climates, possessed some immunity from the diseases that ravaged the Amerindians, and had lower mortality rates in the New World than even the Europeans. By the eighteenth century the British were the main suppliers for this slave

Cerro Rico, the fabulous mountain of silver at Potosí in Bolivia. Potosí itself, at an altitude of 13,700 feet, is one of the world's highest cities. Its population reached 160,000 in 1650 and then declined sharply. [Harvard College Library]

market, followed by the French, but the Portuguese, Spanish, Dutch, Danes, and Americans also participated.

In Spain, the economic effects of its new colonial empire were a mixed blessing. Seville, which enjoyed a monopoly of trade with the colonies, prospered for several centuries. Ultimately, however, its prosperity and economic potential were undermined by the heavy hand of the Spanish government, which overregulated everything, and by the reluctance of the Spaniards to seize the commercial opportunities their empire made possible. The French historian Fernand Braudel has observed:

> **The latent defect in the Spanish imperial economy was that it was based on Seville—a controlled town rotten with dishonest officials and long dominated by foreign capitalists—and not on a powerful free town capable of producing and carrying through a really individual economic policy.[6]**

There was some new manufacturing in Spain, but in general Spaniards continued to rely on France and the Netherlands for their goods. Nor did large numbers of Spaniards emigrate to America, the total number amounting to some 100,000 in the entire sixteenth century. The influx of bullion into Spain, while seemingly a great economic advantage, was so badly mismanaged that for many Spaniards the most direct result was a spiraling cost of living. The quadrupling of prices in the 1500s, in part because of the increase in bullion, adversely affected the living conditions of many Spaniards.

The Impact of Spanish Imperialism

In retrospect, the most dramatic effect of Spanish domination in the New World was the catastrophic decline in the Amerindian population, one of the greatest demographic disasters in history. By 1510 nearly 90 percent of the Amerindians of Hispaniola were dead, while in Mexico the Amerindian population, which had numbered 11 million, fell by more than 75 percent. Famine and ruthless exploitation accounted for some of the deaths, but the biggest killer was disease, especially smallpox. The fact that Europeans introduced universities and printing to the New World and that Spanish law and Christianity ended the Aztec practices of human sacrifice and polygamy was small comfort in the face of such suffering. Although Aztecs and Inca suppressed other Amerindians, the Spanish exploitation of the native inhabitants and the introduction of slave plantations were hardly an improvement, though the Amerindians were treated better than the blacks. Because of the shortage of Spanish women, intermarriage with Amerindians was so frequent that the descendants of mixed marriages—the mestizos—eventually outnumbered both the Spaniards and the Amerindians.

The Portuguese in Brazil

Portugal concentrated on its commercial empire in Asia and paid relatively little attention to Brazil in the early 1500s, particularly since no gold or silver was found there. The region, however, did produce brazilwood, used in making red dye. The threat of Spanish incursion and the intrusion of the French into the brazilwood trade forced the government in Lisbon to act in 1533. It organized Brazil into 15 hereditary fiefs, the holders of which—the *donatários*—enjoyed sweeping powers, including the right to levy internal taxes and bestow grants of land. When most of the *donatários* proved ineffectual, the Portuguese king imposed a centralized administration under the direction of a governor general, who took up duties in 1549. After Spain's conquest of Portugal in 1580, Spanish-style colonial administration, headed by a viceroy, was introduced in Brazil.

As in the Spanish colonies, there was controversy over the treatment of the Amerindians. Jesuit missionaries worked tirelessly to convert and settle them in Christian villages. Their efforts ran counter to the needs of settlers who established sugar plantations in northern Brazil in the late 1500s. Brazil, in fact, became the world's leading producer of sugar in the early seventeenth century. In 1574 the Portuguese government resolved the dispute between the Jesuits and the plantation owners by allowing the former to protect residents of their Christian villages, while giving settlers the right to enslave Amerindians captured in war. Unable to procure sufficient labor in this manner, the colonists increasingly relied on African slaves.

The French, too, were interested in Brazil, and in 1555 they occupied the harbor of Rio de Janeiro. When the colony refused to honor its initial promise of religious toleration, potential Protestant settlers in France and Switzerland lost interest. After the Portuguese captured the French garrison, they founded the town of Rio de Janeiro in 1567. Large numbers of Portuguese Jewish immigrants subsequently settled in Brazil, where they found some freedom for the exercise of their religion.

The North Atlantic States and the Americas

The Portuguese were the first to profit from John Cabot's discovery of the cod fisheries off Newfoundland. For the masses, salted fish was a vital item in the diet, particularly during the winter and on the frequent fast days throughout the year when the Catholic church prohibited the eating of meat. Because the herring fisheries in the Baltic, monopolized by the Hanseatic League of North German merchants, were declining as the fish shifted their spawning grounds to the North Sea, there was a ready market for cod to feed the growing population. Although Portugal claimed Newfoundland, French and English fishermen were soon hauling in catches from its waters. In addition to providing needed food, the development of new fisheries led to the beginning of the fur trade with the Indians and to an increase in the number of ships and mariners capable of sailing the Atlantic.

As their naval expertise improved, the English were determined to participate in the spice trade, the immense profits of which were enjoyed by the Portuguese and the merchants of Antwerp. Unwilling to challenge Portugal's control of the route around the Cape of Good Hope, the English opted to search for a northeast or northwest passage to Asia, encouraged by Magellan's discovery of a southwest route. Accordingly, Sir Hugh Willoughby and Richard Chancellor set out in 1553 to find a northeast passage. Two of the ships became icebound and their crews froze to death, but Chancellor took the third ship through the White Sea to Archangel. From there he traveled overland to the court of Tsar Ivan the Terrible in Moscow. His trip resulted in the establishment of the Muscovy Company (1555), which pursued a small direct trade between England and Russia. Subsequent attempts by the English and the Dutch to find a northeastern passage were unsuccessful, as were English efforts beginning in 1576 to find a northwestern route. The latter, however, led to the discovery of Hudson Strait and Hudson Bay and to additional sources of fur in the adjacent territory.

As the search for a northern passage progressed, the English turned their attention to the possibility of trade with Spain's American colonies, notwithstanding the fact that the Spaniards considered unauthorized trade illegal. In 1562 John Hawkins, son of a Plymouth merchant, launched the English slave trade with the backing of a private syndicate. In Hispaniola he traded the 300 or 400 slaves he had acquired in Sierra Leone for hides and sugar. Impressed by the potential of this trade, Queen Elizabeth I and several of her privy councillors quietly helped finance his successful second voyage in 1564–1565. In the face of mounting Spanish hostility, Elizabeth permitted Hawkins to sail again in 1567, but this time the Spanish fleet captured or destroyed three of his five ships in the Mexican harbor of San Juan de Uluá. As relations with Spain worsened, the English restricted their activity in the New World primarily to privateering—government-approved piracy—for the rest of the century. During his circumnavigation of the globe in 1577–1580, Francis Drake challenged the Spanish sphere of dominion by claiming California, which he called New Albion, for England. In the 1580s Sir Walter Raleigh's pioneering attempt to found an English colony near Roanoke Island (now part of North Carolina) resulted in dismal failure, but the experience proved valuable for later colonial endeavors. The French, whose

activities in the New World in the sixteenth century consisted largely of plundering Spanish shipping, were equally unsuccessful in attempting to establish a colony in Florida in the early 1560s.

The ability of the English, French, and Dutch to make inroads into Spanish America was largely determined by the economic and political events of the late sixteenth century. England's successful war with Spain (1585–1604) severely crippled the latter and provided substantial freedom of action to the Dutch. France, disrupted by a long and bitter civil war, began to build the strong monarchy and economy necessary for colonial expansion only in the 1590s. In all three states, a key to future success in colonial expansion and the emerging global economy was the development of aggressive capitalism.

The Economy in the Age of Exploration

In the fifteenth and sixteenth centuries the European economy underwent dramatic changes that helped chart the course of modern economic development. The most important characteristics of this change involved not only the founding of commercial and colonial empires but also the rapid growth of capitalism and a price revolution triggered by an expanding population.

Merchant Capitalism

Capitalism involves three elements: (1) the acquisition and investment of capital to obtain profit, (2) private ownership of the principal means of production and distribution, and (3) a division in the productive and distributive process between the owners of the capital (the employers) and the laborers. Capitalism cannot exist without the capacity and the willingness to invest and to take risks, which in turn presupposes the possibility of significant profits. The medieval concepts of the just price and the wrongfulness of usury (interest on loans purely for profit) were thus impediments to capitalistic development. Medieval theologians had generally recognized the right of a lender to additional compensation beyond the principal if he incurred a loss by forgoing the use of his money. The acceptability of reasonable interest was gradually extended until, in the sixteenth century, bankers regularly paid interest of 5 to 12 percent on deposits and merchants routinely operated on credit. The expansion of capitalistic activities was also furthered by the increased use of bills of exchange, improved facilities for interregional trade, stable coinage, and an adequate and affordable labor supply. Finally, the rise in prices was a stimulus to capitalistic investment as merchants and others with surplus wealth opted to seek profits through investment rather than to spend their money on consumables.

As the European states centralized in this period, they exercised a threefold influence on capitalism. First of all, their own demands—for weapons, supplies, and luxury items—created an expanding market for merchant capitalists, who were quick to realize the potential for profits. Second, the encouragement of overseas commercial and colonial activity by the governments of the maritime states was a major incentive to invest in such ventures. Finally, these governments introduced economic policies intended to strengthen their respective states. Collectively, these policies constitute what is sometimes referred to as "mercantilism," or the "mercantile system," as Adam Smith called it in 1776.

At the heart of mercantile policy was the principle of state regulation, which was designed primarily for the benefit of the state itself. Free enterprise—the right of merchants and manufacturers to respond to market conditions as they deem best—was not part of mercantile capitalism. Both rulers and merchants who profited from business dealings with the state accepted economic controls as necessary. However, some of these controls, particularly those creating monopolies, became increasingly unpopular in the late sixteenth and seventeenth centuries among the people, who blamed them for high prices. Governments used controls to ensure the availability of strategic items, to provide order in the economy, and to regulate commerce with other states. Economic regulation was thus an important facet of the campaign to impose greater order on the early modern state. The most common controls were tariffs on imported goods, subsidies (grants) to strategic industries, and monopolies, which conveyed the exclusive right to manufacture, sell, or trade in a specific commodity. Some also attempted to regulate the export of raw materials, such as wool and leather. In 1572 French royal edicts banned the export of various raw materials, and England tried a variety of expedients in the sixteenth and early seventeenth centuries to reduce the export of raw wool in order to encourage domestic manufacturing.

Some proponents of mercantile capitalism were convinced that the strength of the state depended on the acquisition of considerable supplies of bullion. To accomplish this, they favored strict controls on foreign commerce in order to produce a favorable balance of trade, whereby the value of exports exceeded the value of imports. The Dutch, who dominated the carrying trade, recognized the sterility of this concept and instead pursued a policy geared to maximize the volume and value of trade. Profit, they recognized, was obtained by increasing trade, not hoarding bullion. The English converted to this view for a time in the 1600s but then reverted to a protectionist policy. The Spanish, who

wanted to amass bullion, had to use it instead to finance their wars and the conspicuous consumption of their elite and to import goods that they were unwilling to manufacture. Supporters of the bullionist theory tried to reduce the export of bullion by encouraging the immigration of skilled artisans, thereby reducing the need of the host country for imports and perhaps even creating new export commodities from the goods the immigrants manufactured.

Government intervention in the economy was not always beneficial, as in the case of most monopolies. An English scheme designed by the merchant Sir William Cokayne to dye and finish cloth before exporting it to the Continent, though supported by the crown, was so disastrous that it helped provoke a depression. Nevertheless, mercantile policies helped France build a stronger economy in the 1600s by expanding trade and assisting farmers, and both the English and the Dutch benefited by allowing religious refugees, especially Huguenots, to immigrate in the sixteenth and seventeenth centuries. Government intervention also had positive results as companies received charters to trade with Asia, Africa, and America; as internal barriers to trade gradually ended (though France was a major exception); and as new industries were subsidized. The implementation of policies was complicated not only by the lack of experience in dealing with a capitalistic economy but also by spiraling prices and corruption.

The Price Revolution

Inflation is a fact of modern life; Europeans in the sixteenth century were unprepared for the rises in prices that occurred, at varying rates, throughout Europe. By today's standards the inflation rate was low, often hovering around 2 percent per year, though in some years the rate was much higher. Moreover, prices varied greatly from region to region, especially over the short run. In Spain prices quadrupled in the sixteenth century, and the figure was nearly as great in England. Inflation began later in Italy, where prices doubled by 1600. The greatest increases came between the 1540s and 1570s when bad weather and crop failures added additional pressures to the inflationary spiral and when the impact of American bullion began to be felt. For a long time many historians attributed the rise in prices to the influx of bullion from the New World, but recent research has confirmed the fact that the main cause was a rise in population and thus in demand without a corresponding increase in output, thereby creating shortages of goods and services. The shortages in turn put pressure on prices, as did the expansion of the money supply because of the large quantities of imported bullion. War destruction, crop failures, and the requirements of expanding governments also contributed to a demand that outstripped production.

Food prices rose approximately twice as much as those of other goods, with wheat costing roughly five times more in the early 1600s than it had in the late 1400s. Rising food prices caused severe hardship for the poor and acted as a brake on population growth by the mid-seventeenth century, but they also spurred the development of the Atlantic fisheries and commercial agriculture. Prices, however, rose faster than agricultural yield. In England in the late 1500s rising grain prices curtailed the earlier trend of converting arable land to pasture. Economic conditions encouraged the Dutch not only to continue reclaiming land from the sea but also to develop the techniques of crop rotation. Traditionally, a third of the land had been left fallow each year on a rotating basis in order to restore fertility, but the Dutch discovered that the same end could be achieved by periodically planting beans or peas (to return nitrogen to the soil) and grazing animals, whose manure acted as fertilizer. The adoption of crop rotation by the English and the French in the late seventeenth and eighteenth centuries was crucial to the growth in agricultural productivity that made the Industrial Revolution possible.

Industrial and Commercial Development

The growth of merchant capitalism led to a major reorganization of the means of producing textiles, the demand for which increased as the population grew. In the cities of the Netherlands and northern and central Italy, merchant capitalists distributed raw wool from England or raw silk from Asia and western Europe to master artisans. These craftsmen, who still belonged to their own guilds, typically owned their shops, though not the materials on which they worked. Then, beginning in the late sixteenth century, English capitalists altered the system by distributing raw wool directly to village workers for spinning, dyeing, and weaving. From the merchants' standpoint, this system of "putting out" the work to villagers had the advantage of bypassing the traditional guilds with their controls over working conditions, wages, and prices. Because the labor was undertaken in the workers' cottages rather than in shops, the merchants' overhead was lower. In contrast to the guild system, however, the workers had no hope of improving their condition by completing an apprenticeship, and the division between employer and worker gradually became permanent. The price revolution provided additional incentive for the expansion of this system as the cost of goods outpaced the rise in wages. Thus the introduction of the domestic system of textile production could bring substantial profits to the merchant capitalists but increasingly sharpened the division between the

The Flemish painter Jan Gossaert, commonly known as Mabuse (c. 1478–1532), depicts a merchant recording his business transactions; other records hang on the cabinet behind him. [National Gallery of Art, Washington, Ailsa Mellon Bruce Fund]

haves and have-nots as workers were exploited. The domestic system, which regularly involved entire families working together in the home, gradually spread throughout western Europe until it was phased out by the introduction of factories in the Industrial Revolution. By that time rural workers were manufacturing not only textiles but cutlery, buttons, gloves, and household goods as well.

Merchant capitalists were also responsible for innovative new forms of business organization intended primarily to take advantage of the trade opportunities with Asia, Africa, and America. The partnerships and family firms of the medieval period were simply not in a position to raise sufficient capital to fund these voyages. With government approval, merchants began banding together as "regulated" companies with a monopoly on a particular item or trade with a given area. Even so, the amount of capital was limited to what the merchants themselves could raise. The solution was the formation of the joint-stock company, an organization of investors rather than an association of traders. Funds came not only from the business community but also from the aristocracy and government officials, and management was in the hands of directors experienced in commercial affairs. The firms were normally awarded monopolies and tended to concern themselves at first with overseas trade and colonization. The English (1600), Dutch (1602), French (1664), and others had East India companies organized on a joint-stock basis by private businessmen with government encouragement. Other companies were formed for such endeavors as colonizing Virginia and Massachusetts and trading furs in North America.

❧ ANTWERP'S GOLDEN AGE

No city more clearly reflected the opportunities and the glory of the age of exploration than Antwerp. In the late fifteenth and sixteenth centuries it stood at the crossroads of Europe, the hub of trade between England and the Continent, the Baltic and the Mediterranean. In terms of international commerce, Antwerp enjoyed the position formerly held by Venice. An awed Venetian envoy observed: "I was astounded and wondered much when I beheld Antwerp, for I saw Venice outdone."[7] Antwerp's dominant position among a host of secondary towns moved the Belgian historian Henri Pirenne to refer to the Netherlands—which in the sixteenth century included what is now Belgium as well as Holland—as its "suburb." Antwerp was a major cultural center as well. The German artist Albrecht Dürer was impressed by the city as well as by the "wonderful works of art" from Mexico that he viewed there on his last visit in 1521. The great Flemish painters Pieter Brueghel the Elder (c. 1525–1569) and Peter Paul Rubens (1577–1640) lived in Antwerp. Rubens, famed for his historical scenes, classical allegories, and sensuous nude figures, was the most eagerly sought-after painter of his time and the first to accumulate a substantial fortune through his art. He served as well as an ambassador from the archducal court of the Spanish Netherlands (later called Belgium), particularly to England.

Antwerp's rise to commercial greatness was facilitated by its geographic advantages. In the late 1400s the preeminence of Bruges as a trading center was undercut when the Zwyn River silted up. Antwerp, situated on the Scheldt River, thereupon became the leading port and commercial center in the Netherlands. Antwerp's rise

◉ Antwerp's Prosperity ◉

When the Florentine traveler Ludovico Guicciardini visited Antwerp in the mid-1500s, he was thoroughly impressed by its commercial activity. Here he tries to explain why the city was so prosperous.

The causes of the great wealth that Antwerp is grown to, are three. The first [is] the two markets that are in Antwerp, the one whereof begins fifteen days before Whitsuntide. . . . The other . . . begins the second Sunday after Our Lady Day in August. . . . Each of these markets endures six weeks, all the which time no man is subject to any arrest for debt. . . . There are also at Antwerp besides these markets two great horse fairs . . . and likewise two of leather and skins of all sorts, which follow immediately after the horse fairs.

The second cause of the wealth of Antwerp is this . . . : The king of Portugal, having partly by love, partly by force, drawn all the traffic of spices in Calicut and the isles adjacent thereunto into his own hands, and having brought them to Lisbon, sent his factor [agent] with spices to Antwerp, by which means it drew all nations thither to buy spices. . . . Afterwards in the year 1516 divers [foreign] merchants . . . departed from Bruges to go and dwell at Antwerp, and after them others. . . .

The third cause of the wealth of Antwerp . . . [is that the citizens have] marvelously fortified their town, for the safety both of it and of all merchants trafficking to it, so that it is now free from all danger and thought impregnable, by means whereof, a great multitude of noblemen and gentlemen come to dwell in the town.

Source: L. Guicciardini, *The Description of the Low Countreys* (London: Peter Short for Thomas Chard, 1593), pp. 26–27 (edited to conform to modern usage).

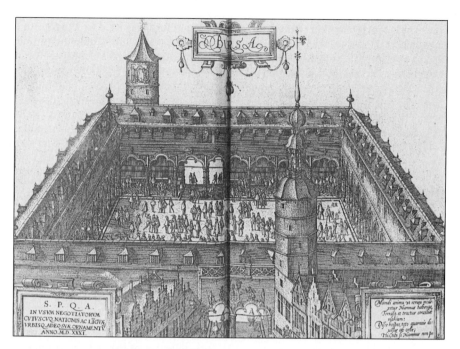

Merchants gathered at the Antwerp Bourse, built in 1531, to transact their business. The portico surrounding the courtyard rested on 38 sculptured columns, each unique, and the upper level housed shops. The building was destroyed by fire in 1581. [New York Public Library]

was also aided by Bruges' insistence on maintaining outmoded commercial regulations; by its hostility to the Burgundian dukes, who turned their attention to Antwerp; and by Habsburg favoritism toward Antwerp in the collection of customs duties. Many of the city's major buildings were constructed in the period of prosperity that ensued, including the great Gothic cathedral of the Holy Virgin (begun in the 1300s), the castle, the Renaissance town hall, and the Bourse, the center of foreign exchange. So great was the expansion that in 1542 a third set of costly city walls had to be constructed. With a population of 100,000 in the mid-sixteenth century, Antwerp was one of the largest cities in Europe.

Commencing in the late 1400s, the shift in the center of European commerce from Venice and the cities of the Hanseatic League brought more than 1,000 foreign businesses to Antwerp. It became the hub of the Portuguese spice trade, the northern headquarters of the Fugger family, and the center for the import of English cloth. Its bustling harbor handled as many as 500 ships a day, and more than 1,000 freight wagons arrived in the city each week carrying the overland trade. Recognizing the amount of capital necessary to participate in the spice trade, as early as 1505 the king of Portugal allowed the merchants of Antwerp to purchase a sizable cargo in the Indies and transport it directly to Antwerp in Portuguese ships. The Fuggers were among those who participated

in this venture and the ensuing expansion of the spice trade. Antwerp also imported large quantities of raw materials for use in its own industries, especially cloth manufacturing and finishing. Antwerp artisans pioneered in the production of "new draperies," a lighter and less expensive material than traditional woolen broadcloth, and they also manufactured silk, velvet, and similar luxury goods. Antwerp designers determined European fashions. Like Geneva, Antwerp was a center of the printing industry, boasting approximately 50 print shops in the mid-1500s. The English Bible translators William Tyndale and Miles Coverdale worked for a time in Antwerp, and by the late sixteenth century its printers were among the leading publishers of Counter-Reformation literature.

Antwerp, facing growing commercial competition from the English, became a casualty of the religious wars that plagued much of Europe in the late sixteenth century (see Chapter 19). In 1576, as the Netherlands struggled against Spanish domination, Antwerp was plundered by Spanish troops, and 6,000 of its citizens were slaughtered. The people rallied, expelled the Spaniards, and were governed by Calvinists until 1585, when the Spanish regained control and exiled the Protestants. Antwerp's troubles enabled Amsterdam to replace it as the leading commercial center of Europe in the seventeenth century.

Antwerp was the first city to serve as the hub of a worldwide commercial network. By the time the city began to decline, the underpinnings of a global economy had been established, and political and economic power was beginning to shift northward from Spain and Portugal to England, the Netherlands, and France. Compared to the tempo of economic change in earlier centuries, the speed with which the global economy developed in this period was remarkable. Europeans experienced a social and economic revolution in the late fifteenth and sixteenth centuries. The emergence of merchant capitalism provided striking opportunities for the acquisition of wealth and power. In England progressive aristocrats recognized this and profited by their association with the business community, whereas in Spain the hidalgos' resistance to commercial activity contributed to that nation's declining economy. Simply put, Spain squandered the opportunities that had been presented by its early dominance in the Americas.

As most western European rulers centralized their states, they adapted to the economic changes by formulating policies designed to control or expand trade. The governments of France, England, and the Netherlands were especially successful, and the resulting wealth was the basis of their growing power in the late 1500s and 1600s. Indeed, one of the effects of the commercial revolution was the increased ability of states to field large, better-equipped armies.

The lives of countless ordinary people changed, slowly but dramatically. The domestic system of manufacturing eventually created significant numbers of workers who had no reasonable prospect of improving their position. Many continued to live at the subsistence level despite shifting from agriculture to manufacturing. To feed the expanding population, commercial agriculture blossomed, aided by the introduction of crop rotation and the further enclosing of land. For many, however, the general living standard declined in the face of bad harvests, higher taxes, the adverse effects of war on the economy, and capitalistic developments, especially on the farms. Colonial expansion, however, brought Europeans new foods—tomatoes (called "love apples" and initially thought to be poisonous), lima beans, maize, squash, potatoes, and chocolate—and in turn the people of the New World were introduced to horses, cattle, and the Eurasian diseases that largely wiped them out. The development of global trade patterns also gave Europeans readier access to such items as tea, coffee, chocolate, and sugar. As sugarcane cultivation spread from the eastern Mediterranean to the eastern Atlantic and then to the New World, so did the slave trade through the agency of the Portuguese and the Spanish. The slave trade was not a European invention, for it was already thriving among the Africans. Nevertheless, for the enslaved Africans and the ravaged natives of America, European expansion often had cruel results. In Europe the discovery of new continents and the increased contact with Africa and Asia forced a rethinking of traditional views. As travelers and explorers documented their observations, a more accurate understanding of the physical world began to replace myth and superstition. The developments of this period also marked the first steps toward a Western hegemony in the world that has lasted into the twentieth century.

Notes

1. C. D. Ley, ed., *Portuguese Voyages, 1498–1663* (New York: Dutton, 1947), p. 28.
2. P. M. Watts, "Prophecy and Discovery: On the Spiritual Origins of Christopher Columbus's 'Enterprise of the Indies,'" *American Historical Review* 90 (February 1985): 102.
3. D. B. Quinn, ed., *New American World: A Documentary History of North America to 1612*, Vol. 1: *America from Concept to Discovery: Early Exploration of North America* (New York: Arno Press and Hector Bye, 1979), p. 97.
4. G. F. Hudson, *Europe and China* (London: Arnold, 1931), p. 201.
5. R. Murphey, *The Outsiders: The Western Experience in India and China* (Ann Arbor: University of Michigan Press, 1977), p. 21.
6. F. Braudel, *Civilization and Capitalism, 15th–18th Century*, Vol. 1: *The Structures of Everyday Life: The Limits of the Possible*, trans. S. Reynolds (New York: Harper & Row, 1979), p. 514.
7. C. Wilson, *The Transformation of Europe, 1558–1648* (Berkeley: University of California Press, 1976), p. 62.

Suggestions for Further Reading

Andrews, K. R. *Trade, Plunder and Settlement: Maritime Enterprise and the Genesis of the British Empire, 1480–1630.* Cambridge: Cambridge University Press, 1984.

Ball, J. N. *Merchants and Merchandise: The Expansion of Trade in Europe, 1500–1630.* London: Croom Helm, 1977.

506 ■ Part Three   The Early Modern World

Boxer, C. R. *The Dutch Seaborne Empire, 1600–1800*. London: Knopf, 1965.

———. *The Portuguese Seaborne Empire, 1415–1825*. New York: Knopf, 1969.

Braudel, F. *Civilization and Capitalism*, trans. S. Reynolds, 3 vols. New York: Harper & Row, 1979–1984.

Cipolla, C. M. *Before the Industrial Revolution: European Society and Economy, 1000–1700*, 2nd ed. New York: Norton, 1980.

———. *Guns and Sails in the Early Phase of European Expansion, 1400–1700*. London: Collins, 1965.

Cole, J. A. *The Potosí Mita, 1573–1700: Compulsory Indian Labor in the Andes*. Stanford, Calif.: Stanford University Press, 1985.

Curtin, P. D. *Cross-cultural Trade in World History*. Cambridge: Cambridge University Press, 1984.

Davis, R. *The Rise of the Atlantic Economies*. London: Weidenfeld & Nicolson, 1973.

Diffie, B. W., and Winius, G. D. *Foundations of the Portuguese Empire, 1415–1580*. Minneapolis: University of Minnesota Press, 1977.

Elliott, J. H. *The Old World and the New, 1492–1650*. Cambridge: Cambridge University Press, 1970.

Gibson, C. *The Aztecs Under Spanish Rule: A History of the Indians of the Valley of Mexico, 1519–1810*. Stanford, Calif.: Stanford University Press, 1964.

Hemming, J. *The Conquest of the Incas*. New York: Harcourt Brace Jovanovich, 1970.

Israel, J. I. *Dutch Primacy in World Trade, 1585–1740*. New York: Oxford University Press, 1989.

Kling, B. B., and Pearson, M. N., eds. *Europeans in Asia Before Dominion*. Honolulu: University Press of Hawaii, 1979.

Kriedte, P. *Peasants, Landlords and Merchant Capitalists: Europe and the World Economy, 1500–1800*. Leamington, England: Berg Press, 1983.

Lockhart, J. M. *The Men of Cajamarca: A Social and Biographical Study of the First Conquerors of Peru*. Austin: University of Texas Press, 1972.

MacLeod, M. J. *Spanish Central America: A Socioeconomic History, 1520–1720*. Berkeley: University of California Press, 1973.

Mannix, D. P., and Cowley, M. *Black Cargoes: A History of the Atlantic Slave Trade, 1518–1865*. New York: Viking, 1962.

McAlister, L. N. *Spain and Portugal in the New World, 1492–1700*. Minneapolis: University of Minnesota Press, 1984.

Meilink-Roelofsz, M. A. P. *Asian Trade and European Influence in the Indonesian Archipelago, Between 1500 and About 1630*. The Hague: Nijhoff, 1962.

Mintz, S. W. *Sweetness and Power: The Place of Sugar in Modern History*. New York: Viking, 1985.

Morison, S. E. *The European Discovery of America: The Northern Voyages, A.D. 500–1600*. New York: Oxford University Press, 1971.

———. *The European Discovery of America: The Southern Voyages, A.D. 1492–1616*. New York: Oxford University Press, 1974.

Murray, J. J. *Antwerp in the Age of Plantin and Brueghel*. Norman: University of Oklahoma Press, 1970.

Nef, J. *The Conquest of the Material World*. Chicago: University of Chicago Press, 1964.

Parry, J. H. *The Age of Reconnaissance*, 2nd ed. New York: New American Library, 1966.

———. *The Discovery of the Sea*, 2nd ed. Berkeley: University of California Press, 1981.

———. *The Establishment of European Hegemony, 1415–1715*. New York: Harper & Row, 1961.

———, ed. *The European Reconnaissance: Selected Documents*. New York: Walker, 1968.

Pearson, M. N. *Merchants and Rulers in Gujarat: The Response to the Portuguese in the Sixteenth Century*. Berkeley: University of California Press, 1976.

Ricci, M. *China in the Sixteenth Century: The Journals of Matthew Ricci, 1583–1610*, trans. L. J. Gallagher. New York: Random House, 1953.

Rice, E. F., Jr. *The Foundations of Early Modern Europe, 1460–1559*. New York: Norton, 1970.

Schurz, W. L. *The Manila Galleon*. New York: Dutton, 1939.

Souza, G. B. *The Survival of Empire: Portuguese Trade and Society in China and the South China Sea, 1630–1754*. Cambridge: Cambridge University Press, 1986.

Spence, J. D. *The Memory Palace of Matteo Ricci*. New York: Viking, 1984.

Tracy, J. E., ed. *The Rise of Merchant Empires*. Cambridge: Cambridge University Press, 1990.

Wallerstein, I. M. *The Modern World System: Capitalist Agriculture and the Origins of the European World Economy in the Sixteenth Century*. New York: Academic Press, 1974.

Maps and Their Makers (I)

One of the most basic tasks of all human communities, from nomad bands to settled civilizations, is to orient the group to the locations of things. To situate resources, to mark off shelter and defense, to establish territorial limits—all are essential to group survival. The idea of accomplishing these tasks by drawing a map evolved long ago among many different peoples. Human beings were making maps long before they developed the ability to symbolize their speech in writing.

From early times, too, maps appear to have been used not only to mark off known places but also to theorize, and sometimes fantasize, about unknown ones. Modern armchair travelers who open maps to stimulate their imaginations about faraway places are exercising the same faculty as ancient mapmakers who populated the scrolls and edges of their charts with dragons and monsters. Maps thus invite us not only to define but also to extend the world. They are the instruments of our curiosity as well as our knowledge, our dreams as well as our science.

The growth of our knowledge has made mapmaking—cartography—an ever more important part of modern civilization. Somewhere in the world at this moment, a topographic or geodesic survey is making our understanding of the earth more precise; somewhere, a telescope is scanning the heavens, and a satellite or a space vehicle is beaming back information about interstellar space that will go into a map. Scientists and physicians speak of mapping the brain and the living cell, and psychologists, the human mind. As a tool as well as a metaphor, mapping is one of the principal functions of our culture, in some ways as basic as speech.

The universality of mapmaking is one of its most striking characteristics. The Eskimos of North America carved coastal maps of extraordinary accuracy on animal skins and wood. The Marshall Islanders of the South Pacific lashed sticks and cane fibers together to indicate wind and wave patterns at sea, inserting stones or pieces of coral to designate islands. The Spanish conqueror Cortés made his advance through Central America with the aid only of native maps, and the British explorer James Cook navigated the South Seas with a chart made for him by a Tahitian that covered nearly 3,000 miles. Australian aborigines made rudimentary maps, and European cave dwellers incised maps on cave walls.

Perhaps the oldest surviving map is a clay tablet found at Nuzi in northern Iraq, dating from c. 2300 B.C. It is a cadastral survey, a map of property lots made for purposes of taxation. Many of the surviving maps from the second millennium B.C. are city plans,

This ingenious map of the Marshall Islands in the South Pacific records wind and tidal patterns. The islands themselves are marked by inserts of coral. [British Museum]

such as the highly detailed one for the city of Nippur on the Euphrates, which shows the major temples, the river itself, the central park and canal, moats, walls, and the city gates. There is no reference to a Chinese map before the seventh century B.C. and none extant before the second century B.C., but the splendid examples excavated in Hunan province in 1974 suggest that Chinese cartography may be as ancient as any, and as sophisticated. Drawn on silk for the king of Changsha, they depict much of modern Hunan and regions as far south as the South China Sea. The first map gives the names of all cities and provinces and indicates major topographic features including more than 30 rivers. The second map, a military one, shows walled fortresses, military encampments, supply depots, and observation towers. Both the detail of the maps and the intricate use of symbols and legends suggest a highly developed tradition of cartography.

The earliest maps, then, were local and functional. The first people to attempt to map the world as a whole appear to have been the Babylonians. Their interest in the earth may have derived from their fascination with the heavens, which had for them, as for most peoples, a deep religious significance. The Babylonians depicted the sky as a vast circle, charting some 5,000 stars. In doing so, they introduced the first systematic measurement into mapping. The Babylonians had long before devised a calendar of 360 days, which they had divided into 60-minute hours and 60-second minutes. They hit on the idea of applying the same number system for measuring the circle, dividing it into 360 degrees, the degrees into minutes, and the minutes into seconds. Applying this to the heavens, they were able to plot the locations of the stars.

The Babylonians likewise conceived of the earth as round. In what appears to be the earliest surviving world map, it is depicted as a flat circular disk with Babylonia in the center and its neighbors, the Assyrians and the Chaldeans, to the east and the southwest, respectively. Beyond that single landmass lay a great, globe-encircling ocean, from which rose seven islands. These in turn formed a bridge to an outer circle or Heavenly Ocean, the abode of the ancient gods. Fanciful and symbolic, this first world map was an exercise in cosmography as much as cartography.

Not long after, the Ionian philosopher Anaximander produced the first world map in the Greek-speaking world. The slightly later map of Hecataeus (c. 501 B.C.), who is credited with having compiled the first manual of geography, was used by Aristagoras of Miletus in soliciting the help of Sparta against the Persian Empire at the time of the Ionian revolt. The Spartan king, Cleomenes, was attracted by the prospect of spoil from Persia's neighbors, but when he learned that they lay three months' journey away, he ordered Aristagoras out of Sparta by nightfall.

Herodotus, the source of this story, himself proposed locating geographic sites by means of parallels and meridians. By the end of the fifth century B.C., the idea of maps had become familiar enough so that a character in Aristophanes' comedy *The Clouds* (produced in 423 B.C.), carried one on stage and pointed out Athens on it. In the next two centuries the geographic horizons of the Greeks expanded considerably, notably through the conquests of Alexander and the travels of Pytheas to Britain and the Low Countries. The actual size of the world remained a matter of conjecture, however, until Eratosthenes (275–194 B.C.), the librarian of Alexandria, conceived the brilliant scheme of measuring the angle of shadow cast by the sun at noon in Alexandria and computing it against the known distance to an-

On the oldest surviving world map, earth, ocean, and heaven are linked. This Babylonian vision of the cosmos dates from the sixth century B.C. [British Museum]

other site on the same meridian in Egypt, where the sun's rays were reportedly vertical at noon on the day of the summer solstice. Assuming (as the ancient mathematician Pythagoras had) that the world was a perfect sphere, Eratosthenes was able to calculate its circumference as 250,000 stadia, or about 28,000 miles. None of Eratosthenes' factual assumptions was quite right—the two sites were not precisely on the same meridian, the distance between them was not measured exactly, and the earth is not a perfect sphere—but his method was basically sound, and his result was only about 3,000 miles off. For the first time, human beings had a tolerably accurate notion of the size of their planet, based not on fancy or guesswork but on scientific measurement. The news was not especially pleasing to Hellenistic geographers, however. It meant that three-quarters of the globe was unknown to them.

This vast expanse, *terra incognita* ("unknown earth"), as the Romans called it, did not remain unpopulated for long. Solinus, a grammarian of the third century A.D., imagined a race of horse-footed men to the east in Asia with ears so long that the flaps covered their entire bodies, making clothes unnecessary. Other men were said to have only one leg with a giant foot. In Germany, Solinus asserted, there were birds whose feathers glowed in the dark, while Libya was the home of the cockatrice, which crept along the ground like a crocodile on its forequarters but was hoisted in the rear by lateral fins. Mythical kingdoms abounded as well, such as that of Prester (Elder) John, a Christian monarch reputedly descended from the Magi who ruled a land in which one of the rivers flowed directly from Paradise. When several expeditions failed to discover this kingdom in the East (Marco Polo reported it conquered by Chinghis Khan), cartographers obligingly shifted it to Africa, where it figured on maps for several centuries. A less benign vision was that of the land of Gog and Magog, whose terrifying hordes, first prophesied by Ezekiel, were feared by Christian and Muslim alike. Some mapmakers placed the savage tribes in southern Russia, while a Syrian tale held that Alexander the Great had sealed them off, presumably in India, behind a wall of iron and brass. Ibn-Khaldun, a fourteenth-century Arab geographer and historian, apparently confused the wall of Gog and Magog with the Great Wall of China.

As the Babylonians had placed themselves at the center of the earth and as medieval Christians placed Jerusalem there, so too did the Chinese regard their "Middle Kingdom" as the center of things. Legend had it that two men had walked from the court of the fabled Emperor Yu, first from north to south and then from east to west, and found the earth equidistant at all points from the imperial palace. We do not know how the Chinese may have embellished their own *terra incognita*, but their high standard of mapmaking was maintained and advanced. P'ei Hsiu (Bei Xiu, A.D. 224–271), author of the *Six Principles of Cartography*, constructed a map of China for the emperor Wu Ti on a scale of about a third of a mile to an inch; it covered 18 sheets. An even more finely detailed map was produced in the eighth century: measuring 33 by 30 feet, it took 16 years to complete. In the eleventh century, Shen Kuo (Shen Guo) produced the first relief map, modeled in wax.

The most important ancient cartographer in the West was Claudius Ptolemy (c. 90–c. 168), who, like Eratosthenes, was the librarian of Alexandria. In his two principal works—the *Almagest*, a compendium of astronomy and mathematics, and the *Geographia*, which, with its large world map and 26 regional ones showing some 8,000 places, was the world's first atlas—he attempted to survey the whole of the cosmos. Like Eratosthenes, Ptolemy had better ideas than information. He devised the notion of dividing maps into areas

of latitude and longitude, and he was the first to orient maps to the north. But he lacked precise instruments for celestial angle measurement and timekeeping that were essential to accurate siting, and he was dependent for much of his information on travelers' reports that, as he well knew, were often both boastful and sketchy. The Ptolemaic world consisted of three continents—Europe, Asia, and Africa. Of these, only Europe was shown in full outline, and even here, guesswork or inaccurate reporting was evident; the shape of Britain (Albion), for example, was grossly distorted, and Scandinavia (Scandia) was shown as an island. Nonetheless, Ptolemy's map was by far the best representation of the known world available to Western or Islamic cartographers for more than 1,300 years, and it became the standard reference, particularly in Arab lands.

Two of Ptolemy's errors were to have fateful consequences. Like most educated people of his time, he rejected the hypothesis of the third-century B.C. astronomer Aristarchus that the sun was the center of the universe and placed the earth there instead. He also underestimated the circumference of the globe, accepting Poseidonius' calculation of 18,000 miles instead of Eratosthenes' older but more accurate one. The result of this, amplified by the expanded idea of Asia brought home by Marco Polo, was to persuade Christopher Columbus that the Indies were relatively close to western Europe. That mistake uncovered the New World, whose inhabitants had their own highly complex systems of mapping and measurement.

The first large map depicting the New World in its relation to Europe was made in 1500 by Juan de la Cosa, who accompanied Columbus on his second voyage. De la Cosa, like Columbus, was still unsure that the New World was not connected to Asia. But in 1507 a German cartographer, Martin Waldseemüller, produced the first map suggesting that "America," as he baptized the southern half of the New World in honor of the explorer Amerigo Vespucci, was actually a continent, separated from Asia by an unknown ocean. Waldseemüller's truncated depiction of the Western Hemisphere was hopelessly inadequate, and his "Ocean Orientalis" was only a fraction of the actual Pacific Ocean. But his daring guess was right. For the first time, even if only in the roughest configuration, the true shape of the world was known. Six years later, Vasco Núñez de Balboa made the first sighting of the western Pacific, and six years after that Ferdinand Magellan undertook the first circumnavigation of the globe. Magellan's heroic voyage cost him his life (he was killed in a skirmish with natives in the Philippines); only one of his five ships survived, and 35 of his 280 sailors. With what they brought back, however, the Portuguese cartographer Diego Ribero was able to produce a map that conveyed not only the true shape but also an approximation of the true proportions of the world.

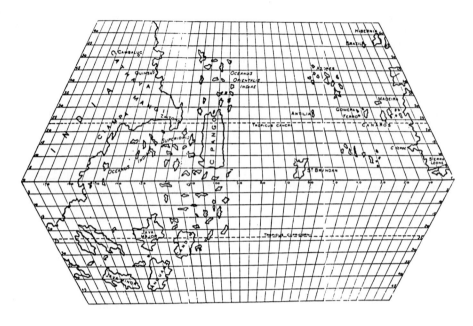

A sketch of the map used by Columbus on his first voyage to the New World in 1492. The cartographer estimated the distance to the "Indies" as little more than that from Portugal to the Azores. "India" and "Cathay" (China) were represented as part of a single undifferentiated landmass. The large island of "Cipango" represents Japan. [Library of Congress]

From this point on, discovery proceeded apace, as explorers and cartographers worked together. The dimensions of Africa had finally been realized in the fifteenth century, when Prince Henry of Portugal—the famous Henry the Navigator—had explored the west coast of Africa, partly in hopes of finding a sea route around it to India, partly in quest of the kingdom of Prester John. The daunting length of Africa had led Columbus to try a crossing of the Atlantic instead, but in 1498 Vasco da Gama sailed around the Cape of Good Hope and reached India. By the mid-sixteenth century the real dimensions of North and South America had begun to appear on maps, and the influence of Ptolemy at last faded. It was no longer permissible, as it had still been only a generation or two earlier, to mix fact and fancy, discovery and tradition. Rulers in quest of gold and merchants of silk and spices demanded accuracy and completeness of their maps. What the historian J. H. Parry has called the age of reconnaissance had begun.

The dependence of mariners on the accuracy of their maps for voyages of increasing distance and duration highlighted a problem that Ptolemy had grappled with: how to represent the reality of a three-dimensional globe on a flat, two-dimensional surface. Ptolemy had divided his world into lines of longitude and latitude, thus forming a grid whose intersections would enable one to plot any point on the globe; but on that globe itself, of course, the lines were curved, not straight, converging in the case of longitude at the two poles and varying widely in length in the case of latitude. Ptolemaic maps had attempted to compensate for this by drawing curvilinear lines, but while this was of some help with lines of latitude, it still left parallel rather than converging lines of longitude. Model globes themselves were helpful, but any large enough to show sufficient detail for navigational purposes were far too large to carry.

A practical solution was devised by a Flemish car-

This huge, splendidly carved Aztec stone calendar, which stood atop the Aztec temple at Tenochtitlán, was used to make complex astronomical measurements, including the calculation of eclipses. [Paolo Koch/Photo Researchers]

tographer, Gerhard Kremer (1512–1594), better known as Gerardus Mercator. Mercator abandoned the Ptolemaic compromise of curving lines to draw a grid of perfectly straight ones. At the same time, he extended the distance between the lines of latitude at an increasing rate from the equator to the poles. This widened the distortion both of distance and of representation, particularly in the polar regions: thus, on a Mercator map, the island of Greenland appears considerably larger than the continent of South America, although in reality it is only one-eighth as big. But the map was of vital advantage to mariners in one respect. It enabled them to plot direction and to chart their voyages from home port to final destination on a straight line. Mercator's new map was first published in 1569, and his system is still in use.

By the late sixteenth century, the shape, dimension, and much of the outline of the world had been revealed. Shortly thereafter, the shape of the heavens would begin to disclose itself as well.

Suggestions for Further Reading

Bagrow, L. *A History of Cartography*. London: Watts, 1964.

Bricker, C., and Tooley, R. V. *A History of Cartography: 2500 Years of Maps and Mapmakers*. London: Thames & Hudson, 1969.

Brown, L. A. *The Story of Maps*. Boston: Little, Brown, 1980.

Harley, J. B., and Woodward, D., eds. *The History of Cartography*. Chicago: University of Chicago Press, 1987.

Kopal, Z. *Widening Horizons: Man's Quest to Understand the Structure of the Universe*. New York: Taplinger, 1970.

Parry, J. H. *The Age of Reconnaissance*. 2nd ed. New York: New American Library, 1966.

Schlee, S. *The Edge of an Unfamiliar World: A History of Oceanography*. New York: Dutton, 1973.

Thrower, N. J. W. *Maps and Man*. Englewood Cliffs, N.J.: Prentice Hall, 1972.

Wilford, J. N. *The Mapmakers*. New York: Knopf, 1981.

State-Building and Revolution

Emboldened by the wealth of its new empire, Spain made a major bid in the late sixteenth century to establish domination in western Europe. This was largely the outgrowth of the determination of both Charles V and Philip II to rule their inherited territories and of the equally strong resolve of the English and the French to prevent the expansion of Habsburg power. The Netherlands, Portugal, England, Italy, and France were all threatened by a militant Spanish imperialism imbued with the spirit of the Counter-Reformation. By the end of the century Philip II had largely failed in his quest, although fighting continued in the Netherlands, and Portugal remained firmly under Spanish rule. Two decades after Philip's death in 1598, the Thirty Years' War erupted. Most of Europe was involved in what proved to be one of the bloodiest wars in the continent's history. The wars, internal tensions and rebellions stemming from the increasing burdens of government centraliza-

A pious, brooding, bookish man, Philip II was described by an English admirer as "the most potent monarch of Christendom." [National Portrait Gallery, London]

tion and taxation, and competing religious ideologies both within and across borders contributed to a series of crises in the mid-1600s that threw almost every major European state into turmoil.

Philip II and the Quest for Spanish Hegemony

Spain's bid for supremacy in the late 1500s was a natural outgrowth of earlier Habsburg policy, the development of political absolutism, the religious zeal of the Counter-Reformation, and the wealth and power created by its new colonial empire. It was also made possible by the division of the vast and unwieldly Habsburg domain between two crowns. When Emperor Charles V abdicated and retired to a monastery in 1556, the imperial crown was bestowed on his brother, Ferdinand I (1556–1564), who also inherited the Austrian Habsburg territories. The Spanish throne went to Philip II (1556–1598), together with the territories of the Netherlands, Milan, Naples, Spanish America, and lesser places. His wife ruled England in her own right as Mary I (1553–1558). Vast though they remained, Spain's dominions still had a clear center of authority in the court of Madrid.

Spanish power in the reign of Philip II became possible in part at the expense of France. Charles V's troubles with the Lutherans and the Turks had prevented him from attaining a permanent victory over his archenemy, King Francis I of France (1515–1547). For most of their reigns the two monarchs quarreled, particularly over northern Italy. After the Habsburg forces captured Francis at the battle of Pavia in 1525, Charles held him prisoner in Spain until he signed a treaty surrendering both the duchy of Burgundy and his Italian claims. When Francis repudiated the treaty, the struggle was renewed. Both rulers had died by the time this phase of the Habsburg quest for dominance ended in 1559 with the Treaty of Cateau-Cambrésis. The treaty, which confirmed Spanish possession of Milan and Naples, ended 65 years of fighting in northern Italy.

In 1559 Philip II's prospects for the extension of Spanish Habsburg hegemony were good. The Treaty of Cateau-Cambrésis, which recognized Spanish mastery in Italy, required Spain to yield nothing of consequence in return. Although Philip's attempt after Mary's death to win the hand of the English queen, Elizabeth I, had been politely rebuffed, the new treaty included a proviso for his marriage to Elizabeth of Valois, the 13-year-old daughter of the French king, Henry II (1547–1559). Henry's accidental death in a tilting match during the treaty ceremonies brought his feeble son, Francis II (1559–1560), briefly to the French throne. Two of his equally weak brothers followed. Not until the late 1590s

would a strong monarch again govern France. Spain was without peer in Europe.

Although the work of centralizing had been under way in the major western European states since the late 1400s, the Spain that Philip inherited was still far from unified. Unlike England, where a single parliament served as a unifying bond, Spain had a separate assembly called the Cortes for Castile, each of the three regions of Aragon, and Navarre. France and the Netherlands similarly had regional states, but in both cases there was an Estates General, albeit weak, to represent the country as a whole. Philip made no attempt to create such a body in Spain but instead governed each of the three states—Aragon, Castile, and Navarre—independently. In Castile, the largest state with 7 million inhabitants, the aristocracy was tax-exempt and thus had little reason to strengthen the Cortes. Because the nobility of Aragon had a tradition of greater independence and political power, Philip seldom summoned its Cortes. The states of Aragon and Navarre, with a population exceeding a million, were in any event less important than populous Castile, whose townspeople and peasants bore the brunt of Philip's taxation. In the end, these taxes virtually destroyed Spanish manufacturing.

Although Philip had no Cortes for Spain as a whole, central authority was administered by local agents appointed by the crown. The English monarchs accomplished this function in the early Tudor period by expanding the authority of the justices of the peace. Similarly, in Castile, Isabella increased the responsibilities of the corregidors, who supervised the town councils.

The distinctive feature of Spanish government was the system of higher councils Philip used to supervise the affairs of his far-flung empire. Although the English sovereigns also used councils, the English conciliar structure was less elaborate and powerful than the Spanish. In England the Privy Council advised the monarch, helped administer the realm, and performed certain judicial functions, and there were councils for the north and for Wales. Philip, whose domain was much more extensive and scattered, had a major council for each region of his empire: Castile, Aragon, the Netherlands, Italy (Milan and Naples), and Spanish America. Viceroys carried out the instructions of these councils. There were also specialized councils to handle such matters as state affairs, finance, war, and the Inquisition. Although the councils convened in Madrid, there were so many of them that Philip rarely attended. Nevertheless, his bookish, bureaucratic temperament moved him to spend long hours poring over the mountain of paperwork his officials produced. Philip became heavily embroiled in the details of government, devoting enormous time to writing marginal comments on the papers he studied. Distrustful of his officials and jealous of his power, he played his officers against each other and set

19.1 Europe, c. 1560

up a system of checks and balances that made Spanish administration ponderous and inefficient.

Although Philip apparently hoped to wield absolute power based on the idea that his subjects owed him unquestioning obedience as a right and a Christian duty, in practice a top-heavy administrative system, a privileged aristocracy, regional traditions, and limited revenues circumscribed his authority. The nobles paid only sales taxes, and though Philip taxed merchants and professionals, there were fewer of them proportionately in Spain than in other western European countries. The bulk of the taxes therefore fell on those least able to pay, the peasants. The result was insufficient revenue, forcing Philip to declare bankruptcy three times during his reign. Because the government protected the ships that transported New World bullion to Spain, it was entitled to a royalty of 20 percent, but smuggling decreased the potential value of this revenue, and the king mortgaged much of what he did receive to finance military campaigns. Like the English monarchs in the early 1600s, he raised some money by selling offices and titles, and he also received income from crown lands and the sale of papal dispensations. None of this, however, compensated for the loss of funds that would have been obtained

by properly taxing the nobility. In Castile alone, 300 tax-exempt nobles owned more than half the land. The king's habitual indebtedness was thus a passive restraint on his power exercised by the nobility.

<hr>

❧
THE SPANISH CITADEL: MADRID AND THE ESCORIAL

<hr>

The development of absolute government and the bureaucracy to administer it made a permanent capital necessary. "It was right," said one observer, "that so great a monarchy should have a city which could function as its heart—a vital center in the midst of the body, which ministered equally to every state in time of peace and war."[1] Unlike Charles V, who frequently moved around his empire, Philip favored a sedentary life, though when he settled the capital at Madrid in 1561, he had no apparent intention of making it permanent. Located on a plateau at an altitude of more than 2,000 feet, its major advantages were its healthy climate and its centrality. The city had a population of only 25,000 in 1561, but by the early 1600s it had quadrupled in size. Madrid's rise adversely affected Valladolid and Toledo, the latter a beautiful medieval city whose population of more than 50,000 decreased by two-thirds during Philip's reign. By the mid-seventeenth century Madrid was the only Spanish city whose population was substantially larger than it had been in the 1500s.

Madrid's growth was not the result of new industry but of bureaucratic expansion and the capital's attraction to younger sons of the nobility, declining hidalgos, and impoverished workers in search of a living. In a futile attempt to curb the growth of the city, the crown ordered the nobles to return to their estates in 1611, hoping the hangers-on would follow. Gypsies were also attracted to the city despite repeated attempts to expel them. Urban growth in Madrid was relatively easy because of ample space. The city was enclosed only with a mud wall to denote its boundaries, and as late as the nineteenth century there was still open space inside the walls. The city's importance as a financial center grew in the 1600s, particularly after the collapse of the large fairs at Medina del Campo. Although Madrid had neither a university nor a bishop, it became a leading cultural center in the early seventeenth century.

The site selected for Philip's massive new palace, the Escorial, was in the rocky hills some 30 miles northwest of Madrid. The building had been planned because of a provision in Charles V's will that his son construct a "dynastic pantheon" to house the bodies of Spanish sovereigns. In the octagonal Pantheon of the Kings, the gray marble coffins now rest four high along the walls. Philip, a deeply religious man, took a direct interest in the design, at one point admonishing one of the architects, Juan de Herrera, to remember the basic ideals of "simplicity of form, severity in the whole, nobility without arrogance, majesty without ostentation." The Escorial took two decades to build (1563–1584). Laid out in the shape of a gridiron, which probably reflected the influence of Italian Renaissance palace architecture, the gray stone building housed a Hieronymite monastery, a royal mausoleum where Charles V was interred, a large domed church inspired by Michelangelo's plan for St. Peter's in Rome, a library, and the royal palace and apartments. From a window in the apartments Philip could look out on the high altar in the chapel.

The Culture of the Spanish Counter-Reformation

The spirit of religious austerity revealed in the Escorial reflected the severer side of the Catholic Reformation. The Spanish Inquisition, founded in 1478, rigorously persecuted Protestants and other suspected heretics, even twice imprisoning Ignatius of Loyola, the founder of the Jesuit order. The extent of its power was demonstrated when it jailed Bartolomé de Carranza, the archbishop of Toledo and primate of Spain, for 17 years on falsified

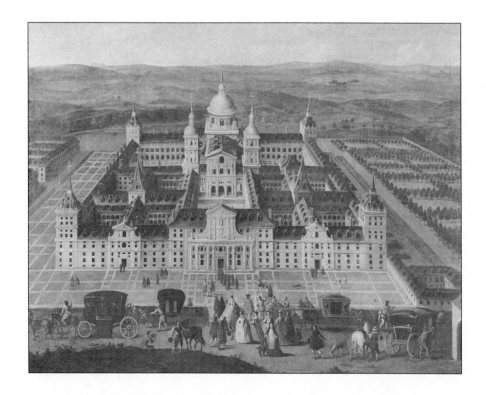

Philip II's palace, the Escorial, as it appeared in the seventeenth century. According to a popular legend, the ground plan symbolized the gridiron on which St. Lawrence, whom Philip admired, was martyred. Philip tried to find the martyr's head to keep at the palace as a relic. [Réunion des Musées Nationaux/Louvre]

charges of heresy. Obsessed with the need to keep the Spanish church pure, Philip supported the Inquisition and on five occasions even attended *autos-de-fé*, or "pageants of faith," religious rites at which sinners and heretics performed acts of penance or were executed. The Spanish Inquisition averaged 1,000 cases a year during his reign. The Inquisition also supervised the converted Jews known as Conversos who remained in Spain. The king himself was anti-Semitic, as reflected in his belief that "all the heresies which have existed in Germany and France . . . have been sown by the descendants of Jews."[2]

When Philip struck at the Moriscos—the Christianized Moors of Granada—by banning their language, customs, and distinctive dress, he incited a rebellion in 1568 that lasted until 1570. Subsequent efforts to assimilate the Moriscos were largely unsuccessful, and in the early 1600s they were deported by the tens of thousands. Altogether the number of Jews and Moors expelled from Spain between 1492, when they were given the option of becoming Christians or going into exile, and 1609 probably exceeded half a million. Philip also exiled the Jews from northern Italy much as his father had expelled them from Naples in 1544. Some 300,000 Conversos survived the threat of the Spanish Inquisition and remained active in professional and commercial activities, though most lived in their own districts.

Despite the brutal repression that characterized Spanish religious policy and comprised an important facet of absolutism, there was a positive side to Spanish piety in this period. This is beautifully manifested in the work of the mystics Teresa of Avila (1515–1582) and John of the Cross (1542–1591), both of whom were of Converso ancestry. Teresa, whose father was a hidalgo and whose seven brothers were colonial officials in America, was a Carmelite nun. Much of her work was devoted to the Carmelite Reform, an order dedicated to recapturing the original spirit of Carmelite austerity. She shared her religious experience in an autobiography, and in writings such as *The Way of Perfection* and *Exclamations of the Soul to God* she described the progress of the Christian soul toward its goal of unity with the divine. John of the Cross, a Carmelite monk who assisted Teresa in her reforming work, expressed his mystical experiences in poetry and in a meticulous analysis of mysticism. Together they inspired humble Spaniards to maintain their devotion to the Catholic church; their emphasis on the spiritual life probably helped the masses cope with their poverty.

Philip's favorite painter was Titian, the late Renaissance Venetian master famous for his sumptuous colors. For more than a quarter of a century Titian supplied Charles V and Philip with paintings. A number of these depicted mythological themes, often including sensuous female nudes. Like most of his contemporaries, Titian and presumably the pious Philip as well saw no contradiction between their veneration of the Virgin Mary and their appreciation of physical beauty in the Venus figures.

Directly as well as through his brilliant successor at Venice, Tintoretto (1518–1594), Titian influenced the painter whose work best captures the spirit of the Spanish Counter-Reformation, Domenico Theotokopoulos (1541–1614), known as El Greco ("the Greek"). Born in Crete, El Greco studied in Venice before moving to Spain in the 1570s. His first work for Philip allegorized the Holy League against the Turks by depicting Philip, the pope, and the doge of Venice kneeling before the "Holy Name" of Jesus. The king commissioned him to paint an altarpiece, the subject of which was the decision of St. Maurice, a commander in the imperial Roman army, to die rather than worship the traditional Roman deities. Displeased with the extent to which El Greco departed from the more straightforward Venetian style, Philip rejected the work. Most of El Greco's paintings convey the tension between the spiritual and material realms through spiral composition—swirling motion that drives the eye upward—and elongated figures. By accentuating color rather than form, he heightened the spiritual sense and created an art more emotional than intellectual or naturalistic. Thus the canvases of El Greco reflect the spiritual ecstasy expressed in the writings of Teresa and John of the Cross.

Although religion dominated much of the culture of Counter-Reformation Spain, other themes were popular as well, especially in literature and drama. The great masterpiece of Spanish literature, *Don Quixote*, was the work of Miguel de Cervantes (1547–1616), a surgeon's son who spent most of his creative life in Madrid. Captured while fighting against the Turks, he was enslaved in Algiers. Following his ransom, he finally turned to writing plays for the Madrid theater, but success eluded him until he published *Don Quixote* in 1605. A satire of the popular chivalric romances, the book entertained readers by humorously juxtaposing the idealist Don Quixote with the realist Sancho Panza. Despite Sancho's warnings, Don Quixote pursued his "righteous warfare" to rid the world of "accursed" giants, which in fact were windmills and sheep—the visions, said Sancho, of one who had "mills of the same sort in his head."

The success that eluded Cervantes on the stage was achieved by the prolific Lope de Vega (1562–1635), author of 1,500 plays by his own count. His works fall into two categories: heroic plays dealing with Spanish history and legend and comedies of manners and intrigue. Several of his plays break down the stereotyped image of the secluded Spanish lady. Some of Lope's women reject love and marriage, pursue careers, and even become outlaws. One of his most important themes deals with the king as the fount of justice and protector of the poor. Reflecting the spirit of his age, his plays demonstrate respect for the crown and the church.

Spain and the Mediterranean

The wars in which Cervantes and Lope de Vega fought—the former against the Turks, the latter against the English—represent the two spheres of military activity that occupied Philip. Attention was focused on the Muslims in the Mediterranean during the first part of his reign and later on the Protestants in the North Atlantic. With the Ottoman Turks already in control of three-quarters of the Mediterranean coastline, their seizure of Cyprus from Venice in 1571 alarmed Europe. Spain, Venice, and the papacy responded by forming the Holy League to attack the Turks. The league's fleet of 300 ships and 80,000 men, most of them Spanish, engaged the Turks near Lepanto in Greece. The league won a decisive victory—the first major one in centuries over a Muslim fleet—in this last great battle between oar-propelled ships. The significance of Lepanto lay primarily in its impact on European morale and its check on Islamic expansion. The Turks, however, quickly rebuilt their fleet and refused to be driven from the western Mediterranean, though henceforth they concentrated on North Africa and never regained the superiority they had once enjoyed.

Philip's second major foreign policy triumph came in 1580 when he annexed Portugal and its empire. The death of the Portuguese king without a direct heir gave Philip, whose mother had been a Portuguese princess, his opportunity. After bribes and promises had won the support of the nobility and higher clergy for his own succession, the Spanish army completed the conquest. Philip ensured peace by leaving Portuguese officials to administer the realm and by generally leaving the people alone. The Spanish, however, failed to exploit their victory by coordinating the economic policy of the two countries and their empires. Spain's failure to unify the Iberian peninsula by anything more than a common crown made it possible for Portugal to recover its independence in the next century. During the period that the two crowns were united, large numbers of Portuguese Jews emigrated to Spain, where persecution had become less intense. The annexation also gave Philip additional ships and Atlantic ports, which were sorely needed for his campaigns in the Netherlands and France and for his armadas against the English.

Rebellion in the Netherlands

The revolt of the Netherlands was the first significant setback to Philip II's dream of Habsburg hegemony in western Europe and the New World. The Low Countries were the wealthiest region in Europe and the center of the developing global economy, and its people were accustomed to considerable local autonomy and religious

The Battle of Lepanto marked the first major European naval victory over the Turks. Some 600 ships were involved. [National Maritime Museum, London]

diversity. Unlike Charles V, who had been raised in the Netherlands, Philip spoke no Dutch, disliked the Netherlands, and did not set foot there after 1559. The roots of the rebellion against Spanish authority were bound up in his attempt to impose a more centralized and absolute government. The first crucial step occurred when the Catholic church in the Netherlands was reorganized. By expanding the number of bishops from 4 to 18 and nominating them himself, Philip strengthened his hold over the church. Determined to impose religious uniformity in the Netherlands, Philip ordered that the decrees of the Council of Trent be enforced. The Protestants responded with the Compromise, a covenant pledging to resist the decrees of Trent and the Inquisition. Leading members of the council of state, which helped Philip's regent, Margaret of Parma, govern the Netherlands, protested in vain. When several hundred nobles presented their grievances to Margaret in 1566, one of her courtiers derided them as beggars. Making the epithet a badge of honor, the rebel battle cry became "Long live the beggars!"

Although the nobles had set the stage for rebellion by their protests, initially they failed to lead it. Instead the first outbreak of violence came in the summer of 1566 when Calvinists attacked the symbols of Catholicism. In a frenzy of iconoclasm—the "Calvinist Fury"—they ransacked Catholic churches, shocking almost everyone by their destructiveness. Unable to keep order, Margaret was replaced by the ruthless duke of Alva, who professed a willingness to destroy the country rather than see it fall into the hands of heretics. Backed by an army of 10,000, he attempted to enforce absolute rule through a special tribunal called the Council of Troubles. Because it executed thousands of heretics, confiscated their property, and imposed heavy new taxes, Netherlanders called it the Council of Blood. Thousands fled.

The heavy-handed Spanish tactics were enormously expensive. With Alva and his successors finally mobilizing 65,000 men and more for their campaigns, the tax revenue from the Netherlands was diverted to the war. Even this was insufficient, but Philip could not provide additional funds from Spain. The result was chronically unpaid troops prone to rebel against their own officers; more than 45 mutinies occurred between 1572 and 1607.

Instead of cowing the Netherlanders, Alva's cruelty prompted them to rally around William the Silent, prince of Orange (1533–1584). William was a *politique*, someone who allowed political circumstances rather than re-

---

◉ The "Calvinist Fury" ◉

The revolt in the Netherlands commenced with an outburst of violent iconoclasm in 1566. An English observer describes the "Calvinist Fury."

When . . . [the priests] should have begun their service, there was a company [that] began to sing psalms, at the beginning being but a company of boys, whereupon the margrave and other . . . lords came to the church and rebuked them. But all in vain, for . . . as soon as they turned their backs, they [went] to it again, and the company increased. . . . They broke up the choir. . . .

After that, they began with the image of Our Lady . . . and utterly defaced her and her chapel, and after [that], the whole church, which was the costliest church in Europe, and [they] have so spoiled it that they have not left a place to sit. . . . And from thence, part went to the parish churches and part to the houses of religion, and made such dispatch as I think the like was never done in one night. . . .

Coming into Our Lady church, it looked like a hell, where were above 1,000 torches burning, and such a noise, as if heaven and earth had gone together, with falling . . . images and beating down of costly works. . . . From thence I went . . . to all the houses of religion, where was the like stir, breaking and spoiling all that there was. Yet, they that did this never looked towards any spoil, but broke all in pieces and let it lay underfoot. So that, to be short, they have spoiled and destroyed all the churches, as well nunneries as others, but as I do understand they neither said nor did anything to the nuns. . . . In divers places in Flanders they have [done] and do the like.

Source: J. W. Burgon, *The Life and Times of Sir Thomas Gresham, Knt.*, vol. 2 (London: Jennings, 1839), pp. 138–140 (edited to conform to modern usage).

ligion to dictate his allegiance. Originally a Lutheran, he had converted to Catholicism as a child in order to receive his inheritance, but he returned to the Lutheran fold in 1567 and became a Calvinist in 1572. As stadholder, or governor, of the northern provinces of Holland, Utrecht, and Zeeland, where Calvinism was strong, he had a natural base of support. He also had the allegiance of a group of pirates and patriots who called themselves "sea beggars" and preyed on Spanish shipping. In the spring of 1572 they captured Brill and other ports in Holland and Zeeland, providing a haven to which Calvinists in other provinces fled. When the Spaniards besieged Leiden the following year, the rebels opened the dikes, forcing the Spanish army to flee before the advancing floodwaters.

The high point of rebel fortunes came in 1576 after unpaid Spanish troops sacked Antwerp. The "Spanish Fury" left more than 7,000 dead and persuaded the largely Catholic provinces in the south to ally with the primarily Protestant areas of the north. All but 4 of the 17 provinces united in the Pacification of Ghent (November 1576), and the others joined in the Union of Brussels (January 1577). The religious question was settled by leaving each region free to make its own policy. The Spanish, however, refused to quit, and by 1579 Philip's new commander, the duke of Parma (Margaret's son), had regained a large degree of control by combining military victories in the south with an appeal to Catholic Netherlanders to stand firm with Spain. The ten southern provinces, organized as the Union of Arras, made their peace with Philip, but under William's leadership the seven northern and largely Protestant provinces, the Union of Utrecht, declared their independence in 1581.

Even as Parma's forces advanced northward, the Dutch cause was jeopardized when a Catholic partisan assassinated William in 1584 with the pope's blessing. Unwilling to see the Protestant cause in the Netherlands crushed, the English stepped into the breach, sending a small army in 1585. The French too provided assistance. Whatever chance Philip had to destroy the Dutch rebels was lost when he became directly embroiled in war against England. By 1593 the Spaniards had been driven out of the northern provinces, though fighting continued until 1609. War resumed in 1621, and not until 1648 did the Spanish formally recognize the independence of the Dutch Republic.

The English Challenge

Well before Elizabeth I's decision to send an army to the Netherlands, relations with Spain had been deteriorating. On the queen's part the reasons for the hostility were less religious than political and economic. The English wanted to trade with Spain's American colonies, and the attack on John Hawkins' third expedition had set off a series of hostile economic moves on the part of both states between 1568 and 1573. The Netherlands were also a source of friction. Although Elizabeth was reluctant to support rebels and was not committed to Dutch independence, she was unwilling to accept either a massive Spanish military presence in the Netherlands or Dutch reliance on the French, which could result in French domination of the entire Channel coast.

Relations between Elizabeth and Philip were further complicated by the problem of Mary Stuart, queen of Scotland (1542–1567), widow of the French king Francis II, and a member of the powerful French Catholic family of Guise. As the great-granddaughter of the first Tudor king, Henry VII, Mary claimed the English throne, insisting that Elizabeth, as Anne Boleyn's daughter, was illegitimate. Mary, however, had fallen on hard times in Scotland because of a scandalous marriage to the earl of Bothwell, the probable murderer of her husband, Henry Lord Darnley. Irate Scottish Protestants, including the reformer John Knox, forced Mary to abdicate in 1567. After her escape to England a year later, she remained under arrest for 19 years in remote castles. Although Elizabeth tried to negotiate her return to the Scottish throne, Mary supported plots for her overthrow. In 1584 a conspiracy involving the Spanish ambassador helped set the stage for English intervention against Spain in the Netherlands. When royal officials intercepted a letter from Mary in 1586 encouraging yet another assassination attempt, Elizabeth agreed to have Mary stand trial. She was unanimously found guilty, and Elizabeth reluctantly authorized her execution in February 1587. Philip had determined to invade England well before Mary's death, but her execution and the Protestantism of her son, King James VI of Scotland, gave him an excuse to claim the English throne as his own. He based that claim on his descent from a granddaughter of the fourteenth-century English King Edward III.

Because Philip had insufficient funds to mount a direct seaborne assault, his plan called for a fleet to control the English Channel while Parma's veterans invaded England from the Netherlands. Preparation of the armada was delayed when Sir Francis Drake's daring attack on Cadiz in April 1587 destroyed some 20 ships and crucial supplies. During the interval, Spain's experienced admiral, the marquess of Santa Cruz, died. His successor, the duke of Medina Sidonia, had neither confidence in himself nor adequate experience. "I am always seasick," he protested, "[and have] no experience of seafaring or war."[3] When the two fleets met in July 1588, they were roughly equal in size, though the English vessels had greater maneuverability and superior long-range guns. Because the Spaniards used a crescent-shaped formation, the English were unable to get into position to use their guns effectively until they finally broke up the enemy formation by launching six burning ships against it. The Spaniards fled north through the Channel, suffering major losses when they rounded northern Scotland and were struck by Atlantic gales. Philip lost nearly half his ships, but an English force sent by Elizabeth to destroy the rest disobeyed her orders, giving Philip a reprieve. In the ensuing years two more armadas were readied to attack England, but storms prevented either from reaching its target. Until peace was officially concluded in 1604, both sides concentrated on helping their allies in the French civil war.

The French Civil War

The struggle in France had begun in 1562 when soldiers of the duke of Guise slaughtered a congregation of Huguenots, or Reformed Protestants, at Vassy in Champagne. The Guise family—patrons of a militant, zealous Catholicism—were political rivals of the Bourbon and Montmorency-Chatillon families, both of whom supported the Huguenots. Because the crown of France was in the hands of a minor, Charles IX (1560–1574), his mother, Catherine de' Medici, exercised authority. To preserve her power, she played a shrewd game of shifting alliances, working first with one and then the other of the factions. Although this helped prevent either side from dominating the other, it also kept France in a state of political and religious instability.

The "wars of religion" in France were at root a struggle for political dominance in which religion, itself a potent and divisive factor, was used to justify the fighting and to attract adherents. The controversy split the aristocracy, more than 40 percent of which was Huguenot. The Protestants also enjoyed a good deal of support in urban areas, though only in Dauphiné and Languedoc

did they comprise a majority of the population. In France as a whole, more than 90 percent of the people were Catholic, but the Huguenots benefited from aristocratic support and a strong religious organization. The religious struggle was marked by intermittent periods of peace, assassinations, and the involvement of foreign troops, including English and German forces who aided the Huguenots in the early years.

The worst atrocity of the war—the St. Bartholomew's Day massacre in August 1572—grew out of Catherine's fear that the Huguenots were becoming too powerful. One of their leaders, Admiral Gaspard de Coligny, had persuaded Charles IX, who had come of age, to intervene in the Netherlands on behalf of the Protestants. Fearful of a Franco-Spanish war, Catherine was determined to reverse this decision. Huguenot power was also on the increase because of the marriage in August of the king's sister, Marguerite of Valois, to a prominent Huguenot, Henry of Navarre. Four days later an assassination plot that had Catherine's blessing wounded Coligny. Fearful of Huguenot reprisals, Catherine persuaded the king to sanction the execution of Protestant leaders on trumped-up charges that they were plotting his overthrow. Shortly before dawn on August 24, Coligny and other leading Huguenots were assassinated, and by daybreak militant Catholics were slaughtering Protestants. At least 3,000 were butchered in Paris, where bloody corpses bobbed in the Seine, and perhaps 20,000 in all of France. News of the massacre pleased Pope Gregory XIII and King Philip II, who celebrated with special religious services.

The massacre temporarily ended French intervention in the Netherlands but failed to destroy the Huguenot cause. As the Huguenots plotted revenge, Henry of

The massacre of a congregation of Huguenots at Vassy by followers of the duke of Guise in March 1562 ignited a civil war in France that lasted until 1596. [Bibliothèque Nationale, Paris]

◉ The St. Bartholomew's Day Massacre: ◉ Papal Reaction

News of the St. Bartholomew's Day massacre in August 1572 prompted rejoicing in Catholic circles, including the papacy itself. An observer describes Pope Gregory XIII's reaction.

Although it was still night, I immediately sent to his Holiness to free him from the tension, and so that he might rise to the wonderful grace, which God had granted to Christendom under his pontificate. On that morning there was a consistory court . . . and as his Holiness had such a good piece of news to announce to the Holy College, he had the dispatches publicly read out to them. His Holiness then spoke about their contents and concluded that in these times, so troubled by revolutions, nothing better or more magnificent could have been wished for; and that, as it appeared, God was beginning to turn the eye of his mercy on us. His Holiness and the college were extremely contented and joyful at the reading of this news. . . .

On the same morning . . . his Holiness with the whole College of Cardinals went to the church of Saint Mark, to have the *Te Deum* sung and to thank God for granting so great a favor to the Christian people. His Holiness does not cease to pray God, and make others pray, to inspire the Most Christian King [Charles IX] to follow further the path which he has opened and to cleanse and purge completely the Kingdom of France from the plague of the Huguenots.

Source: W. F. Reddaway, ed., *Select Documents of European History*, Vol. 2: *1492–1715* (New York: Holt, n.d.), pp. 94–95.

Guise in 1576 organized the Catholic League, which soon received financial support from Philip II. By the mid-1580s the league controlled Paris, forcing King Henry III (1574–1589) to adopt desperate means to save his crumbling authority: the assassination of Henry of Guise and his brother, a cardinal in the Catholic church. Although the king allied with Henry of Navarre in an effort to crush the Catholic League, he was assassinated in July 1589.

With Henry of Navarre now claiming the throne as Henry IV (1589–1610), the civil war entered its final stage. Unprepared to see France governed by Protestants, Philip II not only continued to back the Catholic League but also ordered his army to invade France. Elizabeth I, determined to prevent France from falling under Spanish hegemony, sent her troops to Henry's aid. A *politique* rather than a convinced Huguenot, Henry finally decided in 1593 that peace was possible only if he converted to Catholicism. The pope absolved him of his heresy, and Paris finally opened its gates to him, though Philip continued the struggle until 1598. In the latter year Henry provided some solace to his Huguenot allies by issuing the Edict of Nantes, giving Protestants liberty of conscience, full civil and political rights, and control of 100 fortified towns. Catholicism, however, was rec-

ognized as the official religion of France, and Protestant worship was prohibited in the Paris area.

Although France was saved for Catholicism, from Philip's standpoint the 1590s was a decade of military disaster. Spain had no power in France, the Dutch Netherlands were virtually irretrievable, and the English, exultant in their victory over the armada in 1588, had checked Spain on the seas. By the time of Philip's death in 1598, the Spanish quest for hegemony had been blunted, though the Spaniards retained the southern Netherlands and continued to battle the Dutch until 1609.

The Age of the Queens

The second half of the sixteenth century is notable as an age of unusual political prominence for women in western Europe. Mary I (1553–1558) and Elizabeth I (1558–1603) in England and Mary Stuart in Scotland (whose effective rule was from 1561 to 1567) governed as queens, while other women exercised power as regents: Mary of Guise in Scotland (1554–1560), Margaret of Parma in the Netherlands (1559–1567), and Catherine de' Medici in France beginning in 1560. Women, of course, had governed before, sometimes very successfully, as in the case of Queen Isabella of Castile (1474–1504), cofounder of a unified Spain. Although some Renaissance writers had recognized women's ability to govern, men were still quite reluctant to accept their authority. The classic statement of this view was a treatise by John Knox, architect of the Protestant Reformation in Scotland, titled *The First Blast of the Trumpet Against the Monstrous Regiment of Women* (1558), which argued that female rule was contrary to divine and natural law, though God occasionally made an exception. The queens had their defenders, but even supporters of women's right to rule were unwilling to admit women to governing bodies or deliberative assemblies. No woman sat in the English or Scottish royal councils or Parliaments during the reign of these queens; government remained an essentially male preserve throughout Europe.

Elizabeth I in particular exerted an enormous impact on England, not only by thwarting Spanish ambitions and supporting Protestantism but also by creating an atmosphere conducive to brilliant cultural achievements. The glorious image of her rule, which she assiduously cultivated, is reflected in the literary masterpieces of Edmund Spenser (c. 1552–1599), whose allegorical poem *The Faerie Queene* exalted "the most excellent and glorious person of our sovereign the queen, and her kingdom in Fairy Land," and William Shakespeare (1564–1616). The self-confidence and exuberance that radiated from England after the Spanish were repelled is eloquently expressed in Shakespeare's *Richard II*:

> *This royal throne of kings, this scepter'd isle,*
> *This earth of majesty, this seat of Mars,*
> *This other Eden, demi-paradise,*
> *This fortress built by Nature for herself . . .*
> *This blessed plot, this earth, this realm, this*
> *England.*

In no small measure England's achievements were attributable to its queen. During the early 1600s the image of Elizabeth—more exalted in death than in life—proved to be more than her successors, James I and Charles I, could emulate.

Europe in Crisis

As Spanish ascendancy waned, Europe became preoccupied with the Thirty Years' War and the general crisis of authority that followed it in the mid-1600s. The two problems were directly related, for the unparalleled destruction inflicted in the Thirty Years' War, much of it by undisciplined troops, underscored the need to bring

Elizabeth I, painted by George Gower around 1588. The upper left shows the English fleet; the upper right, the Spanish armada being destroyed by gales. Elizabeth often wore a stylish wig and coated her face with a white cosmetic that blanched the skin. [Marquess of Tavistock, Trustee of the Bedford Estate]

armies and warfare under strict control. Ultimately, monarchs and nobles found it to their advantage to work together to determine policy and implement discipline. By 1660 there was also a consensus that even religious convictions had to be subordinated to the maintenance of order. The period 1600–1660 was thus a major watershed in European history.

The Thirty Years' War

Germany, a patchwork land of some 360 independent political entities, became the killing field of Europe in a great war triggered by a dispute involving the role of the Austrian Habsburgs as Holy Roman emperors. The compromise Peace of Augsburg (1555) that had ended the first round of religious warfare in Germany had given no rights to Calvinists, whose growing strength, particularly in the Palatinate (see Map 19.1), alarmed the Lutherans. There was considerable tension too between Protestants and Catholics because of changes in religious allegiance. When the Catholic rulers of ecclesiastical principalities became Protestant, Catholics demanded that they surrender both their religious office and their lands, but Lutherans refused. After the Protestants organized the Evangelical Union in 1609 and their opponents responded with the Catholic League, Germany was divided into two armed camps.

The event that sparked the fighting occurred when the Habsburg Ferdinand of Styria, king of Bohemia, curtailed religious toleration for Protestants and Hussites. In May 1618, Bohemian nobles registered their protest by throwing two of Ferdinand's advisers out of a castle window in Prague; their lives were saved when they landed in a pile of manure. A year later the rebels deposed Ferdinand as their king and gave the crown to a Calvinist prince, Frederick V of the Palatinate, son-in-law of King James I of England. Had the rebels succeeded in establishing a Protestant on the Bohemian throne, Protestants would have had a majority of the seven votes needed to elect future emperors. Ferdinand, who had become emperor in August 1619, had little choice but to reassert his control over Bohemia.

At first the war went well for Ferdinand. In addition to receiving the help of Catholic armies from Spain and Bavaria, he got the assistance of Lutheran Saxony, whose elector was more interested in acquiring land in the Palatinate than in religious solidarity with his fellow Protestants. After Frederick was defeated at the Battle of White Mountain in 1620, he fled Bohemia, leaving his Protestant supporters to face Ferdinand's wrath. The Dutch, who were alarmed by Spain's presence in the area, provided Frederick with funds to keep fighting, but his small principality was overwhelmed. After the Danes entered the war in 1625, Ferdinand's new general, Albrecht von Wallenstein, invaded Denmark, leaving starvation and destruction in his wake. Danish lands were returned on the condition that Denmark refrain from intervening in Germany.

With Ferdinand on the verge of establishing total control over his empire, the Swedish king, Gustavus Adolphus, invaded Germany. He was supported militarily by Brandenburg and Saxony and financially by the Dutch and the French, both of whom were threatened by Habsburg expansion. Using innovative tactics that increased the mobility of his army, Gustavus Adolphus crushed the imperial forces in 1631. The fighting was carried into Catholic regions, especially Bavaria, whose residents were subjected to calculated brutality—rape, pillage, torture, and murder. In November 1632 the armies of Gustavus Adolphus and Wallenstein confronted each other at Lützen in Saxony in one of the bloodiest battles of the war. The Swedish king was killed, but neither side was strong enough to defeat its enemies in the ensuing months. Wallenstein was assassinated in 1634.

The final and most destructive period of the war (1635–1648) reverted to a dynastic struggle that pitted the Habsburg powers, Austria and Spain, against the French and the Swedes. The real victims were the German people. "Every soldier had his favorite method of making life miserable for peasants," noted one observer, "and every peasant had his own misery."[4] The city of Marburg was occupied no fewer than 11 times. As peasants fled before the marauding armies, the destruction of crops triggered famine. The loss of population was catastrophic: 40 percent in rural areas, 33 percent in the cities. The overall population of the empire decreased by as much as 8 million during the war.

An end to the fighting was finally achieved by the Peace of Westphalia in 1648. The sovereignty of each

The French artist Jacques Callot (1592–1635) created a series of 24 etchings titled *The Miseries of War,* **one of the most moving statements of the horror that gripped Germany in the Thirty Years' War. The etchings reflect a dramatic change of mind on Callot's part, for his earlier works glorify warfare. This etching depicts the hanging of thieves, a vivid reminder of the fate that awaited German peasants unlucky enough to get caught stealing what they needed to stay alive. [New York Public Library]**

German state was recognized; altogether there were now some 300 entities with sovereign rights and nearly 1,500 minor lordships. Each prince, whether Catholic, Lutheran, or Calvinist, could determine the religious beliefs of his subjects, who had no choice but to accept or emigrate. The treaty also recognized the independence of the Swiss Confederacy and the Dutch Republic, but it did not end hostilities between France and Spain, which lasted until the Treaty of the Pyrenees in 1659. Just as Spain's quest for hegemony was doomed by Philip II's defeats in the 1590s and confirmed by the Treaty of the Pyrenees, so the bid of the Austrian Habsburgs to dominate central Europe was wrecked in the Thirty Years' War. Not until 1871 would the Germans achieve political unity. The war also had disruptive effects on the domestic politics of the major European states, thereby contributing to the midcentury crises.

Rebuilding France: Foundations of Bourbon Rule

France's ability to act decisively in the Thirty Years' War and ultimately to impose peace terms on Spain in 1659 was made possible by the rebuilding of its institutions in the aftermath of the Huguenot wars. Beginning with Henry IV, the first Bourbon monarchs pursued a course of absolutism in politics and mercantilism in economics. In the Bourbon view, stability mandated a thoroughly centralized state capable of maintaining order at home and fielding large armies. But absolutism also entailed the recognition that monarchical power was bound up with the preservation of a privileged class of royal officials and landed aristocrats. Continental absolutism was built on the notion of an ascending order of social privilege, at the apex of which was the monarch. Anything that undermined this pyramid of power thus undercut royal absolutism.

Centralization could be accomplished only at the expense of local and special interests, which were sometimes strained severely by the burden of financing a war. The attempt to impose royal absolutism coincided with the costly struggle to prevent the establishment of Spanish or Austrian hegemony. By the 1640s grinding taxation, aristocratic discontent, and resistance to centralized control had built to the crisis point and erupted in a new civil war, the Fronde.

Although no monarch came close to achieving total power in this period, there was growing interest in the concept of absolute rule, particularly in its national, monarchical form. The French political theorist Jean Bodin had stressed the importance of a sovereign power whose authority was beyond challenge, though he also insisted that monarchs were responsible to God for their actions. Building on this traditional notion, various seventeenth-century thinkers asserted that kings and queens derived their right to govern directly from God and were therefore above human law. Seemingly, the apostle Paul had provided the foundation for this theory when he taught that earthly powers were ordained by God. The concept that sovereignty was divinely bestowed suited the needs of rulers intent on centralizing their control, for they were in a position to claim the unquestioning obedience of their subjects as both a right and a Christian duty. Political theorists such as Bodin and the Englishman Robert Filmer drove home the argument for divine right absolutism by likening the monarch to a father. Though widely embraced, divine right theories were applied with more success in France than anywhere else in the 1600s, and even there not without a struggle.

When Henry IV temporarily ended the Huguenot wars in 1598, he revived the goals of the Renaissance sovereigns Francis I and Henry II, who had aimed at centralizing royal authority and expanding French territory. Although he opted not to summon the Estates General after 1593, he took care to secure the support of the more powerful aristocrats—the nobility of the sword—especially by strategic bribes. Offices were traditionally sold in France, but Henry took the practice one step further by allowing his principal bureaucrats, the nobility of the robe, to pay a voluntary annual fee called the *paulette* that made the offices hereditary. These men, most of them members of the bourgeoisie, were thus closely linked to the expansion of the government.

Henry faced daunting economic problems. He was nearly 300 million livres in debt, with annual revenues amounting to only half that amount. His finance minister, the clever duke of Sully, repudiated part of the debt, renegotiated a lower rate of interest on the balance, and rigorously sought new sources of revenue, such as the *paulette*. As a proponent of mercantile policies, Sully established monopolies on salt, gunpowder, and mining. France was already a food-exporting nation, and Sully strengthened agriculture by building more bridges, roads, and canals. To reduce the export of bullion for luxury items, new laws restricted the use of gold and silver, and royal factories were constructed to produce such luxury goods as silk, satin, tapestries, and crystal. By 1601 the budget was balanced.

When Henry was assassinated by a Catholic ideologue in 1610, the throne passed to his 9-year-old son, Louis XIII (1610–1643). The regency was in the hands of Louis' mother, Marie de' Medici. Because she relied on her Italian favorites for advice, disgruntled nobles and troubled Huguenots threatened a resumption of civil strife. Marie tried to defuse the crisis by summoning the Estates General in 1614, but internal feuding rendered it impotent, and it was not called again until 1789. For ten years France lacked an energetic government, but Marie maintained a semblance of peace by lavishing pensions and bribes on the nobles and allowing them a greater role in provincial affairs.

The appointment of Cardinal Richelieu (1585–1642) as the king's chief adviser in 1624 once more meant a strong hand at the controls of government. Nobles who defied royal edicts were imprisoned and some even executed, and their castles were destroyed. Responsibility for local administration was transferred from the nobles to *intendants*, commissioners appointed by the crown who held their posts at the king's pleasure. Their responsibilities included tax collection, the administration of justice, military recruitment, and local defense. To deal with the rebellious Huguenots, Richelieu besieged one of their key strongholds, La Rochelle, for 14 months until it surrendered. Other Huguenot towns were overrun by royal forces. In 1629 Richelieu ended the political and military rights given to the Huguenots in the Edict of Nantes, although they retained religious freedom. Richelieu also enhanced French power by building effective Atlantic and Mediterranean fleets. His policies, however, were expensive and required deficit financing. Occupied with his centralizing schemes and the Thirty Years' War, Richelieu failed to undertake desperately needed tax reform. As the cost of French military involvement in Germany increased, rising taxes underscored the unfairness of the burden on the peasants. Richelieu faced tax riots throughout France, to which he reacted with increased repression.

The death of Richelieu in 1642 and Louis XIII a year later left the 5-year-old Louis XIV on the throne and real power in the hands of Richelieu's protégé, Giulio Mazarin (1602–1661), a Sicilian cardinal and the illicit lover—or secret husband—of the regent, Anne of Austria. A foreigner and a powerful churchman, he was thoroughly disliked. Discontent was especially pronounced because of the effects of centralization on local authority and Mazarin's inability to pay interest on the loans that financed French participation in the Thirty Years' War. So depleted were royal finances that some officials had not been paid for four years. The situation was made worse by famine, especially in the late 1640s, when many peasants lost their holdings to bourgeois creditors.

Against this backdrop of economic dislocation and political unrest, the Parlement of Paris, France's main law court and a stronghold of the nobility of the robe, called for reform, including the abolition of the office of *intendant*, a habeas corpus law, the right to approve taxes, and an end to the creation of new offices. Mazarin arrested the leaders of the Paris Parlement, inciting an uprising that forced the king and the cardinal to flee. Unwilling to sanction popular rebellion, the Parlement of Paris came to terms with Mazarin in the spring of 1649, but the uprising spread nevertheless. The end of the Thirty Years' War enabled prominent nobles of the

◉ Richelieu's Plan for Reform ◉

After Cardinal Richelieu became Louis XIII's principal minister in 1624, he outlined conditions in France and his program of reform.

At the time when your majesty resolved to admit me both to your council and to an important place in your confidence for the direction of your affairs, I may say that the Huguenots shared the state with you; that the nobles conducted themselves as if they were not your subjects, and the most powerful governors of the provinces as if they were sovereign in their offices.

I may say that the bad example of all of these was so injurious to this realm that even the best regulated *parlements* were affected by it, and endeavoured, in certain cases, to diminish your royal authority as far as they were able in order to stretch their own powers beyond the limits of reason.

I may say that everyone measured his own merit by his audacity; that in place of estimating the benefits which they received from your majesty at their proper worth, all valued them only in so far as they satisfied the extravagant demands of their imagination; that the most arrogant were held to be the wisest, and found themselves the most prosperous. . . .

I promised your majesty to employ all my industry and all the authority which it should please you to give me to ruin the Huguenot party, to abase the pride of the nobles, to bring back all your subjects to their duty, and to elevate your name among foreign nations to the point where it belongs.

Source: J. H. Robinson, ed., *Readings in European History*, vol. 2 (Boston: Ginn, 1906), pp. 268–270.

sword to march their forces against Mazarin. Among them was a leading member of the Bourbon family, the prince of Condé. In Bordeaux artisans and lawyers seized control of the city government, and urban and agrarian uprisings broke out elsewhere. Mazarin had to flee again in February 1651; two years passed before he could safely return to Paris. Ultimately, the Fronde collapsed because the *frondeurs* were too fragmented in their goals. The prospect of a France divided into feudal principalities was unpalatable to the nobility of the robe, while neither they nor the nobility of the sword were interested in the plight of the peasants and the urban workers. The crisis in France passed because the leaders of the Fronde, occupied with their narrow self-interests, failed to forge a cohesive movement for reform. The cause of constitutional monarchy in France was then dormant for more than a century.

Spain: Disillusionment, War, and Revolt

As in France, Spain during the reigns of Philip III (1598–1621) and Philip IV (1621–1665) experienced mounting reaction against centralization, economic hardship, and the impact of foreign war, all of which finally triggered open rebellion. The economic problems stemmed from several factors. Seventeenth-century Spain experienced a severe decline in population: Castile and Aragon dropped from 10 million to 6 million, a percentage decrease greater than that in any other European country, including the war-torn German states. The reasons for the decline are not altogether clear, but they include plague, crop failures, mismanaged financial resources, and a decline in the wealth coming from Spain's overseas empire. Between the 1600s and the 1650s, bullion shipments to Spain decreased more than 80 percent, due mostly to the decimation of the Amerindian population and the loss of its forced labor. The Spaniards failed to compensate for this loss of income by developing new industries. When Spain renewed the war against the Dutch in 1621 and subsequently became embroiled in the Thirty Years' War, the government had to squeeze funds from an already overburdened people. The price of elusive glory abroad was grinding poverty at home.

Philip IV's chief minister, the count of Olivares (1587–1645), embarked on a plan of reform designed to increase revenues and rationalize the administration, thereby enhancing Spain's military capabilities. "Kings," he proclaimed, "cannot achieve heroic actions without money."[5] He increased the church's tax burden and reduced the number of officeholders, but in Castile the Cortes blocked his attempt to introduce new direct taxes. Administratively, he wanted to impose uniform laws on the semiautonomous Spanish kingdoms and make each provide its fair share of taxes and troops. Olivares' Union of Arms called for the creation of a reserve army of 140,000 men drawn from every royal dominion. His reduction of regional autonomy and redistribution of some of Castile's burden to other provinces touched off revolts. The first rebellion erupted in the northern province of Catalonia in June 1640, triggered by the billeting of Castilian and mercenary soldiers sent north to repel a French invasion. Rebellious peasants, overtaxed clergy hostile to Castilian domination, and rioting urban mobs joined forces. When Barcelona revolted, the royal viceroy was murdered, but the Catalans had no effective rebel leaders. They tried to establish an independent republic, but dependence on French funds forced them to acknowledge Louis XIII as king. Disillusioned with foreign rule, the insurgents lost heart, and the revolt collapsed when Barcelona's citizen army was defeated in 1652. The Catalan nobles, who had deserted the rebel cause rather than risk their wealth and rank, had their privileges confirmed by Philip IV.

Revolts against Spanish rule also occurred in Portugal, Naples, and Sicily. Resentment against Castilian rule and financial support for Spanish wars triggered a national war of liberation in Portugal in December 1640. The nobles restored the Portuguese monarchy, the Lisbon masses rose in support, and a French fleet provided naval protection. Funded by the profits of the Brazilian sugar fleet, the Portuguese continued defiantly until Spain finally recognized their independence in 1668. In contrast, the government suppressed the 1647 revolts in Sicily and Naples in a matter of months. The Sicilians wanted their local privileges restored and the new taxes abolished, but they were leaderless. The rebellion in Naples began with attacks on anything Spanish and quickly developed into a class war of peasants against landlords. When not even the French were willing to lend support, a Spanish fleet restored order.

The crises of the 1640s made it apparent that Spain could no longer afford the foreign policy of a great power. The Treaty of the Pyrenees in 1659, though it involved only modest territorial losses to France on the frontiers and in the Spanish Netherlands, was nevertheless humiliating. The nobles came to dominate the monarchy, particularly after the inept Charles II became king in 1665. Spanish institutions, however, were sufficiently strong to enable the country to survive Charles' reign and the subsequent accession of a Bourbon dynasty, and in the eighteenth century Spain once again became a major power.

The Dutch Republic and the House of Orange

Although the Dutch had to renew their fight for independence between 1621 and 1648, they were unusual in their ability to keep the state solvent. Severe political tensions existed, but with rare exceptions they were resolved without recourse to violence.

The principal source of friction was the role of the House of Orange in Dutch politics. Because each of the seven Dutch provinces normally chose the prince of Orange as its stadholder, or governor, he was not only the symbol of national unity but often the most powerful man in the country as well. The Dutch had an Estates General to which each of the provinces elected representatives. Delegates to this body traditionally split, some supporting the House of Orange and a militant foreign policy, others favoring a greater degree of provincial autonomy and peaceful relations with foreign countries in order to improve trade. In the early 1600s Jan van Oldenbarneveldt, founder of the Dutch East India Company and the most important representative in the Estates of the province of Holland, challenged Maurice of Nassau, from 1618 the prince of Orange, on the issue of resuming the war with Spain when the truce expired in 1621. The conflict had religious overtones, for Oldenbarneveldt and his supporters opposed the efforts of Calvinists to drive Arminians—Protestants who rejected Calvin's doctrine of predestination in favor of free will—out of the state church and the universities. With the support of the Calvinists, Maurice used the army to purge Oldenbarneveldt's supporters from the town governments in the province of Holland, and in 1619 Oldenbarneveldt himself was executed for high treason.

His main supporters, including the great philosopher and jurist Hugo Grotius (1583–1645), architect of the concept of international law, were condemned to life imprisonment.

The conflict between Holland and the House of Orange erupted again in 1648 when William II became stadholder. Unlike the Hollanders, William opposed peace negotiations with Spain and supported King Charles I of England in his conflict with Parliament. A compromise was reached when William's cousin threatened Amsterdam with an army. After William died unexpectedly in 1650, the Hollanders and their allies took over the government, maintaining their supremacy until a French invasion in 1672 necessitated the return of a strong military leader from the House of Orange.

Although the restoration of the republic in 1650 was a quasi-revolutionary event, the Dutch avoided a civil war and enjoyed continued prosperity. When Antwerp declined in the late 1570s, Amsterdam moved quickly to establish itself as the center of European commerce. By the mid-seventeenth century the Dutch operated more than half of the world's commercial vessels. Using raw materials from Scandinavia, the shipyards of Amsterdam built Europe's most efficient ships, including large vessels for the transoceanic trade and inexpensive flat-bottomed freighters known as *fluiten* ("flyboats"). In addition to trading and shipbuilding, the economy of Amsterdam was based on banking, insurance (including the first life insurance policies), printing, and manufactur-

A meeting of the Estates General at The Hague in the Netherlands in 1651, painted by Dirck van Delen. [Rijksmuseum, Amsterdam]

ing. Artisans finished cloth, made jewelry, brewed beer, dressed leather, processed tobacco, and cut diamonds. Other towns became famous for particular products, such as Delft for ceramics, Haarlem for linens, and Schiedam for gin. The Haarlem area also achieved fame by cultivating tulips, which were first imported from the Ottoman Empire. Jews, who benefited greatly by the normally tolerant religious atmosphere in the Netherlands, played a prominent role in the Dutch business community, especially banking. The Dutch, in short, were economically the most progressive Europeans in the seventeenth century, and the people of Amsterdam enjoyed the highest per capita income in Europe. Although there were a substantial number of poor, whose ranks were swollen by immigrants and refugees, the Dutch provided enough relief to stave off the misery that attended political crises in other European states in the mid-1600s.

Early Stuart England: From Consensus to Conflict

Alone among the European states, England experienced not only a severe crisis but a revolution in the 1640s and 1650s as well. Under Elizabeth I (1558–1603) and James I (1603–1625), who also governed Scotland as James VI (1567–1625), England attained religious stability and a reasonably effective working relationship between crown and Parliament. Elizabeth's Protestant settlement withstood the challenge of Catholics, nearly 200 of whom she executed for treason, and of a handful of radical Protestants who repudiated the state church. James, raised as a Calvinist, disappointed English Puritans who wanted further reforms in the established church, including a better-educated clergy with higher moral standards, stricter sabbath observance, and an end to such "unscriptural" customs as the sign of the cross in baptism and the wedding ring. They also demanded the reform of church courts, especially the High Commission, which could compel accused persons to testify against themselves and tried them without a jury. James agreed only to a Puritan request for a new translation of the Bible into English, the so-called King James version of 1611.

The work of centralization was carried forward, particularly through the appointment of lords lieutenant and their deputies in the counties. Because England had no standing army, local defense was in the hands of these men, but as long as the crown appointed local magnates, the system worked well. Central authority was also enhanced by the use of conciliar courts, especially the Star Chamber, which evolved out of the judicial activities of the king's Council, and the Court of High Commission, which originated in Elizabeth's reign and enforced the laws and doctrine of the Church of England.

Although the war against Spain (1585–1604) was pop-ular, its cost forced Elizabeth to adopt measures that reduced future income, such as the sale of various crown lands. In most respects she handled her Parliaments superbly, though at the end of her reign a controversy over royal grants of monopolies embittered relations as anger over their abuse mounted. Finances were increasingly a problem for James, especially with respect to foreign policy. Dreaming of the glory of the 1580s, his Parliaments were willing to support a naval war against Spain but had little desire to become embroiled directly on the Continent in the Thirty Years' War on behalf of James' son-in-law, Frederick V. Nor did they understand the king's desire to establish an alliance with their traditional enemy, Spain, by means of a marriage involving Prince Charles and a Spanish princess. The proposed match was crucial to James' dream of a partnership between Catholic Spain and Protestant England that could serve as the vehicle to maintain peace in Europe.

James, who thought that kings were "God's lieutenants upon earth" and sat on "God's throne," heightened concern by actions that seemed to challenge traditional constitutional procedures. Chronically short of funds, he sought additional revenue by levying a special import duty, an "imposition," without parliamentary approval. Although the courts decided in his favor on the grounds that import duties were part of his prerogative to determine foreign policy, some members of Parliament were irate. James also provoked controversy by dismissing one of his chief justices, Sir Edward Coke, for attempting to assert judicial independence. The king subsequently imprisoned Coke and a fellow member of the House of Commons for drafting a "protestation" asserting Parliament's right to speak freely on such subjects as "the arduous and urgent affairs concerning the king, state, and defense of the realm, and of the Church of England," including areas that had traditionally been reserved to the crown.[6] Yet when James died in 1625, he left a country whose tensions were still largely contained beneath the surface.

The consensus that Elizabeth had achieved was rapidly undermined by the policies of James' son, Charles I (1625–1649). Unable to conclude an agreement to marry a Spanish princess, he was determined to go to war against Spain, though a distrustful Parliament refused to give him sufficient funds. An expedition that tried to repeat Sir Francis Drake's brilliant 1587 raid on Cadiz not only failed but provoked outrage when the unpaid, sick, and wounded troops returned to the streets of Plymouth. Charles blundered further by going to war against France while still fighting Spain. With his finances depleted, he tried to raise money by forced "loans," billeting his troops in private homes to compel payment. Led by Coke, critics in the House of Commons responded in 1628 with the Petition of Right, which demanded that no taxes be levied without parliamentary consent, no person be imprisoned without knowing the charge, no troops be billeted in private homes without the owners' consent, and martial law not be imposed in peacetime. The king accepted the document in principle in return for further taxes. In 1629, however, a bitter attack on newly appointed Arminian bishops who supported Charles led to Parliament's dismissal, although only after critics held the speaker of the House of Commons in his chair while they passed resolutions condemning Catholicism, Arminianism, and taxes that lacked parliamentary approval. The Arminian position that Puritans and others found so offensive rejected the Calvinist doctrine of predestination, insisted that Christ died for all persons rather than the elect alone, and affirmed the freedom of each person to accept or reject divine grace.

For 11 years Charles ruled without a Parliament, raising revenue by a variety of unpopular expedients that stretched his legal powers. One of these was "ship money," a tax traditionally levied on coastal areas for naval expenses but now extended to the entire kingdom. Charles also sold monopolies, titles, offices, and crown lands. During this period religious grievances continued to mount, with much of the hostility directed at Charles' French Catholic queen, Henrietta Maria, and his Arminian archbishop of Canterbury, William Laud. Committed to the principle that a unified state required unity in religion, Laud vigorously persecuted his Puritan critics. They in turn attacked his Arminian theology and his emphasis on liturgy rather than preaching. When Charles and Laud attempted to force the English liturgy on the Presbyterian Scots, the latter rebelled. The militia units Charles dispatched to restore order were woefully inadequate, and the king was forced to summon Parliament.

The English Revolution

Historians hotly debate the nature and causes of the English revolution. Some contend that it was only a civil war, while others perceive a full-scale revolution that altered the structure of government, religion, the economy, educational thought, and the fabric of society. Lawrence Stone has gone back to the early sixteenth century to find such preconditions of revolution as the crown's failure to establish a standing army and a paid local bureaucracy, Puritan criticism in the state church, the growing wealth and power of the gentry and the decline of many of the greater nobility, and a crisis of confidence in high government officials. Against this background, he argues, the crown precipitated a revolution by encouraging Laud's campaign against the Puritans, curtailing the political role of the gentry, restricting upward social mobility, and enforcing tighter economic controls. The outbreak of civil war was then triggered by military defeat at the hands of the Scots and financial bankruptcy.

Analysts who hold to the more limited notion of a civil war place the origins much later, either in 1637 and 1638,

In the cultural atmosphere of the English royal court, the leading painter was Rubens' disciple Anthony Van Dyck (1599–1641), who painted King Charles I and his queen, Henrietta Maria. Charles, by his ineptitude, and his wife, by her Catholicism, contributed to the outbreak of civil war in England. [Bridgman/AA Resource]

when the Scots rebelled against the English liturgy, or even in early 1642, when the king and Parliament failed to agree on control of the militia. According to this interpretation, the civil war was largely an accident that neither side intended. Marxist historians concentrate on economic factors as the primary cause of the revolution, observing that Parliament drew most of its support from the economically advanced south and east of England, while the king's strength was greatest in the more backward regions of the west and north. Marxists have also tried to demonstrate that most of the aristocracy supported the king, whereas the "middling sort" of tradesmen, merchants, and yeoman farmers allied with Parliament. On any interpretation, however, it is clear that the revolutionary period was the gravest and most sustained political and military crisis in English history.

The "Short Parliament" that met briefly in the spring of 1640 was dismissed when it refused the king's demands for money. After the Scots invaded England, Charles had to call another Parliament in the autumn, the so-called Long Parliament. In a series of striking constitutional measures, Parliament abolished courts such as the Star Chamber and the High Commission, whose authority derived directly from the king; outlawed ship money and other questionable forms of revenue that lacked parliamentary sanction; and provided that no more than three years could elapse between Parliaments. By circumscribing royal authority, this legislation prevented the establishment of absolute government. Parliament also imprisoned and tried the king's principal advisers, the earl of Strafford and Archbishop Laud; both were eventually executed for high treason. Although Charles had little choice but to agree to the constitutional reforms and even to the death of his friend Strafford, he refused to surrender control of the militia, his only real military force. Troops had to be raised to suppress a Catholic rebellion that had erupted in Ireland in 1641, but neither side trusted the other with command. This distrust finally persuaded both sides to take up arms, and the civil war began in August 1642.

The Cavaliers supported Charles, while the Roundheads (so called for their short hairstyles) fought for Parliament. Religion was more important than social and economic considerations in persuading people to support one side or the other; Catholics, Arminians, and conservative conformists backed Charles, while Puritans and sectarians such as the Baptists opposed him. Much of Parliament's support came from the middle social orders, but many other segments of society remained neutral. The fighting divided many families. The two sides were roughly equal in strength, but the Roundheads established military supremacy through an alliance with the Scots, more effective military organization, and greater wealth, owing to the support of London and the commercial southeast. Most members of Parliament were required to resign their commissions, promotion was based on merit rather than birth, and strict discipline was imposed. The Cavaliers were badly defeated at the battle of Naseby in 1645, and a year later Charles surrendered. The price of the Scottish alliance was a promise to make the Church of England Presbyterian, but this was unacceptable to the army, which favored religious toleration for Protestants. The army was also impatient over negotiations with the king. In 1648 civil war broke out again, this time with the Scots on Charles' side. Under the leadership of Oliver Cromwell (1599–1658), the parliamentarian army crushed its enemies. After the victorious army purged Parliament of moderates, the remnant—derisively called the Rump Parliament by its critics—appointed a special tribunal to try the king on charges of treason. Found guilty, he was beheaded in London on January 30, 1649. This act, which shocked all Europe, was, said Cromwell, a "cruel necessity."

The Rump proceeded to make England a republic—the Commonwealth—but refused to provide for new elections. In practice it allowed a good deal of religious toleration, particularly for radical Protestants such as the Congregationalists, Baptists, and Quakers. The Quakers were particularly controversial because they not only rejected the traditional ministry and sacraments but also allowed women to preach. The Rump used the army to crush the rebellion in Ireland and then to suppress the Scots when they rallied on behalf of Charles I's son, hoping to impose a Presbyterian state church on England. The Rump also dispatched the navy to fight an inconclusive trade war against Europe's other major republic, the Dutch Netherlands, in 1652. When Cromwell's patience with the Rump finally ran out in 1653, he forcibly dismissed it.

Although handpicked by army officers with the advice of Congregational churches, a new Parliament—nicknamed Barebones after a quaintly named member, Praisegod Barebone—proved ineffective. In 1654 army officers drew up a constitution called the Instrument of Government that made Cromwell Lord Protector. Cromwell, however, fared no better with his Parliaments than the early Stuart kings had. Dissension raged over the structure of the government, the question of religious toleration, the enormous cost of maintaining a standing army, and the appointment of major generals to maintain order throughout the country. A war with Spain brought England both Dunkirk and Jamaica but simultaneously made Cromwell's financial position desperate despite increased taxation. With the political and economic crisis unresolved at his death in 1658, his son Richard, the new Lord Protector, proved unable to govern. By 1660 the propertied classes, fed up with military rule, were prepared to accept the return of monarchy in order to achieve stability and security. Although a good deal of antimonarchical sentiment and popular support for the republic continued, most of the country was relieved when Charles II returned from exile in May 1660.

Although the monarchy was restored, its position was seriously altered. Absolutism such as existed in France had been rendered impossible. The despotic royal courts of the Star Chamber and the High Commission did not return, and the principle of parliamentary approval for taxes was firmly established. Religious toleration ended in the early 1660s, but the dissenters were now strong enough to survive the sporadic persecution that ensued. The Jews, who had been welcomed to England in the 1650s in the expectation that their return signaled the coming of a millennial age, were not expelled. Moreover, the shakeup in the universities left proponents of the new science firmly established and set the stage for the foundation of the Royal Society in 1660. New directions in political thought had also been initiated by the work of the Levellers, who advocated a moderate form of democracy; by Thomas Hobbes, who developed a theory of secular absolutism; and by Gerrard Winstanley (1609–c. 1676), who advocated a commonwealth based on the abolition of property. Most important, the revolution established the principle in England that there must be a government of laws, not of men.

❧ A WOMAN IN THE ENGLISH REVOLUTION: MARGARET FELL

The collapse of censorship, of the authority of bishops, and ultimately of the monarchy in revolutionary England enabled women who belonged to such Protestant sects as the Congregationalists, Baptists, and Quakers to

◈ Who Should Vote? The Putney Debates ◈

During the English revolution the radicals differed sharply among them-
selves on numerous political and religious issues, one of the most crucial
being the extent of the parliamentary franchise. During a debate in the
army council at Putney in the autumn of 1648, the crucial issue was
whether the right to vote should be limited to male property owners.

Henry Ireton: It is not fit that . . . the persons who shall make the law in the kingdom
. . . have not a permanent fixed interest in the kingdom. . . .

John Wildman: Our case is to be considered thus, that we have been under slavery. . . .
Our very laws were made by our conquerors. . . . We are now engaged
for our freedom; that's the end of Parliaments. . . . Every person in
England has as clear a right to elect his representative as the greatest person in England. I conceive that's the undeniable maxim of government:
that all government is in the free consent of the people. . . .

Ireton: If a foreigner comes within this kingdom . . . that man may very well be
content to submit himself to the law of the land: that is, the law that is
made by those people that have a property, a fixed property, in the
land. . . . A man ought to be subject to a law [to which he] did not give
his consent, but with this reservation, that if this man do think himself
dissatisfied to be subject to this law he may go into another kingdom.
And so the same reason does extend . . . to that man that has no permanent interest in the kingdom. . . .

Edward Sexby: We have engaged in this kingdom and ventured our lives, and it was all
for this: to recover our birthrights and privileges. . . . We have had little
propriety in the kingdom as to our estates, yet we have had a birthright.
But it seems now [that] except a man have a fixed estate in this kingdom,
he has no right in this kingdom.

Source: After C. H. Firth, ed., *The Clarke Papers*, vol. 1 (London: Camden Society, 1891), pp. 317–323.

---

preach and publish their views in a manner hitherto impossible. Of these groups, however, only the Quakers,
with their rejection of a professional ministry and the
sacraments, were relatively comfortable with active female participation in ministerial activities. Quaker
women crisscrossed England carrying their message of
the Inner Light, and the more daring extended their
work as far afield as Ireland, Portugal, Malta, the West
Indies, and the American colonies, including Massachusetts, which expelled or hanged them. Two Quaker
women even went to Adrianople in a futile attempt to
convert the Turkish sultan.

The most influential Quaker woman, as well as one
of the key figures in the Society of Friends, as the Quakers called themselves, was Margaret Fell (1614–1702),
daughter of a Lancashire gentleman. Although she and
her first husband, the attorney Thomas Fell, were
Congregationalists, the Quaker founder George Fox
(1624–1691) persuaded her to adopt his views in 1652,
after which she held Quaker meetings in her home. The
mother of eight children, she was at first unable to become a traveling minister, but she provided the Friends
with an even more important contribution by her extensive correspondence with Quakers of both sexes who
sought her advice on religious questions. Enormously
influential in shaping the Quaker movement and its
ideals, she frequently argued the Friends' case in asser-
tive letters to non-Quaker clergymen and judges.

Fell's wide-ranging activities included the authorship
of numerous pamphlets, several of which were translated into Dutch, Hebrew, and Latin. She pleaded with
Oliver Cromwell and King Charles II for religious toleration, petitioned the Rump Parliament with 7,000 other
women for an end to mandatory tithing, and tirelessly
worked for the release of imprisoned Quakers. She was
jailed several times, once for four years, because of her
religious beliefs. Among her special concerns was the
conversion of the Jews to Christianity, a cause for which
she wrote five pamphlets, including *A Call unto the Seed
of Israel*. Her best-known work, *Women's Speaking Jus-*

CRISIS AND CULTURE, 1598–1670

Wars and rebellions	Writers	Artists and musicians
End of the Anglo-Spanish War (1604)	Cervantes (1547–1616)	Caravaggio (1573–1610)
Russia's "Time of Troubles" (1598–1613)	Shakespeare (1564–1616)	El Greco (c. 1541–1614)
Portuguese revolt (1640)	Lope de Vega (1562–1635)	Rubens (1577–1640)
Catalan rebellion (1640–1652)	Grotius (1583–1645)	Monteverdi (1567–1643)
English civil wars (1642–1648)	Descartes (1596–1650)	
Revolts in Sicily and Naples (1647)	Pascal (1623–1662)	Velázquez (1599–1660)
Dutch crisis (1648–1650)		
Cossack revolt in Poland (1648–1654)	Molière (1622–1673)	Rembrandt (1606–1669)
First Dutch War (1652–1654)	Milton (1608–1674)	Schütz (1585–1672)
Second Dutch War (1665–1667)	Spinoza (1632–1677)	
Cossack revolt in Russia (1667–1670)	Hobbes (1588–1679)	Bernini (1598–1680)

tified, which argued for the right of women to preach and prophesy, helped lay the foundation for the establishment of Quaker women's meetings.

Soon after her husband died in 1658, Fell began traveling throughout England on behalf of the Society. In 1669 she married George Fox, partly to end unfounded rumors of an illicit relationship between them but also to symbolize the union of male and female Quakers. Until her death in 1702 she remained active in the Society's work, particularly its women's meetings. The example that she and other sectarian women set made it difficult to force them back into their traditional places in the home, the shop, and the field. Nevertheless, after 1660, with the revolutionary crisis in England essentially concluded, only the Quakers allowed women to preach. In the 1680s and 1690s a flurry of protofeminist works appeared in England by writers such as Mary Astell, but so successful was the restoration of traditional male authority in the 1660s that the new writers were content to plead only for their spiritual equality with men. Viewed in this context, the work and careers of Margaret Fell and her colleagues were an extraordinary product of the midcentury crisis.

Central and Eastern Europe

Although the institutions of the Holy Roman Empire survived the Thirty Years' War and the Peace of Westphalia, the more powerful German princes subsequently went their own way, leaving the emperors to govern the small German states and their own patrimony in Austria, Bohemia, and Hungary. Increasingly, they concentrated on ruling through ancestral institutions, especially the Austrian Chancellery—where Habsburg policy was formulated—rather than imperial institutions. The result was the gradual establishment of a Danubian state governed from Vienna and mostly Catholic in religion. Because the emperors shared power with the landed aristocracy,

the peasant rebellions of the 1640s and 1650s were doomed, and the empire avoided a serious crisis.

Much of the unrest in central and eastern Europe was sparked by the gradual enserfment of the peasants in the sixteenth and seventeenth centuries. The process of enserfing, carried out by the landed aristocracy with the acquiescence of the monarchs, was intended both to increase agricultural production, particularly for the market in western Europe resulting from the increase in population, and to end the mobility of peasants by binding them to the land. Whereas peasants in western Europe might suffer from heavy debts and eviction from their lands, their counterparts in eastern Europe not only lost their freedom of movement but were also saddled with increasingly heavy burdens, including personal labor on landlords' estates and financial exactions that covered virtually every aspect of their lives. Widespread misery engendered social upheaval.

Social Unrest in Poland

In common with most of the major states in western Europe, Poland and Russia experienced crises in the mid-1600s. In the case of Poland, the centralization of royal authority was not a factor, for the country was thoroughly fragmented. Real power lay in the hands of the nobles, who secured the principle of elective monarchy in 1572. Their assembly, the Sejm, met at least every two years to determine policy. Poland was also religiously split between Catholics, Greek Orthodox, Jews, and adherents of the Uniate church, who recognized the pope but worshiped according to Greek rites. Under Sigismund III (1587–1632), known as the King of the Jesuits, Catholics tried to destroy Polish Protestantism, causing a civil war in which the Orthodox Cossacks allied with the Protestants. The Jews were cruelly victimized by the wave of religious persecution, with as many as 100,000 murdered in the pogroms, or organized massacres, of the decade 1648–1658.

The Cossacks, free herdsmen and peasants, were the

major cause of unrest in both Poland and Russia. In 1648 one of the great Cossack leaders, Bogdan Khmelnitsky, ignited a major revolt against the Polish government, partly in defense of the Orthodox faith and partly because of economic grievances. In 1654 Khmelnitsky and his supporters in the Ukraine offered their allegiance to the Russian tsar and were incorporated into the Russian state. Refusing to accept the loss of the Ukraine, Poland went to war twice until peace was finally achieved in 1667 by partitioning the Ukraine between Russia and Poland.

Russia: Centralization and Turmoil

The roots of Russia's troubles in the seventeenth century stemmed primarily from the imposition of serfdom and the centralizing work of Ivan IV, "the Terrible" (1533–1584). When Ivan assumed control of Russia in 1547 at the age of 16, he was crowned "Caesar (*tsar*) of all the Russias." He ruled by divine right in a land dominated by an Orthodox faith that stressed the subservience of the church to the state. At first he governed well,

consulting with the great nobles, or boyars, formulating a new law code, instituting direct trade with western Europe, and convening Russia's first consultative assembly, the *zemski sobor*. In the late 1550s, however, he became increasingly paranoid and vindictive. Setting aside a portion of Russia exclusively for himself—the *oprichnina*, or "separate realm"—he used the *oprichnina's* black-garbed military force of 6,000 to brutalize his opponents. Boyars who resisted him were summarily imprisoned and executed, and their estates were confiscated. Ivan tortured priests, slaughtered his enemies while they worshiped, and in a rage killed one of his own sons. Towns were burned, and large numbers of people were forcibly resettled on the frontiers. Following his death in 1584, he was succeeded by his weak son, Fedor I, who died in 1598 without an heir. Russia was plunged into a period of turmoil known as the Time of Troubles. While the boyars struggled to regain their power, peasants rioted, and both the Poles and the Swedes intervened militarily.

Dismayed at the civil war and foreign intervention, the *zemski sobor* resolved the feuding over the crown by awarding it in 1613 to Ivan's grandnephew, 17-year-old Mikhail Romanov. The new dynasty would rule Russia

◉ Ivan the Terrible ◉

One of the earliest descriptions of the court of Tsar Ivan IV, "the Terrible," underscores the extent to which he ruled by inculcating respect and fear in his subjects.

This emperor uses great familiarity, as well unto all his nobles and subjects, as also unto strangers who serve him either in his wars or in occupations: for his pleasure is that they shall dine oftentimes in the year in his presence, and besides that he is oftentimes abroad, either at one church or another, and walking with his noble men abroad. And by this means he is not only beloved of his nobles and commons, but also had in great dread and fear through all his dominions, so that I think no prince in Christendom is more feared by his own [people] than he is, nor yet better beloved. For if he bids any of his dukes go, they will run; if he gives any evil or angry word to any of them, the party will not come into his majesty's presence again for a long time if he be not sent for, but will fain . . . to be very sick, and will let the hair of his head grow very long, without either cutting or shaving, which is an evident token that he is in the emperor's displeasure: for when they be in their prosperity, they account it a shame to wear long hair, in consideration whereof they used to have their heads shaven. . . .

   He delights not greatly in hawking, hunting, or any other pastime, nor in hearing instruments or music, but sets . . . his whole delight upon two things: first, to serve God, as undoubtedly he is very devout in his religion, and the second, how to subdue and conquer his enemies.

Source: R. Hakluyt, ed., *The Principal Navigations, Voyages, Traffiques and Discoveries of the English Nation,* vol. 2 (Glasgow: MacLehose & Sons, 1903), pp. 438–439.

Tsar Ivan the Terrible of Russia, as depicted in a contemporary portrait. The period between his reign and that of Mikhail I was an age of turmoil known as the Time of Troubles. [National Museum, Copenhagen]

until its overthrow in the 1917 revolution. Rather than risk their estates in more civil war, the boyars cooperated with the first Romanovs, enabling them to finish the work of bureaucratic centralization. In return the tsars allowed the boyars to complete the process of enserfing the peasants. Together they placed the overwhelming burden of taxation on the peasants, whose rate was 100 times greater in 1640 than it had been a century earlier.

In a period when peasant disorders were endemic, the greatest peasant uprising in seventeenth-century Europe erupted in 1667. Incited by the Cossack Stenka Razin, runaway serfs and Cossacks proclaimed a message of freedom, equality, and land for all. Stenka led his undisciplined followers up the Volga River, inciting peasant uprisings and replacing local governments with Cossack rule. His ships attacked Muslim villages on the Caspian Sea and even defeated a Persian fleet. The tsar's army finally crushed his forces in 1670, a year before Stenka was captured and beheaded. The resulting repression that ended the last of the midcentury crises entailed the death of as many as 100,000 peasants.

Old World Rivalries in a Global Setting

The political struggles that enveloped Europe in the century from 1560 to 1660 had profound consequences for the entire world. By 1660 the two countries that had dominated European expansion in the preceding two centuries—Portugal and Spain—had largely been supplanted by the Dutch, the English, and the French. Spain retained control of most of South and Central America, and Brazil remained in Portuguese hands. North America, however, increasingly became the province of the northwestern European powers who would eventually extend their sway over much of the globe.

The Dutch and English in Asia

The union of Portugal and Spain in 1580 did not materially strengthen what was now their joint effort in the East, but it did highlight the enmity and rivalry between them as Catholic powers and the rising Protestant states of the Netherlands and England. All of the Iberian positions overseas became attractive targets, and Portuguese profits were newly tempting. The Dutch were the first to pick up this challenge effectively in Asia. At this period the Netherlands was a more important center of trade and shipping than England, and Dutch ships had the upper hand in the English Channel. There were more of them, backed by merchant capital earned in trade, and in the course of the sixteenth century they became larger and more powerful, as well as more maneuverable than the Portuguese caravels. Dutch seamen had traveled east on Portuguese ships and learned what they needed to know about sailing to Asia. By the late

1500s their ships began to outnumber those of the Portuguese in Asia, defeating them repeatedly and surpassing them as carriers. Unlike the Portuguese, they concerned themselves only with trade, avoiding any missionary effort or religious conflict, and were generally welcomed as efficient agents to replace the hated Portuguese.

Rival Dutch companies were amalgamated into the Dutch East India Company in 1602, which in the following decades built a highly profitable commercial empire centered on Java, controlling the trade of Southeast Asia far more effectively than the Portuguese had done. Much of this was the work of their able governor-general, Jan Pieterszoon Coen, appointed in 1618, who fixed the naval and administrative capital of the Dutch East Indies at Batavia (now Djakarta), with other bases at strategic points throughout Indonesia and Ceylon, which expelled the Portuguese in 1658. English competitors, excluded from this new empire, increasingly centered their attention on India, while the Dutch successfully competed with them for a share in the trade of mainland Southeast Asia and, more important, at Canton, Formosa, and Nagasaki. Coen and his successors recognized that the long-established trade of Asia would remain in able Asian and Arab hands. They also saw that greater profits could be won by taking whatever part in it they could win, especially in the carrying trade, than by hauling Asian goods to the far smaller European market. The Dutch spice monopoly, however, remained important. Meanwhile, the English East India Company had also been founded, its charter signed by Queen Elizabeth I in December 1600. England was still primarily a country of farmers, unlike the commercially advanced Low Countries, and the scale of its overseas effort was for some time small. The Dutch had little trouble repelling English efforts to break the monopoly of the Asian trade, but the English hung on as minor players at Canton, in some of the mainland Southeast Asian ports, and in India after Dutch attention had shifted to the more profitable East Indies.

The English first concentrated on Surat, where they were obliged to compete with a host of local, Arab, and rival European traders but where much of Indian trade westward was based. The Dutch were not prominent there, and the Mughal governor permitted the English to rent a warehouse. Their ships, though few, were now far more able and maneuverable than those of the Portuguese, and in successive naval battles off Surat in 1612 and 1615 they defeated Portuguese fleets decisively. In 1616 King James I sent Sir Thomas Roe as an ambassador to the Mughal court. Influenced in large part by recent English naval success against both Portuguese and pirates, the emperor, Jahangir, granted the English rights of residence at Surat and limited trade privileges. Roe, however, recognized that the trade goods at Surat were assembled there from all over India, mainly by local merchant networks, and that the most desirable of all, fine cotton cloth of the highest quality and much in demand in Europe, came from Bengal, where the Portuguese and some Dutch traders still had a strong position.

> The number of Portuguese residing there is a good argument for us to seek it; it is a sign that there is good doing. An abbey was ever a token of a rich soil, and stores of crows of plenty of carrion. . . . We must fire them out and maintain our trade at the pike's end.[7]

Thus was foreshadowed the English drive to establish a position in eastern India, the founding of Madras in 1639, and the subsequent rise of English power in Bengal.

Colonial Conflict in the Americas

The Spanish annexation of Portugal in 1580, which was so important for Asia, had less impact on the Americas, where the Portuguese held only Brazil. Because Portuguese settlers, mostly from the islands of the eastern Atlantic, went to Brazil in growing numbers in the seventeenth century, the colonists were strong enough to repulse Dutch and French attempts to establish permanent footholds. Although the Dutch renounced their Brazilian claims in 1661, the French continued their efforts into the eighteenth century, without success. In the meantime, the Dutch began colonizing Guiana, to the north of Brazil, in the 1610s. The Dutch West Indies Company, founded in 1621, subsequently supplied the settlers with slaves for their sugar plantations. The demand for sugar was also a major factor in the colonial efforts of the English and the French in Guiana, the only area in South America where these countries established settlements.

A much stronger challenge to Spanish domination was mounted in the West Indies, strategically important as bases for fleets sailing to and from Mexico and Central America and valuable as well for the raising of tobacco and sugar. The islands attracted so many privateers and smugglers in the late sixteenth century that the Spaniards were forced to build heavy fortifications and organize their shipping in convoys. Beginning with the voyages of John Hawkins in the 1560s, the English intruded themselves into the West Indies trade, though non-Hispanic colonies were not established there until the 1620s. By midcentury the English, Dutch, and French all had colonies in the West Indies, and England added to its holdings when a fleet dispatched by Oliver Cromwell seized Jamaica in 1655. The development of sugar plantations in the mid-1600s meant a growing demand for African slaves, who soon outnumbered Europeans in these "sugar islands."

Apart from Mexico and Florida, where St. Augustine was founded in 1565 to check French incursion, the Spaniards were unable to settle North America. Against a background of deteriorating relations with Spain in the early 1580s, Elizabeth I issued a charter to Sir Walter Raleigh authorizing him to found a North American colony, but his settlement at Roanoke Island lasted only a year. War with Spain prevented further attempts, and not until 1607 did the English establish a permanent colony at Jamestown in Virginia, soon to become famous for its tobacco. Puritan dissatisfaction with the Church of England provided crucial motivation for the founding of colonies at Plymouth (1620) and Massachusetts Bay (1629) in New England, whereas the settlement of Maryland in 1634 was largely made by Catholics. By 1670 English colonies stretched from Maine to South Carolina, the development of which angered Spaniards in Florida.

England's main competitors in North America—the Dutch and the French—could not keep pace. Rebuffed by the Spanish in Florida, the French concentrated their efforts in the north, establishing settlements at Port Royal, Acadia, in 1605, and at Quebec three years later. When France and England went to war in 1627, reverberations were felt in the colonies as Scots from Nova Scotia captured Port Royal and English ships forced Quebec to surrender. Once peace was restored at home, however, both settlements were returned to France in 1632. The decisive struggle for the domination of North America, still more than a century in the future, would not be resolved until 1763.

In the short term the English faced a graver threat from the Dutch, who established New Amsterdam at the mouth of the Hudson River in 1624 and subsequently ended Sweden's bid for a colonial stake on the Delaware River in 1655. Fortunately for the English, however, the Dutch were preoccupied with their Asian trade as well as their African colony on the Cape of Good Hope. The growing commercial and colonial rivalry between the Dutch and the English, which now extended from Asia to the Americas, culminated in a series of three wars, the first of which was instigated by the Rump Parliament in 1652. The Second Dutch War (1665–1667) brought New Jersey and New Amsterdam—henceforth known as New York—to the English and permanently removed the Dutch from North America as a colonial power, though Dutch settlers remained in New York and thousands more made homes in Pennsylvania later in the century. Thereafter, the contest for North America was among the English, the French, and the Spanish, who were exploring northward from Mexico into California. The next three centuries were to demonstrate repeatedly that the struggles for power in Europe could no longer be fought without major ramifications for the rest of the world.

The century that began in 1560 witnessed the failure of Spanish and Austrian attempts to impose hegemony, the former on western and the latter on central Europe. The frequent wars of the period, normally funded by deficit financing and the imposition of onerous taxes on the peasantry, were a major cause of domestic instability. By the mid-1600s every major state in Europe except the Dutch Netherlands underwent a severe crisis: the vicious destruction of the Thirty Years' War in Germany, the Catalan and Portuguese revolts against the government in Madrid, the Fronde in France, the English revolution, and the Cossack uprisings in Poland and Russia. Although the specific conditions differed in each country, certain common themes stand out: reaction against centralized government, the financial burden of war, and, in most areas, religious conflict. Order was restored when monarchs and nobles discovered a common self-interest, though this realization did not lead to political uniformity. Poland retained its feudal monarchy, England brought its sovereign under the rule of law, and France and Russia, their nobles pacified, were governed by absolute monarchs. Of the major European states, only the Dutch Netherlands was a republic, though even there the House of Orange remained very influential. In the end, except for Poland, the costly quest for centralization was successful. With order restored, Europe in the late seventeenth century was threatened by new visions of hegemony, this time in France, but at the same time European expansion around the world offered dramatic new opportunities for commercial and industrial development.

Notes

1. J. H. Elliott, *Imperial Spain, 1469–1716* (New York: New American Library, 1966), p. 250.
2. G. Parker, *Philip II* (London: Hutchinson, 1978), p. 193.
3. D. Howarth, *The Voyage of the Armada: The Spanish Story* (New York: Penguin Books, 1982), p. 23.
4. T. K. Rabb, *The Struggle for Stability in Early Modern Europe* (New York: Oxford University Press, 1975), p. 120.
5. Elliott, *Imperial Spain*, pp. 322–323.
6. R. Zaller, *The Parliament of 1621: A Study in Constitutional Conflict* (Berkeley: University of California Press, 1971), p. 178.
7. J. N. Das Gupta, *India in the Seventeenth Century* (Calcutta: University of Calcutta Press, 1916), p. 212.

Suggestions for Further Reading

Ashton, R. *The English Civil War: Conservatism and Revolution, 1603–1649*. London: Weidenfeld & Nicolson, 1978.

Aylmer, G. E. *Rebellion or Revolution? England, 1640–1660*. New York: Oxford University Press, 1986.

Beik, W. *Absolutism and Society in Seventeenth-Century France: State Power and Provincial Aristocracy in Languedoc*. Cambridge: Cambridge University Press, 1985.

Bergin, J. *Cardinal Richelieu: Power and the Pursuit of Wealth*. New Haven, Conn.: Yale University Press, 1985.

Braudel, F. *The Mediterranean and the Mediterranean World in the Age of Philip II*, trans. S. Reynolds. 2 vols. New York: Harper & Row, 1972–1973.

Buisseret, D. *Henry IV*. London: Allen & Unwin, 1984.

De Vries, J. *European Urbanization, 1500–1800*. Cambridge, Mass.: Harvard University Press, 1984.

Diefendorf, B. *Beneath the Cross: Catholics and Huguenots in Sixteenth-Century Paris*. New York: Oxford University Press, 1991.

Dunn, R. S. *The Age of Religious Wars, 1559–1715*, 2nd ed. New York: Norton, 1979.

Elliott, J. H. *The Revolt of the Catalans: A Study in the Decline of Spain, 1598–1640*. Cambridge: Cambridge University Press, 1963.

————. *Richelieu and Olivares*. Cambridge: Cambridge University Press, 1984.

Elton, G. R. *The Parliament of England, 1559–1581*. Cambridge: Cambridge University Press, 1986.

Fennell, J. L. I. *Ivan the Great of Moscow*. New York: St. Martin's Press, 1961.

Hill, C. *The World Turned Upside Down: Radical Ideas During the English Revolution*. New York: Viking, 1972.

Hirst, D. *Authority and Conflict: England, 1603–1658*. Cambridge, Mass.: Harvard University Press, 1986.

Kamen, H. *Golden Age Spain*. New York: Humanities Press, 1988.

MacCaffrey, W. T. *Queen Elizabeth and the Making of Policy, 1572–1588*. Princeton, N.J.: Princeton University Press, 1981.

————. *The Shaping of the Elizabethan Regime*. Princeton, N.J.: Princeton University Press, 1968.

Maltby, W. S. *Alba*. Berkeley: University of California Press, 1983.

Mattingly, G. *The Armada*. Boston: Houghton Mifflin, 1959.

Parker, G. *Europe in Crisis, 1598–1648*. Brighton: Harvester Press, 1980.

————. *Philip II*. London: Hutchinson, 1978.

————. *The Thirty Years' War*. London: Methuen, 1985.

Pennington, D. H. *Seventeenth-Century Europe*, 2nd ed. London: Longman, 1989.

Rabb, T. K. *The Struggle for Stability in Early Modern Europe*. New York: Oxford University Press, 1975.

Rodriguez-Salgado, M. *The Changing Face of Empire: Charles V, Philip II, and Habsburg Authority, 1551–1559*. Cambridge: Cambridge University Press, 1988.

Rowen, H. H. *John de Witt: Statesman of the "True Freedom."* Cambridge: Cambridge University Press, 1986.

Russell, C. *The Causes of the English Civil War*. New York: Oxford University Press, 1990.

Schama, S. *The Embarrassment of Riches: An Interpretation of Dutch Culture in the Golden Age*. Berkeley: University of California Press, 1988.

Smith, H. L. *Reason's Disciples: Seventeenth-Century English Feminists*. Champaign: University of Illinois Press, 1982.

Stone, L. *The Causes of the English Revolution, 1529–1642*. London: Routledge & Kegan Paul, 1972.

Stradling, R. A. *Europe and the Decline of Spain: A Study of the Spanish System, 1580–1720*. London: Allen & Unwin, 1981.

————. *Philip IV and the Government of Spain, 1621–1665*. Cambridge: Cambridge University Press, 1988.

Tapié, V. L. *France in the Age of Louis XIII and Richelieu*, trans. D. M. Lockie. New York: Praeger, 1975.

Tracy, J. D. *Holland Under Habsburg Rule, 1506–1566*. Berkeley: University of California Press, 1990.

Wilson, C. *The Transformation of Europe, 1558–1648*. Berkeley: University of California Press, 1976.

Zagorin, P. *The Court and the Country: The Beginning of the English Revolution*. New York: Atheneum, 1970.

————. *Rebels and Rulers, 1500–1660*. 2 vols. Cambridge: Cambridge University Press, 1982.

Islamic Empires in the Early Modern World

The sixteenth century witnessed extraordinary events in the Middle East and Asia. Under Suleiman the Magnificent (1520–1566), the Ottoman armies made dramatic advances in Syria and North Africa despite their failure to capture Vienna and strike into the heartland of Europe. Under Suleiman, Ottoman imperial power was rivaled only by the Chinese, and despite the Ottomans' later decline, especially in the eighteenth and nineteenth centuries, they remained a force to be reckoned with into the early twentieth century.

Meanwhile, in India the oppressive rule of the Delhi sultanate gave way early in the sixteenth century to a new Islamic dynasty of conquest, the Mughals, who ruled northern India as well as Afghanistan and parts of southern India from 1526 to 1707. At the height of their power, the Mughals restored and added to India's imperial tradition, brought about a notable flowering of cul-

The coronation of Sultan Selim I, "the Grim." This is a detail from a sixteenth-century manuscript illustration. [Giraudon/Art Resource]

ture, and reestablished a large measure of political unity. The sixteenth century also saw the restoration of imperial grandeur in Iran under the Safavids, particularly Shah Abbas the Great (1587–1629), who freed western and northern Iran from Ottoman control. As in western Europe, the late sixteenth and early seventeenth centuries were a time of cultural brilliance in the Middle East, India, and Iran.

The Ottoman Empire

While the Delhi sultans were at the peak of their power in India, a new dynasty of sultans, the Ottomans, was established among another group of Turks who had moved westward into Asia Minor. For nearly three centuries the Ottomans expanded their conquests, until in 1683 they ranged from Hungary to the Persian Gulf and from the Crimea to North Africa and the coasts of Arabia. The followers of the dynasty's founder, Osman (1299–1326), were mostly ghazis, Islamic warriors who saw their sacred duty in extending the faith by attacking unbelievers. Motivated by religion and a thirst for booty, disciplined by a ghazi code of honor, and aided by the weakness of their enemies, the Ottomans were successful out of all proportion to their relatively small numbers. Their success was also aided by their tolerance of other faiths after their first conquests and by the disgust of many Byzantine subjects with the corrupt and oppressive imperial government (see Chapter 8).

From their newly conquered base in western Asia Minor, the Ottomans began in the 1300s by extending their sway over other Turkish states and Byzantine territories in the rest of Asia Minor and adjoining areas. A request for their help by one of the feuding political factions in Constantinople gave them an opportunity to establish a bridgehead on the European side of the Dardanelles, from which they later refused to retreat. Taking advantage of political chaos in the Balkans as well as their own military superiority, the Ottomans defeated the Serbs, Bulgars, and Macedonians in the late 1300s, opening up the Balkans to Turkish immigrants. Europeans were now sufficiently alarmed to send a crusading army. The Ottoman leader Bayezid I, "the Thunderbolt," who had allegedly threatened to feed his horse at the altar of St. Peter's Basilica in Rome, took only three hours to defeat the Europeans at Nicopolis in 1396. As Bayezid prepared to attack the Byzantine capital at Constantinople, the Ottomans themselves became the victims of a new Turco-Mongol invasion led by Tamerlane, who defeated them near Ankara in 1402.

After Tamerlane withdrew and order was restored, the Ottomans renewed their conquests, defeating the Greeks and finally taking Constantinople in 1453. Under Mehmet II, "the Conqueror" (1451–1481), the city, renamed Istanbul, was rebuilt and repopulated with new immigrants, including Jews and Christians as well as Muslims.

♛ MEHMET THE CONQUEROR

Mehmet hoped to make his new capital the center of a world empire far greater than that to which Alexander the Great and Julius Caesar had aspired. In this imperial state Mehmet ruled supreme. He made war—the vehicle to expand his empire—the dominant preoccupation of Ottoman society.

Because of his imperialistic ambitions and his autocratic rule, Mehmet's life was increasingly endangered by foreign agents as well as domestic zealots. The Vene-

Mehmet II, who conquered Constantinople and renamed it Istanbul, as painted by a contemporary artist. [Topkapi Palace Museum, Istanbul]

tian republic organized at least a dozen attempts to assassinate him, but Mehmet's espionage network successfully protected him. Despite the threats to his life, he frequently rode through Istanbul accompanied by only two guards or walked the streets in the company of his slaves. But the strain eventually took its toll, turning the once affable sultan into a suspicious, reclusive despot, afraid even to eat with his viziers for fear of being poisoned. Stories of his cruelty abound. When the Italian Renaissance painter Gentile Bellini showed Mehmet his painting of the beheading of John the Baptist, Mehmet criticized Bellini for making John's neck extend too far and proved his point by having a slave beheaded in Bellini's presence. A serious offender against Mehmet's laws might have a long, sharp pole driven up his rectum with a mallet; if that failed to kill him, the pole, with the victim on it, was erected. Between his military campaigns and his domestic persecution, Mehmet may have been responsible for nearly 30,000 deaths a year during his reign.

Despite the harsher aspects of his rule, Mehmet was tolerant when it came to matters of religion. Perhaps this was due in part to the fact that his mother, who was of Greek, Slavic, or Italian ancestry, had been raised a Christian. Mehmet himself made some effort to comprehend Christian teachings, at least as a means of understanding the faith of a substantial number of his subjects. His own preference was the Shi'ite version of Islam, but as the ruler of a largely Sunni state, he publicly embraced Sunni tenets. Mehmet treated the Jews well; his Jewish physician, Maestro Jacopo, was also a trusted financial adviser.

The Sufis' religious fraternities, or dervishes, did not fare as well. As mystical religious ascetics roughly akin to Christian monks or friars, they were popular with the masses because of their pastoral concerns, their poverty and charitable work, their mystical rites, and in some cases their cult of saints. Because their popularity made Mehmet suspicious, however, he curtailed their activity and occasionally even exiled their leaders, whom he denounced as insane, and confiscated their property.

Mehmet's personality combined intellectual curiosity with superstition and cold calculation. Given his vast imperial ambition—the state he ruled was roughly equivalent to the Byzantine Empire at its height—it was only natural that he should be interested in the study of geography, history, and military strategy. As he grew older, he increasingly enjoyed the company of poets and scholars. Yet he was also keenly superstitious and hired Persian astrologers to prepare horoscopes for him, sometimes even using their predictions as the basis for military decisions. To an artist such as Bellini, who painted his portrait (which the sultan commissioned in defiance of Islamic law), Mehmet attributed virtually supernatural power. Reinforcing the coldness of Mehmet's personality was the constant threat of assassination as well as his refusal to become involved in long-term relationships with women. Sexually, he enjoyed the company of women and boys, but domestic intimacy he deliberately shunned. Although his modern biographer calls Mehmet's personality "demonic," today many Turks regard the Conqueror as the greatest of the sultans and a holy man who can still intercede with Allah on their behalf.

Selim the Grim, Suleiman the Magnificent, and Ottoman Expansion

In the decades after the fall of Constantinople the Ottoman armies completed the conquest of Greece and the Balkans. They also established a foothold in the Crimea by supplanting colonies founded by the Genoese so that by the late 1400s the Black Sea was virtually a Turkish lake. In the following century two of the greatest sultans, Selim I, "the Grim" (1512–1520), and Suleiman I, "the Magnificent" (1520–1566), made major new advances. Selim first had to turn his attention eastward, where the expansionist Shi'ite regime in Safavid Iran threatened the Ottomans and offended their Sunni orthodoxy. After pushing back the Safavids, Selim overran Syria, Palestine, and Egypt. These conquests forced the sultan to assume responsibility for protecting the Islamic holy places in Mecca and Medina, now threatened by the advance of the Portuguese into the Red Sea and the Indian Ocean in their quest for bases along the route to India.

Suleiman continued his predecessor's expansionistic program. In a series of brilliant campaigns he captured the island citadel of Rhodes; Belgrade on the Danube, gateway to central Europe; and much of Hungary. He besieged Vienna, but his forces lacked both the supplies and the resolve to take the city, and he was forced to retreat in 1529. Elsewhere his armies were victorious in North Africa as far west as Algeria, and in the Middle East, where they captured Baghdad. In the course of these campaigns Suleiman became an ally of France against the Habsburgs. As a consequence France gained special trade privileges in the Ottoman Empire, and later it acted as protector of Catholic subjects in the empire and of the Christian holy places in Palestine.

Ottoman expansion continued for another century, though at a much slower pace because of domestic conflict, a stronger European maritime presence in the Mediterranean, bitter rivalry with Iran, and a succession of ineffectual sultans. After the Ottomans conquered Cyprus in 1570, the Holy League, comprised of Spain, Venice, and the papacy, successfully challenged and defeated the Ottoman fleet in 1571 at Lepanto, off western Greece. The last major Ottoman conquest in the west was the island of Crete in 1669. A second assault on

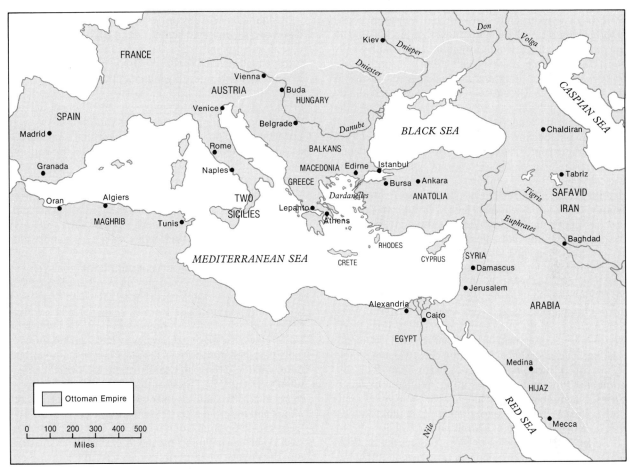

20.1 The Empire of Suleiman I

Vienna failed in 1683 (see Chapter 23), effectively marking the end of Ottoman expansion. From this point on, the Ottomans, now on the defensive and surpassed by European scientific and technological advances, repeatedly lost territory. The remains of their empire finally crumbled after their defeat in World War I.

Ottoman Society

The sultans who presided over the empire had supreme authority in matters civil, military, and religious, subject only to divine law. Interpretation of that law was therefore critical, and for this the sultans turned to the grand mufti of Istanbul, a legal expert who interpreted sacred law and issued legal opinions on the secular decrees of the sultans, with the consensus of other religious leaders. Like their counterparts in Europe and Asia, the sultans ruled with the aid of an advisory council, called the divan, which met regularly to handle petitions and to supervise the affairs of state. Beginning in the late 1400s,

the sultans rarely met with the divan, though they sometimes listened to its proceedings behind a grille in the wall of the council chamber. Presiding over the sessions was the grand vizier, the highest-ranking official in the government after the sultan.

Below the divan a highly centralized and immense bureaucracy administered the affairs of state. Because the sultans had huge harems, the problem of succession was potentially explosive, as in Mughal India and Iran. Mehmet II solved the problem by creating the "law of fratricide," which necessitated that each new sultan execute all but one of his brothers and half brothers; one was usually left alive in case a sultan died without a surviving heir. Perhaps no sultan was more thorough in his adherence to this practice than Selim the Grim, who killed his brothers, nephews, and sons, with the exception of his designated heir, Suleiman. Beginning in the mid-1600s, the Ottomans ended the practice of fratricide in preference for selecting the sultan's eldest son as heir. Other sons were made prisoners in palace chambers called the "cage" and kept politically powerless.

A major responsibility of the sultan was to dispense justice, symbolized by a high "tower of justice" in the imperial palace from which the sultan could theoretically see officials acting unjustly and punish them accordingly. In the divan the grand vizier dispensed justice in the sultan's name. Because the empire was ruled chiefly according to Islamic sacred law, even the sultan's decrees had to be rendered in its spirit, and the judicial system in practice involved a close intermingling of legal and religious principles. The two chief justices, second in legal significance only to the grand mufti of Istanbul, were the leaders of the ulema, a body of learned men that included judges, teachers, prayer leaders known as imams, and muftis, who specialized in interpreting the law for judges and public officials. Although the grand mufti was originally not part of the judiciary in order to ensure his objectivity, in time he came to dominate it, even to the point of naming the chief justice.

These officials were drawn from the sultan's ruling class, and most belonged to an elite group known as the "true Ottomans." This group consisted solely of Muslims who served the state and "knew the Ottoman way"; that is, they were Turkish and conformed to Ottoman customs. Membership in the ruling class was not denied by reason of birth; regardless of origin, one could become an Ottoman by acquiring the stipulated qualifications. In an empire that included a wide variety of races and cultures, this was important in attracting support and conveying a sense of shared power.

Beneath the ruling class were the *reaya*, or "subjects"—peasants, townspeople, and nomads, both Muslim and non-Muslim. They were legally distinct from the ruling class. Because sons of that class generally inherited their father's social status, they perpetuated the oligarchy, provided that they acquired the necessary education to serve the state, although recruits from below could be promoted on merit.

The vast numbers of subject communities enveloped by Ottoman expansion were essentially allowed to govern themselves and to retain their institutions as long as they paid their taxes and provided the sultan with military and administrative personnel. The Ottomans even permitted their subjects to retain their traditional religious loyalties. Non-Muslims, including Jews and Greek Orthodox Christians, were organized into communities known as *millets*, which served as the main agencies for tax collection, education, and civil matters such as marriage and inheritance. To encourage the conversion of non-Muslims to Islam, the Ottomans imposed a special tax on all "infidels." Muslim men were permitted to marry non-Muslim women, who did not have to convert, but the children of such unions had to be raised as Muslims. In general the Ottomans proved more tolerant than Christian monarchs in Europe, who subjected heretics and Jews to forcible conversion and sometimes expelled and even executed them.

A characteristic feature of Ottoman society was the institution of slavery. Slavery, as the Ottomans practiced it, was substantially different from the brutal servitude Europeans imposed on blacks in the New World. It was less menial and offered greater opportunities. As elsewhere in the Middle East and parts of Asia, slaves were employed primarily as personal and household attendants or were given assignments in the military and bureaucracy. Some eventually established themselves as judges, philosophers, and poets. A sixteenth-century sultan typically had between 20,000 and 25,000 civil servants and troops in his household, all nominally slaves; the grand vizier had 1,700 in 1561. Slavery was not necessarily considered demeaning in all its circumstances, for some sultans were sons of slaves in their fathers' harems, and sometimes even the grand vizier was a slave.

Because Islamic law did not permit the enslavement of Muslims, slaves necessarily consisted of prisoners of war, people the Ottomans purchased in North Africa and Spain, and young males from Christian families within the empire who were recruited in a periodic levy. This levy, known as the *devshirme*, was imposed by the sultan's personal authority as a special tax, usually on one household in 40 in order to distribute the burden as equitably as possible. The youths selected had to be unmarried and typically between the ages of 8 and 18; orphans and only sons were exempt. Some parents offered bribes to keep their sons out of the levy; some young men resorted to similar means to get in. Once in Istanbul, the youths were forcibly converted to Islam and circumcised; the most promising were then designated to receive special education so that they might assume appointment to a high government office. Many acquired membership in the janissaries, the most elite unit of the Ottoman army; members became especially proficient in the use of firearms, and originally they were not permitted to marry.

Ottoman society, like nearly all societies of the time, was largely geared to benefit the males. Muslim custom permitted polygamy, and women usually wore veils. In sharp contrast with the Byzantine Empire and the western European states, women were excluded as rulers. Wives of the sultans were instead confined to harems, which were organized hierarchically like the rest of society. Presided over by the sultan's mother, who was assisted by mothers of the sultan's children and royal favorites, harems were guarded by eunuchs, men castrated as boys so as to assure no risk of their plotting to put their sons in power and to prevent them from engaging in sexual misconduct with harem members. From the 1500s onward, virtually all eunuchs in the empire were African blacks.

From their position in the harem, powerful women were sometimes able to dominate the government, particularly in the "sultanate of the women" in the mid-

◉ *Devshirme:* Turks Drafting Christians ◉

Europeans were intrigued and horrified by the Turkish practice known as the devshirme, *by which Christian boys were drafted into slavery by the state. In 1585 a Venetian ambassador described it in these words.*

There are two types of Turks. One is composed of people native-born of Turkish parents, while the other is made up of renegades who are sons of Christians. The latter group were taken by force in the raids . . . on Christian lands, or else harshly levied in their villages from the sultan's non-Muslim subjects and taxpayers. They are taken while still boys, and either persuaded or forced to be circumcised and made Muslims. It is the custom . . . to send men throughout the country every fourth or fifth year to levy one-tenth of the boys, just as if they were so many sheep, and after they have made Turks of these boys they train each one according to his abilities. . . .

Not only is the Turkish army made up of these renegades, but at one time they used to win all the chief positions in the government . . . and the highest commands in the armed forces, because ancient custom forbids that the sons of Turks should hold these jobs. But the present Grand Signor ignores this custom and chooses whatever men he wants. . . .

After they have been taken away as young boys the renegades are sent to different places to be trained according to the jobs they will be given. The handsomest, most wide-awake ones are placed in the seraglio [palace] of the Grand Signor, or in one of two oth-ers . . . and there they are all prepared . . . to rise to the highest government offices. . . .

The other boys . . . [are] in a kind of seminary for the janissary corps. . . . They make them drudge day and night, and they give them no beds to sleep on and very little food. When these boys begin to shave they make them janissaries.

Source: J. C. Davis, ed. and trans., *Pursuit of Power: Venetian Ambassadors' Reports on Spain, Turkey, and France in the Age of Philip II, 1560–1600* (New York: Harper Torchbooks, 1970), pp. 135–136.

1600s. One of the most influential of these women was Turhan, mother of Mehmet IV (1648–1687), who seized power by having the boy's grandmother murdered. Beyond the upper reaches of the imperial harem, however, women were excluded from places of power and even from many of the Islamic religious ceremonies.

Despite their general exclusion from political power, Muslim women in the Ottoman world enjoyed a variety of rights, including the ability to hold and control property without interference from fathers, husbands, or male relatives. This right extended even to property that was part of their dowry, a right not accorded to French women as late as the nineteenth century. Legally Ottoman women could execute wills, defend their rights in court, and testify, although a man's testimony was considered twice as valid. No Muslim woman could be forced to marry, although various pressures could be applied to attain the family's end. Although divorce was rare among Muslims, a woman who received one was entitled to retain her property. Thus, although Ottoman women shared the generally low status of women elsewhere, they did possess some basic economic rights and at least a degree of social choice.

❦ ISTANBUL: "THIS PLACE THAT IS LIKE PARADISE"

Before the Muslim conquest in 1453, the population of Constantinople had declined to some 40,000 inhabitants, and it fell to 10,000 immediately thereafter, but within 25 years it had rebounded to nearly 100,000, including its suburbs. By 1600 Istanbul, as the Turks called it, was larger than any city in Europe, with a population of at least 700,000. The initial impetus for the city's growth came from its conqueror, Mehmet II, who was determined to make his new capital the greatest in the world. To increase the population, he offered to return the property of refugees and to give them freedom to work and worship if they came back, which a great many did.

Mehmet also ordered nearby provincial governors to send 4,000 families to Istanbul (although this goal was never fully achieved), and he attracted merchants and artisans from such conquered cities as Corinth and Argos in Greece and towns in the Crimea. Because of their wealth and trading skills, Jews were also encouraged to emigrate to Istanbul. By 1478 they were the third largest group in the capital, comprising some 10 percent of the population, behind Muslims (58 percent) and Greek Christians (23 percent). To help feed the burgeoning population, Mehmet settled 30,000 captive Balkan peasants, whom he virtually enslaved, in villages near the capital.

Because much of the city had been ruined during the siege, the Ottomans initiated a massive building program that included two palaces and a grand mosque. Around the latter there developed a hospital, an almshouse, and a major center of higher education that provided instruction in theology, law, medicine, and the sciences. The famous Christian church, Hagia Sophia, was transformed into a mosque, minarets were gradually added, the Byzantine mosaics were plastered with a gray limewash, and verses from the Koran were substituted as decorations. The grandest of the new mosques was constructed in the early 1550s at the behest of Suleiman, who employed the leading Ottoman architect, Sinan, de-

signer of more than 300 buildings. When his masterpiece was finished, Sinan reportedly told Suleiman: "I have built for thee, O emperor, a mosque which will remain on the face of the earth till the day of judgment."[1] In addition to such grandiose structures, the Ottomans commissioned many public works, including new roads, bridges, and aqueducts.

The commercial heart of Istanbul was the grand bazaar or *bedestan*, built at Mehmet's command. Consisting of a monumental building with stone domes and iron doors—a secure depository for valuable goods, jewelry, and money—the bazaar was surrounded by groups of shops lining the roads that branched out into the city. Each group of shops housed merchants or artisans who specialized in a particular kind of goods. Mehmet's complex, including the 118 shops in the bedestan and the 984 surrounding it, is today known as Istanbul's covered market.

Crucial to the reconstruction of the capital were the *imarets*, each of which was typically an endowed complex consisting of a mosque, an institution of higher

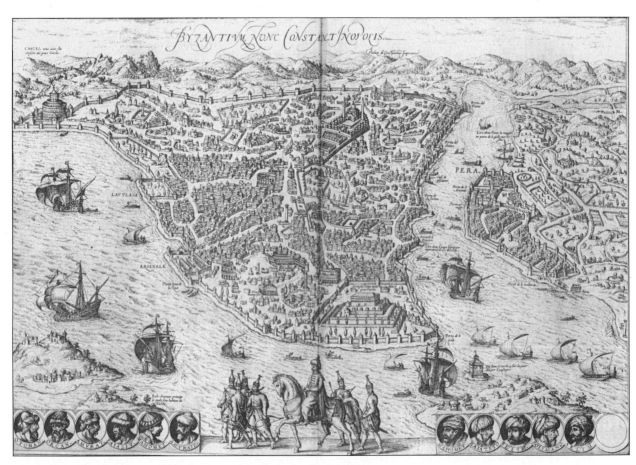

A view of Istanbul in the sixteenth century. Note the natural defenses of the city as well as the wall at the top of the painting. [British Library]

learning or *medrese*, a hospital, travelers' lodgings, and appropriate roads and bridges. In 1459 Mehmet required the most prominent citizens to establish imarets in Istanbul, and in time these complexes became the centers of new quarters or suburbs. Istanbul, in fact, grew so rapidly that in the seventeenth century the sultans tried to restrict its expansion and generally succeeded in slowing the rate of growth. By comparison, the English monarchs Elizabeth I and James I were less successful in their efforts to halt the growth of London. A truly cosmopolitan city unlike anything in Europe, some 40 percent of Istanbul's population in the seventeenth century was non-Muslim.

Urban Life

Though Istanbul was unmistakably the preeminent jewel in the Ottoman crown, a host of other cities contributed to the richness, productivity, and cultural heritage of the empire. Among them by the late 1600s were some of the great cities of antiquity: Alexandria and Baghdad, Athens and Jerusalem. Others, such as Sarajevo and Tatar-Pazarjik in the Balkans, developed from imarets founded in the fourteenth and fifteenth centuries by frontier lords. The largest Ottoman city and commercial center in the Balkans was Edirne (now in European Turkey), which was strategically located on the major overland trade routes between Istanbul and Hungary, Bosnia, and Greece. Its counterpart in Anatolia—Bursa, center of a thriving silk industry—sat astride the overland routes from Europe and western Asia Minor to the Middle East, Iran, and India.

The heart of every major Ottoman city was a great mosque and a bedestan, around which trade centers developed. The endowment of imarets played a key role in the growth of such cities as Edirne and Bursa, underscoring the importance of substantive charitable giving in the expansion of Ottoman urban life and commerce.

Although the people were officially divided into two groups, Muslim and non-Muslim, in practice socioeconomic divisions had little to do with religion. Merchants and artisans in the towns had the same rights, though in theory non-Muslims were required to dress distinctively and were not allowed to ride horses or own slaves. In fact, however, such restrictions were ineffective. Each religious group—Muslim, Jewish, and Christian—was housed in its own quarter, as were the gypsies. Each quarter was typically organized around a religious center or a bedestan and was a community in its own right, its members linked most often by distinctive religious or economic ties. Normally the religious leader of each quarter—imam, rabbi, or priest—was responsible for contacts with the imperial government and would, for example, make the sultan's decrees known to the people. Each quarter had to provide for its own night watchmen, lamplighters, street cleaners, and volunteer firefighters.

Although the Ottoman city was at root a collection of distinctive communities, there were municipal officials who coordinated common services, such as street paving and repair, water supply, building regulations, and refuse disposal. These officials were not, however, representatives of a formal municipal organization, as in modern America, but agents of the imperial government.

Economy and Culture

Economic life in Ottoman cities was organized around the guilds, whose members comprised a substantial part of the population. Like their medieval European counterparts, the Ottoman guilds regulated their activities, including standards, prices, and competition, and cared for the welfare of their members. They also engaged in a wide variety of social activities ranging from processions and festivals to the provision of relief to the needy. Some guilds were restricted to adherents of a particular religious group, while others embraced Muslims, Jews, and Christians. As in Europe, masters trained apprentices, who in time became journeymen and ultimately masters, so long as their number did not become excessive. Some guilds hired women, principally to wind silk and spin cotton. Other guilds, such as that of the weavers in Bursa, relied heavily on slave labor, promising freedom to slaves who wove a stipulated quantity of cloth. As in Renaissance Florence, these guilds also hired free labor.

The range of guilds was extensive, embracing the usual skilled artisans as well as fishermen, minters, scribes, and religious men. There were even guilds in Istanbul that provided snow, ice, and water from the mountains or made sherbet in such exotic flavors as rhubarb, rose, and lotus. All guilds were subject to strict regulations and substantial taxes.

Merchants in the Ottoman cities generally fell into two groups: those who dealt with local products and belonged to guilds akin to those of the artisans and those engaged in caravan and overseas trade, who were essentially free to pursue their businesses as they wished. Some merchants organized partnerships or corporations, sometimes cornering the market in various commodities and driving up the prices to make substantial profits. Guild members were understandably hostile to such merchants, particularly since profit margins in the guilds normally did not exceed 15 percent. Moreover, the great merchants paid relatively little in taxes, though they used their wealth to benefit their communities in other ways. Some procured raw material for workers and exported their finished products, while others endowed charitable institutions.

◉ Jewish Life in the Ottoman Empire ◉

On his tour of the Ottoman Empire in the sixteenth century, Nicolas De Nicolay, chamberlain and geographer to the king of France, described the Jews in this manner.

The number of Jews dwelling throughout all the cities of Turkey and Greece, and principally at Constantinople, is so great, that it is a thing marvelous and incredible. For the number of those who trade and traffic in merchandise, likewise who loan money at usury, doth there multiply so from day to day, that the great haunt and bringing of merchandise which arrives there from all parts as well by sea as by land, is such, that . . . they have in their hands the most and greatest traffic of merchandise and ready money that is in all [the] Levant. And likewise their shops and warehouses, the best furnished of all rich sorts of merchandise which are in Constantinople are those of the Jews. Likewise they have among them workmen of all arts and handicrafts most excellent, and especially of the Maranes [Moriscos] of late banished and driven out of Spain and Portugal, who to the great detriment and damage of Christianity, have taught the Turks divers inventions, crafts, and engines of war, as to make artillery, harquebusses [handguns], gunpowder, shot, and other munitions. They have also there set up printing, not before seen in those countries, by the which in fair characters they put in light divers books in divers languages, as Greek, Latin, Italian, Spanish, and the Hebrew tongue, being to them natural, but are not permitted to print the Turkish or Arabic tongue. They . . . speak and understand all other sorts of languages used in [the] Levant, which serves them greatly for the communication and traffic which they have with other strange nations, to whom oftentimes they serve for Dragomans, or interpreters. . . . The Jews which dwell in Constantinople, Adrianople, . . . and other places of the dominion of the great Turk, are all apparelled with long garments, like unto the Greeks and other nations of [the] Levant, but for their mark and token to be known from others, they wear a yellow Tulbant [a turban].

Source: N. De Nicolay, *The Navigations into Turkie,* trans. T. Washington (London, 1585), fols. 130v–131v (edited to conform to modern usage).

Although charging interest under Islamic law was illegal, merchants of all religious persuasions found ways to provide loans. Among the borrowers were government officials who used the loans to procure higher offices and then rewarded the lenders with such benefits as monopolies or tax farms (the right of private parties to collect taxes for the government). Certain merchants received contracts to establish factories for the production of large amounts of armaments or woolens for the military, thereby depriving the smaller guild shops of business and increasing the friction between merchants and artisans.

The wealthier Ottoman merchants engaged in extensive international trade, particularly from the key centers of Istanbul, Bursa, Edirne, Cairo, and Salonika. Muslim merchants even had their own trading companies in the important cities of northern Italy. The textile merchants of Edirne exported their products as far afield as Florence, Paris, and London and in turn imported European cloth. Cotton from Anatolia, Egypt, Yemen, and India was sold throughout Europe, while the merchants of Bursa exported silk, timber, hides, and ironware to the East. Spices, jewelry, perfume, costly textiles, and dyes were the major commodities in overseas trade. Through the key North African cities of Cairo and Alexandria came ivory, gold, and slaves; Istanbul alone had some 2,000 slave merchants. One of the oddities of the empire was that foreign traders paid fewer taxes than their Ottoman counterparts and thus after the eighteenth century came to dominate international commerce.

Feeding the imperial population, especially the residents of the capital, was a major task. By the mid-seventeenth century Istanbul alone required 250 tons of wheat each day and 2,000 shiploads of food each year. Much of the food, of course, was produced within the empire: wheat from Egypt, Thrace, and especially the Dobrudja region west of the Black Sea; livestock, fish, cereals, and honey from the area north of that sea; wine from the Aegean region; rice, spices, and sugar from Egypt; and cereals from Macedonia and Thessaly. So crucial was the need to find adequate food for the population and sufficient raw materials for the artisans that the imperial government imposed numerous controls. It fixed the price of the food at the point of production, licensed the middlemen who bought it, and supervised its distribution. Smuggling and profiteering were strictly prohibited, and violaters faced the loss of their ships and goods.

Until the end of the sixteenth century the food problem was aggravated by labor shortages in rural areas. The government responded to this by curtailing the mobility of peasants and by offering tax incentives and the right to sell surplus crops on the open market to farmers who brought unused lands under cultivation. Substantial population growth in the sixteenth century finally resolved the labor shortage.

During the golden age of Ottoman culture, which followed the conquest of Constantinople, most leading writers and thinkers belonged to the ulema, although most of the prominent figures in science and medicine were Jews. Ottoman culture was rich and varied, reaching a peak of excellence in the poetry composed for wealthy, powerful patrons. The leading Ottoman poets no longer imitated Persian writers but achieved a creativity of their own, even while extensively borrowing Persian and Arabic words.

The "sultan of the poets," as his contemporaries called him, was Muhammad Abd ul-Baki (1526–1600), a former apprentice to a saddlemaker and hawker of poems in the courtyard of a mosque. His major work was a moving elegy on Suleiman's death:

> Will not the King awake from sleep? The dawn
>   of day has broken.
> Will not he come forth from his tent bright as
>   heaven's display?
> Long have our eyes looked down the road, and
>   yet no news is come
> From yonder land, the threshold of his
>   majesty's array.[2]

Most of Baki's poems urged readers to enjoy the transitory pleasures of life. Almost as revered as Baki, Mehmet ibn Suleiman Fuzuli (1480–1556) explored the unity of creation and mystic love.

> Let your grace, my only Lord, forever be my
>   only guide;
> Lead me not by any path that leads not to
>   where You abide.[3]

There was also poetry for the masses, sung, as in medieval France and Germany, by itinerant troubadours; their themes, however, were mystical rather than secular, as in the West. The greatest of the folk poets was the seventeenth-century minstrel Karacaoglan, whose vigorous verse recounted the lives of the ordinary people of Anatolia:

> The cranes they circle in the air
> The dreams I fear I see anew
> Brave comrades, this I have to say
> She does not love who is not true.[4]

Novels, plays, and short stories became important literary forms in the Ottoman world only in the nineteenth century as the result of Western influence, but earlier prose authors made worthy contributions in essays, biographies, and learned treatises on history, geography, and religion. Recognizing the value of history to buttress their claims to expand the empire, Mehmet II and his predecessor, Murat II (1421–1451), sponsored the earliest Ottoman historians, including Ahmedi, whose *Epic of the Histories of the House of Osman* is the earliest source for the rise of the Ottomans. While the major historical writers of Suleiman's era were chroniclers, the distinguished court historian Mustafa Naima Efendi (1665–1716) not only recorded facts but analyzed them as well. "Historians," he insisted, "should speak frankly and fairly. . . . They should not exaggerate . . . , and if, to attain their end, they must criticize and censure great men of praiseworthy works, they should never be unjust."[5]

Two generations earlier, Mustafa ibn Abdullah, known as Katip Chelebi (1609–1657), demonstrated equal respect for sources in compiling his *View of the World*, a compendium of geography that drew not only on Muslim works but also on such European authors as the Flemish geographer Gerardus Mercator. Western scholarship, which owed so much to the Muslim world, was now beginning to repay the debt.

In the area of religion, Muslim authors continued to debate the relationship between philosophy (reason) and religion (faith), in particular whether the two fields could be reconciled. During the late fifteenth century the ulema officially decided that reason could be used in the study of medicine and mathematics but not religion. Religious writers concentrated on the mystical notion of the unity of existence, a theme popular with many poets as well.

The medrese associated with the mosque founded by Suleiman was a boon to science because of its emphasis on mathematics and medicine rather than religion. Its influence is apparent in the large number of hospitals subsequently established in the empire. One of the most influential Ottoman physicians, Ahi Ahmed Chelebi (1436–1523), founded hospitals in 40 villages, encouraged these institutions to train doctors, and established the first Ottoman medical school. Religious leaders, however, continued to threaten scientific inquiry, as in 1580, when their pressure prompted the sultan to destroy the astronomical observatory in Istanbul. Tensions between religious values and secular movements in education and society have continued in Islamic areas to the present day.

The Decay of the Empire

Beginning in the mid-seventeenth century, the rule of the sultans began to weaken. At the same time the janissaries, who could now marry at will, became more devoted to their families and personal fortunes than to the sultan's welfare. Discipline in the janissary corps eroded, demands for higher pay escalated, and there was a growing reluctance to fight extended campaigns in remote lands. Fortunately for the Ottomans, effective government was restored when Turhan appointed the Albanian Muhammad Kuprili as grand vizier in 1656. Determined to end graft and corruption in the empire, he and his successors dominated Ottoman politics for more than half a century.

After 1716, Ottoman officials, stung by the loss of Transylvania and most of Hungary to Habsburg armies (which had been confirmed in the 1699 Treaty of Karlowitz), began trying to reorganize their decaying army along European lines, but the forces of conservatism, led by the janissaries and the ulema, resisted change. The sultans and some factions at court regularly pressed for reform but were resisted by vested interests and conservative groups. The Ottomans were ultimately unable to stave off the European challenge to their empire. The Treaty of Passarowitz (1718), by which the Ottomans ceded much of Serbia to Austria and Dalmatia to Venice, was a foretaste of things to come.

The Mughals in India

After Tamerlane's bloody invasion of 1398 (see Chapter 11), the Delhi sultanate never regained its earlier control, and the north of India remained fragmented. An Afghan clan, the Lodis, seized power in Delhi in 1451 but could not extend their rule beyond neighboring Punjab. Their continued oppression of the Hindu population, including temple razing, sparked rebellions that could not be put down. These erupted eastward in the central Ganges valley, westward among the Rajputs of Rajasthan (who still defended Hindu India), and finally in Punjab itself.

Babur and the New Dynasty

A rebel governor in Punjab asked for help from the central Asian leader Babur (1483–1530), known already as "the Tiger" and by this time established also as ruler of most of Afghanistan. Babur claimed descent on his father's side from Tamerlane and on his mother's from Chinghis Khan. Like many other central Asian Turks, he had acquired a great deal of Persian culture and was a gifted poet in Persian. Babur's tough, mounted Turco-Afghan troops defeated the numerically superior Lodi forces and their war elephants at the battle of Panipat in Punjab, some 70 miles northwest of Delhi, in 1526. The next year Babur routed the Rajput army, which tried to eject him, and in 1529 crushed the Delhi sultanate's last effort to regain power. Babur was master of the north and proclaimed the Mughal dynasty (the name is derived, via Persian, from *Mongol*), which was to restore imperial grandeur in northern India for nearly two centuries.

The greatness of the Mughal period rested on a fortunate combination of able, imaginative rulers, especially the emperor Akbar (1542–1605), and the new infusion of Persian culture into North India. Under Akbar and his immediate successors, Persian, the official language of court, government, and law, merged with the earlier language of the Delhi-Agra area to form modern Hindi, now the largest single language of India, and Urdu, its close equivalent, now the official language of Pakistan. Persian artistic and literary forms blended with earlier traditions in the north and enriched all of Indian culture. The Mughals reestablished firm central control in the north. Within their empire, agriculture and commerce flourished again. Steady revenues and an efficient imperial administration enabled the Mughals to build a network of roads that linked the empire. This was no small task, given India's previous disunity and regional separatism, as well as its size.

The total population in the empire was probably over 100 million, on a par with China's and almost certainly larger than Europe's. To symbolize their power and wealth, the Mughal emperors built magnificent new capitals at both Delhi and Agra. Only 100 miles apart, the cities served alternately as the seat of government. This area, between the Jumna and Ganges rivers, had long been the key to Hindustan, the Ganges valley, and routes southward (see Chapter 11). Successive Delhis had risen and fallen on the same strategic site, controlling, with Agra as its satellite, the heart of repeated imperial efforts. Both cities were built, like sentinels, on the west bank of the Jumna, which flows into the Ganges below Agra after running parallel to it, like a defensive moat, from well north of Delhi.

Each city was dominated by a great walled fort containing the palace and audience halls. Inside and outside the walls the Mughals also constructed great mosques, gardens, tombs (such as the Taj Mahal at Agra), and other monumental buildings in the Persian style, which they developed further and made distinctively Indian. Literature, music, and the graphic arts flourished under

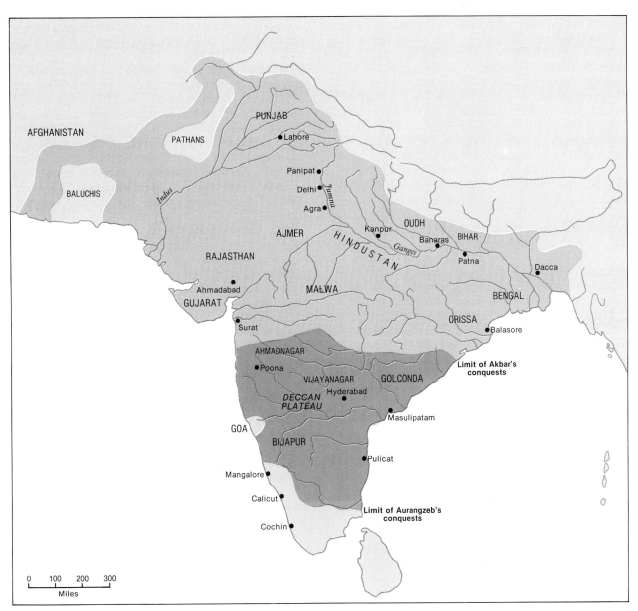

20.2 *India at the Height of Mughal Power*

imperial patronage at both capitals. Strong imperial rule was often oppressive, but it helped ensure an unprecedented period of unity and prosperity that most Indians shared. Hindus too could feel pride in the new imperial grandeur, for they were given an important role in it.

Akbar and His Achievement

Akbar's success in building a truly Indian empire rather than just another alien conquest was the chief foundation of Mughal greatness, but he had first to establish

his rule. Babur died prematurely in 1530, after offering his life to God in exchange for that of his son Humayun, who was deathly ill. But Humayun (1508–1556) was a weakling who was finally driven out of India in 1540 by one of Babur's Afghan generals and forced to take refuge in Iran. A year after he returned in 1555 at the head of a Persian army to reclaim his father's conquests, he fell on the stone steps of his private astronomical observatory and library, light-headed from opium, and died, leaving the throne to his 13-year-old son Akbar, who had been born in exile in 1542.

Immediately challenged upon his accession in 1556,

Akbar's army defeated yet another Hindu effort to drive out the invaders at Panipat. In 1562, at the age of 20, Akbar assumed full charge of the empire from his advisers. In the same year he married a Rajput princess, beginning what was to be a lifelong campaign to blend the many strands of India's ancient cultural, regional, and religious heritage. Akbar was determined to build both an empire and a new culture that was as nearly as he could make it truly Indian, uniting its various elements under firm Mughal control.

He saw himself as an Indian ruler, not a foreign despot, and understood from the beginning that his own success and that of the dynasty depended on commanding the support and participation of all Indians. But he could be ruthless too if his power was challenged. When the chief Rajput faction resisted his diplomacy, he sacked the Rajput capital in 1568 and massacred the surviving defenders. By 1570 all but a small remnant of the Rajputs had sworn allegiance to him; in return, he made a Rajput, whose military skills he knew well, one of his chief generals, and other Rajputs thereafter also played a strong role in the imperial army. This political wisdom solved what would have otherwise been his major military problem. Rajputs became his comrades rather than his implacable enemies. To mark his policy of religious toleration further, for the four wives allowed to rulers by the Koran, he chose two Hindus (including his Rajput bride), one Christian, and one Muslim, thus symbolically embracing India's religious variety.

With his new Rajput allies, Akbar invaded wealthy Gujarat, capturing Surat, the chief seaport of the west coast, in 1573. Three years later he completed the conquest of Bengal in the east and by 1581 had added most of Afghanistan to his empire. For many years his armies raided south into the northern Deccan but were never able to win permanent control, a goal that also eluded his successors. But northern India and Afghanistan under Akbar and his successors remained until the end of the seventeenth century one of history's greatest empires in size, wealth, and splendor. It was divided into 15 provinces, each under a governor but with a separate set of officials responsible for revenue collection. Provinces were subdivided into districts, where representatives of the governor kept order and dispensed justice. Revenue demands were smaller than under the Delhi sultans, and the large number of Hindus employed in the revenue service, as well as at its head, helped keep taxes from becoming exploitive or unfair. Hindu law was applied in disputes between Hindus. Revenue collectors were ordered to remit taxes in districts that had had a poor harvest.

One reform that endeared Akbar to his subjects was his abolition of two hated taxes: on Hindu pilgrims traveling to sacred sites and on all Hindus as infidels (the *jizya*, or poll tax), both of which had been collected by Muslim rulers for centuries. He abolished the practice of enslaving war prisoners and their families and forbade forcible conversion to Islam, long a bitter issue. Hindus were welcomed at court, and their advice was regularly sought. Akbar patronized Persian and Urdu art and literature, but he also appointed a court poet for Hindi and encouraged Hindu literature and art more generally. Most of the greatest court painters were Hindus, producing beautiful portraits, miniatures, and naturalistic bird, animal, and flower paintings. Orthodox Muslims challenged this defiance of the Islamic ban on the depiction of human or animal forms, but Akbar replied that he could not believe God, "the giver of life," would disapprove of the beauty he had made, which was portrayed in true art.

Like the other Mughal emperors after him, Akbar loved gardens, with which nearly all Mughal buildings, including palaces, forts, and tombs, were surrounded in magnificent blendings of green lawns, gaily colored beds of flowers with flowering trees for shade, and an ingenious use of water in fountains, pools, and fluted channels. These devices enhanced the atmosphere of coolness, restfulness, and greenness, creating an effect that was especially striking in the hot, dry surroundings of the plains of North India. Akbar took a personal interest in the planning and care of the imperial gardens. He is often shown by court painters supervising the planting of flower beds and tending his roses.

Akbar was widely curious and loved to discuss philosophy and religion with all comers, Portuguese Jesuits as well as Hindu Brahmins. He had the Christian Gospels translated into Persian and attended mass. But as he came to reject the dogma of Islam as the only true religion, he could not accept the exclusive truth of any one faith, except a universal faith in an all-powerful creator. In later life he increasingly became a Sufi, or Islamic mystic, blending ideas from many religions and symbolizing his mission to merge the best of all the Indian traditions with those the Mughals brought into India. He was a deeply religious person, but his departures from orthodox Islam shocked many Muslim leaders and provoked a revolt against him in 1581. He suppressed it by force and then in deference to Hindu values forbade the slaughter of cattle and became a vegetarian, even giving up hunting, of which he had been very fond. Akbar founded a new faith that he hoped could unite his varied subjects in the common love of God, without need for a sectarian priesthood, but it did not survive him. If he had been followed by rulers like him, his dream of a united India free of strife might have moved closer to realization.

Much has been written about the fascinating Akbar. He was a contemporary of Elizabeth I of England, Henry IV of France, Shah Abbas of Iran, and the Ming Emperor Wan-li. Europeans who had met them all agreed that as both a human being and a ruler, he towered over his contemporaries. He had great strength of intelligence, character, and will, but he also had the good sense to realize that compromise and cooperation work better than force. He was full of energy and imagination but highly sensitive and often prey to melancholy and fits of depression. He seems to have suffered from epilepsy as well, like Julius Caesar and Napoleon. Astonishingly, he also appears to have been illiterate. As a child he preferred hunting and other sports to lessons, but he had a phenomenal memory, like many unlettered people, and was a great listener. From adolescence he appointed courtiers to read to him several hours a day; he had over 24,000 manuscripts in his library, and the learned men who debated with him often found him better "read" than themselves. He had a broadly inquiring mind, but a complicated one; the Jesuits at his court, who came to know him well, could never fully understand it or predict what he might say or do. He kept his dignity with all but had the knack of making the humblest petitioner feel at ease, and he charmed everyone who met him, high and low.

He was remarkably versatile, not only in his interests but in his skills as well. He was an accomplished polo player, metalworker, draftsman (many of his beautiful drawings have survived), and musician. He even invented a lighted polo ball so that the game could be played at night and a gun with a new mechanism that could fire multiple rounds. But his main preoccupation shifted to religion, especially after he had completed his major conquests, and he spent many nights alone in prayer and meditation. In 1575 he built a hall of worship, to which he invited the widest range of philosophers and theologians for periodic discussions, first from Islamic schools of thought and then from all the religions he could gather, including individual holy men, ascetics and mystics, Hindu sadhus and Muslim Sufis, Jesuit priests and Iranian fire worshipers. In time, these "seminars on religion" were held regularly every Thursday evening, while Akbar continued his own private devotions at sunrise, noon, sunset, and midnight. It was typical of him

◉ The Court of Akbar ◉

One of the many accounts of Akbar and the India of his time is that of the Jesuit Antonio Monserrate, who visited the court from 1580 to 1583. Here are some excerpts from the Commentary on His Journey to the Court of Akbar.

This prince is of a stature and type of countenance well fitted to his royal dignity, so that one could easily recognize even at first glance that he is the king. . . . His forehead is broad and open, his eyes so bright and flashing that they seem like a sea shimmering in the sunlight. . . . He creates an opportunity almost every day for any of the common people or of the nobles to see him and converse with him. It is remarkable how great an effect this courtesy and affability has in attaching to him the minds of his subjects. . . . He has an acute insight, and shows much wise foresight both in avoiding dangers and in seizing favorable opportunities for carrying out his designs. . . . Unlike the palaces built by other Indian kings, his are lofty [and] their total circuit is so large that it easily embraces four great royal dwellings. . . . Not a little is added to the beauty of the palaces by charming pigeon cotes. . . . The pigeons are cared for by eunuchs and servant maids. Their evolutions are controlled at will, when they are flying, by means of certain signals, just as those of a well trained soldiery. . . . It will seem little short of miraculous when I affirm that when sent out they dance, turn somersaults all together in the air, fly in orderly rhythm, and return to their starting point, all at the sound of a whistle. [Akbar's] empire is wonderfully rich and fertile both for cultivation and pasture, and has a great trade both in exports and imports. . . . Indian towns appear very pleasant from afar; they are adorned with many towers and high buildings in a very beautiful manner. But when one enters them, one finds that the narrowness, aimless crookedness, and ill planning of the streets deprive these cities of all beauty. . . . The common people live in lowly huts and tiny cottages, and hence if a traveller has seen one of these cities, he has seen them all.

Source: D. Lach, *Asia on the Eve of Europe's Expansion* (Englewood Cliffs, N.J.: Prentice Hall, 1965), pp. 63–69 passim.

Akbar's planned capital at Fatehpur Sikri, near Agra. Shown here is part of the women's quarters, open to the view and the breezes, from which the women could overlook the courtyard in the left foreground, marked off as a giant pachisi (Parcheesi) board. The game was played with live pieces—court ladies and members of the harem—whose moves were directed by court or royal players throwing dice. [Rhoads Murphey]

that although he hoped earnestly that the new mystic religion he founded in 1581 to unite all people would attract a mass following, he never tried to force it on anyone.

Akbar was too intellectually alive and too religiously devout to lapse into the life of extravagant luxury that surrounded him at court, but he was no purist or prude. He enjoyed food and wine, the sherbet brought to him daily by runners from the snowy Himalayas, the dancing girls, the music and plays, and the flourishing literature and art that he so generously patronized. He was, in other words, a truly regal monarch, but a most unusual one in the range of his vision and understanding. It was too much to ask for a succession of others like him, but India was not again to be served by a ruler of his quality until the first prime minister of its modern independence, Jawaharlal Nehru (prime minister, 1947–1964.)

Akbar was still without an heir after six years of marriage. He sought help from a Sufi saint who lived at a place called Sikri, 20 miles west of Agra. A year later his first son was born, and in gratitude Akbar built of red sandstone a magnificent new capital, which he called Fatehpur Sikri, next to the saint's humble cottage. Here he had fresh scope to blend Indian, Persian, Islamic, and Mughal themes in architecture, drawing also on traditional Hindu architecture in the south. But the water supply in this arid region proved inadequate, and Fatehpur Sikri had to be abandoned after only 15 years. The deserted stone city still stands much as Akbar left it, a monument to his vision that still can move visitors.

The last four years of Akbar's life were clouded by the rebellion of his eldest son, whose birth had been such a joyous occasion. The Mughals were never able to work out the problem of succession. From this time on, each emperor was plotted against in his old age by his many sons, who also tore the empire apart by their fighting until the most ruthless had disposed of his rivals. It was a pattern inherited from the Mughals' central Asian origins, and it blighted their otherwise great achievements while also draining the country's resources. In 1605 Akbar reasserted his authority, only to die of poison administered by his rebellious son, who took the throne that year under the name Jahangir ("world-seizer").

Jahangir and Shah Jahan

Jahangir's Persian wife, Nur Jahan, a power in her own right, further entrenched Persian culture at the court and throughout North India. The administrative system inherited from Akbar continued to run smoothly, and revenues flowed in to pay for the brilliance of the court. Jahangir and Nur Jahan preferred Agra to Delhi and adorned it further with new palaces, gardens, and tombs. Court life took on a more luxurious splendor; Jahangir was no mystic like his father. He and his courtiers delighted in silks and perfumes, jewel-decked costumes, wine, song, and the pleasures of the harem. State processions featured troupes of dancing girls and elephants covered with silk and jewels, and monthlong festivities were held to celebrate the marriages of Jahangir's many sons.

The painting of this era became more naturalistic, and the orthodox Islamic prohibition against representing human or animal forms gave way to older Indian traditions, even including nearly nude figures and embracing couples in classic Rajput and earlier Hindu styles, as well as portraits of the emperor, often in his beloved gardens. For all their use of Persian language, culture, and art forms, the Mughals had become Indian rulers and were increasingly seen as such by most Indians. They were following a traditional maharaja lifestyle, and their pretensions to divine authority were familiar to their subjects; like luxurious living, these were expected of royalty.

A resurgent Iran under Shah Abbas began to challenge the Mughal Empire in the west and conquered most of Afghanistan, but Jahangir was too busy with his gardens, wine, and harems to lead his army over the mountains. He had given his son Shah Jahan command of the army, but Shah Jahan refused to leave the capital because he was plotting to seize the throne, having previously poisoned his elder brother. He knew that his real enemy was Nur Jahan, who had manipulated Jahangir, appointed her own father and brother to the highest offices, and even hoped to occupy the throne herself. Jahangir, entranced by her beauty and wit, had named her Nur Jahan, meaning "light of the world," but she became empress in all but name soon after he married her. She arranged the marriage of her brother's daughter, Mumtaz Mahal, to Shah Jahan as an extension of the power of her clan.

But Shah Jahan openly rebelled in 1623, and when Jahangir died late in 1627, he put to death all of his clos-

◙ Festivals in Mughal India ◙

Jahangir's Memoirs *include these descriptions of New Year and birthday festivals.*

The feast of the New Year was held near Agra, and at the time of transit of the sun I seated myself on the throne with glory and gladness. The nobles and courtiers all came forward with their congratulations. . . . I determined that this time I would enter Agra [to visit his father Akbar's tomb] and after that would go on foot on this pilgrimage to the shrine, in the same way that my father, on account of my birth, had gone from Agra to Ajmir [Fatehpur]. . . . At an auspicious hour, I returned to Agra, and scattering with two hands 5,000 rupees in small coins along the way, I entered the august place which was inside the fort. . . . On the ninth of the month the feast for my solar weighing, which is the commencement of the 38th year of my age, took place. According to custom, they got ready the weighing apparatus and the scales. At the moment appointed blessings were invoked and I sat in the scales. Each suspending rope was held by an elderly person who offered up prayers. The first time I was weighed against gold, and then against several metals, perfumes, and essences, up to twelve weighings. Twice a year I weigh myself against gold and silver and other metals, and against all sorts of silks and cloths and various grains, etc., once at the beginning of the solar year and once at that of the lunar. The weight of the money of the two weighings I hand over to the different treasuries for faqirs [holy men] and those in want.

Source: J. N. Das Gupta, *India in the Seventeenth Century* (Calcutta: University of Calcutta Press, 1916), pp. 104–105.

est relatives and pensioned off Nur Jahan. He declared himself "emperor of the world," which is the meaning of his regnal name, with three weeks of extravagant coronation ceremonies. He ruled for three decades. His was the most lavish of all the Mughal reigns, especially visible in the royal passion for monumental architecture inlaid with precious stones. Court life under Shah Jahan was sumptuous, in the pattern set by his father, but he was even more attached to his harem, where 5,000 concubines awaited his pleasure. Nevertheless, he was genuinely devoted to his wife, Mumtaz Mahal, who bore him 14 children. When she died in childbirth in 1631 at the age of 39, he was desolated. "Empire has no sweetness, life has no relish for me now," he said when told of her death.

To honor her memory, he built what may be the most famous structure in the world, the Taj Mahal at Agra, which took 20,000 workmen more than 20 years to complete. Designed by two Persian architects, it beautifully blends Iranian and Indian styles and Indian craftsmanship. The emphasis on water and gardens was characteristically Mughal, whereas the use of Rajput canopies around the base of the dome was traditionally Indian. Before the Taj Mahal was finished, Shah Jahan had begun a new capital city at Delhi, site of so many capitals before, modeled on Akbar's Red Fort at Agra and built of the same red sandstone, with similarly massive walls and battlements but on an even larger scale. Inside were beautiful gardens, palaces, audience halls, harems, barracks, stables, and storehouses, and outside he built India's largest mosque, the Jama Masjid. Both still stand, little altered, and still dominate Delhi, the Mughal name of which was Shah Jahanabad ("Shah Jahan's city").

Monumental building and the opulent court were not Shah Jahan's only extravagances. He ordered campaigns to reclaim Afghanistan and to restore Mughal rule in central Asia. Both failed but exhausted the treasury. From his Red Fort palace, on his Peacock Throne, encrusted with the largest jewels ever found, the emperor doubled Akbar's revenue demands, and the empire groaned. Meanwhile, his many sons were already conspiring against one another, impatient to succeed the ailing ruler. His favorite son, Dara, a philosopher and mystic like his great-grandfather Akbar, might have made a fine ruler, but a younger son, Aurangzeb, was insatiably ambitious.

From 1657 open warfare prevailed among rival brothers. Aurangzeb imprisoned his father, Shah Jahan, in the dungeon of Agra's Red Fort while he completed his gruesome work and then sent the old emperor the head of his favorite son, Dara. The aged Shah Jahan could just see through the barred window of his cell a glimpse of his beloved Taj Mahal. Hearing that this gave the elderly man a little comfort, Aurangzeb is said to have had his father's eyes put out.

The Reign of Aurangzeb: Repression and Revolt

The cold-blooded Aurangzeb ascended the throne in 1658. By poison, intrigue, or assassination he had eliminated a dozen of his own brothers and half brothers, plus uncounted others. He gave as the reason for this slaughter his own devotion to orthodox Islam against the laxer or more tolerant views of his many rivals. But Aurangzeb was also a brilliant and single-minded ruler and admin-

No photograph can do full justice to the Taj Mahal, whose great bulk seems to float weightlessly above the pool that holds its reflection. Mughal cupolas and domes are matched by minarets, the four slender towers on each side in the Islamic tradition, while the central archway beneath the dome is reminiscent of the Persian (Iranian) models on which the archway was based. Inscriptions from the Koran and beautiful inlaid floral patterns cover much of the outer and inner walls. The entire structure is of glistening white marble. [Rhoads Murphey]

istrator and a cunning statesman. Sunni Muslims revered him as much as Hindus hated him. He is said to have had no friends, only servile admirers and bitter enemies.

Civil war on top of Shah Jahan's extravagances had emptied the treasury, but Aurangzeb increased his revenue demands and at the same time extended his own puritanical tastes to the running of court and empire. He stopped all court luxuries, especially the wine, song, and dance forbidden by the Koran, and ended all monumental construction. He also appointed censors of public morals to enforce rigid Islamic law, ordered everyone to pray at the orthodox Islamic intervals every day, tried to abolish gambling and drinking, and began a lifelong campaign to demolish all surviving Hindu monuments and temples. Unfortunately, he largely succeeded in the north, and the only surviving samples of pre-Mughal architecture are in the south, where Aurangzeb never prevailed. Hindus were forbidden to carry arms, forced conversion was resumed for many, and Hindu festivals and public expression were outlawed. Aurangzeb knew the Koran by heart and copied it out twice in his own hand. But his piety and his zealous praying, which mark him as an Islamic zealot, sparked a keen sense of religious intolerance. To increase the revenue needed to maintain his army and to pay for new conquests in the name of Allah, he reimposed the hated *jizya* on Hindus, laid a new tax on Hindu pilgrims, and doubled the taxes on Hindu merchants. When crowds gathered outside the Red Fort in Delhi to protest, he ordered the imperial elephants to crush them to death.

The widespread revolts that arose within a few years merely increased Aurangzeb's pressure for more revenue to put them down. For many years he did so successfully, thanks to his superior generalship and to the fear-induced loyalty of most of his court and army. When revolt failed or the risks of defying Aurangzeb or his tax collectors seemed too great, growing numbers of peasants abandoned their homes and fields and became bandits or joined dissident groups or armies elsewhere, including explicitly Hindu forces such as the Sikhs of Punjab (particularly brutalized by Aurangzeb), the formerly loyal Rajputs, and the Marathas.

Relentless in suppressing rebellion, Aurangzeb was also determined to extend his empire into the south. The last half of his wearily long reign was consumed in bloody but ultimately unsuccessful campaigns into the Deccan, while at the same time his forces tried to stem the rising tide of Sikh, Rajput, Afghan, Bengali, and Maratha revolt. His brief conquests in the south, won at terrible cost in treasure and lives, quickly evaporated. From their mountain fortresses in the northwestern Deccan, the Hindu Marathas became increasingly powerful and took the field to harry Mughal forces retreating from the south near the end of Aurangzeb's reign. His campaigns exhausted the country and left it split among contending powers, who shared an implacable hatred of Mughal rule but were divided by their own differences and rivalries.

Sects and Rebels: Rajputs, Sikhs, and Marathas

Three groups stood out against Aurangzeb's intolerance and military conquests and as his most effective opponents: the Rajputs, the Sikhs, and the Marathas. Unfortunately for them, they never made a common cause, as they also failed to do later against the British.

Aurangzeb broke the alliance that Akbar had prudently made with the Rajputs and eliminated their role in the Mughal army. Throughout most of his reign they were in revolt, maintaining their reputation as courageous fighters, and were never effectively suppressed. The proximity of their base and its fortresses in Rajasthan to the center of Mughal power in the Delhi-Agra region made them highly vulnerable, and they suffered repeated "annihilation" campaigns, but Rajput resistance survived in the margins of Rajasthan. Each campaign against the Rajputs bred new bitterness and new determination to fight. Aurangzeb's religious zeal and conquering ambition called forth resistance in the name of India and of Hinduism against a Mughal order now seen afresh as alien and hateful. It was a sad sequel to Akbar's vision of a multiracial, multicultural, and multireligious India. The Rajputs throughout their history had been quick to spring proudly to the defense of Hindu India, and now they took the field again, convinced of the rightness of their cause.

The Sikhs of Punjab emerged as a religious group with its own separate identity as an outgrowth of the bhakti movement late in the fifteenth century (see Chapter 11). As elsewhere in India where bhakti ideals spread, a series of nonsectarian saint-reformers preached a puritanical form of life and freedom from priestly domination, discarding the more dogmatic and hierarchical aspects of Hinduism, such as caste, but retaining its devotion to nonviolence. The founder of Sikhism, Guru Nanak (1469–1538), tried at first to work out a compromise between Hinduism and Islam and then to purify Hinduism. He preached the bhakti message of a universal God and his love, to whom everyone has access without the need for priests or rituals. Perhaps his best-known saying is "Man will be saved by his works alone; God will not ask a man his tribe or sect, but what he has done. There is no Hindu and no Muslim. All are children of God."[6] Nanak's rejection of priests as essential intermediaries was akin to the view of his European contemporary Martin Luther, although Nanak was not a formal theologian and, unlike Luther, stressed good works rather than faith.

His disciple and successor, Guru Angad (active 1530–

1552), began the compilation of the Sikh holy book, the Granth Sahib, recording all he had learned from Guru Nanak and adding devotional reflections. Successive Sikh gurus continued their opposition to caste and to all forms of discrimination and met with Akbar, who listened to them with interest and granted them a site for their chief temple in Amritsar, near Lahore. The origins of Sikhism were thus wholly peaceful, but in the sixteenth century some Sikhs were drawn into support for one of Jahangir's rebellious sons, hoping that he would be more tolerant of non-Muslims. When the rebellion failed and Jahangir had the Sikh leader executed in 1606, the Sikhs began to develop a defensive military mentality, to maintain their own identity and their territorial base in Punjab.

By 1650 the Sikhs' numbers had greatly increased, and they began to see themselves as a separate state. Sikh gurus urged their followers to eat meat, in distinction from high-caste Hindus but also to give them strength. Martial skills, bravery, and physical strength began to be cultivated as Sikh hallmarks. Shah Jahan left them largely alone, preoccupied as he was with his ambitious building projects and with the luxurious pleasures of his harem and court. But when the Sikhs supported his favored son Dara's bid for the throne, they became Aurangzeb's enemies. His persecutions of them and his efforts to eliminate them as both a power and a community predictably strengthened their commitment and led to their further militarization. Aurangzeb cruelly tortured to death the ninth Sikh guru, Teg Bahadur, in 1675 when he refused to embrace Islam and ignored the guru's warning against the still tiny but foreboding European threat to India. Teg Bahadur's son and successor, Guru Govind Singh (1675–1708), first organized the Sikhs into a real political power and a great military fraternity. He urged them all to adopt the surname Singh ("lion") as he had done, to swear never to cut their hair (which came to be worn knotted up in a turban) or their beards, and to avoid tobacco and alcohol. The practices of purdah (the veiling and seclusion of women) and *sati* (the burning of widows) were rejected. Sikh women were freer and were seen more nearly as coequals than in most other Indian societies. Govind Singh's four sons were captured by Aurangzeb and tortured to death or executed, steadfastly refusing to convert to Islam.

When Govind Singh himself died in 1708, the line of ten guru leaders ended, and the Sikhs were thereafter ruled by political rather than religious leaders. Many Punjabis and others from neighboring areas had adopted Sikhism, and many more now joined its numbers. A former Rajput, Banda Bairagi, ravaged the Mughal forces as leader of the Sikhs until he was betrayed, captured, and executed in 1716. Nadir Shah's invasion from Iran in 1739 finally eliminated the remnants of Mughal power and gave the Sikhs a new opportunity to extend their domination of Punjab. During the re-mainder of the eighteenth century the Sikh kingdom became still stronger and stood finally as the last major obstacle to British rule, overcome only in 1849 after two campaigns against it.

The Marathas were probably the most formidable and effective enemies of the Mughals, and for some two centuries they played a major role in India. For a time it seemed as if they would become the dominant power in the subcontinent and would found a new Indian empire. Their home base was well protected by a mountain range behind Bombay, the Western Ghats; by the hilly Deccan Plateau east of the Ghats; and by the central Indian mountain ranges of the Vindhyas and their spurs to the north and east, which were ideally suited to guerrilla warfare. The Marathas gloried in their hardiness, which they attributed to the relative barrenness of their mountain-girt homeland, rather like the Scots or the Gurkhas of Nepal, and like them had a proud military tradition.

The greatest Maratha leader was Shivaji (1627–1680), who rose to prominence as Hindus were beginning to take up arms against Aurangzeb. Shivaji was brought up as a zealous Hindu but combined Hinduism with his martial background and his determination to free India from the Mughals. From the beginning of Aurangzeb's reign, Shivaji and his commando cavalry raided Mughal territory. The Mughal general sent against him captured Poona, the Maratha capital, in 1663, but was surprised there by Shivaji in a daring night attack and routed. A few months later in 1664 Shivaji attacked and looted Surat, then the richest port in India, and carried off immense booty. A second major Mughal campaign against him ended in negotiations after some of Shivaji's feuding adversaries deserted to the Mughal cause. Shivaji visited Agra, expecting to be offered a high post, but when he complained that Aurangzeb's offer was not good enough, he was imprisoned. He smuggled himself out, concealed in a basket, and rebuilt his forces and resources for what he now saw as an inevitable conflict.

When Aurangzeb ordered all Hindu temples and schools demolished and all Hindu public teaching and practice suppressed, Shivaji renewed his raids in 1670 and over the next ten years more than doubled the territory under his control, rivaling the Mughal territory itself as a state to be reckoned with. This achievement inspired the Marathas with renewed pride, and Shivaji remains their greatest hero. Unlike his successors, he was not only a brilliant military strategist and tactician but also an effective organizer and political administrator. He ruled with a council of ministers, made Marathi and Sanskrit the court languages, and banned the use of Urdu and Persian. For nearly 20 years he defied a series of Mughal armies, a considerable accomplishment in itself. Aurangzeb called him "the mountain rat." "My armies have been employed against him for nineteen years," he said, "and nevertheless his state has always been increasing."

But Shivaji did not live to see the death of Aurangzeb and the collapse of Mughal power, and the son who succeeded him neglected the army and the state and spent his time enjoying the luxuries of court life. He was defeated and captured by the Mughals, who executed him and many other Maratha chiefs in 1689. Shivaji's grandson, the next Maratha ruler, defected to the Mughals and was made one of their high officials, but other Marathas renewed the struggle. A younger descendant of Shivaji reorganized the army and resumed his grandfather's devastating raids. In 1699, after his own generals had failed to put them down, Aurangzeb himself marched against the Marathas, but without success. By 1702 the Mughals were on the defensive, and the Marathas were now led by Tara Bai, the remarkable wife of the ruler, who had died in 1700, although she ruled in name through her son, Shivaji III. She rode a horse with fearless skill and led Maratha cavalry charges in battle.

After Aurangzeb's death, however, and the collapse of his crusade, the Marathas were torn by internal civil war, a continuation of the feuding that was also part of their tradition. Successive leaders after 1712 resumed campaigns to the north, south, and east, extending their territory close to Delhi, conquering most of the peninsular south, and raiding even into Bengal.

The Maratha Confederacy, as it was called, had become by far the greatest power in India, but it lacked the firm hand and the administrative skills of Shivaji and was troubled by chronic factionalism. The Maratha army was used as much to raid and plunder as to fight major engagements, and raids or conquests were seldom followed up by responsible government of the areas acquired. In 1761 the army marched north to meet an Afghan invasion on the historic field of Panipat, northwest of Delhi, and was totally defeated. The short-lived Maratha "empire" was dissolved, and its power was never recovered. The real beneficiaries were the English, since the Marathas had been the only major defenders of India against foreign invaders and the only group with the potential to reunite the country. Internal feuding among themselves, lack of commitment to responsible administration, and the exhausting strain of chronic fighting against the Mughals left them unequal to that enormous task. India itself was exhausted by unending warfare, and the Mughals, Marathas, Sikhs, and Rajputs merely bloodied and drained each other and the country as a whole rather than taking any united stand.

The Mughals and India

By the beginning of the eighteenth century the order and prosperity that had flourished under Akbar and his immediate successors had been fatally weakened. Akbar's carefully designed revenue system, managed by Hindus, had been eroded by the excessive granting of tax-collecting rights for large areas, known as *jagirs*, to people whom the throne wanted or needed to pay off. Especially under Aurangzeb, Mughal attention was concentrated on military conquest, which meant mounting demands for revenue but also decreasing attention to normal administration or its supervision. Hindu revenue officials were eliminated; holders of jagirs (*jagirdars*) became more and more independent and more and more rapacious in extracting everything they could from an oppressed peasantry and merchant class, retaining for themselves any balance beyond the official government tax rates. The same was true for the group known as the *zamindars*, who were also granted tax-collection rights for smaller local areas and used them to enrich themselves, often acquiring the ownership of land from peasants who were unable to pay the tax. This was a disastrous formula for the well-being of most of the agricultural sector, the predominant basis of the economy and the major tax base. The Mughals had built an imperial road system, but it was used mainly for the movement of troops and supplies. Even so, it was not well maintained and became impassable in many sections, especially during the torrential rains of the annual monsoon.

In general, Mughal economic policy concentrated heavily on obtaining revenue and far too little on maintaining or enhancing the system's ability to generate production. In contrast to China, the state did almost nothing to increase irrigation, so badly needed in most of India, or to promote other agricultural improvements. Neglect of agriculture meant neglect of most of the country and its people.

Even before Aurangzeb, what was left over after paying the staggering costs of military campaigns was used primarily for gorgeous display at the capital and the court and for monumental building. The Mughals were at war on a major scale for much more than half of the years from Babur's victory at Panipat in 1526 to Aurangzeb's death in 1707, and fighting continued into the 1750s. Even a prosperous and well-run system would have been fatally weakened by such an outpouring of treasure to no constructive result and by devastation of the countryside on such a scale over two centuries.

Administration as well was increasingly neglected. Court life at Delhi and Agra was sumptuous and brilliant. Officials knew that their money and property would revert to the emperor when they died, and consequently they spent it freely in lavish consumption, with stables full of Arabian horses and harems filled with dancing girls. Massive entertainments and banquets occupied much of their time, complete with music, dance, and poetry readings. Courtiers and the upper classes dressed in magnificent silk outfits, or fine Kashmir wool in the brief northern winter, while the peasants wore coarse sackcloth woven from jute or locally made cottons, if they could afford them. Indian cotton cloth won extensive markets in the rest of Asia and much of Africa as well as in Europe; weavers benefited, but the state's tax collectors benefited still more.

For all the brilliant splendor of court life, however, science and technology were largely neglected after Akbar. What learning there was centered on the Koran and on the cultivation of the arts. There were no changes or improvements in the arts of production, and by the seventeenth century India had fallen behind Europe in science and technology and probably in the productivity of both its agriculture and manufacturing, while at the same time bleeding the economy by virtually continuous warfare. While Shah Jahan was building the Taj Mahal,

at staggering expense, India suffered probably the worst famine in its history, from 1630 to 1632, and another nearly as bad took place in 1702 and 1703 in which over 2 million people died while Aurangzeb was campaigning in the Deccan with a huge army and supply corps.

Aurangzeb had personally moved south in 1683, and for the rest of his life he was primarily concerned with conducting military campaigns from a new capital he established in the Deccan. Annual losses were estimated at 100,000 men and over 300,000 transport animals, mainly requisitioned from the peasantry. Continued Maratha raids and fierce southern resistance sapped his forces. After 1705 he seems to have spent most of his time reading and copying the Koran, preparing himself for death. Until then, he had refused to recognize the

◉ A Westerner Visits Delhi ◉

François Bernier, a French traveler in India from 1656 to 1668, included the following description of Delhi in his Travels in the Mogul Empire.

It is about forty years ago that Shah Jahan, father of the present Great Mogul Aurangzeb, conceived the design of immortalizing his name by the erection of a city near the site of the ancient Delhi. . . . Owing to their being so near at hand, the ruins of old Delhi served to build the new city. Delhi is situated on the Jumna and built on one bank only in such a manner that it terminates in this place very much in the form of a crescent, having but one bridge of boats to cross to the country. Excepting the side where it is defended by the river, the city is encompassed by walls of brick. . . . The suburbs are interspersed with extensive gardens and open spaces. . . . The citadel [Shah Jahan's Red Fort] is defended by a deep ditch faced with hewn stone, filled with water and stocked with fish. . . . Adjoining the ditch is a large garden, filled at all times with flowers and green shrubs, which contrasted with the stupendous red walls produce a beautiful effect. Next to the garden is the great royal square, faced on one side by the gates of the fortress, and on the opposite side of which terminate the two most considerable streets of the city. The tents of such Rajahs as are in the king's pay, and whose weekly turn it is to mount guard, are pitched in this square. . . . In this place also, at break of day, they exercise the royal horses, which are kept in a spacious stable not far distant. . . . Here too is held a bazaar or market for an endless variety of things, which, like the Pont-neuf at Paris, is the rendezvous for all sorts of mountebanks [swindlers] and jugglers. Hither likewise the astrologers resort. These wise doctors remain seated in the sun, on a dusty piece of carpet, handling some old mathematical instruments and having open before them a large book. In this way they attract the attention of the passers-by and impose upon the people, by whom they are considered as so many infallible oracles. . . . Silly women, wrapping themselves in a white cloth from head to foot, flock to the astrologers, whisper to them all the transactions of their lives, and disclose every secret. . . . The rich merchants have their dwellings elsewhere, to which they retire after the hours of business.

Source: F. Bernier, *Travels in the Mogul Empire,* trans. A. Constable (London: Constable & Co., 1891), pp. 241–245 passim.

EARLY MODERN ISLAMIC EMPIRES

The Ottomans	Mughal India	Safavid Iran
Osman (1299–1326)		
Mehmet II (1451–1481)		
Fall of Constantinople (1453)	Babur (1483–1530)	Safavid dynasty founded (1501)
Selim the Grim (1512–1520)		
Suleiman the Magnificent (1520–1566)	Akbar (1542–1605)	Tahmasp I (1524–1576)
Siege of Vienna (1529)		
Battle of Lepanto (1571)		
	Jahangir (1605–1627)	Shah Abbas (1587–1629)
	Shah Jahan (1627–1658)	
Siege of Vienna (1683)	Aurangzeb (1658–1707)	
		End of Safavid rule (1736)

destructiveness of his policies. At least one anonymous letter reached him after he had restored the poll tax on Hindus, which read in part:

> **Your subjects are trampled underfoot; every province of your empire is impoverished; depopulation spreads and problems accumulate. . . . If your majesty places any faith in those books called divine, you will be instructed there that God is the God of all mankind, not the God of Muslims alone.[7]**

In 1705 he confessed to his son: "I came alone and I go as a stranger. I do not know who I am, or what I have been doing. I have sinned terribly and I do not know what punishment awaits me."[8] The Mughals had come full circle from the inspiring vision of Akbar to the nightmare of Aurangzeb.

The effective power of the Mughals ended with Aurangzeb's death in 1707. India slowly dissolved into civil war, banditry, intergroup rivalry, and mounting chaos, a context in which the English traders, present on the fringes for well over a century, began their own path to ultimate power.

Aurangzeb, whose reign had spanned nearly 50 years, was a contemporary of the Manchu emperor K'ang Hsi in China (Chapter 29) and of Louis XIV of France, the Glorious Revolution in England, Frederick I of Prussia, and Peter the Great of Russia. During these years Europe began its modern development of strong centralized states, continued its commercial and colonial expansion overseas, and rode a wave of unprecedented economic growth, which was reflected in the beginnings of major population increases. Manchu China in Aurangzeb's time also experienced a period of prosperity and vigorous economic growth, with major increases in trade and at least a doubling of agricultural output and population. The modern agricultural revolution was beginning at the same time in Europe, and the foundations were being laid for the later Industrial Revolution. European science and technology leapt ahead of the rest of the world with pioneering discoveries of scientists such as Isaac Newton and Robert Boyle. In these years Europe developed a lead that was to widen greatly in subsequent centuries.

If Akbar's open-minded curiosity and zeal for learning and experimentation had prevailed into Aurangzeb's time, India might have taken part in or at least benefited from these important advances. The early European visitors to India had, like Marco Polo, been drawn to and impressed by its wealth and sophistication. In Akbar's time there seems little question that India was not only richer than Europe but at least on a par with it and with China technologically, economically, and politically. Jahangir and Shah Jahan, however, were preoccupied with the pleasures of the court, monumental building, and intrigue. Aurangzeb was a single-minded zealot who cared nothing for the material welfare of his people and bled the empire to finance his wars. Instead of scholars, as at Akbar's court, Aurangzeb surrounded himself with sycophants, servile yes-men who dared not disagree or suggest alternatives and who flattered the emperor into thinking that he and his empire led the world. He did not deign to correspond with other monarchs, as Akbar had done, or to take an interest in anything but his endless military campaigns, undertaken in the name of Islam, to impose his tyrannical rule over all of India, a goal he never achieved. By the time of his death, India was economically and politically a shambles, and technological development was nonexistent. This was to prove a fatal combination of weaknesses, resulting in a situation of virtual anarchy. The now far more effective and technologically advanced Europeans were able to establish footholds from which their power in India could grow.

The Safavids in Iran

By about the year A.D. 1000 the Abbasid caliphate began to break up into separate and rival states. At the eastern end of their former domains, a group of central Asian

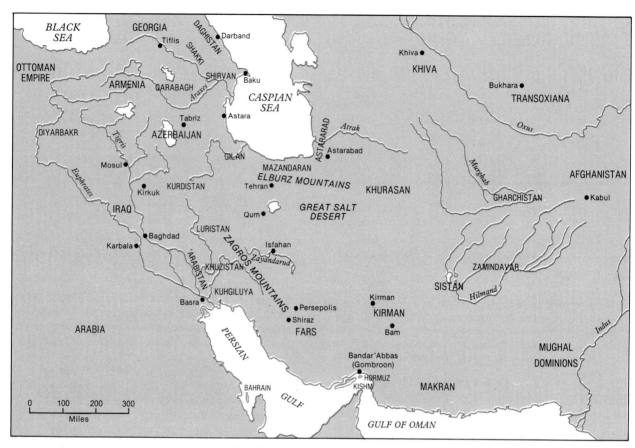

20.3 Iran Under the Safavids

Turks, the Seljuks, took over Iran, accepted Islam, and even captured Baghdad in 1065. The Seljuk rulers of Iran embraced and furthered Persian culture, as did their separate Turkish successors, but all this was swept away by the Mongol onslaught, which also destroyed virtually every city in central Asia in the mid-thirteenth century. A hundred years later, Tamerlane laid waste most of the same area. Through all these catastrophes, Persia's culture and sense of identity survived, much as in China under Mongol rule. Finally, out of the chaos left in the wake of Tamerlane, a new group rose to control Iran and to preside over a new and vigorous period of growth and cultural revival—the Safavids (1501–1736), who claimed descent from a Sufi saint but were in fact founded by yet another central Asian Turkish tribe.

The first Safavid ruler, Ismail, assumed the ancient title of Shah of Iran and briefly incorporated parts of what is now Iraq and southern Russia into his empire. The Safavids were Shi'ite (Shia) Muslims; they forcibly converted the previously Sunni Iranians and came into chronic conflict with the orthodox Sunni Ottomans and with the Mughals in India and Afghanistan.

Shah Ismail's son, Tahmasp I, reigned for 52 years

(1524–1576); defended the plateau of Iran, protected by its mountain borders, against continued Ottoman attacks; and presided over a great flowering of Iranian art, especially in miniature painting. In the familiar central Asian pattern, he was poisoned by his overeager son, who also killed off all his other relatives and rivals, only to die himself a year later, in 1577. After a period of civil war, there emerged the most outstanding of the Safavids, Shah Abbas the Great (1587–1629), who was to restore much of Iran's ancient glory. Its art, literature, and philosophy had long played the leading role in the Middle East, as China's had done in East Asia. Shah Abbas had the strength and vision needed to reunite the country and then to ensure economic prosperity and cultural vigor. He was an efficient administrator and a patron of the arts who made Persian culture once more a model for surrounding peoples. The beautiful capital he built at Isfahan in southwestern Iran remains perhaps the finest example of the medieval Persian style. In a series of campaigns between 1595 and 1612 he drove the Ottomans and their allies out of the parts of western and northern Iran they had occupied during earlier periods of disorder and kept them out for the rest of his reign.

Shah Abbas rebuilt much of the imperial structure

Part of the royal mosque at Isfahan, the capital of Safavid Iran. In Iran a great archway is intended to dominate most monumental buildings, as here. [Marburg/Art Resource]

originally laid down by Cyrus and Darius in the sixth century B.C., including the famous network of roads and bridges that crisscrossed the plateau, penetrated its mountain borders, and connected its cities with ports on the Persian Gulf and the Caspian Sea. Agriculture, trade, and cities grew rapidly under the new conditions. In 1617 Shah Abbas began commercial relations with the newly formed English East India Company and with its help in 1622 drove the Portuguese from the port of Hormuz on the gulf. Silks, ceramics, tapestries, carpets, and other exports from Iran could now be sent directly to England and Europe by sea, avoiding the overland route through hostile Ottoman territory and the tolls exacted along it.

Iran under Abbas became the cultural center of the Islamic world. Persian architecture, painting, literature, and the minor arts flourished and exercised a strong influence on Mughal India and on the Ottoman Empire. Rulers in both countries wrote poetry in the Persian style, had their portraits and court scenes painted in the Persian mode, and built palaces, domes, fountains, pools, gardens, and mosques on Persian models. Much of the credit for Iran's revival must go to Shah Abbas. Persian culture was renowned long before his time, but he inherited a weak, poor, war-torn country and gave it new strength, prosperity, and pride.

By the late seventeenth century the Safavids, Mughals, and Ottomans were experiencing serious problems. The Safavid dynasty would collapse in 1736, yet despite Iran's weakened condition, the Ottomans were unable to subjugate their neighbor. In India the last Mughal emperor was not removed by the British until 1858, but for its final 150 years the dynasty increasingly ruled in name only over a progressively shrinking part of northern India. After the death of Emperor Akbar in 1605, successive rulers were more self-indulgent and more concerned with luxury and power than with responsible administration. With the reign of Aurangzeb, Islamic orthodoxy was reasserted, and the empire's wealth was squandered in bloody but fruitless campaigns to control the south and to subdue the rebellious Rajputs, Sikhs, and Marathas. At Aurangzeb's death India was exhausted, impoverished, and torn by civil war. So weak did India become that in 1739 an Iranian army not only defeated the Mughal emperor but also stole the Peacock Throne (later captured by the Ottomans and taken to Istanbul). Thus the simultaneous flowering of western and south-central Asia in the sixteenth century had turned to decline, and in India's case genuine disaster, by the eighteenth.

The French traveler François Bernier, who visited India in Aurangzeb's time, reported in his Travels that the emperor, after belatedly realizing the potential strength of the Europeans, complained to him that his tutor had told him, "The whole of Feringustan [Europe] was no more than some inconsiderable island, that its kings resembled petty rajahs, and that the potentates of Hindustan eclipsed the glory of all other kings."[9] Bernier's contemporary, the Italian traveler in India, Niccolò Manucci, recorded his impression that Indians believed Europeans "have no polite manners, that they are ignorant, wanting in ordered life, and very dirty."[10] Crude and dirty or not, the Europeans were fast becoming the most effective groups in India, given the ruin of the Mughals and the disorganization of the Marathas and other possible Indian orders. The way was open for the rise of a British-dominated India.

Notes

1. B. Lewis, *Istanbul and the Civilization of the Ottoman Empire* (Norman: University of Oklahoma Press, 1963), p. 110.
2. N. Itzkowitz, *Ottoman Empire and Islamic Tradition* (New York: Knopf, 1972), p. 36.
3. N. Menemencioglu, ed., *The Penguin Book of Turkish Verse* (New York: Penguin Books, 1978), p. 80.
4. Ibid., p. 150.
5. S. Shaw, *History of the Ottoman Empire and Modern Turkey,* Vol. 1: *Empire of the Gazis: The Rise and Decline of the Ottoman Empire, 1280–1808* (Cambridge: Cambridge University Press, 1976), p. 289.
6. D. P. Singhal, *A History of the Indian People* (London: Methuen, 1983), p. 206.
7. J. Sarkar, *History of Aurangzeb*, vol. 3 (Bombay: Orient Longman, 1972), p. 34.
8. W. Hansen, *The Peacock Throne* (New York: Holt, Rinehart and Winston, 1972), p. 485.
9. R. Murphey, *The Outsiders: The Western Experience in India and China* (Ann Arbor: University of Michigan Press, 1977), p. 54.
10. Ibid.

Suggestions for Further Reading

The Ottomans

Babinger, F. *Mehmed the Conqueror and His Time*, trans. R. Manheim. Princeton, N.J.: Princeton University Press, 1978.

Cook, M. A., ed. *A History of the Ottoman Empire to 1730*. Cambridge: Cambridge University Press, 1976.

Frazee, C. A. *Catholics and Sultans: The Church and the Ottoman Empire, 1453–1923*. London: Oxford University Press, 1983.

Inalcik, H. *The Ottoman Empire: The Classical Age, 1300–1600*. London: Weidenfeld & Nicolson, 1973.

Islamoglu-Inan, H., ed. *The Ottoman Empire and the World Economy*. Cambridge: Cambridge University Press, 1987.

Itzkowitz, N. *Ottoman Empire and Islamic Tradition*. New York: Knopf, 1972.

Lewis, B. *Istanbul and the Civilization of the Ottoman Empire*. Norman: University of Oklahoma Press, 1963.

———. *The Muslim Discovery of Europe*. New York: Norton, 1982.

Lewis, R. *Everyday Life in Ottoman Turkey*. London: Batsford, 1971.

Shaw, S. *History of the Ottoman Empire and Modern Turkey*, Vol. 1: *Empire of the Gazis: The Rise and Decline of the Ottoman Empire, 1280–1808*. Cambridge: Cambridge University Press, 1976.

Vyronis, S., Jr. *The Decline of Medieval Hellenism in Asia Minor and the Process of Islamization from the Eleventh Through the Fifteenth Century*. Berkeley: University of California Press, 1986.

Waddy, C. *Women in Muslim History*. London: Longman, 1980.

Mughal India

Blake, S. P. *Shajahanabad: The Sovereign City in Mughal India*. Cambridge: Cambridge University Press, 1991.

Edwards, S., and Garrett, H. L. *Mughal Rule in India*. Delhi: Chand, 1962.

Gascoigne, B. *The Great Moghuls*. New York: Harper & Row, 1971.

Habib, I. *The Agrarian System of Mughal India, 1556–1707*. New York: Asia Publishing House, 1963.

———, et al. *The Cambridge Economic History of India*, Vol. 1: *1200–1750*. Cambridge: Cambridge University Press, 1982.

Majumdar, R. C., ed. *An Advanced History of India*. Delhi: Macmillan, 1973.

Prawdin, M. *Builders of the Mughal Empire*. London: Allen & Unwin, 1963.

Sarkar, J. *Shivaji*. Calcutta: Sarkar & Sons, 1952.

———. *A Short History of Aurangzeb*. Calcutta: Sarkar & Sons, 1962.

Shelat, J. M. *Akbar*. Bombay: Bharatiya Bidya Bhavan, 1964.

Singhal, D. P. *A History of the Indian People*. London: Methuen, 1983.

Srivasta, A. L. *The Mughal Empire*. Agra: Agarwala, 1966.

Subrahmanyam, S. *The Political Economy of Commerce: Southern India, 1500–1650*. Cambridge: Cambridge University Press, 1990.

Wolpert, S. *A New History of India*. New York: Oxford University Press, 1989.

Safavid Iran

Cambridge History of Iran. Cambridge: Cambridge University Press, 1983.

Morgan, D. *Medieval Persia, 1040–1797*. New York: Longman, 1988.

Savory, R. M. *Iran Under the Safavids*. Cambridge: Cambridge University Press, 1980.

Imperial Revival in China

With the expulsion of the Mongols in the mid-fourteenth century, the Chinese imperial tradition was reasserted by the founding of the Ming dynasty in 1368. Pride in regained power and wealth led to the building of magnificent new capitals, first at Nanking (Nanjing) and then at Peking (Beijing), as well as to the resumption of the tributary system whereby lesser Asian states sent regular missions to China, acknowledging its superiority and prostrating themselves before the Son of Heaven. Ming armies reconquered the empire of the T'ang and the Sung, and early in the dynasty a series of seven naval expeditions toured Southeast Asia, India, the Persian Gulf, and as far as the east coast of Africa, acquiring new tributaries, trading in Chinese products, and bringing back curiosities from afar.

The growing commercialization of the economy,

Magnificent paintings of nature continued under the Ming dynasty in the now long established Chinese tradition. This lovely spray of white magnolia is part of a larger painting by the master Wen Cheng-ming (1470–1559). [Metropolitan Museum of Art, bequest of John M. Crawford, Jr.]

aided from the sixteenth century by imports of silver from the Spanish New World, stimulated urban growth and a rich merchant culture. Literature, philosophy, and the arts flourished, and popular culture also expanded into vernacular writing, opera, plays, and woodblock printing. For at least its first two centuries Ming administration was effective and the country was prosperous. But the dynasty became increasingly conservative and traditional. It was plagued by court intrigues, and a series of weak emperors sapped its vigor. Popular unrest mounted as government became less and less able to provide an equitable order or to move with the times. Rebels took Peking and then were replaced by a new set of alien conquerors, the Manchus from Manchuria, who inaugurated the Ch'ing dynasty in 1644. Manchu rule nevertheless rested consciously and purposefully on the Ming heritage, and most of the trends that began under the Ming continued with little break once order was restored.

The Ming Dynasty

By the early 1300s Mongol control of China was weakening under the ineffective successors of Kubilai Khan. Chronic feuding within the imperial clan and pressures from rival clans enfeebled Mongol power, and by 1330 civil war had erupted. Beginning in 1333 successive drought-induced famines racked northern China, worsened by unchecked flooding in the Yellow River where the dikes had been neglected. Most Chinese interpreted these natural disasters as portents of divine displeasure and the loss of the Mandate of Heaven by the Yuan dynasty, a response typical of the declining years of all previous dynasties but further fed in this case by bitter Chinese hatred of the alien Mongols and their oppressive rule.

Banditry and rebellion spread rapidly in nearly every province, and rebel leaders vied for Heaven's Mandate in efforts to eliminate their rivals. Many rebel groups were aided by or belonged to secret societies. The most important of these was the White Lotus, a Buddhist sect originating in the Southern Sung period that consistently opposed the ruling dynasty and hence had to remain secret, with its own private rituals. The White Lotus persisted underground or in association with banditry and rebellion until the twentieth century. Another Buddhist secret society, the Red Turbans, so called from their headdress and similarly with origins in the Sung, rose in revolt and played a major role in the lower Yellow River plain while the White Lotus was active in the Yangtze valley. These and other rebel secret societies recruited supporters from among poor peasants and also drew on anti-Mongol sentiments.

MING CHINA	
1368	Founding of Ming dynasty
1368–1398	Hung-wu
1405–1433	Cheng Ho's expeditions
1472–1529	Wang Yang-ming, philosopher
1573–1582	Reforms of Chang Chü-cheng
1644	Founding of Manchu dynasty
1683	Fall of Taiwan

One of the rebel leaders, Chu Yüan-chang (Zhu Yuanzhang, 1328–1398), rose to a commanding position in the 1350s and went on to found a new dynasty. His forces swept the Yangtze valley by the end of the decade, set up a government at Nanking in 1356, and in 1368 captured Peking, proclaiming the Ming ("brilliant") dynasty, which was to last until 1644. The Ming achievement in rebuilding the empire and restoring Chinese pride ushered in a period of unprecedented economic and cultural growth that went far beyond where the Sung had left off. The population probably rose by at least 50 percent by the end of the Ming dynasty, stimulated by major improvements in agricultural technology promoted by the state. The entire economy commercialized rapidly, accompanied by a rise in the number and size of cities and perhaps a doubling of total trade.

HUNG-WU: THE REBEL EMPEROR

Chu Yüan-chang, the victorious rebel leader who became the first Ming emperor, took the name Hung-wu ("great military power"), by which he is mainly known. Life had been hard for him up to that point. Like Liu Pang, the founder of the Han dynasty, he had been born a peasant. Orphaned early, he entered a Buddhist monastery, where he became literate, and at age 25 joined a rebel band, where his native ability soon brought him to the top. As emperor his strong personality and high intelligence made a deep and lasting impression on the first two centuries of the Ming, whose foundations he largely built. He was an indefatigable worker, concerned with all the details of administering his new empire, but he had few close associates or friends and pursued an austere lifestyle that reflected his difficult and impoverished youth. Having risen to power over rebel rivals, he became paranoid about supposed plots against him and was given to violent rages of temper during which he often ordered harsh punishments for suspected disloyalty or trivial offenses. Irritated by continued Japanese piracy along the China coast, he also wrote to the Ashi-

Emperor Hung-wu (1328–1398), also known more formally as T'ai-tsu ("Great Progenitor"), in a caricature by an unknown fifteenth-century artist, one of a series of caricatures of notable emperors. Hung-wu's rather piglike face, commented on by many of his contemporaries, bore the traces of smallpox, which had nearly killed him as a younger man. The caricature conveys Hung-wu's forceful personality. [Collection of the National Palace Museum, Taipei, Taiwan, Republic of China]

kaga shogun (see Chapter 12): "You stupid eastern barbarians! Living so far across the sea . . . you are haughty and disloyal; you permit your subjects to do evil." The Japanese replied simply: "Heaven and earth are vast. They are not monopolized by one ruler."[1] Hung-wu's re-

action, perhaps fortunately, is not recorded. In his last will, he wrote of himself: "For 31 years I have labored to discharge Heaven's will, tormented by worries and fears, without relaxing for a day."[2] One wonders if he felt that winning the Dragon Throne had really been worth the effort!

Hung-wu increasingly concentrated power in his own hands and in 1380 abolished the Imperial Secretariat, which had been the main central administrative body under past dynasties, after suppressing a plot for which he blamed his chief minister. The emperor's role thus became even more autocratic, although Hung-wu necessarily continued to use what were called the Grand Secretaries to assist with the immense paperwork of the bureaucracy, which included memorials (petitions and recommendations to the throne), imperial edicts in reply, reports of various kinds, and tax records.

This group was later more regularly established as the Grand Secretariat, a kind of cabinet, but in Hung-wu's time he supervised everything and made or approved all decisions. He was concerned about the power of eunuchs, remembering the trouble they had often caused in earlier dynasties, and erected a tablet in the palace that read, "Eunuchs must have nothing to do with administration."[3] He greatly reduced their numbers, forbade them to handle documents, insisted that they remain illiterate, and got rid of those who so forgot their place as to offer comments on government matters. Some eunuchs were considered necessary as guards and attendants for the imperial harem, which the emperor was thought to need so as to ensure male heirs. In time eunuch power was to grow again, until in the later Ming period they became once more a scourge of good government.

One policy of Hung-wu's that shocked the Confucians was his resumption of the Mongol practice of having officials publicly beaten when they had displeased him. Confucian doctrine held that corporal punishment was only for the ignorant masses; the "superior man" was to be exempt, because with him one could reason and could expect him to mend his ways if necessary by following the virtuous example of those above him. Hung-wu was a tough ruler and demanded complete submission despite his praise for the Confucian classics. But as a peasant by birth, he never lost his envy and distrust of intellectuals. He also reorganized the army around a new system of elite guard units stationed at strategic points throughout the empire and along the frontiers. While some of his policies seemed extreme to many and his personality forbidding or fearsome, Hung-wu was a strong emperor whose work provided the Ming with a momentum of imperial power and effectiveness that lasted far beyond his time. His concentration of power in the emperor's hands worked well when the emperor was as able and dedicated as he was. When weaker and less conscientious men occupied the throne, the empire was in trouble, as was to happen disastrously in the last decades of Ming rule.

When Hung-wu died in 1398, the provinces within the Great Wall were secure and Chinese power was again dominant in eastern Sinkiang, Inner Mongolia, and southern Manchuria. Vietnam, Tibet, Korea, and Japan accepted tributary status. Hung-wu built a splendid new capital at Nanking with a city wall 60 feet high and 20 miles around. It was the longest city wall in the world, although like most Chinese city walls, it was intended more for symbolic affirmation of imperial power than for defense. Indeed, the Chinese word for *city* also means "wall," to distinguish it from a mere town. Peking was passed over as a capital because of its association with the Mongols and its location on the northern fringe of the country, far from major trade routes and agricultural centers. The Yangtze valley had long been the economic heart of the empire, and it made sense to put the capital there.

The second Ming emperor, Yung-lo (Yongluo, 1403–1424), was also an able and conscientious administrator. Continued prosperity and the new southern orientation of the Ming stimulated the further expansion of trade. Commerce and city life grew rapidly. Ports on the southeast coast acquired new importance as links with the colonies of overseas Chinese in Java, the Philippines, Vietnam, and elsewhere in Southeast Asia.

Tributaries and Expeditions

To mark the resurgence of empire after the brief Mongol eclipse, the traditional tributary system was enlarged and made more formal. This helped keep peace along the extensive borders as well as assert Chinese overlordship. In theory, Chinese political and cultural superiority was a magnet for all lesser peoples or states. They would willingly acknowledge its greatness and, "yearning for civilization," as the official Chinese phrase went, would model themselves on it. In practice, there was just enough truth in this to warrant saying it. Although, of course, the tributary states had their own pride and culture, they freely recognized that Chinese civilization had a great deal to offer them. Near neighbors such as Korea or Vietnam, and later Burma, Laos, Tibet, and Mongolia, had reason, moreover, to fear Ming military power and hence to accept tributary status. Recognizing China's supremacy cost them little; as long as they did not try to challenge it, they were left to manage their own affairs.

The ritual obeisance to the Chinese emperor required of ambassadors was probably not seen as humiliating, as it might be by a modern diplomat, but in keeping with the way in which they had to deal with their own monarchs at home. Tributary states sent regular missions every few years to the imperial capital, where their representatives knelt before the Son of Heaven in a series of prescribed prostrations known as the *k'e t'ou* (later Westernized as *kowtow*, literally "bang head," placing the head to the floor as a token of respect). They presented a long list of "gifts" and in return were given "presents," often greater in value and number. The missions were in part a polite cloak for trade, combining mutual benefit with diplomacy and the prestige of association with the Celestial Empire. It also fed the Chinese opinion of themselves as the only imperium, the only true civilization, the center of the world, compared with which all other people were barbarians.

At its height, first under the Ming and later in the early Ch'ing period, the tributary system involved over 40 states, including Korea, Vietnam, Tibet, Japan, Java, the Philippines, Burma, Siam, Ceylon, Malacca, and many central Asian kingdoms. The renewed Chinese interest in the wider world was a feature of the first few decades of the Ming, although the tributary system continued into the nineteenth century. The last half or more of Ming rule was, in contrast, a period of retrenchment, preoccupation with the defense of the land frontiers, and cultural conservatism. Such a shift fits the pattern of the dynastic cycle discussed in Chapter 12. All dynasties tended to be open-minded, cosmopolitan, and expansionist in their first century, complacent in their second, and overwhelmed by problems in their third and last, when the effectiveness and vigor of the imperial government deteriorated, corruption mounted, and rebellion spread. The Ming Chinese were no exception to this pattern, and the memory of the Mongol conquest tended in any case to make them antiforeign, conservative in their determination to reaffirm the great tradition of the Chinese past, and inward-centered. All this was understandable and probably benefited the country, at least in the short run, as much as or more than foreign adventuring. China was a huge and productive world in itself. Until late in the 1500s things continued to go well, and general prosperity kept most people content.

Japanese and Korean pirate raids at places all along the coast did worry the Ming, and not only because of what the pirates stole or destroyed. The raids demonstrated that the Chinese government could not keep order locally or defend its people. The raids were regarded as equivalent to rebellion, and the government also knew that a good many renegade Chinese were involved, masquerading as Koreans or Japanese. After much pressure from Peking, the Ashikaga shogunate in Japan, now formally a Ming tributary, suppressed some of the Japanese pirate activity and sent some captured pirates to Peking for execution. A Ming document addressed to the Ashikaga in 1436 acknowledged this and went on to say, in the customary language of the tributary system:

> Since our empire owns the world, there is no country on this or other sides of the seas which does not submit to us. The sage emperors who followed one another had the same regard and uniform benevolence for all countries far and near. You, Japan, are our eastern frontier, and for generations you have performed tributary duties. The longer the time, the more respectful you have become.[4]

From Southeast Asia to Africa

What distinguished the early Ming period was the outreach of imperial pride, manifested especially in remarkable maritime expeditions. The eunuch admiral Cheng Ho (Zhenghe) mounted seven naval expeditions of Chinese fleets between 1405 and 1433, with up to 60 vessels. They toured much of Southeast Asia, the east and west coasts of India (including Calicut, where 90 years later Vasco da Gama was to make his Asian landfall), Ceylon, the Persian Gulf and the Straits of Hormuz, Aden, Jidda (from which seven Chinese went to Mecca), and East Africa. They may have gone as far as the Cape of Good Hope or even around it. They brought back giraffes, zebras, and ostriches to amaze the court, and tributary agreements with gifts from a host of new states. When the king of Ceylon was considered not deferential enough, he was arrested and taken back to Nanking, and Yung-lo appointed a new king in his place. Tributary missions came several times from the Persian Gulf, East Africa, India, and Southeast Asia.

Cheng Ho's many-decked ships carried up to 500 troops but also cargoes of export goods, mainly silks and porcelains, and brought back foreign luxuries such as spices and tropical woods. The economic motive for these huge ventures may have been important, and many of the ships had large private cabins for merchants. But the chief aim was probably political, to show the flag and command respect for the empire, as well as to enroll still more states as tributaries.

Some of the ships were larger than any previously built in the world, 400 feet long and of 500 tons' burden, with four decks. Despite their size, they were reported to be faster sailers than the Portuguese caravels or Spanish galleons of two centuries later, especially with a favorable wind, and they were designed in accordance with the monsoonal wind patterns of Asia and the Indian Ocean. Properly timed voyages could count on going with the wind for about half the year almost anywhere

---

◉ A Ming Naval Expedition ◉

Here is part of a text engraved on a stone tablet in 1432, commemorating the expeditions of Cheng Ho.

The Imperial Ming dynasty in unifying seas and continents . . . even goes beyond the Han and the T'ang. The countries beyond the horizon and from the ends of the earth have all become subjects. . . . Thus the barbarians from beyond the seas . . . have come to audience bearing precious objects. . . . The emperor has ordered us, Cheng Ho . . . to make manifest the transforming power of the Imperial virtue and to treat distant people with kindness. . . . We have seven times received the commission of ambassadors [and have visited] altogether more than thirty countries large and small. We have traversed immense water spaces and have beheld huge waves like mountains rising sky-high, and we have set eyes on barbarian regions far away hidden in a blue transparency of light vapors, while our sails loftily unfurled like clouds day and night continued their course, traversing those savage waves as if we were treading a public thoroughfare. . . . We have received the high favor of a gracious commission of our Sacred Lord, to carry to the distant barbarians the benefits of his auspicious example. . . . Therefore we have recorded the years and months of the voyages. [Here follows a detailed record of places visited and things done on each of the seven voyages.] We have anchored in this port awaiting a north wind to take the sea . . . and have thus recorded an inscription in stone . . . erected by the principal envoys, the Grand Eunuchs Cheng Ho and Wang Ching-hung, and the assistant envoys.

Source: J. J. L. Duyvendak, "The True Dates of the Chinese Maritime Expeditions in the Early Fifteenth Century," *T'oung Pao* 24 (1938): 349–355.

in that vast region and then returning with the opposite monsoon in the other half of the year.

The Expeditions in Retrospect

Cheng Ho's ships, like those of the Sung, were built with double hulls and up to a dozen separate watertight compartments. Despite their far-flung voyages and their many encounters with storms and unknown coasts, few were lost. The crews were provided with detailed sailing directions, at least for the waters near home, and compasses. Their exploits of seamanship and exploration were unprecedented in the world. The grand scale and imperial pretension of the expeditions, as well, perhaps, as their commercial ambition, expressed imperial pride and vigor. However, they contributed little to the economy except temporary employment for shipbuilders and crew and luxuries for consumption, and made no lasting impression on the Chinese except to confirm their sense of superiority as the only civilized empire in the world.

The expeditions were also very expensive. They were stopped after 1433, perhaps mainly for that reason, although abuses and corruption in procuring shipbuilding materials and in contracts with shipyards also attracted official criticism. The emperor may have felt that he had made his imperial point, and it is unlikely that trade profits covered the costs. Another factor was the decision to move the capital to Peking in 1421, better to command the chronically troubled northern frontier against the attempted revival of Mongol power and to assert the tradition of a northern capital. The monumental building of Peking also competed for shrinking sources of timber and labor, as well as for treasury allocations.

But the abandonment of the maritime expeditions, like the move to Peking, was a symptom of the Ming's growing interest in consolidation. There were understandable fears of a Mongol resurgence and deep concern as well about the central Asian conquests of the Turkish leader Tamerlane, who was apparently planning to invade China. Tamerlane's death had ended that threat, but the Mongols were still active. Yung-lo personally led five expeditions into the steppe to combat the Mongol revival and remained preoccupied with the northern defenses for the remainder of his reign. In fact, Mongol tribes were to harass the border areas and raid across the frontier until the mid-seventeenth century. The Ming also promoted the spread of Lamaistic Buddhism to the Mongols in an effort to pacify them, a strategy that seems in the end to have been more effective than military confrontation.

The cost of the anti-Mongol campaigns on top of the building of Peking was a strain, and the extravagant oceanic adventures were a logical area for retrenchment. These excursions had also become politically controversial. Cheng Ho's voyages had been supported by his fellow eunuchs at court and strongly opposed by the Confucian scholar-officials; their antagonism was in fact so great that they tried to suppress any mention of the naval expeditions in the official imperial record.

China's relations by sea had always been given a far lower priority than the empire's land frontiers, and this ancient pattern was now reasserted. The Ming expeditions did not, to the Chinese mind, discover anything worth making greater efforts to exploit, and conquest was never part of the plan. Nonetheless, the scale of Cheng Ho's voyages remains impressive. While the Portuguese were just beginning to feel their way cautiously along the West African coast in sight of land, Chinese fleets of far larger ships dominated the Indian Ocean and the western Pacific and traded in most of their ports. They did not try to cross the Pacific or continue westward to Europe, which they were clearly capable of doing, only because to their knowledge there was nothing in either direction to make such a voyage worthwhile.

If they had reached Europe, they probably would have been no more impressed by it than by what they saw in Southeast Asia, India, the Persian Gulf, or Africa, nor any more than they were to be a century later by the early European arrivals in China. Fifteenth-century North America would have seemed to them too primitive even to mention. Like earlier Chinese innovations in science and technology, these maritime achievements were not followed up. The conquest of the seas, global expansion, and a sea-based commercial revolution were left to the poorer and less complacent Europeans, who from both their own and the Chinese point of view had more to gain thereby. The chief early goal of the European expansion overseas was in fact China, whose riches and sophistication had attracted Europe's mind and ambitions since Marco Polo—indeed, perhaps since the first Roman imports of Chinese silk, that symbol of luxury and wealth.

Prosperity and Conservatism

Meanwhile, the Ming turned inward from their new capital at Peking, rebuilding the Great Wall and its watchtowers in the form it still has today and promoting the development of their own home base. Such domestic concerns had always been the center of Chinese attention. Since Shang times they had called their country the Middle Kingdom, meaning not only that it was the center of the world but also that it combined the advantages of a golden mean, avoiding the extremes of desert, jungle, mountains, or cold around its borders.

In whatever direction one went from China, the physical and cultural environment deteriorated. The Chinese attributed the lack of civilization they noted in all "barbarians" to their far less favorable geographic environment as well as to their distance from the only center of enlightenment. China was indeed the most productive area of comparable size anywhere in the world, especially its great river valleys and floodplains. The empire was bigger than all of Europe in size, held more people, and supported a far greater volume of trade. The Chinese saw their interests best served by embellishing their home base rather than pursuing less rewarding foreign contacts. Domestic and interprovincial trade, between provinces the size of many European states, was far greater than foreign trade and served the world's largest market. Revenues now went increasingly to support domestic projects and to glorify the empire's rulers.

Thus conservatism was growing even before the end of the Ming's first century. Partly this reflected a determination to reestablish the traditional Chinese way in all things after the Mongol humiliation, but it also stemmed from enhanced prosperity. With everything going so well, there was less incentive to seek change or to be innovative, at least in terms of official policy.

The emperors who followed Yung-lo were less able or imaginative and tended to leave policy and administration to the intrinsically conservative Confucian bureaucracy, once again entrenched in power. The imperial censors were revived to keep officials honest and responsible and to keep the capital informed of actual or potential problems. On the whole, this tried-and-true system worked well for another century. In time it became increasingly rigid and less able to respond to change or the need for change, but until the last decades of the Ming, as with other dynasties, it was an impressive form of government that kept order and ensured justice to an admirable degree.

Nor did official conservatism and Confucian-based anticommercialism impede the basic changes at work in the economy. As in every Chinese dynasty, agriculture was regarded as the main source of wealth and worthy of official promotion. Under Hung-wu there was a major effort to rebuild agriculture in the extensive areas devastated by the Mongols and the rebellions against them. Many thousands of reservoirs and canals were constructed or repaired, and depopulated areas were resettled by mass transfers of people. Thousands of acres of farmland were reclaimed. The government undertook new projects to extend irrigation, pave roads, stock public granaries, and construct flood prevention works. Rice yields rose with the use of more productive and earlier-ripening varieties introduced from Southeast Asia and actively promoted by the state. New irrigation and better manuring, plus new land brought under cultivation to feed the growing population, produced a major rise in total output and a marked improvement in average material well-being.

In the sixteenth century new crops, especially maize, peanuts, and sweet and white potatoes, reached China from Spanish America via the Philippines. This increased output still further since the new plants did not replace rice or wheat but grew in hilly or sandy areas little cultivated before.

The Ming government and most of its Confucian magistrates executed duties conscientiously during this period. The tax system was reformed to make it less burdensome for peasants, although the bulk of imperial revenue came from taxes on land and grain in addition to customs duties and the official monopoly taxes on salt and tea. Regular labor service was also required of all districts and households for public works, including the building and maintaining of irrigation and flood prevention systems and the imperial road network. The roughly 2,000 local magistrates, forbidden to serve in their native provinces lest they show favoritism, were necessarily but effectively assisted by a large staff and also by local gentry. The latter were often the major factors in keeping order and ensuring that official policy and projects were carried out. Imperial censors traveling on circuit from the capital watched for irregularities and reported directly to the emperor. A new and comprehensive code of administrative and criminal law was published in 1397.

Food crops were still considered of prime importance, but the state encouraged a boom in commercial crops, such as mulberry (for silkworms) and cotton. Silk was produced in the densely populated Yangtze delta area, where its dependence on intensive hand labor could rest on the family, especially women and older children. The populous Canton (Kwangzhou) area and that of the Red Basin of Szechuan (Sichuan) were other important silk-making regions. All three were close to major urban markets and to navigable waterways to distribute their output throughout the empire at low cost.

Under the Ming, however, for the first time, cotton became the predominant fabric of daily clothing for most people. Cheaper and more durable than silk, it displaced coarser and more laboriously made hemp and linen. Silk remained a luxury item for the wealthy, but cotton became a far larger crop. It was grown and woven in the lower Yangtze, northeastern China, and central China, significantly adding to the income of farmers and providing new employment for weavers and merchants.

Commerce and Culture

For all the ambitious revival of the imperial bureaucracy, it remained a thin and superficial layer at the top. There were only about 2,000 officials outside the capital, far too few to touch most aspects of daily life in a vast country with a population now well over 100 million. Commerce was officially disparaged, but the most significant

21.1 Ming China

changes taking place in Ming China were in the expanding commercialization of the economy. Cheng Ho's expeditions were past, but trade with most of the places he had visited continued to increase, especially with eastern Southeast Asia. Although the largest trade was domestic, new supplies of silver and silver coins came into China to pay for the exports of silk, tea, porcelain, lac-

quer ware, and other goods and heightened the pace of commercialization and monetarization. More and more production was undertaken for sale, in agriculture and in manufacturing. Most of it was consumed in the rapidly growing cities, but some found its way to Korea, Japan, Java, the Philippines, and farther abroad.

Some of the silver flowing back came from Japan, but

more and more of it came from the Spanish base founded at Manila by the end of the sixteenth century, where it was brought from the mines of Peru and Mexico. Spanish-minted silver dollars began to circulate widely in the China market. By about 1450, silver coins, bars, and smaller ingots had driven paper money out; it was abandoned as people came to prefer increasingly plentiful silver over a paper currency that could not be exchanged for metal. Taxes were commuted from a share of the grain harvest and periods of labor on public works projects to silver. A sweeping reform in the sixteenth and early seventeenth centuries attempted, with considerable success, to simplify the tax system. The reform, known as the "single lash of the whip," lumped what had previously been a great variety of exactions into a few categories and collected them at fixed dates in silver, a major step toward a modern revenue system. At least for a time, this greatly reduced the confusion, corruption, and evasion that had bedeviled the former system, and it also increased the government's net income.

Merchant guilds acquired new though unofficial power in many Chinese cities, especially along the lower Yangtze and the southeast coast, the country's most urbanized and commercialized areas. Guilds controlled much nonagricultural production, marketing, and long-distance trade, informally and often through family or hometown networks, but very effectively. Merchants were still considered parasitic rather than productive. They were formally subject to officials and periodically to special government exactions. However, they were able to secure protection, access to favors, and other informal means of assistance, usually through a member of an extended family who had acquired gentry or official status. Indeed, such contacts were the only secure basis for commercial success in this bureaucratic society. Despite the Confucian disdain for their activity, at least on the surface, many merchants grew rich in this expanding economy. Some were able to buy gentry rank, although they were almost never permitted to hold office. Their money enabled them to live in the style if not with the prestige of the scholar-gentry, as literate connoisseurs of sophisticated art and literature in their great town houses.

After 1520 or so, capital investment increasingly moved away from the ownership and rental of land into commercial enterprises: trade and handicrafts. Prices for land continued to fall, and coastal piracy did not apparently discourage the increase of maritime trade as charges rose to cover those risks, although the biggest growth was in domestic commerce. In agriculture too, commercial or industrial crops such as cotton, indigo (for dyeing fabrics), and vegetable oil for illumination became more important. Handicraft production of tools, furniture, paper, porcelain, and art objects for wider sale became common, distributing finished products to

a regional or even national market. Some shops employed several hundred workers—another step toward industrialization.

A major cluster of porcelain workshops that sprang up at Ching Te Chen in the central Yangtze valley made magnificent pieces not only for the imperial household and the court but also for the general domestic market and for export. Iron and steel were made in many places, especially in southern Hopei, in quasi-factories. Large cotton mills producing cloth in major urban centers in the lower Yangtze valley and the highly commercialized delta area sold their output nationwide. There were 50,000 workers in 30 papermaking factories in Kiangsi province alone at the end of the sixteenth century. Skilled workers were in great demand and were recruited over a very wide area. Silk, porcelain, and tea especially, among other products, were exported in growing volume and with great profit. Chinese silk sold in Japan, for example, at five or six times its price in the domestic market, and it continued to be sold in the West at even higher prices.

As would happen two centuries later in Europe, growing commercialization, a widening market, and rising demand for goods provided incentives for improving and speeding up production and the development of new technology to turn out more goods. In the last century of the Ming dynasty a number of technical handbooks were published that show impressive progress in production technology. Some of the new techniques are reminiscent of ones that appeared in eighteenth-century Europe, where the increase in trade and demand helped lead to technological innovation, rising output, and the beginnings of the Industrial Revolution. In Ming China, such innovations included mechanical looms with three or four shuttle winders for producing larger amounts of silk or cotton cloth in less time and without increasing labor requirements. New techniques emerged for the printing of woodblocks in three, four, and five colors to feed the booming market for books and prints. Movable type improved. An alloy of copper and lead made the type sharper and more durable so that it could be used for larger print runs and could be reused many more times. New procedures were worked out even for the manufacture of specially refined grades of sugar, to suit the tastes and the pocketbooks of the greatly increased numbers of the wealthy.

Suspension bridges to carry the booming trade over rivers, making use of iron chains, had been developed by T'ang times. Such bridges became widespread under the Ming dynasty and greatly impressed the early European observers, although they were not successfully copied in Europe until the eighteenth century. The use of a mast and sail on wheelbarrows, important carriers of trade and raw materials on a local scale, especially on the North China plain with its wide expanses of level and treeless areas and its strong winds, also attracted Euro-

◉ A Western View of China ◉

Here is an excerpt from the journal of Matteo Ricci, who observed Ming China from 1583 until his death in 1610.

The Chinese are a most industrious people, and most of the mechanical arts flourish among them. They have all sorts of raw material and they are endowed by nature with a talent for trading, both of which are potent factors in bringing about a high development of the mechanical arts. . . . Their skill in the manufacture of fireworks is really extraordinary, and there is scarcely anything which they cannot cleverly imitate with them. They are especially adept in reproducing battles and in making rotary spheres of fire, fiery trees, fruit, and the like, and they seem to have no regard for expense where fireworks are concerned. When I was in Nanking I witnessed a display for the celebration of the first month of the year, which is their great festival, and on this occasion I calculated that they consumed enough powder to carry on a sizeable war for a number of years. . . . Their method of making printed books is quite ingenious. The text is written in ink, with a brush made of very fine hair, on a sheet of paper which is inverted and pasted on a wooden tablet. When the paper is thoroughly dry, its surface is scraped off until nothing but a fine tissue bearing the characters remains on the wooden tablet. Then with a steel graver the workman cuts away the surface following the outlines of the characters until these alone stand out in low relief. From such a block a skilled printer can make copies with incredible speed, turning out as many as fifteen hundred copies in a single day. . . . The simplicity of Chinese printing is what accounts for the exceedingly large number of books in circulation here and the ridiculously low prices at which they are sold. Such facts as these would scarcely be believed by anyone who has not witnessed them.

Source: M. Ricci, *China in the Sixteenth Century: The Journals of Matthew Ricci, 1583–1610,* trans. L. J. Gallagher (New York: Random House, 1953), pp. 18–21.

pean attention and was soon copied by the Dutch, although the wheelbarrow itself had been invented in Han China, and sails added soon thereafter. A huge network of rivers and canals linked most places from the Yangtze valley south by cheap water transport. In agriculture, new machines were developed under the Ming for cultivating the soil, for irrigation, and even for mechanical sowing, planting, and harvesting. Crops imported from the New World continued to add to total agricultural output. After Hung-wu and Yung-lo, Ming population figures are increasingly unreliable—another symptom of the decline in governmental efficiency—but total population probably increased to something like 130 million by the end of the dynasty.

To serve the needs of an increasingly commercialized economy, guilds of moneychangers and bankers became more important, and some of them developed a national network, with representatives in most major cities and at the capital. Techniques for transferring money through the equivalent of letters of credit, referred to as "flying money," had been used in the Sung dynasty but were refined and greatly expanded in the second half of the Ming period, as were other aspects of banking and the financing of trade. These developments too suggest comparison with what was happening in Europe along similar lines. The Marxist historians of China in the 1970s identified these trends in the Ming era as "early sprouts of capitalism," a description that seems quite reasonable despite the official downgrading of trade and merchants and the state regulation of commerce. Many of the richest merchants in fact grew wealthy through managing what were officially state enterprises or monopolies: supplies for the army, the shipment of rice to feed the capital, and the trade in salt.

Patronage and Literature

Wealthy merchants patronized literature and the arts, decorated their houses lavishly with art objects, and supported an elegant urban culture. Vernacular literature, too, which had had its major beginnings under the Sung, took on new dimensions and variety, appealing now to a growing mass of urban readers. Ming painting was in

In this beautiful work by the mid-Ming artist Lu Chi, painted around 1500, autumn mists veil the rising full moon but do not obscure the white tree peonies or the nearer two of the four wild geese by the edge of the stream. Birds and flowers, especially tree peonies (native to China), were favorite subjects for Ming painters. Like so many others, this painting is deeply restful and at the same time decorative. The detailed plumage of the geese is balanced by the simple and naturalistic single brush strokes of the tall grasses, as much a trademark of the Chinese as their renderings of bamboo. [Collection of the National Palace Museum, Taipei, Taiwan, Republic of China]

and flowers. Ceramics reached a new level of perfection, and beautiful pieces were part of every rich merchant household. This was the period of the famous Ming blue-and-white porcelain, samples and copies of which were prominent among Chinese exports to the West.

Yung-lo commissioned an immense encyclopedia of all knowledge, on which 3,000 scholars worked for five years. It was followed later in the fifteenth century by a great medical encyclopedia and others devoted to geography, botany, ethics, and art. The medical volumes, completed in 1578, listed over 10,000 drugs and prescriptions, most of them unknown in the West, and recorded the use of inoculation to prevent smallpox, far in advance of this discovery in eighteenth-century Europe. A handbook of industrial technology printed in 1637, just before the dynasty collapsed, described methods and tools or machines in the production of rice, salt, porcelain, metals, coal, weaving, paper, weapons, and many other fruits of Chinese industry and ingenuity.

In the popular realm, the theater flourished, but the major advance of Ming literature was in long novels and other stories of adventure and romance. They still make excellent reading and give a vivid picture of the life of the times. Perhaps the best known now is titled *Water Margins* (translated by Pearl Buck as *All Men Are Brothers*), which tells the story of an outlaw band and its efforts to correct wrongs done by unjust officials. Bandits of the Robin Hood variety had the same romantic appeal

A sample of the famous Ming blue-and-white porcelain. [University Museum, Philadelphia]

general less imaginative or innovative than that of the Sung and tended to rework older themes and styles, but the later Ming produced its own great painters, especially gifted in their exquisite representations of birds

in China as in the West, and their life as "men of the greenwood" (a phrase identical to that used in medieval England), meaning, of course, the forest, where they had their protected bases, was idealized. Several centuries later, Mao Tse-tung (Mao Zedong), the revolutionary Communist leader, said that *Water Margins* (the title came from the marshes that surrounded the outlaws' base) was his favorite book, probably because it glorified men attempting to defy and replace the existing government. Another still widely read Ming novel, *The Golden Lotus*, is an often pornographic satire about the amorous adventures of a druggist with servants, neighbors, and other men's wives that seems as fresh as today's bestsellers.

Most of the characters in *The Golden Lotus* are members of the leisure class, servants, or concubines in a wealthy household. The novel is generally interpreted as a critical portrayal of decadence, but since the characters are mainly well educated, including the concubines, it includes scenes in which they recite or improvise classical-style poems or songs. Here is one of them:

> *It is evening.*
> *The storm has passed over the southern hall,*
> *Red petals are floating on the surface of the pool.*
> *Slowly the gentle thunder rolls away.*
> *The rain is over and the clouds disperse;*
> *The fragrance of waterlilies comes to us over the distance.*
> *The new moon is a crescent*
> *Fresh from the perfumed bath, decked for the evening;*
> *Over the darkening courtyard it wanes*
> *Yet will not go to rest.*
> *In the shade of the willow the young cicada bursts into song,*
> *Fireflies hover over the ancestral halls.*
> *Listen. Whence comes this song of Ling?*
> *The painted boat is late returning,*
> *The jade chords sink lower and lower;*
> *The gentlefolk are silent:*
> *A vision of delight!*
> *Let us rise and take each other by the hand*
> *And dress our hair.*
> *The moon lights up the silken curtains,*
> *But there are no sleepers there.*
> *The mandarin duck tumbles the lotus leaves*
> *On the gently rippling water*
> *Sprinkling them with drops like pearls.*
> *They give out fragrance,*
> *And a perfumed breeze moves softly over the flower beds*
> *Beside the summer-house.*
> *How can our spirits fail to be refreshed?*
> *Why crave for the islands of the blest, the home of fairies?*
> *Yet when the west wind blows again, Autumn will come with it.*[5]

The bandit tales collected in *Water Margins* include a well-known story called "The Birthday Gift Convoy," part of which reads as follows:

The road had narrowed to mountain paths, but Yang Chih kept the carriers with their pole loads moving. It was almost noon and the sun [was] directly overhead. The men broke out with "Such hot weather! That deadly sun really kills!" but Yang Chih bore down on them shouting, "Hurry along! We have to cross that ridge. Time to worry about the weather later!"

On attaining the top of the ridge, the men flung down their poles, loads and all, and stretched themselves at full length under the pine trees. Yang Chih tried to beat them into resuming the march, saying, "This very spot is the haunt of bandits, where even in the best of times robberies are committed in full daylight." Suddenly he dropped his cane, grasped his sword, and dashed into the woods, where he saw seven men with seven wheelbarrows. They said they were date sellers on their way to the capital, resting in the woods in the heat of the day. Soon another man appeared, with two buckets of wine hanging from his shoulder pole, who also sat down to rest in the shade. The carriers of the birthday gift convoy begged to be allowed to buy some wine, but Yang Chih adamantly refused, saying the wine might be drugged. Hearing the commotion, the date sellers came out of the woods, and, after some dickering, persuaded the wine seller to let them have one of his buckets, which they drank from with coconut shell ladles they had in their packs. Yang Chih watched all this and observed that even after some time the date sellers did not seem to be much affected by the wine. Realizing that he still had to get his convoy a long way that day and calculating that a little wine might help get his men back on their feet, he grudgingly permitted them to buy some, and even took a little himself. Within minutes, the date merchants, who had been watching these proceedings, pointed their fingers at the entire party and chanted in chorus, "Sink, sink, sink into heavy slumber!" Instantly the carriers and their guards wobbled at the knees and sank to the ground. The seven strange travelers now brought their wheelbarrows out of the woods, emptied out all the dates, transferred the eleven precious loads of gold, silver, and jewels to the seven wheelbarrows, and were soon out of sight.

Yang Chih groaned with rage and bitterness, but his body seemed paralyzed and he could not struggle to his feet. Who were the seven men? Why, they were all famous bandits. How was the wine drugged? Why, by one of the date merchants when he playfully tried to steal another ladleful from the second bucket and in the process added the drug. It was all a carefully worked-out plan to convince Yang Chih and his men, by the date sellers' drinking the first bucket, that the wine was pure. Yang Chih's downfall was like the proverb: Though you be as circumspect as the devil himself, you may unwittingly swallow your own bathwater. Yang Chih tore up his orders. "How can I go back to face my patron? I have no home to return to, no state to serve. Where can I go?" What eventually happened to Yang Chih you will find out in our next chapter.[6]

◉ Folk Wisdom: Maxims from the Chinese ◉

- A wise man adapts himself to circumstances, as water shapes itself to the vessel that contains it.
- Misfortunes issue out where diseases enter in—at the mouth.
- The error of one moment becomes the sorrow of a whole life.
- The gem cannot be polished without friction, nor man perfected without trials.
- A wise man forgets old grudges.
- A mouse can drink no more than its fill from a river. [Enough is as good as a feast.]
- Who swallows quick can chew little. [Applied to learning.]
- What cannot be told had better not be done.
- The torment of envy is like a grain of sand in the eye.
- Dig a well before you are thirsty.
- Better be a dog in peace than a man in anarchy.
- To win a cat and lose a cow—the consequences of litigation.
- Forbearance is a domestic jewel.
- Kindness is more binding than a loan.
- Those who cannot sometimes be unheeding or deaf are not fit to rule.
- Parents' affection is best shown by teaching their children industry and self-denial.
- A truly great man never puts away the simplicity of a child.
- To obtain one leads to wishing for two—enough is always something more than a man possesses.
- If the upper beam be crooked, the lower will be awry. [The example of superiors.]
- One lash to a good horse, one word to a wise man.
- The man who combats himself will be happier than he who contends with others.
- Let every man sweep the snow from before his own door, and not busy himself about the frost on his neighbor's tiles.
- A man need only correct himself with the same rigor that he reprehends in others; and excuse others with the same indulgence he shows to himself.

Source: J. R. Davis, ed., *The Chinese*, vol. 2 (London: Charles Knight, 1845), pp. 235–240.

The West as a whole has still not acknowledged that the novel, in much the same form as we know it today, originated in Asia, as did detective stories. But a few westerners were less parochial in their awareness and their tastes. Here is a conversation between the famous German writer Johann Wolfgang von Goethe (1749–1832) and a friend in 1827:

"During the days when I did not see you," he said, "I have read a great deal, in particular a Chinese novel with which I am still occupied."

"A Chinese novel," I said, "that must be rather curious."

"Not as curious as one might be tempted to think," replied Goethe. "These people think and feel much as we do, and one soon realizes that one is like them."

"But," said I, "perhaps this Chinese novel is a rather exceptional one?"

"Not at all," said Goethe, "the Chinese have thousands of the kind, and they even had a certain number of them

already when our forebears were still living in the woods."[7]

Popular Culture

By the sixteenth century there was a large and growing number of people who were literate or semiliterate but were not members of any elite or of the official Confucian-style gentry. The latter probably never exceeded 2 percent of the population. These nonelite literates and semiliterates lived in the vast Chinese world that was little touched by the imperial system and its canons, most of them outside the big cities and the circles of the rich merchant elites. Popular literature, stories, novels, and plays produced by and for them probably exceeded in volume and circulation the output in the orthodox classical mode, extensive and varied as that was. Much of it was also read, in private, by the elite, who would hide any "undignified" book under the pillow if someone entered the room. For us today, too, most of it is more fun than the restrained, polished, or formal material that the scholarly gentry were supposed to read and write.

In addition were the number of puppet shows, shadow plays, mystery and detective stories (four or five centuries before they appeared in the West), operas, ballads, the oral tradition of itinerant storytellers, and a wealth of inexpensive woodblock prints, many of them dealing with aspects of daily life, others with mythology or folk religion. Opera, which combined drama, music, dance forms, singing, and gorgeous costumes, could appeal also to illiterates, probably still the large majority (although Ming China may have been the most literate society of its time), as could storytellers, balladeers, and plays. Itinerant groups performed in all these media everywhere, even in small towns. Storytellers would be accompanied by musicians or provide their own music and would end each recital at a moment of suspense: "Come back next time if you want to hear the next episode" or "Pay now if you want to know how it all came out!"

Over 300 different local or regional genres of opera have been identified, intended mainly for nonelite audiences. Many operas, plays, and stories centered on the adventures of heroes and villains of the rich Chinese past, not always historically accurate but always entertaining, and appealing to the deep interest of the Chinese in their own history. Most of the common people learned their history from opera, theater, and storytellers, and they learned a great deal of it. The connection with folk religion was close, including folk versions of Buddhism and Taoism as well as local animist cults and deities, and many of the operas, plays, and stories focused on it.

Operas were commonly performed at festivals celebrating a local god or as part of temple rituals, and many of them, as well as shadow plays, had an explicitly religious or ritual content, like the medieval miracle plays of Europe. Still others satirized daily life: henpecked husbands, jilted or faithless lovers, grasping merchants, corrupt officials, overprotective or authoritarian parents, tyrannical landlords, and so on, set in villages or towns rather than in the more sophisticated and urbane world of the cities.

These operas and plays formed in effect a countertradition to the elite culture. They expressed strong sympathy for the powerless, the oppressed, and the underdogs, especially women, who were often major figures. The works express contempt for wealth without compassion, for power without responsibility, and for all forms of hypocrisy, opportunism, and moral compromise. In this extensive genre, individuals are valued and respected for their achievements and their moral virtue regardless of their social position, in contrast to the hierarchical ordering of individuals that Confucian doctrine supported. This rich and varied literature has a universal flavor and many parallels in the popular culture of most other societies around the world, past and present. But it also reveals the basic good sense, humor, and appealing human qualities of the common people of Ming China.

Elite Culture and Traditionalism

In monumental architecture the Ming created new glories in their capitals at Nanking and Peking and in temples in every city and many towns, a further indication of prosperity. But in general, particularly after their first century, the Ming looked to the past for guidance. This accounted for their interest in encyclopedias, which collected the wisdom and experience of previous generations as guardians of tradition.

Most Ming scholars and philosophers were traditionalists, mistrusting speculation or innovation. There were exceptions, of course, but orthodoxy tended to dominate thought, reinforced by the system of imperial examinations. As one Ming writer put it: "Since the time of Chu Hsi [the Sung Confucianist] the truth has been made clear. No more writing is needed. We have only to practice."[8] There were nevertheless some important developments in philosophy, especially in the thought of Wang Yang-ming (1472–1529), a scholar-official who went beyond the Neo-Confucianism of Chu Hsi in urging both a meditative and intuitive self-cultivation, much influenced by Buddhism, and an activist moral role in society. Wang's most famous aphorism stresses the organic connection between knowledge and behavior: "Knowledge is the beginning of conduct; conduct is the completion of knowledge"—a maxim still admired by Confucianists in China, Korea, and Japan.

Before Wang's time, Hung-wu had issued six brief imperial edicts that were posted in all villages and towns in 1397, a year before his death. They ordered people to be filial, to respect their elders and ancestors, to teach their children to do the same, and peacefully to pursue their livelihoods. Local gentry, not in office but functioning as local elites and keepers of order and morality, helped make sure that these prescriptions were carried out. The orthodox Confucian denigration of trade and merchants and their subordination to officialdom helped strengthen official disinterest in commerce. Foreign trade was left largely in private hands or was managed by powerful eunuchs at court, which further devalued it in Confucian eyes.

Grain had to be hauled north from the Yangtze valley to feed the swarm of officials, garrison troops, and commoners as well as the elite of Peking. Japanese piracy prompted Yung-lo to restore the Grand Canal, which had silted up and fallen into disrepair, and to abandon the coastal sea route after 1415. The cost was high, but the canal helped generate further increases in interregional trade and in the production of crafted articles and other consumer goods to supply an enlarged market. It also stimulated the growth of cities along its route. Soochow (Suzhou), in the Yangtze delta just west of Shanghai and until the nineteenth century the major city and port of that area after Nanking, became a national financial and commercial center; it was noted for its fine silk goods, which were distributed to the wealthy all over China, especially in fashionable Peking. Cotton cloth, lacquer, magnificent porcelain pieces, iron cooking pots from Canton, and numerous other goods were carried, mainly by water routes, to an increasingly national market. Hankou (now part of the city of Wuhan) on the central Yangtze grew as a major junction of rivers and a national distribution center as well as a major market in itself. Private Chinese merchants went to Southeast Asia in great numbers and managed an increasing overseas trade from bases on the southeast China coast such as Canton, Amoy, Swatow, and Foochow (Fuzhou) despite official discouragement. Tientsin (Tianjin), the port of Peking, grew also as the chief port for trade with Korea. Other booming cities included Chengdu, the capital of the agriculturally rich province of Szechuan with its many rivers, and Changsha, the capital of Hunan on the Hsiang (Xiang) River, a tributary of the Yangtze, which flowed through the productive lowlands of central China known as "China's rice bowl."

Increasingly conservative official attitudes were reflected in the Ming reform of the imperial examination system. In 1487 a set form was established for the writing of examination papers in eight categories using no more than 700 characters altogether, following a prescribed style of polished commentary on the Confucian and Neo-Confucian classics. This was the notorious "eight-legged essay," which in all likelihood intentionally inhibited individual thought or innovation and encouraged a traditionalist orthodoxy.

Government schools at the county and prefectural levels and private academies and tutors for the sons of the wealthy (daughters were given no formal education) passed on the distilled wisdom of the ages to youngsters fortunate enough to attend and shaped their instruction to prepare them to conform to what the examinations now required. Candidates had to pass preliminary examinations at the county level. Success there enabled them to compete at the prefectural city, where they could obtain the lowest principal degree. That constituted admission to the gentry class with, among other things, exemption from labor service and from corporal punishment. The second level of examinations was held in each provincial capital; it lasted several days, during which each candidate was walled into a tiny cell and provided with food and water. Only about one in every 100 passed, earning a higher degree and the right to compete in the final examination offered every three years

at the imperial capital. Success there was rewarded with the highest degree and an interview with the emperor himself, who could appoint those of his choosing to official posts. The lowest degree could be purchased, especially as the dynasty declined and needed money, but such buyers—merchants or landlords—did not serve as officials. The sale of these degrees (akin to the sale of titles in early Stuart England) served to some extent as a concession to wealthy families that might otherwise become restive.

The basic Confucian message of responsibility and human-heartedness continued to be stressed, with its conviction that human nature is fundamentally good and can be molded by education and by the virtuous example of superiors. The ultimate deterioration and collapse of the Ming, and in 1911 of the entire imperial system, should not obscure its positive aspects, especially during its many centuries of relative vigor. Even up to the last years of the Ming, the growing corruption and ineffectiveness of the court were not much reflected in the continued operation of the system elsewhere in the country, which rested far more on the basic Chinese social fabric of family, gentry, and Confucian principles than on the management or intervention of the few imperial officials. The lives and values of most people had their own momentum. Local freedom and good order had relatively little to do with imperial politics at most times and much to do with the traditional Chinese system of a self-regulating society based on respect for tradition and hierarchy.

Local gentry directed and raised money for public works, especially irrigation, roads, canals, bridges, and ferries. Often they organized and funded schools and academies, orphanages, care for the elderly, and relief measures in hard times or after floods. Many of them compiled the local histories or gazeteers that are still a mine of information about local conditions, events, and notable people. This was all done as a manifestation of Confucian morality, without pay or official appointment. When all went well, perhaps half or more of the time during the 2,000 years of dynastic rule, the local gentry thus served as a major supplement to government and an important cement for society.

<hr />

♨
IMPERIAL PEKING:
AXIS OF THE MING WORLD

<hr />

When Yung-lo decided to move the capital back to the north, Peking was the obvious choice, primarily for its nearness to the most threatened frontiers. It is only about 40 miles from the mountains that surround and protect the city on the west, north, and northeast. The Great Wall runs through them, crossing a narrow lowland strip of coastal plain east of the city that leads to Manchuria and is called Shan Hai Kuan ("mountain sea gate"). Passes to the northwest lead directly into Mongolia. Both areas had been identified by now as the chief trouble spots along the frontier, and it was mainly to guard against them that the Great Wall was rebuilt at tremendous cost.

The Hsiung-nu menace that had plagued the Han had been replaced by that of the Mongols farther east and by early signs of what was to become the next alien conquering group, the Manchus of Manchuria. The gradual eastward progression of China's capital from Chou, Ch'in, Han, and T'ang Ch'ang An (Sian) to Loyang, the Sung move to Kaifeng and Hangchow, and now the Ming choice of Peking reflected these military challenges. The growth of the south, the drought and agricultural deterioration of the northwest, and the provision of canals to bring food from the surplus areas of the Yangtze valley to feed successive northern capitals were also factors in determining where the imperial capital would be located.

The new Peking was designed to make a statement of imperial power and majesty. The older center of the city today is largely a Ming creation, replacing what had been left of the Mongol capital but on a much larger scale. The main outer city walls were 40 feet high and nearly 15 miles around, forming a rectangle pierced by nine gates with watchtowers and outer gates to deter attackers, check permit papers, and awe all who entered.

Inside was the Imperial City, within its own walls, 5 miles in circumference. These enclosed in turn the red inner walls of the Forbidden City, which contained the palace and was surrounded by a moat 2 miles around.

Successive courtyards inside the Forbidden City, dominated by throne halls for different purposes, were set on terraces of white marble with gleaming gold-tiled roofs. These led along a north-south axis to the palace. Outside the Forbidden City (so called because it was closed to all except people with official business), a similar succession of elegant stone-paved courtyards, terraces, and audience halls led to the main gates. The outermost walls enclosed gardens, artificial lakes, and even an artificial hill.

The orientation of the city as a whole, based on astronomical principles, followed a north-south axis, thus aligning the court with the order of the universe. The overall plan and its every detail were designed to awe and impress all who approached or entered its series of walls and courtyards. It still has that effect, and partly for that reason, it has been restored by the People's Republic as the centerpiece of the modern capital. The Ming design was accepted and embellished by their successors, the Ch'ing (Qing). That part of Peking remains one of the best-preserved and most impressive planned capitals anywhere. Its splendid courtyards, the gracefulness and yet strength of architectural and roof lines in all of its buildings, and the lavish use of colored porcelain tiles make it aesthetically as well as symbolically overwhelming.

A less planned city grew up outside the walls, where most of the common people lived, and it soon housed most of Peking's residents. The total population, inside and outside the walls, was probably a little over a million under both the Ming and the Ch'ing, fed in part with rice brought from the Yangtze valley by the Grand Canal. Some space was left clear immediately around the outer

The Imperial Palace inside its own wall, looking south across the courtyards of the Forbidden City. The planned rectangular layout of imperial Peking is evident. [Paolo Koch/Photo Researchers]

Throne room in the Imperial Palace, Peking. Each building in the Forbidden City is fronted by sweeping marble stairs, and courtyards are linked by ornate marble bridges. The buildings are elaborately decorated inside but elegantly simple in their external lines. [Marc F. Bernheim/Woodfin Camp]

walls for better defense, and there were large military barracks. A maze of streets, alleys, and small courtyards covered most of the area outside the walls, including the small walled compounds with their tiny gardens and living space for extended families. Some of these too can still be seen.

The majestic Imperial City and Forbidden City were formally ordered on a grand scale, in sharp contrast to the unplanned alleys and irregular streets of the city around them. But above all Peking was—and remains—an imperial statement in wood, stone, brick, and tile that dominated the entire urban area physically as well as symbolically.

Complacency and Decline

Peking was built in the days of Ming power and pride, but as the decades went by, complacency set in, and a number of growing problems were dealt with inadequately or left unattended. Japanese and Korean pirate attacks on the coast proved impossible to control, and the government's feeble response was to order the re-moval of all settlements 30 miles inland and officially to forbid maritime trade, although the ban was widely ignored. Guns had been in use for centuries, but China had begun to fall behind advances in Western gunnery. Late in the fifteenth century, when a touring censor asked for a demonstration of a garrison's long-neglected cannon, the commander said, "What, fire those things? Why, they might kill somebody!"[9] This may be an exaggerated example, and during most of the dynasty the Ming armies were reasonably effective in keeping the long peace at home and on the frontiers. Yet the failure to control raids by tributary states clearly presaged the decline of the dynasty.

Strangers at the Gates

China had now to deal with Western visitors as well. The Portuguese reached the South China coast by 1514, but their aggressive behavior led to their expulsion from Canton in 1522, where their envoy died in prison. To the Chinese, they were just another lot of unruly pirates, like the Dutch who followed them later, and their numbers and ships were small enough to be brushed off. The Chinese also found the westerners offensively hairy, misshapen, and very smelly, and although a few military commanders noted that their guns were superior to China's, no one in the government took them very seriously.

The westerners had different ideas. The Jesuits had their eye on China as an immense potential harvest of souls and sent a series of missions there beginning with Matteo Ricci in 1582 (see Chapter 18). He and his successors, notably Adam Schall von Bell and Ferdinand Verbiest, were learned men with a good working knowledge of the rapidly developing science and technology of post-Renaissance Europe. Complacency and pride kept the Chinese from learning what would have been most useful from the Jesuits: new European advances in mathematics, geography (despite the great voyages of the fifteenth century, the Chinese picture of the world was still woefully inaccurate and incomplete), mechanics, metallurgy, anatomy, surveying, techniques and instruments for precise measuring and weighing, and gunnery.

The court was instead fascinated by the clocks and clockwork gadgets or toys that the Jesuits brought and used to ingratiate themselves, while their most useful knowledge was passed over. Von Bell, a trained astronomer and mathematician, was able to decipher and explain the use of some remarkable astronomical instruments built under the Yuan dynasty in Peking; by the late Ming period, the Chinese had lost the secret. Their own astronomers had noticed that their calculations no longer accurately predicted the movements of the heavenly bodies, but instead of questioning their assumptions and methods, they concluded that "the heavens

---

◉ Social Customs in Ming China ◉

Matteo Ricci described a variety of social customs, as in these excerpts.

When relatives or friends pay a visit, the host is expected to return the visit, and a definite and detailed ceremony accompanies their visiting. The one who is calling presents a little folder in which his name is written and which may contain a few words of address, depending on the rank of the visitor or the host. These folders or booklets consist of about a dozen pages of white paper, with a two inch strip of red paper down the middle of the cover. . . . One must have at least twenty different kinds on hand for different functions, marked with appropriate titles. . . . Men of high station in life are never seen walking in the streets. They are carried about enclosed in sedan chairs and cannot be seen by passers-by, unless they leave the front curtain open. . . . Carriages and wagons are prohibited by law. . . . The whole country is divided up by rivers and canals. People here travel more by boat than we in the West, and their boats are more ornate and more commodious than ours. . . . Sometimes they give sumptuous dinners aboard their yachts and make a pleasure cruise of it on the lake or along the river. . . . Because of their ignorance of the size of the earth and the exaggerated opinion they have of themselves, the Chinese are of the opinion that only China among the nations is deserving of admiration. They look on all other people not only as barbarous but as unreasoning animals.

Source: M. Ricci, *China in the Sixteenth Century: The Journals of Matthew Ricci, 1583–1610,* trans. L. J. Gallagher (New York: Random House, 1953), pp. 61, 81, 167.

---

were out of order." All these were symptoms of an increasing tendency to ignore new ideas or troublesome problems or to gloss them over with confident-sounding pronouncements.

Politics and Corruption

At the capital, decline in administrative effectiveness was clear by the end of the sixteenth century. The court was filled with intriguing factions, including the eunuchs. This was to become a curse of the imperial system. Because they had no heirs, eunuchs were often trusted, given the care of imperial sons, and granted ready access to the emperor and to powerful wives and concubines. The eunuchs also commanded the palace guard and often won high military posts as commanders or served as imperial inspectors in the provinces. They controlled the workshops that made luxury products for the court and supervised the tribute sent by the provinces and foreign countries. Eunuchs were also often appointed to head official missions abroad.

All this gave the eunuchs certain opportunities for graft, which they used to enrich themselves. Eunuchs gained control of the fearsome secret police and used its power to blackmail and corrupt. This was a burden on the treasury as funds were siphoned off from normal revenues. Another serious drain was the huge allowances paid to the numerous relatives of the imperial family and the nobility, altogether many thousands of people and their dependents. By the late sixteenth century these allowances alone consumed over half of the revenues of two provinces, which provides some measure of their gargantuan scope.

Other heavy expenses, including the cost of the expedition to Korea to repulse the invasion of the Japanese warlord Hideyoshi, drained financial resources still further. Subsidies to Mongol and other central Asian princes to keep them quiet and to deter them from new uprisings or raids on Chinese territory added to the financial strain. The already high taxes were raised still more, inciting both urban and rural revolt. The tax burden fell disproportionately on the poor since many families with money and connections had managed to get their names off the tax registers. Peasants also had to perform heavy labor service, including the rebuilding of the Grand Canal and the Great Wall. Many became so desperate that they melted away into the countryside or the towns or became bandits.

Strong rulers, like Hung-wu, could control the eunuchs, but under weaker rulers the eunuchs often assumed real power, which they usually did not use responsibly. Hung-wu had warned his ministers: "Anyone using eunuchs as his eyes and ears will be blind and deaf."[10] After Yung-lo came a succession of undistinguished emperors, most of whom kept to the pleasures of their palaces and left the running of the empire to the eunuchs and the bureaucrats, a disastrous pattern in a system where authority and responsibility had been so heavily centralized in the person of the emperor.

Banditry and piracy proliferated, a response largely to growing poverty but also to the still growing trade, especially with Japan. The Japanese often alternated as traders and as pirates, like their approximate contemporaries Francis Drake and John Hawkins in Elizabethan England. When the Chinese government in 1530 canceled permission for the official Japanese trading missions to Ningpo (Ningbo) on the coast south of Shanghai, piracy and smuggling multiplied. Pirates and smugglers had their major base for the central coast in the Chusan Islands off the mouth of the Yangtze River, conveniently near Ningpo, then the dominant maritime trade center for populous and highly commercialized central China. Other pirate and smuggling bases were scattered along the much indented coast of the south, shifting from one to another as government pressures or other circumstances required.

From the Yangtze southward, the coast was almost impossible to patrol adequately, and it had a long history of piracy. Mountains come down to the sea in most of this area, which meant that there were limited opportunities for agriculture or trade on land but ample forest cover for concealment and timber for ships. Like the shores of much of the Mediterranean, the Dalmatian coast of the Adriatic, or the Caribbean, the southern Chinese coast combined motives and bases for piracy with tempting opportunity: a golden stream of seaborne trade passing just offshore. In fact, piracy along this coast was not finally put down until after 1950, and smuggling continues still.

As an early-twentieth-century report by the Chinese Maritime Customs Office put it, speaking of the south coast, "Piracy and smuggling are in the blood of the people." When hard pressed by the authorities, pirates and smugglers from Amoy or Swatow southward could cross the border into nearby Vietnam, where they could find sanctuaries, supplies, and Vietnamese colleagues. Hainan Island off the coast opposite the border was long notorious as a pirate and smuggling base for desperadoes from both countries, and even modern China has had trouble preventing large-scale smuggling there. The people of the South China coast were the country's principal seafarers in any case, and many earned their living as fishermen and traders. The fleets of Cheng Ho were built in those harbors, using local timber, and their sailors were recruited from this region. As the power of the central government weakened under the later Ming dynasty and as poverty worsened after the fifteenth century, piracy and smuggling once again grew out of control. By the late Ming period, most of the pirates were not Japanese or Korean but Chinese.

A briefly successful effort at reform was led by Chang Chü-cheng (Zhang Juzheng), who became Grand Secretary from 1573 to 1582. Emperor Wan-li had ascended the throne as a boy in 1572 and was guided for some time by Chang, who as a distinguished Confucian scholar stressed the need for economy, justice, and responsibility. Chang tried to increase the now shrinking imperial revenue by once more reforming the tax system to restore exempted lands and families that had slipped off the rolls after the earlier tax reform. He also tried to limit the special privileges and extravagant expenses of the court and the imperial family and to rebuild the authority of the censors to check abuses. But after Chang's death in 1582, Wan-li abandoned all pretense at responsibility and indulged in more extravagance and pleasures, leaving the court eunuchs to run the empire. He avoided even seeing his own ministers for many years and refused to make appointments, conduct business, or respond to abuses.

Unfortunately, he lived and reigned until 1620, and the 15-year-old who succeeded him on the throne was mentally deficient and spent most of his time tinkering with carpentry in the palace. He gave control of the government to an old friend of his childhood nurse, a eunuch named Wei who had been a butler to his mother. Wei then almost certainly poisoned the emperor, although this was never proved; by then people were reluctant to challenge him. Wei put together a small eunuch army to control the palace and set up a spy network all over the empire. By unscrupulous plotting and force he eliminated all his official enemies—most of the Confucianists at court—filled their places with his opportunist supporters, and extorted new taxes to pay for his luxurious lifestyle. There ensued a general persecution of intellectuals, who were branded as "conspirators," and many hundreds were executed. Most of the academies were closed, half the government offices were left vacant, and petitions went unanswered. A group of Confucian scholars calling themselves the Tung Lin (Donglin, from the name of a famous academy) attempted a moral crusade against these evils. Wei responded with terror tactics after the Tung Lin leader accused him of murders, of having forced abortion on the empress, and 24 other "high crimes." In the end Wei won out, and most of the Tung Lin scholars were disgraced, jailed, or beaten to death before he himself was assassinated in 1627.

It was late for reform, and the eunuch stranglehold on the palace was now too strong to break. Eunuch power at court undercut and then virtually eliminated the power and even the role of the imperial censors. Many censors were killed when they dared to speak up. Palace eunuchs went on making most policy, or not making it, after Wei's death. By the 1630s most of the country had lost confidence in the imperial order. The state treasury, drained especially by extravagances at court,

◉ An Earthquake at Peking, 1626 ◉

The Chinese interpreted earthquakes and other natural disasters as symbols of Heaven's displeasure. When they coincided with popular discontent and dynastic decline, they were seen as warnings. Here is a description of an earthquake in 1626 at Peking, in the last corrupt years of the Ming. The partisans referred to were palace eunuchs.

Just when the . . . partisans were secretly plotting in the palace, there was a sudden earthquake. A roof ornament over the place where they were sitting fell without any apparent reason and two eunuchs were crushed to death. In a moment there was a sound like thunder rising from the northwest. It shook heaven and earth, and black clouds flowed over confusedly. People's dwellings were destroyed to such an extent that for several miles nothing remained. Great stones hurtled down from the sky like rain. Men and women died by the tens of thousands [a phrase that in Chinese means "a great many"]. Donkeys, horses, chickens, and dogs all had broken or cracked limbs. People with smashed skulls or broken noses were strewn about—the streets were full of them. Gunpowder that had been stored in the Imperial Arsenal exploded. This alarmed elephants, and the elephants ran about wildly, trampling to death an incalculable number of people. The court astrologer reported his interpretation of these events as follows: "In the earth there is tumultuous noise. This is an evil omen of calamity in the world. When noise gushes forth from within the earth, the city must be destroyed. . . . The reason why the earth growls is that throughout the empire troops arise to attack one another, and that palace women and eunuchs have brought about great disorder."

Source: C. O. Hucker in D. Lach, *Asia on the Eve of Europe's Expansion* (Englewood Cliffs, N.J.: Prentice Hall, 1965), p. 133.

never fully recovered. The results for the efficient operation of all state systems were disastrous.

Inflation aggravated the problem. Officials and local magistrates had to cope with a much larger population, increasingly troubled by discontent, banditry, and even rebellion. Their salaries were increased and special allowances given to discourage them from diverting official funds or taking bribes, but none of this made up for the far heavier work demands, which necessitated their hiring larger and larger staffs to assist them. These aides, though essential, were not official employees, and their wages were not provided by the state, leaving mag-

Street people of the Ming: beggars and hawkers, painted by Chou Ch'en (active c. 1500–1535). [Cleveland Museum of Art, John L. Severance Fund]

istrates and other officials to meet the costs out of their own inadequate salaries and allowances. The inevitable result was increased corruption and bribery, since the greatest of all traditional Confucian virtues was responsibility for one's own family. More and more, the rest of the Confucian morality disappeared as individuals and families strove simply to survive.

The Ming army did not distinguish itself in Korea. It drove the Japanese back but then was ambushed near Seoul, the Korean capital, and the rest of the campaign was largely a stalemate until Hideyoshi providentially died and his army promptly returned to Japan. A few years later, Matteo Ricci found the Ming army unimpressive: "All those under arms lead a despicable life, for they have not embraced this profession out of love of their country or love of honor but as men in the service of a provider of employment."[11] Many Chinese were now saying, "Good iron is not used for nails or good men for soldiers."

Much of the Ming army by this time was composed of ex-prisoners, drifters, former bandits, and idlers. Its size had doubled since the beginning of the dynasty, but its effectiveness had diminished sharply. Military contracts had become an open and expanding field for graft and corruption, and the quality of equipment and other supplies had deteriorated, as had military morale and leadership. One of the reasons for the failure to drive the Japanese out of Korea was what had become the inferiority of most Chinese weapons, including swords, spears, and guns. The Japanese had quickly noted and copied the Portuguese improvements in cannonry, and the development of an early version of the rifle, the harquebus, a cumbersome muzzle-loading weapon that was, however, devastating in close combat.

At the capital under the dissolute Emperor Wan-li, and progressively elsewhere in the empire, effectiveness and morale likewise declined. Despite Chang Chücheng's reforms, corruption had again removed much land and other wealth from the tax rolls, and the new taxes imposed by the eunuch Wei and his successors, together with a growing population, created widespread economic hardship and a rapid growth of tenancy, lawlessness, and regional famine. Banditry, local revolts, and secret societies, always a barometer of impending collapse, multiplied. There was open talk that the Ming had forfeited the Mandate of Heaven.

The incompetent government now faced two major revolts. A famine in Shensi (Shaanxi) in the northwest in 1628 led to arbitrary government economies instead of the needed relief. A postal clerk named Li Tzu-ch'eng (Li Zicheng) was laid off and joined his uncle, a bandit in the nearby mountains. Li and his forces raided widely among three or four adjoining provinces, attracted more followers, set up a government, distributed food to famine victims, appointed officials, and proclaimed a new dynasty. Early in 1644 he advanced on Peking, meeting only weak resistance. Hearing the news that the city had fallen, the last Ming emperor hanged himself in the palace garden, after failing to kill his oldest daughter with a sword.

A rival rebel leader named Chang (Zhang) had meanwhile been raiding and plundering much of northern China. In 1644 he invaded Szechuan, set up a government, and moved to claim the throne. His power plays and his terror tactics, however, lost him the support of the gentry, and without them his cause was lost. Neither Li nor Chang was fated to create a new dynasty; it came instead, as in Mongol times, from the steppe beyond the Great Wall.

The Manchu Conquest

A non-Chinese steppe people, the Manchus, descendants of the Jurchen, had risen to power in Manchuria despite Ming efforts to keep them divided. A strong leader, Nurhachi (1559–1626), united several previously separate tribes and founded a Chinese-style state, taking the title of emperor and promoting the adoption of the Confucian system and its philosophy. His capital was established at Mukden (now called Shenyang) in southern Manchuria, where his two sons, also capable leaders, succeeded him and continued the Sinification of the Manchu state and culture.

By 1644 the Manchus were for all practical purposes politically and culturally indistinguishable from the Chinese, except for their spoken language. Their administration and army included large numbers of Chinese, who saw them as a coming power. The Manchus made vassals of the Mongols of Inner Mongolia and the Koreans after expeditions had conquered both. They were consciously building their power to take over China, and in 1644 they had their opportunity.

A Ming general invited the Manchu armies waiting on the border at Shan Hai Kuan to help him defeat Li Tzu-ch'eng, who with his army now occupied Peking. The Manchus did so and remained to found a new dynasty, rewarding a number of Chinese collaborators with grants of land. Some of these collaborators later rebelled but were suppressed in heavy fighting. Finally, in 1683 the new dynasty conquered the offshore island of Taiwan, which had clung to the defeated Ming cause, a situation with parallels in the twentieth century. It thus took nearly 40 years before the Manchu conquest was complete. Unlike the Mongols, however, the Manchus ushered in a long period of domestic peace and unprecedented prosperity.

The Manchus called their new dynasty Ch'ing (Qing), a title adopted by Nurhachi's son and continued by his grandson, K'ang Hsi (Kangxi, 1661–1722). *Ch'ing* means "pure," and the name was intended to add legitimacy to an alien rule. But the Manchus had learned their Chinese lessons well. They honored and continued the best of the imperial tradition and could plausibly represent themselves as liberators restoring China's glorious past. While this made them, like the Ming, conservative stewards rather than innovators and in time helped harden them against change, they too presided over a brilliant period in Chinese history for their first two centuries. Ch'ing was the China most westerners first knew well. Although already in its declining years in the nineteenth century, westerners still found it impressive, built as it was on the long foundation of imperial greatness that had preceded it.

The Ming dynasty ended in ineptness and disgrace, but the positive aspects of its achievements were valued and preserved by its successors. Having begun with great vigor and success, the Ming went on to administer effectively for two centuries or more a new wave of prosperity, cultural growth, commercial and urban development, and the further refinement of taste. Popular culture, aided by cheap printing, enjoyed a notable boom, and in the larger cities rich merchants patronized and participated in elite culture. Although the dramatic maritime expeditions of Cheng Ho were abandoned, private Chinese trade multiplied with Southeast Asia, and domestic commerce thrived. Agriculture was made more productive, in part under state direction, and the population increased substantially. Ming Peking still stands as a monument to the dynasty's wealth and power. But the highly centralized system of government begun under Hung-wu helped sap administrative effectiveness under later and weaker emperors as power came increasingly into the hands of court eunuchs, with disastrous results. In the end the Ming dynasty was easy prey for the far better organized Manchus, who had learned the Confucian lessons that the Ming had forgotten.

Notes

1. J. K. Fairbank, E. O. Reischauer, and A. Craig, *East Asia: Tradition and Transformation* (Boston: Houghton Mifflin, 1989), p. 197.
2. Ibid., p. 182.
3. Ibid.
4. W. Bingham, H. Conroy, and F. Ikle, *A History of Asia*, vol. 1 (Boston: Allyn & Bacon, 1964), p. 459.
5. After W. McNaughton, *Chinese Literature: An Anthology* (Tokyo: Tuttle, 1959), pp. 697–698.
6. After H. C. Chang, *Chinese Literature* (Edinburgh: Edinburgh University Press, 1973), pp. 166–177.
7. J. W. von Goethe, *Conversations with Eckermann*, in J. Gernet, *A History of Chinese Civilization*, trans. J. R. Foster (Cambridge: Cambridge University Press, 1985), p. xxvii.
8. C. O. Hucker, *China's Imperial Past* (Stanford, Calif.: Stanford University Press, 1975), p. 373.
9. C. O. Hucker, *China to 1850* (Stanford, Calif.: Stanford University Press, 1980), p. 139.
10. Fairbank et al., p. 182.
11. J. Gernet, *History of Chinese Civilization*, p. 431.

Suggestions for Further Reading

Berliner, N. *Chinese Folk Art*. Boston: Little, Brown, 1986.

Chang, S. H. *History and Legend: Ideas and Images in the Ming Historical Novels*. Ann Arbor: University of Michigan Press, 1990.

De Bary, W. T., et al. *Self and Society in Ming Thought*. New York: Columbia University Press, 1970.

Duyvendak, J. J. L. *China's Discovery of Africa*. London: Probsthain, 1949.

Eberhard, W. *Moral and Social Values of the Chinese*. Taipei: Chengwen Publishing Co., 1971.

Fairbank, J. K. *The Chinese World Order: Traditional China's Foreign Relations*. Cambridge: Harvard University Press, 1968.

Farmer, E. L. *Early Ming Government: The Evolution of Dual Capitals*. Cambridge, Mass.: Harvard University Press, 1976.

Gernet, J. *A History of Chinese Civilization*, trans. J. R. Foster. Cambridge: Cambridge University Press, 1985.

Hayden, G. *Crime and Punishment in Medieval Chinese Drama*. Cambridge, Mass.: Harvard University Press, 1978.

Huang, R. *Taxation and Government Finance in Sixteenth Century Ming China*. Cambridge, Mass.: Harvard University Press, 1974.

Hucker, C. O., ed. *Chinese Government in Ming Times.* New York: Columbia University Press, 1969.

Idema, W. L. *Chinese Vernacular Fiction.* Leiden: Brill, 1974.

Johnson, A., Nathan, A., and Rawski, E., eds. *Popular Culture in Late Imperial China.* Berkeley: University of California Press, 1985.

Lach, D. F. *China in the Eyes of Europe: The Sixteenth Century.* Chicago: University of Chicago Press, 1968.

Levenson, J. R. *European Expansion and the Counterexample of Asia, 1300–1600.* Englewood Cliffs, N.J.: Prentice Hall, 1967.

Loewe, M. *The Pride That Was China.* New York: St. Martin's Press, 1990.

Mote, F. W., and Twitchett, D., eds. *The Cambridge History of China*, Vol. 7: *The Ming.* Cambridge: Cambridge University Press, 1987.

Parsons, J. B. *The Peasant Rebellions of the Late Ming Dynasty.* Tucson: University of Arizona Press, 1970.

Rawski, E. S. *Agricultural Change and the Peasant Economy of South China.* Cambridge, Mass.: Harvard University Press, 1974.

Ricci, M. *China in the Sixteenth Century: The Journals of Matthew Ricci, 1583–1610*, trans. L. J. Gallagher. New York: Random House, 1953.

So, K. W. *Japanese Piracy in Ming China During the Sixteenth Century.* East Lansing: Michigan State University Press, 1975.

Struve, L. *The Southern Ming.* New Haven, Conn.: Yale University Press, 1984.

Van Gulik, R. *The Chinese Bell Murders.* Chicago: University of Chicago Press, 1984.

The Societies of the Early Modern World

The richness and variety of the world's societies is abundantly revealed in the period of transition between the medieval and modern worlds that extends from approximately 1400 to 1800. Throughout the Western world in particular, social structures, behavioral patterns, and value systems underwent important changes that helped determine the character of today's societies. The institution of the family also altered, again mostly in the West, whereas in Asia the traditional family remained the bulwark of social hierarchy and stability. The age of women's rights lay in the future, but throughout the world women made significant contributions to their societies, sometimes by exercising political power at the highest levels of government. Women ruled, or were powers behind the throne, in societies as different as western Europe, Africa, and the Ottoman Empire.

The dress and many of the pursuits of the aristocracy—such as hunting, lawn bowling, and formal afternoon promenades—set them apart from the other social classes. This is a detail from *Le Rendez-vous pour Marly* **by Moreau le Jeune. [The Metropolitan Museum of Art, Harris Bisbane Dick Fund, 1933]**

The early modern period saw dramatic educational expansion in the West and a printing revolution in both the West and Asia. For the most part, neither Africa nor the Ottoman Empire effectively shared in these developments. Although patterns of trade became worldwide in the early modern period, most people lived at or near the subsistence level. To alleviate misery, Asians looked primarily to the family; Europeans, to religious, civic, and charitable institutions. In many respects, however, people responded to their social needs in similar ways, as reflected, for example, in the resort of the desperate in virtually all societies to banditry. This was particularly so in areas where governmental power was weak and resentment of urban wealth was strong. Beyond the threads of common human experience, however, differing value systems, rooted in religion and tradition, shaped early modern societies into distinct entities.

Social Hierarchies

Traditional Asian civilizations were hierarchically based, marked not only by the uniquely Indian institution of caste but also by the status groupings associated with kinship, feudal-style relations, occupation, age, gender, and levels of literacy and learning. In general, apart from caste, the importance of the social hierarchy and the emphasis on achieving status through learning remains a distinctive aspect of Indian, Chinese, Korean, and Japanese civilizations to the present day. Perhaps more than any other characteristic, this emphasis on seeking status and advancement through education distinguishes them from most societies elsewhere. For many Asians, an individual's place in the hierarchy is still the most important single determinant of how to behave, and the proper observance of hierarchical rules remains the most basic means of preserving social and political harmony.

Southeast Asia has always been fundamentally different from China, Korea, India, and Japan, partly because of the influences of Buddhism and Islam, both of which stress equality, and partly because of the indigenous nature of Southeast Asian culture. Kingship and the hierarchies related to it, however, were common in Southeast Asia too.

Caste and the Social Order in India

In contrast to the merit system of China and its variants in Vietnam, Korea, and Japan, caste was decreed by birth in India. Caste is a sociocultural practice with some religious concepts woven into it. Since it is also practiced by South Asian Muslims, Christians, and Buddhists (in Sri Lanka), it is clearly separable from Hinduism as a nonreligious system evolved later as a means of ordering an otherwise disordered society. The lack of a strong central state was accompanied by chronic disruption. Caste provided a system of social organization, a mutual-benefit society, a trade guild, and a sense of group identity. Ritual pollution and purity became the essence of caste, but its operative units were and are "subcastes," or *jatis,* commonly linked to occupation: potters, weavers, farmers, and so on. Each *jati* was and is endogamous (that is, it restricts marriage to fellow *jati* members), and members are forbidden to eat with or accept food or water from members of other *jatis*. One cannot change one's caste any more than one can change the place where one was born, although caste distinctions seem not to have been observed rigidly until relatively late in Indian history, well after the time of Harsha (seventh century A.D.). However, it has always been possible to escape from caste through religious devotion, again underlining the nonreligious nature of the caste system. The ascetic sadhu, or holy man, was beyond caste and honored by all, regardless of his earthly origins. Such mystics were, and like priests remain, far more numerous in India than elsewhere. South Asians have known for many centuries which *jati* they were born into, but this is not really part of their religion, any more than ancestry, social class, or occupation is for Christians in the West.

Caste has remained a highly flexible system. Although individuals are born into a given *jati*, by sustained group effort the members of a *jati* can raise its status, often by adopting religious, dietary, and other practices of higher-status groups. This process is called "Sanskritization," from the use of Sanskrit rituals associated with the Brahmins. In addition, the power of group action can be a potent weapon, especially in politics. This is particularly characteristic of Asian societies, where the individual is important primarily as a member of a group, be it family, clan, caste, guild, or regional or linguistic division.

Caste also served the need for some form of hierarchical order in a region of complex divisions. As new religions, cultures, and languages came into India, no single one emerged as permanently dominant. In this bewildering context caste provided a sense of group identity, a means of support and defense, and a cultural vehicle as well, since each caste was necessarily local and shared a common language. Occupational associations for most subcastes meant that they also functioned as the equivalent of guilds and mutual-help societies, serving to arbitrate disputes. Caste was less a matter of religious than of social ordering, and the hierarchy it entailed was perhaps less important than the day-to-day support it gave and the social mobility it made possible for group members.

◉ Aristocratic Behavior in Japan ◉

The importance of hierarchical order in Japan is revealed in this 1615 decree of a shogun regulating the behavior of the feudal lords, or dai-myo, and their retainers, the samurai. Note the obligation to be aristo-crats rather than mere soldiers.

Literature, arms, archery, and horsemanship are to be the favorite pursuits. Literature first, and arms next to it, was the rule of the ancients. They must both be cultivated concur-rently. . . . Drinking parties and gambling amusements must be kept within due bounds. . . . Offenders against the law are not to be harbored in the feudal domains. Law is the very foundation of ceremonial decorum and of social order. To infringe the law in the name of reason is as bad as to outrage reason in the name of the law. . . .

The distinction between lord and vassal, between superior and inferior, must be clearly marked by apparel. Vassals may not . . . wear silk stuffs. . . . Miscellaneous persons are not at their own pleasure to ride in palanquins. . . . Lately even sub-vassals and henchmen of no rank have taken to so riding. This is a flagrant impertinence. . . . The *samurai* through-out the provinces are to practice frugality. Those who are rich like to make a display, while those who are poor are ashamed of not being on a par with others. There is no in-fluence so pernicious as this, and it must be kept strictly in check. . . .

Source: D. Lach, *Asia on the Eve of Europe's Expansion* (Englewood Cliffs, N.J.: Prentice Hall, 1965), pp. 157–160 passim.

Social Hierarchy in East Asia

Despite the uniqueness of caste, Indian society con-formed in other respects to the dominant Asian social model, of which China is the principal example. Under the empire in China, which lasted from the third century B.C. to 1911, power, responsibility, and status formed a pyramidal structure, with the emperor at the top as a truly absolute monarch. Below him were appointed of-ficials in a series of grades: councillors, provincial gov-ernors, and generals, down to the district magistrates in some 2,000 counties, all of whom were selected from the ranks of the scholar-gentry who had passed the third level of the imperial examinations.

But this was not merely a political pyramid, and it did not act alone. The emperor and his officials had as their highest duty the setting of a good example, of "virtuous conduct." They were seen, and saw themselves, as fath-ers to the people, since the family was the basis of social order in all of Asia to an even greater extent than in most other societies. In theory, if the emperor and his officials behaved properly and responsibly, others in the social hierarchy would do so as well. In practice, social order—in Chinese parlance, the "Great Harmony"—was pre-served primarily by the family system; this operated in much the same way in the rest of Asia. Younger people deferred to their elders, wives to husbands, and social "inferiors" to "superiors." This was the Confucian for-mula for human happiness and social harmony, but it was accepted in Hindu and Muslim India, too, as well as in Korea and Japan as Confucianism spread.

Social Hierarchy in Europe

Europeans likewise attached a great deal of significance to a hierarchical society, which they believed was or-dained by both divine and natural law. Civic and reli-gious leaders alike insisted that the duty of each person was to accept his or her place in the social order, an ideal intended to promote social stability and domestic tran-quillity. The hierarchical societies of early modern Eu-rope were not, however, structured according to a class system in which groups were defined by similar levels of income and lifestyles, as in the modern West. In the early modern period the common basis of aristocratic power—landed wealth and the control of labor—was modified by the source of one's wealth, the antiquity of one's title, and the number of armed and paid retainers at one's disposal. A noble, though possibly not as rich as an urban businessman, outranked the latter in pres-tige—so much so that business families often tried to marry their daughters to landed aristocrats as a means of enhancing their social status.

The European system was divided, though less formally than in Asia, into *estates*, or social groups defined by degrees of fixed status, that is, by the dignity and respect with which each group was regarded by society in general. The aristocratic estate was generally expected to possess significant wealth in order to fulfill its social function as leader, exemplar, local ruler, maintainer of order, and reliever of the poor. Whereas in Asia many of these functions resided primarily with the family, in Europe—and among the Aztecs in Mexico—they were largely the province of the aristocracy. It was the duty of the lower orders, both religious and political, to accept the rule of the upper, though in reality there was often resentment and occasionally rebellion. Good behavior demanded deference to superiors, courtesy to equals, and kindness to inferiors. More was expected of, but also tolerated from, the higher orders, where gentility was supposed to entail a combination of birth, breeding, and virtue.

There are some parallels between social hierarchy in the East and the West, including the importance attached to the idea that status entailed responsibility. Europeans too used the analogy of paternal authority to justify monarchical power, especially in the 1600s, but never to the same degree as in Asia, where the family exercised a greater role in the maintenance of social order. In the West the function of the extended family in this regard declined in the early modern period as the emphasis gradually shifted to the nuclear family on the one hand and the state on the other. With the general exception of the Dutch, both Europeans and Asians tried to reinforce the social hierarchy by reserving distinctive styles of dress for the upper orders.

In Europe social distinctions were also reflected in numerous other ways, such as the number of a noble's retainers or clients or the number of coaches in his procession. Even funerals were distinctive pageants designed to reflect the social status of the deceased and their families.

The privileged life of the European aristocracy is reflected in Peter Paul Rubens' portrait of Marchesa Brigida Spinola Doria (1606) clad in a sumptuous gown. [National Gallery of Art, Washington, Samuel H. Kress Collection]

The European Aristocracy

Prior to the mid-sixteenth century, the aristocracy generally improved its social position and became more involved in public affairs at the local or state level. Most nobility strove to acquire more land, usually by strategic marriages, or greater status, normally by obtaining more elevated titles of nobility. To meet the demand for status, titles such as duke, marquis, and viscount were created, and new chivalric orders, including the Knights of the Garter in England and the Order of the Golden Fleece in Burgundy, were founded. New nobles were usually recruited from the landed gentry (the lesser aristocracy) rather than the bourgeoisie (the upper merchant and professional class), especially in France and England. On the Continent an administrative aristocracy developed in the early modern period. In France and Milan, for example, officials acquired aristocratic privileges and became known as the nobility of the robe, after their gown of office.

Conditions among the gentry varied widely. Whereas the more successful among them could be as wealthy and powerful as some nobles, others, especially on the Continent, sometimes turned to banditry to improve their sagging fortunes. A notorious gang of English robbers followed the lead of two lesser aristocrats, Sir William Bussy and Sir John de Colseby, while in France similar groups tried unsuccessfully in 1560 to end the political dominance of the Guise family, the head of which, the duke of Guise, was the king's chief adviser. Disaffected knights often supported reform movements, including Lutheranism in Germany and Calvinism in France, hoping to better their position.

Beginning in the mid-sixteenth century, the aristocracy entered a period of difficulty. Incomes from landed estates did not keep pace with excessive expenditures on elaborate dress, rich food, fine jewelry, lavish hospitality, and luxurious buildings. Some governments, especially in France and Spain, pressed the nobility for cash to repay war debts. Raising funds by selling land only reduced the income from rents. Nor did rents keep pace with the rising cost of living due to inflation, especially since many rents were fixed by custom, and in some areas tenants held long-term leases. The position of the aristocracy was further undermined by the growing reliance of governments on talent rather than rank, though no Western country came close to establishing a meritocracy such as existed in China.

The prestige of the older aristocracy was harmed when sovereigns in France, Spain, and England sold titles to raise funds and accommodate the demand for status among newly wealthy elites. The upper aristocracy normally suffered more from these problems than the lower; in England much of the gentry improved their position in this period through careful land management, advantageous marriages, and the purchase of lands from the monasteries dissolved during the Reformation.

Urban Society

The social eminence of urban merchants, or patricians, stemmed from their involvement with long-distance trade, their ownership of city property, and their control of town government. Patricians intermarried to preserve the exclusiveness of their privileges, though some married off their daughters to aristocrats merely to acquire the unique prestige that went with ownership of the land. Townsfolk treated the patricians as a noble class, particularly in republican Venice, where the absence of a monarch or a landed aristocracy elevated their status. In the Netherlands and the German states too the wealthy patricians were virtually a noble class, though their supremacy was disputed by the landed nobility. In Russia the growth of an autonomous bourgeoisie was delayed by the feudal structure of that society.

In contrast to the patricians, the guildsmen continued, as in the medieval era, to concern themselves primarily with local production and services. In most towns they had considerably less influence than the patricians but were better off than the artisans and unskilled workers, who were poorly organized and had little voice in town government. Only by joining with the guildsmen could the artisans and laborers bring about change. Another urban group, the lawyers, found their services in increased demand as commerce expanded, land trans-

actions became more complex, and landowners sought ways to evade the fiscal payments that were still part of feudal land tenure. Together these middling and upper urban groups began insisting on a greater share of political power in early modern Europe, particularly in France and England, where their demands contributed to the outbreak of civil war in both countries in the 1640s.

Marriage and the Family

Throughout the early modern world, the family was the basic unit of social organization. The western European aristocracy began to distinguish itself in this period by moving away from the extended family, which remained common in Asia and Africa, toward the conjugal or nuclear family, which was probably already the norm among the lower social orders in Europe. Although family structures varied substantially between Muslims and some Africans and Amerindians, with their polygamous marriages, and Asia and Europe, where monogamy prevailed, all societies valued children for a variety of reasons, including, among the lower orders especially, their function as laborers and eventually as providers for elderly parents. Protestant Europe, by establishing the principle of divorce as we now understand it, planted the seeds for the eventual weakening of the family as the fundamental social unit.

The Family in Asia

The Asian family was a hierarchical structure in which group welfare took precedence over individual preferences. The father was like a little emperor, with absolute power but also with absolute responsibility. Filial obedience was the cardinal Asian virtue; loyalty and obligation to parents and elders was rigid and inflexible, but it produced a tight-knit unit. In family relations age was the major determinant. Three generations commonly lived under one roof, and the grandfather was thus the dominant figure, although his place might be taken after his death by his widow. Younger sons were subject to their older brothers, wives and sisters to their husbands and brothers, and all to the eldest male. Individual initiative other than by the patriarch was not tolerated; the welfare of the family as he interpreted it came first, and all decisions were accordingly made by the elder members.

A new Asian bride was the servant of the husband's family and was often victimized by a tyrannical mother-in-law. More so than in the West, Asian girls could be married against their wishes and had little or no right of refusal—except suicide. An entire genre of Asian stories was devoted to this theme. In a typical story, an unwilling bride is carried in an enclosed cart or sedan chair to her new husband's family; when the curtains are opened, she is found to have killed herself. Marriage was seen as a business arrangement between families, not as an individual choice or a love match. In later centuries the custom of foot-binding spread through the Chinese population, inflicting dreadful pain on growing girls and emphasizing their role as erotic playthings while reducing them to a hobble that effectively kept them at home. About the same period, the practice of purdah, the veiling and sequestering of women, spread with the Muslim conquerors even through Hindu northern India.

Few Asians questioned the family hierarchy. The family operated as a collective entity; each member was both socially and legally responsible for the behavior of all other members. Collective responsibility, family pride, and the shame of family disgrace are still credited for the relatively low rate of crime in much of Asia. Government from higher levels was far less necessary. Asian societies have been called self-regulating, and to a very large extent that is true. The price of this has been the sacrifice of individual initiative, independence, and self-fulfillment so prized by the modern West and now increasingly attractive in many parts of modern Asia.

Individuals moved through life only as members of families, as did members of larger groups such as castes, clans, or guilds. Yet there was a surprising amount of vertical mobility in Chinese society. Judging from the numerous biographies of successful examination candidates, as many as a third of the gentry group in each generation represented new blood. In Asian countries families and sometimes villages, clans, or guilds squeezed their resources to support promising boys through the lengthy education needed for entry to the scholarly ranks, in effect as their representative and as one who could bring prestige and profit.

The larger society offered few support mechanisms. Without a family or descendants to care for them, the sick, the poor, and the elderly could not survive. In the Hindu and Buddhist countries minimal shelter and food were available to all at temples, as they still are, but in all of Asia the production of offspring, especially sons, was the overriding goal for simple self-preservation. People who did well in life were bound to help not only siblings but also uncles, aunts, cousins, and their families.

The bonds of obligation and collective responsibility reached throughout the extended family, which in Asia included all paternal and maternal relatives, or at least those with whom a given nuclear family was in touch. Each Asian society had a complex variety of name designations for each of these graded kin relationships; one did not refer merely to "brother," "sister," "uncle," "aunt," or "grandmother" but to elder or younger brother, first, second, or third paternal aunt, maternal grandfather, and so on. This extended network of relationships put a heavy burden on individuals but also provided mutual support.

The Family in Europe

Extended family linkages were important in Europe as well at the level of the aristocracy, where patterns of ownership, inheritance, and status were complex. Below this level the conjugal or nuclear family was a more or less self-contained unit. Except in eastern Europe, most couples married late, in their mid-twenties, by which time they were usually in a position to establish their own households. A widowed parent might subsequently take up residence with a married child, in contrast with the Asian practice of newlyweds moving in with the bridegroom's parents. The prevalence of the nuclear family pattern at the lower social levels was disadvantageous in the sense that mistreated spouses received less kin support, and smaller family units were more vulnerable to economic hardship if a spouse became unemployed.

The large family network common in Asia provided an important support system that commoners in the West often lacked. Conversely, however, the smaller family units in the West presumably made it easier for many couples to make the personal adjustments necessary for a successful marriage without the intervention of relatives and in-laws.

The nature of the Western family underwent a significant change in the sixteenth and seventeenth centuries, particularly among the aristocracy. The late medieval aristocratic family, in return for loyalty and personal attendance by its retainers and servants, provided patronage and hospitality. The aristocratic household was large because it included not only family members and relatives but also a collection of servants and retainers that might number in the hundreds. The importance of preserving the family's status and property led to the practice of the arranged marriage. Often a young person had no choice in the determination of a partner, for matrimony was a collective decision of the family and kin in which the key issues were property and power. Protestant reformers generally favored the arranged marriage as a means to discourage young people from selecting spouses on the basis of sexual attraction. Some parents allowed their children a veto over the proposed spouse, and occasionally headstrong young people defied the system by eloping, but only at the risk of losing their inheritance. Young men's acceptance of the arranged marriage was aided by the knowledge that once an heir was born, mistresses could be enjoyed. There was a double standard, however, for wives were denied such freedom and were expected to remain sexually loyal to their husbands.

An arranged marriage, in this instance between the son of a financially strapped nobleman and the daughter of a wealthy merchant hungry for social prestige, is the subject of one of the scenes from William Hogarth's series of six paintings titled *Marriage à la Mode* (1744–1745). [National Gallery, London]

Daughters were often an economic liability among the propertied classes since a dowry had to be provided for marriage; in turn, the groom's father guaranteed the bride an annuity if her husband died before she did. As heirs and potential fathers of future heirs, firstborn sons usually married earlier than other young men. In sixteenth-century England men normally wed at about age 28, but aristocratic heirs typically married at 22 in order to facilitate property settlements and enhance the prospects of providing a male heir in the next generation. Because a younger son had considerably less property and wealth than his elder brother, who benefited in England and parts of western Europe from the practice of primogeniture (bequeathing a landed estate to the eldest son), he faced a decline in social position unless he could find a wealthy bride.

About the middle of the sixteenth century the nature of the family began to change among the upper social orders. On the one hand, more significance was attached to the nuclear core (parents and children), and on the other, affection between spouses apparently became more important as a determinant of family relationships. The decline of kinship dominance was manifested in both decreasing hospitality and the diminishing sense of kin responsibility for individual acts. As states such as France, Spain, and England expanded their control of justice, protection, and the preservation of property, the responsibility for social control shifted from kin to state. Simultaneously, Protestantism increased the significance of the nuclear family by stressing marital affection and by treating the family as a miniature parish, with distinct religious responsibilities in instruction and worship. These changes brought about a greater and greater divergence from the Asian model and its associated lack of state control.

In contrast to the modern nuclear family, patriarchal authority was reinforced. The Renaissance state supported the domination of the husband-father on the grounds that his authority was analogous to that of a sovereign over his subjects. The decline of kinship could increase the wife's subordination to her husband by leaving her more exposed to exploitation in the nuclear family. Capitalizing on this, the state relied on husbands to keep their wives law-abiding. Yet the development of the nuclear family could also facilitate better relations between spouses by providing them with more time to be alone, away from the prying eyes of relatives, retainers, and servants.

Marriage in Asia

In the societies of early modern Asia marital patterns were similar in many ways to those in Europe, particularly with respect to the arranged marriage, the premium placed on sons, and the use of dowries, although considerably less so in areas such as divorce and remarriage. In Asia, however, the average age at marriage was lower than in the West—approximately 21 for males and 17 for females in China; 16 and 14, respectively, in India; and 20 and 16 in Japan and Southeast Asia.

Except for parts of Southeast Asia and a small region of South India, marriage was and remains patrilocal; that is, the bride, who was almost invariably recruited from

◉ "Surplus" Daughters ◉

In the eyes of both Asians and Europeans, daughters were much less desirable than sons. To avoid the expense of providing dowries, Catholic parents sometimes sought to dispose of "surplus" daughters by coercing them into becoming nuns. Some clergymen strongly protested this practice.

You have no right to dispose of your children by forcing a vocation on them. . . . It would cost money to establish this daughter: reason enough to consecrate her as a nun. . . . But she has no trace of religious calling: the present state of your finances is calling enough for her. . . . And so the victim is led to the temple, hands and feet tied: by which I mean against her will, dumb with fear and awe of a father whom she has always honored. Such murderous fathers are far from imitating Abraham . . . who was ready to sacrifice his son to God: instead they sacrifice their children to their own estate and to their own cupidity.

Source: L. Bourdaloue, *Œuvres complètes*, in *Collection intégrale et universelle des orateurs sacrés*, vol. 15 (Paris, 1845), cols. 374 ff.; English translation in *Not in God's Image*, ed. J. O'Faolain and L. Martines (New York: Harper Torchbooks, 1973), p. 270.

another village to avoid inbreeding, left her family and became a member of her husband's family, where she was the lowest-status member until she had borne a son. She might visit her parents occasionally, but she was lost to them as a family member and cost them heavily in dowry. Girls were often loved as much as boys, but on practical grounds they were of far less value, although they were desirable domestic helpers to their mothers. Sons were essential for family continuity and security. Since life was an uncertain business and death rates were high, especially in the early years of life, most families tried to produce more than one son. Girls might be sold in hard times as servants or concubines in rich households.

The childless family was truly bankrupt and might even pay relatively large sums to acquire a son by adoption. A wife who failed to produce a son after a reasonable amount of time was commonly returned to her parents as useless, for the primary purpose of marriage was perpetuation of the male line. It was not understood until quite recently that the sex of a child is determined by the father or that childlessness may result as often from male as from female sterility. In time, however, most women became willing and even enthusiastic members of their husbands' families, passing on these attitudes to their children. Eventually they might become household heads and oldest survivors, thereby sometimes achieving considerable power.

All members of the society regarded marriage as a contract between families for the furthering of their interests. Virtually all marriages were arranged by the families, usually through a go-between. Bride and groom had usually not met before their wedding. Sometimes they might be allowed to express preferences, although these might be overruled in the family interest. Compatibility was rarely considered, and love marriages were extremely rare, although affection might grow in time.

There was a similar willingness to suppress individual wishes among the Inca of South America, where state officials chose mates for young people slow to act on their own. At times the Inca arranged mass marriages. The rulers themselves could marry only their sisters, making the royal family a product of considerable inbreeding.

Divorce in Asia and Europe

Divorce was rare in Asia, difficult but not impossible. Unlike the West, remarriage was even more difficult, and that knowledge probably helped people try harder to make their marriages work. It doubtless helped too that romantic expectations were not as high as in the modern West. People were trained to put individual wants second to family interest. Biographies, memoirs, popular literature, and legal records bear out that most marriages were successful on these terms and that husbands and wives valued and even loved each other and worked together in the family unit to reproduce the dominant social pattern. Divorce was relatively rare in the Islamic world as well.

There was no divorce in the modern sense in the medieval West since the canon law of the Catholic church deemed marriage an unbreakable sacrament. If the existence of an impediment or bar to a marriage could be demonstrated, the marriage could be annulled, but any children resulting from the union were thereby made illegitimate. Annulments were granted in such cases as marriage to relatives or in-laws, impotence, or forced marriage. The only other alternative, separation, did not bastardize the children, but neither did it leave the spouses free to remarry. In cases of wife beating, church and state courts in Spain and France permitted legal separation.

The Reformation reduced the grounds for annulment but established divorce in the modern sense in some areas, including the Lutheran states, Zurich, and Geneva. Catholic states retained the medieval canon law, with its absolute prohibition of divorce, until modern times, apart from a brief period during the age of the French Revolution and Napoleon. Among Europe's poor, some unhappy spouses ran away; others committed bigamy. From the medieval period into the nineteenth century a dissatisfied husband in England occasionally put a halter around his wife's neck, took her to the local cattle market, and sold her. The practice underscored the notion that a wife was the property of her husband, although common law never recognized this. In rural Greece well into the twentieth century, a bride might simply be returned to her family if she was discovered or believed to have lost her virginity before marriage.

Marriage and the Family in Africa

Like the Muslims, Aztecs, and Inca, many African tribes practiced polygamy. A man demonstrated his wealth by having several wives, although in reality women, who typically worked beside men, produced so much by their labor that they virtually supported themselves. The perception of wealth was derived from the fact that a man had to pay "bridewealth"—usually livestock—to a woman's father in order to marry her. As in western Europe, men married relatively late, usually about the age of 30, though brides were typically in their late teens. A new wife would be added at fairly regular intervals of a year or two, and because of the importance attached to fertility, the result was normally a large family.

The high birthrate helped offset the large number of deaths of infants and children and also ensured support for parents in their old age, an ideal no less valued in Asia. Like the early Hebrews, many Africans accepted the practice of leviratic marriage, by which the brother of a deceased man married the widow. In the African family no function was more important for the wife than bearing children, but beyond that she exercised a criti-

cal role in providing the food supply and in some instances even conducting local and regional trade.

The Status of Women

Although many women might have had powers within the family, their role in general was subordinate. There is no question that theirs was a male-dominated world and that their chief claim to status was as breeders of sons. They were less valued from birth virtually everywhere. Females were subject first to their fathers and brothers, then to their husbands and their husbands' male relatives. A new bride was under the authority most directly of her mother-in-law, who was sometimes tyrannical. A wife's status in her husband's family rose only when she produced a son. In time she became a mother-in-law herself, often the role of true power in the family.

Women in Asia

Much is revealed about the status of women in Asian countries by examining the fate of widows. Unlike their counterparts in the West, Asian widows were not supposed to remarry or even to have male friends. Given the high death rate and the unpredictable fortunes of life, many women—often no more than girls—were thus condemned to celibacy, loneliness, and poverty for most of their lives. "Chaste widows" were praised, and though some managed a little life of their own, most conformed to the expected model and suffered. Some widows committed suicide in China and in the Islamic world; this was carried to its extreme in India, where it often came to be expected among the higher castes. Hindu funeral practice includes the burning of the corpse; a surviving widow was supposed to throw herself on her husband's funeral pyre, a ritual known as *sati* (suttee). Perhaps as many as one-fifth of all childless Indian upper-caste widows actually sacrificed themselves in this way.

As in the West, in hard times female infants might be killed soon after birth so that the rest of the family might survive; Asian female babies could also be sold as servants or potential concubines. The selling of children seems especially heartless, but such a girl might have a better life as a slave-servant or concubine in a wealthy household than starving to death with her own family. Women were rarely given any formal education, and although some acquired it, they were primarily instructed by their mothers and mothers-in-law in how to be good, subservient wives, mothers, and daughters-in-law.

Power within the family brought women rewards that were especially important in this family-centered society. Their key role in ensuring family continuity brought much satisfaction. In most families women, as the chief raisers of children, shaped the future. More directly, they managed most families' finances, as they still do in Asia. Some women achieved public prominence as writers, reigning empresses, and powers behind the throne as imperial consorts or concubines. In India, China, and Southeast Asia, as in England and Scotland, a few women became rulers in their own right, such as the T'ang empress Wu. But only in India could one find women who were brilliant generals and cavalry fighters, such as the Rani of Jhansi. Admittedly, these were a tiny handful within Asia and Europe as a whole. In East and West alike, the crucial role of women in what mattered most—the family, its well-being, and its perpetuation—was, within clear status limits, recognized. Among the peasantry, the overwhelming mass of the population, women played a crucial role in helping with the agricultural labor and were usually the major workers in cottage industries, producing handicraft goods for sale or barter. Upper-class women lived a generally idle life and commonly turned their children over to nurses or tutors.

It remained for the twentieth century, spurred by Western influence, to discourage the traditional subjugation of women in Asia and begin the movement toward equality, or at least more equitable treatment. Southeast Asia has traditionally been freer of sex discrimination than India, China, Korea, or Japan, and most of its regional cultures included some matrilocal marriage, female control and inheritance of property, and female dominance within the family. In the rest of Asia the traditional patterns were formed 4,000 years ago and persisted largely unchanged until this century. (See Chapters 39 and 40.)

Women in the Middle East and Africa

In the Islamic societies of the Middle East and North Africa, women were discouraged from participating in activities outside the home by the conviction that females should be secluded as well as veiled. The latter practice was obviously a practical way of enforcing anonymity on them when they did appear in public. Women who engaged in trade or educational pursuits were rare exceptions. As in Asian cultures, the woman's primary task was to marry and raise children, especially boys.

Religion was used, as in the West, to legitimate the subordination of women. This point was succinctly stated by a seventeenth-century Iranian theologian, who asserted that a wife's principal spiritual duty was subservience to her husband: "A wife must obey her husband, never disobey his commands, never leave the house without his permission." As early as the 1200s Islamic society was characterized by a separate social

life for men and women, though a small number of women were sometimes able to exert political power in both Ottoman Turkey and Safavid Iran.

In sub-Saharan Africa some tribal societies accorded prominent roles to women. In contrast to the Western world, West African tribes such as the Igbo and the Yoruba in Nigeria were organized on a "dual sex" system in which each sex governed its own affairs at all levels of society. One group of Igbo was ruled by dual monarchs, one female and the other male, each with its own advisory group. The female monarch, or *omu* (literally "mother"), was different from a queen in the Western sense, for she was neither the king's wife nor the reigning daughter of a deceased king who had no male heir. The *omu* represented all women and had special responsibility for the marketplace. Igbo women also had their own organizations at the village level, which functioned as political pressure groups.

Although most African societies were dominated by men, there were important exceptions. Women, for instance, could be chiefs among some of the tribes of West Africa. A number of other West African tribes followed the custom of female descent, by which the throne descended not to the king's son but to the son of his sister. In precolonial African societies, which had no permanent political structure, important matters were routinely decided by a meeting of the heads of households, but because women rarely exercised this responsibility, they were not prominent in making community decisions.

The subordinate role of most African women was underscored by the predominance of patrilineal and patrilocal customs, which traced lineage through the male line and required brides to live in the villages of their husbands. There were exceptions, such as the Senufo of West Africa, whose wives could remain in their native villages and whose divorced women retained custody of the children because the latter belonged to the maternal kin. Generally, however, the traditional African societies treated women as the economic and social dependents of males, as elsewhere.

Women in Europe

In late medieval Europe aristocratic women were regarded largely as bearers of children, sexual companions, and comrades in social functions. Few administered family estates or raised their own children, a task left to nurses and tutors. Nurturing an infant was turned over to a wet nurse, typically a peasant woman hired for the occasion and often blamed for subsequent medical or psychological problems. Wet nursing freed the mother from the inconvenience of nighttime feeding, it did not interrupt her social engagements, and it permitted her to serve the father's sexual appetites, as nursing mothers tended to shun intercourse for fear that breast feeding would starve an embryo. However, wet-nursing declined sharply in the 1700s.

Aristocratic women had relatively little to occupy their time apart from such leisurely pursuits as reading, social visits, cardplaying, and theatergoing, especially since many had stewards to run their households as well as nurses and tutors to care for their children. However, women of the landed gentry often played a major role in the household economy and managed the family estates when their husbands were away. Because of her social status, a gentlewoman or a merchant's wife had little choice of occupation, for manual labor was incompatible with her position, and the professions were closed to women. Some became ladies-in-waiting to aristocratic women, some governesses of children, and a few, such as the English dramatists Aphra Behn and Susan Centilivre, authors. Two aristocratic English women—Margaret Cavendish, duchess of Newcastle, and Anne, Viscountess Conway—wrote about the new science, and Katherine Boyle, sister of the chemist Robert Boyle, took an active part in it. Some women, such as Judith Leycester (1609–1660) of the Netherlands and Artemisia Gentileschi (1593–c. 1652) of Italy, were accomplished painters. Catholics, of course, had the option of joining a convent or a teaching order.

Near the lower levels of society, the wives of craftsmen and peasants had to labor with their husbands to survive, for most Europeans lived at or near subsistence. As in Asia, Africa, and the Americas, peasant women engaged in virtually every aspect of farming from plowing and spreading manure to reaping and threshing and also handled the household chores and cared for any poultry or dairy animals. In both urban and rural areas many wives supplemented the family income by weaving or other side employments, occasionally even prostitution.

Late medieval craft guilds allowed masters' wives to share in their work, and they often carried on the business when the men died. Although women had been admitted to the guilds, the new forms of business organization were almost exclusively male, and there was mounting hostility to women in the trades because they worked for lower pay. Apart from the cloth industry, women were being pushed out of many trades, such as brewing, at one time largely a female preserve. In England men even moved into the occupation of midwife. Women could practice folk medicine and compete with barber-surgeons, but they were generally excluded from the professions of physician, attorney, and minister. Although women found it increasingly difficult to compete for jobs in most trades, they found employment in the cottage industry concerned with cloth manufacturing, but the pay was poor and the hours long. Life was also difficult for single women. Some worked in the coal and iron mines, where they typically received lower

A self-portrait of the Dutch artist Judith Leycester, one of the most prominent women painters of the seventeenth century. [National Gallery of Art, Washington, gift of Mr. and Mrs. Robert Woods Bliss]

wages than their male peers. Most single women earned their living by spinning yarn, a practice that gave rise to the term *spinster* for an unmarried woman.

In certain respects the legal position of European women declined in the late medieval period. French women could no longer participate in public affairs, testify before various courts, or even act in place of an absentee or insane husband. The laws of Saxony and England prohibited women from undertaking legal actions; an English wife had to be represented by her husband, while a Hamburg statute of 1603 stipulated that "women can neither bring a matter up before the court nor transfer or hand over property without a guardian." Bavarian law prohibited a woman from selling anything without her husband's consent, though beginning in 1616 an exception was made for goods specified for her personal use. In England a husband enjoyed absolute control over his wife's personal property and could profit by leasing her real estate to others.

In the seventeenth century, however, marriage contracts guaranteed the wife "pin money" for her personal expenses, and the courts increasingly recognized the existence of her "separate estate," a handy device if her husband was sued for bankruptcy. French courts similarly began to demonstrate greater concern for a wife's rights, including control over her dowry. A French wife whose husband mismanaged her property could win a legal separation, the most she could expect in a society without divorce. By the eighteenth century Russian noblewomen and the wives of artisans and merchants became the heads of their households when their husbands died, although only in urban areas. Legally, then, the decline in women's rights bottomed out in Europe in the 1500s and improved slowly in the seventeenth and eighteenth centuries.

Sexual Customs

Sexual customs give us insight into cultural values and provide a benchmark for tracking changes in those values up to modern times. For example, Asian women have always been expected to be modest and chaste. They seldom appeared in public, and any open display of affection with their spouses was taboo. At the same time, the elite Asian cultures, unlike those in the West, are famous for their erotic literature and art and for the development of a courtesan (prostitute) tradition older than any other living civilization. The geisha tradition of Japan and its original, the "singsong" or "flower boat" women of China, are well known, as is the cult of ritual sex among Indian temple priestesses and the orgies of Tantric Buddhism. Explicit portrayals of sex appear in Indian art, and the classic Indian sex manual, the *Kama-sutra*, is world famous. But this behavior was reserved for the privileged few.

In contrast to the Judeo-Christian West, India, Tibet, and parts of Southeast Asia had a religious tradition in which sex was used as ritual, in some ways rather like the ancient cult of Dionysus in classical Greece. Representations of sex in Indian sculpture and painting use gods and goddesses as subjects, not ordinary mortals, and celebrate the divine life force, creation. Tantric Buddhist and some Hindu temple sex rites had the same purpose. Western art, beginning in the Renaissance, was less explicit than Indian art but depicted sensuous nudes in the guise of classical deities. All of this—the pleasures of the elite dallying with their concubines, singsong girls, erotic pictures, and the joys of Islamic rulers in their harems—was beyond the experience of the lower social orders, although at least in the West they might find an outlet for their sexual desires in traditional festivals, such as May Day or, in Asia, other celebrations, when promiscuous behavior was reportedly common.

A relationship between sex and religious ritual existed in some African societies, especially in connection with puberty rites. The Kikuyu, who lived in the region of Mount Kenya, not only circumcised boys as part of

such rites but also removed the clitoris from girls. This practice is still widespread in eastern Africa today. In both cases the act of cutting symbolized the rite of passage into adulthood. In the case of the Masai, however, puberty initiation for girls involved elongating the labia by massage and teaching the girls movements to enhance their sexual performance.

Figure of a dancing woman, in painted pottery, from a T'ang dynasty tomb. The elaborate dress and hairstyle and the long floppy sleeves suggest that the figure represented a courtesan-dancer. It was from T'ang China that the Japanese imported much of their culture, and here is, in effect, the origin of the Japanese geisha. [The Nelson-Atkins Museum of Art, Kansas City, Missouri (Nelson Fund)]

European attitudes toward sex were generally determined by the teachings of the church, although these were often merely a veneer imposed on centuries of folk custom and were frequently ignored. For the masses of East and West, sex appears to have been largely oriented toward procreation and usually confined officially to marriage or engagement, although Japanese, Southeast Asian, and Polynesian young people of both sexes were encouraged to experiment with sex before marriage. In the eyes of the medieval Christian church, sexual relations were acceptable only within marriage and were intended primarily for procreation. Little attention was attached to love in a sexual context, and lust was condemned.

During the Reformation, Protestants began to treat love and procreation as related and to regard sexual pleasure in marriage as a legitimate expression of the conjugal relationship. Among the propertied orders, sexual relations before marriage were regarded with disapproval, largely because of the importance of bearing a legitimate heir. Because a woman was regarded as the sexual property of a man, her value diminished if she had been "used" by another male. Despite the church's official disapproval, males of the propertied elite frequently engaged in premarital sex, normally with women from professional or merchant backgrounds whose families had fallen on hard times. The same freedom did not extend to women of their rank. A woman's honor was based on her reputation for chastity, a man's on his word. A wife who committed adultery insulted not only her husband's virility but also his ability to govern her, which resulted in dishonor. In this respect the elites of East and West shared the acceptance of a double standard that enhanced male dominance.

Among the lower orders in Europe, pressure for premarital sex was created by the late ages at which people wed—typically in their upper twenties. Late marriage helped hold down population growth, but figures for illegitimacy indicate relatively little sexual activity apart from engaged and married couples, probably due to religious and socioeconomic pressures. Infanticide may also have contributed to low bastardy levels. The bastardy rate was 3 percent in rural England in the 1590s and 2 percent at Frankfurt in the early 1700s, despite considerable sexual activity by engaged couples. Approximately 21 percent of English brides were pregnant at their weddings in the late sixteenth century.

Because the Catholic church considered the sexual act primarily procreative, it regarded most attempts at contraception as mortal sin. By the sixteenth century, however, many Catholics accepted coitus reservatus—withdrawal before ejaculation—as a permissible technique for the economically destitute, and people did use a variety of physical contraceptives. The church condemned coitus interruptus—ejaculation outside the vagina—as unnatural on biblical grounds, although it became increasingly widespread in the 1700s.

In Protestant lands, religious leaders discouraged birth control methods, believing they were contrary to the biblical command to be fruitful and multiply. Instead, they argued, children should be accepted as blessings from God, means to maintain the commonwealth and the church, and opportunities for women to recover the honor lost to their sex when Eve disobeyed God.

For women with unwanted pregnancies, medical manuals provided information on how to induce abortion, typically through the ingestion of vegetal or mineral poisons, all of which were dangerous to the mother. Interest in the use of birth control methods was undoubtedly strong among women who wanted relief from the repeated cycle of pregnancies that often brought death. In the sixteenth and seventeenth centuries, perhaps one out of every ten pregnancies ended in the mother's death, and 30 to 50 percent of all children died before the age of 5. In France as many as 30 percent were dead before their first birthday.

Because abortion could be as dangerous to the mother as to the fetus, infanticide was a common alternative, particularly since it could be disguised as accidental "overlaying," or accidental suffocation. The problem was so prevalent that in 1784 Austria made it illegal for parents to take children under 5 into bed with them. The punishment for infanticide was often harsh: in the German town of Bamberg a convicted person was drowned or buried alive and then speared. Infanticide figures for Renaissance Florence indicate that more girls than boys died, presumably reflecting the greater value placed on males, though in eighteenth-century Paris there was no significant discrepancy among victims.

Many poverty-stricken parents simply opted to abandon their children in the streets. More foundling hospitals were built to deal with the problem. Milan and Venice had established theirs in the medieval period, and new ones were built in Florence (1445), Paris (1670), London (1739), and St. Petersburg, where two former palaces of the nobility were used to house the children. The availability of the houses seems to have encouraged more parents to abandon their infants. In the 1770s and 1780s the number of children abandoned in Paris reached 4,500 per year, more than double the number at the beginning of the century. By the 1770s more than one out of every five children baptized in Paris had been abandoned. Conditions were so bad in these homes that at times no more than 5 percent of the infants admitted in Paris survived to adulthood.

Catholic and Protestant leaders alike denounced homosexuality. In England the Tudor Parliaments of the sixteenth century made it a capital offense, though the statutes seem not to have been enforced. Magistrates there were more concerned with heterosexual intercourse outside marriage because it could lead to illegitimate children and thus place a financial burden on the community. Homosexuals were found in the court of Elizabeth I and even more extensively in that of her successor, James I, himself bisexual. Homosexuality appears to have been common in secondary schools, where boys often shared beds, and in universities. It was probably also common among servants and in tiny rural communities where access to persons of the opposite sex was severely restricted. In London there were homosexual prostitutes as well as "molly houses" where homosexuals gathered for entertainment. Although Islamic religious writings typically disapproved of homosexuality, the practice itself was generally treated with indifference. In Asia homosexuality was generally considered shameful, and people who were caught at it were condemned or punished, in part because it was held to be unnatural and could not produce offspring, the prime goal of marriage and of society. To Confucius, having no descendants was the ultimate disloyalty to one's parents. Homosexuality was, however, more common and tolerated among the samurai of Japan, many of whom remained unmarried.

By the 1600s organized prostitution was common in European cities such as Paris, Berlin, and Toledo, often with the tacit acceptance of authorities. In Seville brothel keepers and prostitutes were licensed by the city, which even leased houses for this purpose. Church officials tried to close down the brothels, but the city fathers would do no more than require the prostitutes to attend church on Sundays and holy days. In 1676 Cambridge had 13 brothels catering largely to the university community. Many women drawn into a life of prostitution were economically destitute, including unwed mothers and cast-off mistresses, while others opted for it in preference to a 14- to 16-hour day as a seamstress. Some domestics as well were forced out of service and into prostitution when their employers got them pregnant. Other prostitutes were wives whose families were economically destitute or young girls introduced to this life by their mothers, themselves often former prostitutes. Prostitution was typically treated as a criminal offense for which women were pilloried, flogged, imprisoned, and sometimes expelled from a city, though usually to little effect. Nor were punitive measures effective against operators of houses of prostitution.

The late ages at marriage as well as the proximity of family members in small houses tempted some Europeans to commit incest. Apprenticing male children and placing girls in other homes as servants were safety valves, but incest was still sufficiently common to trouble church authorities. Perpetrators caught in the act were usually punished by shaming (public penance), as in the case of other sexual offenses. Usually confined to the lower orders, shaming typically required the offender to appear in church clad only in a white sheet or to ride through town in a cart with a sign proclaiming the offense.

Parents of bastards were treated more harshly because their misdeed was a potential drain on the community's funds; such persons were regularly stripped to

Brothels such as this one, which catered to the aristocracy, became commonplace in early modern Europe. Note that the nobleman is casually giving alms to a beggar. This drawing by Thomas Rowlandson is titled *Charity Covereth a Multitude of Sins.* [Trustees of the British Museum]

the waist, whipped, and placed in the stocks. In keeping with the double standard of the age, mothers but not fathers of bastards were often subjected to punishment, although there were growing efforts to hold fathers fiscally responsible for their illegitimate children. Whether suffering from the double standard or undergoing frequent pregnancies, sexual experience for the early modern woman was fraught with hazard and anxiety and was potentially life-threatening as well.

The dangers sexual intercourse posed to a woman were real whether she lived in Europe, Asia, Africa, or the Americas. Nevertheless, sex was widely valued as the means for procreation. The way in which sex was viewed varied considerably, depending especially on religious traditions. Whereas Roman Catholicism, for instance, exalted the celibate life, sexual elements were incorporated into religious ritual in parts of Africa, India, Tibet, and Southeast Asia, while Hindu elites kept concubines and their Muslim counterparts had harems. Although all societies embraced sex as a life force, for procreative purposes, there was considerable disagreement as to whether it should properly serve as a vehicle for pleasure or for religious expression.

Education, Literacy, and the Printed Word

Attitudes toward education and learning varied sharply among early modern societies. Until the arrival of Europeans, schools were nonexistent in the Americas and sub-Saharan Africa, while in the Islamic world education was narrowly confined and provided to the few by schools linked to the royal palace or the mosques. The advent of the printing press and the Protestant and Catholic Reformations in Europe spurred the founding of schools, the growth of literacy, and a growing appreciation of learning that has generally continued in the West to the present. Yet nowhere in the early modern world was respect for learning greater than in Asia, both as a means to preserve its philosophical and religious traditions and as a path to achieve worldly success.

Learning in Asia

Respect for learning was universal in Asia. Written texts in particular or even scraps of paper with writing on them were to be treated reverently and preserved. This was partly due to the importance of the philosophical, moral, and religious texts that played so great a part in each Asian cultural tradition but partly also because literacy and learning were the surest and most prestigious paths to worldly success. In the cultures where religion was more centrally important than in China, especially in India and Buddhist Southeast Asia, literacy and learning also led to an honored status as priest or monk; such persons were second only to the ruler in the status hierarchy. The Indian Brahmin combined the role of scholar and priest, while in Buddhist countries the monkhood has remained the most honorable calling of all. Scholars, priests, and monks were exempt from manual labor, whereas in Europe many clergymen farmed to make ends meet, and monastic labor was often a deliberate part of the ascetic regime. In East and West alike, lip service was paid to the worth and importance of peasant labor and agriculture, but the rewards and status went to people who had risen above the necessity of physical work. In Asia even kings and emperors deferred to the learned holy man or the upright scholar.

Freedom from manual labor for the educated was marked by dress, lifestyle, and the deference of others. In Europe and Asia alike, it was the duty of the rest of society to support monks and priests by regular donations and alms and to finance their temples and rituals. Their activities were connected with ordinary life, including weddings, namings of children, funerals, and religious festivals. Officials, drawn from the ranks of the learned, also wore distinctive clothing and enjoyed special privileges, including exemption from corporal pun-ishment. Especially in China, the masses treated them with respect in deference to their awesome authority as the direct representatives of the emperor. The Chinese gentry, from among whom officials were selected, wore the long blue scholar's gown, hem touching the ground and loose floppy sleeves hanging from the arms. Since no physical exertion could be performed in such a garment, it was in effect a badge of their freedom from manual labor. The scholar-gentry also frequently let their fingernails grow to extreme length, sometimes protecting them with special covers, to make that same point. Throughout Asia and Europe, sumptuary laws prohibited the wearing of upper-class clothing or the use of carriages by the lower orders, the great bulk of the population.

There were three grades of gentry in China, reflecting the three levels of the examination system. Only members who had passed the third level could be selected as officials, but those in the two lower grades were also recognized as educated men and adopted gentry lifestyles and dress. Many of them served as teachers of the next generation of candidates, running both private and government-financed schools where Chinese boys learned their characters and worked their way through the Confucian classics under stern discipline. Most gentry did not become officials but formed an unofficial local elite, serving as teachers, arbiters of disputes, and managers of local enterprises, deferred to by all below them.

Merchants too needed at least some literacy in all Asian cultures, especially since in most of them merchants also had to deal with the state and the official bureaucracy. In any case, they had to keep records and accounts and communicate over long distances. Some of them also acquired a good deal of classical education, and certainly they read poetry and fiction, both classical and popular, as did the scholars. We have no accurate means of measuring literacy in traditional Asian societies. It may have been as high as a quarter of the population, at least in terms of the most basic ability to read and write. Literacy was much higher in Japan after about 1600, and by 1800 it probably reached 50 percent for males. But even a literacy rate of 25 percent would be remarkable, considering the difficulty of learning Chinese characters, which were also the basis of the Japanese, Korean, and Vietnamese written languages.

The gentry group in China, and comparable elites in other Asian societies, probably never constituted more than about 2 percent of the population. To these must be added merchants and petty traders (who often had at least some degree of literacy), clerks and scribes, and some village elders. Despite the fact that they did not attend the regular schools, women sometimes acquired literacy from their brothers or fathers or occasionally on their own. The best evidence is probably the respectable number of female Asian authors, including the famous Lady Murasaki, Japanese author of the world's earliest psychological novel, *The Tale of Genji*. Court ladies such as Lady Murasaki had the leisure to learn to read and write. Literacy was expected of them, as were accomplishments in music, painting, and dance. In the Buddhist countries of Southeast Asia the monkhood claimed virtually all young men for at least two years and at any one time may have included, with older monks, 10 or 15 percent of the population, all of whom were literate. In India the Brahmins, as the sole performers of ritual and the keepers of the Great Tradition, had to be literate.

Paper and printing were both invented in China, the former by the first century A.D. under the Han, the latter by T'ang times. Movable type appeared in the Sung dynasty by about A.D. 1100 and shortly thereafter in Korea. These inventions spread rapidly to Japan, more slowly to India, Southeast Asia, the Islamic areas, and the West. The importance of sacred texts and commentaries for Hinduism, Buddhism, and Islam meant that even before printing, large numbers of copies were made by scribes. As in the West, the spread of printing greatly increased the reading public. The most important result was the increased circulation of literature, first in China, then progressively in other parts of Asia. This included copies of the classics; philosophical and religious texts; epic tales, such as the Indian *Mahabharata* and the *Ramayana*; and similar epics and accounts of heroic deeds from the classical traditions of China, Japan, and Korea.

Literature for a mass audience was being printed by T'ang times in China (A.D. 600–900) and soon thereafter in the rest of Asia, including plays, short stories, poetry, and the first novels. Well before the T'ang period in China, in the splendor of Guptan India (A.D. 300–500), the court poet and playwright Kalidasa had created a brilliant series of dramas. With the spread of printing, his plays and poems were made available to a mass audience. Throughout Asia printing also meant that what had long been present as an oral tradition of storytelling and drama took on new life. Much of it has been lost or is available only in much later printed versions, but from T'ang times on there was a vigorous popular literature in the vernacular, less lofty and more down-to-earth than the classics. Stories and plays about universal human foibles—akin to Chaucer's *Canterbury Tales* in the West—were read avidly by a growing number of people, including scholars to whom such works were supposedly prohibited and who hid them under their pillows. In China there were even detective stories. India produced similar tales, and some of the works of Kalidasa are in this genre. Accounts of adventure and intrigue flourished throughout Asia.

Learning in the West

Respect for learning in the West was not as pronounced as in the East, though in the early modern period there was a notable increase in literacy, in the number of schools, and in the continued development of the universities. In keeping with their broad range of intellectual and cultural interests, Renaissance humanists not only founded new schools but also reformed the traditional curriculum by challenging its heavy reliance on Aristotle. The success of Protestant reformers ultimately rested on the ability to educate younger generations in their religious principles, and in turn the Catholics relied heavily on education to thwart Protestant expansion and to provide the foundation for their missionary work.

Both religious groups looked to the universities to provide intellectual leadership. The Protestant stress on Bible reading, especially with the availability of new vernacular translations in the sixteenth century, was a powerful incentive to education. The scientific revolution, with its rapid communication of ideas, was also highly dependent on learning, and the rapid growth of state bureaucracies increased the demand for skilled officials, particularly those with some legal training. In England the early modern period was the golden age of the Inns of Court, where aspiring young men studied the common law.

As in the East, many Western educational developments were closely linked to religion. Catholic orders such as the Jesuits and the Ursulines are famous for their educational work, but other groups were active too. The Oratory of Jesus, a society of priests, established colleges and seminaries throughout France, mostly for children of the French nobility, which rejected physical punishment as an educational tool. So did reforming Catholic Jansenists, whose "little schools" normally had no more than 25 boys in classes of six or less. Several Catholic organizations were established in France in the late 1600s to teach the children of the poor. Although Protestants had no teaching orders, they too actively founded schools, including "charity schools" for children of the poor; their curricula concentrated on reading, writing, and religion. One of the greatest Protestant successes was the founding of the University of Halle in eastern Germany in 1694 by Pietists, whose evangelical, devotional faith troubled orthodox Lutherans. By its emphasis on independent thinking, the faculty at Halle helped pioneer the development of modern academic freedom.

The Jewish communities of eastern Europe and Spain were keenly interested in education. At the elementary level, education was mandatory for all boys, and some girls were taught to read, especially after the appearance of printed vernacular literature. Gifted male students were directed into the fields of medicine and religion, the latter being a specialty of rabbinical academies. Because of the importance of rabbinical law in the ghettos, legal studies as well as religion were an important part of the curriculum. Nonreligious subjects often had to be learned from private tutors.

Progress in the founding of schools and the increase of literacy was pronounced in early modern Europe. Between 1580 and 1650 more than 800 schools were en-

Note the use of corporal punishment as a learning device in this 1592 woodcut of a German classroom. [Bettmann Archive]

dowed in England and Wales. By the late seventeenth century the number of parishes with schools was near 90 percent in the diocese of Paris and the lowland counties of Scotland, though the figure was only 42 percent in the diocese of Verdun and even less in some areas. French literacy rates were perhaps 20 percent overall in the seventeenth century, but a third of the population was literate by 1789. The reformer John Knox proposed a program of universal education in the 1560s, but the Scottish Parliament refused to fund it. Nevertheless, a century later Scotland had an impressive system of parish schools where even the poor were welcome.

Universal education effectively began when Prussia made attendance at elementary school mandatory in 1717. The founding of new schools was accompanied by substantial increases in literacy. By 1800 the literacy rate for males approached 90 percent in Scotland and 67 percent in France, whereas in 1600 only one in six Frenchmen had been able to read. Among women, whose educational opportunities were more restricted, literacy rates generally rose more slowly. Only 5 percent of the women in the English counties of East Anglia were literate, compared to 35 percent of the men in the period from 1580 to 1640. In Amsterdam, where literacy greatly enhanced employment opportunities, the rates were 57 percent for men and 32 percent for women in 1630. Because the Swedes required literacy for confirmation and marriage, by the 1690s at least one Swedish diocese had achieved a rate approaching 100 percent, though for many this may have represented little more than the abil-

ity to sign one's name. As in the East, the growth of literacy helped spur the printing industry, which published inexpensive books, ballads, and newspapers, these last appearing for the first time in the seventeenth century. The dramatic increase in Western literacy was not matched in Asia; in Japan, which had the best record, 45 percent of the men and only 15 percent of the women were literate as late as the mid-nineteenth century.

Education in the Ottoman Empire

Unlike eastern Asia or the West, the Turks, who opposed the publication of Islamic religious literature, did not allow printed books until 1728 or 1729, with the exception of a small number of presses in the non-Muslim communities. The first Turkish newspaper did not appear until 1861. Religious influence dominated the Turkish educational system; most schools were attached to mosques, and the ulema typically supplied the teachers. The Jewish and Christian communities had some schools, but generally the Ottomans discouraged education for their subject peoples. Even among the Muslims, education was essentially the preserve of the well-to-do or the politically important, since the Turks were convinced that too much learning threatened Islam.

Beyond the elementary schools, the more capable Muslim students could pursue the study of Islamic theology, law, and some humanities and science in theological schools known as *medreses*. Here the curriculum lasted as long as 12 years. The sultan also maintained five preparatory and four vocational schools where a full course of study could be as long as 15 years. These palace schools had some Christian teachers, though most of the faculty belonged to the ulema. The curriculum included the study of Turkish, Persian, and Arabic as well as the liberal arts, physical education, calligraphy, and vocational training in such areas as architecture, shipbuilding, and military affairs. There was instruction too in Islam and Turkish etiquette. But the *medreses* and the palace schools were only for the few. The expansion of Islam into North Africa and the Sudan meant that there too education was not encouraged for the masses.

Poverty, Crime, and Social Control

It is impossible to measure levels of well-being for most periods in the past. We can calculate living standards only roughly, using such evidence as travelers' accounts, estimates of population and production, trade figures, stories reflecting lifestyles, famine records, and remedial measures. Before the modern period these records are fullest for China, where we have a wealth of official and local documents and an extensive literature. Generally, most Chinese seem to have been materially better off in diet, housing, and clothing than most people elsewhere in the world until perhaps as late as the mid-nineteenth century. But the only real defense against absolute poverty was the family system in Asia, which provided its own mutual-assistance network.

Authorities in France and England in the late 1600s probably exaggerated in estimating that over half of their people lived at or below the subsistence level, but the number was high. In the late 1400s more than two-thirds of the taxpayers in Basel and Augsburg were too poor to survive serious economic adversity. The large number of poor seriously strained the ability of religious and civic authorities to provide assistance. In the plague year of 1580, more than half the population of Genoa was on poor relief. In the last decades of the sixteenth century some 20 percent of the inhabitants of Lyons, France's second largest city, needed assistance.

For the poor the greatest problem was often the uncertainty of the food supply, which was frequently threatened by inflationary pressures as well as natural disasters. Malnutrition and disease were the principal reasons for a life expectancy in Europe of only 25 years as late as 1700. Most of the world's population still lived in rural areas in the early modern period, often in mud huts with thatched roofs. Living quarters were severely cramped;

an entire family often lived in a single room. In towns the poor were victims of polluted water and filthy living conditions.

The diet of the poor was simple and, even in Europe, usually devoid of meat. The more fortunate peasants might occasionally have a little mutton or pork, but the poor usually had to survive on a diet of dark bread, peas, beans, and soup. Each day a typical adult peasant ate 2 to 3 pounds of bread made from wheat, rye, barley, or oats; wheat was the most expensive grain. Bread was a valuable source of carbohydrates, vitamins, proteins, and minerals. Many European peasants kept stock simmering in a pot, adding to it whatever foods were available each day. Sometimes cheese, butter, or curds were consumed, but milk was shunned because it was thought to be unhealthy. In general, the lot of the rural poor was marginally better than that of their urban counterparts, since many of the former were able to raise some of their own food. This was not usually true of landless day laborers, who amounted to as much as half the population of some districts in Spain and Switzerland. As the general population increased, it was imperative to find means to relieve the destitute.

Causes of European Poverty

Various factors contributed to the severity of poverty in early modern Europe. As the population grew, landlords improved the efficiency of their farms to provide additional food, but industry did not expand rapidly enough to absorb the surplus labor displaced as landowners switched from raising crops to grazing sheep. Inflation itself took a heavy toll as rents and prices rose faster than wages, leaving urban workers particularly vulnerable. Short-term increases in poverty were caused by extreme fluctuations in the cloth industry, which was adversely affected by such things as plague, war, and bad harvests. Whereas rural textile workers might weather a slump by finding temporary farm work, urban laborers were typically reduced to poor relief or begging. When harvests failed, the plight of the poor often became desperate. In England from the late fifteenth to the early seventeenth century, harvests failed on an average of every four years. When the harvests were bad several years in a row, the problem was more acute, and food riots were common. Finally, as the size of European armies expanded in the early modern period, the number of demobilized and often unemployable soldiers increased, adding burdens to relief rolls.

Poor Relief in Europe

There were various attempts to deal with the poor in this period. In the late 1400s local authorities ordered beg-

◎ Peasant Poverty: France, 1696 ◎

*The famous French military engineer Sébastien Le Prestre, marquis de
Vauban, wrote a moving description of the poor peasants in France in
1696.*

All the so-called *bas peuple* [mean people] live on nothing but bread of mixed barley and
oats, from which they do not even remove the bran, which means that bread can sometimes be lifted by the straw sticking out of it. They also eat poor fruits, mainly wild, and a
few vegetables from their gardens. . . .

The general run of people seldom drink [wine], eat meat not three times a year, and
use little salt. . . . So it is no cause for surprise if people who are so ill-nourished have so
little energy. Add to this what they suffer from exposure: winter and summer, three-fourths
of them are dressed in nothing but half-rotting tattered linen, and are shod throughout the
year with *sabots* [wooden shoes], and no other covering for the foot. . . .

The poor people are ground down in another manner by the loans of grain and money
they take from the wealthy in emergencies, by means of which a high rate of usury is enforced, under the guise of presents which must be made after the debts fall due, so as to
avoid imprisonment. After the term has been extended by only three or four months, either
another present must be produced when the time is up, or they face the *sergent* [debtors'
bailiff] who is sure to strip the house bare.

Source: Vauban, "Description géographique de l'élection de Vézelay," in P. Goubert, *The Ancien Régime:
French Society, 1600–1750,* trans. S. Cox (London: Weidenfeld & Nicolson, 1973), pp. 118–119.

gars to leave their districts, although exceptions were
sometimes made for local beggars who were handicapped, ill, or elderly. In Brabant, France, and Venice,
vagabonds provided oarpower for the galleys, while in
England a 1495 law ordered that the idle be whipped,
placed in the stocks for three days, and then returned
to their parishes of origin. Intended to keep the destitute
from flooding into the towns, virtually all early measures
to deal with the poor relied on some form of coercion
but failed to provide organized means to relieve the
needy.

The widespread social unrest sparked throughout
Europe by the harvest failures of the 1520s brought
major changes in social policy. Between 1531 and 1541
some 60 cities reformed their welfare policies, and the
state imposed reforms in the Netherlands, England,
France, Scotland, and Spain. The governments of the
first three states prohibited begging and insisted that
the able-bodied poor work. Funds for those unable to
work were raised through taxes or donations, but there
was a clear shift in emphasis from private charity to public welfare. The English Poor Law of 1601, for example,
prohibited begging, required the able-bodied poor to
work on local projects, centralized poor relief, and provided for the education of paupers' children. Where
there was industry to employ the able-bodied at low
wages, as in Flanders, France, and England, the new

system achieved some success. In Scotland and Spain,
however, there was little need for the labor of unskilled
paupers, and licensed begging was used in an attempt
to keep them under control. But since licenses could
easily be forged, this system was ineffective.

Because employment could not always be found for
the able-bodied poor, many European cities established
workhouses to discipline the poor as well as to provide
job training and moral instruction. Although these institutions could not accommodate all the able-bodied poor,
officials hoped to coerce the remainder into finding employment. Some workhouses, such as Bridewell in London and those founded by the papacy in Rome, became
little more than places of punishment, while others, such
as those in the Netherlands, Scandinavia, and Germany,
were sources of cheap labor for private employers.
French workhouses at first were used to benefit private
business, but after 1640 they were employed primarily
to control rebellious peasants and workers. The inmates
of these institutions rarely benefited from their enforced
stays.

Poor Relief Outside Europe

The towns of coastal West Africa similarly developed a
system of poor relief in the late sixteenth and seven-

In early modern Europe, many indigent persons took to the highways in search of employment, but in so doing they risked severe punishment as vagabonds. This 1520 engraving is by Lucas van Leyden. [Staatliche Museen Preussischer Kulturbesitz, Berlin, Kupferstichkabinett/Jörg P. Anders]

teenth centuries. As the rural poor fled to the towns in search of better opportunities, the number of the indigent was often as high as 40 percent, and in the port of Shama on the Gold Coast it reached 70 or 80 percent.

There were, however, no professional beggars because of a rather extensive system of poor relief. The wealthy took some of the poor into their personal service, while others received assistance from special funds raised by taxes or court fines. Some of the offerings given to priests made their way to the poor as well. Local authorities were required to provide gainful employment for young men, the physically handicapped, and the elderly, usually in the crafts, food processing, and market vending. Because the rural poor who faced severe economic hardship sometimes opted for banditry rather than migration to the towns, in the early 1600s brigandage reached near-epidemic levels in parts of West Africa. By striking at the trading caravans transporting rural produce to the towns, the brigands effectively symbolized the resentment of peasants at their growing subservience to urban merchants, a development that was also common in much of Europe and Asia.

In South America the Inca addressed the problem by systematic regimentation and care of the needy. The state itself owned the land and apportioned it to families based on their size, with a substantial portion of the crops going to storehouses to supply the nobility, the military, state workers, and priests. The government also took much of what the artisans produced. Although the masses were thus deprived of both freedom and initiative, in times of famine or natural disaster the state provided them with food from the public warehouses.

The larger Asian society had pitifully inadequate means beyond the family level to intervene on behalf of the poor. In China the imperial bureaucracy did what its limited local powers allowed, including the remission of taxes, the control of floods, the keeping of order, and the storing of grain for distribution in lean years at un-inflated prices, a policy called the "ever-normal granary system." Such efforts flagged or failed when the dynasty was weak or collapsed—perhaps a third of the time—and even in strong periods the state could not cope with a major catastrophe. In India and Southeast Asia, and to a lesser degree in the Buddhist areas of Korea and Japan, temples provided some refuge for the destitute, but this too was inadequate. In general, the family system of mutual support could keep most people from total destitution most of the time, but no means were adequate to deal with the recurrent large-scale disasters to which all premodern societies were subject, such as drought-induced famine, major flooding, or long periods of civil disorder. In the Islamic world, the poor could look to social-service institutions funded primarily by charitable legacies and the obligatory tax, or *zakat*, which was one of the principal duties of a Muslim.

Crime and Poverty

One of the most striking differences between East and West was in the treatment of crime. In general terms, Asian thought made no place for the Judeo-Christian concept of sin. Correction and, if possible, reform through reeducation or renewed piety were stressed more than repayment or punishment, although these were certainly used and frequently harsh. The incidence of crime or social deviance was almost certainly less in Asia than in other areas, thanks to the self-regulating mechanism of the family and the deterrent power of the shame that individual misbehavior might bring on the group. It is sometimes said that whereas Western societies emphasized individual sin and guilt, the East stressed the unacceptability of antisocial behavior and used shame to enforce moral codes. In addition to the social stigma of misbehavior, public shaming was commonly used as an official punishment both in Asia and in Europe. Both Asian and European criminals were publicly exhibited, often paraded through the streets carrying placards indicating their offenses, and sometimes executed.

As the living standards of European workers and peasants deteriorated, criminal activity increased, especially from the mid-1500s on. In rural areas there was a clear connection between crime and destitution. Records for the Spanish province of Toledo show that nearly all defendants in larceny cases came from the lower ranks of society. Theft was often the most common crime; in the English county of Sussex in the early 1600s stealing accounted for nearly two-thirds of all indictments. Theft was a capital offense, though the death penalty was rarely applied. Most rural felons were common laborers who did not repeat their criminal activity after their initial arrest.

The type of larceny changed somewhat in the early modern period. In medieval times thieves stole mostly subsistence items—food, clothing, and tools—but later they began to prefer luxury goods, increasingly available in the expanding towns. Whereas the poor had hitherto stolen mostly from other poor people, they now increasingly robbed the rich. A major exception to this pattern of crime occurred during the unsettled times of fourteenth- and fifteenth-century Europe when bands of lawless nobles and gentry engaged in robbery and extortion. Victims who refused to pay often had their crops destroyed and their homes burned. Not even the wealthy were immune, for they provided tempting targets for kidnapping and extortion. Known as "fur-collar criminals" because of their noble garb, the culprits thrived until governments were strong enough to stamp most of them out in the 1500s.

Banditry did not cease with the decline of fur-collar crime, but henceforth nearly all bandits were from the lower social orders and included many men unable to find employment. In Granada some of the bandit groups were led by women. As major roads were more effectively patrolled by the seventeenth century, most of these bandits were forced into remote areas. Russia, however, experienced considerable turmoil throughout the 1600s because of large roving bands. Russian bandits were commonly viewed as heroes and defenders of the common people, particularly since most victims were bureaucrats, tax collectors, and wealthy merchants.

In Asia, too, banditry was a common response by people reduced to absolute poverty. It was especially frequent in periods of political disorder and hence virtually endemic in parts of India, while its incidence rose and fell in China with the changing effectiveness of the imperial government and the levels of peasant distress. Bandits operated most successfully on the fringes of state-controlled areas or in frontier zones between provincial jurisdictions, areas that were often mountainous or forested. Bandits exacerbated the poverty of their prey. Although their prime targets were the rich and the trade routes, these were often better protected than the common people and their villages. Some bandit groups turned into rebels, who built on the support of the disaffected majority to overthrow the government and found a new order that could better serve mass welfare. Much popular fiction dealt with the adventures of bandit groups, often depicted as Robin Hood–type figures but in any case regarded as heroes rather than criminals.

In the West a new literary form, the picaresque novel—celebrating the adventures of an urban rogue, or *picaro*—developed in connection with a trend toward more sophisticated urban crimes. In addition to the usual larceny, physical assault, homicide, and arson, early modern towns were increasingly troubled by business fraud and swindlers. By the mid-1600s novels about these rogues were popular in Spain, from whence they spread to Germany and England.

Another facet of urban crime in the larger European cities was the growth of neighborhoods where a genuine underworld existed. In Paris the criminal sector near the Porte St.-Denis was so extensive that officials dared not enter it until it was subdued by an army detachment in 1667. Curtailing crime in the cities was nearly impossible because the poor were packed into grossly overcrowded slums where shanties filled even the narrow alleys and where criminals could easily hide.

Controlling Crime

European states responded to the rise in crime by reorganizing the personnel and procedure necessary to control it. In the medieval period criminal control was based on the existence of small populations in compact, mostly isolated areas. As the population expanded and interregional contacts increased, it became imperative to develop more effective government controls beyond the local level. The French met this need by expanding the powers of the royal *procureur*, who handled the prosecution in criminal proceedings. In England the Tudors, who had no police force, enlarged the role of the justices of the peace, who, as unpaid agents of the crown, had the authority to arrest, indict, and grant bail. They also enforced labor codes and social laws that governed such things as alehouses and unlawful games. By the late sixteenth century justices of the peace were responsible for enforcement of the poor law.

Throughout Europe revised criminal procedures had the effect of depersonalizing the judicial process and treating criminal activity as an offense against society rather than the individual. Punishment became more severe. In contrast to the medieval system, where justice was intended to settle disputes between persons, the new criminal proceedings punished the guilty but ignored compensation for the victim. Unlike medieval justice, corporal punishment became more widespread,

◉ Capital Punishment and Cruelty ◉

European justice entailed not only the use of torture to extract confessions but also the application of capital punishment for various crimes against property as well as human life. Here is the account of a French observer sensitive to the cruel suffering inflicted on criminals in eighteenth-century Paris: note his opposition to capital punishment as contrary to natural law.

I went home by way of rue Saint-Antoine and the Place de Grève. Three murderers had been broken on the wheel there, the day before. . . . As I crossed the square I caught sight of a poor wretch, pale, half dead, wracked by the pains of the interrogation inflicted on him twenty hours earlier; he was stumbling down from the Hôtel de Ville supported by the executioner and the confessor. These two men, so completely different, inspired an inexpressible emotion in me! I watched the latter embrace a miserable man consumed by fever, filthy as the dungeons he came from, swarming with vermin! And I said to myself, "O Religion, here is your greatest glory! . . ." I saw the other as the wrathful arm of the law. . . . But I wondered: "Have men the right to impose death . . . even on the murderer who has himself treacherously taken life?" I seemed to hear Nature reply with a woeful no! . . . "But robbery?" "No, no!" cried Nature. "The savage rich have never felt they devised enough harsh safeguards; instead of being friends and brothers, as their religion commands, they prefer the gallows. . . ." This was what Nature said to me. . . .

Source: Nicolas-Edmé, Restif de la Bretonne, *Les Nuits de Paris, or The Nocturnal Spectator,* trans. L. Asher and E. Fertig (New York: Random House, 1964), pp. 7–8.

though a status distinction was generally made in meting out justice; the rich were often fined, the poor imprisoned, flogged, or mutilated. The increased severity of punishments was intended to discipline the lower orders and curb the increase in crimes by the poor against the rich. Public punishment thus had a twofold purpose: to deter crime and to demonstrate the authority of the state to regulate the behavior of its citizens and command their obedience.

In both Asia and Europe criminals were tried and laws and punishments enforced by civil courts run by the state and presided over by magistrates, rulers or their representatives, community elders, or learned men. In Asia and sometimes in Europe there was no prior assumption of guilt or innocence; judgment was made and sentences arrived at on the basis of evidence, including the testimony of witnesses. Asians had no lawyers standing between people and the law; plaintiffs and defendants spoke for themselves. In China and most of the rest of Asia, people charged with criminal behavior could be found guilty and punished only if they confessed their guilt. If they refused to do so despite the weight of evidence against them, they were often tortured to extract a confession. Torture was also used in early modern Europe, though confession was not essen-

tial for a conviction. Asian law and the system of official justice, like its European counterpart, was designed to awe all who appeared before its majesty. Plaintiffs, defendants, and witnesses knelt before the magistrate or judge and could be whipped if they were not suitably reverential—another expression of a strongly hierarchical, authoritarian society.

In both Asia and Europe punishment for major crimes of violence was almost invariably death, commonly by beheading or strangulation. Death could also be imposed for many minor crimes. For especially dreadful crimes, such as parricide, treason, rebellion, or, in Asia, other forms of filial and political disloyalty, more gruesome punishments were used: dismemberment, the pulling apart of limbs by horses, the Chinese "death of a thousand cuts," or in India impalement or trampling by elephants. In Europe dismemberment by "drawing and quartering" (sundering limbs from the body) was imposed for treason.

Punishments were seen as deterrents to would-be criminals; the heads of the executed were exhibited on poles until they rotted. For lesser offenses Asian criminals were displayed in painfully small cages or mutilated, practices also used in Europe, or forced to wear a heavy wooden collar that prevented them from feeding them-

Chinese punishment for minor offenses. The heavy wooden collar, the *cangue*, was a burden to support and also prevented the criminal from reaching his mouth with his hands, which meant that he would starve if not fed by others. This man's crime is recorded on the inscription, but all that can be read here are the official title and seal of the imperial magistrate at Shanghai in 1872. [John Thomson/Harvard-Yenching Library, Harvard University]

selves. In East and West alike prisons were often dreadful places where inmates might starve if they were not fed by relatives. For what we might call misdemeanors, Asian sentences tended to stress reeducation and reform. Criminality, or at least misbehavior, was seen as potentially correctible, especially with family help.

People naturally worried about falling into the machinery of the law and the courts, especially in criminal cases. Two important points need to be made. In Asia probably considerably fewer than 10 percent of disputes and minor crimes—perhaps most crimes of all sorts—ever reached the courts since they were settled through family, village, gentry, or other local networks. Second,

modern Western scholars conclude that justice was done by that system, perhaps more consistently than in the West. Most magistrates were judicious, diligent with evidence, and concerned to see justice done, not only to avoid the censure that could ruin their careers but also because of the sense of responsibility they bore. But there was, particularly in the West, a double standard of justice, which was much harder on the poor, whose crimes generally stemmed from poverty, than on their social betters. Laws were made and administered by elite groups, whose interests in the preservation of their privileged status and property were at least as great as their devotion to justice.

Surveying the societies of the early modern world, perhaps most striking is the contrast between the relative stability of Asian society and the volatility of Europe. As Europeans made crucial economic, political, and educational advances in the early modern period, Western society altered substantially, beginning in western Europe and spreading to the Americas through colonization. Nevertheless, the strikingly numerous social parallels between the different parts of the world in this period underscore the common-ality of much historical development and human experience. Societies were structured hierarchically and embraced the principle that social status entailed special responsibility. In Asia and Europe alike, arranged marriages were common, and precedence was accorded to sons. Capital punishment was commonly imposed for major crimes, and some of the poor in all societies periodically resorted to banditry. Moreover, in their treatment of women, most Asian and Western societies were alike in not granting even a modicum of social equality to women until the twentieth century.

Conflicting religious tenets were responsible for some of the most basic social differences in the early modern world. Religious considerations explain at least in part why Aztecs, Inca, Muslims, and some Africans practiced polygamy, whereas non-Muslim Asians and Europeans were primarily monogamous. Religion was also a key factor in views on sex. Many East Asians and Africans, unlike Christians, for instance, linked sex and religious ritual. Religious changes were responsible for altering the way some westerners viewed marriage: divorce (other than through annulment) was not possible in Europe until the Protestant Reformation in the sixteenth century; in Asia, divorce did occur, though rarely. The relative importance attached to education, particularly in Asia, stemmed partly from the desire to preserve its religious and philosophical traditions. The same can be said of Judaism and later of Christianity.

Suggestions for Further Reading

Buxbaum, D., ed. *Chinese Family Law and Social Change.* Seattle: University of Washington Press, 1978.

Cahn, S. *Industry of Devotion: The Transformation of Women's Work in England, 1500–1660.* New York: Columbia University Press, 1987.

Ch'u, T. *Law and Society in Traditional China.* Paris: Mouton, 1961.

Cohn, B. S. *India: The Social Anthropology of a Civilization.* Englewood Cliffs, N.J.: Prentice Hall, 1971.

Davidson, B. *The African Genius: An Introduction to Social and Cultural History.* Boston: Little, Brown, 1969.

Dumont, L. *Homo Hierarchicus: An Essay on the Caste System,* trans. M. Sainsbury. Chicago: University of Chicago Press, 1970.

Fildes, V. *Wet Nursing: A History from Antiquity to the Present.* Oxford: Blackwell, 1988.

Foucault, M. *The History of Sexuality,* trans. R. Hurley. New York: Pantheon, 1977.

Fraser, A. *The Weaker Vessel: Woman's Lot in Seventeenth-Century England.* London: Weidenfeld & Nicolson, 1984.

Freedman, M., ed. *Family and Kinship in Chinese Society.* Stanford, Calif.: Stanford University Press, 1970.

Goody, J. *The Oriental, the Ancient and the Primitive: Marriage and the Family in the Preindustrial Societies of Eurasia.* Cambridge: Cambridge University Press, 1990.

Goubert, P. *The French Peasantry in the Seventeenth Century,* trans. I. Patterson. Cambridge: Cambridge University Press, 1986.

Greaves, R. L. *Society and Religion in Elizabethan England.* Minneapolis: University of Minnesota Press, 1981.

Hanawalt, B. A., ed. *Women and Work in Preindustrial Europe.* Bloomington: Indiana University Press, 1986.

Hinsch, B. *Passions of the Cut Sleeve: The Male Homosexual Tradition in China.* Berkeley: University of California Press, 1990.

Houston, R. A. *Literacy in Early Modern Europe: Culture and Education, 1500–1800.* New York: Longman, 1988.

Hunt, D. *Parents and Children in History: The Psychology of Family Life in Early Modern France.* New York: Basic Books, 1970.

Kamen, H. *European Society, 1500–1700.* London: Hutchinson, 1984.

Kea, R. A. *Settlements, Trade, and Politics in the Seventeenth-Century Gold Coast.* Baltimore: Johns Hopkins University Press, 1982.

Ladurie, E. L. *The French Peasantry, 1450–1660.* Berkeley: University of California Press, 1986.

Lannoy, R. *The Speaking Tree: Indian Culture and Society.* New York: Oxford University Press, 1971.

Laslett, P. *The World We Have Lost Further Explored,* 3rd ed. London: Methuen, 1983.

Le May, R. S. *The Culture of Southeast Asia.* London: Allen & Unwin, 1954.

Lewis, R. *Everyday Life in Ottoman Turkey.* New York: Putnam, 1971.

Macfarlane, A. *Marriage and Love in England: Modes of Reproduction, 1300–1840.* New York: Blackwell, 1986.

Mandelbaum, D. G. *Society in India: Continuity and Change.* 2 vols. Berkeley: University of California Press, 1970.

Maynes, M. J. *Schooling in Western Europe: A Social History.* New York: State University of New York Press, 1985.

McKnight, B. *The Quality of Mercy: Amnesties and Traditional Chinese Justice.* Honolulu: University Press of Hawaii, 1981.

Naquin, S., and Rawski, E. S. *Chinese Society in the Eighteenth Century.* New Haven, Conn.: Yale University Press, 1988.

Norberg, K. *Rich and Poor in Grenoble, 1600–1814.* Berkeley: University of California Press, 1985.

Ozment, S. *When Fathers Ruled: Family Life in Reformation Europe.* Cambridge, Mass.: Harvard University Press, 1983.

Pollock, L. A. *Forgotten Children: Parent-Child Relations from 1500 to 1900.* Cambridge: Cambridge University Press, 1984.

Rawksi, E. S. *Education and Popular Literacy in Ch'ing China.* Ann Arbor: University of Michigan Press, 1979.

Rose, M. B., ed. *Women in the Middle Ages and the Renaissance: Literary and Historical Perspectives.* Syracuse, N.Y.: Syracuse University Press, 1986.

Schalk, E. *From Valor to Pedigree: Ideas of Nobility in France in the Sixteenth and Seventeenth Centuries.* Princeton, N.J.: Princeton University Press, 1986.

Shorter, E. *The Making of the Modern Family.* New York: Basic Books, 1977.

Slack, P. *Poverty and Policy in Tudor and Stuart England.* New York: Longman, 1988.

Stone, L. *The Family, Sex, and Marriage in England, 1500–1800.* New York: Harper & Row, 1977.

———. *Road to Divorce: England, 1530–1987.* New York: Oxford University Press, 1991.

———, and Stone, J. C. F. *An Open Elite? England, 1540–1880.* New York: Oxford University Press, 1984.

Traer, J. F. *Marriage and the Family in Eighteenth-Century France.* Ithaca, N.Y.: Cornell University Press, 1980.

Wakeman, F., ed. *Conflict and Control in Late Imperial China.* Berkeley: University of California Press, 1975.

Wiesner, M. E. *Working Women in Renaissance Germany.* New Brunswick, N.J.: Rutgers University Press, 1986.

Woodbridge, L. *Women and the English Renaissance: Literature and the Nature of Womankind, 1540–1620.* Champaign: University of Illinois Press, 1984.

The Age of Absolutism

The sixteenth century had witnessed the emergence of the nation-state in western Europe. The seventeenth and eighteenth centuries saw its consolidation. By the end of the Thirty Years' War, it was clear that the future lay with the powers capable of mobilizing their resources most effectively for both war and peace. From the middle of the seventeenth century to the end of the eighteenth, the major states of Europe embarked on a variety of programs designed to increase centralized political and economic control. On the political level, this process generally took the form of absolutism; on the economic level, that of mercantilism. Each of the major states took a somewhat different path to these ends. What proved workable in the France of Louis XIV required a different approach in England or in the Russia of Peter the Great. But by the mid-eighteenth century, every major power

Louis XIV of France, known to contemporaries as the Sun King, epitomized divine right kingship and the power of the monarchical state in early modern Europe. [Réunion des Musées Nationaux (France)]

had succeeded in its program of centralization—or had paid the price of failure.

This process was not accomplished without difficulty. Merchants generally welcomed the economic initiatives of the state and in some cases actively sought them. The landed aristocracy, fearful of losing its privileges and jealous of its traditional authority, often opposed centralization. Workers demanded wage and price controls, a dependable supply of bread, and restrictions on cheap imported labor. Peasants sought relief from the onerous burdens of taxes and traditional obligations. Thus the state's quest for political unity and economic control raised a host of demands from competing constituencies. It sharpened the differences between social groups and led eventually to the demand for political representation. By the eighteenth century some European rulers frankly regarded themselves as arbiters between the competing interest groups in their countries. But the centralizing states were not always able to control the forces they had unleashed. By the late eighteenth century, absolutism had created the conditions that would lead to its demise and its replacement by the modern state.

France Under Louis XIV

Of all the absolute monarchs, none stamped his age as decisively as Louis XIV (1643–1715) of France. No other Western European ruler exerted greater or more uncontested control of his country during the 1,000-year period between the reign of Charlemagne and the French Revolution of 1789. Yet even Louis faced daunting obstacles and resistance in his efforts to bend the people and institutions of France to his will, and even he was forced to acknowledge the limitations of his power.

Provincial Autonomy and Central Control

The France of Louis XIV was not a unitary state but a patchwork of widely varying provincial customs and powers. In many respects, the crown's relations with the larger and older provinces, called *pays d'état* because they had their own representative assemblies or estates, resembled treaties with quasi-sovereign powers. These provinces set their own tax rates and passed laws independent of and often at odds with those of the central government. As late as 1661 Louis was acknowledged as no more than count of Provence and duke of Brittany in those two provinces. Many of the towns not only set up their own councils and magistrates but also levied their own customs duties and raised their own militias. A good

number of them were wholly exempt from the basic property tax of the realm, the *taille*. So were whole classes of the population, notably the clergy and, in at least some of the forms in which it was levied, the nobility. However, the taille was imposed directly and unilaterally on the newer provinces. The hated excise tax on salt, the *gabelle*, was applied so unequally that the price of this vital commodity was as much as 25 times higher in one province than in another.

Armed rebellions often broke out when the central government attempted to impose a new tax. Some of these rebellions went on for years and cost the government far more to suppress than it could ever have hoped to gain in revenue. The only constant in the system was that it bore most heavily everywhere on the poor, particularly the peasantry. Thus it combined both the greatest unfairness and the greatest inefficiency.

The basis for a policy of effective centralization was clear: standardization of laws and taxes, reduction of internal tariffs, promotion of key industries, and the neutralization of seigneurial courts and provincial legislatures. The foundations for this policy had been laid in the previous two reigns. Henry IV had curbed the power of the provincial estates and established government monopolies over mining and the production of gunpowder and salt. Louis XIII's minister, Cardinal Richelieu, had dispatched special agents, the *intendants*, to oversee provincial administration. Both Henry IV and Louis XIII had studiously ignored the national representative assembly, the Estates General, which met only twice during their combined reigns. The revolt of the Fronde (see Chapter 19), in which the nobility had made its last serious attempt to assert power on a national level, had ended in failure.

Divine Right Monarchy

It was Louis XIV, however, who most successfully exploited the powers of personal monarchy to create a centralized state. For Louis, increasing the power of the state was not merely a matter of policy. It was a natural consequence of his authority as a divine right king. Whether Louis actually made the famous statement attributed to him, "I am the state," he clearly lived by the thought. Louis identified himself wholly with the French state. Even his private life was lived in public, among a throng of courtiers; for him, there was no distinction between the man and the monarch. Fortunately, Louis had the ideal temperament for a king. He was highly conscious of his dignity; it was said that even as a child he seldom laughed. But Louis did not experience the cares of state as a burden. "The calling of a king is great, noble, and delightful," he said. In 54 years of active rule, he never lost his zest for governing.

For Louis, the aim of the state was *gloire*—glory.

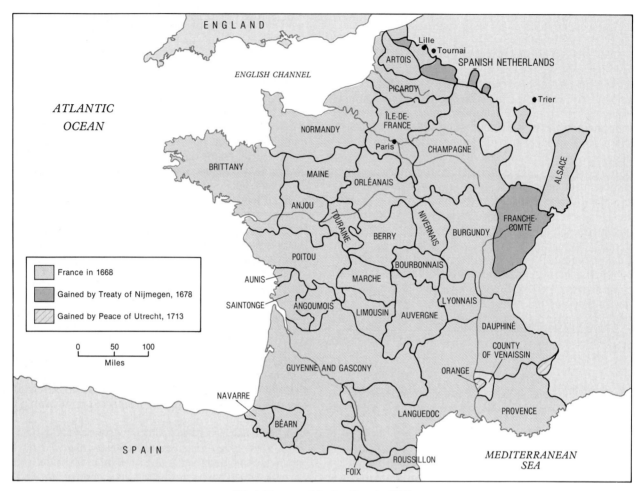

23.1 France Under Louis XIV

Gloire was both an attribute of persons—the dignity of a nobleman, the majesty of a king—and the collective aspiration of a nation. The glory of France was in its wealth and productivity, its technology and engineering, the splendor of its arts. Even more, in an age that valued military prowess above all else, its glory was measured by its power. France was already the richest and most powerful state in Europe at the accession of Louis XIV. For Louis that was only the measure of its potential for further achievement and greater *gloire*.

❧ JEAN-BAPTISTE COLBERT, MINISTER OF FINANCE

The king assembled around him a small group of ministers recruited not from the nobility but from the bour-geoisie. Chief among these was Jean-Baptiste Colbert. The son of a draper, Colbert shared his master's vision of glory. From 1661 until his death in 1683 he was the most important man in the kingdom after Louis himself.

Colbert had entered government service when not yet 20, and his talents and capacity for hard work soon commended him to the secretary of state for war, Michel Le Tellier, who made Colbert his private secretary. By 1649, at the age of only 30, Colbert had himself become a councillor of state, and two years later he entered the service of Cardinal Mazarin, who had succeeded Riche-lieu as the dominant figure in French politics. Mazarin at first treated the upstart young bourgeois with reserve, if not disdain, but he soon found Colbert's services in-dispensable, as Le Tellier had. As the cardinal's health began to fail, Colbert took on more and more responsi-bility. By the late 1650s he was charged with suppress-ing a major revolt of the nobility in Normandy, Anjou, and Poitou, while at the same time he drafted an ambitious new plan for reform of the king's finances that directly undercut his chief rival, Nicholas Fouquet.

Fouquet learned of Colbert's scheme through his friend the postmaster general of Paris, who opened the letter that contained it. But Colbert's position was now unassailable, and at Mazarin's death in 1661 Colbert had the professional and no doubt personal pleasure of arresting Fouquet. The fallen minister, who had grossly enriched himself, narrowly escaped execution. Colbert also used his position to gain wealth for himself and his numerous family, but with a difference: he enriched the king as well.

Colbert's title was controller of finances, but his mandate embraced the economy as a whole, including trade and commerce, the merchant marine and the navy, the colonies, and internal security. Colbert found that the crown's deficit was nearly a third of its income and that its revenues were pledged as much as three years in advance. Worse still, barely a third of the taxes levied by the crown found their way into the treasury due to fraud and evasion.

While actually decreasing the taille, Colbert was able to double the overall tax yield within six years by curbing the abuses of tax collectors, tightening exemptions, exploiting the royal demesne more efficiently, and compelling the *pays d'état* to increase their share of taxes. He presided over a council of commerce consisting of prominent merchants, which charted a course for France's commercial and industrial supremacy. Disdainful of agriculture, he pointed to the example of the Dutch, who had gained wealth and world power by commerce despite a land area and population barely a tenth the size of France. He established and subsidized hundreds of new workshops and factories, either under direct royal control or licensed as monopolies. His agents scoured Europe to recruit the most skilled technicians—dyers, glassblowers, gun founders. At home, meanwhile, he tried to organize all French craftsmen into guilds, subject to minute regulations and supervised by an army of state inspectors.

The purpose of new industry was to provide material for commerce; the purpose of commerce was to amass wealth; and the purpose of wealth was power. Economic activity was thus for Colbert, as for Louis, both a preparation for war and a kind of warfare in itself. By fostering new trades and erecting tariff barriers, France would reduce its dependence on imports and prevent the drain of its bullion. By increasing production, expanding the navy, and creating large overseas trading companies, it would penetrate markets, drive off rivals, and extend French power on a global scale. To all of this, centralized organization and control were the key. "If your Majesty could constrain all your subjects into these four kinds of profession," Colbert wrote the king, "agriculture, trade, war by land or by sea, it would be possible for you to become the master of the world."[1]

Jean-Baptiste Colbert, the consummate bureaucrat, in a portrait by Lefebvre. Colbert's financial and organizational genius made the splendor of Louis XIV's reign possible. [Giraudon/Art Resource]

Colbert was particularly active on behalf of maritime trade and warfare. Within France, he built canals and modernized ports. He created a flotilla of trading companies for both the West Indies and the East Indies that were designed to extend French power and wealth no less than its fleet. He was the real founder of the French navy, and he searched the prisons and poorhouses of France to man his new ships. In some cases he commuted death sentences to procure sailors, but in many others he arbitrarily lengthened prison terms, compelled judges to sentence convicts to the galleys, and forcibly impressed beggars and vagrants. Such actions showed the darker side of a man obsessed with the goals of power. Assiduous in cultivating his superiors, he seemed a tyrant to many when at last he had no superior but the king. When he died in 1683, his body was buried secretly lest his tomb be desecrated by his enemies. Yet he was France's greatest economic statesman, and perhaps its greatest cultural patron as well.

Louis XIV and the Bureaucracy

Ironically, the chief obstacle to the king's dreams appeared to be his own bureaucracy. According to one contemporary estimate, the number of government offices in France had increased by 50,000 during the first half of the seventeenth century. There were nearly 2,000 officers in the Court of Chancery and almost 1,000 tax collectors for the taille (at least on paper) in the province of Normandy alone.

The reason for this explosion of bureaucrats lay in the nature of officeholding itself. Each occupant of a venal office bought and owned it. In return for his investment, he acquired a blue-chip property that yielded a handsome income in fees and had a resale value very likely to appreciate. There was status value too, since even minor offices often entitled the holder or his heir to ennoblement.

The entire system constituted a form of indirect taxation. Purchasers advanced a lump sum to the crown and recouped their outlay by charging the public for their "services." For the financially pressed monarchy, the lure of ready cash was irresistible. Administratively, however, the system was a nightmare. The number of offices created bore no relation to function or need. The public business was intolerably delayed, and the king's own edicts were lost in the maze of clerkships. Once entrenched, the officeholders resisted any attempt at accountability or reform. In return for short-term financial relief, the crown had created long-term political paralysis.

In contrast to this bloated bureaucracy, Louis XIV gathered around him a tiny nucleus of advisers. Besides Colbert, the only important ministers were Lionne for foreign affairs and Le Tellier for war. The king made all decisions of state with these three. Another 30 councillors of state and fewer than 100 masters of requests prepared material and executed orders, assisted by scribes, ushers, and other minor functionaries. All in all, the royal executive consisted of fewer than 1,000 persons.

By streamlining his government at the top, Louis was able to act swiftly and in secret and to keep all major threads of policy in his own hands. If there was chaos at the extremities of the state, the king was determined to counteract it by command at the center.

The key to the royal strategy was the revived use of

◉ On the Nature of Majesty ◉

Jacques-Bénigne Bossuet, bishop of Meaux and tutor to the royal family, was the foremost spokesman for the divine right of kings in seventeenth-century France and its last great apologist in Europe. In this characteristically titled work, Politics Derived from the Words of Holy Scripture *(published posthumously in 1709), Bossuet describes the quality of "majesty" in kingship as the reflection and transmission of the power and glory of God on earth.*

By majesty, I do not mean that pomp which surrounds kings, or that show of brilliance which dazzles the vulgar. This is but the reflection of majesty, and not majesty itself.

Majesty is the image of the glory of God in the prince. God is infinite; God is all. The prince, in his capacity as a prince, is not considered an individual man: he is a public person, the whole state is in him, the will of the whole people is contained within his own. As all perfection and all virtue are united in God, so is the entire power of individual persons united in the person of the prince. What greatness is it for a single man to hold such power!

God's power makes itself felt in an instant from one end of the world to the other. Royal power acts simultaneously throughout the realm. It keeps the whole realm in its proper state, just as God does for the whole world. Let God withhold his hand, and the world would collapse again into nothingness; let authority cease in the realm, and everything would be in confusion.

Source: K. M. Baker, ed., *Readings in Western Civilization*, vol. 7 (Chicago: University of Chicago Press, 1987), p. 39.

intendants, who were handpicked from among the masters of requests. At first, as under Richelieu, they were sent out on specific assignments to the provinces. Later, however, they took up permanent residence. Their commissions were all-embracing, and their powers superseded those of all other officials, including the provincial governor. Not since Roman times had central authority exerted such continuous and effective control at the local level.

By such means Louis was able to cut through his own bureaucracy and impose his will on France. To be sure, he often met stubborn resistance. Local noblemen, jealous of their independence, made common cause with local officials to frustrate his intentions. Proud Brittany did not submit to the yoke of an intendant until 1689. But in the last analysis, there could be no disputing the command of a divinely anointed king. As God's representative on earth, his will was supreme. Bishop Bossuet (1627–1704), Louis' chief spiritual adviser, went so far as to declare that the king was God himself. It is not recorded that Louis denied it.

Versailles: The Sun King Enthroned

For the king's power to be felt, it had to be visible. Louis had his architects and decorators turn the royal hunting lodge at Versailles, 10 miles from Paris, into the most splendid palace in the Western world. Surrounded by formal gardens and artificial lakes, it stretched in a great semicircle for more than a quarter of a mile. Fountains and statues adorned it on all sides. Inside, a hall of mirrors lit by thousands of candelabras led to the main apartments. Louis himself was portrayed in triumph everywhere, ruling over Europe, Asia, and the Americas in the frescoes that lined the halls of state or garbed as a Roman emperor surrounded by classical gods and goddesses. The king had taken the sun as his personal emblem early in the reign, and every aspect of Versailles, from the smallest decorative details to the long, tree-lined avenues that spread out from the palace like the rays of a great orb, reflected the solar theme. An army of workmen and engineers the size of a city—36,000 were counted on the site at one time—toiled to construct this ultimate monument to *gloire*, digging trenches and canals, erecting pagan temples, stocking the game parks, and trimming the gardens to create a perfect world where nature as well as man obeyed an absolute ruler.

This hothouse paradise enclosed one of the most artificial societies ever created. The most distinguished noblemen of France vied for the honor of living in the cramped and squalid conditions of an overcrowded court. Proximity to the king determined one's status. Personal attendance on him was the most coveted honor of all. Great dukes fought for the right to serve as his footmen, adjusting his livery or holding his candlestick. Louis lived in Versailles not as a man but as an idol, displaying himself to the privileged few permitted to worship him in person. In this way he tamed his nobility. Absorbed in etiquette, obsessed with their own vanity,

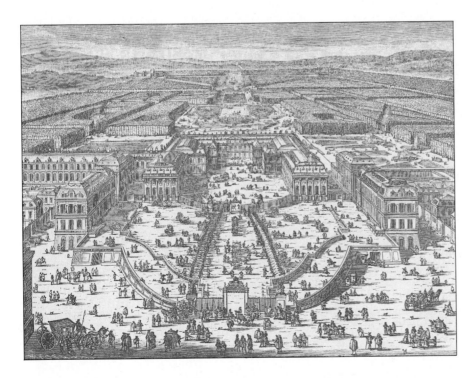

This contemporary engraving of the palace at Versailles conveys the vast size of the royal complex and grounds and the throngs of courtiers, suitors, officials, and ladies of fashion that made up its daily traffic. [Bettmann Archive]

they neglected the most important aspect of status: power.

As Voltaire remarked, "Louis liked the ladies, and it was reciprocal." The prominence of women in the court life of Versailles reflected the general softening of manners that had come to the French court with its increasing refinement and sophistication of taste. But royal favor, once withdrawn, could be devastating. Louis' first mistress, Louise de la Vallière, had to endure the ignominy of watching him pass through her apartments to visit his new favorite, Madame de Montespan, until she was permitted to retire to a Carmelite nunnery.

The king was finally tamed by a remarkable woman, Madame de Maintenon (1635–1719). Born Françoise d'Aubigné, she was taken to the Caribbean island of Martinique as a child and left penniless at her father's death. She struggled back to France with her mother and, soon orphaned, escaped the fate of a poor relation by marrying the poet Paul Scarron. After Scarron's death, a chance connection brought her the estate of Maintenon and a position at court, where she became governess to Madame de Montespan's bastards and eventually the king's confidante. When Queen Marie-Thérèse died in 1683, Louis secretly married the woman now called Madame de Maintenon, and although the wedding was never acknowledged, she was the dominant presence at Versailles until his death.

Under Maintenon's influence, the court, still brilliant, took on a more pious and sober tone. Remembering the hardships of her own life, Maintenon had begun to educate poor children as early as 1674, and in 1686 she opened a school exclusively for the daughters of impoverished nobility, St. Cyr. For the remainder of her life she visited it nearly every day, directly overseeing the development of its curriculum and the welfare of its pupils. St. Cyr was an immense success, a training college whose graduates spread the spirit of reform into old-fashioned convent schools and a milestone in the history of women's education. Maintenon was buried in the school's chapel, beside her beloved children. St. Cyr itself was closed during the French Revolution, and in 1794 some workmen, engaged in demolishing the chapel, discovered her grave, pulled out her preserved body, dragged and kicked it about the grounds, and threw it into a pit.

The Wars of Louis XIV

If Versailles was the image of *gloire*, war was the practice of it. Louis waited until Colbert had filled the treasury before embarking on his first military adventure, an attack on the Spanish territories of Flanders and the Franche-Comté, which he claimed by right of inheritance through his wife, Marie-Thérèse. This brief contest, the so-called War of Devolution (1667–1668), gained him a dozen towns, including the important commercial centers of Lille and Tournai. It also provoked an alliance between England and the Netherlands, which had only recently completed a war of their own.

The Dutch War (1672–1678)

For Louis, the Dutch were both commercial rivals whose defeat would open up their lucrative carrying trade to French shipping and religious heretics whose Calvinism he was planning to suppress among his own Protestant subjects, the Huguenots. The Dutch had personally offended him at the end of the Flanders campaign with a cartoon that portrayed his sun emblem eclipsed by a wedge of Dutch cheese. More important, the Dutch alone stood between Louis and his long-range goal of dominating the Low Countries and Germany, and even—as a book published under royal sponsorship in 1667 declared—reviving the empire of Charlemagne in the West.

William of Orange, stadholder (governor) of the Netherlands and later, as William III, king of England, was the heart and soul of European opposition to Louis XIV for 30 years. [Scala/Art Resource]

Louis struck in the spring of 1672. The French occupied three of the seven Dutch provinces, and Amsterdam was saved only by opening the dikes and flooding the province of Holland. The Dutch offered to concede all their strongholds in Flanders and to pay an indemnity of 10 million livres. This would have given Louis victory and left the Dutch frontier defenseless. But Louis demanded a virtual surrender of sovereignty: major territorial concessions within the seven provinces themselves, French commercial and religious penetration, an indemnity of 24 million livres, and most insulting of all, an annual embassy to present a medal in tribute to Louis, like a Roman client state acknowledging its emperor.

These humiliating demands may have been the worst mistake of Louis' career. The Dutch dug in, determined to resist to the end. The republican Regime of True Liberty that had governed the Netherlands since 1650 was overthrown; its leader, Jan de Witt, was torn to pieces by an angry mob, and the 22-year-old Prince William of Orange was summoned as stadholder and captain general of the army. Louis thus raised up his own worst enemy, for the dour but capable William was to be the heart and soul of European resistance to Bourbon France for the next 30 years. With French troops stalled by the floodwaters, he gained support from Spain and Austria. By 1674 the French had withdrawn from Dutch soil. The Treaty of Nijmegen (1678) not only affirmed Dutch independence but forced the French to lower their own tariffs against Dutch goods. Louis had lost the war.

Aggression Without War: Louis Against Germany

Despite this check, the French state, with its army of 250,000 men, was the strongest not just in Europe but probably in the world. The Dutch were exhausted, the Spanish enfeebled under their last Habsburg king, the ailing and incompetent Charles II, and the Austrians preoccupied by a new Turkish advance along the Danube that brought Ottoman armies under the grand vizier, Kara Mustafa, to the gates of Vienna in 1683 for the first time in a century and a half. Only a relief army commanded by the king of Poland, Jan Sobieski, saved the imperial capital. Louis, meanwhile, continued his war of nerves along the Rhine. He claimed any area on or near his borders that had ever been French by law or custom, a tactic not unlike the one Hitler employed in Germany in the 1930s. Accordingly, French troops occupied large parts of Flanders, Luxembourg, Alsace, and the Saarland after 1680, as well as the free city of Strasbourg. Even Casale Monferrato in northern Italy admitted a French garrison.

Louis insisted that these actions were in accordance with the treaties of Westphalia and Nijmegen. He certified each claim in special courts set up for that purpose, the Chambers of Reunion. In the absence of any international court of arbitration, what better title could be established? But as his courts and armies pushed farther and farther into the heartland of Germany, the princes

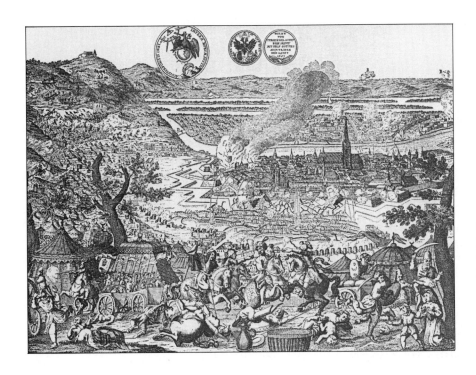

The 1683 siege of Vienna, here depicted in a composite view, marked the last great Muslim advance in Europe, although the Turks remained a presence on the continent until the early twentieth century. [Austrian National Library, Vienna]

of the Holy Roman Empire became alarmed. Alarm turned to panic when, in 1685, Louis revoked the Edict of Nantes, which had guaranteed freedom of worship to French Protestants. If the French king's worst diplomatic miscalculation was to have rejected the Dutch peace terms of 1672, the revocation of the Edict of Nantes was his greatest domestic blunder. The thousands of refugees who fled across the border with their tales of persecution were among Louis' most productive subjects, and their skills as artisans and merchants were soon enriching his enemies. Meanwhile, under Habsburg leadership, the German princes hastily formed a defensive alliance, the League of Augsburg (1686).

The War of Five Continents

When Louis entered the Rhenish Palatinate in September 1688 to support his claims in the region, he began a war that was to outlast all the protagonists but himself. Ranging over five continents and lasting 25 years, it was the first truly global war in history. No war of comparable scale was to be seen again until the twentieth century. For the first time, the quarrels of Europe became the affair of the world.

The conflict had two distinct phases. The Nine Years' War (1688–1697) was fought largely along the disputed frontiers of Flanders and Germany, though it reached as far afield as North America, where it was known as King William's War. At first the French had the advantage. But Louis had too many enemies now to win a decisive victory. The Anglo-Dutch alliance was revived in the most dramatic way when William of Orange, responding to a secret invitation from a coalition of English lay and religious leaders, sailed to England in November 1688 and deposed James II. William became king of England (as William III), reigning jointly with his wife Mary (1689–1695), James' elder daughter, while continuing to govern the Netherlands through his able regent, Antonius Heinsius. With such a base, William soon brought Spain, Austria, and Savoy together in a grand anti-French alliance. By the end of the war virtually all of Europe east of the Elbe was fighting France. Louis could not be dislodged from his strong defensive position. But the war took a terrible toll within France itself. Poor harvests, soaring grain prices, and military requisitions caused a devastating famine in 1694–1695. Be-

◉ The Disasters of War ◉

In 1695, at the height of the great famine, which had been induced by a combination of bad harvests, wartime requisitions, soaring inflation, and speculation and hoarding, a remarkable open letter circulated among elite circles in France. Addressed to Louis XIV, it was probably the work of an outspoken clergyman, François Fénelon (1651–1715). Its view of the king's pursuit of gloire *is a very different one from that offered by Bossuet.*

Your people, Sire, whom you should love as your children, and who up to this time have been so devoted to you, are dying of hunger. The land is left almost untended, towns and countryside are deserted, trade of all kinds falls off and can no longer support the workers; all commerce is at a standstill. . . . For the sake of getting and keeping vain conquests abroad, you have destroyed half the real strength of your own state. Rather than take money from your poor people, you ought to feed and cherish them. . . . All France is now no more than one great hospital, desolate and unprovided. . . . And it is you, Sire, who have brought these troubles on yourself. . . . Little by little the fire of sedition catches everywhere. The people believe that you have no pity for their sufferings, that you care only for your own power and glory. They say that if the king had a father's heart for his people, he would surely think his glory lay rather in giving them bread and a little respite after such tribulations than in keeping hold of a few frontier posts which are a cause of war.

Source: P. Goubert, *Louis XIV and Twenty Million Frenchmen* (New York: Pantheon, 1970), p. 220.

fore it had run its course, 2 million French subjects—one-tenth of the population—had died. It was a man-made disaster comparable in its effects on France only to World War I.

The Treaty of Ryswick (1697) compelled Louis not only to restore almost all the territories he had occupied since 1678 but also to withdraw recognition from his hapless guest and pensioner, the former James II, and to acknowledge his archenemy William III as king of England. But a new round of warfare was in the offing, for even higher stakes. For a third of a century, the dynastic politics of Europe had swirled about the fate of the Spanish throne, whose feeble and childless occupant, Charles II, had presided helplessly over the ruin of a once-great power. When Charles died at last in 1700 his government was so impoverished that it could not pay for masses for the repose of his soul. Yet Spain still held much of the southern Netherlands and most of Italy, as well as its great empire in the Americas. In the hands of a competent ruler, it might still regain its former glory; in the hands of a foreign one, it was an incomparable asset.

So thought both Louis XIV and his Habsburg contemporary and antagonist, the Austrian emperor, Leopold I (1658–1705). Since neither was willing to concede control of the whole Spanish patrimony, they had begun, by themselves or through dynastic proxies, to negotiate for Spain's division as early as 1668. As Charles II's death at last became imminent, an effort was made to find a compromise candidate for the throne. This failed, however, and when Charles died, he unexpectedly willed his throne and all his dominions to the Bourbon claimant Philip of Anjou, Louis' grandson, who became Philip V of Spain (1700–1746).

Britain and France: The Contest for Empire

The result was the second phase of the great war of France against Europe, the War of the Spanish Succession (1701–1713). Louis moved quickly to consolidate his hold on Spain and its possessions. It was a foregone conclusion that Austria would resist. England and the Netherlands were even more directly menaced. With the occupation of the Spanish Netherlands, the last buffer between French and Dutch territory had been stripped away. The English found their access to the Mediterranean cut off and their empire in the New World threatened.

William III swiftly organized a new Grand Alliance against Louis. It was his last achievement. In March 1702 he died following a fall from his horse, to be succeeded in England by James II's younger daughter, Anne (1702–

THE SPANISH SUCCESSION

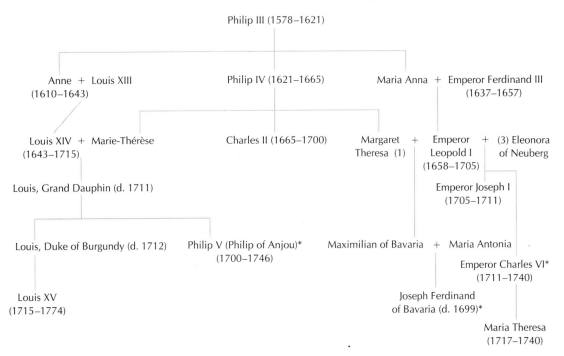

*Designated heirs of Charles II.

1714), while in the Netherlands Heinsius remained the dominant figure until his death in 1720. The Anglo-Dutch alliance held, though England was now decidedly the senior partner. The English general John Churchill, duke of Marlborough (1650–1722), the greatest soldier of his age, turned back Louis' thrust into Bavaria at Blenheim (1704) and crushed French armies at Ramillies (1706) and Oudenaarde (1708) in Flanders. Meanwhile, the superior Anglo-Dutch fleet kept France at bay in the New World and Africa. By 1709 Louis' position was desperate. Allied armies were poised on the borders of France itself, the treasury was empty, and famine ravaged the land. A bitter parody of the Lord's Prayer circulated at court: "Our father who art at Versailles, whose name is no longer hallowed, whose kingdom is no longer large, give us our daily bread. . . ."

Louis held out, stiffened by demands not only that he surrender all the conquests of his reign but that he help drive his grandson from the Spanish throne as well. At Malplaquet, the bloodiest battle on European soil up to that time, he blunted the allied advance. Thereafter, the Grand Alliance dissolved and the war wound down. The cluster of treaties known as the Peace of Utrecht (1713) left Spain and its overseas dominions to Philip V, though on condition that his throne never be united with that of France. Spain's possessions in the Netherlands and Italy were given to Austria, partly to compensate it for the lost Spanish throne and partly as a buffer against French expansion, though the Dutch received so many concessions in the former area that they actually dominated it. England's prizes reflected its increasing concern with empire. Gibraltar and Minorca gave it control of the Mediterranean, Nova Scotia and Newfoundland entrenched it on the North American coast, and trading concessions offered a foothold in the lucrative slave trade of Spanish America.

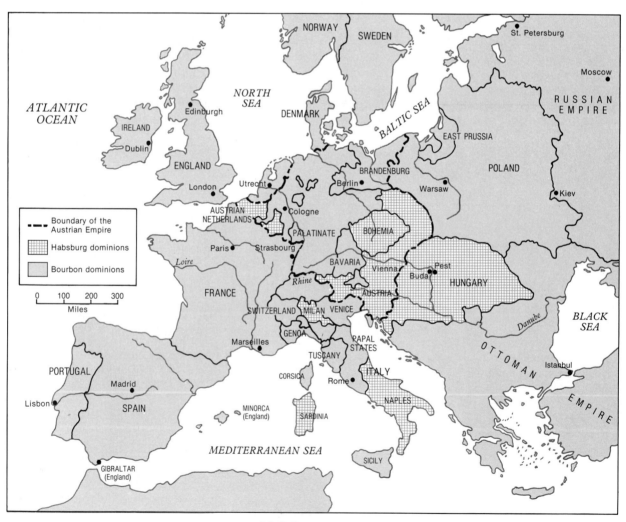

23.2 Europe in 1714

The wars of 1688–1713 were fought to contain the territorial ambitions of the French in Europe. In retrospect, however, they marked the first stage in the great contest of empire between England and France that, resumed in the war cycles of 1740–1763 and 1792–1815, would end only with Wellington's defeat of Napoleon at the Battle of Waterloo. They marked as well the final eclipse of Spain as a great power. The Austrians gained the most territory in Europe itself, but their greatly distended borders were to prove more of a burden than an asset in the long run.

Louis XIV and the Climax of Absolutism

Despite its defeat, France was still the greatest power on the European continent. When Louis XIV died on September 1, 1715, he had reigned longer than anyone else in the history of the world and had dominated his time more completely than anyone since Charlemagne. If he had failed ultimately to impose his will on Europe, it had taken the united strength of his adversaries to contain him. Yet the sum of Louis was more than his parts. He was neither a great soldier nor a genuine innovator. His economic views were firmly rooted in the rigidly protectionist doctrines of mercantilism, and his persecution of the Huguenots drove away many of his most productive subjects. Although he personified divine right kingship, his religion was conventional and often opportunistic. Even his administrative reforms looked backward to the traditions of personal monarchy rather than forward to the modern bureaucratic state. If he showed what could be accomplished by a determined royal absolutism, he showed the limitation of such a system as well. It was left to his archrivals, the English, to develop on a large scale what the Dutch polity had already suggested: that a politically stable oligarchy with a moderate representative base could be a far more effective instrument of government than an absolute monarchy dependent on the will and energy of a single man.

Peter the Great and the Emergence of Russia

As forceful as Louis XIV and far more despotic, Peter I (1682–1725), called "the Great," consolidated autocracy in Russia and brought his country into the European state system. From its modest beginnings in the fourteenth-century duchy of Muscovy, Russia had become the largest state in the world by Peter's time.

Three times the size of Europe, it spanned the Eurasian landmass from the Polish steppe to the Pacific Ocean, embracing some 5.7 million square miles. Much of this expansion had taken place in the seventeenth century, culminating in the first Russian settlement on the Pacific (1647), the reconquest of the ancient Rus capital of Kiev (1654), and the pacification of the Siberian tribes.

The Tsarist State

This vast land had a population of only 14 million, one-fortieth the density of France or Italy. Grain yields were comparable only to those of pre-Carolingian agriculture in the West, compelling almost the entire population to farm; only 2 percent lived in towns. The tsarist state and its nobility had undertaken to control this scarce labor supply since the late fifteenth century, first restricting and at last completely eliminating all freedom of movement. By the seventeenth century the Russian peasantry had been fully enserfed except in some frontier areas and for all practical purposes enslaved. The great law code, or *Ulozhenie*, of 1649, which served as the basis of Russian society for the next 200 years, formalized its rigid, castelike divisions. Each person's status was fixed by law down to the last detail. Townsmen as well as peasants were bound to their dwellings and occupations. The nobility had become a civil service class since, apart from the clergy, only nobles who performed state service were permitted to own land. Few societies have ever been more tightly controlled. The concept of personal rights, so important to the development of the West, simply did not exist. Authority could be questioned only by authority. The tsar alone was free, and his freedom—that is, his power—was absolute. What an Austrian ambassador to Russia said in the early sixteenth century was if anything even more true at the end of the seventeenth:

> In the sway the tsar holds over his people, he surpasses all the monarchs of the whole world. . . . He uses his authority as much over ecclesiastics as laymen, and holds unlimited control over the lives and property of all his subjects; not one of his counsellors has sufficient authority to dare to oppose him, or even differ from him, on any subject. They openly confess that the will of the prince is the will of God, and that whatever the prince does he does by the will of God.[2]

Peter and the West

This was the throne that passed to Peter the Great. Like Louis XIV, he experienced a turbulent minority. At the death of his father, Alexis (1645–1676), his half brothers Feodor (1676–1682) and Ivan (1682) succeeded, but both were incompetent, and in 1682 the nobility pro-

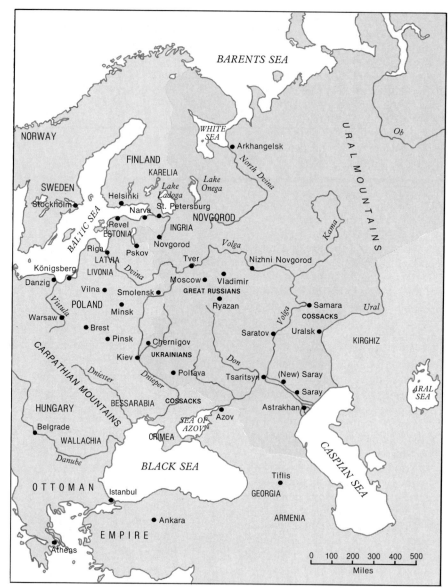

23.3 *Russia in the Age of Peter the Great, 1689–1725*

claimed the 9-year-old Peter tsar instead. The country was saved from civil war only by Peter's sister, Sophia, who ruled in his name until 1689. The Peter who came to young manhood then needed no help from anyone. Nearly 7 feet tall and with strength and appetites to match, he was no less ambitious than the ruler of Versailles but far less prudent. All but one of his 36 years of active rule were spent at war. Military expenditures consumed more than 80 percent of his revenue. Even church bells were melted down into cannon. The Russian state was turned into a gigantic battering ram, and it was aimed west.

At the same time, Peter was deeply impressed by the advanced technology and warcraft of the West. He studied tactics and fortifications and built a standing army of 300,000 that, despite Russia's acute manpower shortage, was made up largely of his own subjects, whom he conscripted for life. In 1697–1698 he became the first Russian prince to visit the West, where he and his entourage made a sensation. A bemused William III was his host in Holland and England, where he ignored protocol by touring and even working in foundries and dockyards. The ruler of the world's largest landmass was fascinated by the sea and proudly flourished a certificate declaring him a master shipwright. William invited him to attend a session of England's Parliament. Peter was impressed by the sight of subjects speaking openly to their sovereign, but constitutional monarchy was not one of the Western innovations he brought home with him.

Peter's first military efforts were directed against the Ottoman Turks, from whom he wrested Azov on the Black Sea in 1696. His attention then turned to the Baltic. Here, 1,000 miles from Moscow, he built a new capital, St. Petersburg, whose royal residence, the Winter Palace, rivaled Versailles in its splendor.

But Peter still lacked a secure northern seaport except at Archangel (Arkhangelsk) on the White Sea, whose harbor was frozen nine months a year. Access to the Baltic was blocked by Sweden, whose territory enclosed it on three sides. The eastern end of the Swedish triangle included the traditionally Russian Karelian peninsula, which Sweden had occupied during the Time of Troubles. Tsar Alexis, Peter's father, had failed to recapture it. The time now appeared ripe. Sweden's hardy but scattered population of 1.5 million seemed insufficient to defend it against a concerted attack. Its new ruler, Charles XII (1697–1718), was still a boy. With Denmark, Poland, and Brandenburg-Prussia as allies, Peter declared war.

The result was the Great Northern War (1700–1721). After swiftly dispatching Denmark, the warlike Charles, not yet out of his teens, humiliated Peter at Narva (1700), crushing an army five times the size of his own. Muscovy lay defenseless before him. But Charles turned to secure his rear in Poland, giving Peter time to rebuild. By 1704 Peter had retaken Narva. Not content merely with fighting a major war, however, he was simultaneously building his new capital and attempting to join the Don and Volga rivers by a canal, thus giving full access to his port at Azov.

Peter's insatiable demands on the country at last provoked revolt. Invoking the name of the populist rebel Stenka Razin, who had dreamed of establishing a peasants' state in the seventeenth century, the Cossack chieftain Kondraty Bulavin rose in 1707. He burned villages along the whole length of the Don, and cannon were mounted on the Kremlin walls. At the same time, Charles began his long-awaited invasion, striking south into the Ukraine. Peter himself lay ill. Desperately seeking help, he turned to his old ally, England. But the English, fighting their own war with Louis XIV and fearing that Charles might turn against Austria if not otherwise occupied, sent Marlborough the length of Europe personally to persuade the Swedish king to concentrate on Russia.

Victory at Poltava (1709) saved Peter. While Charles was forced to seek refuge in Turkey, Peter overran Karelia and the Baltic provinces of Ingria, Estonia, Latvia, and Livonia, securing the ports of Revel and Riga. These gains were confirmed by the Treaty of Nystadt (1721), which established Russia as the major power in the Baltic. Peter celebrated by assuming the titles of father of his country and emperor and accepted formally the appellation of "the Great." "By our deeds in war," he exulted, "we have emerged from darkness into the light of the world."

The Reforms of Peter

Peter dreamed of yoking the great rivers of Russia together by a system of canals, thereby linking the vast expanses of his realm to his new outlets on the sea. Azov was lost to the Turks in 1711, and with it ten years' labor on the Don-Volga canal. Undaunted, Peter linked the Volga to St. Petersburg's river, the Neva, thus uniting the Caspian Sea with the Baltic. Thousands of lives were lost on the project, but within a decade of Peter's death, flotillas of flat-bottomed barges were moving the grain and oak timber of central and southern Russia steadily to market.

Peter reorganized his government on the latest Western models. He replaced the old boyar Duma (council of nobles) with a nine-member senate, in effect a supreme council of state, and reduced the 40-odd ministries to 12, each headed by a "college" of senior officials reporting to the senate. The countryside was also divided into new provinces and districts. The purpose of the whole, as Peter straightforwardly told the senate, was "to collect money, as much as possible." In this it was successful; tax revenues tripled over the course of the reign.

Foreigners were at first brought in to coordinate the new system and even to staff it. But Peter had always intended that his boyars be bound, as before, to state service. To learn Western ways, he compelled them to adopt Western food and dress and to shave their beards, personally shearing off any he saw in his presence. There were grislier acts of submission as well. When his palace guard, the Streltsi, rebelled in his absence, Peter forced the palace nobility to participate in their executions.

In 1722 Peter capped his administrative reforms with the Table of Ranks, which created a new hierarchy of 14 military and civil service grades. It permitted commoners as well as nobles to enter state service, ennobling them either upon receiving an officer's commission or attaining the civilian rank of collegiate assessor. In this way Peter broadened the base of the landowning class and gave room to talent from below, though the most privileged positions were still reserved for the old nobility. This system remained essentially intact down to 1917.

The church was also thoroughly restructured. The office of patriarch, assumed by the metropolitan of Moscow in 1589, had in the hands of such men as Philaret (1619–1633) and Nikon (1652–1666) rivaled the power of the tsar, as Peter himself complained. In 1700 he per-

◉ Law and Justice Under Peter the Great ◉

Ivan Pososhkov (1652–1726) was a Russian merchant and entrepreneur who was frequently in trouble with the law and ultimately died in prison. This passage reflects both his own frustration with an often arbitrary and capricious judicial system and the horrific abuses to which it could easily give rise.

There is no man more excellent and judicious than Prince Golitsyn, yet in 1719 I petitioned him for permission to build a distillery and for a license to supply vodka for sale, but he had me put under arrest for no known reason. I remained in custody for a whole week and began to get impatient at being there so long without knowing why. On the eve of the Lady Day fast I asked the corporal of the guard to inform the Prince of my case and Prince Golitsyn said: "Has he been in custody long?" And the corporal said: "A whole week, Sir." And he at once ordered my release. Now I am not entirely without position, I think, and Prince Golitsyn knows me personally; yet I was detained for a whole week for no reason at all. How much worse is the case of a man of no account who will be arrested and forgotten about? In this way a great number of innocent folk languish in prison and die there before their time. . . . I am truly astounded that judges are in the habit of holding men in prison for five or six years or more. If judges and governors were to inspect the new prisoners daily this would no longer happen and there would be no possibility of an innocent man being imprisoned or kept in custody.

Source: I. Pososhkov, *The Book of Poverty and Wealth* (Stanford, Calif.: Stanford University Press, 1987), p. 207 (modified slightly).

mitted it to lapse, and in 1721 he replaced it with the Holy Synod, a body closely tied to the state. He reduced the number of monasteries and nunneries as well and diverted much of their income into his own coffers, though they were too much a part of the fabric of Russian life to be done away with altogether, as he would probably have wished. For Peter, all idle hands were useless, and praying hands were idle.

There were perhaps 3,000 foreigners in Russia at the beginning of Peter's reign, many of whom lived in the so-called German suburb of Moscow. Peter brought in many more to staff his ministries and run his new technical schools and fledgling industries. Their heathen mores aroused the ire of churchmen and nobles, and native merchants resented their privileges; they even sometimes inspired actual panic in the countryside. At one point a wild rumor circulated that Russian men would be forbidden to marry for seven years so that foreigners imported by Peter (himself viewed by many as the Antichrist) could take their women instead. One of the rallying cries of the Cossack rebellion was a demand for the expulsion of all foreigners.

Despite this, Peter persisted in his attempts to westernize Russia. He reformed the calendar and rede-signed the alphabet, ordered translations of the Greek and Roman classics, and hired a German troupe to perform French comedies in the Kremlin Square. In 1703 he introduced the first newspaper into Russia, which he edited himself. He built the first Russian greenhouses and laboratories and in 1724 established the Russian Academy of Sciences, though its first members were all Germans.

Peter died in February 1725, leaving an unsettled succession and an exhausted realm. But he had created the foundations of a modern state and economy and made Russia a permanent part of Europe. The Western powers were not slow to recognize this. Peter's ambassador in Vienna reported after Poltava, "It is commonly said that the tsar will be formidable to all Europe, that he will be a kind of northern Turk." By 1711 Prussia was already proposing an anti-Russian alliance, and the British fleet appeared in the Baltic to challenge Peter's presence.

In many ways, Peter's life was a struggle to tame himself as well as Russia. The young tsar who loved to trick his courtiers by signing decrees with pseudonyms became the statesman who introduced orderly, bureaucratic government to his realm. The man who corre-

Peter the Great, himself clean-shaven after the fashion of the West, decreed that his nobility must shear off the beards that were a traditional mark of their status. Recalcitrant nobles were fined or, as here, subjected to compulsory barbering. [Granger Collection]

sponded on politics with the great philosopher Leibniz had ungovernable fits of rage, beat his ministers, and put his son Alexis to death. As a foreign visitor observed, "He is a prince at once very good and very bad; his character is exactly that of his country." In his passionate contradictions, Peter mirrored the conflicts of a Russia torn between the isolation of its past and the world presence of its future.

Austria: The Dynastic State

After the division of the Habsburg crown in 1555 between its Spanish and Austrian branches, the Austrian monarchy consisted of three major units, the hereditary provinces of Austria itself; the so-called crown of St. Wenceslas, comprising Bohemia, Moravia, and Silesia; and the crown of St. Stephen, including Hungary, Transylvania, and Croatia. Bohemia and Hungary had become part of the Habsburg dominions in 1527 after the Battle of Mohács, though much of Hungary was still contested. Indeed, only the continuing threat of the Turks in southeastern Europe could have united so disparate a group of peoples—Germans, Czechs, Magyars, Croats, Slovaks, Slovenes, Italians, Romanians, Ruthenians—under a single head. Turkey may in this sense be said to have engendered the Austrian monarchy; nor was it a coincidence that the final expulsion of Turkey from Europe in the early twentieth century should have been followed shortly after by the collapse and dismemberment of the Habsburg empire. The histories of Turkey and Austria rose and fell together.

Austria in the seventeenth century might be described as a power but not a state. The imperial title was recognized only in the Austrian provinces proper; the Habsburg emperor was separately king of Bohemia and Hungary. The chief unifying factor in this strange entity, whose ruler lacked a single title and whose lands lacked a common name, was the person of the monarch himself. His government was actually a series of ongoing negotiations with the provinces of his realm, whose noble estates possessed extensive powers, including the right to veto imperial taxes and, in Hungary, even to rebel.

After the failure of Ferdinand II's attempt to reassert his power as Holy Roman emperor in the Thirty Years' War, his successors, Ferdinand III (1637–1657) and Leopold I, concentrated on achieving internal consolidation. The Counter-Reformation in Austria was, in its political dimension, a struggle against the Protestant nobility who were dominant in Bohemia and Hungary. Bohemian Protestantism had been ruthlessly suppressed after 1620, and the native nobility was replaced by Catholic loyalists. A similar policy was applied in Hungary after 1671 following an abortive rebellion. While the zeal to root out heretics tended to diminish in states that had achieved political stability, the Habsburgs continued their efforts to impose religious uniformity and, with it, centralized control. Such persecution fell most heavily on the Jews, who were expelled from all of Lower Austria as a pious act by Leopold I despite the fact that his principal financier, Samuel Oppenheimer, was and remained a Jew.

Religious orthodoxy was linked to what the Habsburgs saw as their special mission: the defense of Christian Europe against the menace of the Ottoman Turks. After a period of quiescence following the Treaty of Sitva-Torok (1606), the Turks crossed the Danube in strength in 1663, ravaging Hungary, Moravia, and Silesia. Repulsed at St. Gotthard by a papal-sponsored and

Austrian-led army, they acceded to the Truce of Vasvar (1664). This treaty formally divided Hungary, which, though nominally a Habsburg principality, had long enjoyed semi-independence as a border region between the two great powers. When the Turks renewed the war in 1683 with an army of 200,000 men, the Hungarians, preferring the Ottoman yoke to what they had seen of the Habsburg, joined forces with the invaders. The Turks were also assisted by Louis XIV, who saw the attack as a welcome opportunity to divert Leopold's attention from his own aggression on the Rhine, though he temporarily suspended aid as a gesture to European public opinion when the Turks stormed up to the very gates of Vienna, subjecting it to a two-month siege.

The relief of the Habsburg capital by Jan Sobieski of Poland (1673–1696) was hailed throughout Europe as a miraculous deliverance. It was a historic moment, for it marked the last great thrust of Muslim power that had threatened Europe for nearly 1,000 years. In the war that ensued, climaxed by Prince Eugene of Savoy's great victory at Zenta (1697), the Turks were driven permanently from the Danube basin and back upon the Balkans. They might have been expelled completely from Europe had France heeded the appeal of Pope Innocent XI to join the Habsburg alliance. But the bitter rivalry between Bourbon and Habsburg prevented any such union, leaving a significant Turkish presence on the continent for more than two centuries.

The Treaty of Karlowitz (1699) gave the Habsburgs possession of virtually all of Hungary, Transylvania, and Croatia. Hungary's crown of St. Stephen was declared hereditary in the Habsburg family (1687). The Magyar nobility was not purged, as in Bohemia, and it was permitted to retain its provincial assemblies and national diet. But its power was curbed, and non-Magyar nobles were settled in the new lands, as well as German and Slavic peasants. The result was a new Magyar rising under Prince Ferenc Rakoczi, which lasted from 1703 to 1711. The defiant Magyars, with their proud sense of isolation among the surrounding Slavic populations, remained the most refractory of the Habsburg empire's many peoples.

The Habsburgs thus faced three major problems during the long reign of Leopold I and after: in Germany, to contain Louis XIV and to restore the influence if not control of the emperor; in the east, to defend the frontier, first against Turkey and later against Russia; and at home, to assert the imperial authority over a fractious and independent nobility. Each of these tasks seemed beyond their strength. French influence appeared well on the way to replacing Austrian in Germany. The timid Leopold had fled Vienna at the approach of the Turks, and only the courage of a foreign prince had saved the empire. The monarchy's plight at home was symbolized by the efforts of Charles VI (1711–1740) to gain support for the Pragmatic Sanction, which tried to establish the principle of a common succession in all Habsburg lands and thus ensure a single rule.

Yet the unwieldy Habsburg state continued to grow. Its victories against the Turks had doubled its effective size during the reign of Leopold I. The Treaty of Rastadt (1714) brought it the Spanish Netherlands and most of Italy. Another brief war with Turkey (1716–1718) pushed its borders into the Balkans. Even Prince Eugene, who conducted this campaign, expressed misgivings about the acquisition of so much territory. A swollen empire now stretched from the Carpathian Mountains to the North Sea. The Habsburgs had multiplied their subject populations but had devised no strategy for integrating them.

Prussia: The Garrison State

A very different course was pursued by Prussia, which emerged from the rubble of post-Westphalian Germany to become a major European power and the ultimate unifier of Germany as a whole. Prussia had its origin in the electoral mark of Brandenburg, a flat, sandy terrain south of the Baltic coast that passed in 1417 to the princely house of Hohenzollern. In 1618 the elector of Brandenburg acquired the duchy of Prussia, then a fief of Poland, giving the dynasty its first access to the sea. At about the same time (1614) he fell heir to Cleves, a small duchy on the Rhine. These three entities were widely separated on the map. Their populations, half German and half Polish, half Lutheran and half Catholic, half serf and half free, had nothing in common but their ruler. During the Thirty Years' War, all three territories were overrun by foreign armies. Brandenburg was occupied between 1627 and 1643, and the population of its capital, Berlin, fell from 14,000 to 6,000. Many towns were destroyed completely.

Under these circumstances the 20-year-old Frederick William (1640–1688), later known to history as the "Great Elector," succeeded to the Hohenzollern legacy. By 1648 he had built up an army of 8,000, a small force but one sufficient to obtain for him a part of the coastal region of Pomerania and the ecclesiastical principalities of Magdeburg and Halberstadt at the Conference of Westphalia. Frederick William had the means of a prince but the ambition of a great dynast. When Pomerania and East Prussia were menaced by a war between Sweden and Poland in 1655, he ignored the refusal of the Brandenburg estates to vote new taxes and collected them by force. Though he lacked a royal title, he considered himself as much a divine right ruler as Louis XIV, demanding recognition of this from the estates of Prussia

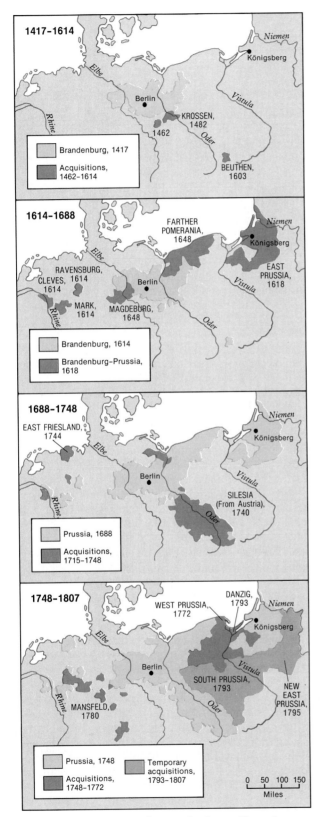

23.4 The Rise of Brandenburg-Prussia

and landing 2,000 troops in its capital, Königsberg, to enforce his claim. Frederick William found the key to state-building in the maintenance of a standing army, which he swelled to 30,000. The army was both his excuse for raising taxes and his means of compelling payment. His soldiers collected taxes directly and exercised police powers as well. Thus from the first, the Great Elector broke down the distinction between civilian and military functions.

Frederick William was not uniformly successful. He made no further territorial gains after 1648 despite participating in two major wars and was thwarted in his lifelong goal of connecting Prussia with the rest of his dominions, a task not accomplished until 1772. Though he tripled his tax revenues, he remained dependent on foreign subsidies to maintain the army. To conciliate the nobility, he exempted them from his new taxes. These fell mainly on the towns instead, thereby frustrating his goals of commercial and industrial development. Like Peter the Great, however, he required service of the nobility, particularly in the army. Thus while curtailing the nobility's privileges on a political level—that is, their power to obstruct him—he confirmed their social preeminence and integrated them into his absolutist state.

The elector Frederick III (1688–1713) was recognized as King Frederick I of Prussia in 1701 in return for his participation in the War of the Spanish Succession against Louis XIV, though Prussia contributed little. The task of state-building was resumed by his eccentric but capable successor, Frederick William I (1713–1740). The Great Elector had seen the army as an instrument of state power; under his grandson and namesake, the army to all intents and purposes became the state. With the establishment of the General Directory in 1723, which combined the functions of the war and finance councils, the entire governing apparatus down to the lowliest tax collector or quartermaster in the provinces revolved about the needs of the army. Frederick William divided the country into recruitment districts and regimental cantons. The army was not segregated in barracks but billeted among the general population, so that civilians, particularly in the towns, were continuously exposed to the impress of military discipline and drill. No sight in Prussia was more common than a parade. In addition to the regular career army, every Prussian male was subject to three months of military service a year. By this means Frederick William was able to maintain a standing army of 80,000 men on a population base of only 1.5 million. Not since ancient Sparta had a society lived so completely by the military ideal.

Under Frederick II (1740–1786), also called "the Great," Prussia reached the full status of a great power. Frederick was the most impressive monarch of the eighteenth century, and at least for the first half of his reign he dominated continental politics almost as completely as Louis XIV had done. Frederick broke with the personal austerity and Calvinist piety of his father. He was a son of the Enlightenment who flirted with atheism and entertained the philosopher Voltaire; a soldier-king whose armies, like Louis XIV's, held off half of Europe. In his social policies, however, he adhered closely to the practice of his father. Each class was assigned its duties from above. The higher ranks in the army and the state bureaucracy were reserved for the nobility. Merchants and townsfolk were obliged to accept a subordinate position. They could neither purchase noble land nor aspire to noble status. Frederick had kind words for the peasantry, which, he declared, deserved the greatest respect because it carried the heaviest burdens. He did little to relieve those burdens however, even in East Prussia, where peasants were enserfed and in many respects little better than enslaved by the local nobility, known as Junkers.

Eastern European Absolutism in Context

Vast Russia, divided Austria, and militarized Prussia took different routes after 1650 toward a common goal: the centralization of authority. All three were landlord states where peasant labor was largely unfree and trade and industry were largely undeveloped. All three lacked suitable outlets to the sea until the eighteenth century, and despite the efforts of Peter the Great to build a Russian navy, none became a true maritime power. Thus the commercial pressures that spurred the development of centralized (though not necessarily absolutist) authority in western Europe were not directly present. But the impressive wealth and power of the Atlantic states— England, France, and the Netherlands—were very much on the minds of Romanov, Habsburg, and Hohenzollern sovereigns. Peter the Great's visit to the West in 1697–1698 determined him to modernize his country. The Great Elector had been educated in the Netherlands and dreamed, though in vain, of emulating its commercial success. The Habsburgs, too, sought to encourage mining and industry and even attempted to establish overseas trading companies as the Dutch and English had done. Mercantilist doctrines that equated the amassing of treasure and the increase of state power took hold in the east just as they had begun to give way to more sophisticated models in the west. In England, particularly, a more flexible political and financial system emerged in the wake of a second rebellion to give it a signal advantage in the new global context of European state competition.

England: The Triumph of Parliamentary Government

The Stuart monarchy had been restored in 1660 under a formula that defined the government as consisting of king, lords, and commons. But it was not clear where the balance of authority lay among these three elements. A newly constituted Convention Parliament, composed chiefly of nobles and other great landowners, compelled Charles II (1660–1685) to accept its terms. The crown could no longer create special courts outside the jurisdiction of the common law, nor could it collect taxes not authorized by Parliament. The king was obliged to issue a general amnesty for all but those directly responsible for his father's death. In all, 13 persons were executed, an astonishingly small number in view of the scale of the rebellion and the customs of the age. Finally, Charles agreed to exchange his traditional feudal revenues for a permanent grant of customs and excise taxes, thus freeing the magnates from all restrictions on the ownership of their estates and shifting the tax burden from the landed classes toward the towns.

Charles was not even able to reward those who had supported him. Royalists whose estates had been confiscated during the revolution were permitted to sue for their recovery, but those who had sold them, even under duress, received no compensation. This too confirmed the rebel gentry in their gains and accelerated the tendency toward concentration of land ownership. Charles' promise of religious toleration was swept away by his first elected parliament. This "Cavalier" Parliament, as it was nicknamed for its initially reactionary tone, restored the supremacy of the Anglican church and placed severe restrictions on all other forms of worship. Some 1,200 ministers were ejected from their parishes for refusing to accept a new prayer book and to take an oath of conformity, creating a schism within English Protestantism that persists to the present day.

Charles' return was generally popular at first, though a republican underground persisted. But his honeymoon was short-lived. An unsuccessful war with the Dutch resulted in the fall of his chief minister, the earl of Clarendon (1667), and a similar fate befell his successor, the earl of Danby (1678). Charles' most persistent problem was money. The grant of taxes he had received in 1660 was calculated to meet his expenses. It proved insufficient, however, and he remained financially and therefore politically dependent on Parliament. Charles sought to escape this dependence by obtaining a French subsidy in return for supporting Louis XIV's war against the Netherlands (Treaty of Dover, 1670). But Charles also agreed secretly to announce his conversion to Catholicism and, if necessary, to accept French troops to impose it on the country. The rumor of this agreement poisoned the remainder of his reign. Parliament responded in 1673 by passing the Test Act, which barred all religious dissenters from public office. The real object of attack was the king's younger brother and prospective heir, the openly Catholic duke of York. After a wave of anti-Catholic hysteria following allegations in 1678 of a Jesuit plot to assassinate Charles, three successive Parliaments attempted to ram through an act excluding the duke of York from the throne. The country seemed again on the verge of civil war. But the opposition party, called the Whigs, was divided in its aims, some members favoring alternative candidates to the throne and some the establishment of a republic. The king was able to rally his own supporters, the Tories, behind the principles of direct hereditary succession and divine right. The leading Whigs were banished or executed, and, on his deathbed, Charles was finally received into the Catholic church.

The Glorious Revolution and the Revolutionary Settlement

The duke of York succeeded peacefully as James II (1685–1688). He promised to preserve the constitution and the supremacy of the Church of England. He was already 51 and without a male heir. The country hoped that his brief Catholic reign would pass without serious incident.

But James soon revealed his true intentions. He placed Catholics in key civil and military positions. This violated the Test Act, but James claimed that he was not bound by former acts of Parliament. He camped Irish troops above London, allowed Jesuits to proselytize freely, and imprisoned seven Anglican bishops for refusing to read a proclamation giving freedom of worship to Catholics and Protestant nonconformists. When James reported the birth of a son in June 1688, thus opening the possibility of a Catholic dynasty, Whigs and Tories swiftly united. They called on William of Orange to free the country.

William's invasion was one of the great gambles of history. Victory meant the possibility of combining England and the Netherlands into a force capable of resisting Louis XIV; defeat meant the loss of his fleet and, most likely, his country. Landing on the coast of Devon in the southwest on November 5, William was hailed as a liberator. Most of James' army deserted, and James was forced to flee into exile.

William summoned Parliament, which declared him jointly sovereign with his wife, Mary. Over the next dozen years they built a new constitutional order that, much modified by time and circumstance, has remained both the basis of English government itself and the primary model of representative government the world over. The Bill of Rights (1689) declared the supremacy of all laws passed by Parliament. Henceforth, no king could levy taxes, maintain an army, or create new organs of government without Parliament's consent. No Englishman could be arrested without a legal warrant, detained by excessive bail, or subjected to "cruel and unusual punishments"—words incorporated directly into the American Bill of Rights a century later. Though they lacked the phrase for it, the framers of this new order—which came to be known as the Revolutionary Settlement—worked to contain executive authority by a separation of powers. The king might not tamper with elections or interfere with free speech in Parliament, nor might royal officials sit in the House of Commons. Similarly, judges could no longer be removed by the king, only through parliamentary impeachment. Some of these ideas proved unworkable, such as the ban on electioneering and the exclusion of officials from Parliament, and others were modified in practice. But the essential principles of legislative and judicial independence remained.

The new system worked awkwardly at first. With the threat of James removed, Whigs and Tories fell out with each other over the spoils of power. There were genuine differences between them as well, however. Though both derived from the landed gentry, the Whigs tended to embrace the great London merchants who believed in commercial and colonial expansion and eagerly supported parliamentary supremacy. The Tories, by contrast, were reluctant revolutionaries, rural and isolationist, who regarded 1688 as a necessity rather than an opportunity. William naturally tended to rely on the Whigs, and with their support he chartered the Bank of England (1694). Private banks had been in operation in England since the 1650s, and the Bank of Amsterdam (1609) was the most important commercial institution in Europe. The Bank of England, however, represented a new kind of marriage between private capital and government. It was established for the specific purpose of lending William £1.2 million—nearly a year's ordinary revenue—to help finance the war against Louis XIV. By borrowing rather than taxing, William was able to tap an almost limitless source of funds. Thus was born the idea of a permanent national debt and with it the power of modern government.

By 1713 the public debt stood at £54 million, nearly 100 times more than in 1688. This was the money that defeated Louis XIV. Some feared that without the need to rely on Parliament for taxation, the monarchy would soon become independent of any control. But the Whig magnates who funded William through the bank were

◉ The Right to Alter Government ◉

In 1688 England deposed a king for the second time in 40 years. Writing to justify the right of a sovereign people to alter its institutions of government, John Locke (1632–1704) offered what would become a classic defense of revolution.

The reason why men enter into society is the preservation of their property, and the end why they choose and authorize a legislature is that there may be laws made and rules set as guards and fences to the properties of all the members of the society. For since it can never be supposed to be the will of the society that the legislative should have a power to destroy that which everyone designs to secure by entering into society and for which the people submitted themselves to the legislators of their own making: whenever the legislators endeavor to take away and destroy the property of the people or to reduce them to slavery under arbitrary power, they put themselves into a state of war with the people. . . . By this breach of trust they forfeit the power the people had put into their hands for quite contrary ends, and it devolves upon the people, who have a right to resume their original liberty and the establishment of a new legislative (such as they shall think fit), to provide for their own safety and security, which is the end for which they are in society. . . . What I have said here, concerning the legislative in general holds true also concerning the supreme executor, who having a double trust put in him, both to have a part in the legislative, and the supreme execution of the law, acts against both when he goes about to set up his own arbitrary will as the law of the society.

Source: J. Locke, *Two Treatises of Government*, ed. P. Laslett (Cambridge: Cambridge University Press, 1964), pp. 430–431 (spelling and punctuation modernized).

---

the same men who supported him in Parliament. The struggle between crown and Parliament had ended in the discovery of common interests: war, empire, and profit.

The only thing that threatened this new partnership was the fragility of the Stuart line in England, represented by Queen Mary. At William III's death, he was succeeded by Mary's sister Anne (1702–1714), none of whose 16 children had survived. Parliament settled the succession on the electoral house of Hanover in Germany, distantly related to the Stuarts through the daughter of James I. At the same time, it declared that no Catholic could ever sit on the throne of England, thus barring James II and his son, James Edward. As a further precaution, the Whigs united Scotland with England in 1707, thus creating the modern Great Britain. When Anne died, some Tory leaders, unwilling to relinquish divine right, rashly backed an invasion attempt by James Edward. The Whigs, who staunchly supported the new dynasty, were more firmly entrenched than ever and remained the dominant political force in the country until 1760.

❧ LATE STUART AND HANOVERIAN LONDON

If Paris was the cultural capital of Europe and Amsterdam its financial center, London's time was fast approaching in the late seventeenth century. With a population of between 500,000 and 600,000 by 1700, it was one of the largest cities in the world. Whereas only one of every 40 or 50 Frenchmen was a Parisian, however, one of every ten Englishmen lived in London, fully half the urban population of the country.

The magnet of London was trade. People engaged in commerce and manufacturing averaged four times the income of those who farmed. The wealth and produce of the entire country flowed daily into the city: great droves of turkeys who walked the roads from Norfolk and Suffolk, sheep from Lincoln and Leicester, cattle from Wales and the Scottish Highlands, corn from the midland counties, cheese from Cheshire, fish from Kent, coals from Newcastle, stones from Dorset. London "sucks the vitals of trade in this island to itself," wrote Daniel Defoe, the author of the immensely popular *Robinson Crusoe* (1719). Daily, 3,500 boats and barges plied London's river, the Thames; in 1700 fully 77 percent of England's foreign trade and nearly 60 percent of its shipping passed through the city.

By the late seventeenth century a lively business culture had grown up around a new London institution, the coffeehouse. Over 500 of them flourished in the reign of Queen Anne. Merchants wrote maritime insurance at Lloyd's, and brokers traded stocks and securities at Jonathan's and Garraway's in Exchange Alley (a formal stock exchange was finally licensed by the government in 1697; the first crash followed in 1720). Noblemen and men of fashion, artists and scholars had their favorite houses too. Here men exchanged news and gossip; read the daily newspapers, which, beginning with *The Daily Courant*, had reached a circulation of 67,000 by 1714; and avidly consumed political pamphlets and the popular periodicals, *The Tatler* and *The Spectator*. But the new climate of business so evident after 1688 predominated. As Defoe, himself the editor of an influential journal, *The Review*, put it simply, "the main affair of life" appeared to be "getting money."

The face of London also changed in this period. The Great Fire of September 1666 burned down 13,000 of the city's old timbered houses. Most were rebuilt with brick and mortar, many in the classical style popularized by Sir Christopher Wren (1632–1723), England's greatest architect. The new West End suburbs of Bloomsbury, Piccadilly, and St. James's were marked by splendid squares and esplanades down which the rich and fashionable paraded or were carried in coaches or sedan chairs. But the vast majority of the population lived quite otherwise, in one-room tenement apartments without water or sanitation on streets so crowded and obstructed by carts, overhangs, basements, and open sewers that movement was next to impossible. The working poor of the city—porters, coal heavers, dockworkers, scavengers, domestics—lived hand to mouth in squalor and filth. An underworld of thieves and cutthroats preyed on this population, their activities all but uncontrolled in a world where life was cheap, riot common, and policing virtually nonexistent. (By contrast, Paris had instituted an effective police force as early as 1667.) The introduction of cheap gin in the second quarter of the eighteenth century sent the death rate soaring, particularly among the destitute. The London magistrate and reformer Henry Fielding observed that gin was "the principal sustenance . . . of more than a hundred thousand people in this metropolis." A man too poor to eat could drink himself into a stupor for a penny. Even after an act of Parliament regulated the consumption of gin, 1,000 people a year starved to death in the richest city of the world.

Gin Lane, **William Hogarth's devastating portrayal of the poverty and degradation that lay at the heart of Britain's imperial capital and their consequences. A besotted, pox-ridden mother is oblivious as her infant falls over a wooden rail; an emaciated drunk is on the brink of death by starvation, while another hangs himself in an exposed tenement; and the very walls of the city begin to topple. *Gin Lane* was one of the earliest examples of the power of social propaganda: a year after it was published, the consumption of cheap gin was sharply curtailed by law. Little was done, however, about the underlying squalor and despair of which gin drinking was only a symptom. [Lauros-Giraudon/Art Resource]**

᭤   ᭤   ᭤

The state system of Europe in the second half of the seven-teenth century and the first half of the eighteenth was char-acterized by the tension between monarchies that attempted to extend and centralize their authority, often by appeal to divine right, and landed aristocracies that generally re-sisted them, seeking to reassert traditional privileges. In most cases the monarchies prevailed to a greater or lesser extent, sometimes by coercion, sometimes by cooptation, and sometimes with the assistance of a new elite of mer-chants, bankers, and bureaucratic officeholders. In France, the leading power on the Continent throughout the period, this process was clearly visible in the policies of Louis XIV, who placed men of bourgeois origin in the most important offices of state and kept his nobility in opulent idleness at

Versailles. In England, by contrast, the landed and mer-cantile elites united to create through revolution a uniquely successful partnership between limited monarchy and a broad governing class. In Russia the absence of constitu-tional tradition enabled Peter the Great to subordinate his nobility and to replace Sweden as the major power in the north, while the retreat of Turkish power left Habsburg Aus-tria, despite its diffuse political structure, dominant in southeastern Europe. The most extraordinary example of state-building was in Prussia, where a series of able and determined rulers welded a scattered and unpromising pat-rimony into a formidable military machine. These new pat-terns of power produced a Europe more politically complex, competitive, and interdependent than ever before.

Notes

1. G. Treasure, *Seventeenth Century France* (New York: Barnes & Noble, 1966), p. 334.
2. R. K. Massie, *Peter the Great* (New York: Knopf, 1980), p. 177.

Suggestions for Further Reading

Anderson, P. *Lineages of the Absolutist State*. London: N.L.B., 1974.

Baxter, S. B. *William III and the Defense of European Liberty, 1650–1702*. New York: Harcourt, Brace & World, 1966.

Blum, J. *Lord and Peasant in Russia from the Ninth to the Nineteenth Century*. Princeton, N.J.: Princeton University Press, 1961.

Carsten, F. L. *The Origins of Prussia*. Westport, Conn.: Greenwood Press, 1981.

Clark, G. N. *The Later Stuarts, 1660–1714*. 2nd ed. Oxford: Clarendon Press, 1958.

————. *War and Society in the Seventeenth Century*. Cambridge: Cambridge University Press, 1958.

Evans, R. J. W. *The Making of the Habsburg Monarchy, 1550–1700*. New York: Oxford University Press, 1979.

Goubert, P. *Louis XIV and Twenty Million Frenchmen*. New York: Pantheon, 1972.

Greaves, R. L. *Deliver Us from Evil: The Radical Underground in Britain, 1660–1663*. New York: Oxford University Press, 1986.

————. *Enemies Under His Feet: Radicals and Nonconformists in Britain, 1664–1677*. Stanford, Calif.: Stanford University Press, 1990.

Hatton, R. M., ed. *Louis XIV and Absolutism*. Columbus: Ohio State University Press, 1977.

Hellie, R. *Slavery in Russia, 1450–1725*. Chicago: University of Chicago Press, 1982.

Hutton, R. *Charles the Second: King of England, Scotland and Ireland*. Oxford: Oxford University Press, 1990.

Kamen, H. *Spain in the Later Seventeenth Century*. London: Longman, 1980.

Kann, R. A. *A History of the Habsburg Empire, 1526–1918*. Berkeley: University of California Press, 1974.

Kenyon, J. P. *Revolution Principles: The Politics of Party, 1689–1720*. Cambridge: Cambridge University Press, 1977.

Laslett, P. *The World We Have Lost*. London: Methuen, 1965.

Massie, R. K. *Peter the Great*. New York: Knopf, 1980.

Plumb, J. H. *The Growth of Political Stability in England, 1675–1725*. London: Macmillan, 1967.

Riasanovsky, N. V. *The Image of Peter the Great in Russian History and Thought*. New York: Oxford University Press, 1985.

Rosenberg, H. *Bureaucracy, Aristocracy, and Autocracy: The Prussian Experience, 1660–1815*. Cambridge, Mass.: Harvard University Press, 1958.

Rudé, G. *Paris and London in the Eighteenth Century*. New York: Viking Press, 1971.

Rule, J., ed. *Louis XIV and the Craft of Kingship*. Columbus: Ohio State University Press, 1970.

Spielman, J. P. *Leopold I of Austria*. London: Thames & Hudson, 1977.

Sumner, B. H. *Peter the Great and the Emergence of Russia*. New York: Macmillan, 1951.

Wolf, J. B. *Louis XIV*. New York: Norton, 1968.

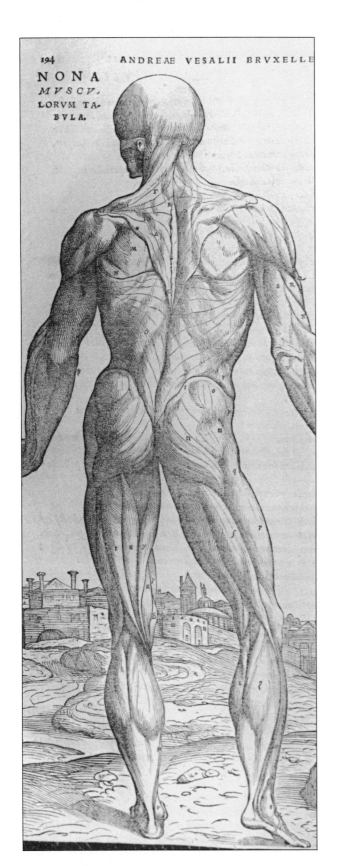

Europe's Century of Genius

Science is the systematic attempt to understand the physical world and to adapt it to human uses. As such, it is as old as culture itself. The establishment of the first major civilizations was concurrent with the Neolithic revolution that occurred about 8000 B.C. The advances made in China between the third and thirteenth centuries A.D. may be considered a second scientific revolution. But the development of modern science that began in Europe in the sixteenth and seventeenth centuries and, having spread across the globe, continues today at an accelerating pace has transformed not only our relation to the environment but the environment itself. It thus stands as one of the most momentous changes in human history.

This illustration from Vesalius' *De Fabrica* (1543), the first great textbook of modern anatomy, shows the sheaths of muscle beneath the skin. The body is posed upright against a typical Renaissance landscape, as if to emphasize the relationship between a human's natural elements and those of the world. [Lynn Mooney/College of Physicians and Surgeons]

633

From Ancient Science to the Copernican Revolution

It is often assumed that the scientific revolution was a sudden breakthrough that cleared away the mists of legend, superstition, error, and ignorance with which the human imagination had cloaked the world and revealed the physical universe in its true light. Nothing could be further from the truth or indeed further from the nature of modern science itself. The scientific revolution was the product of particular historical circumstances and imperatives and the culmination of a rich and varied intellectual tradition. Without the circumstances and the tradition, its achievement would have been impossible.

The Legacy of Antiquity

Classical antiquity had bequeathed a rich scientific heritage to Western civilization. Mathematics, astronomy, biology, and medicine were all highly developed. Much about the physical world was accurately known, and many modern theories had their origin in Greek science. Pythagoras had deduced that the earth was a sphere in the sixth century B.C., and Eratosthenes in the third century B.C. measured its diameter to within 90 percent accuracy. Anaximander, a contemporary of Pythagoras, offered the first theory of the earth's evolution, based on his discovery of fish fossils in mountain areas far removed from the sea. A century later, Leucippus and Democritus put forward the first atomic theory of matter. These theories were not universally accepted, however. Aristotle put the great weight of his authority behind the rival theory of Empedocles that matter consisted not of complex structures of atoms but of compounds of the four primary elements of earth, air, fire, and water. Similarly, the third-century B.C. speculation of the astronomer Aristarchus that the sun rather than the earth was the center of the universe was rejected in favor of the geocentric view Aristotle sponsored, which was given its classical expression in the work of Ptolemy of Alexandria (second century A.D.).

The Romans made little contribution to scientific theory, although their technological achievements—dams, irrigation, road building, engineering, plumbing, and heating—were unequaled in the West until the Renaissance. The period after the fall of the Roman Empire in the West, with its erosion of civic life and loss of records, interrupted the literate culture and the social and state patronage on which scientific development depended. The heritage of Greek science was continued in Byzantium, however, and even more intensely in the Arab world. Following the Arab conquests of the seventh century, Islam served as a focal point for Greek, Egyptian, Persian, and Indian traditions of thought. The introduction of paper from China provided the means of transforming the largely oral Arab culture into written form. The result was an enormous diffusion of knowledge. Whereas the sixth-century A.D. Roman historian Cassiodorus had access to only one treatise by Galen (c. 130–200), the greatest physician of the ancient world, by 900 the Arabs had translated some 129 of his works. Arabic science improved on Greek measurements and astronomical calculations and built the world's first observatories in the ninth century. It culminated in the career of Ibn Sina, or Avicenna (c. 980–1037), whose breadth of interest and learning in philosophy, medicine, natural history, physics, chemistry, astronomy, mathematics, and music rivaled that of Aristotle. (See Chapter 8.)

The Medieval World Picture

By the twelfth century Arab science had begun to decline, in part because of the breakup of what had been a unified empire into warring principalities. Shortly after that, however, a revived and expanding western Europe began to cull its fruits. Arab scientists and their Greek predecessors were both translated into Latin. Aristotle's prestige was so great in the medieval West that he was referred to simply as "the Philosopher," as if no rival could exist, and indeed none challenged him until the sixteenth century.

Reassimilating Greek science into the western tradition meant reconciling it with Christian doctrine. Fortunately, Ptolemy's geocentric model of the universe proved readily compatible with Christian notions about man's central position in the divine order. The cosmos was held to consist of an arrangement of ten concentric spheres rotating around a fixed, motionless earth. The first two of these spheres carried the moon and the sun. The next five were occupied by the known planets, and the eighth, like a giant diadem, carried all the stars. The last two spheres were dark, but their rotation was held to account for apparent changes in the positions of the stars. Beyond the tenth sphere, whose distance from the earth was estimated by Campanus of Novara (c. 1205–1296) at 73 million miles, was the throne of God, surrounded by his angels and the souls of the righteous. The spheres themselves were moved by angels, since according to Aristotle all bodies not activated by a constant external force would come to rest. In keeping with the perfection of the heavens, the celestial bodies were composed of a pure, unchangeable substance, the quintessence. For this reason any alteration among the celestial bodies, such as the appearance of a comet or the great explosion of the Crab nebula in 1054, was looked upon as a divine portent, since they could not naturally alter by themselves. On earth, humans were locked in the prison of time and decay, but when they looked up, they could see the image of eternity.

This view of the heavens was deeply satisfying. It combined a credible explanation of the natural world with a religious view of the cosmos as the theater of human redemption, in which humankind was the center of God's concern just as the earth was the center about which the heavens revolved. Medieval maps showed Jerusalem as the center of the earth and therefore of the universe, completing the perfect symmetry of the cosmos. It was true that certain details refused to fit in. Some physical bodies, such as projectiles, failed to behave as the Aristotelian theory of motion said they should. Some of the planets and fixed stars appeared to be wayward in their orbits. But these problems did not seem enough to shake an edifice built up over the centuries, hallowed by tradition, and deeply entwined with the belief and value systems of Christianity.

However, new currents were running beneath this placid surface. The fourteenth and fifteenth centuries saw serious challenges to the authority of the church during the Babylonian Captivity and the Great Schism. The French philosopher and bishop Nicholas of Oresme (c. 1323–1382) observed that it was fortunate that faith instructed people that the earth could not rotate on its axis and that there could be no bodies beyond the fixed stars, for it could not be demonstrated either by argument or observation. Oresme's comment illustrated the loss of confidence in the belief of men such as Thomas Aquinas that reason and revelation both disclosed the same truth about the world. A century later, the German Nicholas of Cusa (1401–1464) asserted the rotation of the earth despite official doctrine. With the Reformation, there was no longer a single authority to interpret the Christian faith. By the early seventeenth century the Jesuit Cardinal Robert Bellarmine (1542–1617) felt obliged to concede that in cases where reason and the Bible differed about the natural world, reason must be accepted. For the first time in the history of the church, faith was no longer the final arbiter of knowledge.

The Hermetic Challenge

At the same time, the authority of Aristotle was being questioned as well. The Greek scholars who fled after the fall of Byzantium in 1453 brought with them texts not previously known in the West. Prominent among these were the writings of Hermes Trismegistus ("thrice-great"), believed to be an Egyptian who had received divine revelations about the physical world at the time Moses had been given the Ten Commandments. In fact, Hermes was fictitious, and his texts were the product of third-century A.D. Neoplatonists working in Alexandria. The so-called Hermetic doctrine viewed the material world as an emanation of divine spirit. All ob-

This mosaic from the cathedral in Siena, Italy, depicts the legendary lawgiver of ancient science, Hermes Trismegistus, with a figure who is probably meant to be Moses, giver of the moral law. The paired sphinxes in the lower-right-hand corner represent Hermes' allegedly Egyptian origins. The mosaic dates from the 1480s, when the Neoplatonic revival that so influenced Copernicus was at its height. [Alinari/Art Resource]

jects were related to each other by sympathy or antipathy through the energies of this spirit, which could be released and manipulated by those who knew how to pair the right objects. Humans, the highest compound of matter and spirit, were destined to command the forces of the natural world by learning to read the book of nature and to decipher its hidden codes.

The Hermetic doctrine greatly stimulated interest in chemistry, botany, metallurgy, and astronomy, since the celestial bodies were believed to be the agency by which the divine spirit was transmitted. The sun, as the most important of these, was held to be at the center of the universe, rather than the earth, as in Ptolemaic theory. Hermeticism thus revived the heliocentric theory of Aristarchus, although on a mystical rather than a mathematical or mechanical basis. But mathematics was crucially important for the Hermeticists too. They believed, as Plato and Pythagoras had, that the universe was ultimately constructed in terms of mathematical proportions and harmonies. As the medieval mystic had sought to know the God of love by prayer and meditation, the disciples of Hermes sought to understand the Divine Mind through the mathematical harmonies by which it expressed itself. Mathematics was the highest form of understanding, both of the physical world and of the God who manifested himself in it.

Much of Hermeticism tended to degenerate into the cruder forms of magic, alchemy, and astrology. But the image of man as a natural magician calling forth the hidden powers of the world had great appeal. It suggested that there was still much to be learned about the world beyond the categories of Aristotelian science. Shakespeare's hero Hamlet reflects this new sense of possibility when he tells his loyal but conventional friend, "There are more things in heaven and earth, Horatio, than are dreamt of in your philosophy," and Prospero, the hero of his last play, *The Tempest* (1611), is a portrait of the Renaissance man as a Hermetic magician.

The Neoplatonic revival was only one element that contributed to the crisis of knowledge and belief in the sixteenth century. The Reformation had deeply unsettled people's assurance about the nature of grace and salvation and undermined their faith in those who had interpreted spiritual knowledge. The discovery of the New World shattered their faith in the adequacy of their knowledge of the physical world as well. The scientific revolution was a product of this upheaval and shared in its difficult birth the tensions and contradictions of the age.

The New Order of Knowledge

The most important convert to the Hermetic doctrine was the Polish astronomer and mathematician Nicholas Copernicus (1473–1543). Born in Toruń on the Polish-German frontier, he imbibed Hermeticism in the course of a ten-year sojourn in Renaissance Italy. Copernicus was convinced that the majesty of the cosmos demanded that the sun be at its center rather than the earth. As he explained his conception:

> In the middle of [the cosmos] sits the Sun enthroned. . . . Could we place this luminary in any better position from which he can illuminate the whole at once? He is rightly called the Lamp, the Mind, the Ruler of the Universe; Hermes Trismegistus names him the visible God. . . . So the sun sits as upon a royal throne ruling his children, the planets which circle around him.[1]

Copernicus devoted the rest of his life to proving not only that the heliocentric theory of the Hermeticists was preferable to that of Ptolemy on aesthetic and religious grounds but also that it offered a better account where Ptolemy's theory was weakest, in explaining celestial motion. This claim was reflected in the title of his trea-

JOHANNIS HEVELII
COMETOGRAPHIA.

This engraving from Johannes Hevelius' *Cometographia* (1608) shows the excitement generated by Copernican astronomy. In the foreground, three scholars compare their calculations: in front of them is an armillary sphere representing the celestial globe, together with a sextant. On the roof of the building in the background, observers train a telescope and measuring devices on the heavens and the comet coming into view. Comets were of intense interest for both scientific and superstitious reasons, as they were held to portend great events. [Stanford University Libraries]

tise, *On the Revolution of the Heavenly Spheres,* whose publication he authorized only on his deathbed in 1543. Copernicus assumed that only the earth and the five planets actually moved. The sun was motionless at the center of the universe as the fixed stars were at the periphery, their apparent motion being accounted for by the rotation of the earth. This was a great theoretical simplification, although the mathematics necessary to calculate the actual position of the stars relative to a moving earth were hardly less complex than Ptolemy's. Copernicus was also able to dispense with the idea of giant crystalline spheres moved by angels, which Christian doctrine had superimposed on Ptolemy's original theory. Heavenly bodies moved and rotated because it was their nature to do so; put a globe in space, Copernicus argued, and it will spin. Such an idea contradicted the Aristotelian notion that bodies not externally propelled would come to rest, but it did not explain why some bodies—the earth, the moon, and the planets—were in motion, while the sun and the stars were not.

The Copernican theory offered a credible but not compelling alternative to the Ptolemaic system. Its cal-culations of the celestial orbits were no less complex, and it created as many mathematical and physical problems as it solved. Martin Luther's reaction was typical. "That is how things go nowadays," the great German reformer said. "Anyone who wants to be clever must not be satisfied with what others do. He must produce his own theory as this man does, who wishes to turn the whole of astronomy upside down."[2] No other astronomer accepted Copernicus, and his theory was kept alive only in Hermetic circles. One convert, the Italian philosopher Giordano Bruno (1548–1600), argued that the sun around which the earth revolved was only one of innumerable suns in an infinite universe, each of which might harbor planets and species like our own. Bruno fell into the hands of the Inquisition and was burned at the stake. Such were the perils of unguided speculation on the basis of Copernicus' theory. Catholics and Prot-

---

◎ On the Infinity of the Universe ◎

The Copernican displacement of the earth from the center of the universe led the Italian philosopher Giordano Bruno to question the very notion of a "center" in space and to contend for the idea of an infinite universe that reflected the infinite power and glory of God.

How is it possible that the universe can be infinite? . . . I say that the universe is entirely infinite because it has neither edge, limit, nor surfaces. But I say that the universe is not all-comprehensive infinity because each of the parts thereof that we can examine is finite and each of the innumerable worlds contained therein is finite. I declare God to be completely infinite because he can be associated with no boundary and his every attribute is one and infinite. And I say that God is all-comprehensive infinity because the whole of him pervades the whole world and every part thereof comprehensively and to infinity. . . . What argument would persuade us that the Agent capable of creating infinite good should have created it finite? And if he has created it finite, why should we believe that the Agent could have created it infinite, since power and action are in him but one?

The influence of Bruno's daring hypothesis can be seen in the work of a contemporary scientist, William Gilbert.

Who has ever made out that the stars which we call fixed are in one and the same sphere, or has established by reasoning that there are any real and, as it were, adamantine spheres? No one has proved this, nor is there a doubt but that just as the planets are at unequal distances from the earth, so are these vast and multitudinous lights separated from the earth by varying and very remote altitudes. . . . How immeasurable then must be the space which stretches to the remotest of fixed stars! How vast and immense the depth of that imaginary sphere! How far removed from the earth must be the most widely separated stars and at a distance transcending all sight, all skill, all thought!

Source: D. W. Singer, *Giordano Bruno: His Life and Thought* (New York: Schuman, 1950), pp. 66–67, 250, 257, 262.

estants alike condemned it. The greatest astronomer of the late sixteenth century, Tycho Brahe (1546–1601), explicitly rejected it.

But the Copernican theory did not die. The appearance of a bright new star in the sky in the 1570s, followed by a brilliant comet, reminded people that there were phenomena not explained by Ptolemy's static system. Tycho Brahe's meticulous celestial observations served a young German astronomer, Johannes Kepler (1571–1630), who had come to Copernicus through his own Hermetic beliefs. Kepler made the crucial discovery that the orbits of the planets were not circular, as both Ptolemy and Copernicus had assumed, but elliptical. This enabled him to simplify Copernicus' calculations, giving him for the first time a decisive advantage over Ptolemy. Ironically, however, Kepler's discovery was itself rejected by the man whose work finally undermined the Ptolemaic theory, Galileo Galilei.

Galileo and the Copernican Triumph

Galileo (1564–1642) was born in Pisa, Italy. After completing studies in mathematics and natural philosophy, he joined the faculty of the University of Padua, where Copernicus had studied a century before. Galileo was the first important figure to accept Copernicus outside the Hermetic circle. His own inspiration was the ancient Greek mathematician Archimedes (287–212 B.C.), whose works had been republished in 1543. Archimedes, like Pythagoras, had attempted to describe the world in purely mathematical terms. Unlike Pythagoras, however, he attributed no mystical significance to the mathematical proportions he found in nature, and unlike the Neoplatonists, he posited no spiritual basis in matter. For him, and for his latter-day disciple Galileo, the world was best thought of as a gigantic machine operating by simple principles expressible in geometric ratios.

In such a world there was no room either for Aristotle's mythical quintessence or for the medieval angels who moved the stars. Galileo's own most important work was his discovery of the principle of accelerated motion, in which he brilliantly connected velocity and distance to the variable of time. But he caused a sensation when in 1609 he turned a newly invented instrument, the telescope, on the heavens. Galileo discovered four moons in orbit around the planet Jupiter, and so many hundreds of previously undetected stars that he declared them to be innumerable. This seemed to suggest a startling confirmation of Bruno's belief in an infinite universe. Galileo also demonstrated that the surface of the moon was rough and eroded, thereby demolishing the theory of a perfect and unchanging heaven.

Galileo's espousal of Copernican theory and his own celestial discoveries were decisive in gaining acceptance for the new astronomy, and his strict adherence to a mechanistic view of the cosmos purged it of lingering Hermetic elements. [Art Resource]

Copernicus had disclosed his findings only with great caution during his lifetime, but Galileo, armed with his new observations, rushed boldly into print. He claimed that the truth of the Copernican theory had now been established, and when confronted with the familiar scriptural story of Joshua making the sun stand still, he retorted that the Bible might be adequate for ignorant laymen but could hardly qualify as a scientific treatise. This was too much for the Catholic church. Despite the burning of Bruno, it had never officially condemned the Copernican theory. It did so now, however (1616), and when Galileo defiantly published a further defense of Copernicus in his *Dialogue Concerning the Two Chief World Systems* (1632), he was arrested by the Inquisition, threatened with torture, and obliged to recant his belief in the heliocentric system. But though Galileo might be silenced, his challenge to received authority could not. What he represented was not the familiar problem of the heretic who challenged Christian doctrine on its own terms but a rival system of truth that bypassed it as irrelevant to the description and understanding of the physical world. For Galileo, observation was the guide, experiment the test, and mathematics the language of physical reality. No other form of understanding was necessary, no other authority acceptable.

Thus Copernicus, who believed that the sun was the lamp of nature and the image of God, was vindicated by the mystic Kepler, who believed that the planets and stars were souls who danced to the music of the spheres, and by the rationalist Galileo, who banished spirit and purpose from the world of matter and left only physical bodies obeying the mechanical laws of motion. What all three held in common was the language of mathematical proof. It was by mathematics that Copernicus turned the Neoplatonic doctrine that the sun was the center of the universe into a plausible description of the actual cosmos, by mathematics that Kepler was able to demonstrate the superiority of that description to its rivals, and by mathematics that Galileo was able to begin constructing the new physics of motion that the Copernican universe required.

Other Scientific Advances

If the common language of mathematics made astronomy and physics the cutting edge of the scientific revolution, chemistry, medicine, anatomy, and biology all advanced as well. As in the case of astronomy, the impetus for development often came from Hermetic and Neoplatonic doctrine. The Swiss-born German physician Theophrastus Bombastus von Hohenheim (1493–1541), called Paracelsus, launched a one-man crusade against the influence of Aristotle and Galen in medicine. Paracelsus was imbued with the spirit of medieval and Renaissance magic. He believed that occult forces were at work everywhere in nature and that demons could even divert the courses of the stars. It would be hard to imagine a mind further removed from the cool, rational skepticism of Galileo. Yet Paracelsus' very belief in the omnipresence of magical forces led him away from the traditional textbooks—he is said to have burned all the medical classics before delivering his introductory lecture at the University of Basel in 1527—and back to nature. In accordance with Hermetic doctrine, he believed that the structure of the human organism was directly analogous to that of the natural world and that specific organs of the body were sympathetically related to specific plants, minerals, chemical substances, and even stars. The disorders of the body came from disturbances in the natural harmony between the body and the world, and their remedies were thus to be sought in identifying and applying substances that could correct the balance. This meant constant search and experimentation. "A man cannot learn the theory of medicine out of his own head," Paracelsus declared, "but only from that which his eyes see and his fingers touch. . . . Theory and practice should together form one, and should remain undivided."[3]

The emphasis on direct observation of nature produced the first great textbook of anatomy, *De Fabrica* (1543) by the Fleming Andreas Vesalius (1514–1564), and the discovery in the West of the circulation of the blood (1628) by the Englishman William Harvey (1578–1657), though anticipated in Han China in the second century B.C. The results of these discoveries, as in the case of astronomy, proved contrary to the theories that had originally inspired them. Vesalius believed that the structure of the human head, as the temple of reason, was necessarily different from that of animals, and Harvey saw the heart as the source of spiritual as well as physical life. What they showed instead was that the anatomies of humans and animals were similar in structure and function. Harvey became an enthusiastic disciple of comparative anatomy, remarking tartly that had the anatomists paid as much attention to animals as to humans, the mysteries of the body would have been solved long before. Indeed, the last element in the circulation of the blood unsolved by Harvey himself, the transfer of blood from veins to arteries by capillary action, was discovered in 1661 by the Italian Marcello Malpighi (1628–1694), who examined a frog's lungs with the aid of another optical instrument, the microscope.

New Technology

New inventions and techniques were stimulated not merely by the requirements of scientific curiosity but also those of practical activity. The great voyages of trade and discovery that began in the late fifteenth century are a case in point. Until that time, European ships seldom ventured out of sight of land and could proceed by pilotage, or reckoning by coastal landmarks. But when they sailed out into open and uncharted seas, they required navigation, or reckoning by the sun and the stars. For this purpose seamen adapted instruments previously used by astronomers, the quadrant and the astrolabe. The problem of plotting straight-line courses on two-dimensional maps representing a three-dimensional earth was solved by the Fleming Gerhard Kremer (1512–1594), called Mercator, whose map was first published in 1569 and in modified form is still used today. In 1484 King John III of Portugal appointed a commission of mathematicians to work out tables of latitude, and when Gresham College was founded in England in 1597, one of its three scientific chairs was reserved for an astronomer whose duties included the teaching of navigation. Sixteenth-century interest in theories of the cosmos thus had a very practical basis. In similar fashion, the development of the cannon took ballistics, the science of calculating the trajectory of missiles, out of the realm of academic theory and onto the battlefield, and the extraction of gold and silver from the Indies stimulated the development of chemical separation processes and mining technology such as subsurface ventilation and hydraulic pumps.

Science at the Crossroads

The new scientific theories were disturbing to established authority, particularly in the universities and the churches. The new ideas were often associated with political subversion and black magic, inflammatory charges in an age marked by civil unrest and witchcraft persecution. Galileo had already been driven from the University of Padua before his arrest by the Inquisition, and Kepler was expelled from the Protestant faculty of the University of Tübingen. Jewish elders were hostile to the Kabala, a system akin to Hermeticism that claimed to decode secret meanings in the Old Testament.

The authorities' concern about the new science and the esoteric doctrines that swirled about it was not unfounded. The confidence of educated laymen in the traditional picture of the world had already been eroded by the late sixteenth century. "The more I think, the more I doubt," the Jesuit Francisco Suárez confessed in 1581, and 30 years later the English poet and minister John Donne summarized the anxieties many people felt about humanity's loss of its privileged place in the cosmos in "An Anatomy of the World" (1611):

> *And new philosophy calls all in doubt;*
> *The element of fire is quite put out,*
> *The sun is lost, and the earth, and no man's wit*
> *Can well direct him where to look for it*
> *And freely men confess, that this world's spent*
> *When in the planets and the firmament*
> *They seek so many new; then see that this*
> *Is crumbled out again to his atomies*
> *'Tis all in pieces, all coherence gone;*
> *All just supply and all relation.*

Donne's poem is remarkable in demonstrating the speed with which scientific ideas were circulating, since Galileo had announced his discovery of new celestial bodies only a year before. His familiarity with the dispute about "the element of fire" (challenged by Paracelsus and his followers) and with the revival of interest in Democritus' theory of atoms can also be glimpsed in his lines.

Doubt and Faith: Descartes and Pascal

More extreme reactions to the new science can be seen in the Frenchmen René Descartes (1596–1650) and Blaise Pascal (1623–1662). As Descartes himself related his experience, he was assailed one night by a sudden paralyzing doubt about the possibility of knowledge. The senses, he felt, deceived us, faith was undermined by doubt, and the authorities were only people like ourselves. How could one be sure of the existence of the world, of God, or even of oneself? Descartes' famous reply—"I think, therefore I am"—was the starting point of his extraordinary attempt to reconstruct all knowledge from the ground up on the basis of simple, self-evident propositions.

Pascal, a brilliant mathematician and a man of great religious sensitivity, felt the vast new spaces of the Copernican universe as a terrible silence in which humans were alone with their frailty and doubt and God had become a remote conjecture. He was one of the first men of his time to realize that the traditional conception of God no longer fit the world revealed by science. But he argued, in his famous "wager" with skeptics, that it was better to affirm the existence of a just and merciful God in whom one might no longer fully believe than to deny him, since there was everything to gain if he did in fact exist and nothing to be lost if he did not.

Conflicting Roads to Truth

Science itself had arrived at a crossroads by the mid-seventeenth century. The scientific enterprise was a Babel of languages from which no common grammar had yet emerged. The Aristotelian tradition was largely in shambles, but nothing had appeared to replace it. An English participant in an early scientific meeting has left us a catalog of the subjects discussed that suggests both the excitement and confusion of the new science:

> **We discoursed of the circulation of the blood, the valves in the veins, the *venae lacteae*, the lymphatick vessels, the Copernican hypothesis, the nature of comets and new stars, the satellites of Jupiter, the oval shape (as it then appeared) of Saturn, the spots in the sun, and its turning on its own axis, the inequalities and selenography of the Moon, the several phases of Venus and Mercury, the improvement of telescopes, and the grinding of glasses for that purpose, the weight of air, the possibility, or impossibility of vacuities [vacuums], and nature's abhorrence thereof, the Torricellian experiment in quick-silver, the descent of heavy bodies, and the degrees of acceleration therein; and divers other things of like nature.[4]**

Especially lacking was a common standard of judgment and proof. Although important discoveries had been made by scientists working from both Hermetic and mechanistic assumptions, in the last analysis they were incompatible as ways of seeing the world. The cosmos could be a living organism or an enormous machine, but not both. A similar division existed regarding scientific method. The English philosopher and jurist Sir Francis Bacon (1561–1626), Lord Chancellor under King James I, argued for the inductive or empirical method, by which knowledge was gained through systematic observation of the world and tested by experiment. The deductive method was championed by Des-

◉ Pascal on Humankind's Place ◉ in the Universe

The notion of an unlimited cosmos seemed to reduce humanity to insignificance and to call into question the idea of God's love and purpose for humankind. Such feelings were given unequaled expression by the great seventeenth-century mathematician and philosopher Blaise Pascal.

When I consider the brief span of my life absorbed into the eternity which comes before and after—*as the remembrance of a guest that tarrieth but a day*—the small space I occupy and which I see swallowed up in the infinite immensity of spaces of which I know nothing and which know nothing of me, I take fright and am amazed to see myself here rather than there: there is no reason for me to be here rather than there, now rather than then. Who put me here? By whose command and act were this time and place allotted to me? . . .

The eternal silence of these infinite spaces fills me with dread.

Source: B. Pascal, *Pensées*, trans. A. J. Krailsheimer (Baltimore: Penguin Books, 1966), pp. 48, 95.

cartes, who, as we have seen, rejected the senses as a basis for knowledge and argued that reality could be known only by reasoning from axiomatic principles. Descartes took a step that was decisive in the intellectual history of the West. He divided reality into two distinct entities, spirit, characterized by the power of thought but without physical properties, and matter, substance extended in space through motion. In doing so, he completely separated matter and spirit, rejecting the Hermetic vision of the world as a fusion of the two. He was thereby able to treat the material world in completely mechanical terms, while reserving an independent realm for spirit. Spirit meant in effect intelligence for Descartes, and the greatest intelligence was that of God, who had created the physical universe of matter in motion and designed the laws by which it operated. By studying and understanding those laws, humankind could understand God. Thus Cartesianism, as Descartes' philosophy came to be called, made science into a religious quest, but one that proceeded in terms not of theology but of mechanical engineering and mathematical reasoning.

The immediate importance of Descartes' work was that it gave impetus to the mechanistic conception of the world, where the most fruitful line of scientific advance actually lay, while avoiding the charge of black magic on the one hand and of atheism on the other. Cartesian science itself had serious drawbacks. It was well suited for physics but completely useless for biology, since it could provide no convincing explanation for the phe-

The great French skeptic René Descartes in a confident pose by Frans Hals. Descartes' separation of mind from matter marked the beginning of a crisis in Western thought. [Lauros-Giraudon/Art Resource]

nomenon of life. It relegated observation and experiment to matters of secondary detail at best, thus failing to provide an independent standard of proof for anyone who did not accept the premises of the system. Brilliant strategically as a means of breaking the impasse between Hermeticism and mechanism, it was still inadequate as a general model for science itself.

The Newtonian Synthesis

Sir Isaac Newton (1642–1727) finally carried out the task Descartes had set: to provide a clear and comprehensive explanation of the physical universe in mathematical terms, a universe created by the will of God but fully subject to the laws of nature. Newton's work was a synthesis of all the elements of the scientific tradition. His solution to the problem of gravity, which he had made the key to his system, illustrates this. In Aristotelian physics, gravity was the inherent tendency of physical bodies to fall toward the earth as the center of the universe. The Englishman William Gilbert (1540–1603) had advanced the argument by his discovery that the earth itself acted as a magnet, drawing bodies to itself. But this left a serious problem in a Copernican universe where the sun was the center of the cosmos or (as both Descartes and Newton assumed) there was no center at all. Even granting the principle of inertia—that bodies set in motion would continue along the same path—how could it be explained that heavenly bodies did not simply drift randomly through space but described regular orbits about one another? Descartes rejected the idea of gravity as attraction at a distance because it seemed to him too close to the Hermetic idea of a force inherent in matter emanating from a divine source. Newton, however, had no trouble accepting such a notion, provided that it could be given an adequate mathematical basis—that is, provided that it could be shown to describe the actual orbits and positions of heavenly bodies. But classical mathematics, like classical physics, had always assumed the existence of a stable center. There was no mathematics capable of describing the interaction of independently moving bodies. Newton thereupon invented a new mathematics, called calculus, to deal with these relations.

Using the assumption of gravity as a universal constant, Newton was able to reduce the movement of all bodies in heaven or on earth to three basic laws: (1) objects in motion continue so unless acted on by an external force (such as friction), (2) changes in motion are proportional to the force applied, and (3) every action produces an equal and opposite reaction. The elements of the system were as simple as the proofs were painstaking and complex. When Newton published his findings in his *Mathematical Principles of Natural Philosophy* (1687), he completed the work begun by Copernicus a

century and a half earlier in replacing the Ptolemaic system. But Newton's model was even further from that of Copernicus than the latter's had been from Ptolemy's. Copernicus had still assumed that the universe had a definite center and a final boundary. Newton's cosmos was infinite and centerless. The speculation for which Bruno had been burned at the beginning of the seventeenth century had become scientific orthodoxy by its end.

The great success of Newton's synthesis was to reconcile not only the conflicting traditions of the new science but its competing methodologies as well. The conceptual simplicity of his system was a triumph of inductive logic, yet it was fully supported by the most up-to-date astronomical observations. This combination brought about ultimate acceptance of his system after the initial skepticism of men like the German mathematician Gottfried Wilhelm von Leibniz (1646–1716), who had independently worked out calculus at the same time as Newton but rejected his notion of gravity. The Newtonian model was not only mathematically convincing as Descartes' was not, but for the next 200 years every empirical observation and experiment confirmed it in detail. After Newton, scientific method was a matter not of theory or of observation but of both. By the time of his death in 1727, his prestige was so great that the poet Alexander Pope could write:

> *Nature and nature's laws lay hid in night;*
> *God said, Let Newton be! and all was light.*

The Scientific Method

Newton himself remarked, "If I have seen further [than others], it is by standing on the shoulders of giants." Indeed, the most impressive aspect of the scientific revolution was less an increase in knowledge about the world than the creation of a new method for understanding it. The ancient world had stressed the primacy of reason as a means of knowledge. The Middle Ages, while accepting reason, had insisted on the primacy of God's word as revealed in the Bible and interpreted by the church. The Reformation had changed that. Faith in God's word might be as strong as ever, but faith in its interpretation by the clergy was not. No longer was a single standard of truth acceptable to all.

The result, in part, was a return to reliance on reason. Descartes was a clear and radical example of this. What he wanted of reason was what he could no longer find in faith: certain and irrefutable truth. But the scientific method, as it had actually developed, offered both something less and something more. It was something less because science could not claim, even with Newton, to have arrived at a final truth about the world (though some of his eighteenth-century admirers would assert

◉ The Scientific Method ◉

As received ideas of truth and knowledge were cast into doubt by the scientific revolution, a new method for ascertaining truth slowly evolved, stressing the importance of observation, experiment, and mathematical reasoning. The English philosopher Sir Francis Bacon stressed the importance of controlled experiment.

But by far the greatest impediment and aberration of the human understanding proceeds from the dullness, incompetency, and errors of the senses; since whatever strikes the senses preponderates over everything, however superior, which does not immediately strike them. Hence contemplation mostly ceases with sight, and a very scanty, or perhaps no regard is paid to visible objects. The entire operation, therefore, of spirits enclosed in tangible bodies is concealed, and escapes us. . . . Again, the very nature of common air, and all bodies of less density . . . is almost unknown; for the senses are weak and erring, nor can instruments be of great use in extending their spheres or acuteness. All the better interpretations of nature are worked out by instances, and fit and apt experiments, where the senses only judge of the experiment.

Of equal importance, the Frenchman René Descartes stressed the use of deductive reasoning.

By [deduction] we mean the inference of something as following necessarily from some other propositions which are known with certainty. . . . This distinction had to be made, since very many facts which are not self-evident are known with certainty, provided they are inferred from true and known principles through a continuous and uninterrupted movement of thought in which each individual proposition is clearly intuited. This is similar to the way in which we know that the last link in a long chain is connected to the first: even if we cannot take in at one glance all the intermediate links on which the connection depends, we can have knowledge of the connection provided we survey the links one after the other, and keep in mind that each link from first to last is attached to its neighbor.

Sources: F. Bacon, *Novum Organum,* in *Great Books of the Western World,* vol. 30 (Chicago: Encyclopaedia Britannica, 1952), p. 111; *The Philosophical Writings of Descartes,* trans. J. Cottingham, R. Stoothoff, and D. Murdoch, vol. 1 (Cambridge: Cambridge University Press, 1985), p. 15.

---

as much). It was something more because it amounted to a redefinition of truth itself. Henceforward, truth was not something to be revealed at once and in its entirety, whether by the sacred word or by direct intuition. Rather, truth was to be discovered and refined piecemeal, with each new stage in understanding serving as a step toward the next one. Through individual trial and error, collective truth was to be won.

For this reason, science became more and more a collaborative effort after the mid-seventeenth century. The first scientists had worked alone, like Copernicus and the reclusive Tycho Brahe, who built an observatory on his private island and jealously guarded the results of his work. Gradually, these isolated individuals became linked by chains of correspondence, such as the one set up in Paris in the 1630s by the friar Marin Mersenne (1588–1648), an enthusiast of the new science and a friend of Galileo's. From this grew scientific meetings and finally formal societies. Among the first of these latter was the Royal Society of London for Improving Natural Knowledge, founded in 1662, of which Newton was an early member and later president. Four years later Colbert founded the French Academy of Sciences under state patronage, and similar societies were soon established in Berlin, Uppsala, Stockholm, Copenhagen, and St. Petersburg. By the last decades of the seventeenth century we can speak of a scientific world, international in scope and cosmopolitan in character, in which knowledge could be systematically communicated, new theories debated, and new talent recognized.

THE SCIENTIFIC REVOLUTION

Scientific milestones	Social reactions
Copernicus, *On the Revolution of the Heavenly Spheres* (1543); Vesalius, *De Fabrica* (1543)	Montaigne, *Essays* (1580)
Tycho Brahe discovers a new star (1572)	Shakespeare, *Hamlet* (1600)
Galileo's law of falling bodies (1591)	Bruno burned at the stake (1600)
Galileo discovers Jupiter's moons (1609)	Shakespeare, *The Tempest* (1611)
Kepler's third law of motion (1609)	Donne, "An Anatomy of the World" (1611)
Bacon, *Novum Organum* (1620)	Galileo cautioned by the papacy (1616)
Harvey discovers the circulation of the blood (1628)	
Galileo, *Dialogue Concerning the Two Chief World Systems* (1632)	Galileo forced to recant by the Inquisition (1633)
Descartes, *Discourse on Method* (1637)	Royal Society founded in England (1662)
Newton, *Principia Mathematica* (1687)	Pascal, *Pensées* (1670)

Philosophy: The Age of Reason

In the seventeenth century no strict distinction was made between philosophy—inquiry into the limits of human knowledge as such—and science, the branch of knowledge that addressed itself to the natural world. In that sense, the attack on Aristotle, Ptolemy, and Galen that characterized the scientific revolution was part of a wider movement in European thought that questioned traditional authority in general. But there can be no doubt that the success of science in dethroning medieval cosmology gave impetus and urgency to the development of critical philosophy as a whole.

The two traditions of philosophy that were most influential in the seventeenth and eighteenth centuries were the English and the French. German philosophy, which began its modern career with Leibniz and Samuel Pufendorf (1632–1694), began to dominate European thought only in the late eighteenth and nineteenth centuries. In English and French philosophy, speculation adhered to the norms set down respectively by Bacon and Descartes. The English tended to begin from concrete observation of the world, the French from a priori assumptions about it.

Another broad distinction between English and French philosophy can be drawn in terms of subject matter. The English, preoccupied with the revolutions of 1640 and 1688, concentrated on the problem of people's relation to the civic orders of state and society, whereas the French, inheriting the skepticism of Descartes, focused on humanity's relation to the cosmos.

Thomas Hobbes and the Natural Man

The Englishman Thomas Hobbes (1588–1679), writing in the tumultuous 1640s, produced in *Leviathan* (1651) the most important work of Western political philosophy since *The Prince*. Hobbes argued that human beings are social by necessity rather than by nature, as Aristotle had thought. He started from the mechanistic assumption that humans, like all other entities, could be described in terms of matter and motion and that their thoughts, feelings, and desires could be explained as responses to external stimuli, differing in degree but not in kind from those of animals. Even reason, the glory of the mind, was only a complex form of calculation, and the will, which attested to human freedom, was defined simply as the last appetite before choice. Hobbes professed to believe in God, the soul, and the workings of Providence, but, like Descartes (whom he knew and admired), he separated the realms of matter and spirit so sharply that his view of society appeared purely secular. That, combined with the fierce anticlericalism that ran through all his political writings, led to his condemnation as an atheist.

In Hobbes' view, human beings strive to maximize pleasure and minimize pain. This brings them into conflict with others who, acting on the same principle, compete for scarce goods. The result, Hobbes declared, was a "war of all against all," a condition in which the life of men was, in his pithy phrase, "solitary, poor, nasty, brutish and short." To avoid this, they gave up their natural freedom and entered society, as rational animals might enter a zoo. Hobbes' zookeeper was the sovereign, who had absolute power to order all social arrangements, allotting each person a share of goods and duties. Only in this way, he believed, could order be guaranteed and the anarchy of the natural human condition avoided. Society was in effect a contract in which freedom was exchanged for security, or at least the hope of security, since the subject, in surrendering all natural rights, had also surrendered the means to enforce the bargain. To critics who complained that this created a license for tyranny, Hobbes replied that it was better to be subject to the arbitrary will of a single individual than to the potential violence of all.

Hobbes insisted that his theory was not an abstract

The famous frontispiece of Hobbes' book *Leviathan* shows his absolute sovereign as a giant who incorporates the entire body politic. The Latin quotation at the top, from the Book of Job, reads: "There is not his like upon earth." [Granger Collection]

blueprint but an actual description of power in society. Whether monarchy, aristocracy, or democracy, the core of every government was an absolute, unchallengeable sovereignty that could not be divided or infringed without destroying the state and consequently the social order. He therefore rejected all theories of "mixed" government or separation of powers as a confusion between real and delegated powers.

Hobbes' theory scandalized everyone. Liberals rejected it because it left no place for political dissent. Conservatives liked it no better because, although Hobbes condemned rebellion as the greatest of political evils, he accepted all changes of government in a spirit of pure pragmatism. The only test of a regime was its ability to provide security. A government that could not do so forfeited all claim to loyalty, while any government that could possessed a sufficient title to be obeyed.

John Locke and the State of Nature

Writing 40 years later, John Locke (1632–1704) took a very different view of human society. Locke started from the premise that human beings in their natural condition—what had come to be called the state of nature—were not competitive but cooperative. Such persons entered society to gain the benefits of communal organization. Their natural rights were not surrendered but rather enhanced in society. Government on this view was merely an instrument of common social purpose, and the ruler was entrusted with such powers as were necessary to provide for the general welfare but no more. Should he abuse this trust, he might be replaced or deposed without doing violence to the constitution and certainly without dissolving society as Hobbes had thought. This was what had happened to James II in 1688, and English society, far from being destroyed or hurled back into anarchy, had been strengthened and renewed.

Locke's view of politics derived from his assumptions about human psychology, expressed in the *Essay Concerning Human Understanding* (1690). Taking a radically empirical stance, he argued that the mind at birth was a *tabula rasa*, or blank slate, on which experience inscribed itself. It followed from this that careful education could develop the mind in almost any desired direction. Thus, although reason in the state of nature suggested the desirability of human cooperation, people could easily be trained to obey the far more complex rules of society.

French Skepticism

In France a vein of skepticism ran through philosophy from the essayist Michel de Montaigne (1533–1592) to Descartes to Pierre Bayle (1647–1706). Descartes dealt with his own crisis of belief by asserting the power of reason to validate the world, including the existence of God. The idea of an infinite being, he argued, is spontaneously present in the human mind; yet since it would never have occurred of itself to a finite, limited consciousness, it could only have been placed there by God. But Descartes insisted on excluding God from any direct responsibility for the material universe, remarking that his readers could substitute "the mathematical order of nature" for "God" wherever he used the latter term.

For Blaise Pascal the absence of God from the material universe was the very source of human despair.

◈ The Institution of the Commonwealth ◈

The English philosopher Thomas Hobbes described the origin of the state in the agreement of sovereign individuals to merge their natural rights in a single person acting in the name of all.

It is manifest, that during the time men live without a common power to keep them all in awe, they are in that condition which is called war, and such a war, as is of every man, against every man. For war consisteth not in battle only, or the act of fighting; but in a tract of time, wherein the will to contend by battle is sufficiently known. . . . The only way to erect such a common power, as may be able to defend [individuals] from the invasion of foreigners, and the injuries of one another . . . is to confer all their power and strength upon one man, or upon one assembly of men, that may reduce all their wills, by plurality of voices, unto one will: which is as much as to say, to appoint one man, or assembly of men, to bear their person. . . . This is . . . a real unity of them all, in one and the same person, made by covenant of every man with every man, in such a manner, as if every man should say to every man, *I authorize and give up my right of governing myself, to this man, or to this assembly of men, on this condition, that thou give up thy right to him, and authorize all his actions in like manner.* This done, the multitude so united in one person, is called a commonwealth. . . . This is the generation of that great Leviathan, or rather (to speak more reverently) of that mortal God, to which we owe under the immortal God, our peace and defense.

A very different view of the state as originating in force and fraud was offered by Hobbes' contemporary Gerrard Winstanley (c. 1609–c. 1676).

In the beginning of time, the great creator Reason, made the earth to be a common treasury, to preserve beasts, birds, fishes, and man, the lord that was to govern this creation; for man had domination given to him, over the beasts, birds, and fishes; but not one word was spoken in the beginning, that one branch of mankind should rule over another. . . . But . . . selfish imagination taking possession of the five senses, and so ruling as king in the room of Reason therein, and working with covetousness, did set up one man to teach and rule over another, and thereby the spirit was killed, and man was brought into bondage, and became a greater slave to such of his own kind, than the beasts of the field were to him.

Sources: T. Hobbes, *Leviathan*, ed. A. R. Walter (Cambridge: Cambridge University Press, 1904), pp. 83, 118–119 (modernized); G. H. Sabine, ed., *The Works of Gerrard Winstanley* (Ithaca, N.Y.: Cornell University Press, 1941), pp. 251–252.

Descartes' cool, rational conception of a God who made himself known as an idea but could not be reached as a person had no interest for him. Pascal contended that Descartes, by exalting the powers of the mind, had excluded God, reducing him to a meaningless abstraction. It was only by admitting one's frailty and need that it was possible to reach the Christian God who had extended himself to humankind by his own suffering.

Pascal was closely associated with the religious circle at Port-Royal, a Cistercian abbey a few miles southwest of Paris that had embraced the teachings of the Dutch theologian Cornelius Jansen (1585–1638). Jansenism was a reaction against the scholastic tradition maintained by the Jesuits. Stressing individual piety and personal election rather than outward good works and conformity to church doctrine, it was viewed as a "protestant" heresy within Catholicism, although Jansen claimed his inspiration from St. Augustine rather than Calvin. Opposed by Richelieu and Louis XIV no less than by a succession of popes, it maintained itself as a religious and political counterculture well into the eighteenth century.

The skeptical tradition nonetheless continued to gain ground in France. In his *Critical History of the New Testament* (1678), the Oratorian priest Richard Simon subjected the Bible to an exhaustive textual scrutiny, exposing hundreds of errors and discrepancies. Shocked by the audacity of anyone—no less a priest—treating Holy Writ by the standards of ordinary literature, Bishop Bossuet ordered the book burned. Simon protested that his aim was not to cast doubt on the essential truth of the Bible but to purge it of human error. No such redeeming purpose could be attributed to Pierre Bayle, who satirized biblical and pagan figures side by side in his *Historical and Critical Dictionary* (1697). For Bayle, whose book profoundly influenced such eighteenth-century skeptics as Voltaire, reason and religion were mortal enemies fighting "for possession of men's souls."

The great Jewish philosopher Baruch Spinoza saw God and nature as indivisible. Contemporaries found his ideas "frightening," but he was a hero to later generations. [Municipal Museum, The Hague]

❦
THE LENS GRINDER OF AMSTERDAM, BARUCH SPINOZA

The philosophical and religious issues of the seventeenth century were perhaps nowhere better epitomized than in the life of Baruch Spinoza. Spinoza was born in Amsterdam in 1632, the son of a prosperous Jewish merchant whose family had emigrated from Portugal at the end of the sixteenth century. The Amsterdam of his youth was the most cosmopolitan city in Europe. The Jewish community mixed freely with the general population, adopting its manners and dress (as portraits by Rembrandt show), intermarrying, and imbibing liberal social and religious ideas. This freedom created great tension within the Jewish community itself, which conservative members feared would soon lose its identity. The brilliant young Spinoza was a case in point. While the elders of the community supported the House of Orange and the Dutch East and West India companies, Spinoza backed the republican revolution of 1650 and advocated the dissolution of the trading companies and the abolition of their privileges. Above all, he rejected his Jewish heritage, abjuring the synagogue and denying that the Jews were a chosen people. The Amsterdam synagogue responded by excommunicating him in 1656. He was formally cursed, and Jews were forbidden all contact with him. Spinoza renounced the career in commerce he had begun and earned his living by grinding and polishing lenses, a job of deliberately low status but symbolically appropriate for a man determined to see the world by no light but his own.

In his major work, the *Ethics*, Spinoza proposed a radical solution to the central seventeenth-century question of the relation between God and nature. Traditional philosophy had distinguished between substance, the stuff of the universe, and cause, the external agency that acts on it and shapes it. Spinoza rejected this distinction as false. There could be no separation between God as cause and nature as substance. It followed that God *was* the world, which was contained in him though he was not confined by it.

It is hard to imagine an idea more calculated to give offense. Religious thinkers had speculated that the human soul might be regarded as a spark of divinity within humankind. Spinoza denied the existence of the soul, since there could be no distinction between matter and spirit; yet he asserted that God was present not only in humans but in the lowest and most degraded phenomena of the world as well. To accept God was to accept everything, and once that was done, false categories such as sin and salvation, which separated man from God, lost all meaning and fell away. Descartes, daring as he was, never left the Catholic church. Spinoza's metaphysics made all religious doctrine irrelevant.

Spinoza's political ideas were equally radical. Like Hobbes, he argued that sovereignty was absolute and indivisible and denounced clerical influence in the state; unlike Hobbes, Spinoza demanded complete freedom of thought. "The rights of the individual," he declared, "extend to the utmost limits of his power," and freedom was the final, indispensable human value:

> He that knows himself to be upright does not fear the death of a criminal, and shrinks from no punishment; his mind has no remorse for any disgraceful deed: he holds that death in a good cause is no punishment, but an honor, and that death for freedom is glory.[5]

Spinoza was not entirely isolated. He had friends and even disciples in the Netherlands and carried on a wide correspondence. Leibniz, who visited him, professed admiration for the rigor of his thought but finally concluded that the *Ethics* was "a frightening work" and spoke of the "monstrous opinions of this Jew expelled from the Synagogue." When Spinoza died from a long-standing tubercular condition in 1677, he had no defenders, and his work fell into obscurity until Goethe rediscovered it in the eighteenth century and the Romantics made him a hero in the nineteenth. Since then he has found his place among the great Western philosophers and the champions of freedom—honored at last, but still alone.

Literature: The Triumph of the Vernacular

Latin was still the language of educated Europeans in the sixteenth and seventeenth centuries, the language of international diplomacy, of scholarship, and of the Catholic church. As late as the early eighteenth century, when the elector of Hanover came to Britain to reign as King George I with no knowledge of the English language, he conversed with his chief minister, Sir Robert Walpole, in Latin. But the sixteenth century saw the beginning of a sustained tradition of vernacular literature, that is, literature in the popular spoken tongue. It began in Italy with the immensely popular chivalric poems of Ludovico Ariosto (1474–1533) and Torquato Tasso (1544–1595); in France with the prose epics of François Rabelais (1494–1553), *Gargantua* and *Pantagruel*; and in Germany with Luther's translation of the Bible, which went through 377 printings in his own lifetime. But the development of vernacular literature was particularly associated with the theater, the most popular of all art forms. The late sixteenth and seventeenth centuries were a golden age of theater in England, France, Spain, and the Netherlands, unrivaled from the time of ancient Greece and unequaled since.

The first of these national theaters was the English, where licensed companies of actors appeared from 1574. Two years later James Burbage built the first public theater in London, a roofless wooden amphitheater similar to the open spaces in inns and bull- and bear-baiting arenas. Large enclosed theaters were built in the 1590s, of which the most famous were the Swan (1596) and the Globe (1599), which boasted seating capacities of 3,000. The basic price of admission was a penny for "groundlings" or standees; a seat in the lower galleries cost 2 pence, one in the upper ones 3, and a private box, usually reserved for a nobleman, 6. The audience thus represented every element of Elizabethan society, and what it saw was the reflection of its own world, from cobblers to kings: Thomas Dekker's *Shoemaker's Holiday* (1599) depicted an upwardly mobile craftsman who becomes Lord Mayor of London; Thomas Middleton's *Chaste Maid in Cheapside* (1613), a goldsmith; Ben Jonson's *Bartholomew Fair* (1614), Puritans and pickpockets. Well might the greatest of these playwrights, William Shakespeare (1564–1616), whose imaginative world was perhaps larger than that of any person who ever lived, boastfully declare:

> *All the world's a stage,*
> *And all the men and women merely players.*
> *They have their exits and entrances,*
> *And one man in his time plays many parts.*[6]

The English stage exhibited not only great variety but also astonishing boldness and freedom. Topical and political satire abounded. Jonson was in trouble early in the reign of James I for attacking the vices and corruption of the court, as was Middleton later on for a thinly veiled attack on the king's foreign policy. Shakespeare himself was paid to perform *Richard II*, his play about the fall of the fourteenth-century English tyrant, on the eve of the earl of Essex's rebellion against Queen Elizabeth in 1600. Actors, authors, and producers were often just a step ahead of the censor, until at last the Puritans, so often the butt of the London stage, closed it down at the outbreak of the English civil war in 1642.

Civic theater also flourished in the Netherlands, where it produced a major figure in Joost van den Vondel (1587–1679), a committed republican who protested against the rigidities of Dutch Calvinism. The playwrights of the Spanish school—Lope de Vega (1562–1635), Tirso de Molina (1571–1648), and Pedro Calderón de la Barca (1600–1681)—were immensely prolific; Lope claimed to have written over 1,500 plays, and the titles of nearly 1,000 survive. Performances were held outdoors in the public square, with seats arranged around the stage and rooms rented in private houses to provide the equivalent of boxes for noblemen and ladies. Male and female spectators were strictly segregated, and though the monarchy was often the subject of the Spanish theater, it was considered improper for the king and queen to attend. The French theater of Pierre Corneille (1606–1684) and Jean Racine (1639–1699), in contrast, was court-sponsored and reflected its patronage in its choice of classical themes, its emphasis on honor and the renunciation of the passions, and its formal, chiseled verse line. But the French produced their comic genius too in Jean-Baptiste Poquelin, called Molière (1622–1673), who mocked the social pretensions of his own bourgeois class, although he stopped carefully short of satirizing his aristocratic audiences.

The seventeenth century saw the entry of women into literature for the first time, particularly in France. Women writers of note, such as Christine de Pisan, Marguerite of Navarre, and the English mystic Juliana of Norwich, had occasionally emerged before, as had even the stirrings of a feminist literature in Elizabethan England, but not until the accession of the Bourbon dynasty in France did women begin to occupy an important place in literature and literary life. Madeleine de Scudéry (1607–1701) created a new genre with her *Grand Cyrus* (1649–1653), a historical romance that portrayed the protagonists of the Fronde in the fictional guise of ancient Persians. Similarly, Marie de Sévigné (1626–1696) established letter writing as a literary art; her volumes of correspondence, ranging in their description from court life at Versailles to peasant rebellion, are the most rounded portrait we possess of life in the age of Louis XIV. No less important to the emerging cultural prominence of women was the literary salon, pioneered by the elegant Catherine de Rambouillet (1588–1665), at whose private gatherings aspiring writers came to establish their reputations. Even so, however, literature was not yet a respectable pursuit for women; Scudéry's *Grand Cyrus*, certainly the most popular and influential French novel of its time, was published under the name of her brother George, a mediocre playwright.

The last of the great epic poets was the Englishman John Milton (1608–1674), a lonely figure despite his service in the revolutionary regimes of the 1650s. Milton's *Paradise Lost* (1667), a poem not surpassed since in any language for its breadth and ambition, looked back to the model of Dante in its account of the fall of Adam and Eve, although its powerful portrayal of the character of Satan anticipates the rebellious Romantic hero of the nineteenth century. A new medium for narrative had begun to emerge, one that would dominate the literature of the West as it had the literature of China: the novel. The rambling adventure tales of Rabelais had anticipated the form in the sixteenth century, but the first true European example is Miguel de Cervantes' *Don Quixote* (1605). Cervantes intended to satirize the chivalric tales still popular in his native Spain, but he

accomplished much more. His two wandering heroes, the idealistic nobleman Don Quixote and his worldly but faithful servant, Sancho Panza, are not mere stock figures on which a tale of adventures can be strung but living, individual characters whose success arises from their vivid contrast of temperament. The English drama was accomplishing much the same thing at the same time, but 100 years were to pass before anyone was able to capture the necessary balance of character and plot again in prose. With Daniel Defoe's enormously popular *Robinson Crusoe* (1719), however, a story not for the old world of chivalry but for the new one of capital formation and commercial enterprise, the age of the novel had begun.

The Age of the Baroque

The origin of the term *baroque* is obscure, but it may come from the Portuguese *barroco*, an irregularly shaped pearl. It has come to define the very distinctive art of the seventeenth century, though originally, like the adjective *Gothic*, it was a term of derision. Certainly, to those whose ideal was the serene beauty of a Raphael or the monumentality of a Michelangelo, the dramatic, swirling lines of baroque architecture and the darkened palette of baroque painting, with its abrupt contrasts of light and shadow and the brooding intensity of its portraits, could not but seem strained, distorted, and profoundly disturbing. Yet the baroque, like every major art style, had complex and subtle affinities to the wider culture of the age. In its restless, probing, and essentially theatrical nature, it reflected a period of conflict, exploration, and doubt, while in its bold redefinition of space it suggests a response to the vision of Copernicus, Bruno, and Galileo.

The baroque originated as a style in Italy. Its first patrons were the Jesuits, and Gesù, the church of the order in Rome, is commonly accepted as the first full-fledged example of baroque architecture. Certainly the sense of spiritual quest and renewal emphasized by the Jesuits can be seen in such works as the *St. Theresa in Ecstasy* of Gianlorenzo Bernini (1598–1680) or the somber ecclesiastical portraits of Francisco de Zurbarán (1598–1664), but the baroque soon stepped across national and religious frontiers. The spiritual and the sensual, moreover, often blended into one another, as Bernini's *St. Theresa* vividly illustrates, or settled down happily side by side, as in the fleshily exuberant biblical scenes of the Flemish painter Peter Paul Rubens (1577–1640).

Dutch painters carried the new chiaroscuro style of the Italian Michelangelo Merisi, called Caravaggio (1573–1610), back from Rome. Caravaggio's work, with its dramatic interior lighting, often from no visible source, was soon reflected in the work of artists all over Europe, including Diego Velázquez (1599–1660) in Spain and George de la Tour (1593–1652) in France, but it found its apotheosis in the Dutch Mennonite artist Rembrandt van Rijn (1606–1669). Rembrandt was the greatest of a remarkable series of painters who captured the variety and vitality of seventeenth-century Dutch society, leaving an unmatched record of the everyday life of their time. Rembrandt's own work reveals this same curiosity about the unusual and even (by classical standards) the bizarre, as in his *Anatomy Lesson of Dr. Tulp* (1632), in which an anatomist dissects the cadaver of an executed criminal before the Surgeons' Guild of Amsterdam. But his genius was too impatient for the landscape and genre scenes preferred by his contemporaries; as his drawings reveal, he could capture the essence of a landscape more surely in a few quick strokes of brush or pen than most of them in elaborate and painstaking canvases. He spent his own immense gifts of color and composition on individual portraits, including a series of self-portraits that, begun in a vigorous and commercially successful youth, continued up to the year of his death when, unfashionable and destitute, he painted largely for himself alone. In Rembrandt's portraits, something of what Spinoza may have meant by the "soul that lives in all things" is visible, for no other artist has ever revealed so much of our common humanity.

The music of the baroque, like its art and architecture, tended toward the dramatic. Sung texts and spoken words had largely existed apart before Claudio Monteverdi (1567–1643), who fused them into a new theatrical form, the opera. By the 1630s Italian opera had become a lavish spectacle; Cardinal Barberini sponsored one performance at his palace in Rome before an audience of 3,500, with stage designs by Bernini. Much of seventeenth-century music remained dominated by Italian models, particularly in the secular forms of the oratorio, the cantata, and the concerto. In Germany the tradition of church music introduced by the hymns of Martin Luther produced a series of important composers, including Heinrich Schütz (1585–1672). Later baroque music developed in the direction of elaborate ornamentation and contrapuntal complexity, reaching its climax in Johann Sebastian Bach (1685–1750), in whom the Lutheran tradition achieved a universality that, like the art of Rembrandt, reaches across all ages and cultures.

The state gradually superseded the Catholic church in the role of patron of baroque art. Rubens was commissioned to paint a series of allegorical portraits glorifying Marie de' Medici of France and her husband, Henry IV, and he was also employed (with his younger colleague Anthony Van Dyck) in making equestrian portraits of the ill-fated Charles I of England, who took the extraordinary step of knighting Van Dyck for his services. It was Louis XIV, however, who saw most clearly the possibilities of bringing art to the service of the state. In Versailles the dramatic, heaven-storming qualities of baroque art (suitably refined by French taste) and the pomp of divine right monarchy came together in an image of absolute secular power. Other rulers rushed to follow his example—Leopold I in Austria, Charles XII in Sweden, Peter the Great in Russia, Frederick the Great in Prussia, Augustus the Strong in Saxony, and a host of lesser princelings, neither great nor strong, who felt that no reign could be complete without a palace to attest to its *gloire*.

ROME: THE REBIRTH OF A CAPITAL

Rome, for most of the population of Europe still the center of Christendom, recovered slowly from the sack of 1527 and the subsequent Spanish occupation. With the new energies of the Counter-Reformation, however, the city began to revive. Work on St. Peter's Basilica, still without a façade or a dome, was the first order of priority. Pope Sixtus V, working men around the clock for 22 months, finished Michelangelo's dome in 1590. The architect Carlo Maderna (1556–1629) designed the new façade, and Bernini spent nearly a decade (1657–1666) completing the great colonnaded square in front. Maderna departed radically from Michelangelo's original designs, widening and opening the central nave and replacing Michelangelo's façade with columns whose variable spacing produced a fluid effect. Bernini's undulating columns in the nave and his daringly open square—the first such space in any European city—completed with baroque exuberance and novelty the great edifice that had been begun in the High Renaissance. In no other building is the contrast between the aims and aspirations of the two epochs more strikingly visible.

With St. Peter's in progress, Popes Paul V (1605–1621) and Urban VIII (1623–1644) undertook the reconstruction and beautification of Rome, giving it the squares and fountains—many designed by the ubiquitous Bernini—that still distinguish it today. With these came new churches as well, notably Bernini's San Andrea al Quirinale (1658–1670) and Francesco Borromini's San Carlo alle Quattro Fontane (1638–1641), whose interior represents the first completely undulating wall space since the reign of the Roman emperor Hadrian. In Borromini (1599–1666), the greatest Italian architect of the century, the flowing space of the baroque—like the post-Copernican universe, itself never defined by any single perspective—achieves its most characteristic form.

By the early eighteenth century the rebuilt city had

The revival of Rome was marked by completion of the colonnaded square of St. Peter's, the masterpiece of the greatest architect and sculptor of the baroque, Gianlorenzo Bernini. St. Peter's Church, seat of the Vatican, is at the left rear. [Granger Collection]

become a major tourist attraction for Protestants and Catholics alike, an obligatory stop on the grand tour by which elegant young ladies and gentlemen put the finishing touches to their education. One such traveler, the French magistrate Charles de Brosses, declared that Rome was "the most beautiful city in the world" and St. Peter's "the finest thing in the universe." Like a jewel's, the church's facets were endlessly fascinating: "You might come to it every day without being bored. . . . It is more amazing the oftener you see it." Most impressive of all, he thought, were the fountains and firework displays that played constantly and gave the city an air of perpetual festivity. This impression was not far from wrong, as Rome celebrated no fewer than 150 holidays a year, not to mention occasional pageants, local processions and fairs, and weekly summer festivals that included water jousts and mock sea battles in the flooded Piazza Navona.

Rome's population grew steadily during this period, from approximately 80,000 in 1563 to 118,356 in the census of 1621 to about 150,000 by 1709. This included some 8,000 priests, monks, nuns, and other religious who staffed the almost 400 churches of Rome and a nearly equal number of monasteries, convents, and seminaries. The papacy dominated the political and economic life of Rome just as the dome and square of St. Peter's did its skyline. It governed the city as the capital of the so-called Papal States, a band of territories that stretched across the middle of Italy, and was far and away its chief employer, dispensing charity and relief as well to the poor. What the papacy did not provide directly it did indirectly, in the services that were needed for the hordes of pilgrims, estimated at 100,000 per year in 1700, that formed the bulk of the tourist trade. The result was that Rome's was almost entirely a service economy, living on papal wealth and foreign income. Life was casual if not indolent; even at the Vatican, washing was hung out to dry from the windows. At the bottom of the social scale, Rome's easygoing ways tailed off into squalor, and its poor, favored at least by the climate, spent as little time

The restless, aspiring spirit of the baroque is well illustrated in the detail of the curving façade of Borromini's church of San Carlo at the Four Fountains in Rome. Massive but supple form and a dramatic use of interior space characterized the architecture of the baroque. [Wim Swann]

as possible in their wretched hovels. The very openness of life acted as a safety valve for discontent; there was always distraction in the street, even for the most extreme misery, and, in a city full of wealthy strangers, always opportunity as well.

One group that stood apart from the ministrations of the church was the Jewish community. Yet it, too, was noted in the papacy's ubiquitous accounts, and when Paul V planned his new fountains for Rome, one was duly provided for the city's synagogue. A more curious and less benevolent example of Rome's uneasy relationship with its Jews was in the ceremony that opened the Roman Carnival, the eight-day pre-Lenten celebration that was the most elaborate and tumultuous holiday of the year. The Jews were taxed the cost of the prize money for the horse races and, assembled as a group, were thanked for their "gift" to the city by a pretended kick in the small of the chief rabbi's back.

The seventeenth century has rightly been called the century of genius. Shakespeare, Milton, Cervantes, Rembrandt—these men shaped the image of humankind in the West and still stand at the frontier of its cultural heritage, their works undimmed by time. Bacon, Hobbes, Descartes, Pascal, and Spinoza shaped the modern quest for knowledge, and the questions they posed, about humankind and the cosmos, about freedom and government, are still alive today. Copernicus, Kepler, Galileo, Newton, and many others of lesser ability created the scientific revolution and with it transformed humankind's capacity to know, to create, and to destroy.

The effects of the changed intellectual climate were visible by the end of the century. The triumph of the mechanistic vision of nature over Aristotelian physics and cosmology and the rival tradition of Hermetic natural magic had a decisive influence on popular superstition as well as educated thought. The beginning of the century had seen the last upsurge in witchcraft persecution, affecting some 100,000 persons between 1580 and 1650. By the end of the century belief in witchcraft itself was largely extinct, and

faith in astrology and magic healing had declined sharply. The view of the cosmos as a web of hidden affinities and powers on which such beliefs depended was no longer credible, and so they silently faded away.

The cultural shock that greeted humanity's dethronement from its position at the center of the universe gradually gave way to a new pride in the power of human knowledge. Until the nineteenth century the scientific revolution had little practical consequence, and few of the technological advances of the 1700s owed themselves to the abstruse physics of Newton. Nonetheless, the new science came to symbolize faith in the improvement of the human condition, a faith that for some in the eighteenth century took on the quality of religious conviction itself. At the same time, the mathematized God of Newton and Descartes was gradually detached from science. For them, God had still been the ultimate guarantor of the truth of their universe. A century later, asked why he had omitted God from his system, the French astronomer Pierre Simon de Laplace (1749–1827) would answer coolly, "I have no need of that hypothesis."

Notes

1. T. S. Kuhn, The *Copernican Revolution* (Cambridge, Mass.: Harvard University Press, 1957), p. 128.
2. H. F. Kearney, *Science and Change, 1500–1700* (New York: McGraw-Hill, 1971), p. 101.
3. A. R. Hall, *The Scientific Revolution, 1500–1800* (Boston: Beacon Press, 1956), p. 132.
4. Martha Ornstein, *The Rôle of Scientific Societies in the Seventeenth Century* (Chicago: University of Chicago Press, 1938), p. 95.
5. *The Chief Works of Benedict de Spinoza*, ed. R. H. M. Elwes (London: G. Bell, 1917, 1919), vol. 2, p. 263.
6. *As You Like It*, act 2, scene 7.

Suggestions for Further Reading

Butterfield, H. *The Origins of Modern Science*. New York: Macmillan, 1957.
Cohen, I. B. *The Birth of a New Physics*. New York: Norton, 1985.
Feuer, L. S. *Spinoza and the Rise of Liberalism*. Boston: Beacon Press, 1966.
Friedrich, C. J. *The Age of the Baroque*. New York: Harper, 1952.
Gillespie, C. C. *The Edge of Objectivity: An Essay in the History of Scientific Ideas*. Princeton, N.J.: Princeton University Press, 1960.
Hall, A. R. *The Scientific Revolution, 1500–1800*. Boston: Beacon Press, 1956.
Jacob, M. C. *The Cultural Meaning of the Scientific Revolution*. New York: Knopf, 1988.
Kearney, H. F. *Science and Change, 1500–1700*. New York: McGraw-Hill, 1971.
Koyré, A. *From the Closed World to the Infinite Universe*. Baltimore: Johns Hopkins University Press, 1957.
Krautheimer, R. *The Rome of Alexander VII, 1655–1667*. Princeton, N.J.: Princeton University Press, 1985.
Kuhn, T. S. *The Structure of Scientific Revolutions*. Chicago: University of Chicago Press, 1970.
MacPherson, C. B. *The Political Theory of Possessive Individualism: Hobbes to Locke*. New York: Oxford University Press, 1964.
Mesnard, J. *Pascal, His Life and Works*. New York: Philosophical Library, 1952.
Nash, J. M. *The Age of Rembrandt and Vermeer: Dutch Painting in the Seventeenth Century*. New York: Holt, Rinehart and Winston, 1972.
Ornstein, M. *The Role of Scientific Societies in the Seventeenth Century*. Chicago: University of Chicago Press, 1928.
Palisca, C. V. *Baroque Music*. Englewood Cliffs, N.J.: Prentice Hall, 1981.
Popkin, R. *History of Skepticism from Erasmus to Spinoza*. Berkeley: University of California Press, 1979.
Santillana, G. de. *The Crime of Galileo*. London: Heinemann, 1958.
Spear, R. E. *Caravaggio and His Followers*. Cleveland, Ohio: Cleveland Museum of Art, 1971.
Strauss, L. *The Political Philosophy of Hobbes*. Chicago: University of Chicago Press, 1966.
Thomas, K. *Religion and the Decline of Magic*. New York: Scribner, 1971.
Warnke, F. J. *Versions of Baroque: European Literature in the Seventeenth Century*. New Haven, Conn.: Yale University Press, 1972.
Westfall, R. S. *Never at Rest: A Biography of Isaac Newton*. Cambridge: Cambridge University Press, 1980.
Wilson, M. D. *Descartes*. Boston: Routledge & Kegan Paul, 1978.
Yates, F. A. *Giordano Bruno and the Hermetic Tradition*. Chicago: University of Chicago Press, 1964.

PART · FOUR

Toward the Modern World

The modern world that came of age in the eighteenth century was marked by rapid and revolutionary change. In Europe a century of imperial expansion and development abroad and unprecedented social criticism at home was climaxed by the French Revolution, which at a stroke abolished feudal tenures and the hierarchy of orders in the Continent's most powerful state. The French Revolution paved the way for economic modernization and political centralization throughout Europe, the latter also assisted by the rising sentiment of nationalism. By the late nineteenth century the two largest territorial blocks in central Europe, Germany and Italy, had been unified politically for the first time since the Middle Ages, while the growing power of Russia, the protracted collapse of the Ottoman Empire, and the increasing demands for national independence among the minorities of the Austrian Empire had created an unstable zone of contending powers and client states. These complex power realignments, tied to imperial and commercial rivalry, resulted in a conflict of global magnitude, World War I.

While these changes were taking place, a far wider transformation of the human situation was under way. Beginning in the mid-eighteenth century, the population began to expand. At the same time, new sources of mechanized power exploiting steam, coal, and other natural elements were being devised in Britain, which, closely tied to the imperatives of capitalism and state power, produced the most significant development in human technology in 10,000 years, the Industrial Revolution. That process, like the population explosion, has now become a global phenomenon that continues to transform our material culture.

The advantage lent to Europe by its aggressive organization and superior technology was translated into global hegemony in the nineteenth century. European states claimed large portions of Africa and Asia as colonies, protectorates, or spheres of interest. The British completed a conquest of India begun in the mid-eighteenth century and fanned out to dominate much of Southeast Asia and the Middle East, creating the largest empire the world had ever known. China was forced to accept humiliating infringements of its economic and territorial sovereignty. Weakened by a civil war in the mid-nineteenth century that undermined the Manchu dynasty, it took the first painful steps toward modernization. Only two major states remained outside the European orbit: the United States, founded by rebellion in the late eighteenth century and, by the end of the nineteenth, the dominant force in the Western Hemisphere and the world's greatest industrial power, and Japan, which, startled from feudal isolation by the imperial challenge, rapidly transformed itself into the equal of any European state.

These changes in politics and technology were accompanied by far-reaching transformations of the social order. Slavery was formally abolished in Africa and the Americas, although other forms of labor coercion remained. In Europe and later in the Western Hemisphere the industrial working force began to organize in its own behalf under the banner of a new doctrine, socialism, which consciously opposed itself to the capitalist and imperialist order. The movement for gender equality known as women's liberation began in the industrial nations and spread rapidly across the globe. In Europe the Jews were emancipated after centuries of enforced isolation, and other minorities began to claim their rights to equality and free expression. By 1900 a majority of the population in the leading industrial nations lived in cities, creating a new and distinctive urban culture, and despite the continuing economic struggle of many, improvements in sanitation and health care had begun to increase the average life expectancy in developed countries. ■

Europe and the Americas

By the eighteenth century the economy of western Europe had become worldwide in scope. Large regional economies, integrated by trade patterns and dominated by strong states, had existed since ancient times. China had long been the center of such an economy in East Asia. The Indian Ocean and Red Sea area constituted another large system. In Europe itself, the Mediterranean had provided a natural focus of economic integration under the successive dominion of Egyptians, Phoenicians, Greeks, Romans, Arabs, Venetians, and, most recently, Spaniards.

But Spain had begun to decline in the seventeenth century, and by the early eighteenth the Mediterranean was dominated for the first time by a power not based geographically in the region, Britain. At the same time, the center of European gravity had shifted to the Atlantic states. Not only were Britain, France, and the Dutch

William Pitt the Elder, Britain's choleric but brilliant statesman and architect of its North American empire. A contemporary described him as "imperious, violent, . . . implacable, . . . despotic" yet also "a man of veracity and a man of honor." [National Portrait Gallery, London]

Netherlands the dominant economic powers of Europe, but their scattered overseas possessions, a source of persistent though relatively peripheral rivalry in the seventeenth century, became the focus of much more intense competition in the eighteenth. Those possessions, increasingly consolidated in political terms and increasingly valuable in economic ones, became themselves the springboard for further expansion and conquest. The slave trade directly linked four continents—Europe, Africa, and North and South America—in a complex and highly coordinated relationship. After 1750 India and to a lesser extent Indonesia were drawn more and more into the web of European-dominated exchange, and by the end of the century the British were knocking at the gates of China. As the importance of the world market grew, Britain and France clashed repeatedly for control of it. After three major cycles of warfare spread across 125 years, the British emerged victorious, though shorn of what had been their largest New World colony, the newly independent United States of America.

The Old Colonial System

The new global economy consolidated by Europe in the eighteenth century had its roots as far back as the crusades, when the potential for profit in overseas trade first became apparent. This economy was based on the establishment of colonies, used both as forward bases for trade, exploration, or further conquest and as passive markets and sources of raw materials. The crusader colonies in Palestine, Cyprus, and Greece were prototypes of the later and much larger Spanish, Portuguese, Dutch, and English colonies in the New World, Africa, and Asia. A second type of colony, developed by the Genoese in the fourteenth century, was based on control by a private trading company operating under a government charter. The English and Dutch East India companies, founded in 1600 and 1602, respectively, administered large territories under such arrangements, as did the Virginia and Massachusetts Bay companies on the Atlantic seaboard of North America. Yet a third type of colony was based on an agreement between individuals for the settlement of a territory; the Mayflower Compact was an example.

The nature of a given colonial enterprise depended on the territory to be settled and the general approach of the colonizing center, or "metropolis." In the New World tiny bands of adventurers such as those commanded by Cortés in Mexico and Pizarro in Peru, exploiting native rivalries, were able to conquer vast areas through mobile tactics, skillful use of Indian auxiliaries, and technological superiority. The urban civilizations of the Aztecs in Mexico and the Inca in Peru were in many

respects the equal of Europe's, but their weapons were those of the Stone Age. Elsewhere in the Americas, Europeans confronted only scattered tribes, which were quickly exterminated, enslaved, or driven into wilderness areas.

The peoples of Africa were nearly as vulnerable to European penetration as those of the Americas. The Portuguese established their influence along the Congo and Zambesi rivers in the early sixteenth century, but the unattractiveness of the climate for Europeans deterred large-scale settlement except at the Cape of Good Hope on the southern tip of the continent, where Dutch colonists arrived in the seventeenth century. For the most part, Europeans were content to barter for slaves, gold dust, and ivory with African middlemen, and apart from establishing coastal bases for commerce they made little attempt to explore the continent.

In Asia, where Europeans possessed no significant technical or military advantage except in ship design, conquest and hence colonization were out of the question. Here the Portuguese and the Dutch competed with Asian and Arab merchants for a share of the lucrative spice trade, often financed by piracy. At the beginning of the eighteenth century, however, the European presence in Asia was still marginal.

Spain and the New World

Spain ruled its colonies in the New World through its Council of the Indies, although its powers were gradually dispersed among other ministries in the eighteenth century. With the immense bureaucratic patience typical of the Spanish Old Regime, it attempted—for the first time in Europe in 1,000 years—to govern a territory and population far exceeding its own, a challenge compounded by the distance of several thousand miles of ocean. From Madrid it sent out an endless stream of edicts covering the minutest details of colonial life; by 1700 over 400,000 of these were still technically in force, and a digest of the most important ones contained 11,000 laws.

To ensure conformity with its regulations, the council relied on the *residencia*, a review of all senior colonial officials at the end of their service, and the *visita*, irregular inspections that might produce temporary improvements but more often, as one viceroy put it, did little more than raise the dust on the streets. The empire was formally divided into the viceroyalties of New Spain and Peru, the former encompassing Mexico and most of the western two-thirds of the present-day United States. In addition, there were three captaincies general, Santo Domingo, Guatemala, and New Granada, the last of which, centered in what is now Colombia, became a viceroyalty in 1739. The viceroyalties were divided into provinces, but the basic unit of administration, as in Spain itself, centered on the municipality, governed by an official usually called the corregidor. The corregidor was the backbone of the colonial system, and the day-to-day lives of most of the population depended on his performance.

The primary purpose of the empire was the exploitation of its wealth. This required the mobilization of its inhabitants. In the early years of the sixteenth century the Spaniards enslaved the island populations of the Caribbean and worked them literally to extinction in the gold mines; by midcentury the population of Hispaniola had been reduced from several hundred thousand to a few hundred. The inhabitants of Cuba and Puerto Rico suffered a similar fate, while smaller islands, which the Spanish did not bother to settle, were stripped of their populations by raiding parties. Reports of these atrocities, and the complaints of Spanish priests that the native population was dying off before it could be converted to Christianity, prompted the Spanish government to issue an edict regarding its treatment:

> **Because of the excessive liberty the Indians have been permitted, they flee from Christians and do not work. Therefore they are to be compelled to work, so that the kingdom and the Spaniards be enriched, and the Indians Christianized. They are to be paid a daily wage and well treated as free persons, for such they are, and not slaves.[1]**

These instructions had no discernible effect on the extermination of the Caribbean Indians. In Mexico labor was at first directly enslaved. This was modified by the introduction of the *encomienda,* a type of manorial system whereby Spanish settlers were given responsibility for protecting and "civilizing" native communities in return for their labor. As mining developed in Mexico and particularly in Peru, the system proved inadequate to the demands for a mobile labor force that could be transported from site to site and was supplemented by a conscript system, the *repartimiento,* in which Indian community chiefs were required to provide a stipulated amount of labor to the authorities, who distributed the workers to Spanish contractors. Nominal wages were paid, but they were so low that they were often a mere pretext to force Indian workers into debt and peonage. Although conditions varied from region to region with the requirement of a work force (being worst where economic activity was most intense), the *repartimiento* tended to become indistinguishable from forced labor. In its brutally efficient regimentation of labor, it became the prototype of colonial capitalism, and its techniques eventually found their way home to the metropolis with the advent of the Industrial Revolution.

Gold and silver brought Europeans to the Americas in the sixteenth century. The great silver mountain at Potosí, in Bolivia, 10,000 feet above sea level, gave rise

◉ Conscript Labor in Spanish Mexico ◉

A seventeenth-century Spanish commentator, Antónío Vásquez de Espinosa, describes the operation of a textile mill in the city of Puebla.

There are in this city large woolen mills in which they weave quantities of fine cloth, serge, and grogram, from which they make handsome profits. . . . To keep their mills supplied with labor . . . [the operators] maintain individuals who are engaged and hired to ensnare poor innocents. Seeing some Indian who is a stranger to the town, with some trickery or pretext, such as hiring him to carry something, like a porter, and paying him cash, they get him into the mill. Once inside, they drop the deception, and the poor fellow never again gets outside that prison until he dies and they carry him out for burial. In this way they have gathered in and duped many married Indians with families, who have passed into oblivion here for 20 years, or longer, or their whole lives, without their wives and children knowing anything about them. . . . And although the Royal Council of the Indies . . . has tried to remedy this evil with warrants and ordinances . . . and the Viceroy of New Spain appoints mill inspectors to visit [the Indians] and remedy such matters, nevertheless, since most of those who set out on such commissions aim rather at their own enrichment . . . and since the mill owners pay them well, they leave the wretched Indians in the same slavery . . . as if it were not a most serious mortal sin.

Source: A. V. de Espinosa, *Compendium and Description of the West Indies* (Washington, D.C.: Smithsonian Institution, 1942), pp. 133–134.

to a city whose population eventually reached 160,000, rivaling at one point the size of London and exceeding that of Madrid, Paris, and Rome. Its 36 churches, with their splendid baroque ornamentation, were matched by 36 gambling casinos, no less grandly adorned. Its mines consumed the lives of an estimated 8 million Indian workers before they gave out.

Gold and the Expansion of the European Economy

The importation of massive quantities of precious metals, ferried home by an annual treasure fleet, had a profound effect on the European economy. The Mediterranean region, whose weak bullion base had been further eroded by the decline of imports from its previous supplier, the Sudan, suddenly burgeoned. From Seville to Antwerp, the ports of western Europe teemed with new shipping and trade, presaging the great shift of power to the Atlantic economies that occurred within the next two centuries. Transatlantic trade multiplied

A woman weighing gold looks pensive in this painting by Rembrandt. Gold was vital to commercial and industrial expansion in early modern Europe and the chief spur to exploration and colonization in the Americas. [Marburg/Art Resource]

eightfold between 1510 and 1550 and tripled again between 1550 and 1610. Through trade and smuggling, a considerable quantity of the new bullion found its way to Asia and the Levant, and at one time a direct transpacific trade developed between Acapulco and Manila in the Philippines. Gold and silver from the New World created a network of worldwide commerce on a scale and of a complexity never seen before.

The gradual exhaustion of the mines of Mexico and Peru brought this first, precocious global economy to an end. Asia had no interest in Western goods comparable to the European demand for silks and spices, which therefore had to be paid for almost entirely in bullion. As new supplies tapered off, the Asian trade dwindled. At about the same time, the European economy, so powerfully stimulated by the influx of precious metals, began to contract. European states blamed the prolonged depression that set in between 1619 and 1622 on their shrinking bullion reserves, although this was only one factor in a complex process of overproduction, diminished population growth, and a long-term pattern of severer climate. The anxiety of states to protect their bullion supplies led to import restrictions, thus hindering trade and deepening the slump. This in turn heightened the tensions surrounding the Thirty Years' War, which itself produced ruin in much of Europe.

Merchant Capitalism and the Growth of the State

Nonetheless, the great sixteenth-century boom had permanent effects. The sharp rise in profits and prices enriched the merchant bourgeoisie, whose new political importance was clearly manifested in Britain, France, and the Netherlands. The value of estates and rents tended to fall, thus putting pressure on the landed nobility. In eastern Europe the demand for foodstuffs and raw materials to stoke the expanding Atlantic economies stimulated the enserfment of scarce peasant labor, an apparently backward step that was, like the regimentation of Indian labor in the Americas, in significant part a response to growth in the core economies of the West. The results of this were profound. The peasant population was immobilized, which stunted urban growth and confirmed the power of the landed nobility at a time when it was under challenge in the West. From the sixteenth century onward, the development of eastern and western Europe increasingly diverged; their twentieth-century political and economic divisions were a consequence.

The growth of the economy was linked to that of the

state. The expansion of the latter was most visible in palace building and the development of a court-based culture, which reached their climax in the Versailles of Louis XIV. These self-conscious displays of power were accompanied by a proliferation of state offices and the gradual transformation of royal attendants serving the king's pleasure into bureaucratic functionaries performing regular and prescribed duties. At the same time, the state took a greater interest in economic development, which provided it with a larger tax base. The fiscal demands of the state stimulated the growth of banking and credit, and these in turn expanded the state's capacities further.

The development of merchant capitalism and of centralized political authority was thus reciprocal. The establishment of centralized authority was essential to peaceful commerce at home and the protection of colonial ventures abroad. Often, as in the development of the silk and glass industries in France or of mining in Austria and Hungary, the state allied itself directly with business interests, and the entire process of exploration and colonization in the sixteenth century may be considered a partnership between the state and private entrepreneurs in which the state provided venture capital in return for a fixed share of the profits. War itself took on a more overtly commercial tone as states fought over trade routes, commercial privileges, and control of profitable or potentially profitable territories.

This did not mean that the interests of rulers and merchants were necessarily harmonious. Their partnership was always an uneasy one, and by the eighteenth century some merchants felt that the state had become unduly restrictive and even oppressive, hampering rather than fostering economic development with its rigid controls and regulations. On balance, however, the state and merchant capitalism were mutually supportive during the first stages of global economic growth in the West. If the merchant bourgeoisie had developed to the point where state intervention was perceived as a handicap, it was only because state power had nurtured it to the point of self-generating growth.

The Economy of the Americas

The principal economic activity of Spanish America, even in the headiest days of gold and silver production, was agriculture. Spanish colonial society quickly reproduced the patterns of the home country, with large estates worked by native labor. The government made land grants of immense size as a means of encouraging new settlements, and great cattle herds pushed the frontiers of New Spain beyond Mexico into what is now the southwestern United States. The Spaniards supplemented the native crops of maize, beans, and squash with wheat and a variety of fruits. Sugar was grown from early on in the Caribbean islands and on the Mexican lowlands, and olive and vine culture was successfully established in Peru. Cortés, seeking a profitable crop, introduced the silkworm into Mexico in 1523. The most successful export over the next three centuries of Spanish dominance in America, however, was cochineal, a red dye made from insects.

In Portuguese Brazil, where no precious metals were discovered until 1690 and the native population was inadequate as a labor force, a plantation society quickly developed based on sugar, tobacco, cocoa, and cotton, employing black slave labor. This pattern was repeated by the British, French, and Dutch in the Caribbean and the southern colonies of North America, where similar climatic and demographic conditions prevailed. Farther up the North American coast and along the rivers of the interior, notably the Mississippi and the St. Lawrence, a settler society developed in the absence of readily exploitable labor or natural resources. The most populous of these settlements were the British colonies along the Atlantic seaboard, although the most far-flung geographically was the long arc of French trading stations and fortifications that extended from the Gulf of Mexico to Hudson's Bay. The principal Dutch base on the North American mainland was New Amsterdam, at the mouth of the Hudson River. From here the Dutch conducted a lucrative fur trade and an even more profitable smuggling operation until the settlement was conquered by the British in 1664, who renamed it New York.

The Settlement of North America

British settlement in North America proceeded fitfully. After several false starts, a small colony was established at Jamestown on the Potomac River in 1607. By 1733 the number had grown to 13 colonies along the coast and the adjacent river valleys from New England to Georgia. The northernmost of these colonies, particularly Massachusetts, Rhode Island, and Connecticut, were essentially subsistence economies of slight value to the mother country. They served, together with the Quaker colony of Pennsylvania, primarily as a dumping ground for religious and political dissidents, some 20,000 of whom migrated to New England between 1629 and 1642 in the wave of repression that preceded the English revolution. In the Middle Atlantic and southern plantation colonies, indigents and convicts (frequently transported as an alternative to hanging) joined religious exiles as settlers, together, of course, with imported slave labor.

Since Britain's mainland colonies were at first perceived largely as a safety valve for excess population or unwanted social groups, the crown exerted relatively little control over them. The French, in contrast, never thought of allowing their colonies to be peopled by paupers, felons, and dissidents. Great efforts were made to procure suitable migrants, down to the provision of tools, seed, stock, and even free passage to Canada for women willing to marry settlers. The crown first subsidized and controlled the companies formed to plant settlements and then, under Jean-Baptiste Colbert, relieved them of all administrative responsibility, placing each colony under a military governor. Nonetheless, the combined French and British presence in the New World in the seventeenth century was only a fraction of Spain's in size, population, and wealth—and that in spite of the loss in Spanish America, mostly to epidemic disease, of some nine-tenths of its preconquest population of 20 million or more, in one of the greatest demographic extinctions in history. It was not, however, the vast expanses of the North American continent that were to make the New World profitable for Britain and France in the late seventeenth and early eighteenth centuries but the small sugar-producing islands of the Caribbean.

Sugar and Slavery

Sugar had been grown in the New World almost from the beginning of European colonization. As early as the 1510s sugar cultivation had been introduced into the Caribbean islands, where it was harvested by black slaves imported from Africa to replace an Amerindian population already decimated by white settlers. The Portuguese were the first to introduce sugar on a relatively large scale in Brazil, where some 60 mills were in op-

The phases of sugar harvesting and processing are shown here in a print representing a plantation in the West Indies. At right, raw cane is being brought in from the fields: it is crushed in a roller mill, mixed with lime and egg white, and left to crystallize. The profitability of sugar—and of the slave trade that supplied the labor it demanded—resulted in one of the greatest forced migrations in history. [Bettmann Archive]

eration by 1580. Most of the export trade was carried on by Dutch merchants, one of whose spokesmen, Willem de Usselincx, farsightedly pointed out that plantation crops such as sugar had a far greater long-range profit potential than the Spanish bullion that so dazzled his contemporaries. The Dutch themselves were driven out of Brazil by 1654, but their role in spreading the sugar trade in the West Indies by means of shipping and selling the product, introducing the processes that turned brown sugar into the much more popular white variety, and supplying African slaves, was crucial.

The replacement of the Dutch as middlemen and their defeat as competitors marked the coming of age of the British and French imperial systems. The British moved swiftly to consolidate control of their colonial trade. The Navigation Acts of 1651 and 1660 provided that colonies could trade certain "enumerated" products—sugar, tobacco, cotton, indigo, ginger, and dyewoods—only with the mother country or other British colonies and only on British ships. In return they were to accept manufactured goods from Britain. This closed system of trade exemplified the economic theory of mer-

cantilism, which sought to enhance the wealth of the mother country by acquiring a captive source of supply for its commodity needs and a compulsory outlet for its manufactures. The French were never able to develop a system as fully integrated as that of the British, partly because of the absence of a mainland population sufficient to promote intercolonial trade, but as commodity suppliers alone their major West Indian possessions—Guadeloupe and Martinique, settled in 1635, and Santo Domingo, acquired from Spain in 1697—had an increasing impact on the metropolitan economy.

Of all British and French colonial products, sugar was by far the most important. Its cultivation required not only suitable colonies but also a heavy investment in land and labor. Wealthy royalist exiles from the English civil wars provided this in the 1640s and 1650s, driving out poorer white settlers and consolidating their land into large plantations. By 1673 sugar production on tiny Barbados was one-quarter that of Brazil's, and by 1700 the economic value of the West Indian islands exceeded that of all the mainland colonies combined. Jamaica, acquired by Britain in 1655, did not develop into a major

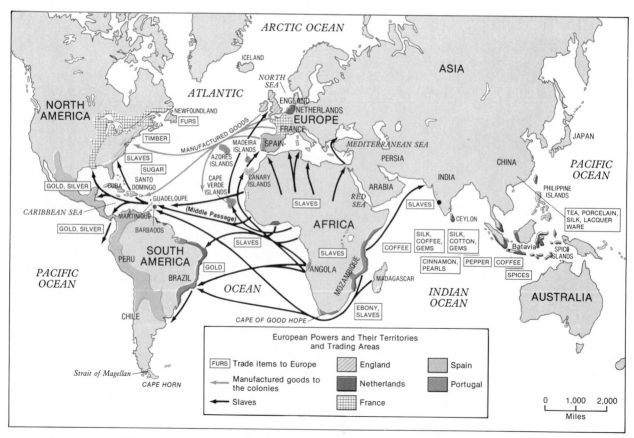

25.1 *Overseas Trade in the Seventeenth and Eighteenth Centuries*

supplier until the early eighteenth century, but by 1770 it was producing half of all British sugar and was incontestably the single most valuable colonial territory in the New World. Despite some price fluctuation, the demand for sugar remained extraordinarily high for well over a century, particularly in Britain itself, where per capita consumption was eight times that in France. Overall, the production of sugar in the Americas rose from 20,000 tons per year in 1600 to 200,000 tons on the eve of the American Revolution.

The Slave System

The labor required for sugar cultivation on this scale could have come only from slaves, and as the pace of importation quickened, the free white population of the West Indies fell dramatically; some 30,000 whites left Barbados alone between 1650 and 1680. Seen in this perspective, the "settlement" of the New World in the seventeenth, eighteenth, and much of the nineteenth century was overwhelmingly by African blacks. A million blacks had been imported into the Americas by 1700, and 6 million more arrived in the course of the eighteenth century, a number nearly equaling both the partly recovered Amerindian population and that of white settlers combined. Half of this number was funneled into the West Indies alone, where the permanent British and French population was less than 100,000. Yet despite the 3 million black men, women, and children who entered the Caribbean during this period, the net population increase was only 700,000. The vast majority of slaves perished within ten years of arrival. In part this may be accounted for by disease, the major factor in the destruction of the native population in the sixteenth century. But the primary reason was exploitation: blacks were systematically worked to death.

At first glance this appears difficult to explain. Slaves were an expensive investment; they accounted for 90 percent of the capital value of Jamaican plantations in the eighteenth century, exclusive of land. Nonetheless, in the calculus of profit, they were expendable. It was cheaper to replace than to maintain them, which meant supporting those too young and too old to work.

The Slave Trade

The mechanism of replacement, the great wheel that turned all of eighteenth-century colonial commerce, was the slave trade. Slaving was a textbook example of what mercantilist economists called the "triangular trade." Ships from ports such as Liverpool or Nantes exchanged cheap textiles, gunpowder, or gin for slaves provided by native traders at stations on the West African coast. As new cargo, the slaves were transported to the West In-

dies. Allowing for a 15 to 20 percent mortality rate en route, the survivors would sell for approximately five times their original purchase price. The ships would then fill up with sugar and return home.

The transatlantic voyage, known euphemistically as the "middle passage," took two months. The slaves were segregated by sex and packed together below decks in chains, helpless amid vermin and rats. In fair weather they were exercised on deck, under the lash; when seas were rough, they were kept below with the portholes shut. The tensions of the voyage provoked insane acts of cruelty. The captain of one ship flogged a 10-month-old child with a cat-o'-nine-tails for refusing to eat, then plunged it into scalding water, tied it to a log, flogged it again to death, and forced its mother to throw it into the sea.

Once ashore, the slaves in Britain's Caribbean colonies possessed neither legal nor moral rights. A planter who flogged a 14-year-old girl to death was actually tried for murder in Jamaica but was acquitted on the ground that "it was impossible [that] a master could destroy his own property." The Spaniards had tried to justify their conquest of the Americas by the necessity to convert the heathen, but eighteenth-century missionaries were forbidden to proselytize among blacks, and one slave caught going to church in Grenada was given 24 lashes.

In assessing the mutual dependency of sugar and the slave trade and its overall economic impact, it would be a mistake to focus too narrowly on the calculations of the plantation owner, crucial though they were. Only by bringing profitable cargo into the New World on a large scale and a regular basis could the European sugar market be developed, since merchant fleets would not risk the journey across the Atlantic with empty hulls, and the sugar islands were hardly major consumers of manufactured products. Thus slaves were vital not only to the production of the tropical economy but also to its marketing process. If black mortality in the New World had not exceeded reproduction, a saturation level would have been reached, and the slave trade would have died. From this perspective, the sugar market could have been sustained only by genocide.

Much attention has been focused on the economic marginality of the slavers themselves. It is true that while the opportunity for great profit existed, the risk of great loss was also present, as on any long-distance voyage. The significance of the triangular trade itself, however, did not lie in the reliability of profit in any single component but in the profit-generating capacity of the whole. The existence of the trade meant a steady demand for shipping; the feeding and clothing of millions of slaves was a major stimulus to textiles and agriculture. The capital spinoff into the European economy was therefore of considerable importance, and it was with the mechanization of the textile industry, financed in part by the slave trade, that the Industrial Revolution began.

◉ A Slave's Experience ◉

Olaudah Equiano (c. 1745–1797), an Ibo born in eastern Nigeria, near Benin, was abducted into slavery at the age of 10. He survived a transatlantic crossing and a series of masters, eventually bought his own freedom, worked as a barber, a domestic servant, and a sailor, and in 1789 published, in English, a two-volume memoir of his life as a slave, from which these excerpts are taken.

The first object which saluted my eyes when I arrived on the coast was the sea, and a slave ship which was then riding at anchor and waiting for its cargo. These filled me with astonishment, which was soon converted into terror when I was carried on board. I was immediately handled and tossed up to see if I were sound by some of the crew, and I was now persuaded that I had gotten into a world of bad spirits and that they were going to kill me. Their complexions too differing so much from ours, their long hair and the language they spoke (which was very different from any I had ever heard) united to confirm me in this belief. . . . When I looked round the ship too and saw a large furnace or copper boiling and a multitude of black people of every description chained together, every one of their countenances expressing dejection and sorrow, I no longer doubted of my fate. . . .

The stench of the hold while we were on the coast was so intolerably loathsome that it was dangerous to remain there for any time, and some of us had been permitted to stay on the deck for the fresh air; but now that the whole ship's cargo were confined together it became absolutely pestilential. The closeness of the place and the heat of the climate, added to the number in the ship, which was so crowded that each had scarcely room to turn himself, almost suffocated us. This produced copious perspirations, so that the air soon became unfit for respiration from a variety of loathsome smells, and brought on a sickness among the slaves, of which many died. . . . This wretched situation was again aggravated by the galling of the chains, now become insupportable, and the filth of the tubs, into which the children often fell and were almost suffocated. The shrieks of the women and the groans of the dying rendered the whole a scene of horror almost inconceivable.

Source: P. Edwards, ed., *Equiano's Travels: His Autobiography* (New York: Praeger, 1967), pp. 25, 28–29.

❀ LIVERPOOL IN THE AGE OF SLAVERY

Even before industrialization, the influx of slave-generated wealth was very evident. Liverpool, an English coastal town on the Irish Sea with a population of barely 500 in the sixteenth century and only 28 streets in the late seventeenth, became the chief slave port of Europe, carrying at its height almost two-thirds of the British and nearly half of the total European slave trade. The town's rise to success was in part the result of the bankrupting of the London slave merchants in the financial crash of 1720. Enterprising Liverpudlians soon took over from them, taking advantage of the port's westerly location.

The profitable War of the Austrian Succession in the 1740s also enabled trade, in the words of a local merchant, "to spread her golden wings." By 1750 a flotilla of nearly 200 ships directly served the slave trade, and four years later a splendid new exchange opened on Castle Street—as if to emphasize the alliance of commerce and government, it also housed the town hall. No expense was spared as the town fathers sought to emulate the Greek columns and the imposing cupola of the Royal Exchange in London. A week of boat races, public breakfasts, and balls celebrated its opening. An observatory and an academy of arts came soon after, a regular stagecoach run to London, and in 1768 representation in Parliament, the ultimate mark of status.

Fourteen banks graced the town by midcentury as well, none with fewer than £200,000 in assets. Most banks were founded by the slave merchants, who also

Liverpool was the chief port of terminus for the sugar and slave trades, and it prospered accordingly. The corner of Tithebarn Street is shown, with the back of the town hall at the right. Behind the hall, space is being cleared for a new commercial exchange, in which project the man with the wheelbarrow is presumably employed. [Liverpool Public Library]

operated their own insurance companies, collected the excise, and guaranteed the municipal finances. They were, in fact, Liverpool. The city maintained its traditional trade with Ireland, chiefly in cattle, and it produced pottery, glassware, and salt. But these activities were dwarfed by the slave and sugar trade and gradually strangled by it. The banks, the warehouses, and the dockyards formed a commercial trinity that dominated the city's life as it did its skyline. Until 1772 it was also possible to see slaves in their iron collars being sold for domestic use at the city market, but in that year Lord Chief Justice Mansfield ruled in the court of King's Bench that no person could be subjected to slavery in Britain. Liverpool's slave market disappeared, but not its slave trade; it was to be 61 years before the slaves in Britain's colonies were likewise freed.

From Liverpool the prosperity produced by the slave and sugar trade spread visibly across the English landscape in the form of great country houses and the merchant mansions of London and Bath. As early as 1729 the pamphleteer Joshua Gee noted that "all the great increase in our treasure proceeds chiefly from the labor of negroes in the plantations." But conspicuous consumption by the rich was not the principal result of the commerce in human lives. The new wealth was to lay the ground for Britain's rise to world power.

From the sixteenth century on, the European economy had become significantly entwined for the first time with that of a region thousands of miles away that provided it with the means of capital expansion, first through the importation of bullion from Spanish America and later primarily through the trade in sugar and slaves. The importance of this new global economy was great. So, too, was its human cost. It destroyed by direct or indirect means much of the native population of two continents and substantially depleted that of a third.

The First Age of Global War

"It is a notorious fact that the history of colonial expansion is also the history of incessant warfare," the historian Walter Dorn observed.[2] The wars of the early modern period, particularly in what has sometimes been called the era of the second Hundred Years' War (1689–1815), were fought for a variety of reasons, including religion, dynastic rivalry, and positional advantage on the European continent. Increasingly, however, the major wars of Europe involved conflict in four overseas areas as well—North America, the West Indies, Africa, and India. By the time of the Seven Years' War (1756–1763) these external theaters had become more important than the European struggle itself.

The wars of Europe, then, were in part the effect of expansion, but they were a cause of it as well. The use of firearms and cannon in European warfare became decisive between 1460 and 1540, and during that time iron production rose by as much as 500 percent and copper by even more. The mechanization of war made it the monopoly of the state. As heavy field pieces replaced horses, armor, and crossbows as the major capital investment in warfare, private noblemen could no longer afford the personal armies that had been the hallmark (and often the bane) of the late medieval period. A modern arsenal containing furnaces, forges, foundries, gunpowder mills, and saltpeter shops might employ, as the French arsenal at St. Étienne in the early seventeenth century did, 700 workers or more. The building of warships, which carried two or three banks of cannon and often exceeded 1,000 tons, was an even more complex activity, requiring specialized skills and materials that might come from halfway around the world. The state alone possessed the resources for such investment, and this in turn spurred its own growth. The increasing scale of warfare, the expanding role of the state, and the widening arc of commerce were all part of the dynamic that made Europe's wars, as well as its economic activity, worldwide.

The New Balance of Power

The wars of Louis XIV marked a turning point in the European balance of power. France remained, as it would for the next century and a half, the dominant land power on the Continent. Its main rival, however, was no longer Spain, its great antagonist in the Thirty Years' War, or Austria, the chief barrier to its expansion in Germany, Italy, and the Low Countries, but Britain. Britain owed its new international prominence to its naval supremacy, its commercial wealth, and, perhaps most important, its access to that wealth through the working partnership of the landed elite, the financial community, and the organs of government.

Walpole, Britain's First Prime Minister

The stability of the new system was epitomized by the man who made it function for two decades, Sir Robert Walpole (1676–1745). The son of a prosperous Norfolk squire, Walpole rose steadily through the Whig hierarchy. He sat in Parliament for 40 years, held high office for 30, and for 20—from 1722 to 1742—was the effective ruler of the country, the first prime minister of Britain in fact if not in name.

Walpole grasped the fact that the Glorious Revolution of 1688 had settled the basic issues of seventeenth-century British politics, creating a limited monarchy firmly subject to the wishes of the landed gentry. What remained, with rising prosperity and a stable dynasty on the throne, was to organize the division of spoils. Walpole's command of the system was based on his control of its three major components, the crown, Parliament, and patronage. The support of the first two Hanoverian kings, George I (1714–1727) and George II (1727–1760), was his anchor. He consulted their wishes, cultivated their prejudices, and flattered their mistresses; through them, he consolidated and controlled all honors, promotions, offices, and contracts, scrupulously rewarding his friends and punishing his enemies. This monopoly of favor enabled him in turn to ensure a comfortable majority in Parliament, for although the principle of ministerial responsibility—that the king's ministry must retain a working majority in the House of Commons—was not firmly established until the nineteenth century, it was already true that no government could survive for long without such support. That this support was based more or less openly on bribery and corruption did not bother Walpole. If corruption was required to ensure stable government and general prosperity, he argued, then corruption was a political virtue, if not a moral one.

The Triumph of the Elite

The real stability of the British system, however, was in the unchallenged dominance of the landed elite, particularly its uppermost stratum. The government of eighteenth-century Britain, superficial political scrimmaging apart, rested securely with some 400 families, who controlled one-quarter of the arable land in the country. This striking concentration of ownership, which had been achieved largely since the Restoration of 1660, was the result of several interrelated factors. Large estates were

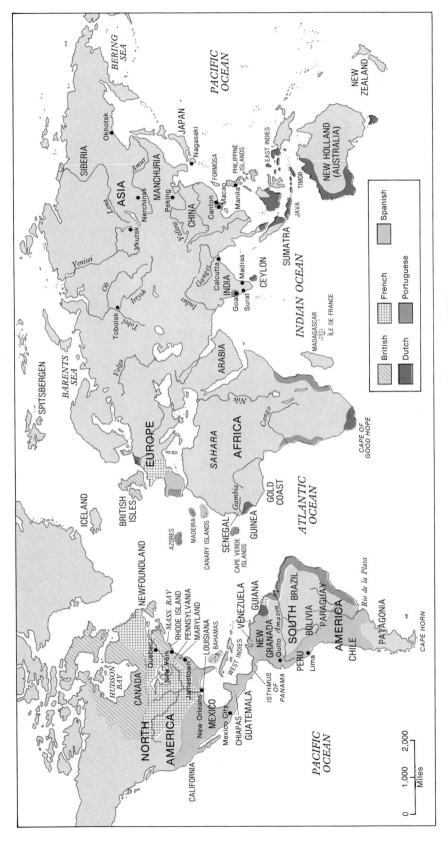

25.2 *The Expansion of Europe, 1715*

Legend:

British
Dutch
French
Portuguese
Spanish

Map labels include:

NORTH AMERICA, SOUTH AMERICA, EUROPE, ASIA, AFRICA

CALIFORNIA, CANADA, NEWFOUNDLAND, HUDSON BAY, QUEBEC, NEW YORK, MASS. BAY, RHODE ISLAND, PENNSYLVANIA, MARYLAND, LOUISIANA, New Orleans, Jamestown, MEXICO, Mexico City, CHIAPAS, GUATEMALA, ISTHMUS OF PANAMA, WEST INDIES, BAHAMAS, VENEZUELA, NEW GRANADA, GUIANA, Quito, PERU, Lima, BOLIVIA, BRAZIL, PARAGUAY, CHILE, AMERICA, PATAGONIA, CAPE HORN, Rio de la Plata, Amazon

ICELAND, SPITSBERGEN, BRITISH ISLES, BARENTS SEA, Volga

AZORES, MADEIRA, CANARY ISLANDS, CAPE VERDE ISLANDS, SENEGAL, Gambia, GUINEA, GOLD COAST, SAHARA, ARABIA, Nile, Congo, CAPE OF GOOD HOPE, MADAGASCAR, ÎLE DE FRANCE

SIBERIA, Okhotsk, Lena, Amur, MANCHURIA, Nerchinsk, Irkutsk, Tobolsk, Ob, Irtysh, Tobol, Yenisei, Yellow, Ganges, Indus, Peking, CHINA, Canton, Macao, FORMOSA, JAPAN, Nagasaki, Manila, PHILIPPINE ISLANDS, EAST INDIES, INDIA, Calcutta, Madras, Goa, Surat, CEYLON, SUMATRA, JAVA, TIMOR, NEW HOLLAND (AUSTRALIA), NEW ZEALAND

PACIFIC OCEAN, ATLANTIC OCEAN, INDIAN OCEAN, BERING SEA

Scale: 0   1,000   2,000 Miles

The way to favor under Sir Robert Walpole's rule was graphically illustrated in this contemporary print. [Culver Pictures]

protected from partition by laws that required that they be passed on to a single heir, who was prohibited from selling off parcels except under strict conditions. The value of land had been enhanced by increased productivity, in part the result of agricultural improvements, in part of laws that encouraged the cultivation of grain for export. This spurred the process known as enclosure, by which common grazing land and individual farm plots were fenced in by wealthy landowners armed with sheriffs' writs or private acts of Parliament. By 1840 fully 6 million acres had been enclosed in this fashion, bringing another quarter of Britain's farmland under elite control. The small independent farmer or yeoman, once the backbone of English agriculture, had become an endangered species by the eighteenth century and virtually extinct by the nineteenth, disappearing into the mass of wage laborers and tenant farmers who worked the great estates of the few.

Such a far-reaching and traumatic centralization of ownership might have been expected to produce unrest and even rebellion, yet Britain's countryside was for most of the eighteenth century among the most peaceful in Europe. This was partly due to the unique nature of its aristocracy. Only about 200 families in England held formal titles of nobility (as opposed to half a million each in France and Spain), and the only distinct advantage such titles conveyed was the right to sit in the House of Lords. It entailed no legal privileges such as marked off continental elites from the mass of the population, particularly exemption from taxation. Indeed, the difference between Britain and the other European monarchies might be summarized by saying that whereas on the

Continent the landed elite tolerated royal control of taxation on the condition that it fall chiefly on others, in Britain it accepted the burden of taxation in return for the right to control it through Parliament.

The absence of a status system based primarily on graded titles of nobility and distinguished by special privileges meant that wealth itself was the basic criterion for membership in the British elite. This encouraged entrepreneurship and investment in mining, industry, canal building, and urban real estate as well as colonization and agriculture, and the ever-expanding wealth of this elite provided the sinews of empire. At the same time, it was a true governing class that controlled and unified the instruments of social order from the pay of the local justice of the peace to the provision of the Royal Navy. Few aristocracies in history had exercised so clear and thorough a dominion over their societies as that of eighteenth-century Britain.

France Under Louis XV

The situation of France was quite different. Louis XIV had devoted much of his energy to reducing the nobility to political impotence. He had worked all his life to create a system of government dependent on the will and capacity of the sovereign, only to leave his throne to a 5-year-old boy, Louis XV. Power devolved on his elder cousin, Philip, duke of Orléans, as regent. With a nobleman heading the government, the aristocracy reasserted its claims to power, with disastrous results for central authority. By 1723 Louis XV had proclaimed his majority, but he never really assumed the reins of power. Though bright and served by some able ministers—Cardinal Fleury, the duke of Choiseul, and René de Maupeou—he lacked the discipline and the character to impose his will on the government, and so faint was his impress on the history of his long reign (1715–1774) that the age is better remembered for a shrewd and vivacious royal mistress, Madame de Pompadour, than for its titular ruler. Without forceful leadership, the bureaucracy became slack and unresponsive, the intendants pursued policies at variance with those of the government, and the parlements openly defied the crown, supporting opposition groups such as the Jansenists and successfully resisting all efforts to raise taxes.

Taxation and Finance

A pair of similar incidents early in the reigns of Louis XV and George I demonstrated the growing difference between the pace of development in France and Britain. In 1716, while Orléans was regent, he gave permission to a Scottish speculator, John Law (1671–1729), to found a private bank whose notes could be used as legal tender to pay taxes. Orléans hoped in this way to centralize tax collection and to avoid the rapacity of the tax collectors, who even under Louis XIV had kept a third of all receipts for themselves. At the same time, Law was given a chartered monopoly of all overseas French commerce, the Mississippi Company, whose profits were to secure the bank's notes. Wild reports of gold and diamonds in French Louisiana, some deliberately fabricated, drove the price of Mississippi stock up from 500 to 15,000 livres. By 1720 Law had been appointed controller general of France, with virtual control of the nation's economy. His fall was as dramatic as his rise. The profits of overseas trade lagged behind expectations, and the rumor of a bonanza in Louisiana was soon dispelled. Mississippi stock plummeted, Law's bank collapsed, and by year's end he had fled the country, leaving French finances as before in the hands of the tax collectors.

What the French had sought in Law's bank was to emulate the success of the Bank of England in providing regular, low-interest credit to the crown. It failed in part because of opposition by the tax collectors, who preferred to siphon off one-third of French tax revenues rather than settle for the 8 percent per annum paid by the Bank of England, and in part because of the suspicion of the nobility that Law's scheme was simply a device to abolish their tax privileges. In Britain, where the landed elite controlled the taxing power and taxes were received directly instead of through collectors, there were no vested interests to overcome or privileges to be protected.

What did concern Britons, however, was the size of the public debt, which had risen from £644,000 in 1688 to £54 million in 1713. This represented more than the gross annual product of the economy, and many Englishmen wondered how they as a nation could owe more than they were worth. It was at this point that the South Sea Company, a trading company set up to exploit the South American slave trade, put forward an audacious proposal to assume the entire public debt from the Bank of England on the strength of its anticipated profits and to pay it off by establishing a sinking fund equivalent to 2 percent of the value of the debt per year. For a time it appeared that the company might replace the bank as the leading credit institution of the country. Its board of directors included prominent Whig politicians, and George I himself consented to become its honorary head. But as with Law's Mississippi Company, the profits on which its scheme was to be capitalized proved illusory, and after a similar run-up, the value of its stock collapsed in the spring of 1720. The company went into receivership, and a number of smaller firms set up by using its stock as collateral failed, ruining thousands of investors. Thus the first two great financial panics of modern times occurred almost simultaneously in Paris and London. Their consequences, however, were far different. The Bank of England, having weathered the challenge to its supremacy, emerged stronger than ever, and the expanding British economy absorbed the effects of the panic with relative ease. In France, the failure of Law's bank set back the development of modern credit for 70 years, condemning the crown to an escalating spiral of debt.

The Wars of Midcentury

Europe enjoyed a generation of relative calm after the Peace of Utrecht. But the death of two kings brought war again in 1740. Frederick II succeeded to the throne of Prussia, where his father, Frederick William I, had drilled and perfected an army he had never used. Maria Theresa (1740–1780) became empress of Austria and queen of Hungary, the first female sovereign in the history of the Habsburg dynasty. Her father, Charles VI (1711–1740), had spent the better part of his reign trying to get the princes of Europe to recognize her right to succeed him through the document known as the Pragmatic Sanction. Their promises were worthless. Charles Albert, the elector of Bavaria, immediately claimed the Austrian throne. Bavaria, in turn, was considered a mere stalking-horse for Austria's archrival, France. At the same time, Frederick II sought to take advantage of Austria's disarray by seizing the rich province of Silesia, which Prussia had long coveted. This was the signal for a general conflict, the War of the Austrian Succession (1740–1748).

The war soon turned into another chapter in the great imperial war of the century between Britain and France.

◙ The First Stock Market Crash ◙

The rage for speculation and the lust for profit, which at its height inflated stock values on the London Exchange to five times the estimated cash reserves of the entire continent of Europe, was well described by a contemporary observer, William Chetwood. Shortly after, the South Sea Bubble collapsed, ruining thousands and threatening the Bank of England itself.

The whims of the stocks in this kingdom [are] of late so far cultivated and improved from a foreign example [Law's Mississippi Company in France], that one might reasonably conclude the numerous inhabitants of this great metropolis had for the most part deserted their stations, business, and occupations; and given up all pretensions to industry, in pursuit of an imaginary profit.

If your occasions are never so urgent for a mercer, a tailor, a shoemaker, etc., they are nowhere to be met with but at the Royal Exchange. If you resort to any public office or place of business, the whole enquiry is, How are the stocks? If you are at a coffee-house, the only conversation turns on the stocks. . . . If you repair to a tavern, the edifying subject (especially to a philosopher) is the South Sea Company; if you wait on a lady of quality, you'll find her hastening to the House of Intelligence in Exchange Alley. . . . Even smocks are deposited to help make up the security for cash; jewels pawned to raise money for the purchase of ruin—and, perhaps, wives and daughters have been mortgaged for the very same purpose.

Source: L. Melville, *The South Sea Bubble* (London: O'Connor, 1921), pp. 78–79.

Britain entered it on the side of Austria, while France supported Prussia and Bavaria. The Anglo-French conflict once again extended to North America, where fighting ranged from the isthmus of Panama to Cape Breton Island off the coast of French Canada. In Europe the chief battles were fought in Flanders, where the French sought to dislodge Austria. In the end, France's success on land was checked by Britain's supremacy at sea. The Treaty of Aix-la-Chapelle (1748) restored Britain and France to their original positions, as the British surrendered Fort Louisburg, taken by colonial militia, in return for their trading station at Madras on the east coast of India. The only belligerent to come out ahead was Frederick of Prussia, who, having realized his objective in the conquest of Silesia, had dropped out of the war six years before.

The Seven Years' War

The absence of a clear winner ensured an early resumption of the conflict. The Seven Years' War (1756–1763) marked the decisive triumph of the British Empire over that of France on all fronts, in North America, Africa, and India. It also marked the end of the rivalry between

Habsburg and Bourbon that had been the polestar of European politics for the previous 2½ centuries. This was the achievement of Count Wenzel von Kaunitz, who was to direct Austrian foreign policy until his death in 1794. Kaunitz' chief objective was the recovery of Silesia from Prussia. Austria's former allies, Britain and the Netherlands, had forced it to give up Silesia and to fight instead for Flanders, a policy that suited their interests but not Austria's. The solution was simple. In return for French troops and money against Prussia, Austria would cede Flanders, a territory it could neither usefully exploit nor properly defend. Thus the alignment of the previous war was completely reversed. All former friends were now enemies, all former enemies friends.

Kaunitz completed the diplomatic isolation of Prussia by entering into an alliance with Russia, which thus joined the European concert of powers for the first time. For five years Frederick fought a war of survival against apparently hopeless odds, earning the appellation "the Great." Each year defeat seemed inevitable; each year—at Rossbach, Leuthen, Zorndorf, Leignitz, Torgau—he staved it off with a last-ditch victory. The toll on Prussia, fighting virtually alone against the three largest powers in Europe, was immense. The Prussian army was reduced from 150,000 in its first campaign to 90,000 in its last. Frederick himself despaired of the final outcome. "To tell the truth," he wrote a minister, "I believe all is lost. I will not survive the ruin of my country."

For Britain, too, the war at first went badly. The French began their drive into the Ohio valley in North America two years before the formal outbreak of hostilities in Europe. They built a line of forts to block British expansion in the region and repelled expeditionary forces sent against them under General Edward Braddock and a young colonial colonel, George Washington. While Indian raids harassed the British frontier, the French seized Oswego on Lake Ontario and captured the strategic Mediterranean island of Minorca when Admiral John Byng abandoned its defense. The British hanged Byng, "to encourage the other admirals," as Voltaire remarked dryly, and in June 1757 replaced the inept ministry of the duke of Newcastle with one headed by William Pitt (1708–1778).

Pitt, the son of a great merchant in the Indian trade, was a leader born for crisis. Magnificent in debate, possessed by his vision of Britain's imperial destiny, he had been for 20 years the most dominant personality in the House of Commons. Yet power had eluded him. Harsh and uncompromising, often ill and frequently unstable, he had none of Walpole's managerial skills, and George II despised him. In the crisis of 1757, however, no one else would do. For the next four years he ruled with almost dictatorial powers and brought Britain victory.

Pitt's strategy was to keep Frederick the Great in the field against the French and the Austrians while he applied Britain's naval superiority against France's North American empire and plundered its trade. In effect, while the French refought the Hundred Years' War in Flanders, Britain would fight for everything else. The French fleet was bottled up in Brest and Toulon and was destroyed at Quiberon Bay and at Lagos off the coast of Portugal when it attempted to break out. Relief expeditions to North America were turned back, and the sheer weight of numbers—the 13 colonies now had a combined population of 2.5 million, against only 70,000 permanent French settlers—told at last. The French forts on the Great Lakes and the St. Lawrence River fell, and the Ohio valley was evacuated. Quebec was captured after a daring campaign in 1759, and with the fall of Montreal in 1760, the last French army in North America surrendered. The West Indian island of Guadeloupe was taken too, as well as the African slaving stations of St. Louis and Gorée. French aggression also backfired in India, where the British found themselves after their victory at Plassey in 1757 in possession not only of the rich Carnatic coast but of the entire hinterland of Bengal as well.

Pitt resigned in 1761 when his cabinet balked at his plans to conquer the whole of the French West Indies. The Peace of Paris (1763) reflected the view of more cautious men that Britain could not hold on to all it had conquered (which now included Havana and Manila, taken from Spain in 1762) and that any attempt to do so would shortly provoke another war. Guadeloupe was restored to France, its sugar having proved a glut on the British market, and the French were permitted again to trade in India and to fish off Newfoundland, though not to maintain garrisons. Havana and Manila were returned to Spain in exchange for Florida. From his seat in Parliament, Pitt denounced the treaty as a betrayal of Britain's blood and treasure. Nonetheless, victory over France was complete and decisive. Britain had gained all of Canada, doubling the size of its American territories. France would never, it seemed, pose a threat to its hegemony in the New World again. The significance of the unexpected British victory in India would prove even greater, as India's wealth provided much of the capital for the Industrial Revolution a generation later. If Britain had not achieved all that Pitt desired, it had accomplished more than anyone but Pitt would have thought possible.

With the hope of winning Flanders gone, the French deserted their Austrian allies. Russia too pulled out in 1762. With no hope of accomplishing alone what it had failed to do with two powerful allies, Austria reluctantly made peace with Prussia (1763). Frederick the Great retained Silesia, although it had cost him the near-destruction of his country to do so, and the remainder of his reign was spent largely in rebuilding it. The transfer of this single province from the Habsburg to the Hohenzollern crown was the only territorial result of two great wars in Europe. Those wars were the last to be fought over questions of dynastic succession and among the first to be fought for the high stakes of overseas empire.

The Birth of the American Republic

If the map of Europe had been little altered by the Seven Years' War, that of North America had been substantially redrawn by the British capture of Canada from France and Florida from Spain. The British prepared to exploit and extend their new conquests, but they failed to take into account the existing colonies, whose inhabitants, themselves largely of English and Scots-Irish stock, had reached a point of economic and political maturity at which they were no longer prepared to subordinate their interests to those of the mother country, with which they had already begun aggressively to compete. The result was rebellion and the creation of the first independent nation in the New World, the United States of America.

25.3 The British Empire in 1763

The American Colonies and Britain

By 1763 the 13 colonies of the Atlantic seaboard had become an important market for British manufactures, and if they could not yet compete with the West Indian sugar islands in sheer profitability, their size and the potential for expansion opened up by the conquest of Canada ensured that they would eventually dominate Britain's American empire. Yet within 13 years those colonies would begin the first successful rebellion in the New World, within 13 more they would have established the first indigenous non-European republic in history, and little more than three decades later, with their example and in part with their support, the whole of the Western Hemisphere south of Canada would have thrown off the European yoke brought in with the Spanish conquest.

It might be said with justice that the cause of the 13 colonies' rebellion was Britain's attempt to govern them. Until 1763 they had enjoyed an extraordinary degree of independence. Though theoretically subject to the British Parliament, they were exempt from British taxation

and had their own assemblies, legal systems, and finances. Instead of serving the home economy as envisioned by mercantile theory, the colonists competed with British ships in the Newfoundland fisheries, built their own vessels in competition with British shipyards, and carried on a lively smuggling trade with the West Indies. The crown had made sporadic attempts between 1685 and 1714 to revoke colonial patents and charters with a view to governing the colonies more directly, but these had foundered on the refusal of Parliament to tamper with what it regarded as property rights. The American colonists saw this as a vindication of their autonomy. They considered themselves not a subject people but Britons with the same rights and entitlements as anyone living in Britain itself.

The crown viewed matters differently. It regarded the colonies as a dominion or possession, united to it like Ireland but distinct from the realm of Britain itself, which after 1707 had consisted of England, Wales, and Scotland. Ireland too had its own lawmaking assembly, the Irish Parliament, but its subservience to the acts of the British Parliament had been spelled out in the Declaratory Act of 1719. Whereas Ireland was a plantation economy in which an Anglo-Scottish minority ruled a subject population of Catholic tenantry, the Middle Atlantic and New England colonies in particular consisted largely of independent freeholders and a mobile class of wage earners. And while Ireland was in Britain's shadow, the American colonies were 3,000 miles away.

America's distance from Britain made it difficult not only to control but also to defend. Even after the defeat of the French, the western frontiers were insecure, as the general rising of Indian tribes under Pontiac in May 1763 made clear. In theory, the colonial militias could have looked to their own defense, but their performance in the war against the French had been reluctant and halfhearted. Moreover, the British government was anxious to prevent uncontrolled settlement beyond the Appalachian Mountains, which was certain to provoke further Indian attacks. Accordingly, it placed the trans-Appalachian west under direct royal control, although several of the colonies had already claimed the Mississippi River as their border. At the same time, it proposed to maintain a permanent army of 10,000 to guard the frontier and levied new taxes, notably on all stamped or licensed paper, to help pay for it.

Protest and Rebellion

The British were quite unprepared for the explosion of protest that greeted these acts. Rioters burned the official stamps and formed resistance groups called the Sons of Liberty, merchants boycotted British wares, the colonial assemblies passed resolutions denouncing taxation without representation in Parliament, and nine colonies sent representatives to a Stamp Act Congress in New York. The British reacted uncertainly. On the one hand, they affirmed parliamentary control of the colonies, arguing that the colonists were "virtually" represented in Parliament in the same way as Britons at home who lived in boroughs that lacked a parliamentary franchise. On the other hand, they repealed the Stamp Act and reduced the much hated customs levy on sugar to a token penny per gallon.

Britain's policy continued to vacillate in the next several years, in part because of a rapid turnover of ministries until 1770, when the new king, George III (1760–1820), finally settled on the conciliatory but ineffective Frederick Lord North to serve as prime minister. The American colonies were importing almost £2 million more in British goods by 1770 than they were shipping back across the Atlantic. If they could not recoup that sum in trade with the West Indies, legally or illegally, their economy, particularly that of the mercantile Northeast, could not survive. Britain's vague but alarming gestures in the direction of new taxes and import duties as well as its sweeping assertions of jurisdiction over colonial trade threatened America's economic viability. Concern for prosperity merged with concern for legal rights. The closing of the western frontier and the policing of the Caribbean menaced two freedoms that Americans valued highly indeed: freedom of movement and freedom of trade.

A clash between British soldiers and a mob in Boston that left five colonists dead sobered both sides momentarily. North withdrew all British taxes except that on tea and announced that no further ones would be levied. When in 1773 he permitted the East India Company to dispose of a tea surplus in America, however, it was promptly interpreted as a new attempt to raise revenue. The Bostonians dumped the company's tea in their harbor. North responded by closing the harbor and imposing martial law on Massachusetts. At the same time, Parliament passed the Quebec Act, extending the Canadian frontier southward to the Ohio River. Unrelated in British eyes, these actions signaled to the colonials a new campaign of repression. As a sympathetic Englishman, Edmund Burke, observed, "Any of these innumerable regulations, perhaps, would not have alarmed alone; some might be thought reasonable; the multitude struck them with terror."[3]

Events now moved swiftly. An assembly of all the colonies calling itself the Continental Congress met in Philadelphia in September 1774. Although it still acknowledged the authority of the crown, its very meeting was regarded as an act of rebellion in Britain. Sporadic fighting broke out in Massachusetts in the spring of 1775, and in May the Continental Congress voted to raise an army in defense of the colonies. Much of the hardening on the British side came from George III himself. Burke and others opposed the drift to war, but North, who lacked the stomach to fight it, found himself without a politically acceptable way to back down.

The Revolutionary War

On July 4, 1776, the Continental Congress declared the independence of the 13 colonies in a document, drafted largely by Thomas Jefferson of Virginia, whose tone was more of sorrow than of anger. The colonials had little choice but resistance or surrender. Strong forces had already landed from Canada, with reinforcements from Britain. Inferior in numbers and training, with British troops in possession of Boston, New York, and Philadelphia, the colonial army fought at first merely to survive. But in October 1777 a British army unit of 7,000 men under General John Burgoyne, intended as part of a pincer movement to cut the northern colonies in two, blundered into a trap in the wilderness near Saratoga, New York, and was forced to surrender.

This defeat changed the character of the war. Until Saratoga, France and Spain had limited themselves to offering aid and financial credits to the rebels. Now they entered the war actively, France in 1778 and Spain a year later. America's war for independence had become an international struggle in which Britain found itself rapidly isolated. Control of not only the Atlantic seaboard but also the West Indies, the Mediterranean, and even India was at stake. Gibraltar withstood a three-year siege (1779–1782) that was, militarily, the largest operation of the war, and a French thrust at Jamaica was repelled by Admiral George Rodney in the great naval Battle of the Saints (1782). But the French fleet, temporarily gaining control of the waters off Virginia, forced the surrender of another large British army at Yorktown in October 1781.

With their empire threatened on all fronts, the British could no longer continue the luckless and draining struggle in America. The independence of the colonies was recognized in the Treaty of Paris (1783); Minorca and East Florida were returned to Spain, and the French recovered some West Indian islands and their former strongholds in Senegal. A shattered Britain was left to redirect its imperial energies toward India and East Asia, where in 1788 it began to colonize Australia. The French could now reflect that the loss of Canada had at least been balanced by the separation of the 13 colonies from Britain. But victory would prove dear. France's habitually insolvent treasury, taxed by the demands of another major war while still burdened with the debts of previous ones, soon tottered into bankruptcy, bringing the French state, and with it the entire Old Regime in Europe, to crisis.

Forming a Nation

Having won their independence, the 13 colonies set about the task of forming themselves into a nation. The Declaration of Independence had boldly asserted that "all men are created equal"—a revolutionary sentiment in a world ruled by monarchy and nobles, although America had never had a hereditary aristocracy—yet the new nation was clearly dominated by a landed and mercantile elite, and one-fifth of its total population (one-third in the plantation states of the south) consisted of black slaves. But the revolution liberalized white American society to a significant degree. Primogeniture and entail, which protected large estates from division, were swept away; Anglican and Congregationalist churches lost their privileged positions, paving the way for the complete separation of church and state that would be one of the most radical features of the American constitution; and the electoral franchise was widened in a number of states. These represented concessions won by workers, farmers, frontiersmen, and religious dissidents in return for support of the rebellion.

Though America was far from having achieved true egalitarianism and though the cloud of slavery, already troubling to many, hung over its future, it was incontestably the most democratic state in the world and the

first since the short-lived English Commonwealth of the 1650s to proclaim the sovereignty of the people, or at least those who were free and male. As such, it was a potent inspiration for reformers in Britain and elsewhere in the Old World, a unique experiment that embodied much of the advanced political thought of the century.

From Confederation to Commonwealth

At first the 13 states were individually sovereign entities that associated themselves loosely under the so-called Articles of Confederation. Each state had its own constitution, civil laws, militia, and currency. The Continental Congress continued as a national organ, but it lacked the power to tax or to raise an army and could order nothing without the approval of all 13 states. There were no central courts to resolve disputes between the states, most of which had rival territorial claims, and no agency existed to provide for common trade policy, diplomacy, and defense. As John Adams of Boston remarked, trying to provide for any collective interest was like trying to get 13 clocks to chime at once. In addition, the elites feared that continued popular pressure on weak state governments for political and economic reform would lead to anarchy. In 1786 farmers threatened by foreclosure rebelled in Massachusetts under a former militia captain, Daniel Shays. To men such as the Virginia patrician Edmund Randolph, Shays' rebellion was a perfect example of "the turbulence and follies of democracy."[4]

The result was a convention that met in Philadelphia in the summer of 1787 with the approval of the Continental Congress to amend the Articles of Confederation. The leading members of the convention, including George Washington (1732–1799), the former commander in chief of the revolutionary army, who chaired it, and James Madison (1751–1836), a brilliant young lawyer and fellow Virginian, scrapped the articles completely and, defiantly exceeding their mandate, devised an entirely new constitution. This created a new federal entity, the United States of America, with a bicameral legislature composed of a House of Representatives and a Senate empowered to levy taxes, raise an army, regulate commerce, fix a uniform national currency, and, in a sweeping grant of authority, "make all laws necessary and proper for carrying into execution" these powers. A strong executive was also provided, consisting of a president and a vice-president, as well as the foundation of a national court system. In a frankly revolutionary gesture, the convention discarded the requirement that any act at the national level have unanimous consent, declaring that approval by any nine states would ratify the constitution. If there had been a national government worthy of the name, the actions of the convention would have constituted a coup d'état against it.

Historians of the American Revolution have been divided ever since the publication of Charles A. Beard's *Economic Interpretation of the Constitution* in 1913 over whether the U. S. constitution was a betrayal of the democratic promise of the new republic by a cabal of rich men anxious to protect their property through a strong government. Unquestionably, the new system reflected suspicion if not hostility toward popular democracy. It was warmly welcomed by the elites and viewed with skepticism by wage earners and small farmers. But the inconveniences of the Articles were real, and some of the more drastic proposals at the convention—such as the abolition of the states altogether and life terms for the president and the members of the Senate—were rejected. Madison, the constitution's most articulate defender, argued that no lesser degree of centralized authority would suffice to govern a state larger than any in Europe except Russia and larger than any republic in history. After turbulent debate, the constitution was ratified (in the event by every state), and the new republic was inaugurated in 1789 with George Washington as its first president.

American and Canadian Expansion

The United States contained 3 million persons at its first census in 1790, including 600,000 African-Americans, most of them slaves. Approximately three times as many American Indians were dispersed within its borders and across the remainder of the North American continent. The new nation was expansionist from the start. As early as 1787 plans were laid in the Northwest Ordinance for the development of new states in the territory west of the Alleghenies, and new land was systematically acquired, by purchase (Louisiana, Florida, Alaska), annexation (Texas), settlement and negotiation (Oregon), and conquest (New Mexico, California). By the mid-nineteenth century Americans had fulfilled what they called their "manifest destiny" of becoming a transcontinental power with a larger territorial mass than any other nation save Russia and China.

The chief obstacle to the expansion of the United States was the native Amerindian population. Although less sophisticated than the Maya, Aztecs, and Inca of pre-Columbian America, the Indians of North America were far from primitive: they farmed as well as hunted, formed complex political and commercial networks, and often lived in towns. The Iroquois Confederation under Pontiac had allied with the French in an effort to resist British expansion during the Seven Years' War, and 50 years later the Shawnee chieftain Tecumseh (1768–1813) allied with the British during the Anglo-American War of 1812 to resist the United States. Tecumseh dreamed of a united Indian nation strong enough to

drive whites off the continent altogether, but the withdrawal of the British ended all realistic hopes of resistance. The Indians were devastated by war, forced migration, disease, and starvation, and by 1890 only a million were left in the territorial United States.

Visiting the United States in the 1830s, the French observer Alexis de Tocqueville ventured the bold prediction that the United States would have a population of 100 million within 100 years and would be, with Russia, the great power of the twentieth century. America, Tocqueville asserted, represented the triumph of equality and of the democratic revolution that he believed was destined to sweep the globe. By almost every yardstick, the new society appeared to be a success: "While all the nations of Europe have been ravaged by civil strife," he wrote, "the American people alone in the civilized world have remained pacific. Almost the whole of Europe has been convulsed by revolutions; America has not even suffered from riots."[5] But immigration, industrial development, and sectional antagonisms between the urban north and the plantation society of the south, particularly over the issue of the westward expansion of slavery, undermined the seeming tranquillity of the Union. In 1861 it collapsed, following the secession of the ten southern states, in a civil war that left more than 600,000 dead.

Many former Loyalists—supporters of the British cause in the American Revolution—had fled to Canada at the conclusion of that war. The British, attempting to deal with a still preponderantly French population, divided Canada into two jurisdictions in 1791. English-speaking Upper Canada, the future province of Ontario, retained English laws and institutions, while French-speaking Lower Canada, now Quebec, kept French law, seigneurial land tenures, and an officially recognized Catholic church. An invasion by the United States during the War of 1812 united the inhabitants of both Canadas briefly, but a steady stream of immigrants from Britain aroused French fears of cultural submergence. Following the Durham Report in 1839, Britain reunited Upper and Lower Canada over the latter's opposition, and the British North America Act of 1867 created the Dominion of Canada, a fully self-governing entity within the British Empire. This voluntary granting of independence, called "devolution," was to be applied later to Australia (1901), New Zealand (1907), the Union of South Africa (1910), India and Pakistan (1947), and the other former colonies in the Caribbean, Africa, and Asia that remain associated in what is today the British Commonwealth of Nations.

Canada expanded rapidly westward after 1867, linking both oceans by rail in 1885. Comparable in size to the United States, its population has never been more than a tenth as large, with most of it clustered in the more temperate coastal regions and the southern plains. Generally stable and prosperous, its chief problems have been intercommunal tensions with the French-speaking minority of Quebec and the economic and cultural dominance of the United States.

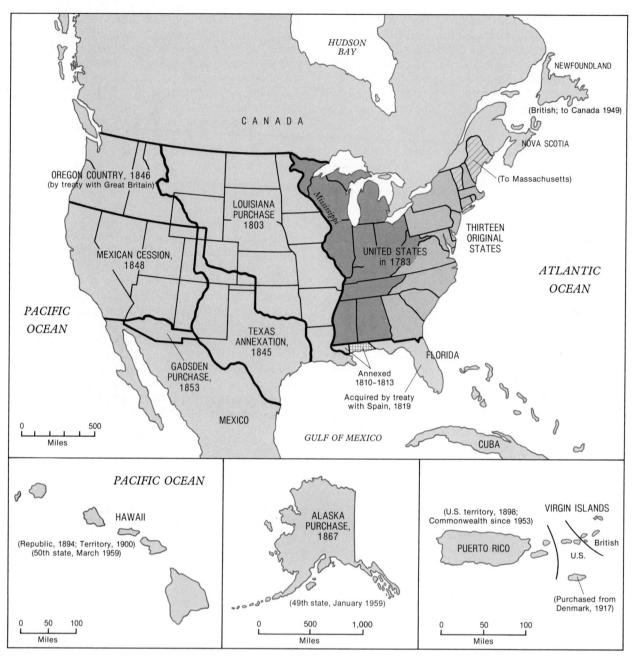

25.4 *The Expansion of the United States*

The Abolition of the Slave Trade and the Emancipation of Spanish America

The last quarter of the eighteenth century witnessed a revulsion against the Atlantic slave trade. Testimony before the British Parliament in 1788 laid bare the inhuman conditions under which millions of slaves had been transported, and revolutionary France in the 1790s found slavery incompatible with its professions of universal brotherhood. The slaves, for their part, were unwilling to wait for the enlightenment of their masters; a major rebellion broke out in Jamaica in 1760, and in 1791 half a million blacks under Toussaint L'Ouverture drove the French out of Haiti. At the same time, the profitability of the slave trade declined sharply with the collapse of sugar prices in the 1790s. The framers of the American constitution agreed to abolish the slave trade after 1807, and Britain outlawed it as well in that year, soon to be followed by most other European states. Slavery itself, however, remained legal in the British Empire until 1833, in the United States until 1863, and in Brazil and Cuba until 1886 and 1888, respectively. The slave trade continued to flourish illegally for most of the nineteenth century, and a British commission reported in 1844 that more slaves were being transported than at any time in the previous century.

What doomed the slave trade—at least in the West Indies, where the advanced economies of Britain and France predominated—was the obsolescence of the old colonial system itself. As the Scottish economist Adam Smith argued persuasively in *The Wealth of Nations* (1776), free trade was far more profitable to a state such as Britain than a rigid protectionism that tied down capital, engendered pointless wars, and leaked away profits in smuggling. With the loss of the 13 colonies by Britain and of Haiti by France, the futility of a closed labor and commercial system became apparent.

The economy of Spanish America had gradually been reorganized in response to pressures from the more advanced imperial powers, but politically it was as tightly ruled from Madrid as before. Despite earlier rebellions in Peru and Colombia and the spread of republican ideas among some of the Creole (American-born) class, however, disaffection was not widespread until disaster struck the mother country itself. That disaster was Napoleon's conquest of Spain in 1808. For the next six years the American colonies refused to recognize the occupation ruler, Joseph Bonaparte, and were left to fend for themselves. When the Bourbon ruler Ferdinand VII was restored in 1814, most of the colonies swore renewed allegiance to him. In the six years of Ferdi-

Toussaint L'Ouverture was the leader of the second successful colonial rebellion in the Americas and the first great black revolutionary of modern times.
[Mansell Collection]

nand's absence, however, they had come of age politically. Competing parties and improvised organs of government, or juntas, had been formed, the latter often based on extensions of the municipal councils traditionally dominated by Creoles. The experience of self-government had changed the chemistry between Spain and its colonies. When Ferdinand, blind to the new situation, attempted to reimpose royal government and commercial monopoly in its old form, there was widespread resentment.

❦

SIMÓN BOLÍVAR, THE LIBERATOR

Disillusionment with Ferdinand was exploited by republican nationalists, who had staged several abortive re-

Proud, imperious, and mercurial, Simón Bolívar liberated South America from three centuries of foreign rule and lived to regret his own work. [Granger Collection]

uprising at Caracas in 1810, in which he played a leading role. After toying with the idea of accepting a commission in the British army in Spain, he raised a new rebel army, declaring war to the death against the Spanish empire. By January 1814 he had returned to Caracas, declaring Venezuela a republic with himself as its head. Rather than choosing a more conventional name as head of state, he adopted the title of "liberator," symbolizing his commitment to the freeing of all of New Granada. Driven out by the Spaniards six months later, he fled to Jamaica but returned to Venezuela in 1817 and, raising an army of native forces and British soldiers of fortune, staged a daring invasion of Colombia. By August 1819 the entire province was in his hands, and three months later he proclaimed a constitution for the United States of Colombia, including Venezuela, where the last pro-Spanish resistance was extinguished in 1821. Ecuador fell in 1822, and Peru was conquered in 1824.

Bolívar hoped to unite this entire area—virtually all of South America apart from Brazil, Argentina, and Chile—into a single great republic. His enemies attacked him for his apparently boundless ambition; "I am tired," he complained to Bernardo O'Higgins, the liberator of Chile, "of hearing men call me tyrant, that I wish to make myself King, Emperor, the Devil." But his brutal methods of conquest, the indiscipline of his armies, and his undoubted dictatorial tendencies ultimately defeated what remained a noble if tarnished dream. By his death in 1830 the provinces of what he called Gran Colombia had splintered again into their old imperial configurations. "He who serves a revolution," he wrote in one of his final letters, "ploughs the sea."

volts during the interregnum of 1808–1814, notably in Mexico, Venezuela, and Argentina. Though formally professing loyalty to Spain, the Argentines refused to readmit the old royal officials and declared independence under their leader José de San Martín (1778–1850) in 1816. By 1821 San Martín had occupied Lima and declared Peru liberated. Royalist forces soon retook it, however, and the real work of revolution was left to another Creole leader, Simón Bolívar.

Bolívar was born in Caracas, Venezuela, in 1783, the fourth child of one of the oldest and wealthiest noble families in the city. Orphaned at an early age, Bolívar was fired as a young man by the republican ideals of the American and French revolutions. Like most Creole aristocrats, he completed his studies in Europe and was present in Paris when Napoleon was crowned emperor. He brought a young wife, Maria Teresa del Toro, back with him from Madrid, but she died of yellow fever. Bolívar kept his vow never to marry again, although it did not prevent him from enjoying a number of passionate love affairs.

Bolívar began his revolutionary career in an abortive

The End of Empire

Backward Brazil, a slave society with few cities worthy of the name, had an even more passive revolution. The regent John had come to it in exile after Napoleon's conquest of Portugal, returning to Lisbon in 1821 and leaving his son Pedro behind to serve as regent. When John attempted to recall Pedro to Portugal, the Brazilians refused to let him go, raising him to the position of emperor and driving Portuguese troops out of the country. In 1822 Brazil became an independent state.

In the viceroyalty of New Spain, a rebellion that had broken out in Mexico in 1810 under the leadership of a Creole priest, Father Hidalgo, was brought to completion in 1821 by a renegade royalist, Agustín de Iturbide, who proclaimed himself emperor. The remaining provinces of New Spain—Honduras, Nicaragua, Salvador, and Costa Rica—all became independent at the same time, rejecting union with Mexico or each other.

Within ten years Spain had been divested of an empire it had ruled with remarkable equanimity for three

25.5 Latin American Independence

centuries, retaining only Cuba and Puerto Rico of its former possessions in the New World. Unlike the newly fledged United States of America, Spain's colonies were neither prepared for independence nor particularly desirous of it. External events had weakened Spain's grip on the New World, and when it attempted to reimpose it without suitable consideration for the developments that had taken place in the interim, it was easily shaken off. The Spanish were never able to send large forces to combat the rebels, and the wars of liberation were essentially fought between native loyalists and republicans. The factor that tipped the balance in favor of the latter was the support of the British, who, seeking to break up Spain's commercial monopolies for good and

⊕ Bolívar's Message to ⊕ the Congress of Angostura

Simón Bolívar's message to the congress that had gathered in 1819 to consider a proposed constitution for the new state of Venezuela reflects the disillusionment he already felt for the revolution he had led and his foreboding for the future stability of the South American republics.

America, in separating from the Spanish monarchy, found herself in a situation similar to that of the Roman Empire when its enormous framework fell to pieces in the midst of the ancient world. Each Roman division then formed an independent nation in keeping with its location or interests; but this situation differed from America's in that those members proceeded to reestablish their former associations. We, on the contrary, do not even retain the vestiges of our original being. We are not Europeans; we are not Indians; we are but a mixed species of aborigines and Spaniards. Americans by birth and Europeans by law, we find ourselves engaged in a dual conflict: we are disputing with the natives for titles of ownership, and at the same time we are struggling to maintain ourselves in the country that gave us birth against the opposition of the invaders. Thus our position is most extraordinary and complicated. But there is more. As our role has always been strictly passive and our political existence nil, we find that our quest for liberty is now even more difficult of accomplishment; for we, having been placed in a state lower than slavery, had been robbed not only of our freedom but . . . we were deliberately kept in ignorance and cut off from the world in all matters relating to the science of government.

Source: V. Lecuna, comp., and H. A. Bierck, Jr., ed., *Selected Writings of Bolívar*, vol. 1 (Caracas: Banco de Venezuela, 1951), pp. 175–176.

for all, permitted irregular land and naval forces to assist Bolívar and San Martín openly and threw up a virtual blockade against the feeble Spanish navy. Britain, having lost its own most important American colonies in a bitter and protracted war, thus emerged, ironically, as the patron of liberation. But the new societies of Central and South America, where a 20 percent white minority continued to perpetuate oligarchic rule over a majority population of native and mixed (mestizo) blood, subsided into a period of political oppression, governmental instability, and economic exploitation from which they began to emerge only in the twentieth century.

ᛙᚢᛁ   ᛙᚢᛁ   ᛙᚢᛁ

The colonies of the New World became a critical element in the advanced European economies of the eighteenth century, and the character of European warfare was gradually reshaped by the struggle for possession of them. By the end of the first quarter of the nineteenth century, most of those colonies had gained their independence, and what remained in European hands—Canada and most of the West Indies—had become relatively insignificant in economic terms. Nevertheless, the wealth derived from them was a crucial factor in the development of the new global economy and of capitalist enterprise, particularly in Britain. The transportation of millions of blacks across the Atlantic constituted the largest involuntary migration in human history up to this time, and their settlement throughout North and South America profoundly altered the demographic and social structure of the New World.

Notes

1. R. Davis, *The Rise of the Atlantic Economies* (Ithaca, N.Y.: Cornell University Press, 1973), p. 43.
2. W. D. Dorn, *Competition for Empire, 1740–1763* (New York: Harper, 1940), p. 13.
3. D. K. Fieldhouse, *The Colonial Empires: A Comparative Survey from the Eighteenth Century* (New York: Delacorte Press, 1967), p. 109.
4. W. U. Solberg, ed., *The Federal Convention and the Formation of the Union* (Indianapolis: Bobbs-Merrill, 1958), p. xc.
5. A. de Tocqueville, *Democracy in America* (New York: Anchor Books, 1969), p. xiv.

Suggestions for Further Reading

Brown, P. D. *William Pitt, Earl of Chatham: The Great Commoner.* London: Allen & Unwin, 1978.

Butler, R. *Choiseul.* New York: Oxford University Press, 1981.

Curtin, P. *The Atlantic Slave Trade: A Census.* Madison: University of Wisconsin Press, 1969.

Davis, D. B. *The Problem of Slavery in the Age of Revolution.* Ithaca, N.Y.: Cornell University Press, 1966.

de Vries, J. *The Economy of Europe in an Age of Crisis, 1600–1750.* Cambridge: Cambridge University Press, 1976.

Dickson, P. G. M. *The Financial Revolution in England: A Study in the Development of Public Credit, 1688–1756.* London: Macmillan, 1967.

Dorn, W. D. *Competition for Empire, 1740–1763.* New York: Harper, 1940.

Fieldhouse, D. K. *The Colonial Empires: A Comparative Survey from the Eighteenth Century.* New York: Delacorte Press, 1967.

Fox-Genovese, E., and Genovese, E. D. *Fruits of Merchant Capital: Slavery and Bourgeois Property in the Rise and Expansion of Capitalism.* New York: Oxford University Press, 1983.

Frank, A. G. *World Accumulation, 1492–1789.* New York: Monthly Review Press, 1978.

Heckscher, E. *Mercantilism.* New York: Macmillan, 1955.

Lynch, J. *The Spanish American Revolutions, 1808–1826.* London: Weidenfeld & Nicolson, 1973.

McDonald, F. *We the People: The Economic Origins of the Constitution.* Chicago: University of Chicago Press, 1958.

McKeown, T. *The Modern Rise of Population.* New York: Academic Press, 1976.

Madariaga, S. de. *Bolívar.* New York: Farrar, Straus & Cudahy, 1956.

Mintz, S. W. *Sweetness and Power: The Place of Sugar in Modern History.* New York: Viking Press, 1985.

Morgan, E. S. *Birth of the Republic, 1763–1789.* Chicago: University of Chicago Press, 1977.

Nef, J. U. *War and Human Progress.* New York: Russell & Russell, 1968.

Parry, J. H. *Trade and Dominion: European Overseas Empires in the Eighteenth Century.* New York: Praeger, 1971.

Plumb, J. H. *Sir Robert Walpole.* 2 vols. Boston: Houghton-Mifflin, 1956, 1960.

Scammell, G. *The First Imperial Age: European Overseas Expansion, 1400–1715.* New York: HarperCollins, 1990.

Shennan, J. H. *Philippe, Duke of Orléans, Regent of France, 1715–1723.* London: Thames & Hudson, 1979.

Wallerstein, I. *The Modern World System.* 2 vols. New York: Academic Press, 1974, 1980.

Wood, G. S. *The Creation of the American Republic, 1776–1787.* Chapel Hill: University of North Carolina Press, 1969.

The Enlightenment

The eighteenth century was characterized by a wide-ranging critique of the social and intellectual bases of European culture to which contemporaries gave the name of the Enlightenment. Unlike other movements of renewal and reform in the West since the advent of Christianity, the Enlightenment did not take the form of a religious revival. It grew instead out of the new methods of inquiry bequeathed by the scientific revolution and the questions that its view of the cosmos posed to traditional religion. The thought of the Enlightenment was frankly secular and rationalist, and this, in a society where all art, science, morality, and political authority had acknowledged the primacy of religious truth for 1,500 years, posed a revolutionary challenge to the social order. At the same time, the Enlightenment was a response to economic and political changes at work in European society. Some of the most influential thinkers of the Enlightenment were men of bourgeois origin. Unattached to church or court, they heralded the coming of a new secular society, and their demands for freedom and toleration, their conception of a worldwide human community, and their contempt for inherited privilege

A lady leaving a circulating library, in a mezzotint by J. R. Smith (1781). [British Museum]

echoed the interests of free trade, unfettered enterprise, and an expanding global economy.

The rulers of the eighteenth century could heed or censor their Enlightenment critics, but they could not ignore them. Some monarchs attempted to incorporate Enlightenment principles into an essentially traditional style of governance, with varying results. Other critics, troubled by the divorce of reason from emotional and spiritual values in much of Enlightenment thinking, urged a new emphasis on feeling and intuition, and a popular religious revival breathed new life into Christian worship. The call to accommodate both intellectual clarity and emotional depth was perhaps best answered in music, whose eighteenth century masters achieved a balance of feeling and design that has never been surpassed.

The Roots of the Enlightenment

The scientific revolution gravely undermined a set of closely interlocked assumptions on which the traditional social order rested. According to the traditional view, all created things had their place on the universal ladder of existence that ultimately led to God. The angels were subordinate to God as humankind was to the angels, beasts to persons, and inanimate to living matter, in a descending scale of natural value. Each order of being had its own internal hierarchy as well. There were superior and subordinate angels, higher and lower animals, and nobler and baser persons. The human order was part of the harmony ordained by God for the universe, and anyone who attempted to disturb it was defying God as well as humankind. The historian Arthur O. Lovejoy has named this complex of ideas the "great chain of being."

In social terms, the great chain of being entailed a general principle of subordination, by which women and children were subject to the authority of men, commoners to noblemen, and all subjects to their rulers. This notion culminated in the idea of the divine right of kings. Monarchs received their authority directly from God as a means of enforcing his will on earth. Since kings had no superior but God, their actions could not be questioned by anyone on earth, and their commands must be treated as if coming directly from God. If a king were a tyrant, he should be regarded as a scourge sent by God to chastise people for their sins. God would hold the tyrant accountable, but subjects could not.

In practice, the absolute power of kings was often subject to challenge. The church of the Counter-Reformation insisted that heretical rulers might be deposed or even killed; in 1570 Pope Pius V absolved

Queen Elizabeth I's English subjects of their allegiance to her, and in 1610 Henry IV of France was assassinated by a deranged priest. The English in 1649 had executed their own king, Charles I, after trying him before an extraordinary tribunal, and even Louis XIV had known rebellion in the early years of his reign. Further down the social scale, desperate peasants rebelled frequently against oppressive taxes and other burdens, and such customs as the English practice of ducking in the local pond or river scolds who beat or abused their husbands showed that women did not always passively accept the roles imposed on them.

Although resistance might be offered in particular cases, most women continued to regard their subservience to men, and peasants to their lords, as part of the natural order of things. This pattern of submission, called deference, was instilled in the lower orders of society from an early age. Here is the journalist Richard Steele's description of the proper attitude of the tenant farmer, written in 1672: "A just fear and respect he must have for his landlord, or the gentleman his neighbor, because God hath placed them above him and he hath learnt that by the father he ought to honor is meant all his superiors."[1]

These words were written in England. Even there, where the attempt to impose absolute monarchy had been curbed by the revolutions of 1640 and 1688, the social supremacy of the nobility was not merely undiminished but greater than ever. This was generally true of the privileged orders throughout eighteenth-century Europe. Beneath the surface, however, the Old Regime was not only being reshaped by the stresses of imperial competition and the emerging global economy but also being undermined by the intellectual consequences of the scientific revolution.

The most immediate of these consequences was a weakening of faith in the traditional Christian God of salvation, at least among the more educated classes. It was true that nothing in the new science directly contradicted the tenets of Christianity. But it was difficult to reconcile the biblical God who regularly manifested his presence in the world through signs, wonders, and miracles with the expanded Newtonian universe of self-regulating mechanical motion. Such a God seemed not so much incompatible with this universe as irrelevant to it.

The revolution in the Western concept of space was soon matched by a corresponding revolution in the concept of geologic time. Just as the cosmos had been thought to be contained within the ten heavenly spheres of the Ptolemaic universe, so its age, reckoned by the creation of Adam and Eve, was thought to be no more than 6,000 years. A seventeenth-century English theologian, James Ussher, calculating by biblical genealogies, had even announced the precise date of creation to have been October 23, 4004 B.C.

The God of Reason

As scientists began to turn their attention to the natural history of the earth, it was soon apparent that a far longer span was necessary to account for the evolution of its features. The God who had already been exiled to the outer edges of a vast and perhaps boundless universe now seemed to recede as well from the intimate scale of human history to that of a remote, geologic time. Such a God might be conceived of as a creator, but in what sense was he still a father? This led to a further difficulty, for if the idea of a paternal God had begun to lose its credibility, divine right monarchs could not plausibly justify their rule. The theories of Newton might have seemed very far removed from the glitter and pomp of Louis XIV's court, but their implications for royal absolutism and noble privilege were serious and ultimately fatal. In pulling the linchpin of a traditional Christian God from the great chain of being, the new mechanical universe had called into question the entire justification for the social order that rested on it.

For some thinkers, such as Pascal, the erosion of faith in a personal God of salvation was profoundly disturbing. But for many others in the late seventeenth and eighteenth centuries, the biblical God died a natural death with the view of nature and the cosmos of which he had been part, to be replaced by one more in keeping with the rational world of the new physics. Thus was born what was called "natural religion," or Deism. Deism rested on a variant of the old scholastic argument from design. The rational universe revealed by science, the Deists contended, could never have organized itself by accident and was thus necessarily the product of a rational, divine mind. Having created an orderly and self-perpetuating universe, this intellectual God had no need to intervene in it, and his apparent absence from it reflected merely his repose in its perfection. What God did in the world, in effect, was to contemplate it. He had no need to force notice of himself on it, since his presence was implicit throughout its design. It followed that the proper way to worship such a God was to study the world itself.

Deism appeared on the surface to reject and even scorn Christianity. For the cultural outsider Spinoza or for a cool, rationalist skeptic such as the third earl of Shaftesbury (1671–1713), this was a matter of indifference if not pride. But many people anxious to embrace Deism wished to save as much as possible of Christianity within it. They found their spokesman in John Locke, who argued in *The Reasonableness of Christianity* (1695) that Christian ethics reflected divine reason. What Christianity could not claim to possess was an exclusive revelation of truth. All religions reflected the "natural religion," which recognized and worshiped the divine intelligence in the world. This was the valid core of each faith, underneath the impurities of dogma and superstition. For this reason, as Locke argued in *An Essay on Toleration* (1689), all religions were worthy of respect, none of priority. Toleration thus emerged as a positive virtue, not merely a truce in a war to the death between rival systems of belief.

The argument that each religion should be sifted for the truth it possessed was akin to the method of science in testing different theories by experiment. Common to both was the assumption that truth was not discovered all at once through external revelation but rather acquired slowly by applying reason to the facts of experience, in the manner of fitting together the pieces of a jigsaw puzzle. The scientific revolution itself was the most triumphant demonstration of this process. Newton's synthesis, "the true system of the world," as an eighteenth-century admirer called it, had been built on the earlier theories of Copernicus, Galileo, and Kepler, each of which had contributed its partial truth to the final discovery of the whole. If the truth about the physical cosmos, obscured even to the greatest minds of antiquity, had been disclosed at last by this method, what mystery could not be made to yield to it? Reason, perfected by the method of science, seemed poised to unlock the final secrets of heaven and earth.

The Idea of Progress

The upshot of these developments was the idea of progress, a notion that changed an entire civilization's conception of itself. For more than 2,000 years, the West had thought of its world as the shrunken remnant of a glorious past. The Greeks had looked back to a mythical world of gods and heroes, the Romans of the empire to the virtue of the republic, the Middle Ages to the sanctity of the apostles, and the Renaissance back again to Rome. Most important of all was the Judeo-Christian myth of humankind's fall from grace in the Garden of Eden. In the Jewish version of the fall, redemption was still conceived in secular terms as a return to the promised land. But for Christians, human sin could not be eradicated in historical time; indeed history, time itself, was the punishment inflicted on humanity for its sins.

The notion of secular progress, the improvement of the human condition in the world through human effort alone, thus required a radical transformation in Western thinking. The scientific revolution, and the Deist faith in a rational God to which it gave rise, provided the basis of this transformation. The success of the scientific method in explaining the cosmos generated great confidence in its ability to resolve social, political, and even moral problems as well. If humankind could unlock the secrets of the natural world, why should it be unable to master its own human one? At the same time, the God of Deism freed humankind from the Christian preoccupation with sin, and it became possible to think of human nature positively. The human race was not born with an innate propensity to sin, but it could be animated, even in the absence of divine grace, by feelings of benevolence and a disinterested desire for the welfare of others. "I have seen some take on the feelings of others," declared the French poet Saint-Lambert, "espouse the interests of others, and enter into their situation to the point of losing their own feelings, of forgetting their own interests and situation."[2] A Deist, Saint-Lambert believed that contemplating the goodness of God was necessary to the cultivation of moral sentiments. Established churches, however, were actually harmful to them, since they substituted formal duties and barren rituals for natural and spontaneous feeling.

The possibility of progress was the subject of a famous literary debate in late-seventeenth-century France, the so-called quarrel of the ancients and the moderns. The ancients upheld the view that modern man could never duplicate the achievements of classical Greece and Rome, while the moderns asserted that the age of Louis XIV was the equal if not the superior of any pre-

vious period in history. The most persuasive of the moderns' spokesmen, Bernard de Fontenelle (1657–1757), argued that whereas great works of art required only individual genius, the growth of knowledge was a collaborative effort and thus cumulative over time. Although history suffered periods of reversal as well as advance, the attainments of the past always remained to be built on and surpassed by the present. An enthusiastic popularizer of the new science, Fontenelle believed that his own time represented a new summit of human achievement. In the perspective of centuries to come, he declared, the fifth century before Christ and the seventeenth after would both be seen as peaks on a line of ascending progress. The time of Christ himself was pointedly absent from this reckoning.

If each period could build on the past, each individual represented a new and untested set of possibilities. The traditional Christian view had assumed that the individual was born in a state of sin and that the primary task of education was to control a natural inclination to evil. In the view suggested by Deism, however, humankind was morally neutral if not instinctively good, and the

The idea of progress spawned a number of amusing fantasies, such as this alleged flight from "Pazentia" to "Coria" in Spain. By the end of the eighteenth century, balloon flights had already been made and observation balloons were being used in battle. [Bulloz/Musée Carnavalet, Paris]

proper function of education was to maximize society's potential for progress by developing each individual talent to the fullest. Once again, John Locke provided the most popular account of this new psychology. In *An Essay Concerning Human Understanding* (1690) he argued that the mind at birth was a blank slate that registered the experience of the senses passively. These sensations were organized by simple categories and processed by reflection. The result was a product called knowledge or understanding. Locke viewed the mind of the child as fluid and malleable. Bombarded by sensory impressions and relatively unorganized, it was, he said, "as easily turned this way or that, as water itself." This meant that education was critical in determining human development. Properly guided, the mind could realize its full powers, both for its own benefit and that of society. Deprived of such guidance, or purposely misled, it was prey to superstition, intolerance, and tyranny.

Locke and Liberty

John Locke (1632–1704) was a member of the Whig opposition to Charles II and James II and for a time went into exile under an assumed name. After the Glorious Revolution, he published *Two Treatises of Government* (1690), intended to defend the deposition of James II and to refute the theories of Thomas Hobbes.

Hobbes had argued that people contract with a sovereign whose unchallengeable authority erects a society that protects them from one another. Although Hobbes, like Locke, explained human psychology from a materialistic standpoint, his view of the antagonism between individuals reflected traditional Christian pessimism about the depravity of human nature. For Locke, humans were innately peaceful, rational, and gregarious in the state of nature, enjoying their natural rights to life, liberty, and the fruit of their own labors. They entered society not from fear but from the desire to increase their wealth and happiness by cooperation with their fellows. The social contract thus involved not a surrender of natural rights but the protection and enhancement of them. Society itself was the voluntary association of free, equal, and separate individuals as free, equal, and united members of a group.

The first task of society was to establish a rule-making authority or government. Locke rejected Hobbes' assertion that sovereignty must reside in a single person or institution. As each individual had been sovereign over himself or herself in the state of nature, so all were now jointly sovereign over the society they had created together. This was the very meaning of their union as a people. It followed that government was first and foremost an instrument of the people's will. If the particular government they had chosen proved tyrannical or otherwise defective, they might amend it or cast

it off. Thus the right of rebellion was implicit in the formation of society itself. Far from dissolving the social order, as Hobbes had argued, rebellion was a means of renewing and reaffirming the ends for which it had been instituted. Nothing could dissolve the union of a free people as long as they elected to remain together.

Locke's *Treatises* provided what still remains the classic foundation of the liberal state, with its emphasis on associative community, representative government, and natural rights. His view of society as an act of collective decision making by free and unconstrained individuals reflected both the Deist vision of man as a rational being and the values of an emerging secular society with its emphasis on choice and satisfaction. His influence on the American Revolution, with its claim to a people's right to rebel on behalf of their inalienable rights, was obvious, and the convention of the founders who drafted a constitution for the 13 former colonies might almost have stepped from the pages of the second *Treatise* as an illustration of society in the making.

Locke's views remained open to objection however. His picture of the human mind as a bundle of sensations acted on by "reflection" did not explain how the capacity to reflect could arise. By locating political sovereignty in the people as a whole, he begged the question of how power is actually exercised in society. In asserting that natural rights disclosed themselves intuitively, he assumed that everyone would agree what they were. But the English revolutionary Gerrard Winstanley had already rejected one of Locke's rights, the right of property, as incompatible with true liberty, and the abuse of property was to be denounced by Jean-Jacques Rousseau and others in the eighteenth century as well.

Philosophy in Action

The Enlightenment was a broadly based intellectual movement whose avowed goal was to apply reason to society for the purpose of human betterment. It was led by the philosophes, a loose coalition of thinkers and critics who were not philosophers in the traditional sense but social activists for whom knowledge was something to be converted into reform. Many of the leading philosophes were French, but they came from virtually every country in Europe, and their ideas carried everywhere. The philosophes saw themselves not as subjects of a particular country but as citizens of the world, or, in Peter Gay's phrase, as "the party of humanity." They claimed to speak on behalf of all oppressed by tyranny or blighted by ignorance, and their goal was nothing less than a world where reason alone was sovereign.

The philosophes prided themselves on their political

and intellectual independence. The bible of their movement, Denis Diderot's *Encyclopedia*, defined the philosophe as one who, "trampling on prejudice, tradition, universal consent, authority, in a word all that enslaves most minds, dares to think for [himself and] . . . to admit nothing except on the testimony of his experience and his reason." The philosophes did not seek specific political reform so much as fundamental changes in values and attitudes that would bring reform about. Their motto, coined by the German philosopher Immanuel Kant, was "Dare to know," and their object, Diderot boasted, was to make "a revolution in men's minds."

Voltaire

The most famous and influential of the philosophes was François-Marie Arouet (1694–1778), known to history by his pen name, Voltaire. Born in Paris, Voltaire was, like many of the philosophes, of bourgeois origin; his father was a notary. He began his career as a satiric playwright but ran afoul first of the regent, who imprisoned him for 11 months in the Bastille, and then of a prominent nobleman, the Chevalier de Rohan, who had him caned in the street and imprisoned again when he protested. Forced into exile, Voltaire spent three years in England. This experience was the turning point of his career. Voltaire was deeply impressed by the relative freedom he found in England, and his *Philosophical Letters on the English Nation* (1734) praised that nation's institutions. He was influenced as well by Lockean psychology and Newtonian physics, and his *Elements of the Philosophy of Newton* (1738) is one of the clearest and most direct links between the scientific revolution and the thought of the Enlightenment.

Unable to publish freely in France, Voltaire accepted an invitation from an admirer, Frederick the Great of Prussia, at whose court he spent two years (1749–1751). He then retired with his niece and mistress, Madame Denis, to an estate at Ferney, just over the French border in Switzerland, where he spent the last third of his life. There he functioned as a one-man republic, entertaining a steady stream of visitors, firing off as many as 30 letters a day, and carrying on a tireless series of campaigns for justice. The most famous of these was to clear the name of Jean Calas, a French Protestant put to death on the trumped-up charge of having murdered his son to prevent his conversion to Catholicism. As a Deist, Voltaire had no more use for one form of Christianity than another; his interest was in exposing the consequences of bigotry. *"Écrasez l'infâme!"*—crush the infamy!—he cried, and no one did more, by anger or ridicule, to expose intolerance and to undermine the authority of established religion in Europe. The compliment was returned: his last major work, the *Philosophical Dictionary* (1764), was burned in Paris, Geneva, and Rome, and Vol-

Frederick II of Prussia visits Voltaire in his study during the writer's residence at Frederick's court. In this extraordinary image, it is Voltaire, pen in hand, who remains seated while his royal host bends forward in greeting. Only the rearing horse outside conveys the image of bridled majesty and hints at the stormy rupture that was to part the men later. [Bettman Archive]

taire observed wryly that the authorities would gladly have burned the author as well.

Satire was Voltaire's special forte, and his wit was turned against his friends as well as his enemies. His novel *Candide* (1759), the most popular and enduring of all his works, was a satire on the faith of his contemporaries in automatic or unlimited progress. There was a dark side to Voltaire; that God was good, he believed, did not protect humankind from evil. What people could do was to minimize the evil they inflicted on one another, and they could do this best by coming to understand their common heritage. In a sense Voltaire is the father of this book; his *Essay on Custom* (1756) was the first survey of the history of world civilization, beginning with that of ancient China. As always, Voltaire's purpose was didactic, to show that no culture had a monopoly on beauty or value, just as no religion had a monopoly on truth. In his last years he was able to return to Paris in triumph. He described himself as bowed down with every infirmity of old age; but nothing, he added, "can deprive me of hope."

The Enlightenment and Society

When the philosophes put their own society under the lens of reason, they found it seriously wanting. Superstition abounded; free thought was stifled; education was in the hands of the established churches. Idleness had been elevated to a way of life by the aristocracy, while the efforts of the most productive class, the bourgeoisie, were for the most part scorned.

At the same time, the idea that the structure of society reflected the hierarchical order of the universe was under attack. "No society can exist without justice," Voltaire had written; yet could a God of reason have created a society where justice was so perverted? Some of the more radical philosophes had already gone beyond Deism, however. For such openly avowed atheists as the Frenchmen Denis Diderot (1713–1784) and Julian La Mettrie (1707–1747) or the Baron d'Holbach (1723–1789), a wealthy German nobleman living in Paris, the idea of God itself was the last superstition. Humankind, they declared, was alone in the universe, the author of its own destiny. Society, its own creation, should respond to its needs. If it did not, the answer to the problem had to be sought in humankind itself, for the only law to which humanity was subject was that of its own nature.

Rousseau and the Social Contract

These questions led the philosophes to investigate the origins of society. The most radical analysis was offered by Jean-Jacques Rousseau (1712–1778). Born in Geneva, Rousseau was, unlike most of the philosophes, poor and ill-educated. He ran away from home at the age of 16 and remained a misfit all his life, betraying friends and even abandoning his own children. Rousseau's personal discontents were reflected in his view of society. "Man is born free," he declared, "yet everywhere we find him in chains." Society had not fulfilled human nature but perverted it. In his *Discourse on the Origin of Inequality* (1755), he found the origin of injustice in the institution of property:

The first man who, having enclosed a piece of ground, bethought himself of saying *This is mine*, and found people simple enough to believe him, was the real founder of civil society. From how many crimes, wars and murders, from how many horrors and misfortunes might not someone have saved mankind, by pulling up the stakes and filling in the ditch, and crying out to his fellows, "Beware of listening to this impostor; you are undone if you once forget that the fruits of the earth belong to us all, and the earth itself to nobody."

Rousseau depicted the state of nature as an idyllic primitive communism, corrupted by the sin of possession. That original transgression created the basic institution of society, property. This in turn led to greed, the source of all oppression. The love of gain made sons wish for the death of their fathers and helped speculators profit from plague, famine, and war. Far from being an absolute natural right, as Locke had thought, property, when perverted by greed, was the evil that usurped and destroyed all other rights.

The solution, Rousseau argued in *The Social Contract* (1762), was to create a society in which private interest was subordinated to the common good. This, he asserted, could be accomplished only if each individual agreed to give up the final determination of his interest to the collective whole. Rousseau saw in this not loss but a gain of freedom. Since each person, while giving up his own rights, received at the same time the surrender of everyone else's, his original rights were actually returned many times over. Yet since everyone had made the same exchange, all persons remained exactly equal to one another. This was the true meaning of the social contract. In Hobbes' version of it, all persons were equal in their subordination to an absolute ruler, but none were free. In Locke's version, all persons were free to pursue their private interests, which led inevitably to inequity, oppression, and the loss of freedom. Only by guaranteeing both freedom and equality, Rousseau believed, could the conditions for a just society be met.

Rousseau called the collective entity in which all individual rights were vested the general will. Rousseau took the general will (as opposed to the will of any segment, including a majority) to mean both the permanent interest of the entire community and the course of action that represented its best interest at any given moment.

Ideally, the general will would be enacted by the unanimous consent of the entire community. In practice, however, it could not be expected that all citizens would be able to transcend their private interests, and to wait for unanimity on every question would, Rousseau admitted, reduce the social contract to an empty formula. It would therefore be necessary at some point to oblige dissenters to comply with the general will, for their own good as well as the community's. In the last analysis, Rousseau declared, citizens who could not recognize where their real freedom lay must "be forced to be free."

State and Utopia

Rousseau's insistence that freedom and equality were inseparable was echoed in the famous assertion of the

◈ Rousseau on the Social Contract ◈

Rousseau, agreeing with Hobbes that society had been founded by compulsion but with Locke that it ought to be founded on consent, argued that a properly constituted social order was the instrument for converting natural into civil freedom.

Man is born free, and everywhere he is in chains. One thinks himself master of others, but is himself the greater slave. How did this change take place? I do not know. What can render it legitimate? I believe I can answer this question.

   If I were to consider nothing but force and its effects, I should say: "As long as a people is compelled to obey, and does so, it does well; as soon as it can shake off the yoke, and does so, it does even better; for in recovering its liberty on the same grounds on which it was stolen away, it either is right in resuming it, or was wrongly deprived in the first place." But the social order is a sacred right which serves as the basis for all others. And yet this right does not come from nature; thus it is founded on conventions.

Source: J. J. Rousseau, "The Social Contract," in *Rousseau: Political Writings,* trans. and ed. F. Watkins (Edinburgh: Nelson, 1953), pp. 3–4.

American Declaration of Independence that all men were created free and equal. But Rousseau never clearly explained how the general will was to be recognized. The American founders therefore turned instead to the ideas of another philosophe, the Baron de Montesquieu (1689–1755), who argued in *The Spirit of the Laws* (1748) that liberty was best secured by a separation of the powers of government. Montesquieu's influential notion found its way not only into the checks and balances of America's constitution but also into the French constitution of 1791, the Prussian Code of 1792, the Spanish constitution of 1812, and the short-lived revolutionary constitutions of 1848.

   If Montesquieu had the more practical effect on political reform, Rousseau expressed the more fundamental tension that lay at the heart of Enlightenment thought. If men were created equal in rights and yet unequal in the wealth, power, and interest by which those rights were to be enjoyed, how was society to achieve justice and promote the common welfare? For the Abbé Morelly, author of the *Code of Nature* (1755), the only answer was to abolish all property and commerce and to establish a rigidly egalitarian society in which each individual was allotted a specific quota of production and consumption. The late Enlightenment figure Simon-Henri Linguet, a lawyer disbarred for his attacks on the property system, predicted a widening gap between rich and poor that would lead to general revolution: never, he wrote, "has Europe been nearer to a complete upheaval."

   The majority view, expressed by Bernard de Mande-ville (1673–1733) and Adam Smith (1723–1790), remained optimistic. In his *Fable of the Bees* (1714), Mandeville argued that just as bees building a hive contributed to the greater good without being aware of it, so even vices such as vanity, envy, and pride were useful because they promoted commerce and industry and gave employment. Adam Smith, expounding a similar view more systematically in *The Wealth of Nations* (1776), asserted that public wealth (and thereby private benefit) was maximized by allowing each individual to pursue his or her own selfish interest. Just as the Newtonian universe produced balance and harmony by obeying its own laws without the need of special divine intervention, so the market was a self-regulating mechanism that functioned best when left alone. As Alexander Pope expressed it in verse, "God and Nature link'd the gen'ral frame, / and bade Self-love and Social be the same."

The Philosophes and Their Public

The philosophes spoke to and largely for the new commercial classes and their interests. But their ideas were also disseminated in the salons of the liberal aristocracy. At these large and semipublic social gatherings, where wit rather than birth was the criterion for admission, they held forth as the guests of such influential tastemakers as Madame du Deffand and Madame Geoffrin. The salons served to domesticate the ideas of the En-

A lively conversation among the philosophes, dominated as usual by Voltaire, whose arm is raised. International celebrities, the philosophes in this print are identified by number. Diderot, the editor of the *Encyclopedia*, is seated at Voltaire's left. [Mansell Collection]

lightenment and also to make them more acceptable. These ideas in turn undermined the social dominance that the French court had enjoyed in the days of Louis XIV and thus some of its power as well. The salons gave the leading figures of the Enlightenment both prestige and an entrée into circles of the highest influence they could not have attained without them, a point ruefully acknowledged later by the conservative Joseph de Maistre when he remarked that "an opinion launched in Paris was like a battering ram launched by thirty million men."

Literacy and Censorship

The principal vehicle of Enlightenment thought, however, was the printing press. In the 100 years before the French Revolution, 18 more men and 13 more women in every 100 became literate in France, and comparable increases were recorded in England, Austria, Denmark, and parts of Germany. The philosophes rode the crest of a great wave that created a new kind of public in Europe: the reading public. For the first time in the West, literature had not merely a circulation but a market, and this market created a new profession, that of the independent writer. Newspapers and periodicals flourished, among them the remarkable *Journal des Dames* ("Ladies' Journal"), whose feminist tone was ringingly set by its first female editor, Madame de Beaumer: "Be silent, all critics, and know that this is a *woman* addressing you!"

One indication of the burgeoning appetite for serious discussion, particularly in France, was the emergence of provincial literary academies that sponsored essay competitions on such subjects as the nature of the passions,

the influence of Christianity, and the condition of philosophy. Rousseau himself first gained recognition through a competition offered by the Dijon Academy, and the future revolutionary Robespierre was secretary of the one at Arras in the 1780s. Lower down on the social scale, but still appealing primarily to a bourgeois audience, were less formally organized reading clubs and social groups such as the Freemasons, a social brotherhood dedicated to celebrating human dignity whose members included figures as diverse as Mozart and Benjamin Franklin.

The governments of the Old Regime tried vainly to stem the spread of new and seditious ideas through the licensing of printers and booksellers, censorship, confiscation, and in the case of notorious figures such as Voltaire, burning books by the common hangman. In Austria under Maria Theresa, even foreign ambassadors had their luggage searched for forbidden books, and Prussia under Frederick William I exiled its foremost philosopher, Christian Wolff. Nor did governments alone exercise censorship; the Catholic church maintained its *Index of Prohibited Books*, and such bodies as law courts and universities could also order the suppression of printed works. Universities, with few exceptions, played little part in the Enlightenment. The Austrian reformer Joseph von Sonnenfels lamented that the universities in his country were a century behind the times, but the same could be said for Paris, Cambridge, and Oxford.

The philosophes used great ingenuity in getting around the various forms of censorship. Some of them used the device of the fictional reporter, as Montesquieu did in his *Persian Letters*, or science fiction, as Voltaire did in his Utopian fantasies *Zadig* and *Micromégas* and

As this charming portrait by Jean-Honoré
Fragonard suggests, literacy was still largely
the privilege of the elite. But a wider middle-
class public was begining to read too,
and it was this public that made the
Enlightenment possible. [National Gallery
of Art, Washington]

the satirist Jonathan Swift (1667–1745) in *Gulliver's
Travels*. A large underground book trade also flourished,
fed by presses in Switzerland and the Low Countries that
supplemented their business in serious social criticism
with scandal, gossip, blasphemy, and pornography. One
enterprising Spanish editor even established a journal
called *El Censor*.

The *Encyclopedia*

The most important and embattled publishing project of
the Enlightenment was the great *Encyclopedia*, conceived and edited by the versatile Diderot. The son of a
provincial artisan and himself the author of philosophical
and mathematical treatises as well as plays, essays, and
novels, Diderot commissioned a veritable Who's Who of
the Enlightenment, including Voltaire, Rousseau, and
Montesquieu, to contribute thousands of articles on
every aspect of human knowledge. The result was the
largest publishing venture up to that time in Western

history. The first volume, containing controversial articles on atheism and the human soul, appeared in 1751.
It was pounced on by the censors, who first suspended
and later revoked the publisher's license. The attorney
general of France denounced it as a conspiracy against
public morals, and the pope declared anyone buying or
reading it to be excommunicated. When the coeditor,
Jean d'Alembert, dropped out, Diderot continued alone,
issuing further volumes despite the ban, filling in the
gaps when contributors defaulted, and even setting up
the plates himself. By 1765 the 17 volumes of text were
complete, and in 1772 the last of 11 volumes of illustrations appeared. In the end, the *Encyclopedia* was a great
commercial success, although Diderot himself saw little
of its profits. By 1789 an astonishing 20,000 full sets had
been sold, and many more circulated in abridgments,
extracts, and pirated editions. Modern public opinion—
the reaction of an audience too large and too independent to be controlled by any institution of church or
state—was born in the eighteenth century. No single
book did more to create and mold it than Diderot's
Encyclopedia.

The Enlightened Despots

One of the most remarkable aspects of the Enlightenment was the adoption and espousal of many of its ideas
by some Old Regime rulers themselves, a phenomenon
known as "enlightened despotism." This was less surprising than it might seem. The Enlightenment was a
general movement that penetrated the most entrenched
bastions of tradition and privilege; even rulers were not
immune to new ideas. Moreover, some monarchs saw
the philosophes as potential allies in their struggles with
the nobility, which almost everywhere resisted the centralizing tendencies of royal governments. Thus it was
that Voltaire could be the guest and companion of one
king at the same time that his works were being burned
by order of another.

For their part, the philosophes welcomed enlightened despotism as the most efficient means of realizing
their objectives. Although Locke and Rousseau had
championed popular sovereignty, neither was a demo-
crat; Rousseau, despite his humble origins, scorned the
masses. Most philosophes were ready enough to welcome a despot, provided that he was willing to use his
power in the service of reason and reform.

Catherine the Great

Russia, still in many respects on the margins of European society, seemed a particularly unlikely setting for
enlightened despotism. In the 37 years following the

In addition to its often provocative articles, Diderot's *Encyclopedia* offered hundreds of unique illustrations of the industrial and mechanical arts of the eighteenth century, such as the brass foundry pictured here, whose workers seem dwarfed by the giant machines and implements they ply. The horse pictured at left turns wheels that crush crude zinc with copper to make brass. The brass is then stamped in a mold and cut by giant shears. [Granger Collection]

death of Peter the Great, it had had six rulers, including a boy of 12, an infant, and a half-wit. Some observers believed that the country was headed toward the kind of aristocratic anarchy that had befallen Poland, whose elective king was a mere figurehead. The Russian nobility had largely emancipated itself from the code of state service Peter imposed on it, and the status of the peasantry had deteriorated even further. The criminal

◈ From Diderot's *Encyclopedia* ◈

Denis Diderot, whose multivolume Encyclopedia *was the largest, most daring, and most influential single work of the Enlightenment, here defends his project against the censors.*

We have already remarked that among those who have set themselves up as censors of the *Encyclopedia* there is hardly a single one who had enough talent to enrich it by even one good article. I do not think I would be exaggerating if I should add that it is a work the greater part of which is about subjects that these people have yet to study. It has been composed with a philosophical spirit, and in this respect most of those who pass adverse judgment on us fall far short of the level of their own century. I call their works in evidence. It is for this reason that they will not endure and that we venture to say that our *Encyclopedia* will be more widely read and more highly appreciated in a few years' time than it is today. . . . Some . . . were once praised to the skies because they wrote for the multitude, following the prevailing ideas, and accommodated their standards to those of the average reader, but they have lost their reputations in proportion as the human mind has made progress, and they have finally been forgotten altogether. Others, by contrast, too daring for the times in which their works appeared, have been little read, hardly understood, not appreciated, and have long remained in obscurity, until the day when the age they had outstripped had passed away and another century, to which they really belonged in spirit, overtook them at last and finally gave them the justice their merits deserved.

Source: D. Diderot, *Encyclopedia*, ed. and trans. S. Gendzier (New York: Harper & Row, 1967), p. 95.

code of 1754 listed serfs only under the heading of property; they had lost even the legal status of human beings.

Strong rule returned to Russia in 1762 when Catherine the Great (1762–1796), the German-born wife of Tsar Peter III, organized his assassination and seized the throne for herself. Few rulers have ever matched Catherine's blend of cosmopolitan charm, instinct for publicity, and ruthless opportunism. She described herself, somewhat disconcertingly, as "every inch a gentleman," but certainly there were at least a few areas that were not: she had 21 attested love affairs during her reign, and doubtless more of briefer duration.

In the early years of her sovereignty, Catherine was oriented almost wholly toward the West. She founded new schools and stimulated the nascent publishing industry. While neighboring states were banning the philosophes, she read Voltaire openly and admiringly, and she subsidized the publication of the *Encyclopedia*. In 1767 she summoned a legislative commission of 560 delegates, of whom half were commoners, including peasants, to revamp the Russian legal code. Catherine herself drafted an elaborate "instruction," including long passages cribbed from her favorite philosophes, expressing her commitment to reform.

The Instruction was a remarkable document in many ways, although some of its more liberal provisions, especially concerning the reduction of serfdom, were cut out of the final draft. The sections on legal procedure were particularly novel. Catherine declared that all persons should be equal before the law. Reflecting her reading of the seminal reform treatise by Cesare Bonesana, marquis de Beccaria, *Of Crimes and Punishments* (1764), she called for the abolition of torture and the reduction of capital punishment. The Instruction was translated into the major languages of Europe; Voltaire received a personal copy. Catherine's fellow enlightened despot, Frederick the Great, was so delighted with it that he made her a member of the Berlin Academy. The most flattering response came from France, where it was banned as subversive.

Despite this fanfare, the legislative commission was a disappointment if not a fiasco. The delegates, most of them inexperienced in public affairs, were bewildered as to what was expected of them, as well they might have been, since Catherine's proposals would have stood much of Russian society on its head. The commission divided bitterly over the issue of serfdom, with the peasants and a few of the liberal nobility opposed stoutly by the landed interest, and produced only minor reforms in provincial administration. It was adjourned at the outbreak of war with Turkey in 1768 and never reconvened.

The Russo-Turkish war of 1768–1774 marked a turning point in Catherine's reign. Her dalliance with reform was now over, and she devoted herself instead to the more familiar business of power politics. In this and a subsequent war with Turkey (1787–1792), Catherine an-

nexed the north shore of the Black Sea, although her goal of conquering Istanbul itself—the oldest and hardiest of all Russian imperial dreams—remained unfulfilled. The false hopes of reform Catherine raised were also largely responsible for the great rebellion of Emilian Pugachev (1773–1774), a Cossack chieftain who declared himself to be the murdered Tsar Peter, set up a court with the "true" Catherine, and promised an end to serfdom, taxation, and conscription, as well as the abolition of the landed aristocracy. For a time much of southern Russia was aflame, and refugees streamed into Moscow; but Pugachev was defeated at last in a series of pitched battles, brought to Moscow in a cage, and, like Stenka Razin a century before, quartered in the Kremlin Square.

Pugachev's rebellion confirmed the mutual dependence of Catherine and her nobility. As the nobility needed the strength of absolute despotism to protect their privileges, so they alone stood between the empress and peasant anarchy. Their common interest was sealed in the Charter of the Nobility (1785). The charter completely freed the nobility from imperial service, giving it instead sole responsibility for provincial administration. In this way the nobility, in looking after their own interests as landowners, exercised direct political control of the countryside on behalf of the state. Content with their powers, they ceased to meddle in palace affairs, while the imperial government no longer concerned itself with serfdom, human and political rights, and other unpalatable subjects. The few intellectuals who still did, such as the educational reformer Nikolai Novikov (1744–1818) and Alexander Radischev (1749–1802), author of the bitterly critical *Journey from Moscow to St. Petersburg* (1790), soon found themselves in exile or in prison. It was of no avail for Radischev to point out that he had said nothing that Catherine herself had not affirmed in her days of Enlightenment. In the end, she even banned her old friend Voltaire.

Frederick the Great

A far more sophisticated example of enlightened despotism was Frederick the Great of Prussia. Frederick was the most admired monarch of the eighteenth century. He dominated it, by reputation if not by the actual strength of his country, much as Louis XIV had dominated the Europe of his time. Frederick liked to encourage the parallel, although he was certainly Louis' superior both as a soldier and as a man of intellect. Not only did Frederick speak the rhetoric of the Enlightenment, but he was also a philosophe of sorts himself. He scorned divine right kingship, declaring that his power rested on his service to the people; a ruler, he said in a famous phrase, was only "the first servant of the state." In effect, Frederick replaced the divine right notion of a

---

◉ Frederick the Great ◉ on the Enlightened Despot

Frederick here offers the classic justification for the traditional sovereign who, by comprehending all interests, is alone qualified to promote the common interest.

The sovereign is attached by indissoluble ties to the body of the state; hence it follows that he, by repercussion, is sensible to all the ills which afflict his subjects; and the people, in like manner, suffer from the misfortunes which affect their sovereign. There is but one general good, which is that of the state. . . . The sovereign represents the state; he and his people form but one body, which can only be happy as far as united by concord. The prince is to the nation he governs what the head is to the man; it is his duty to see, to think, and act for the whole community, so that he may procure it every advantage of which it is capable. . . . Such are in general the duties imposed upon a prince, from which, in order that he may never depart, he ought often to recollect that he himself is but a man, like the least of his subjects. If he be the first general, the first minister of the realm, it is not so that he should shelter in the shadow of authority, but that he should fulfil the duties of such titles. He is only the first servant of the state, who is obliged to act with probity and prudence; and to remain as totally disinterested as if he were each moment liable to render an account of his administration to his fellow citizens.

Source: Frederick the Great, *An Essay on Forms of Government,* trans. T. Holcroft, in E. Weber, ed., *The Western Tradition,* 3rd ed. (Lexington, Mass.: Heath, 1972), pp. 539, 544.

---

mystical relation between the ruler and God with an equally mystical relation between the ruler and his people. He identified the king with what Rousseau was to call the general will, for the monarch alone, he argued, standing above all parties and interests, could legislate for the common good. For that reason too, although the monarch's power derived from the people and was exercised solely on their behalf, they could never recall or revoke it. Their interests being partial, they could never be in a correct position to judge the whole; only the ruler could see the common interest.

Such a ruler, restrained by neither God nor man, might turn tyrant with impunity. But having already all the power he could desire and all the wealth he could consume, Frederick argued, he was beyond ordinary temptation. Frederick himself seemed the perfect illustration of this. He built a palace at Potsdam in imitation of Versailles but found little time to enjoy it. No breath of scandal ever touched him; he had no private vices and, it almost seemed, no private life. His energies, apart from philosophy, literature, and music, were wholly absorbed in Prussia. He drained its swamps, encouraged its industry, and expanded its agriculture. Within the country, he promoted education, welcomed religious refugees of every stripe, and undertook a codification of the laws. "My chief obligation," he wrote, "is . . . to make

[my people] as happy as human beings can be, or as happy as the means at my disposal permit."

The people Frederick wished to serve were not the free and equal citizens of Rousseau's commonwealth, however, but the hierarchically defined subjects of an Old Regime society. Prussians were not free; although Frederick, like Catherine, was opposed to serfdom in theory, he did little to alleviate it. Nor were Prussians equal. Frederick favored the nobility even more than his father had, reserving the officer corps of the army and the upper levels of the civil service exclusively for them. Because the army and the bureaucracy dominated Prussian society between them, this meant that little initiative and less authority was left for the fledgling merchant class. At Frederick's death, Prussia was the most aristocratically controlled society in Europe. The long-term consequences of this, for Prussia and for Germany, were severe.

If Frederick believed in service to inferiors, he had few behavioral scruples toward his fellow monarchs. Even Louis XIV had attempted to rationalize his aggressions by legal claims, but when Frederick attacked Silesia in 1740, he blandly justified it on the grounds that it was in the nature of states to expand up to the limit of their ability. In 1772 he joined Catherine and Maria Theresa of Austria in carving up a helpless Poland in

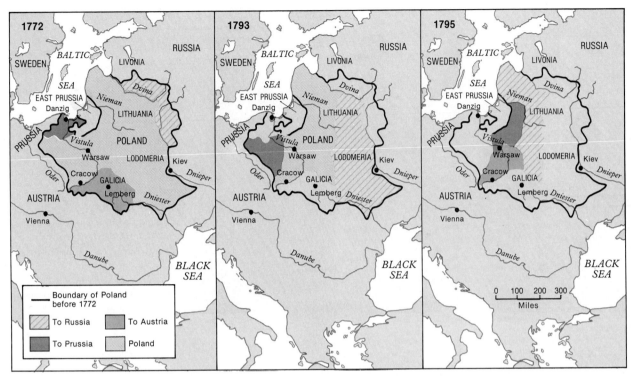

26.1 The Partitioning of Poland, 1772–1795

order to "adjust" the balance of power in eastern Europe in the wake of Catherine's gains against Turkey. Poland lost a third of its territory and half its population in this so-called Partition Treaty. Despite desperate attempts to strengthen itself by constitutional reform, it was wholly swallowed up by the subsequent partitions of 1793 and 1795 and ceased to exist as an independent nation. Enlightened despotism might sometimes aim at making states more rational and efficient; it did not make them more peaceful.

Joseph II:
The Revolutionary Emperor

If Catherine and Frederick were essentially conservative rulers who used the rhetoric of the Enlightenment to maintain traditional autocracy, the Austrian emperor Joseph II (1780–1790) was the one sovereign who seriously embraced its principles and unreservedly attempted to put them into effect. The eldest of Maria Theresa's 16 children, Joseph grew up unhappily in the shadow of a court whose dull and devout propriety was far removed from the witty, urbane skepticism of the philosophes. In 1765 he became Holy Roman emperor and coregent of Austria, but his desire for reform was frustrated during his mother's lifetime. When he suc-

ceeded her at last, he had a 15-year backlog of projects and ambitions.

The empire Joseph inherited was a crazy quilt of territories and populations that spread across Europe from Flanders on the North Sea to the borders of Russia and Turkey. Its various peoples—Flemish, Italian, German, Czech, Croatian, Magyar, Polish—had little in common, and their loyalty to the Habsburg throne had been purchased only by conceding a large measure of self-rule, especially in Hungary and Bohemia. Joseph set out to compress this explosive mixture into a single political and social order and to transform some of the most backward regions of Europe into instant models of progress and enlightenment.

In her quiet way, Maria Theresa had done much to put the Austrian empire on the path to modernization. Administration had been centralized in Austria proper and Bohemia, creating a model for the whole empire. Guild monopolies and tariff barriers had been overthrown, establishing the largest free trade zone in Europe. Church land had been expropriated, and despite Maria Theresa's own hostility to secularism, the church's grip on education had been broken. For Joseph, however, the work of reform had barely begun with these steps. In ten years of ceaseless activity, he issued 6,000 edicts covering every aspect of life in the empire. What Catherine and Frederick had only talked

Joseph II and Catherine the Great, two of the enlightened despots and rivals in power politics as well as in reform, met in 1787. By this time Catherine had long abandoned her liberal pose and Joseph's attempt to remodel the Austrian Empire had driven many of its provinces to the verge of revolt. [Historisches Museum der Stadt Wein]

of doing, Joseph decreed with the stroke of a pen. Serfdom was abolished, censorship lifted, and freedom of religion instituted. Jews were given civil rights and permitted to intermarry with Christians. Marriage itself was declared a civil contract, to the horror of conservatives and the outrage of the church. Apostasy and witchcraft were stricken from the legal code. Capital punishment was limited, and judicial torture was abolished. Equality before the law was not only proclaimed but enforced; Vienna was shocked by the sight of a young nobleman sweeping the streets in a chain gang.

There can be no doubt of the sincerity of Joseph's intentions. Although many of the changes he introduced were similar to those of other centralizing eighteenth-century monarchies, he regarded his power as an instrument for the betterment of humanity. He considered the existence of serfdom an "incredible and inexpressible evil," was outraged by bigotry and intolerance, and viewed the task of reform as an almost holy calling. "The service of God is inseparable from that of the state," he declared, and he wrote to one of his ministers, "Hasten everything that brings me nearer to the accomplishment of my plans for the happiness of my people."

Joseph brushed privilege, tradition, and special interests aside in the spate of his reform, boasting that he had made philosophy alone the legislator of his empire. The result was to unite the nobility, the church, and the provincial estates against him. Even the peasants, bewildered by the mass of edicts meant for their benefit and often sympathizing with the local priest or noble whom Joseph declared to be their oppressor, failed to support him.

Faced with almost universal opposition, Joseph re-

doubled his efforts. He reimposed censorship in an effort to dampen criticism, suspended due process, and set an army of spies on the population. The reactionary Count Pergen, his minister of police, became the most powerful man in the government and ultimately the only one Joseph trusted. Rebellion flared in Hungary, the Tirol, and Flanders, and by the end of Joseph's reign, large parts of the empire were held down only by force. He died a broken man at 48, and within a few years the entire edifice of his reforms collapsed. Serfdom was restored, to survive in parts of the empire as late as 1867, and the nobility and clergy resumed their sway.

Enlightened Despotism in Perspective

The creed of enlightened despotism was best summed up in the motto of another reforming monarch, Charles III of Spain (1759–1788): "Everything for the people, nothing by the people." The enlightened despots represented a stage in the transformation of the personal monarchy of the old dynastic states to the impersonal rule of modern bureaucracies. Their very success in consolidating the power of the central state proved to be their undoing. It was true that the nobility and the church had frequently stood in the way of their ambitions. But in the long run absolute monarchy depended on these institutions as much as they did on it. Together, the church, the aristocracy, and the crown had made up the hierarchical order of authority whose ultimate expression was the divine right of kings. In undermining the foundations of that order, the enlightened despots eroded the ground on which they stood. There was no particular reason why their functions could not be exercised by someone else, and in fact similar programs—freeing trade, secularizing education, curbing privilege, modernizing the law, and guaranteeing basic rights—were carried out in Portugal and Denmark by ministers rather than by the feeble monarchs they served. When the French Revolution broke out in 1789, Joseph II condemned it bitterly, even though its authors sought many of the same goals as he. Joseph, who had wanted to do so much for the people, could not accept the fact that they might at last do something for themselves.

The Counter-Enlightenment

Reason was not triumphant everywhere in the eighteenth century, nor were its claims accepted uncritically. In his enormously popular novels, *The New Heloise* (1761) and *Émile* (1762), Rousseau argued that feeling was as important as intellect in the development of moral sentiments. He praised nature not merely as a clever mathematical arrangement but also as a source of beauty and wonder whose effect on human emotions was as crucial as the operation of its laws on reason. *The New Heloise* went through 70 editions by 1789 and became the bible of people who saw in unspoiled nature a haven from the corruptions of society and a model for the pure and simple life. *Émile,* by stressing the importance of developing each child's individual character and ability and the role of the teacher as a sympathetic guide rather than as a taskmaster, inspired a new movement in education, carried forward by the Swiss reformer Johann Heinrich Pestalozzi (1746–1827) and the Germans Johann Basedow (c. 1742–1790) and Friedrich Fröbel (1782–1852), and eventually a new view of childhood altogether. Instead of seeing the child as an immature and refractory adult, these educators emphasized the unique and distinctive character of childhood and the various phases of the child's development.

The middle and upper classes sought relief from the rationalism of the Enlightenment in a cult of sentiment, fed by popular novels such as Samuel Richardson's *Pamela* and *Clarissa* and Pierre de Marivaux's *Marianne.* But the official culture left deeper needs unmet. Established religion, buffeted by attacks on the tenets of its faith no less than on its wealth and privilege, was everywhere on the defensive. The Jesuits were so fiercely assailed that their order was temporarily dissolved in 1773, while theologians such as Samuel Clarke (1675–1729) and Joseph Butler (1692–1752) in England tried to anchor morality in reason and prudence rather than revelation.

The Revival of Religion

Such ideas were cold comfort to Europe's laboring millions, who sought in religion the promise of salvation and the only hope and consolation in their lives. What they could no longer get from their betters they soon began to make for themselves. Grass-roots religion—a phenomenon previously associated with periods of upheaval such as the Reformation or the English revolution—spread out from late-seventeenth-century Germany across Protestant Europe and even to the New World. As Pietism in Germany, Methodism in England, and the Great Awakening in America, it had one general goal: to revitalize religion by encouraging personal piety, good works, and a communal, often highly emotional experience of worship.

The roots of Pietism lay in the German mystical tradition, revived in the early seventeenth century by Jakob Böhme (1575–1624) and popularized by the evangelist Philip Jakob Spener (1635–1705). As with popular religious movements during the midcentury English revolution, Spener's preaching was attacked by the clerical establishment; the University of Wittenberg found 250 alleged errors in his doctrine. Nonetheless, by the end of the century Pietism had become the dominant spiritual movement in Protestant Germany. It found academic support in the newly established University of Halle (1694) and an aristocratic patron in Count Nicholas von Zinzendorf (1700–1760), who sheltered the Moravian Brethren, a radical Pietist sect, on his estate. It was a Moravian Pietist who counseled the spiritually troubled young English clergyman John Wesley (1703–1791), who with his brother, Charles, and a charismatic preacher, George Whitefield, took the evangelical message to the mine pits and the open fields when the churches closed their doors to him. Wesley's conversion experience was typical. On an evening in May 1738, he wrote, "I felt my heart strangely warmed. I felt I did trust in Christ, Christ alone, for salvation, and assurance was given me that . . . saved me from the law of sin and death." Never faltering in this conviction thereafter, Wesley tramped the English countryside for 50 years, delivering by his own estimate some 40,000 sermons. His followers, called Methodists, embraced the lower-middle-class virtues of thrift and toil, but their social horizons were limited, and they tended to be hostile to Catholics and Jews.

Catholicism produced its own reform movements, beginning in the seventeenth century with Quietism in Spain and Jansenism in France, Flanders, and Italy. Because of the greater organizational unity of the Roman church, these movements, unlike the various forms of Pietism, were of elite rather than popular origin, although in some areas they spread more widely among the population; in spite (or perhaps because) of papal

The charismatic John Wesley was one of the most important figures in the religious revival that spread among people whose spiritual hunger was served neither by the established churches nor by the Deist God of Reason. [National Portrait Gallery, London]

and royal opposition, two-thirds of Paris was Jansenist in 1730. Like Pietism, the Catholic reform stressed personal faith, emancipation from dogma, and the right of individual conscience.

Skepticism and Idealism

Reason itself was subjected to criticism by the Anglo-Irish philosopher George Berkeley (1685–1753) and the Scotsman David Hume (1711–1776), who cast doubt on the simple model of sensation and reflection proposed by Locke. Both stressed that ideas developed in the mind on the basis of sensory impressions did not necessarily correspond to the world as it actually existed. Immanuel Kant (1724–1804), the greatest philosopher of the age, went even further. Kant argued that the mind imposed its own structure on experience, creating a picture with which it then lived. This picture could be tested and refined—for example, by science—but the mind could never go beyond it to know what the world was really like in itself. Kant's idealism, as his philosophy

came to be called, was devastating to the more exaggerated claims of both science and religion; neither faith nor reason, he suggested, could lead to a knowledge of reality in itself.

Both skeptical philosophy and popular religion stressed the subjective experience of the individual, and both laid the ground for the new Romantic sensibility that began to develop in the eighteenth century. We must not, however, think of the Enlightenment in terms of rationalism and the reaction against it. Rather it must be seen as a great current whose very strength created countercurrents that are inseparably linked to it. In this respect, its most characteristic figure is perhaps Rousseau, who dreamed of an ideal community yet found himself always an outsider and insisted on the submission of the individual to the general will while exalting the rights of personal feeling and a liberated human nature. If the eighteenth century has with justice been called the age of reason, it was also a time that knew, in the words of Pascal, that "the heart has its reasons, which reason knows nothing of."

The Emancipation of the Jews

The decline of traditional Christian faith among the elite, the general questioning of the political and social order, and the concept of a secular brotherhood that animated the Enlightenment at its best led to a gradual reassessment of groups that had long been on the margins of European society. Prominent among these were the Jews. There were perhaps a million Jews in eighteenth-century Europe. The overwhelming majority were the Ashkenazim, who lived mainly in the small towns and villages of eastern Poland and Lithuania and spoke the mixed German-Polish dialect called Yiddish. Confined in ghettos, shunned and subjected to periodic outbreaks of looting and massacre known as pogroms, and for the most part desperately poor, they lived in almost complete isolation from the surrounding Christian community, marked off by their distinctive dress, beards, and speech, striving to live by their ancient biblical and rabbinical precepts and nourishing the secret, never-extinguished hope of a messiah who would lead them out of exile and back to the Holy Land.

By contrast, the Sephardim, mostly the descendants of Jews expelled from Spain and Portugal in the sixteenth century and settled largely in such urban centers as Amsterdam, Venice, London, Frankfurt, and Bordeaux, were more prosperous and cosmopolitan. But Jews everywhere, still commonly blamed for Jesus' death and disliked for their distinctive practices, were subjected to restrictions and prohibitions of every kind.

◙ The Romantic Reaction ◙

*The rationalism and skepticism of the philosophes produced a powerful
reaction in favor of emotion and religious sensibility, expressed in these
verses by William Blake (1757–1827).*

Mock on, Mock on Voltaire, Rousseau:
Mock on, Mock on: 'tis all in vain!
You throw sand against the wind,
And the wind blows it back again.
    And every sand becomes a Gem
Reflected in the beams divine:
Blown back they blind the mocking Eye,
But still in Israel's paths they shine.
    The Atoms of Democritus
And Newton's Particles of light
Are sands upon the Red Sea shore,
Where Israel's tents do shine so bright.

Source: W. Blake, *The Commonplace Book.*

They were periodically driven from any place where their numbers seemed alarming, as in Vienna in 1421 and 1669 and Prague in 1557 and 1744. Elsewhere they were restricted by quota; the city of Ulm permitted exactly one Jewish family to reside there. In central and eastern Europe, Jews were forbidden to engage in agriculture and most ordinary trades and were confined to banking, commerce, moneylending, and peddling. They were subject to special taxes and assessments and often pure blackmail: Maria Theresa forced the Jews of Bohemia to pay 3 million florins to spare the community from expulsion. They were barred everywhere from public office, and a bill to naturalize British-born Jews in 1753 was withdrawn in the face of a violent public outcry.

A few Jewish financiers attained great wealth and on occasion political influence. The so-called court Jews of the seventeenth century were merchants and bankers who played a vital role in raising credit, supplying armies, and serving as financial advisers to rulers in Spain, Germany, and Austria. Samuel Oppenheimer (1630–1703) of Heidelberg organized the defense of Vienna against the Turks in 1683. The river fleet he constructed enabled the Austrian army to besiege Budapest and Belgrade, and when the victors brutally sacked the Jewish communities there, he provided for their relief. During the 1690s, as imperial armies fought both Louis XIV in Germany and the Turks in Hungary, Oppenheimer was given the title of director general of war supply. This so scandalized the Viennese that a mob was permitted to attack and loot his mansion, though not, to be sure, until the war was over.

The Sephardic Jews in the west were spared the more horrific experiences of their eastern brethren, such as the pogrom at Uman near Kiev in 1762, when 20,000 Poles and Jews were massacred by peasants and Cossack tribesmen. But all Jewish communities lived in perpetual fear and anxiety. When in 1665 a charismatic Jew of Syrian origin, Sabbatai Zevi (1626–1676), proclaimed himself the messiah, a wave of millennial fervor swept over European Jewry. It gripped not only the poor and downtrodden Ashkenazim of eastern Europe but the wealthiest Jewish families of Amsterdam and Hamburg as well. Tens of thousands of Jews sold their belongings and prepared to march east. Their hopes were tragically disappointed. The Turkish sultan, alarmed at the commotion Zevi's activities had aroused in his dominions, forced him to convert publicly to Islam on pain of death, and his movement collapsed.

Traditional anti-Semitism was at first reinforced by the Enlightenment. Christian anxiety at the weakening of faith was easily deflected toward the Jews; the Hebraic scholar Johann Andreas Eisenmenger (1654–1704) published a 2,000-page anti-Semitic tract in 1699, *Judaism Discovered*, a source frequently mined by later authors. Many of the philosophes were unsympathetic toward the Jews as well, taking up Spinoza's attack on their adherence to the Mosaic law as an enslavement to a dead past. But others, such as Locke and Montesquieu, promoted their cause as victims of the church. In *The Persian Letters*, Montesquieu's fictional correspondent upbraided the conduct of Christian Europeans: "You Christians complain that the Emperor of China roasts all

This French engraving shows a Portuguese Jewish family celebrating Passover at their home. [Brotherton Library, University of Leeds]

Christians in his dominions on a slow fire. You behave much worse toward the Jews, because they do not believe as you do." The German playwright and critic Gotthold Ephraim Lessing (1729–1781) made a Jew the hero of his drama *Nathan the Wise* (1779). Joseph II saw toleration in more practical terms: "It is our purpose," he wrote, "to make the Jews more useful and serviceable to the state." Though even this most enlightened of despots did not grant Jews full equality, he removed most of the customary disabilities against them, encouraged them to enter agriculture and the crafts, and permitted them to enroll at academies and universities. The poll tax levied against Jews was remitted in France in 1784 and in Prussia in 1787, and the marquis de Pombal, the reforming minister of Joseph I of Portugal, promulgated the first laws against anti-Semitism.

Jewish emancipation was a special case of the more general extension of religious toleration in eighteenth-century Europe. After a long crusade, French Protestants regained in 1787 the civil rights and freedom of worship they had lost by the revocation of the Edict of Nantes in 1685, while in England the first legal Roman Catholic chapel since the mid-sixteenth century opened in Westminster in 1792. The Prussian Law Code of 1794 summed up the fruits of a century of agitation by declaring that "every inhabitant of the state must be granted complete freedom of conscience and religion."

But toleration was a two-edged sword for the Jews. Some embraced it fully, such as the philosopher Moses Mendelssohn (1729–1786), a colleague of Kant's and reputedly the model for *Nathan the Wise*. Mendelssohn founded the Haskalah movement, which attempted to reconcile Enlightenment thought with Jewish tradition.

Conservatives, however, viewed such overtures with horror. They feared that what centuries of persecution had failed to do, toleration would at last achieve instead: the destruction of the Jewish community and its assimilation into the dominant Christian culture. The fear of losing Jewish identity also stimulated the growth of Hasidism, a popular religious movement akin to Pietism that emphasized the aliyah, or return to Israel. But neither tradition nor nostalgia nor the revival of Judaism's most ancient dream could prevent the incursion of the new secularism into even the most closed quarter of European society. After centuries, the Jews were being forced out of their isolation into a future of uncertain promise.

The assimilation Mendelssohn favored was the main goal of the Reform movement of the early nineteenth century. The first Jewish Reform temple was founded in 1810 in Brunswick, in northern Germany; the service was conducted in German as well as Hebrew, and an organ was used, a musical instrument hitherto associated with Christian churches.

The aim of the Reform movement was to demonstrate that the Jews had lost any sense of nationalism and had become a purely religious sect. Within the movement itself there was considerable debate about the authority of the Hebrew Bible and the Talmud, together with the value of retaining the use of the Hebrew language in religious worship. This challenge to tradition provoked strong reactions, with those who upheld the traditional point of view becoming known as Orthodox. In its present form, Orthodox Judaism combines a strict observance of traditional beliefs and observances with an awareness of their applicability to modern living.

An attempt at compromise inspired the development of the Conservative movement, which began in the United States at the end of the nineteenth century. Both Reform and Conservative Jews worship in synagogues in which the sexes are not segregated and in which prayers in the vernacular are used. Conservative Jews follow the Orthodox tradition of accepting the entire rabbinic tradition of the Talmud, although they interpret it more flexibly; they also promote Jewish aspirations to be recognized as a nation.

An offshoot of the practical aims of Conservatism was the development of the Reconstructionist movement, whose members interpret Jewish traditional practices as folkways acquired over the centuries and religion as only one aspect of the Jews' existence as a people. The Reconstructionist God, far from being the supreme creator and legislator of the Old Testament, is perceived as a cosmic process. Like other splinter movements, Reconstructionism has generally failed to establish itself on a widespread basis, and most practicing Jews today are either Orthodox or Reform, except in the United States, where Conservatism has a large number of followers.

The Abolitionist Movement

The contradiction between the ideals of freedom and equality expressed by the Enlightenment and the reality of eighteenth-century practice was most glaringly evident in the case of slavery. This contradiction was explained away by the assumption of black inferiority. Blacks, it was held, were less developed than whites both biologically and intellectually; thus they felt physical and mental hardships far less keenly. Perpetual children, they were incapable of taking independent responsibility for their lives and hence of genuine liberty. Their management by whites was actually a kindness; one slave ship was piously named the *Social Contract*.

The myth of the happy slave ran aground on the fact of black rebellion. The critic Samuel Johnson shocked a literary gathering at Oxford by offering a toast to the next slave revolt in the colonies. The pamphleteer Thomas Paine asked Americans in 1775 how they could rebel against the British while still keeping slaves themselves. But it was not until nearly the end of the century

◉ The Revulsion Against Slavery ◉

The opposition to slavery, muted at best in the writings of the philosophes, gained ground in the late eighteenth century and culminated in the abolition of the slave trade in the early nineteenth. The new revulsion was well expressed in this letter of 1778 describing a slave auction in Kingston, Jamaica.

Early this morning a Negro went through all the streets ringing a little bell. He had a slip of paper in his hand and called out something for sale. I asked what he was calling out, and someone answered: "People."

I got dressed and went to the market. There a whole mass of black people was standing about, old and young, men and women, all stark naked, just as God had made them. Each had a card hung around his neck with a number written on it.

Dear God, I thought, here people sell human beings just as we sell geese and pigs.

By nine o'clock, everything was sold, and everyone made his preparations to carry off his newly acquired goods. The little black girl kissed her little brother once again and cried; the old Negroes embraced one another and howled their goodbyes. As they were going, there suddenly started up a dull roaring among them. At first I thought it was just more howling. Then I realized they were singing a song in their Guinea language which would go something as follows:

> Far from my homeland
> I must languish and die,
> Without comfort, amidst struggle and shame.
> O the white men, so clever and handsome!
> Yet I have done these pitiless white men no harm.
> You, there, in heaven, help me, a poor black man!

Source: A. L. von Scholzer, "A New Year's Letter from Jamaica," trans. R. Gay, in P. Gay, ed., *The Enlightenment: A Comprehensive Anthology* (New York: Simon & Schuster, 1973), pp. 688–689.

Am I Not a Man and a Brother? **This
medallion, struck by Josiah Wedgwood
and adopted as the seal of the Slave
Emancipation Society, may be regarded
as a prototype of the modern political issue
button. It was a powerful propaganda
weapon in the abolitionist campaign of the
late eighteenth century. [Culver Pictures]**

that a movement to abolish slavery and the slave trade
gathered force. Significantly, it was led not by the philosophes but by dissenting English Protestant groups
such as Quakers and Baptists as well as a group of Anglicans seeking to revitalize their church, the Clapham
sect. The sect's leaders, William Wilberforce (1759–
1833) and Thomas Clarkson (1760–1846), lobbied Parliament and campaigned vigorously in the press and in
the pulpit, demonstrating again the growing importance
of popular opinion. Clarkson, the first reformer to make
abolitionism a professional career, interrogated seamen
on the Liverpool docks and tracked down witnesses who
could testify to the evils of the slave trade. Not to be
outdone, the republican leaders of France's National
Convention declared slavery abolished outright and all
former slaves citizens in 1794, although this edict was
never put into effect, and Napoleon later reestablished
slavery in the colonies. British abolitionism proved a
longer-lasting cause. It gave religious dissenters their
first major social cause in 100 years and a chance to
show that Christianity too could take its place in the vanguard of progress. If the actual achievement of abolition
owed more to the decline of slavery's profitability than
anything else, the abolitionist role in forging the political
consensus necessary to act was a crucial one.

The Rights of Women

John Adams, replying in 1776 to a suggestion from his
wife, Abigail, that the American revolutionaries "remember the ladies" in their new charter of rights, observed

with uneasy humor that her letter "was the first intimation that another tribe more numerous and powerful
than all the rest were grown discontented." The debate
on the rights and status of women already had a long
history when Abigail Adams spoke up to her husband.
As early as 1589, a woman suitably named (or calling
herself) Jane Anger had written a spirited defense of
women. During the English revolution some women had
preached from the pulpits of Independent congregations, and the colonist Anne Hutchinson (1591–1643)
was expelled from Massachusetts Bay for demanding
religious freedom; she and five of her children were later
murdered by Indians. By the end of the seventeenth century a number of women, including Aphra Behn, Susan
Centlivre, Mary de la Rivière Manley, and Eliza Haywood had begun to earn independent livings as writers.
Catherine Macaulay (1731–1791) wrote an eight-volume
history of England as well as pamphlets denouncing the
British monarchy and defending the French Revolution,
and the educational reformer and abolitionist Hannah
More (1745–1833) earned more than £30,000 by her
writings. These, however, were exceptions to the norm.
Although Daniel Defoe had urged wives to participate
actively in their husbands' businesses and a remarkable
article in *The Gentleman's Magazine* in 1739 by an anonymous woman writer deplored the fact that the economic helplessness of women forced them to marry
against their will, respectable tradesmen preferred to
keep their spouses at home, and working women were
severely stigmatized.

As we have noted, some women played important
roles as hostesses of salons during the Enlightenment,
and writers such as Locke, Montesquieu, and Voltaire
occasionally commented on the legal disabilities of
women. Significant changes were also taking place in
the most important institution that touched on women,
the family. The emphasis on romantic love and companionship first advanced by writers such as the poet John
Milton had become general by the late eighteenth century, and with it, women's expectations in marriage had
begun to rise. At the same time, the attack on divine
right hierarchy shook traditional notions of male dominance in the family. The entry for "Women" in the *Encyclopedia* pointed out that marriage was a legal contract
with mutual rights and responsibilities. The extension of
the idea of a contract to marriage and the family had
profound social implications. Its consequences are still
unfolding today.

But the status of eighteenth-century women, even of
the most privileged classes, is better summarized in the
careers of two Englishwomen, Lady Mary Wortley
Montagu (1689–1762) and Mary Wollstonecraft (1759–
1797). Montagu, a woman of great energy and independence, associated on terms of equality with such
leading literary figures as Alexander Pope and edited a
journal supporting Sir Robert Walpole. Her husband was

British ambassador to Istanbul, and in her "Turkish letters," which she circulated only in manuscript, she contrasted the freedom of Turkish women to carry on adulterous affairs under their veils with the restraints on women of her own class and nation. Montagu's intention, like Montesquieu's in *The Persian Letters*, was of course satiric, but she had a serious purpose underneath. Before her marriage she had written to her fiancé that wealthy young women were sold by their fathers into marriage "like slaves, and I cannot tell you what price my master will put upon me." Montagu's father had in fact attempted to force her to marry a man she could not love. She had educated herself against his wishes, and when she eventually separated from her freely chosen husband, she was forced to live the remainder of her life in Italy. Her own experience of oppression gave her sympathy for that of others, and she praised the Roman critic Longinus for having chosen as examples of the best writing of antiquity the work of "a Jew . . . and a woman."

John Opie's portrait of the great English feminist Mary Wollstonecraft shows a powerful, mature woman in her mid-thirties whose introspective expression is tinged with sadness and disillusion. Wollstonecraft may have been pregnant with her second child when this portrait was painted. [National Portrait Gallery, London]

❦ MARY WOLLSTONECRAFT, FEMINIST

Mary Wollstonecraft was the daughter of a tradesman who squandered an inheritance and abused his wife. From an early age she showed signs of rebellion against the conventions of dress and behavior expected of respectable girls. She was also precociously aware of the ill treatment of servants, widows, and the poor generally. Leaving home, first as a lady's companion and then as a schoolmistress, she struck up a passionate friendship with a girl two years her senior, Fanny Blood. It was the first of her many attempts to find the affection and understanding that had been so painfully absent in her family.

At this time too Wollstonecraft began to find the first adult role models with whom she could identify herself. Respectable society had been shocked by the elopement of Lady Eleanor Butler and Sarah Ponsonby, who set up house together in a remote Welsh valley where they received selected visitors in an exquisitely arranged house and garden. For Wollstonecraft and for many other young Englishwomen, they represented an ideal of companionship and personal freedom.

Escape to Wales was impracticable, but in the London suburb of Newington, Wollstonecraft met the Unitarian minister and political radical Richard Price, whose circle included women writers such as Ann Jebb and Anna Barbauld. Like Lady Montagu, Wollstonecraft soon found her professional outlet in writing. Her first essay, *Thoughts on the Education of Daughters*, was largely conventional in tone, but it contained a bitter complaint against the lack of occupations open to women that clearly echoed her own situation. This was followed by an autobiographical novel that she called simply *Mary*. In it the author advocates both social reform and sexual liberation, and in an uncompleted second novel, *Maria, or the Wrongs of Women*, Wollstonecraft makes the latter point even more strongly: "When novelists and moralists praise as a virtue a woman's coldness of constitution and want of passion, I am disgusted."

Like many other British radicals, Wollstonecraft placed great hopes in the French Revolution. Her eye, however, was as much on what could be done in Britain as on what was happening in France. In *A Vindication of the Rights of Man*, written in answer to Edmund Burke's attack on the revolution, she called for the breakup of large estates as a means of relieving urban poverty and denounced Burke's notion of liberty as a cloak for the defense of property interests. She traveled alone to Paris in December 1792 to observe the revolution at first hand and returned to publish a defense of it. "The will of the people," she declared, "is always the voice of reason."

Wollstonecraft's most famous and most important work, however, was *A Vindication of the Rights of Woman*, published in 1792 and now regarded as the true beginning of the modern women's movement. The *Vindication* is a work of passionate indignation; Wollstonecraft declares that women have been as brutalized as black slaves and degraded almost beneath the status of reasonable beings:

> The *divine right* of husbands, like the divine right of kings, may, it is to be hoped, in this enlightened age, be contested without danger . . . . I love man as my fellow, but his sceptre, real or usurped, extends not to me, unless the reason of an individual demands my homage; and even then the submission is to reason, and not to man.

It was time, she asserted, not to make place for "a small number of distinguished women" in society but to demand liberation for all.

Wollstonecraft won support in radical circles, but Horace Walpole's denunciation of her as "a hyena in petticoats" was typical of conservative reaction. Her personal life also shocked respectable opinion. She bore a daughter out of wedlock in 1794 and lived openly with the anarchist William Godwin (1756–1836), who opposed marriage on philosophical grounds but agreed to a wedding upon learning of her second pregnancy. Wollstonecraft died ten days after the birth of another daughter, Mary. The scandals of her personal life, revived by the publication of Godwin's memoirs, led nineteenth-century feminists such as Harriet Martineau to shun her as an unsafe example for the women's movement. It was not until 1889, when Susan B. Anthony and Elizabeth Cady Stanton published the first volume of their *History of Woman Suffrage*, that Mary Wollstonecraft's name was redeemed and given first place among the pioneers to whom the book was dedicated.

The Arts: From Rococo to Neoclassical

The dramatic style of the baroque gave way in the eighteenth century to the smaller-scaled and more refined rococo. With its often elaborate ornamentation, rococo was most effective in intimate, interior forms, and it is for the elegance of its aristocratic drawing rooms, furniture, and porcelain that the period is best remembered. The hold that French culture had taken on Europe during the reign of Louis XIV continued up to the

French Revolution. French painting at last displaced Italian and Spanish in the work of Antoine Watteau (1684–1721), Pierre Chardin (1699–1779), François Boucher (1703–1770), and Jean-Honoré Fragonard (1732–1806) and in the vogue enjoyed by the earlier landscape painter Claude Lorrain (1600–1682). Élisabeth Vigée-Lebrun (1755–1842), whose subjects included Queen Marie Antoinette, established herself as one of the leading portrait painters of the age. Watteau, Boucher, and Fragonard have left us a pictorial record of what Baron Talleyrand meant when he said that no one who had not lived before 1789 had tasted the true sweetness of life. Their aristocratic lords and ladies disport themselves against a pastoral background from which all hint of those on whose labor they existed has been removed. French, too, was the language of the Enlightenment. By

Élisabeth Vigée-Lebrun (1755–1842), here depicting herself, was one of the most celebrated and sought-after painters of her age. Among the subjects of her more than six hundred portraits were Marie Antoinette, Madame de Staël; Lady Emma Hamilton, the paramour of Admiral Nelson; and the poet Byron.

the end of the seventeenth century it had already begun to replace Latin as the language of diplomacy and learning, and it was a disgrace to be unable to speak it in society. Its influence was particularly strong in countries such as Poland, Russia, Sweden, and the German states, whose national literatures were just beginning to develop.

The chief rival to French culture was that of Britain. The brilliant satirist of London life, William Hogarth (1697–1764), showed a world in all its strength and brutality that the French court painters had so carefully eliminated, although Britain's aristocracy too had its chroniclers in Thomas Gainsborough (1727–1788) and Sir Joshua Reynolds (1723–1792). Defoe's *Robinson Crusoe* was translated into French, German, and Swedish, and the novels of Samuel Richardson (1689–1762), Henry Fielding (1707–1754), Laurence Sterne (1713–1768), and Tobias Smollett (1721–1771) had great success. Italy was still regarded as the ultimate finishing school for the cultured European, and a fresh revival of interest in antiquity led to the first excavations of Herculaneum and Pompeii and the beginnings of modern archaeology. European taste was growing more sophisticated and for the first time conscious of artistic history as a sequence of styles and traditions, each with its own value. This led to the emergence of a new kind of literary authority, the critic, whose task was to give perspective to cultural experience and to shape public taste. The critics Gotthold Ephraim Lessing, Johann Joachim Winckelmann (1717–1768), and Johann Gottfried von Herder (1744–1803) did much to shape an emerging national consciousness in Germany, while Samuel Johnson (1709–1784), whose biography, faithfully chronicled by his admirer James Boswell, is one of history's best-known lives, reigned for more than two decades as the literary dictator of London. Johnson, stung by the rejection of an early aristocratic patron, exemplified the new bourgeois man of letters who made his own way and owed his position to his native wit and force.

The heroic period of European exploration was largely over, to be replaced by an age of travel. One of the fruits of this was the great enthusiasm for China and its civilization displayed by Leibniz, Voltaire, Diderot, Christian Wolff, and others, a compliment, to be sure, that the Chinese did not return. On an artistic level this expressed itself in a craze for all things Chinese, particularly fine silks and porcelain, that went by the name of chinoiserie. Wallpaper and watercolor paints were also introduced from China, and the influence of Chinese painting was particularly evident in the work of Watteau. The European conception of China, based on reports by earlier Jesuit missionaries, was hardly an accurate one; Confucius, who was translated and widely admired, was read as a kind of philosophe. Nonetheless, the fascination with China marked a stage in Europe's expanding consciousness of the outside world; a global culture, as well as a global economy, was taking its first uncertain steps.

Vienna and the Golden Age of Western Music

Of all the forms of art, the only one that produced names to rank with the greatest figures of the seventeenth century was music. The baroque forms that had culminated in Johann Sebastian Bach and Georg Friedrich Handel (1685–1759), who adapted the Italian forms of the opera and the oratorio to northern tastes with great success, gave way to a more linear, less ornamental style in the works of Jean-Philippe Rameau (1683–1764) in France and Christoph Willibald von Gluck (1714–1787) in Germany. Bach's eldest son, Carl Philipp Emanuel (1714–1788), in his lifetime far better known than his father, was a crucial link in the development of what came to be called the classical style. This style, which came to fruition in the latter half of the century, was based on the elaboration of an old seventeenth-century form, the sonata. As applied in the orchestral forms of the symphony and the concerto, it produced a music that combined wit, elegance, and formal symmetry in a manner that reflected the balance of intellectual thrust and emotional restraint characteristic of much of eighteenth-century culture. Yet it was capable, too, in the hands of its greatest masters, of achieving extraordinary poignancy and depth, much of it in the setting of religious texts such as the mass for which there remained a steady demand.

The leading exponents of the new style were the Austrians Franz Joseph Haydn (1732–1809) and Wolfgang Amadeus Mozart (1756–1791), the latter an astounding prodigy who composed musically mature works from the age of 9 and works of profound originality from his teens. Haydn, slower to develop but immensely prolific in every form of the period, was employed by the greatest noble family of Hungary, the Esterhazys, who maintained a private orchestra for his use. Haydn remained with the Esterhazys all his life, although in later life he traveled widely and accepted commissions from all over Europe. Mozart's patronage was much less secure, and he depended for his living on a fickle public, for whom he turned out music with astonishing speed.

For both men, the Viennese public was the ultimate test of success. The growth of the bourgeoisie in the later reign of Maria Theresa and that of Joseph II had stimulated the development not only of music halls and

THE ENLIGHTENMENT

Principal works	Other arts	Related events
John Locke, *An Essay on Toleration* (1689); *An Essay Concerning Human Understanding* (1690)	Climax of baroque art: Rembrandt (1606–1669); Bernini (1598–1680)	Glorious Revolution in England (1688); English Bill of Rights (1689)
Pierre Bayle, *Historical and Critical Dictionary* (1697)	Molière satirizes the bourgeoisie; building of Versailles	Revocation of the Edict of Nantes (1685); wars of Louis XIV (1688–1713)
Montesquieu, *Persian Letters* (1721); Voltaire, *Philosophical Letters on the English Nation* (1734), *Elements of the Philosophy of Newton* (1738)	Rococo art: Watteau, Boucher; climax of baroque music: Bach (1685–1750), Handel (1685–1759)	Death of Newton (1727); Regency France; Pietism in Germany, Methodism in England
Montesquieu, *The Spirit of the Laws* (1748); David Hume, *An Enquiry Concerning Human Understanding* (1748)	Hogarth, *Marriage à la Mode, Gin Lane*; Handel, *Messiah*	War of the Austrian Succession (1740–1748); Voltaire at the court of Frederick the Great
Diderot's *Encyclopedia* (1751–1772); Rousseau, *Discourse on the Origin of Inequality* (1755); Voltaire, *Essay on Custom* (1756), *Candide* (1759)	Classical art: Chardin, Fragonard, Johnson's *Dictionary* (1755); rise of the English novel: Richardson, Fielding, Sterne, Smollett	Voltaire at Ferney; Lisbon earthquake; *Encyclopedia* banned in France (1759)
Rousseau, *Émile* (1762); *The Social Contract* (1762); Beccaria, *Of Crimes and Punishments* (1764)	*Sturm und Drang* movement in Germany; beginnings of Romanticism in England and France	Calas affair; Voltaire's *Philosophical Dictionary* burned (1764); enlightened despotism in Russia, Spain, Portugal
Abbé Raynal, *History of the Two Indies* (1770); Adam Smith, *The Wealth of Nations* (1776)	Goethe, *The Sorrows of Young Werther* (1774)	Cook explores the Pacific; United States declares independence (1776); deaths of Voltaire and Rousseau (1778)
Rousseau, *Confessions* (1781); Kant, *Critique of Pure Reason* (1781)	Golden age of Viennese music: Haydn, Mozart, Beethoven	Enlightened despotism in Austria; abolitionism in England; Jewish emancipation; outbreak of the French Revolution (1789)
Wollstonecraft, *A Vindication of the Rights of Woman* (1792)	Blake, *Songs of Innocence* (1789); Coleridge, *Lyrical Ballads* (1798)	Revolution in France; war in Europe (1792–1815)

theaters but also of a very lively salon culture. What verbal display and wit were to the salons of Paris, music was to those of Vienna. There were thousands of amateur musicians and singers in the city, and a British traveler remarked on provincial schools full of young children learning to read, play, and write music. The young Ludwig van Beethoven (1770–1827) came to Vienna at the age of 16, returned to stay permanently at 21, and dominated Viennese musical life for 30 years. His death, and that of Franz Schubert (1797–1828), the only native Viennese among these composers, marked the end of the golden age of Vienna's music. For Beethoven, who burst the bounds of classical tradition to forge the new Romantic style and who commanded an audience throughout Europe, Vienna was merely a stage; but Schubert, who lived his short life in the shadow of his great elder contemporary, was nurtured by the salon culture and the small circle of friends and admirers for whom he wrote his songs, sonatas, and chamber works.

The Enlightenment had a profound and lasting effect on Western culture. It called into question the basic institutions of European society, subjecting them to the test of reason and condemning whatever fell short by its measure. On the surface, it seemed the work of a small, self-appointed band of critics, the philosophes, who for the most part lacked status and position and were frequently hounded, censored, and even imprisoned. Yet the philosophes themselves represented only the cutting edge of the great transformation of Western thought that had begun with the Reformation, the commercial expansion of Europe, and above all the scientific revolution. If they succeeded despite such apparent odds, it was largely because their conservative opponents had capitulated to their values and ambitions or found it imprudent to resist. This was most evident in the phenomenon of enlightened despotism. If the seventeenth century had marked the triumph of a new order of the universe, the eighteenth produced a new vision of humanity to complement it. To many, this vision was troubling. But even those who continued to seek comfort in a traditional Christianity were forced to redefine it in terms of achieving secular progress on earth.

Notes

1. R. Zaller, *Europe in Transition, 1660–1815* (New York: Harper & Row, 1984), p. 12.
2. L. G. Crocker, *An Age of Crisis: Man and World in Eighteenth-Century French Thought* (Baltimore: Johns Hopkins University Press, 1959), p. 328.

Suggestions for Further Reading

Beales, D. *Joseph II*, vol. 1. Cambridge: Cambridge University Press, 1987.

Bernard, P. P. *Joseph II*. New York: Twayne, 1968.

Besterman, T. *Voltaire*. New York: Harcourt, Brace & World, 1969.

Cassirer, E. *The Philosophy of the Enlightenment*. Boston: Beacon Press, 1951.

Comini, A. *The Changing Image of Beethoven*. New York: Rizzoli, 1987.

Crocker, L. G. *An Age of Crisis: Man and World in Eighteenth-Century French Thought*. Baltimore: Johns Hopkins University Press, 1959.

Darnton, R. *The Business of Enlightenment: A Publishing History of the Encyclopedia, 1775–1800*. Cambridge, Mass.: Belknap Press, 1979.

———. *The Literary Underground of the Old Regime*. Cambridge, Mass.: Harvard University Press, 1982.

Ferguson, M., ed. *First Feminists: British Women Writers, 1578–1799*. Bloomington: Indiana University Press, 1984.

Gay, P. *The Enlightenment: An Interpretation*. 2 vols. New York: Knopf, 1966, 1969.

Gelbart, N. R. *Feminine and Opposition Journalism in Old Regime France: Le Journal des Dames*. Berkeley: University of California Press, 1987.

Gough, J. W. *The Social Contract*, 2nd ed. Oxford: Clarendon Press, 1957.

Hazard, P. *The European Mind, 1680–1715*. New Haven, Conn.: Yale University Press, 1935.

Israel, J. I. *European Jewry in the Age of Mercantilism, 1550–1750*. New York: Oxford University Press, 1985.

Jacob, M. *The Radical Enlightenment: Pantheists, Freemasons and Republicans*. Boston: Allen & Unwin, 1980.

Jones, R. E. *The Emancipation of the Russian Nobility, 1762–1785*. Princeton, N.J.: Princeton University Press, 1973.

Krieger, L. *An Essay on the Theory of Enlightened Despotism*. Chicago: University of Chicago Press, 1975.

Lough, J. *The Encyclopedia*. New York: McKay, 1971.

Madariaga, I. de. *Russia in the Age of Catherine the Great*. London: Weidenfeld & Nicolson, 1981.

Manuel, F. *The Eighteenth Century Confronts the Gods*. Cambridge, Mass.: Harvard University Press, 1959.

Rendall, J. *The Origins of Modern Feminism: Women in Britain, France, and the United States, 1780–1860*. New York: Macmillan, 1984.

Ritter, G. *Frederick the Great: A Historical Profile*. Berkeley: University of California Press, 1968.

Rogers, K. *Feminism in Eighteenth-Century England*. Urbana: University of Illinois Press, 1982.

Scott, H. M. *Enlightened Absolutism*. Ann Arbor: University of Michigan Press, 1990.

Shklar, J. *Men and Citizens: A Study of Rousseau's Social Theory*. London: Cambridge University Press, 1969.

Spencer, S. I., ed. *French Women and the Age of the Enlightenment*. Bloomington: Indiana University Press, 1985.

Tomalin, C. *The Life and Death of Mary Wollstonecraft*. New York: New American Library, 1974.

Wade, I. O. *The Intellectual Origins of the French Enlightenment*. Princeton, N.J.: Princeton University Press, 1957.

Wilson, A. *Diderot*. 2 vols. New York: Oxford University Press, 1957, 1972.

The French Revolution and Napoleon

Great transformations had taken place in Western society between the beginning of the sixteenth century and the end of the eighteenth. The Reformation had shattered the unity of Christendom, and the Enlightenment had challenged the roots of Christian belief itself. The European economy had acquired a global dimension through the conquest and exploitation of the New World and the expansion of its markets in Asia and Africa. The scientific revolution had reordered Western perceptions of the cosmos and of Western society itself. Yet the political order of Europe had remained relatively static. The nations of Europe were still governed by kings and princes. The nobility was still predominant, its privileges seemingly more entrenched than ever.

An engraving of the Abbé Sieyès, a pamphleteer and power broker who was a major force in the atmosphere of intrigue that surrounded the French Revolution in its last days. [Granger Collection]

The French Revolution challenged all that. Within a matter of weeks in the summer of 1789, a social and political edifice that had stood for 1,000 years was torn down, and for a generation all of Europe was caught up in the convulsive changes that ensued. From the very beginning, the revolution was recognized as the most important event of the age. In its turmoil and agony the shape of the modern world first became visible. Two centuries later, historians are still debating its nature and its impact.

The Crisis of the Old Order in France

The revolution began as an uprising not by the poorest segment of French society but by its richest and most privileged one. It was inevitable that the nobility would react against the autocratic rule of Louis XIV and seek to reassert their power. The long reign of the indolent Louis XV (1715–1774) provided them with an opportunity to do so. Thus while in most other places the privileges of the nobility were being reshaped and in many cases curtailed by enlightened despots, in France they remained unchecked. The intendants whom Louis XIV had sent to break the nobles' control of the provinces had been neutralized. The nobility's monopoly on the best and most lucrative offices in the church, the army, and the government was growing more and more restrictive; by the 1780s, for example, it required four generations of noble blood to qualify for an army commission. The parlements, the chief courts of the realm, had regained much of their old power to challenge and obstruct royal edicts, claiming broad powers of judicial review. By the 1760s they had grown bold enough to imprison provincial governors and military commanders who attempted to execute royal orders that the parlements held to be illegal.

Of all their privileges, the one the nobility defended the most stubbornly was their exemption from most forms of taxation. Attempts to levy even token amounts in 1726 and 1749 met with furious resistance and had to be dropped. For the nobleman, taxation was the ultimate insult: like public flogging, it was something properly inflicted only on commoners. The bourgeoisie or upper merchant and professional class—a steadily expanding group in the eighteenth century—also sought to avoid taxation as a mark of status and in large part succeeded. The result was that while the privileged classes grew richer, the state became poorer, obliged as it was to rely on the poorest and most depressed sectors of the economy for support.

Reform and Reaction

Stung by the open defiance of his authority, Louis XV at last attempted to act. Guided by a reforming minister, René Charles de Maupeou (1714–1792), he took the daring step of abolishing the parlements outright and exiled their former judges to remote parts of the country. In their place he created new courts whose members would no longer have life tenure in office but could be removed at pleasure. At the same time, he undertook reforms to reduce the public debt to manageable proportions and to put the state's finances in order.

These measures were greeted by a storm of protest. Louis and Maupeou were attacked as despots bent on overthrowing the constitution. The king, however, remained firm. After nearly 60 years, he had finally decided to govern. It was too late. His death in 1774 brought his 20-year-old grandson, Louis XVI (1774–1792), to the throne. Louis was an affable, pious young man, fond of hunting and gardening and eager to please. He was soon persuaded to abandon his father's reforms and to restore the old parlements.

The Fiscal Crisis

The new king was ably served by his chief ministers, the philosopher Turgot (1774–1776) and the banker Necker (1776–1781). Both had connections to the Physiocrats, a circle of economic reformers who advocated liberal trade and fiscal policies. The two ministers sought to relieve the chronic indebtedness of the crown by easing trade restrictions, abolishing guild monopolies, and raising new taxes. The need for reform was clear and had now become urgent. The 26 provinces of France represented a hopeless tangle of conflicting laws and jurisdictions. Taxes levied in one place were prohibited in another. Commerce was impeded everywhere by customs and tolls; even a uniform system of weights and measures was lacking. But Turgot and Necker found themselves stymied. The revived parlements rejected their proposals out of hand, and factional intrigue undermined their position at court. Each in turn was forced from office, having accomplished nothing of substance.

The crown's plight was worsened by its participation in the American war of independence, which added considerably to the debt burden. By 1786 interest payment on the existing debt amounted to half the royal budget, and the treasury was borrowing to meet that. At last it could obtain no further credit at any price. The king's controller, Charles de Calonne, informed his master that the state was bankrupt.

A new tax was the only possible solution. To circumvent the inevitable opposition of the parlements and to appeal directly to the more liberal nobility, Calonne proposed that Louis call a handpicked Assembly of Notables. This body convened in February 1787, but, suspicious of Calonne's motives and unwilling to bypass the parlements, it refused to support his program. Louis dismissed Calonne and dissolved the assembly.

The Constitutional Crisis

The financial crisis now became a constitutional one. The parlements insisted that new taxes could be granted only by the representative assembly of the whole realm, the Estates General. This ancient feudal body had not met since 1614, but the judges made it into a symbol of popular liberty. Adopting the language of the Enlightenment, they insisted that law was the expression of reason, the general will, and the rights of man. It could no longer be accepted as the will of a single individual.

The crown found itself isolated, the natural focus of all discontent. The nobility feared it as the usurper of its privileges. The peasantry, ground under by taxes, resented it as the expropriator of its labor. The bourgeoisie saw it as a barrier to wealth and status. Its problems were blamed not on genuine need but on the extravagance of the court. Whereas the pomp of Versailles under Louis XIV had reflected the glory of France, it now symbolized the decadence of personal monarchy.

Louis finally attempted to suppress the parlements as his father had done and set up new courts in their place. But the tide of reform could no longer be stopped by a show of force. Rioting and near-rebellion broke out in the provinces, and committees of correspondence were formed on the model of the American Revolution. The clergy threatened to reduce their annual "gift" to the treasury, and the king's own courtiers opposed him. Louis backed down. In July 1788 he recalled the parlements, whose judges returned as heroes, and agreed to summon the Estates General. The revolt of the nobility had triumphed.

Progressive opinion now looked for a system of constitutional government to emerge, with the Estates General evolving into a more or less modern representative body like the British Parliament or the American Congress. But the progressives were in for a shock. The judges of the parlements may have spoken the language of Rousseau and Thomas Jefferson, but they had no intention of sharing the powers they had pried from the crown. The Parlement of Paris ruled at once that the new Estates General must have the same form as the old, with three separate chambers representing the clergy, the nobility, and the commoners of the realm. Because

---

◎ France on the Eve of the Revolution ◎

The English traveler Arthur Young gives a vivid impression of the ferment in prerevolutionary France in his account of a dinner party in 1787.

Dined today with a party, whose conversation was entirely political. . . . One opinion pervaded the whole company, that they are on the eve of some great revolution in the government: that everything points to it: the confusion in the finances great; with a deficit impossible to provide for without the states-general of the kingdom, yet no ideas formed of what would be the consequence of their meeting: no minister existing, or to be looked to in or out of power, with such decisive talents as to promise any other remedy than palliative ones: a prince on the throne, with excellent dispositions, but without the resources of a mind that could govern in such a moment without ministers: a court buried in pleasure and dissipation . . . a great ferment amongst all ranks of men, who are eager for some change, without knowing what to look to, or to hope for: and a strong leaven of liberty, increasing every hour since the American revolution; altogether form a combination of circumstances that promise ere long to ferment into motion, if some master hand, of very superior talents, and inflexible courage, be not found at the helm to guide events, instead of being driven by them.

Source: A. Young, *Travels in France During the Years 1787, 1788, and 1789*, ed. C. Maxwell (Cambridge: Cambridge University Press, 1950), pp. 84–85.

each chamber voted as a separate unit, the two privileged orders could always outvote the Third Estate of the commons, which in fact was made up of merchants, financiers, petty officials, and members of the professions, the group loosely referred to as the bourgeoisie. Except in theory, none of these groups represented the actual majority of peasants and workers who made up four-fifths of the population.

The Bourgeoisie and the Third Estate

The situation now boiled down to a three-cornered struggle among the king, the nobility, and the bourgeoisie. The resentment of this last group was of long standing. The bourgeoisie regarded themselves as the most productive element in society. They chafed at economic restrictions that they saw as largely designed to protect the interests of the nobility and, though some of them had acquired fortunes as great as any nobleman's, they were bitter at their exclusion from the highest echelons of status and power. As the political debate widened, they also came to see themselves as speaking, through the Third Estate, for the nation as a whole. Their position was eloquently summarized in a pamphlet circulated early in 1789 by a liberal clergyman, the Abbé Sieyès (1748–1836), which asked:

> *What is the Third Estate? Everything.*
> *What has it been thus far in the political order?*
>   *Nothing.*
> *What does it demand? To be something.*[1]

The Third Estate's discontent was the king's opportunity. If he could exploit it properly, he could outflank the opposition to tax reform and break the back of the nobles' revolt. Urged on by Necker, who had been restored to power, Louis decreed that the Estates General be popularly elected: nobles by nobles, clergy by clergy, and the Third Estate by all other males over 25 whose names appeared on the tax rolls. With a stroke of the pen, the king had enfranchised millions of Frenchmen for the first time.

In deference to this greatly expanded electorate, Louis agreed to "double the Third," that is, to permit twice as many representatives to be chosen for the Third Estate as for the other two orders. But this did not affect the voting balance of the three estates. Each order would still vote as a separate unit. In terms of actual power, therefore, the Third Estate's position remained that of a minority.

Louis' position was bound to leave the Third Estate unsatisfied. But the concessions he had made also aroused fierce opposition from the nobility, the Parlement of Paris, and even the royal family. The king was caught between a bourgeoisie he dared not trust and a nobility he dared not abandon.

In the meantime, election fever swept over France. In 40,000 electoral districts all over the country, lists of grievances were compiled to be sent along with the delegates; the lists revealed widespread dissatisfaction with the social system. The same demands were repeated insistently: popular representation, legislative control of taxation, and a limitation of the monarchy. The lists also attacked church tithes; traditional payments by peasants to the local lord, which ranged from a tenth to a third of the value of their crop; and hunting rights that enabled the nobility to trample across fields and vineyards in pursuit of game. The lists of the Third Estate were virtually unanimous in demanding full civil equality for all Frenchmen.

In these grievances and demands lay the seeds of a social revolution. The nobility had wanted to protect its privileges, the bourgeoisie to share them. What arose from the countryside was a cry of protest at the exploitation that the peasantry had suffered at the hands of both. Throughout the eighteenth century noble and bourgeois landholding increased, as the peasants were squeezed onto smaller and smaller plots and sometimes entirely off them. In the region of Toulouse in the south, for example, where a capitalist, market-oriented agriculture had developed, wage-earning laborers made up a majority of the rural population 50 years before the revolution. Many of those peasants who still owned land could not produce enough on it to feed themselves and their families, and they too depended on wage labor for survival. This meant that more of the French were vulnerable to a subsistence crisis—crop failure compounded by price rises and hoarding—than ever before.

As it happened, the worst political crisis in the nation's history coincided with the worst subsistence crisis of the eighteenth century. Following a period of expansion in midcentury, France had entered a long cycle of depression after 1770. This was aggravated by a series of bad harvests, culminating in that of 1788. Starving peasants fled to the towns, swelling the urban unemployment rate to as high as 50 percent. Even people who had work found up to 80 percent of their earnings consumed by the price of bread. By the spring of 1789 there were violent uprisings against grain prices and shortages, and wandering bands roved the countryside, attacking the castles of the nobility.

The Revolution of 1789

France had known periods of disorder before, but the circumstances that now converged on it—a constitutional crisis that was a thinly veiled struggle for power among contending political and economic groups, a monarchy enfeebled not only by an incompetent ruler but also by attacks on its fundamental legitimacy, a widespread sense of social injustice and an assumption that radical change was inevitable—all combined to bring about the collapse of the government, the destruction of the manorial order, and the replacement of a society based on the division of estates and orders into one predicated, at least in theory, on the legal and political equality of all citizens. This was the revolution of 1789.

From the Estates General to the National Assembly

The 1,165 delegates to the Estates General were the focus of all hopes when they came together at Versailles on May 5, 1789. The First Estate of the clergy consisted of 291 delegates, of whom 46 were bishops; the majority were hardworking and underpaid parish priests, close to

the peasantry they served and sympathetic to reform. The 270 nobles of the Second Estate also included a vociferous reform group. Among its number was the marquis de Lafayette (1757–1834), already celebrated as a hero of the American Revolution. Of the 578 commoners who comprised the Third Estate,* well over half were lawyers, most of whom also held government jobs, and another quarter were merchants, businessmen, and rentiers, persons who lived off the profits of feudal dues. Despite the wide franchise, not a single worker or peasant had been elected. This was partly because the final selection of delegates took place at only 200 district assemblies, where the influence of local notables predominated, and partly because of the traditional deference of the electorate to its social superiors. The result was that the full Third Estate was represented only by its narrowest elite, although an elite angry and embittered at its rebuff by the nobility.

Had the crown been able to assert itself at this point,

*The remaining 26 delegates were unclassified.

Louis XVI presides from his raised throne at the opening of the Estates General on May 5, 1789. Louis' failure to provide a credible reform program or to resolve the issue of whether the estates would vote by number or by order ended the last royal hope to control events. [Bulloz]

a compromise might still have been found. But Louis and Necker had no program to present, no solution to offer. The king spoke of caution, his minister of deficits. Leaderless, the Estates General fell to wrangling over the question of voting by orders, with the Third Estate insisting that the three orders merge into a single body. As this not only would have given the Third Estate a numeric voting majority but would also have abolished the principle of separate orders on which the privileges of the clergy and the nobility rested, it was stoutly resisted. On June 17, after weeks of deadlock, the Third Estate took the decisive step toward revolution: it declared itself an independent body, the National Assembly, with the right to legislate alone in the public interest. Three days later the members of the Third Estate found themselves locked out of their chamber. They gathered in a nearby indoor tennis court, where in great passion and excitement they vowed not to disband until they had given France a constitution.

Louis now acted. He told the Estates General that he would give it a permanent place in the state, with wide though unspecified rights over the administration and the budget. In this he seemed to accept the principle of a limited monarchy that had been demanded on all sides. But he also declared the self-created National Assembly (whose numbers had now been swollen by dissident clergy and nobility) null and void and ordered the Estates to return to their separate chambers. The nobles were elated. The king had come down for the principle of blood privilege on which his own throne ultimately rested. But the Third Estate remained defiant. Facing mutinous soldiers and an angry populace, Louis backed down. On June 27 the first two Estates united with the Third. The National Assembly was now a fact.

The Popular Revolution

The revolution now moved into the streets. The workers and tradesmen of Paris, fearing both rural mobs and military repression, broke into the civic arsenals and armed themselves. On July 14 they stormed the ancient fortress

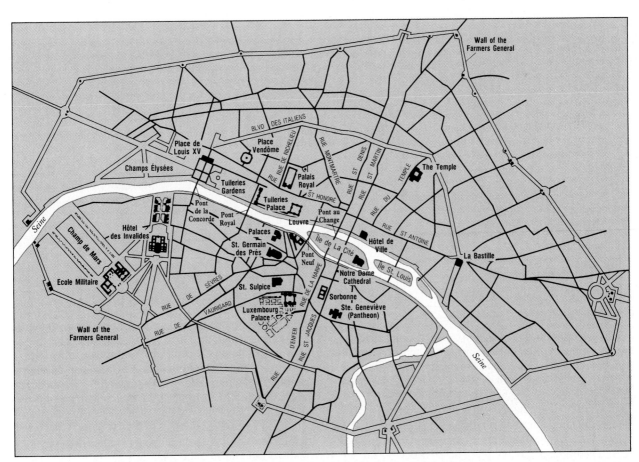

27.1 Paris at the Outbreak of the French Revolution

◉ The Fall of the Bastille: ◉
An Eyewitness Account

Jean-Baptiste Humbert, a Parisian watchmaker who claimed to have been the first to scale the walls of the Bastille on July 14, 1789, provides a vivid account of the excitement and confusion of that day.

I followed the crowd, to get to the cellar where the arms were kept. On the staircase leading to the cellar, seeing a man armed with two muskets, I took one from him, and went up again; but the crowd at the top of the stair was so great that all those who were climbing up were pushed down again, and fell right into the cellar. . . . In spite of this horrible tumble, the crowd persisted in going down the stairs, and as nobody could get up again, there was such a crush in the cellar that people were shrieking and gasping for breath. . . . Afterwards I went to the cannon that stood just above the drawbridge of the Bastille, in order to push it off its guncarriage and render it unusable. But as I stood for this purpose with my shoulder under the mouth of the cannon, someone in the vicinity fired at me, and the bullet pierced my coat and waistcoat and wounded me in the neck; I fell down senseless; the Swiss soldier whose life I had spared dragged me on to the staircase, still clutching my gun, so he told me. . . . On my way home I remembered some friends who lived in the rue de la Ferronnerie; I had left them that morning, and they had seemed anxious about the dangers which they foresaw my zeal might lead me into. I went to their house, and four armed bourgeois escorted me to the rue du Hurepoix. I was greeted with praise wherever I went; but when we reached the Quai des Augustins, we were followed by a crowd of people who mistook me for a malefactor, and twice attempted to put me to death. As I could not explain things to everyone, I was about to be seized, when I was recognized by a bookseller on the Quai, who rescued me from the hands of the crowd and took me into his own home. . . . I rested until about midnight, when I was woken by repeated cries of *to arms! to arms!* Then I could not resist my longing to be of some further use. I got up, armed myself, and went to the guardroom, where I found M. Poirier, the Commanding Officer [of the National Guard], under whose orders I remained until the following morning.

Source: J. Godechot, *The Taking of the Bastille, July 14th, 1789,* trans. J. Stewart (New York: Scribner, 1970), pp. 281–286 passim.

---

of the Bastille and seized its weapons after a pitched battle in which 98 of the attackers were killed. This event, still celebrated annually in France, was of enormous symbolic significance. It gave the revolution its baptism of blood and resulted in the final collapse of the king's authority. Riots broke out and arsenals were pillaged in Bordeaux, Lyons, and other large cities. In some eastern towns, such as Sedan, Nancy, and Troyes, there were violent clashes, but elsewhere, as in Strasbourg and Rennes, the army defected en masse. In many places the intendants and municipal officials simply fled, leaving the local population to organize citizen militias and revolutionary committees, or communes, on the model already established in Paris.

Disorder broke out simultaneously in the countryside, often triggered by a wave of rumor and hysteria, the so-called Great Fear, which centered around reports of advancing royalist or bandit armies. From town to town the cry went up, "The brigands are coming!" Since there were enough bandits in the best of times, these fears were not without foundation. They soon became a pretext for looting, and by late July a full-scale agrarian insurrection was in progress. Peasants broke into the manor houses of the nobility, systematically destroying the legal records of debts and feudal dues. What went up in flames was more than paper. In the high summer of 1789 the Old Regime itself was dying in a thousand bonfires throughout France.

The Abolition of Privilege and the Declaration of the Rights of Man

The bourgeois members of the National Assembly were far from pleased with this wholesale destruction of property rights. But they quickly moved to ratify what they were powerless to prevent. On the night of August 4 two liberal noblemen, coached by leaders of the Third Estate, moved to abolish all compulsory labor service, such as road maintenance, and to offer redemption for all other dues and obligations. What can only be described as a psychological stampede ensued. Member after member arose to volunteer renunciation of his own privileges and those of cities, corporations, and provincial estates. Hoarse and exhausted, the delegates adjourned at 2 A.M. with the declaration, "Feudalism is abolished." By morning many had repented their enthusiasm and tried to reinstate various qualifications and exemptions. It was too late. The people of France took them at their most generous word and simply ceased to pay all former dues.

The assembly's next step was to issue a constitutional blueprint, the Declaration of the Rights of Man and the Citizen (August 26). Its 17 brief articles summarized the political principles of the Enlightenment. All men, it stated, "are born and remain free and equal in rights." Those rights were defined as "liberty, property, security, and resistance to oppression," which it was the duty of every state to preserve. Sovereign power was declared to be vested in the nation as a whole, and law was to be the expression of the general will. Freedom of speech and religion were guaranteed, and liberty—the right "to do anything that does not harm another person"—could be abridged only by due process of law, before which all men were to be regarded as equal. The declaration was to remain the basic document of the revolution, however far subsequent regimes departed from its principles in practice. At one stroke it eliminated the archaic, cumbersome divisions of French society. It replaced the system of orders by one based on formal civil equality and cleared the ground for the modern political and economic development of France. It also made devastating propaganda. Translated into every major European language, it shook the established order and galvanized demands for reform across the Continent.

The king alone remained passive and aloof in the face of these developments. This led to the last of the revolutionary tremors of 1789. On October 5 a contingent of Parisian housewives, having previously invaded the mayor's office to protest food shortages and the continuing high price of bread, marched to Versailles and demanded that Louis return to the capital. They were soon

Classical and biblical symbols entwine in this engraved representation of the Declaration of the Rights of Man. The preamble and the 17 articles of the document are depicted as the tablets of a new Mosaic law, and two female deities appear against a sky whose parting clouds reveal the light. The figure on the left holds the broken chains of privilege; the winged figure on the right holds the staff of popular sovereignty. A luminous eye representing the God of Reason completes the trinity. [Historical Pictures Service, Chicago]

backed up by the arrival of the newly formed National Guard under Lafayette, 20,000 strong. Virtually defenseless, the royal family was forced to accompany this motley procession back to Paris, where they took up residence in the Palace of the Tuileries. The National Assembly followed a few days later, and Louis gave his unhappy consent to the August 4 decrees and the Declaration of the Rights of Man.

The New Order, 1789–1791

The poet Chateaubriand was later to remark that the nobility had begun the revolution and the people had finished it. But despite the slogan that now epitomized the goals of the revolution—"Liberty, fraternity, equality"—there was no single "people" of France, only groups with divided and often bitterly contending interests. On one extreme were the 20,000 people, mostly aristocrats, who had left the country and rejected the revolution. On the other were those, especially the *sans-culottes** or working class of the towns, who had gained theoretically but not materially from it and continued to demand both relief from high prices and scarcity and representation of their interests. In between were the great mass of the peasants, who wished chiefly to consolidate the fruits of their rebellion in July, the destruction of the manorial regime and the freeing of their title to the lands they farmed.

The Bourgeoisie in Power

Actual power was in the hands of none of these groups, however, but rather those of the bourgeoisie, the unexpected beneficiaries of the collapse of royal authority and the abolition of the order of the nobility. The bourgeoisie dominated the National Assembly or, as it called itself from October 1789, the Constituent Assembly. The assembly had two crucial tasks: to write a new constitution for France and to govern the nation while doing so. Having achieved power and control of the king by mass action, it wanted no further interruption of its business by the sans-culottes. Its first acts from its new base in Paris were to declare martial law and censorship of the press, and on October 21 a young laborer, Michel Adrien, was hanged for sedition. The honeymoon of the Third Estate was over.

The assembly's desire to insulate the new government against undue popular influence was reflected in the constitution of 1791. Contrary to Article 6 of the Declaration of the Rights of Man, the constitution distinguished between "active" and "passive" citizens. Both groups enjoyed full civil rights, but only active citizens, those meeting a minimum property qualification, had the right to vote for some 50,000 electors, who in turn chose the 500 representatives of the Legislative Assembly. About two-thirds of the adult male population qualified for active citizenship and fewer than half of it for nomination as electors. This was still a far wider franchise than in England, and the property qualification for voting was lower than in some states in America. But since the electors were obliged to spend several days choosing representatives at their own expense and often at a considerable distance from home, the process ensured that they would necessarily be men of means and leisure—in short, men of the bourgeoisie.

The Reorganization of Church and State

The most pressing issue before the Constituent Assembly was the unresolved crisis of the public debt. The simplest recourse was to repudiate it as a legacy of the discredited Old Regime. As a substantial portion of the debt was owed to members of the bourgeoisie, however, there was no question of doing that. Instead, the assembly decided to pay the debt off by selling the lands of the church, which it declared to be confiscated in the name of the nation. A special currency called assignats was issued to facilitate the purchase of these lands. In this way some 10 percent of the real estate of France was redistributed to deserving—that is, chiefly bourgeois—revolutionaries.

This massive transaction destroyed the financial independence of the church and made it a ward of the state. Clergymen became salaried officials, chosen from a qualified slate by popular election like other state functionaries. Archbishoprics were abolished, and the number of bishops was reduced from 135 to 83. Monasteries and nunneries were dissolved, and the taking of religious vows was prohibited. The pope was to be informed as a matter of courtesy when a bishop was installed, but his authority was in no other way recognized.

These changes were embodied in the Civil Constitution of the Clergy (1790). They were less drastic than they seemed, since clergymen's salaries were to be nearly doubled under the new dispensation. The problem was ratification. The church wanted to adopt the Civil Constitution on its own authority, thereby affirming its continued identity as a corporate body. To the assembly, this would have been tantamount to recognizing the existence of a First Estate again, when all estates and orders had been abolished. It therefore promulgated the new constitution alone and backed it up with an oath of allegiance that all clergy were required to swear.

The assembly perhaps could not have acted otherwise, since Pope Pius VI, whose antagonism to the revolution was fanned by émigré agents in Rome, was preparing to denounce the Civil Constitution. The result, however, was to divide the French church. Half the lower clergy—and all but seven of the bishops—refused

---

*Literally, "without breeches." For practical reasons, workingmen wore long pants instead of the silk or muslin stockings and breeches of the nobility and the bourgeoisie.

to take the new oath. The "refractory" or "nonjuring" clergy, as they were called, emigrated or went underground, where, protected by loyal parishioners, they formed a natural focus of resistance to the revolution. Far from becoming an obedient servant of the state, the church would henceforth be its bitterest enemy.

Equally far-reaching was the assembly's reorganization of administration and government. All former courts and jurisdictions were abolished. A uniform code of administration was instituted for the 44,000 rural and urban districts of the country. The 26 old provinces, many of them rich with history (and memories of previous rebellions), were replaced by 83 "departments," all newly named and democratically equal in size. An independent judiciary was established, with elected judges and juries for criminal trials. Yet, although the administration was thus radically standardized, it was actually less centrally controlled than under the Old Regime. Local and regional officials were to be elected from below rather than appointed from above, and they were left essentially on their own in the work of government. In this respect, the Constituent Assembly's reforms did not go nearly far enough. Anxious to avoid the charge of despotism leveled at the Old Regime, it left the implementation of its decrees in the hands of officials over whom it had little effective control. Had the revolution been securely established, such a system might have been workable. As matters stood, with an embittered nobility, a divided church, a suspicious peasantry, and an unsatisfied proletariat, it was an open invitation to resistance. Counterrevolutionary disturbances broke out in the region of the Midi around Toulouse, Nîmes, and Montauban in the spring of 1790, precursors of full-scale rebellion to come.

The status of the king posed a difficult question. It was inexpedient to depose Louis, as republican members of the assembly wished. He was the only remaining link between the old France and the new and the only valid symbol of authority for millions of French citizens. At the same time, despite his grudging approval of the Declaration of the Rights of Man and the Civil Constitution of the Clergy, his hostility to the revolution was plain. His powers were therefore restricted to a three-year suspensive veto over the Legislative Assembly.

But Louis refused to play the role assigned him. On June 20, 1791, he attempted to flee the country with the royal family. Captured by peasants at the border town of Varennes, they were forced to return to Paris in a humiliating procession. The assembly accepted the fiction that the king had been "kidnapped." It was clear to all, however, that even before its formal adoption, the new constitution had been repudiated by the man intended to serve as its head of state.

In the long run, the work of the Constituent Assembly was of great importance. It dissolved and replaced the institutions of the Old Regime and laid the foundations of the modern French state. But it failed to solve almost all the immediate problems before it. It passed out of existence on September 30, 1791, leaving behind a sharply polarized nation, mounting political and economic chaos, and a constitution that, satisfying no one, survived it by barely ten months.

The Revolution and Europe

At first many people outside France greeted the revolution with enthusiasm and even rapture. "How much the greatest event that has happened in the world, and how much the best!" exulted the British politician Charles James Fox. The poet William Wordsworth later recalled the sense of liberation and almost limitless hope inspired by the French revolution:

> *Bliss it was in that dawn to be alive*
> *But to be young was very heaven!*

Elsewhere, too, the reformers rejoiced. In Germany the elderly philosopher Kant and the young nationalist Johann Fichte both sang the revolution's praises, and the bourgeoisie of Hamburg turned out to celebrate the first anniversary of the fall of the Bastille. Societies and clubs in support of the revolution were founded in Switzerland, Savoy, the Netherlands, and Britain, and many of them engaged in revolutionary activities themselves. An uprising in the Austrian Netherlands drove the imperial army out of Brussels in December 1789, while in the Rhineland peasants refused to pay seigneurial dues to their lords. Not content to admire from afar, many activists gathered in Paris to participate directly in the revolution, including the American pamphleteer Tom Paine and the Prussian Anarchasis Cloots, who styled himself the "representative of the human race."

Not all reaction was favorable, however. The British statesman and orator Edmund Burke (1729–1797), who had supported the American Revolution, criticized the tenets of the new regime in his *Reflections on the Revolution in France* (1790), which remains to this day a classic statement of the conservative view of history. Burke argued forcefully against the assumption that all men possessed identical natural rights. Not men, he contended, but nations were the basic units of history. Each nation was a unique cultural entity shaped by its distinctive historic experience. Reforms that respected the time-tested institutions of the nation were right and proper. But for a single generation to destroy those institutions and to attempt to substitute some abstract formula of justice for the collective wisdom of all its predecessors was an act of folly and arrogance, a "fond election of evil" that could bring only ruin.

The émigrés who fled France brought their own tales of horror, and the monarchies of Europe were soon alert to the danger the revolution posed. Bavaria, Sardinia, Spain, and Portugal took steps to suppress all expressions of revolutionary solidarity within their own borders, and Spain posted troops along its frontier to keep out the "French plague." Not until August 1791 were the two largest Continental powers able to agree on a joint statement of policy toward France. The Declaration of Pillnitz, issued by Frederick William IV (1786–1797) of Prussia and Leopold II (1790–1792) of Austria, stated as its goal the restoration of the French monarchy, by force if necessary. A declaration of war without an actual call to arms, it served only to strengthen the republicans in France, who argued that the revolution would never be complete or secure as long as Louis remained king.

❧
PARIS AND THE
FALL OF THE MONARCHY

Paris was the nerve center of the revolution, the seat of national government, and the home of the volatile sans-culottes, who comprised half its population of 600,000. The city had enjoyed its own revolution in July 1789 when it overthrew its royal administration and improvised, almost on the spot, a new governing authority, the Commune, based on the electoral districts set up to choose delegates to the Estates General. These districts, subsequently reorganized into 48 "sections," remained the heart of the city's political activity. Although the Constituent Assembly attempted to restrict the franchise to the communal assembly, which was the city's official governing body, to so-called active citizens, the section assemblies themselves, open in practice to all comers, were at their best schools of democracy in which, in the words of a contemporary petition, "there reigns that equality, that fraternity of the golden age that our benevolent laws are seeking to restore."

Political activism in the city spilled over into numerous popular clubs and societies, of which the most famous, the Jacobins,* had more than 400 provincial affiliates by 1791 and debated before audiences of up to 2,000. By 1793 half a million people were enrolled in such clubs. Some of them functioned as interest groups or embryonic political parties; the Jacobins themselves had originated as a caucus of liberal members of the National Assembly. To such groups were added the *fédérés*, or "federations," spontaneously formed unions of

---

*So named from their original meeting place in the former convent of the Jacobin order.

the municipal councils and militias of the provinces that converged on Paris on the first anniversary of the fall of the Bastille to affirm their loyalty to the revolution. When not gathered in the large crowds and assemblies so characteristic of the revolution, Parisians themselves avidly consumed the scores of newspapers, pamphlets, and petitions that poured forth daily from the press.

One of the first newspapers, *l'Ami du Peuple* ("The Friend of the People"), was founded by Count Mirabeau (1742–1791), who, boycotted by his fellow noblemen, had won election as a member of the Third Estate and emerged as a leader of the National Assembly. Other journalists such as Camille Desmoulins and Jean-Paul Marat (1743–1793) won wide public followings and often exercised considerable political influence. Thus was born the modern power of the press, whose nickname, the "Fourth Estate," still attests to its revolutionary origins.

The Parisian sans-culottes were the most radical element in the revolution, in part because of the idealism with which they embraced their first experience of politics and self-government, in part because their concrete interests clashed with those of the bourgeoisie who dominated the Constituent Assembly. The assembly, as we have seen, had sought to deny sans-culottes the vote; by the Le Chapelier law (1791) it had outlawed all workers' unions, and, in a direct confrontation, 15 sans-culottes had been killed in an antimonarchical demonstration on the civic parade ground, the Champs de Mars, in July 1791.

By the summer of 1792 the revolution had reached a new flashpoint. Swept on by a combination of ideological fervor and traditional anti-Habsburg sentiment, the new Legislative Assembly had declared war on Austria in April. It was a disastrous decision. The army was bereft of commanders, two-thirds of its officers (all former nobles) having deserted or quit. The country was in the grip of renewed inflation, in part the result of the government's failure to remove assignats from circulation as church lands were sold off. As their value depreciated, peasants refused to accept them as payment for their crops, creating food shortages and riots. When the war proved a fiasco, the public mood turned grim. Amid a general breakdown of order, there were rumors of counterrevolutionary plots. The Jacobin republicans blamed the failure of their crusade on Louis. How, they demanded, could a war against all kings be led by a king?

By the end of July, 47 of the 48 Paris sections had declared against the monarchy. The city was in an uproar as military recruits from the provinces mingled with the sans-culottes. Agitation was particularly severe in the district of St.-Antoine, whose working-class inhabitants had led the assault on the Bastille. The Jacobin leadership, alarmed by the prospect of a new popular insurrection, now backtracked and offered Louis support. But a more radical faction, led by Maximilien Robespierre, threw its lot in with the crowd. On August 10, Louis and his entourage were driven from the Tuileries by an armed mob, with heavy loss of life. It was an event as crucial as the fall of the Bastille. A new revolutionary council, composed largely of sans-culottes and lesser bourgeoisie, seized control of Paris. The constitution was suspended, the Legislative Assembly was dispersed, and a new National Convention was summoned to create a republic.

The Radical Revolution, 1792–1794

The National Convention, elected by all French males, met on September 20 in an atmosphere of near anarchy. Earlier in the month hysterical mobs had rampaged through the prisons of Paris in search of "counterrevolutionaries," killing as many as 1,400 inmates, including 37 women. A Prussian army had penetrated deep into northern France and was stopped at Valmy, only 200 miles from Paris, on the very day of the convention's first meeting. The convention had deliberately taken its name in reference to the Constitutional Convention, which had written the modern world's first democratic constitution in the United States five years earlier. But Paris in the early autumn of 1792 bore little resemblance to Philadelphia in the summer of 1787.

Reform and Regicide

Nevertheless, the convention set to work undaunted. It abolished not only the monarchy but also the calendar, declaring September 22 the first day of Year I of the republic. Later it scrapped the entire Christian calendar of months and days, commissioning a poet, Philippe Fabre d'Églantine, to rename them. Fabre decided to call his months by their seasonal characteristics; thus July 27 was to be the ninth of Thermidor, the month of heat; November 10 became the eighteenth of Brumaire, the month of fog; and so on. The year was to consist of 12 equal months of 30 days each, with five leap days at the end to be celebrated as revolutionary holidays. Each month consisted of three weeks or "decades" of ten days each, which meant, among other things, a nine-day workweek. Saints' days, used for festivity and rest, were eliminated as well. This calendar remained in effect until 1804, although it was never adopted beyond official circles.

The convention's faith in the future was soon repaid. French armies, fired by patriotic ardor and reorganized under officers promoted from the ranks, drove the Austro-Prussian invaders out and swept across the border,

A satirical print titled *Exercise of the Rights of Man and of the French Citizen* depicts the violence that erupted at the fall of the monarchy in September 1792. Murder is attempted by every means: shooting, hanging, stabbing, clubbing. The victims in the foreground include a gentlewoman, a bishop, and a child; in the background, a nobleman's house and a church are burning. [Bulloz]

occupying Frankfurt and Brussels. In two months they conquered more territory than Louis XIV had in 50 years. The convention decreed feudal dues and services abolished in all areas occupied by French forces and offered "liberation" to any people wishing it. On February 1, 1793, war was declared on Britain, Spain, and the Dutch Netherlands.

The king remained to be dealt with. Alive, he was a magnet for counterrevolution, and his incriminating correspondence with the Austrians had been discovered. Placed on trial for treason, he was condemned to death by a single vote in the convention, 361 to 360. On January 21, 1793, Louis went to the guillotine. Ten months later, his Austrian queen, Marie Antoinette, followed him.

The condemned queen, Marie Antoinette, dressed in a prisoner's smock and ironically crowned with a liberty cap, was sketched by Jacques-Louis David on her way to execution. [Bulloz]

The revolution now entered its climactic phase. It was a time of great passions and great excesses. The men who ruled France often worked around the clock, facing political, military, and economic crises all at once. At the same time, they were conscious of living at a historic moment and making decisions that would stamp generations to come. Out of what they did, and what they failed to do, came much of the shape of the modern West.

The center of this activity was the National Convention. Only 286 of its 750 members had served in the two earlier assemblies of the revolution, although socially they had the same predominant makeup of lawyers, merchants, businessmen, and officials. Despite the fact that the convention had been created by the insurrection of the sans-culottes, it contained only two workers, a munitions maker and a wool comber. The peasants, who comprised 80 percent of the population, had no representative at all.

Politically, the convention was divided between what had emerged as the two warring factions of the Jacobin club, with the great mass of delegates in the middle. The Girondins, so called because many of their leaders came from the southwest department of the Gironde, had been the war party of the Legislative Assembly, but in the eyes of their opponents their revolutionary purity had been compromised by their attempt to deal with the king the previous summer. The more radical faction was the Montagnards (the "mountain men"), so called because they sat in the upper tiers of the convention, whose base of support was among the sans-culottes of Paris. Their leaders were Robespierre, the journalist Marat, and the worldly politician Georges Danton. The two parties were separated by no great issues or principles. Both accepted the republic, both had shed the king's blood, and both believed in the mission of the revolution to liberate Europe. But the Montagnards proved more adept at riding the tiger of mass politics that the second revolution of August 1792 had unleashed. On June 2, after a spring of military reverses, renewed inflation, and a major royalist uprising in the western region of the Vendée, Robespierre led a purge of Girondist leaders by the sans-culottes.

The Montagnards were now in power, though largely at the sufferance of their working-class allies, who came daily to the convention to harangue them. The sans-culottes demanded, and for the first time got, price controls on bread, flour, and other commodities, as well as a general increase in wages. The speech of the radical street leader and ex-priest Jacques Roux on June 25 was typical:

> Liberty is nothing but a figment of the imagination when one class can deprive another of food with impunity. Liberty becomes meaningless when the rich exercise the power of life and death over their fellow creatures by means of monopolies. . . . Have you outlawed speculation? No. Have you decreed the death penalty for hoarding? No. Have you defined the limits to the freedom of trade? No. . . . Deputies of the Mountain, why have you not climbed from the third to the ninth floor of the houses of the revolutionary city? You would have been moved by the tears and sighs of an immense population without food and clothing . . . because the laws have been cruel to the poor, because they have been made only by the rich and for the rich . . . [but] the salvation of the people . . . is the supreme law.[2]

The deputies of the convention were shocked by this oration, because Jacques Roux was telling them that their revolution had accomplished nothing of substance and that liberty without bread was a fraud. Roux was removed bodily from the convention and later committed suicide in prison. But his challenge would remain to haunt the politics of liberal democracy.

Robespierre and the Terror

Maximilien Robespierre now emerged as the most conspicuous figure of the revolution. Robespierre was born in 1758 in the coastal town of Arras, the son of a lawyer and a brewer's daughter. Abandoned by his father at the age of 8, he was raised by aunts and educated in the school of the Oratorian order. Robespierre was nicknamed "the Roman" by his classmates, for both his gravity of manner and his command of Latin. He grew up a reserved and serious young man, followed his father's profession, and became a judge in the local episcopal court. Fond of pets, he kept pigeons but had no close friends. He remained unmarried, and his sister Charlotte kept house for him. Elected to the Estates General in 1789, he caught the eye of Mirabeau, who remarked cynically, "He will go far; he believes everything he says." Above all, Robespierre believed in himself: "You have no idea," he said, "of the power of truth or the energy of innocence when sustained by an imperturbable courage."

Robespierre's ability to formulate and even personify the ideals of the revolution brought him to prominence. He lived for the revolution and had no life apart from it. By the end of 1792 he was the dominant figure in the

Maximilien Robespierre, the leading figure in the National Convention and the main architect of the Terror. [Mansell Collection]

◉ Robespierre on the Principles ◉ of Revolutionary Government

In this, one of his many speeches to the National Convention, Robespierre attempts to define the nature of the revolutionary government.

The defenders of the Republic must adopt Caesar's maxim, for they believe that *nothing has been done as long as anything remains to be done.* . . .

The object of constitutional government is to preserve the Republic; the object of a revolutionary government is to establish it.

Revolution is the war waged by liberty against its enemies; a constitution is that which crowns the edifice of freedom once victory has been won and the nation is at peace.

The revolutionary government has to summon extraordinary activity to its aid precisely because it is at war. It is subjected to less binding and less uniform regulations, because the circumstances in which it finds itself are tempestuous and shifting. . . .

Under a constitutional government little more is required than to protect the individual against abuses by the state, whereas revolutionary government is obliged to defend the state against the factions that assail it from every quarter.

To good citizens revolutionary government owes the full protection of the state; to the enemies of the people it owes only death.

Source: G. Rudé, ed., *Robespierre* (Englewood Cliffs, N.J.: Prentice Hall, 1967), pp. 58–59.

Jacobin club; by the following summer he stood at the forefront of events. The convention had just finished drafting the new Constitution of the Year I. It provided for the most democratic system of government since that of ancient Athens, with a broader definition of natural rights, a ballot based on universal manhood suffrage, and a popular referendum. As Robespierre himself declared, it contained "the essential basis of public happiness." But with foreign armies still pressing against French borders and armed resistance to the government flaring across three-quarters of the country, there was no question of putting it into effect. The convention, like the Constituent Assembly before it, had attempted to govern the country by a system of councils and committees. To one of these, a body with rather vague supervisory functions called the Committee of Public Safety, Robespierre was elected on July 27. Galvanized by his presence, it soon became the focal point of the revolution.

Steps were now rapidly taken to put down the revolts in the Vendée and elsewhere. Draconian punishment was meted out to rebels, as at Lyons, where nearly 2,000 people were executed in the wake of a Girondist uprising. So-called representatives on mission, armed with almost unlimited authority, struck terror into the provinces. At the same time, a *levée en masse*, or general conscription of all able-bodied men, was decreed. Of all the acts of the convention, this was perhaps the most significant. War was no longer to be the sport of kings and nobles but the sacred cause of the nation, a mass mobilization of all human and material resources. Young men who could not fight were to make weapons, munitions, clothing, and banners; women were to serve as nurses; elderly men were to make patriotic speeches.

Out of this fevered atmosphere was born the Terror, a systematic attempt to root out and destroy all enemies of the revolution. To catch these enemies, special tribunals were set up and new categories of counterrevolutionary offense established so broad as to include almost everything. A certain Monsieur Blondel was arrested, for example, for "thoughtlessness and indifference," a Citizen Lachapelle because he "did not lose much sleep over the revolution." These denunciations were made not by secret police but by zealous sansculottes who were genuinely puzzled that anyone could lack enthusiasm for the revolution. Who but an enemy of the republic would not lose sleep over it?

Robespierre defended the Terror in a famous speech: "If the basis of popular government in time of peace is virtue, the basis of popular government in time of revolution is both virtue and terror: virtue without which terror is murderous, terror without which virtue is powerless." Terror was merely inflexible justice applied to the enemies of the people and so "an emanation of virtue." As Robespierre's young colleague Saint-Just put it more succinctly, "Between the people and its enemies there is only the sword." In the ten months between September 1793 and July 1794 perhaps 300,000 people were arrested and 40,000 executed. Of these, only 15 percent were ex-aristocrats or priests and another 15 percent bourgeois, mostly members of the Girondist resistance in the south. The overwhelming majority were ordinary workers and peasants caught up in the whirlwind of revolutionary self-purification.

The Terror had another aim: to centralize all authority in the revolutionary government and to eliminate all opposition and dissent. By the law of 14 Frimaire (December 4, 1793), all subordinate authorities were placed under the direct control of the Committee of Public Safety, to which they were ordered to report every ten days. All local officials became "national agents," subject to immediate removal by Paris. Committees of surveillance—teams of spies—were placed over government functionaries at every level. The law of 14 Frimaire became the real constitution of France.

The Republic of Virtue

The revolution produced not only a new political apparatus but a new political culture as well, the "Republic of Virtue." Styles of dress, which had indicated differences of social position under the Old Regime, now proclaimed differences of political position as well. The color of one's clothes or the length of one's trousers might touch off a quarrel or even a riot. Even common objects such as plateware, calendars, or playing cards became ways of displaying commitment, and the popular symbols of the revolution—the red, white, and blue ribbons or "cockades" worn on the hat, the liberty trees planted by the tens of thousands all over France—became enduring badges of republican affiliation that long outlived the revolution itself. The government soon began to channel spontaneous activities such as dances and celebrations into organized festivals. These centered at first around mass loyalty oaths but soon became replacements for the old religious festivals on which the regime now frowned. Thus the veneration of the Virgin Mary was deflected into that of the goddess of Liberty, popularly called Marianne, and the worship of the Christian God became that of a Deist supreme being or, even more abstractly, Reason itself. As patriotic outlets, as propaganda forums, and as a means of surveillance, the festivals were no less important than the guillotine in maintaining political discipline.

By the spring of 1794 order had been restored, and the armies of the *levée en masse*, 850,000 strong, poured victoriously again into the Low Countries. Yet the Terror, like a mindless machine, ground on. Danton and Desmoulins went to the guillotine for suggesting that too much blood had been shed, the ultraleft Enragés and their leader, Jacques Hébert, for complaining that there had been too little. The Enragés were to get their wish. The law of 22 Prairial (June 10) declared spreading rumors and defaming patriots to be capital crimes and limited the Revolutionary Tribunal to two verdicts: acquittal or death. In the next six weeks more people were guillotined in Paris than in the entire preceding year. Even the members of the all-powerful Committee of Public Safety walked in fear of one another, especially of Robespierre. A group of them conspired to denounce him before the convention on 9 Thermidor (July 27). Robespierre attempted to defend himself but was shouted down and arrested. The next day he and Saint-Just were executed.

His enemies called Robespierre a tyrant who sought absolute power for himself. When he participated in the Festival of the Supreme Being, an attempt to set up a Deist god of reason as a revolutionary religion, many were convinced that he aimed to be not merely the dictator of the revolution but its high priest as well. Yet he never held any title but delegate to the convention, and his estate at his death came to barely 100 livres. A disciple of Rousseau, he believed that he embodied the general will. Among the corrupt and disillusioned, and even at last the horrified, he retained absolute faith in the justness of the revolution. As its tragedy unfolded, he foresaw his own martyrdom. "The founders of the Republic," he wrote, "can only find peace in the tomb."

Madame Roland, the most politically influential woman of the French Revolution and a prominent victim of the Terror. [Bulloz]

❦
MADAME ROLAND: A WOMAN IN THE REVOLUTION

Few women not of royal blood came closer to the center of political power in the eighteenth century than Marie-Jeanne Phlipon (1754–1793), better known by her married name, Madame Roland. The daughter of a Parisian engraver, Manon—as family and friends called her—exhibited her gifts early and was taught to read before the age of 4. Profoundly influenced by Rousseau, she found a kindred feminine spirit as well in the writings of Madame de Sévigné. The American Revolution fired her enthusiasm as a war against kings, and she followed its progress eagerly. At about the same time, she composed an essay deploring the gulf between the rich and the poor in France, the absence of representative government, and the monarchy's use of force to stifle dissent, which, in a prophetic phrase, she denounced as a "reign of terror." In revolution alone did the 20-year-old Manon see any hope for her country's future.

In 1780 Manon married Jean-Marie Roland de La Platière, the inspector of manufactures for the province of Picardy, a man 20 years her senior. With characteristic frankness, the young bride described her wedding night as "surprising and disagreeable," but a daughter, Eudora, soon resulted from the union. Madame Roland threw herself into her husband's career, collaborating on his technical studies and polishing his awkward literary style. When Roland was transferred to Lyons, she was appalled at the condition of the local peasantry, tending so assiduously to the sick among them that Roland feared for her own health.

From the moment the revolution began in 1789 Madame Roland lived for little else. She chafed at her provincial isolation, wrote to warn her friends in Paris of the reactionary tendencies of the smaller cities, and urged from the beginning the abolition of the monarchy. The Rolands returned to Paris in 1791, where Manon, with her vivacity, ambition, and charm, created a salon that attracted such figures as Robespierre and Tom Paine. Roland became minister of the interior and a member of the war party led by his patron, Jacques Brissot. In June 1792 he delivered a letter to the king, actually written by Manon, demanding that he revoke his veto of the legislation against nonjuring priests. Louis responded by dismissing Roland, and the entire Girondist ministry soon fell. This triggered an attack on the royal palace and, following a summer of heated intrigue in which

Madame Roland took an active part, the fall of the monarchy, the September massacres, and the summoning of the National Convention.

When it was moved in the convention that Roland be invited to resume his ministry, Georges Danton, a political opponent, suggested that the invitation be extended to Madame Roland as well. The convention, knowing her influence, burst into laughter. But Roland's star was already on the wane, while Manon, appalled by the September massacres and now deeply distrustful of Robespierre, began to waver for the first time in her belief in the revolution. She so triumphantly acquitted herself of charges of conspiring with royalist émigrés that she received a standing ovation from the convention, but six months later she was arrested in the coup of June 1793. Imprisoned for five months, she hastily composed her memoirs, knowing that she would be permitted no other defense. Condemned and executed on the same day, November 8, she showed great courage and composure on the scaffold and uttered before the guillotine fell what have come down as the most famous words of the French Revolution: "O Liberty, what crimes are committed in thy name!" Roland, who had gone into hiding, committed suicide at the news of her execution.

Madame Roland was a heroic figure to nineteenth-century historians, with their tendency to idealize women of passion and character. Her powers were not always matched by her judgment, but her integrity was unquestioned, and her career was astonishing and unprecedented. Not until the emergence of organized feminist politics in the late nineteenth century would any woman put a comparable stamp on the events of her time.

Conquest and Reaction, 1795–1799

The fall of Robespierre was followed by a sharp swing to the right, known as the Thermidorian reaction. Men were tired of terror and virtue alike. Political opportunists, money men, and speculators abounded. Aristocratic styles and even sentiments returned to fashion among the *jeunesse dorée*, or "gilded youth," of the bourgeoisie. Ex-Robespierrists in the provinces were purged by a semiofficial White Terror that rapidly degenerated into a brutal settling of scores with radicals in general. The democratic Constitution of the Year I was shelved for good, and with surviving Girondists readmitted to the convention, a new constitution was devised in 1795 that reinstated the old system of electors, with a property qualification so high that only 20,000 men in France met the test. The electors chose all department officials and

a new Legislative Assembly, which in turn chose a five-member executive, the Directory, from which the new regime was to take its name. As a precaution against future reprisal, the convention decreed that two-thirds of the new assembly must be made up of its own members.

These events spelled final defeat for the sans-culottes. The convention removed economic controls, prices skyrocketed, and the bread ration was cut to 2 ounces a day. Concluding not unreasonably that they were being deliberately starved into submission, the sans-culottes stormed the convention in May 1795, crying, "Bread or death!" It was less a demand than a simple statement. But loyal units of the National Guard dispersed them, and, leaderless, they were henceforth spent as a political force.

Despite this, however, the Directory was inherently unstable. It had neither the ideological attraction of Jacobinism nor the traditional appeal of monarchy. It was particularly vulnerable to attacks from royalists, who denounced its bourgeois leadership as a would-be aristocracy without the courage to choose its king. A royalist uprising in October was put down only by the presence of mind of a decommissioned young brigadier of artillery named Napoleon Bonaparte who happened to be in Paris at the time, but the threat remained. When elections in April 1797 produced startling gains for the right, the results were annulled, and the Directory declared that anyone advocating either the monarchy or the democratic constitution of 1793 would be shot on sight. With this it shed its last pretense to legitimacy. What remained was simply a cabal in search of a strongman.

Despite its difficulties at home, the revolution went from success to success abroad. Its conquering armies annexed the Austrian Netherlands, the left bank of the Rhine, and the Mediterranean principalities of Nice and Savoy to France outright and turned the proud Dutch republic into a satellite state after exacting an indemnity of 100 million livres. A daring foray by Napoleon in 1796 produced a string of new satellite republics in Italy, all grandiloquently named: the Cisalpine (Milan), the Ligurian (Genoa), the Roman (the Papal States), and the Parthenopean (Naples). The Swiss cantons were also herded into the so-called Helvetic Republic. Austria was compelled to recognize these conquests, as well as the annexation of its province in the Netherlands, by the Treaty of Campo Formio (October 1797). As a sop, the Austrians received Venice, thus extinguishing the independence of Europe's oldest republic.

Propped up by this success, the Directory drifted on for two more years. But the outbreak of war again in 1799 made a strong government imperative. A group led by the Abbé Sieyès put forward Napoleon Bonaparte, whose rapid rise to military prominence seemed to make him an ideal front man for a reorganized and strengthened executive. A coup in November 1799 ousted the

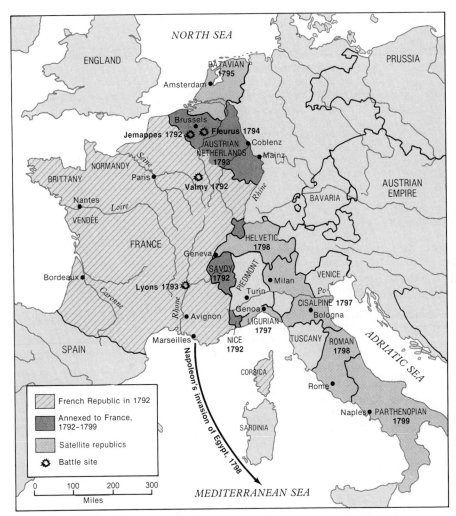

27.2 The Expansion of Revolutionary France, 1792–1799

Directory and dispersed the Legislative Assembly. It was the eighth major change of power in the revolution. Napoleon rapidly dispensed with his civilian allies and assumed complete power. For the next 15 years he governed France alone as first consul, consul for life, and finally emperor of the French. The revolution was over.

The Legacy of the Revolution: Conflicting Interpretations

The men and women who experienced the French revolution can be broadly classified into three groups. Some wished it had never occurred and wanted only to turn the clock back before 1789; some were satisfied with their gains at a given point and wished it to go no further; and some felt that it had not yet accomplished its task. The first group was composed chiefly of the nobility and the nonjuring clergy, the second of the peasants and the bourgeoisie, and the third of the sans-culottes and their allies among the liberal nobility and bourgeoisie. From these differing attitudes emerged the right, center, and left of nineteenth-century European politics.

Historians too, depending on their own political sympathies, have seen in the revolution either a great calamity, a necessary adjustment to changing circumstances, or a vision of social justice as yet unrealized. The first view was best represented in the nineteenth century by Hippolyte Taine (1828–1893), who feared a new revolution in his own time and wished to warn his fellow countrymen of the evils he felt it would unleash, and in more modern form by J. L. Talmon, who saw in the revolution a false dream of secular salvation that could lead

THE FRENCH REVOLUTION

From revolution to republic: 1789–1792

May 5, 1789	Estates General convenes at Versailles
June 17, 1789	Third Estate proclaims itself the National Assembly
July–August 1789	Storming of the Bastille (July 14); Great Fear in the countryside; abolition of legal orders (August 4); Declaration of the Rights of Man (August 27)
October 5–6, 1789	Women's march on Versailles; Louis XVI returns to Paris
July 1790	Civil Constitution of the Clergy
June 16, 1791	Louis XVI attempts to flee France
April 20, 1792	France declares war on Austria
August 10, 1792	Insurrection of the Paris Commune; Louis XVI arrested
September 1792	September massacres; National Convention declares France a republic (September 20)

War and Terror: 1792–1795

Autumn 1792	French armies repel allied invaders, occupy Antwerp (January 21, 1793)
January 21, 1793	Louis XVI executed
February 1793	France declares war on Britain, Spain, and the Netherlands
June 2, 1793	Montagnard coup brings Robespierre to power; Girondists purged
September 1793	Reign of Terror begins; thousands executed throughout France
July 27, 1794	Robespierre executed; Thermidorian reaction begins
July 1794–October 1795	White Terror purges radicals; satellite regime established in the Netherlands

The Directory: 1795–1799

October 1795	Directory established
1796	Napoleon campaigns in Italy; Manifesto of the Equals
September 4, 1797	Coup of Fructidor annuls French elections
October 17, 1797	Treaty of Campo Formio
November 9, 1799	Coup of 18 Brumaire; Napoleon seizes power

only to tyranny. The second view is identified with Alexis de Tocqueville (1805–1859), who argued in his highly influential book *The Old Regime and the French Revolution* (1856) that the revolution was not so much a break with the Old Regime as a development of the tendencies toward centralization and bureaucracy already inherent in it. From this perspective, the constructive work of the revolution was essentially complete by 1791, and the radical or Jacobin phase was an aberration caused by the instability of the constitutional monarchy that the Constituent Assembly had attempted to set up.

The third view, associated with the work of Jules Michelet (1798–1874) and, later, Albert Mathiez and Albert Soboul, argues to the contrary that the Jacobin republic was the climax of the revolution, which, by exposing the hollowness of a formal political equality unaccompanied by a redistribution of the wealth on which actual political power depends, set the agenda for modern mass politics and the demand for social justice. This view was first put forward during the revolution itself by the left-wing ideologue and conspirator Gracchus Babeuf (1760–1797), who predicted in his *Manifesto of the Equals* (1796) that "the French Revolution is but the forerunner of another, far more grand, far more solemn, which will be the last."

The group least satisfied by the revolution was women, particularly those of the urban working class. Although women bore the brunt of the revolution's hardships at all times and at least at one point, in the march on Versailles in October 1789, played a critical role in events, their interests were not addressed by any of the dominant factions of the revolution. The actress Olympe de Gouges demanded civil equality for women in a tract pointedly titled *Declaration of the Rights of Women and Citizenesses* but met only ridicule. Very few women were in the position of Madame Roland, whose salon was a center of revolutionary intrigue; most spent their days on ration lines, often to receive spoiled or unpalatable goods or nothing at all. Women and children were the first to succumb to starvation or malnutrition, as local records clearly show, and one can only imagine the desperation of the mothers of Masannay who in May 1794 demanded the elimination of all people over 60 so that the young might be fed enough to survive. When the women of Paris tried to organize their own clubs, they were shut down by the procurator of the Commune, who observed that sans-culottes had a right to expect their wives to keep house while they attended political meetings.

The legacy of the French revolution remains a matter

◉ A Revolutionary's Plea ◉ for the Rights of Women

In On the Admission of Women to the Rights of Citizenship, *the marquis de Condorcet, one of the few French noblemen to give his unqualified support to the revolution, chided the authorities for failing to provide for the rights of women as well as those of men.*

Is there a stronger proof of the power of habit, even among enlightened men, than to hear the principle of equality invoked in favor of 300 or 400 men deprived of their rights by an absurd prejudice [against counting all votes in the Estates General equally] and forgotten in the case of some 12 million women? . . .

Women are superior to men in the gentle and domestic virtues. Like men, they know how to love liberty, although they do not share all its advantages; and in republics they have often been known to sacrifice themselves for it. They have demonstrated the virtues of citizens whenever chance or civil troubles have brought them upon a scene from which the pride and the tyranny of men have excluded them in all nations.

Source: Marquis de Condorcet, *Selected Writings*, ed. K. M. Baker (Indianapolis: Bobbs-Merrill, 1976), pp. 97, 99.

of debate among historians as they continue to discuss the precise composition of the groups we call "bourgeois," "aristocratic," and "sans-culotte," the complex interactions and alliances among these groups, and the relationship between Paris and the countryside and between France and Europe. There are still many questions to be answered about the actual redistribution of land, wealth, and power in the revolution; about the functioning of revolutionary institutions, especially outside Paris; and about the effect of those institutions on conquered territories abroad. Some conclusions, however, seem unlikely to be seriously modified.

The revolution destroyed the localism of Old Regime France, welding it into a single political and economic unit and opening it to the forces of market capitalism while giving impetus to similar developments elsewhere. It produced the first citizen army of modern times and showed for the first time what an entire society mobilized for war and driven by ideology could achieve. It introduced modern mass politics and made the sovereignty of the people, already proclaimed in America, the fundamental legitimating principle of Western governments. It also introduced in the name of the people the suspension of all legal rights and forms and the elimination of all dissent by genocide, a practice that began with the Jacobins but was equally characteristic of the Directory and has since become an increasingly casual weapon of modern regimes. In that respect the revolution may be said to have opened up the Pandora's box of modern politics in which, as the Russian novelist Feodor Dostoevsky remarked, "everything is permitted." But it also, like Pandora, gave the great mass of the human race what it had never had before except from religion: hope.

The Napoleonic Era

It was not immediately clear that Napoleon's coup d'état would be very different from the previous changes of government of the past ten years, let alone that it would usher in a new era both for France and for Europe. As Napoleon slowly but firmly drew the reins of power into his own hands, however, and as his campaigns of conquest brought more and more of the continent under French sway, it became apparent that France had a master, and Europe a ruler, such as neither had known before.

From Republic to Empire

The Abbé Sieyès had brought Napoleon to power under the slogan "Confidence from below, authority from above." Napoleon took the slogan and dropped his ally. Born in 1769 into a family of impoverished minor nobility on the island of Corsica, he was barely 30 when he became master of France. Italian by descent (Napoleon dropped the *u* in the family name Buonaparte when he invaded Italy in 1796), he was French only by virtue of Corsica's annexation to France in 1768, and his first adventure was fighting for his island's independence in 1789. Soon swept up in the revolution on the mainland, he gained notice by taking the royalist port of Toulon in 1793, and after the stroke of luck that put him in Paris during the revolt of October 1795 he became a central figure in the political upheavals of the Directory. His brilliant campaign in Italy made him the man of the hour, and despite the failure of a campaign against the British in Egypt in 1798, his reputation was undimmed.

Napoleon promulgated a new constitution, which created an enfeebled legislature whose three chambers could respectively debate, enact, and veto laws but do nothing together and which centralized executive authority in the hands of three "consuls." Napoleon took the title of first consul, with full authority to appoint all officials and magistrates, conduct diplomacy, declare and wage war, and protect the public safety. Napoleon had vowed to keep the republic, but all that remained of it was a façade. The powers he gave himself made him an uncrowned king. In a masterful stroke of public relations, he submitted the constitution to a popular referendum, although he had already proclaimed it in effect. The result was predictably lopsided, with a count of 3,011,007 votes for and 1,562 against. Napoleon could now claim his "mandate" from the people. In 1802 he extended the term of his consulship from ten years to life, and in 1804, after making peace with the church, he assumed the title of emperor. Both acts were ratified by popular referendum, but for his coronation Napoleon summoned Pope Pius VII to Paris, and in a gesture deliberately reminiscent of Charlemagne's at his coronation as Holy Roman emperor 1,000 years before, he took the crown from the pontiff's hands and placed it on his own head. Shortly afterward he created an aristocracy, mostly from the upper bourgeoisie. The revolution against kings, priests, and nobles had come full circle.

Napoleon ruled through propaganda, press censorship, the highly efficient secret police, and, on occasion, acts of political terrorism such as the kidnapping and execution of the young Bourbon duke of Enghien in 1804. Yet his popularity was genuine, and he enjoyed the broad support of all classes almost to the end. Only diehard royalists and republicans refused to accept him. Simply stated, Napoleon gave the rich what they wanted, the poor what they would accept, and, through an un-

---

◎ Napoleon on Himself ◎

Napoleon's cynicism is clearly reflected in his many statements, a sample of which are presented here.

My policy is to govern men the way the great majority wants to be governed. This, I believe, is the only way in which it is possible to acknowledge the sovereignty of the people. By making myself Catholic I brought the war in the Vendée to an end. By becoming a Muslim I established myself in Egypt. By acting ultramontane I won the minds of the Italians. If I governed a nation of Jews, I should restore the temple of Solomon. Thus I shall talk freedom in the free part of Santo Domingo; I shall confirm slavery in the Île de France and even in the slave part of Santo Domingo—with the reservation that I shall soften and limit slavery wherever I maintain it and shall restore order and discipline wherever I maintain freedom.

You must know that I am not in the least afraid of committing an act of cowardice if it were useful to me. Look here, at bottom there is nothing either noble or base in this world. My character possesses all those qualities that are capable of strengthening my power and of deceiving those who imagine that they know me. Frankly, I am a coward, indeed I am—essentially a coward. I give you my word of honor that I would not experience the least repugnance toward committing what the world calls a dishonorable action.

Don't talk to me of goodness, of abstract justice, of natural law. Necessity is the highest law; public welfare is the highest justice. Unto each day the evil thereof; to each circumstance its own law; each man according to his own nature.

Source: J. C. Herold, ed. and trans., *The Mind of Napoleon* (New York: Columbia University Press, 1955), pp. 79, 160.

precedented career of conquest, a measure of glory to everyone such as Louis XIV had only dreamed of.

Napoleon centralized political control as thoroughly as the Jacobins had ever done in the days of the Terror. All officials from the lowest level were responsible to the national state and ultimately the emperor himself through a clear chain of command. The judiciary, declared independent in 1791, was brought back under executive control. The economy was similarly taken in hand. Napoleon applied price controls as he saw fit, promoted new industry, and built an extensive network of roads and canals. The Bank of France was chartered in 1800 to free the government from reliance on private credit. Thus the French began to catch up with the fiscal system developed by the English more than a century before.

Napoleon capped his reforms with the Civil Code of 1804, known, with later additions and modifications, as the Napoleonic Code. The code was the culmination of efforts to produce a digest of French legal and administrative principles dating back to the sixteenth century, and it became the most influential code of secular law outside the Anglo-Saxon tradition since Roman times. The main principles of the early revolution—civil and legal equality, religious toleration, and the abolition of feudal obligations and legally privileged orders—were confirmed. Beneath the veneer of formal equality, however, the code envisioned a hierarchical society based on subordination to wealth and gender. The emphasis, as in the Old Regime, was on the flow of authority downward from the state to the patriarchal family. Women were enjoined to obey their husbands and prevented from acquiring property without written consent and from administering joint property. Children might be imprisoned for up to six months on the mere word of their father and had to gain his consent to marry up to the age of 30. A similar hierarchy was established in the workplace; for example, the word of an employer automatically prevailed over that of a worker in court. The code was extremely detailed in its guarantees of property rights and its provisions for contracts and debts, but as for labor, denied as before the right of association, it was merely "free"—free to survive or perish as market conditions might dictate.

Napoleon's other major settlement was with the church. By the Concordat of 1801, the Vatican recognized the confiscation of its lands and tithes as permanent, thereby accepting the role of the clergy as salaried employees of the state. It even consented to a catechism in which disobedience to Napoleon was declared to be grounds for eternal damnation, something no divine right monarch had ever succeeded in making a part of religious instruction. In return for his concessions, the pope was recognized as head of the church, and Catholicism was declared to be the religion "of the majority of Frenchmen." By this careful formulation, Napoleon stopped short of making Catholicism the official state church, thus preserving the principle of religious toleration; yet it served that function in effect. With the Concordat, the empire, and the code, his structure of authority was complete.

France Against Europe

Napoleon inherited command of the war France had been fighting since 1792, which by 1815 ranged over the entire globe and brought such consequences as the conquest of India, the liberation of South America, and the doubling of the size of the United States. Despite its complexity, however, it had, like the wars of Louis XIV a century before, a single dominant element: the containment of France.

The French had gone to war in 1792 to extend the revolution abroad and to maintain its momentum at home. By 1795 this initial enthusiasm was largely spent, and the French pursued the war for more traditional imperial and commercial goals. They were opposed by a shifting coalition whose only stable member was Great Britain. The Continental powers were slow at first to react to the French threat. Informed military opinion, far from considering France a menace, dismissed the revolutionary army as a leaderless mob. It was a measure of their preoccupation with more important matters, such as the partition of Poland, that Austria and Prussia did not even think this defenseless France worth attacking and confined themselves at first to diplomatic gestures such as the Declaration of Pillnitz.

The success of French forces took Europe wholly by surprise. No one had ever seen an army like this, which broke all the rules of military practice yet kept on winning. New recruits picked up their training on the march, discipline was negligible, and supplies were always short. Promotions were made on the basis of merit rather than birth: Napoleon's marshals included former coopers, millers, masons, and stable boys. Their average age was about 30; most of Prussia's generals were over 60.

But Europe could not long tolerate a French frontier that ran from the North Sea to the Ionian. Backed by British money and Russian troops, a second coalition drove the French back on a broad front in 1799. If the original revolutionary impetus of the French army was exhausted, however, it was now replaced by an equally powerful force: Napoleon's own dream of world empire. Napoleon smashed the Austrians at Hohenlinden and Marengo, forcing them to sue for peace (Treaty of Lunéville, 1801) on even worse terms than at Campo Formio, and with the fall of the 18-year ministry of William Pitt the Younger, the son of the hero of the Seven Years' War, the British made a reluctant peace at Amiens in 1802.

Full-scale war resumed in 1805 with Britain, again under Pitt, subsidizing Russian troops to the tune of £1,250,000 per each 100,000 recruits. But at Ulm on October 15 an Austrian army, completely outgeneraled, surrendered without firing a shot, and six weeks later, on the first anniversary of his coronation (December 2), Napoleon won the greatest of all his battles over a combined Austro-Russian force at Austerlitz. Prussia, neutral since 1795, blundered into war alone in 1806, only to have its reputedly invincible army destroyed in two simultaneous battles 12 miles apart at Jena and Auerstadt. The French now pursued Russia along the Baltic shore into East Prussia, where after bloody battles at Eylau (February 1807) and Friedland (June), Tsar Alexander I (1796–1825) too offered peace. Napoleon was unsuccessful only at sea, where his plan for invading Britain was dashed by the fleet under Lord Horatio Nelson at Cape Trafalgar off the coast of Spain. Nelson sank or captured 18 French ships without the loss of a vessel but was himself slain in the battle.

The Grand Empire

European politics had long been predicated on maintaining a balance of power between its major states. This principle was formally incorporated into the Peace of Utrecht (1713), and it appeared so self-evident to eighteenth-century commentators that one even likened it to gravity as a law of nature. The French Revolution had challenged it with the idea that all states might be compelled to respect natural rights, if necessary by force. Napoleon openly rejected the balance of power. "Europe," he declared, "cannot be at rest except under a single head who will have kings for his officers." Clearly he saw himself as that head.

After the defeat of the Third Coalition in 1805, Napoleon began to construct his Grand Empire. The debris of petty German principalities was swept away, to be replaced by the Confederation of the Rhine, a satellite entity whose 38 members acknowledged Napoleon as their protector and agreed to furnish troops for his army. The 1,000-year-old Holy Roman Empire, once the symbol of German nationality and latterly of Austrian domination, was summarily abolished in 1806. Only Prussia retained its nominal independence, but shorn of half its territory and with its army reduced to a mere 42,000 men. Prussian Poland was reconstituted as the Grand Duchy of Warsaw, another satellite. Napoleon created a kingdom of Italy for his stepson Eugène, later annexing some of it to France and imprisoning Pius VII when he objected to the occupation of the Papal States. Similarly, a kingdom of Holland was created for Napoleon's brother Louis but absorbed outright four years later. Using his siblings essentially as prefects, Napoleon made his brother Jérome king of the German satellite of Westphalia in 1807 and his brother Joseph king of Spain in 1808, deposing the reigning Bourbon dynasty.

By the time this structure of satellite kingdoms was complete, however, Napoleon considered it obsolete. National entities, even ruled as the private preserve of the emperor's own family, were still too insubordinate, too conscious of their separate historical identities. As the Constituent Assembly had abolished the old provinces of France, so Napoleon decided to abolish the nations of Europe, replacing them with a single imperial administration. But events overtook him, and this last design was never carried out.

The Napoleonic Code was used as the basis of administration in the Grand Empire, from whence its influence spread throughout Europe and beyond, reaching places as distant as Bolivia, Egypt, and Japan. By abolishing serfdom, dissolving the Old Regime system of orders, and introducing public education, it opened careers in commerce, industry, and government to men of talent. If the code represented the revolution at its least liberal, it was still often startlingly new and progressive elsewhere in Europe, and its importance as a solvent of feudal structures and as a model of modern society can scarcely be exaggerated.

Despite the order and prosperity Napoleonic government introduced, it provoked reactions ranging from passive resistance to outright rebellion everywhere. The chief common grievance was the Continental System, an attempt by Napoleon to close the ports of the empire to British commerce. This exposed such ports to reprisals by the British, who wholly dominated the seas, as well as to a counterblockade that had a crippling effect on European commerce. The deeper reason for resentment, however, was the suppression of national culture in the subject territories, the dominance of French officials and the presence of French troops and police, and the exploitation of the wealth and resources of a continent for the benefit of a single nation and ultimately a single family. In the Dutch Netherlands, where French aggression had been resisted for centuries, the occupation was particularly severe. The use of Dutch was discouraged, and all books were rigidly censored. Unhappy Westphalia rebelled no fewer than seven times against Napoleonic rule, and Rome bitterly resented the humiliation of the papacy. But by far the most serious resistance came from Spain. Spaniards of all classes rose up spontaneously against the French occupation and for six years waged a fierce guerrilla war whose atrocities were recorded for all time by the painter Francisco Goya. Spain was the stanchless wound in Napoleon's side. He thought that 20,000 men could hold the country; ten times that many failed. A British army under Arthur Wellesley, later duke of Wellington, linked up with the Spaniards through Portugal in what came to be known as the Peninsular War. By early 1814 southern France

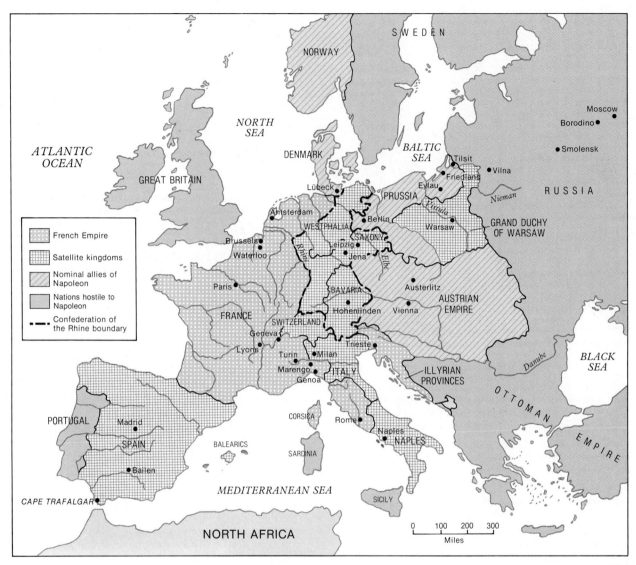

27.3 Europe in 1810

itself was under attack. The war ended with the British in Toulouse.

A more lasting effect of the Napoleonic occupation was the stimulation of national feeling, particularly in Italy and Germany. Passed from hand to hand since the sixteenth century, Italy had been parceled out in bits and pieces by Napoleon to in-laws and even cabinet ministers. But despite heavy taxes and a general distaste for the French presence, Italian commerce and industry benefited from the abolition of tariff barriers, the building of new roads, and the introduction of uniform weights and measures. It is significant that many of the future leaders of the movement for Italian unification were descended from families that became rich under

Napoleon. These new industrialists and financiers were not prepared to return to the inefficiencies of the traditional economy after 1815, and they chafed under its reimposition.

National consciousness had been promoted in eighteenth-century Germany by the philosopher Johann Gottfried von Herder, who argued that each people had a separate and unique historical destiny shaped by its *Volksgeist*, or national spirit. But most German intellectuals of the Enlightenment prided themselves on a lofty cosmopolitanism instead. Their ideal was the tiny, idyllic dukedom of Weimar, whose ruler, Karl August (1775–1828), had gathered around him a brilliant court crowned by the great poet Goethe. They despised Prus-

And They Are like Wild Beasts: **Spanish women, virtually unarmed, battle Napoleon's troops in this print from Goya's series of etchings *Disasters of War*. No other artist has ever captured so directly the naked ferocity of war. [Metropolitan Museum of Art, Rogers Fund, 1922]**

sian militarism in particular, and many initially welcomed the Napoleonic invasion; on the eve of the Battle of Jena the philosopher Hegel, himself a Prussian, wrote, "As I [did] formerly, now everybody wishes success to the French army."

The collapse and dismemberment of the Prussian state changed all that. Defeat brought Prussia what victory never had: a sense of nationhood. As French troops paraded through the streets of Berlin, the philosopher and publicist Johann Gottlieb Fichte (1762–1814) delivered a series of "addresses to the German nation" in which he argued that the German Volksgeist was intrinsically superior and must protect itself from contamination by outside cultures. Fichte denounced the petty sectionalism of German politics and called for a national movement to drive out the French oppressor. The dramatist Friedrich von Schiller also preached national liberation in his patriotic odes and plays, and freedom from oppression was the thinly veiled message of Beethoven's opera *Fidelio*. In Prussia itself, meanwhile, the crown ministers Baron Stein and Prince Hardenburg initiated significant land reforms, including the abolition of serfdom, liberalization of land tenures, and the reform of the bureaucracy.

For the moment, however, liberation seemed far away. From the Atlantic to the Polish steppe, from the Baltic to the Mediterranean, Napoleon ruled or dominated the whole of Europe. A swollen France itself stretched from the north German port of Lübeck to

south of Rome. When Austria, which like Prussia had been reduced to dependent status, rebelled in 1809 and called on the former states of the Holy Roman Empire to assist it, not a single one responded. The Habsburg army was quickly crushed at Wagram, and it was now Vienna's turn to entertain a triumphal parade of French troops.

Yet Napoleon's empire was inherently unstable. As the flush of idealism and reform it had borrowed from the revolution wore away, the cynical and exploitive nature of its administration was increasingly apparent. It preached human equality but demanded permanent subjection. It violated the entire history and tradition of the European state system. It was not even in the interest of France, whose distended borders now resembled a jaw open on the whole continent. As early as 1808 Napoleon's foreign minister, Talleyrand, had made secret overtures to Tsar Alexander. Even at the height of the empire, Talleyrand did not believe it would last.

Napoleon himself was aware of the weakness of his position. He became obsessed with founding a dynasty. When his first wife, Joséphine de Beauharnais, failed to provide him with an heir, he divorced her in favor of Princess Marie-Louise of Austria. In 1811 she bore him a son, whom Napoleon grandly called the king of Rome. But nothing could obscure the fact that Napoleon, who had so often humiliated Austria, felt compelled to buy legitimacy by mixing his blood with that of the Habsburgs.

The Collapse of the Napoleonic Order

Of the major states of Europe, only Britain and Russia remained outside the Grand Empire. Britain continued its struggle with Napoleon alone, resulting in a war with the United States over its naval blockade of the Continent in 1812. Russia, by contrast, was formally a French ally. By the Treaty of Tilsit (1807), which the tsar and the emperor had negotiated in person on a barge in the middle of the Niemen River, Alexander agreed to join the Continental System if his efforts to mediate between Britain and France failed, and he also accepted French intercession in his conflict with the Turkish sultan. Superficially, this seemed to be an agreement between equals to assist each other in disputes with their neighbors; in reality, it obliged the tsar to recognize the Napoleonic order while giving Napoleon an entrée into a traditional Russian sphere of interest.

An uneasy truce prevailed for the next five years as both sides probed for each other's weaknesses. Alexander attempted to gain control of the Grand Duchy of Warsaw, which under Napoleonic rule was a dagger pointed at Russia itself. Napoleon in turn sought influence in Istanbul, which he regarded as the "center of world empire," an empire presumably to be controlled by himself.

When Russia reopened trade with Britain and erected tariffs against French goods, Napoleon resolved on war. In June 1812 he crossed the Niemen into Russia with over 600,000 men, the largest army ever assembled for a single campaign. Napoleon envisaged a quick victory. His troops carried only four days' rations and the supply convoys three weeks' more. But the Russians gave ground instead of fighting, leaving behind only scorched earth. They surrendered Moscow after an indecisive but bloody battle at Borodino, and Napoleon entered unopposed on September 14. What had been a city of 300,000 was all but deserted. Fires had already begun, and within a week three-quarters of it had burned down. Without food or shelter, Napoleon could not winter in the devastated city. On October 19 he began a retreat. Mired in snow and mud, dogged by Russian snipers, his army laid a 1,000-mile track of corpses along its way. More than half a million men died, deserted, or disappeared.

Abandoning his army to its fate, Napoleon raced back to Paris. He raised a new army of 250,000 to face a revived coalition of Russia, Prussia, Austria, and Sweden, with Britain as usual footing the bill. After several indecisive victories, Napoleon's forces were defeated outside Leipzig in the great three-day Battle of the Nations (October 1813) and thrown back upon France. The Austrian foreign minister, Count Klemens von Metternich, alarmed at Prussia's new nationalism and eager to have

the Russians out of Europe, offered to guarantee the French borders of 1792, including the former Austrian Netherlands and the left bank of the Rhine. Napoleon refused. For the emperor of the French, the only stakes were all or nothing. Allied armies now poured into France from Belgium, the middle Rhine, and Switzerland, with Wellington attacking from the south. Napoleon's defensive campaign was the most brilliant of his career, but the result was foregone. On April 4, 1814, he abdicated as emperor in favor of his 3-year-old son, a day after his Senate had deposed him.

The Bourbon Restoration

The victorious allies, aided by Talleyrand, restored the Bourbon dynasty in the person of Louis XVIII, count of Provence,* who signed the Treaty of Paris on May 30 that ended France's 22-year war with Europe. Wishing to support the new monarch, the allies demanded no indemnities or reparations. France was simply required to return to its prewar boundaries. Even Napoleon was treated leniently. He was exiled to the island of Elba off the west coast of Italy but permitted to retain the title of emperor and granted a pension of 2 million francs a year.

Louis XVIII was in theory an absolute king, but he confirmed the revolutionary land settlement and the Napoleonic Code and issued the Constitutional Charter, which provided for a bicameral assembly chosen by a restricted suffrage of large landowners. But thousands of vengeful émigrés returned with him who would be satisfied by nothing less than a complete restoration of the Old Regime. The activities of these Ultraroyalists, or Ultras, as they were popularly called, together with economic depression and the inevitable letdown from the excitement of Napoleon's reign, cost the Bourbon regime whatever credibility it had. Napoleon, sensing his opportunity, returned with a small flotilla and with 1,000 veterans marched unopposed on Paris. The Bourbons fled to Belgium, and the emperor declared himself restored "by the unanimous wish of a great nation."

The allies, who had gathered in Vienna to discuss the settlement of postwar Europe, promptly declared Napoleon a public outlaw. Napoleon himself, courting support at home, made conciliatory gestures both to the right and to the left. But only a trial by battle could reestablish him. Raising an army, he crossed into Belgium, where on June 18, 1815, he met a combined force under the duke of Wellington and the Prussian general Gerhard von Blücher at Waterloo on the road to Brussels

---

*The son of Louis XVI, who died in prison at the age of 10 without ever reigning, was recognized as Louis XVII.

and was defeated in daylong combat. Returning to Paris, he was met with a stony demand for abdication. His second reign had lasted exactly 100 days.

Napoleon was now exiled to St. Helena, a bleak, tiny island in the south Atlantic, 4,000 miles from Europe, where in 1821 he died of stomach cancer. His legend lived on in France, where a veritable cult grew up around him that was climaxed by the return and reentombment of his body in 1840.

Napoleon himself said that the man of genius is a meteor who illuminates his time but does not transform it. Talleyrand, who knew him as well as anyone, thought that he had squandered an opportunity to create a lasting political equilibrium in Europe. Yet Napoleon did leave a permanent legacy. His code became the basis of modern French society. His conquests stimulated both anti-French nationalism and aspirations for a liberal society on the French model. His suppression of the Holy Roman Empire was the first step toward the unification of Germany. If the ideas he spread were those of the revolution rather than his own, they might never have traveled as far as they did without him. Napoleon failed to make Europe a province of France, but he did much to make the French Revolution European.

The quarter century between 1789 and 1815 marked the climax of French domination in Europe and the watershed of the modern age. Fired by the hopes and ideals of the Enlightenment and frustrated by a political system that seemed unresponsive to the needs of a new society, the French embarked on a career of revolutionary transformation at home and conquest abroad unmatched in European history. They succeeded at first through the power of ideas no less than the force of arms, but as the revolution at home began to lose its way they relied more and more on military strength, which in the hands of Napoleon produced a vast but unstable empire. If Napoleon carried the core principles of the revolution across Europe, he awakened resentment and resistance that at last united the continent against him. In the end Europe returned largely to its old boundaries, but neither they nor the old order on which they were founded would ultimately survive the shock of the revolutionary decades and the profound forces they both unleashed and reflected.

Notes

1. J. H. Stewart, *A Documentary Survey of the French Revolution* (New York: Macmillan, 1951), p. 42 (modified slightly).
2. R. Zaller, *Europe in Transition, 1660–1815* (New York: Harper & Row, 1984), p. 130.

Suggestions for Further Reading

Applewhite, H. B., and Levy, D. G., eds. *Women and Politics in the Age of the Democratic Revolution.* Ann Arbor: University of Michigan Press, 1990.

Bergeron, L. *France Under Napoleon.* Princeton, N.J.: Princeton University Press, 1981.

Blanning, T. C. W. *The Origins of the French Revolutionary Wars.* London: Longman, 1986.

Cobb, R. C. *The People's War.* New Haven, Conn.: Yale University Press, 1987.

Cobban, A. *The Social Interpretation of the French Revolution.* Cambridge: Cambridge University Press, 1964.

Doyle, W. *Origins of the French Revolution.* Oxford: Oxford University Press, 1980.

Furet, F. *Interpreting the French Revolution.* New York: Cambridge University Press, 1981.

Geyl, P. *Napoleon: For and Against.* New Haven: Yale University Press, 1967.

Godechot, J., Hyslop, B., and Dowd, D. *The Napoleonic Era in Europe.* New York: Holt, Rinehart, and Winston, 1971.

Hampson, N. *A Social History of the French Revolution.* Toronto: University of Toronto Press, 1963.

Hunt, L. *Politics, Culture and Class in the French Revolution.* Berkeley: University of California Press, 1984.

Jones, P. M. *The Peasantry in the French Revolution.* Cambridge: Cambridge University Press, 1988.

Jordan, D. *The Revolutionary Career of Maximilien Robespierre.* New York: Free Press, 1985.

Kennedy, M. *The Jacobin Clubs in the French Revolution.* 2 vols. Princeton, N.J.: Princeton University Press, 1981, 1988.

Lefebvre, G. *The French Revolution.* 2 vols. New York: Columbia University Press, 1962, 1964.

———. *The Great Fear of 1789: Rural Panic in Revolutionary France.* New York: Pantheon, 1973.

———. *Napoleon from Tilsit to Waterloo, 1807–1815.* New York: Columbia University Press, 1969.

May, G. *Madame Roland and the Age of Revolution.* New York: Columbia University Press, 1970.

Palmer, R. R. *The Age of the Democratic Revolutions.* 2 vols. Princeton, N.J.: Princeton University Press, 1959, 1964.

———. *Twelve Who Ruled: The Year of the Terror in the French Revolution.* Princeton, N.J.: Princeton University Press, 1970.

Rose, R. B. *The Making of the Sans-Culottes: Democratic Ideas and Institutions in Paris, 1789–92.* Manchester: Manchester University Press, 1983.

Rudé, G. *The Crowd in the French Revolution.* Oxford: Oxford University Press, 1959.

Schama, S. *Citizens: A Chronicle of the French Revolution.* New York: Knopf, 1989.

Soboul, A. *The Sans-Culottes and the French Revolution.* Princeton, N.J.: Princeton University Press, 1980.

Thompson, J. M. *Napoleon Bonaparte: His Rise and Fall.* New York: Oxford University Press, 1969.

Venturi, F. *The End of the Old Regime in Europe, 1776–1789.* Princeton, N.J.: Princeton University Press, 1991.

Death and the Human Experience (II)

Throughout history, every society has grappled with the fact of death and speculated about what may lie beyond the grave. Thus death is a common human bond, linking the most primitive societies with the most advanced. Though all of the major world religions have offered explanations of death and hypotheses about subsequent existence, each has, in practice, been forced to accommodate its tenets to folk customs and popular mores. In so doing, religion has borne witness to the universal human effort to find a satisfying way to cope with death and dying. Reformers, in their quest to purify religion, have periodically attempted to purge funeral rituals of these culture-bound practices, thereby forcing their followers to rethink the question of death. Missionaries made similar efforts, attempting to replace folk customs with their own conceptions of death and the afterlife. Thus history is in part the story of conflicting attitudes about the common human experience of mortality.

The fundamental need to render death less fearful led orthodox Muslims to embellish the tenets of the Koran. Gradually Muslims came to believe that as a believer neared death, white-faced angels descended and sat before him. When he died, the Angel of Death gently extracted his soul from the corpse and gave it to other angels. They in turn carried the soul, wrapped in a perfumed shroud, to the seventh heaven, where the beliefs and deeds of the deceased were recorded. The soul then rejoined the body in the grave for an interrogation on those beliefs and deeds by two blue-eyed, black-faced angels named Munkar and Nakir. To prepare the dead person for this Trial of the Grave, mourners sometimes whispered advice—the Instruction of the Deceased—to the corpse at the funeral. After the Trial of the Grave, the soul was comforted by Munkar and Nakir and allowed to enjoy a virtually limitless garden before its resurrection from the grave.

For an unbeliever the routine was superficially similar, though the angels attending him were black-faced and his soul could only be dragged from his body with enormous difficulty. The soul, bound in haircloth that reeked like rotting flesh, was borne only to the gate of the lowest heaven. Following the questioning by Munkar and Nakir, this soul would be sentenced to a period of torment in a grave filled with heat and smoke. The point of adding these details was to help the living deal with the demise of others as well as to prepare for their own deaths. Such details made the account more memorable as well as more familiar in experiential terms.

This mask from the Ikoi tribe in Nigeria expresses belief in life after death, representing death as the dark male face to the left, with eyes closed, and life as the lighter female face to the right. [Werner Forman Archive]

A comparable phenomenon occurred in Japan as traditional folk belief was blended with Buddhism. According to folk religion, death occurred when the soul left the body; hence as a person lay dying, his or her friends beseeched the soul not to depart. Following death, a bowl of cooked rice for sustenance and a sword or other sharp object for protection were placed beside the corpse. As happens occasionally in the West, family members sat with the corpse the night before the funeral. The service itself was conducted by Buddhist priests, one of whom gave the deceased a new name for use in the afterlife seven days after his or her death. Formal mourning lasted 49 days, on the last of which a commemorative service was held. As in Roman Catholicism, requiem masses were observed for the deceased at specified intervals. The last of these, held 33 or 49 years after the person's death, marked the point at which the spirit lost its individuality and merged with the ancestral diety (*kami*), following which reincarnation in a newborn child could occur. The family of the deceased could take comfort that through its ritual observances the soul of the dead could enhance its status until it united with the ancestral *kami*. Thus not only was death familiarized, but the bereaved could find comfort in their efforts to aid the soul in the afterlife, much as Roman Catholics pray for the speedy passage of souls through purgatory.

Thus people sought to familiarize death by blending spiritual tenets with folklore. Periodically, reformers tried to purge religion of these customs. In Europe, for example, the Protestant reformers of the sixteenth century denounced requiem masses, prayers for the dead, monthly and yearly "minds" (commemorative services for the dead), purgatory, and extreme unction (the anointing of the seriously ill) on the grounds that they were superstitious and without foundation in the Bible. In India the bhakti movement, a religious renewal in the fifteenth and sixteenth centuries, similarly deemphasized ritual in favor of devotion to the Godhead.

An eighteenth-century illustration of the Hindu practice of *sati*. [Granger Collection]

The poet-reformer Kabir (died 1518), for instance, criticized traditional Hindu death rituals, holy places, and the doctrine of reincarnation. Taking a less extreme position, devotional cults in northern India retained simplified funeral rites but insisted that they were meaningful only if infused with love for God.

Colonial expansion brought Europeans into contact with many new perceptions of death and, to them, exotic burial customs. But there were also some striking resemblances. African folklore, for instance, included numerous myths to explain the origin of death, some of which were similar to Judeo-Christian concepts. As in the ancient Hebrew belief in a fall from a pristine state, some Africans suggested that death was the consequence of a fall from morality or disobedience to specific commandments. A number of African myths are essentially variations of the "forbidden fruit" theme of Genesis, but others attribute the origins of death to such things as family discord, disease, sexual intercourse, or a natural longing to die.

The spread of Western imperialism starkly juxtaposed Christian beliefs and funeral rites with those of other religions. In northern India the imposition of British rule beginning in 1763 actually sparked a revival of Hindu funerary practices, including pilgrimages to holy places associated with death rituals. But the British in turn tried to prohibit "unnatural" funerary customs. Among them was suicide at holy places, which could be undertaken for a variety of reasons, including a desire to be reincarnated in a higher state or, for Muslims, entry into paradise. British authorities also tried to limit the practice of *sati*, insisting that a widow could not be forced to cast herself into the flames of her husband's pyre. British Baptist missionaries in Bengal attempted to stop the Hindus from leaving the terminally ill beside a river without food or shelter. From a Hindu perspective, to allow such a person to die in a home would mean lengthy and expensive purification rites. Though in some respects colonial rule brought modifications in burial customs, Indians who resented imperialism clung resolutely to traditional rites, at least in part to defy their colonial overlords.

The Indonesian island of Sumba provides another illustration of the conflict between Christian and native burial customs. Like the Chinese, the Sumbanese believed that the dead engaged in social relations with the living; in fact, the dead enjoyed greater power because they could enforce supernatural sanctions in dealings with their descendants. Missionaries discouraged such beliefs, especially when Sumbanese diviners began reporting that deceased converts to Christianity were demanding reburial according to traditional customs, including interment of their corpses in megalithic tombs. The diviners buttressed their claims by blaming illness and hardship among descendants on their failure to bury their ancestors in the traditional manner. Numerous converts finally left the church in order to reinter their forebears in their ancestral villages.

Sometimes the customs associated with death shocked westerners. In the seventeenth century, French Jesuits were scandalized by the practices of the Huron Indians of southeastern Canada. According to the Hurons, at death the soul is separated from the body and enters an afterlife akin to the world of the living. It was therefore important to participate in a ritual known as the Feast of Courage to enable one's soul to be powerful in the afterlife. In this feast the Hurons drank the blood and ate the flesh of an enemy warrior who had died valiantly after being cruelly tortured; by this act, they believed, they incorporated his courage within themselves.

The Hurons also observed the Feast of the Dead, which was held every 10 or 12 years with the intent of binding the people together. At heart the ritual entailed a second burial. Family members began by retrieving the bodies of deceased relatives that had been stored on scaffolds in a cemetery, after which the women cleaned any remaining skin and flesh from the bones. The bones were then wrapped in furs and taken back to the village houses, where the families dined in their

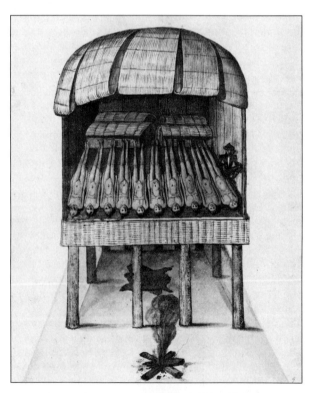

Like the Hurons, the Natchez Indians dried their corpses on frames, as shown in this watercolor by John White. [British Museum]

presence. Only then were the bones taken to a circular burial pit, over which they were suspended on poles for as long as a week while the people played games, gambled, danced, and feasted. After an elaborate ritual, the bones were buried in the pit along with various gifts. When the Hurons were defeated by the Iroquois, they began to lose faith in the Feast of Courage, and when, in the nineteenth century, they were forced to move to reservations in Oklahoma, they left behind their dead and thus their sense of identity as a people.

The use of death to heighten the sense of community is present in other cultures. This is true, for example, of the Christian community's commemoration of the death and resurrection of Christ, a ceremony sometimes linked to passion plays and realistic reenactments of the crucifixion. Among Shi'ite Muslims, the annual performance of rites to commemorate the death of Muhammad's grandson, Husein, underscores the historical continuity of the Shi'a movement and deepens its sense of community.

In the Iraqi cities of Nejev and Karbala, pilgrims honoring Husein annually crowd the streets. Their buildings are draped in black, and the cafés, bars, and theaters are closed as religious processions command attention. As in Christian lands, there are dramatic reenactments of the last days and death of the religious leader. The public ceremonies climax with a procession reputedly bearing Husein's head, followed by flagellants, bare to the waist, thrashing themselves with chains. Other ritual sufferers bear swords, periodically striking themselves on the forehead or scalp until blood gushes forth. Some worshipers have died, among them actors who, for the sake of realism, had depicted Husein's decapitation by burying their own heads or bodies in the scorching sand. Others engage in knifing rituals, the object of which is to stab oneself in the stomach without bleeding, thereby demonstrating a higher spirituality.

The ultimate self-punishment is, of course, suicide, as sometimes occurred among Hindus in India or believers in other countries who burned themselves to death to dramatize their message. The public suicide of Buddhist monks in Vietnam helped bring about the fall of the American-sponsored Diem government in 1963. Closely related to these practices is the deliberate courting of martyrdom. In Islam this has been a means of immediate entry to paradise and has been fairly common among such diverse groups as modern terrorists and Iranian soldiers willing to sacrifice themselves in the Iran-Iraq war. From time to time Christianity too has experienced this phenomenon, particularly during the period of the church's persecution in the late Roman Empire and again during the crusading movement that commenced in the 1090s. Thus many have courted death at the hands of others to advance their cause or obtain spiritual rewards.

Martyrdom of a different sort has been practiced among the Jews, who, though in no sense seeking death, have confronted a death inflicted by others with a commandment known as the *Kiddush Hashem*, the sanctification of God's name. During the Holocaust there were numerous instances of Jews going to their death singing religious songs, radiating spiritual ecstasy, or performing ritual dances. As one rabbi wrote in 1939, "Every Jew [is prepared to] be killed for *Kiddush Hashem*, happy in the privilege of sanctifying, by his own means, the Name of Heaven."[1]

For many modern westerners, death has become something to shun or even deny. The roots of this attitude can be found in a number of complex changes that occurred in the early modern era. During the Reformation, Catholics, Lutherans, and Puritans called for simple funerals and greater attention to the spiritual truths involved in death and resurrection; physical death was deemphasized. At the same time, artists and writers began consciously linking death and love, sometimes in an openly sensual way, making death at once a thing of beauty and a sudden rupture between this world and an alluring afterlife. In the seventeenth century, baroque playwrights staged love scenes in tombs, and Bernini's statue of St. Theresa's mystical union with God simultaneously depicted physical death and a spiritual ecstasy suggestive of sexual fulfillment. Death and resurrection, death and ecstasy—the tendency of the new sensibility was to play down the cruder physical aspects of dying by associating death with life and especially pleasure.

During the Enlightenment this trend culminated in attempts to suppress the awareness of death. Mourning, said the Abbé Coyer, a French priest, only encourages a cruel image of death, when in fact dying is "agreeable." Some chose to speak not of death but of a journey, a voyage, a refuge, a harbor, or sleep. Efforts were made to halt burials in churches and churchyards within the cities, partly for health reasons, thus symbolically expelling the dead from the community of the living. Corpses were to be interred in public cemeteries, enabling families to visit specific grave sites as distinct from vaguer burials under church floors or in charnel houses. The grave plot became in effect a piece of family property, keeping the deceased "at home." In rare instances this was carried to the point that bodies were preserved for viewing in huge containers of alcohol or as mummies in the home. More often, loved ones contented themselves by keeping an embalmed heart at hand; it was the wish of one Frenchman that his be kept in his mother's sewing basket.

Attitudes shifted again in the late eighteenth and nineteenth centuries, primarily due to the rise of the modern nuclear family with its heightened sense of personal affection. Concern now focused more on the family survivors than on the deceased. Even wills changed, becoming merely a record of the disposition of property, as in our time; the more personal elements, such as expressions of religious faith or decisions about burial, were discussed with family members, who thus became more intimately involved in the process of dying.

A change also occurred with respect to the manifestation of grief. From the late medieval period to the eighteenth century, mourning was socially controlled: excessive grief was frowned on, but some manifestation of sorrow was expected even if it was not genuine. In the nineteenth century the restraints were dropped, sometimes leading to hysterical mourning. Unleashed feeling was but one manifestation of the emotion so fundamental to Romanticism. Another was the exaltation of death as a thing of eerie beauty, a means to attain reunion with loved ones, a path to eternal peace. The English author Emily Brontë wrote:

> Oh, not for them should we despair,
> The grave is drear, but they are not there;
> Their dust is mingled with the sod,
> Their happy souls are gone to God![2]

The age of Romanticism also produced the cult of the hero, and this too was reflected in funerary practices, including the Pantheon in Paris and the monuments to George Washington, Thomas Jefferson, and Abraham Lincoln in Washington, D.C., to Victor Emmanuel II in Rome, and to Lord Nelson in London.

The Romantic vision of death as at once emotional, beautiful, and perhaps heroic could not survive World War I. Death in the trenches was indescribably ugly, as reflected in soldiers' memoirs:

> Each body was covered, inches deep, with a black fur of flies which blew up into your face, into your mouth, eyes, and nostrils, as you approached. The bodies crawled with maggots. . . . We worked with sandbags in our hands, stopping every now and then to puke.[3]

It was again time to rethink death. Dying became ugly, death itself a taboo. Efforts were made to protect the dying person from a knowledge of his or her condition, and the place of death was transferred from the home to the hospital or sanitarium. As belief in life after death declined, there was a growing tendency to downplay the reality of death itself. Mourning was sharply curtailed as too upsetting, a sign perhaps of mental instability; tears were banished to the privacy of solitude. The practice of cremation, which had revived amid considerable controversy in the late nineteenth century, became popular. As the founders of the Cremation Society of England candidly asserted, this method of disposing of corpses did not offend the living and rendered the remains "innocuous." Especially in America, people began to "depart" rather than die; their corpses became "remains" taken to "funeral homes" or "parlors," from there to be placed in "memorial parks" for their "eternal rest." But the effort to hide from death is simply one more manifestation of the diverse human experience in coping with an inescapable fact of nature.

The Funeral of Attala by Girodet illustrates the Romantic tendency to make death both sensual and eerily beautiful. [Art Resource]

The romanticized image of death had no relevance in the trenches of World War I. Shown here is the corpse of a German soldier killed at the Battle of the Somme. [Imperial War Museum, London]

Notes

1. F. E. Reynolds and E. H. Waugh, eds., *Religious Encounters with Death: Insights from the History and Anthropology of Religions* (University Park: Pennsylvania State University Press, 1977), p. 174.
2. P. Ariès, *The Hour of Our Death*, trans. H. Weaver (New York: Knopf, 1981), p. 438.
3. S. Cloete, *A Victorian Son: An Autobiography, 1897–1922* (London: Collins, 1972), p. 237.

Suggestions for Further Reading

Abrahamsson, H. *The Origin of Death: Studies in African Mythology*. New York: Arno Press, 1977.

Ariès, P. *The Hour of Our Death*, trans. H. Weaver. New York: Knopf, 1981.

———. *Images of Man and Death*, trans. J. Lloyd. Cambridge, Mass.: Harvard University Press, 1985.

———. *Western Attitudes Toward Death: From the Middle Ages to the Present*, trans. P. M. Ranum. Baltimore: Johns Hopkins University Press, 1974.

Gillon, E. V. *Victorian Cemetery Art*. New York: Dover, 1972.

Gorer, G. *Death, Grief and Mourning in Contemporary Britain*. Garden City, N.Y.: Doubleday, 1965.

Greaves, R. L. *Society and Religion in Elizabethan England*. Minneapolis: University of Minnesota Press, 1981.

Harrah, B. K., and Harrah, D. F. *Funeral Service: A Bibliography of Literature on Its Past, Present and Future, the Various Means of Disposition and Memorialization*. Metuchen, N.J.: Scarecrow Press, 1976.

Kipp, R. S., and Rodgers, S., eds. *Indonesian Religions in Transition*. Tucson: University of Arizona Press, 1987.

McManners, J. *Death and the Enlightenment*. Oxford: Oxford University Press, 1981.

Miller, A. J., and Aeri, M. J. *Death: A Bibliographical Guide*. Metuchen, N.J.: Scarecrow Press, 1977.

Mitford, J. *The American Way of Death*. New York: Simon & Schuster, 1963.

Morley, J. *Death, Heaven and the Victorians*. Pittsburgh: University of Pittsburgh Press, 1971.

Perlove, S. K. *Bernini and the Idealization of Death*. University Park: Pennsylvania State University Press, 1990.

Reynolds, F. E., and Waugh, E. H. *Religious Encounters with Death: Insights from the History and Anthropology of Religions*. University Park: Pennsylvania State University Press, 1977.

Stannard, D. E. *The Puritan Way of Death*. Oxford: Oxford University Press, 1977.

———, ed. *Death in America*. Philadelphia: University of Pennsylvania Press, 1975.

Watson, J. L., and Rawski, E. S., eds. *Death Ritual in Late Imperial and Modern China*. Berkeley: University of California Press, 1987.

Whaley, J., ed. *Mirrors of Mortality: Studies in the Social History of Death*. London: Europa, 1981.

Wolf, A. P., ed. *Religion and Ritual in Chinese Society*. Stanford, Calif.: Stanford University Press, 1974.

Early Modern India and Iran

The collapse of Mughal power in India after 1707 was not followed by the rise of a new Indian order. The subcontinent's legacy of cultural diversity and intergroup rivalry worked against unity, and there was no single effective successor to the Mughals. In this confused setting, the English East India Company began to extend the position it had slowly built up as a trading agent on both coasts, first to protect its merchants, trade partners, and goods against banditry and civil war, then to take on the actual function of government. By 1800 or so the Company was the most powerful single force in the country, and it had become the real sovereign over most of India. In the course of the next half century, a series of military campaigns, more peaceful takeovers, and

Colonel James Todd, an English East India Company official on tour "upcountry" around 1800, by an Indian artist. Many Company officials took on the trappings of traditional Indian potentates and assumed many of their functions, such as hearing cases and settling disputes. [E.T. Archive]

treaties with local Indian rulers left the Company as the direct administrator of about half the subcontinent and indirectly the dominant power in the rest. The development depended to a large degree on Indian collaboration, but in 1857 dissidents joined forces in supporting a mutiny by some of the Indian troops in the Company's army. This was put down after much bloodshed, and the British asserted dominance over the whole of India.

Iran in the eighteenth century had to withstand powerful Ottoman efforts to conquer the country, which the orthodox Sunni Ottomans considered a stronghold of heretical Shi'ite Islam. After early Ottoman successes, Nadir Shah came to the Iranian throne in 1736 and regained the lost territories but presided over a bloody period of internal repression. His successor, Karim Khan, restored peace until his death in 1779, when Iran was again torn by internal rivalries.

The Mughal Collapse

India had been left in chaos at the death of Aurangzeb in 1707. His military campaigns in the south and his continued persecution of Hindus and Sikhs had brought most of the country to rebellion. His successors on the throne at Delhi were far weaker men. Aurangzeb's three sons fought each other in the usual battles of the Mughal succession. After 2½ years of civil war, the victor was then virtually besieged by a Sikh uprising that swept the Punjab and by guerrilla warfare to the west and south. His death in 1712 brought on another struggle for the throne among his sons. They were outmaneuvered by a cousin, who captured and killed the Sikh leader only to be poisoned by his own courtiers in 1719.

The authority of the once great Mughals was by now irretrievably lost, and it no longer mattered to most people what feckless creature sat on the Peacock Throne, dreamed away his days in the imperial harem, or smoked hashish or opium. But even Aurangzeb could never have reestablished control over Rajasthan, Maharashtra, Gujarat, Punjab, or Bengal, let alone the Deccan or the south. Only a remnant of the former empire remained around Delhi and Agra. Most of the rest of India was also torn by factional fighting, civil war, and local banditry, with widespread raiding by Maratha cavalry all over the Deccan and into the north.

Aurangzeb's immediate successors had officially recognized the Maratha Confederacy (so called, although it never really achieved unity) and its extensive conquests in Mysore and on the southeast coast. The Marathas were made nominally tributary allies of the Mughals but controlled their own territories and revenues.

◉ India in Turmoil ◉

The Muslim Indian historian Khafi Khan, writing in the 1720s, gives a vivid picture of the chaos following the death of Aurangzeb in 1707.

It is clear to the wise and experienced that . . . thoughtfulness in managing the affairs of state and protecting the peasantry . . . have all departed. Revenue collectors have become a scourge for the peasantry. . . . Many townships which used to yield full revenue have, owing to the oppression of officials, been so far ruined and devastated that they have become forests infested by tigers and lions, and the villages are so utterly ruined and desolate that there is no sign of habitation on the routes.

This is matched by English descriptions of late seventeenth-century Bengal, which had broken away from Mughal control.

Bengal is at present in a very bad condition by means of the great exactions on the people. . . . There are no ways of extortion omitted . . . [which] makes merchants' business very troublesome. . . . The king's governor has little more than the name, and for the most part sits still while others oppress the people and monopolize most commodities, even as low as grass for beasts . . . nor do they want ways to oppress people of all sorts who trade, whether natives or strangers.

Sources: I. Habib, *The Agrarian System of Mughal India* (New York: Asia Publishing House, 1963), p. 186; H. Yule, ed., *Diary of William Hedges*, vol. 2 (London: Barlow, 1887), pp. 237, 239.

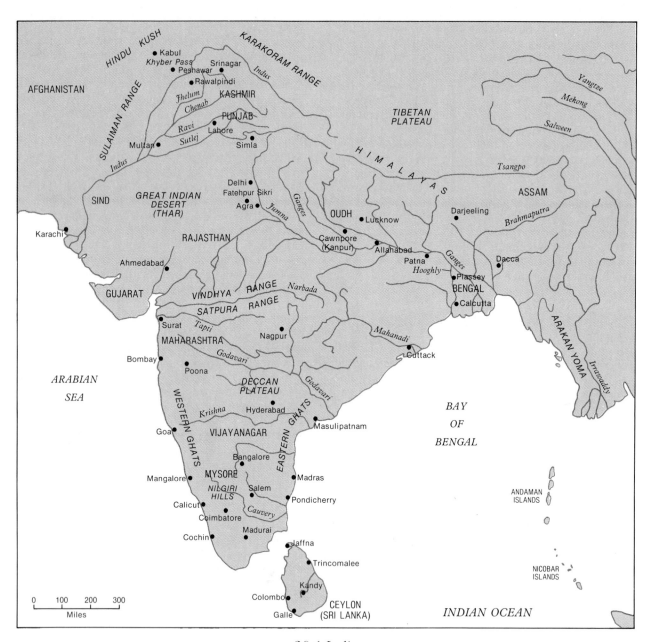

28.1 India

They were in effect given thus both the means and the license to extend their raids or conquests into still more of central, southern, and eastern India, whose revenues could further augment their power. They continued to nibble away at the remaining shreds of Mughal authority in the north and Hindustan, ultimately raiding Agra and Delhi itself as well as deep into Bengal as far as Calcutta, though English defenses kept them out of the city.

For a time it looked as if the Marathas might inherit the former Mughal position, but they proved incurably divided into contending factions, and no leader emerged who might have welded them into a coalition. The Maratha cavalry operated more and more as bandits and plunderers, rarely attempting to set up any administration in the areas they swept for loot and then left in chaos. In the south, Hyderabad became a large and wealthy kingdom independent of both the Mughals and the Marathas, while in the central Ganges valley the independent kingdom of Oudh with its capital at Lucknow also emerged from the breakup of the once great empire. In many parts of India cultivated areas were abandoned by peasants unable to defend their crops or their homes against raiders and bandits. Trade dwindled, famine increased, and India slipped further into impoverishment and anarchy. At the same time there was a revival of trade in other areas, especially in the north, with the collapse of Mughal control, and some economic growth.

The last shreds of Mughal power were swept away when a Persian army sacked and looted Delhi in 1739, massacred its inhabitants, and took back with them the famous Peacock Throne. Iran's powerful ruler, Nadir Shah, upon seizing the Persian throne in 1736, asked for Mughal help to crush Afghanistan, formerly a part of the Mughal Empire. But the Mughals were by now hard pressed to defend even Delhi against Maratha raiders. In 1738 Nadir Shah, acting alone, conquered Afghanistan and went on to Lahore and Delhi, leaving them in smoldering ruins. The dynasty continued in name, and successive Mughal emperors sat in state in Delhi's Red Fort until 1858, when the last of them was banished by the British.

After 1739 few people in India or elsewhere took the Mughals seriously. This was the harvest of Aurangzeb's cruel reign, which had condemned most of India to chronic civil war, local disorder, and impoverishment. Unfortunately, Rajputs, Marathas, Sikhs, Gujaratis, Bengalis, and other regional groups who had fought against the Mughals saw each other as rivals and indeed as enemies rather than as joint Indian inheritors of power. Their languages, though related like those of Europe, were different, and they differed culturally as well. Their divisions now made it possible for the English and French to make a place for themselves and to increase their commercial and political power.

Westerners in India

The story of the arrival of the Portuguese in India and their establishment of a major base at Goa on the west coast was briefly told in Chapter 18. For about a century after Vasco da Gama's voyage to Calicut in 1498, the Portuguese dominated Western trade with India, as well as with Southeast Asia, China, and Japan. In India they competed with Indian and Arab traders and increasingly after the end of the sixteenth century with Dutch and English merchants and their ships. But no westerners even thought about contending for political power in India for another 250 years, until the latter half of the eighteenth century. Although the Portuguese arrived well before the establishment of the Mughal Empire in 1526, they were a tiny handful with no effective means of confronting any of the Indian states of the south, let alone the soon-triumphant Mughals.

Westerners fought among themselves for control of the sea routes, but their objectives in India were purely commercial, except for the early Portuguese interest in converting the few Indians they encountered to Catholicism. In their competition for trade, the Europeans offered local rulers guns and naval help for use against their neighbors, together with a share of their profits, in exchange for commercial privileges or the use of a port. Small numbers of Europeans might involve themselves on opposite sides of such inter-Indian conflicts, seeking further influence or advantage. Once the Mughals became the dominant force in India, such power brokering largely subsided, and European merchants became humble petitioners before the Peacock Throne, whose influence was so much greater than their own.

The Portuguese were first in India and hence obtained the largest number of concessions, including a base at Goa. Concessions elsewhere included the rights to warehouses, residences, and commercial rights-of-way at small ports on both east and west coasts, as well as at sites inland in Bengal, source of the finest cotton textiles for export and the richest and biggest market. By the early seventeenth century, however, the Portuguese were rapidly losing ground to Dutch and English traders. Portugal's ships were outclassed in size, speed, maneuverability, firepower, and numbers, and its poor and tiny home base could no longer sustain the effort of maintaining an overextended commercial empire. The Portuguese also suffered from political miscalculations. Vijayanagar, for example (see Chapter 11), actively sought Portuguese help in its efforts to fight off its ultimate conquest by a coalition of Muslim sultanates in the northern Deccan. The Portuguese had earlier provided Vijayanagar with imported horses and cannon and had benefited commercially from their association with this dominant state of the south, but the ruler's urgent request for more aid in his greatest hour of need was shortsightedly refused. After the defeat of Vijayanagar in 1565, Portuguese trade and the Portuguese position in India rapidly declined.

The Dutch and later the English were able to move into the Indian market by making their own agreements with local rulers or with the Mughals and to begin to establish their own trade bases. The interest of the Dutch in Asia was from the beginning centered on the spice trade and its sources in the Indonesian archipelago, but they established several bases in small ports along the east coast of India, retaining many of them until late in the eighteenth century. There they competed vigorously against the Portuguese and later the English. The Dutch involvement in Ceylon, however, was far more extensive. The Portuguese had fortified a base at Colombo some years after arriving there in 1502 and controlled large parts of the lowland west coast of the island, including the profitable trade in cinnamon bark from the Colombo area. Their efforts to extend

their control inland were repelled by the Sinhalese*
kingdom of Kandy in the central highlands, which had
become the chief power in Ceylon after the collapse of
the classical and medieval state based at Anuradhapura
and Polonaruwa (see Chapter 11). But the Portuguese
did succeed in converting many of the west coast Sinhalese to Catholicism, at first often by force, and Portuguese surnames remain widespread there, as in parts of
Southeast Asia.

The Dutch drove the Portuguese out between 1640
and 1658 and established their own more extensive position in Ceylon, including bases on the east coast as well
as the west coast. Although they too failed in several
attempts to conquer the mountain-girt Kandyan kingdom, they made Ceylon an even more profitable commercial enterprise, setting up a plantation system for
coconuts and later for coffee, imported from their territories in Java. Like the Portuguese, they often intermarried with the Sinhalese, producing a Eurasian group still
known as "Burghers." By the 1630s Dutch ships dominated the Indian Ocean and its approaches and were
even able to blockade Goa. Ceylon was an obvious prize,
both for its trade profits and for its strategic role along
the route eastward from India, in sight of the southern
tip of the subcontinent and only three or four days' sail
from Goa. The Dutch were to remain in control of the
trade of Ceylon from their several coastal bases until the
Napoleonic wars, when the British took over the island
and in 1815 finally conquered the Kandyan kingdom.

The Early English Presence

England, like other European trading nations, learned
about Portuguese profits in India and began to seek a
northeast passage to India by sea around Russia and
Siberia in 1553. The expedition was found two years later
frozen into the Arctic ice, all aboard dead. A later effort
to run the Portuguese blockade in 1583 in the ship *Tiger*
ended in the Portuguese capture of the vessel, but one
of the English merchants aboard, Ralph Fitch, escaped
and went on to India, where he visited Akbar's capitals
of Agra and Fatehpur Sikri as well as Goa, returning to
London in 1591 with firsthand accounts of India's wealth.
Portugal was dynastically united with Spain in 1580, but
this tended to weaken rather than strengthen the Portuguese effort in Asia, and with the defeat of the Spanish

*The Sinhalese are the dominant inhabitants of Ceylon (Sri Lanka),
having invaded and settled the island, probably from northern India, in the sixth century B.C.

Armada in 1588 the way eastward was more open to
England.

The English East India Company was founded in
1600. Its first two ventures were aimed at the spice trade
in Southeast Asia, but the third went to India, reaching
Surat, the major port of Gujarat, in 1608. Gujarat had
been absorbed into the Mughal Empire in 1573, and
Captain William Hawkins, who commanded the fleet of
three English ships, carried presents and a letter from
King James I to the Mughal emperor, Jahangir, requesting a trade treaty. Hawkins claimed that the Portuguese,
especially the Jesuits who were already ensconced at the
Mughal court, conspired against him, but in any case he
was kept waiting for over two years and was finally
obliged to return home empty-handed. A second English
envoy reached Agra in 1612 but was sent away even
more summarily after the Jesuits there urged the emperor not to deal with him.

However, later in 1612 a single English ship defeated
and dispersed four Portuguese galleons and a number
of frigates off Surat, in view of shore, a feat that was
repeated in 1615. Indians now saw that the English were
more valuable clients than the Portuguese and better
able to defend Indian shipping and coasts from pirates
and from rival Europeans, whose tactics were often indistinguishable from those of pirates. The Indian market
had little or no interest in trade with England and was
not impressed by the samples of goods it was offered
from what was, after all, a much less advanced economy.

The lack of goods attractive to the Eastern market
was indeed to hamper European and American trade in
India, China, and the rest of Asia until well into the nineteenth century. The Mughals, however, had no navy and
had to depend on foreigners for protection against piracy; of these, it now seemed clear, the English were the
least troublesome and the most effective. In 1616 King
James sent another ambassador, Sir Thomas Roe, who
finally won permission from Jahangir for the East India
Company to build a warehouse in Surat. Seven years
later the Dutch massacred ten English merchants who
had been sharing the spice trade of eastern Indonesia,
signaling the end of the Netherlands' willingness to allow any European competition in what thus became
their private preserve. The English were obliged to abandon their effort to penetrate Dutch territory and to concentrate on India.

Territorial Bases

From Surat, English ships completed the elimination of
Portuguese power at sea, and English merchants became the main traders in the port. They then sought
bases on the east coast and in Bengal, where they could
buy the finest-quality cottons more directly as well as
the indigo and saltpeter produced in the lower Ganges

valley. After their early attempts had been driven off by the Dutch, English negotiations with a local ruler to the south led to their purchase of land in 1639 around a small harbor that later became the city of Madras. Here they immediately built Fort St. George. Madras became their chief base in eastern India, from which they had access to South Indian cottons and other goods. From Madras they made repeated efforts to trade directly in Bengal and finally established a warehouse upriver near the provincial capital. They found, however, that such proximity to the Mughal and Bengali authorities exposed them to arbitrary taxation and even sometimes expropriation, and on at least one occasion the Company's agent was publicly whipped and expelled. Accordingly, the English sought a more secure position. They had traded periodically at a small market half a day's sail up the Hooghly River, one of the lesser mouths of the Ganges, and in 1690 decided to make a settlement there where they felt their ships could protect or rescue them if needed. It also put them at a greater distance from Indian authority. Soon thereafter they received permission to build a fort. The new settlement, called Fort William (after the English monarch William III), was shortly to be known as Calcutta.

At Surat the English remained among many merchant groups and were dependent on the fickle pleasure of Mughal and Gujarati powers. But Bombay, originally a chain of small islands enclosed in a large bay, was ceded to the English crown by Portugal in 1661 as part of the marriage contract of the Portuguese princess Catherine of Braganza and Charles II. The Portuguese had built no settlement there and used it only occasionally, since it was vulnerable to piracy, cut off from landward access to markets by the rampaging Marathas, and had a harbor too big for the small ships of the time. But the quite different drawbacks of Surat and the attractions of a more nearly independent and protected base, as at Madras and Calcutta, led the Company to move its western India headquarters to Bombay in 1687.

With the founding of Calcutta in 1690, the English now had three small territorial footholds, well placed to tap the trade of India in each of its major segments, west, south, and east. But like all other foreigners in India, they remained petitioners, dependent on the favors of the Mughal state or of local rulers and liable to be driven out, expropriated, or denied trading privileges. No one as yet anticipated the imminent collapse of Mughal power.

Even after the death of Aurangzeb, there was little recognition of the changed situation. The East India Company sent an embassy to the by then virtually powerless Mughal emperor in 1714; the embassy's leader

Bombay about 1790: Western sea power and one of its early beachheads. Note the fortifications, the ship in the foreground firing a salute, and the Western-style architecture, including a church (center).

◉ Why Calcutta? ◉

Before the founding of Calcutta, the English had tried to use several other harbors on the seaward edge of the Ganges delta. Here is a 1689 description of the problems at Ballasore, one of those harbors, and of the plan to make a base instead at Calcutta.

Our ships in Ballasore road do generally ride in a hard and dangerous roadstead and many of our men come to sickness and death by the constant labor of rowing so far in such a rough sea, which we would willingly prevent all that in us lies, and therefore if the Moors [Mughals] will allow us to fortify ourselves at Chutanutee [the village that became Calcutta] where our ships may go up and ride within the command of our guns it would be much better for us, though it should cost us a bribe of thirty or forty thousand rupees to the great men to be paid when we are possessed of the Mughal's Phirmaund [charter of trading privileges] for that and for the twelve articles made with Mr. Charnock [the Company's chief agent in Bengal], but the confirmation of these articles we insist on in right and will not purchase them.

But Calcutta had other problems. Here is a description in 1703.

[Mr. Charnock chose the site] for the sake of a large shady tree, though he could not have chosen a more unhealthful place on all the river, for three miles to the northeast is a salt water lake that overflows in September and October and then prodigious numbers of fish resort thither, but in November and December when the floods are dissipated those fishes are left dry and with their putrefaction affect the air with thick stinking vapors which the northwest winds bring with them to Fort William [where] they cause a yearly mortality.

Sources: C. R. Wilson, *Old Fort William in Bengal* (London: Murray, 1906), p. 5; J. N. Das Gupta, ed., *India in the Seventeenth Century* (New Delhi: Associated Publishing House, 1976), p. 232.

prostrated himself before the throne as "the smallest particle of sand," giving "the reverence due from a slave" and asking for additional trade privileges. Significantly, however, the agent also sought the right to collect revenues in the immediate areas around Madras and Calcutta, where the Company was by now the de facto government. The embassy was largely ignored and would probably never have been even acknowledged if the emperor had not fallen ill and asked for treatment from the embassy's English doctor. His success led to the embassy's reception, and in 1717 all its requests were granted.

The Mughal and Post-Mughal Contexts

The Mughals, like many premodern states, were used to such arrangements with various groups or individuals to whom they in effect farmed out the collection of taxes and the administration of local areas that the taxes supported. In their view, the English were little different from scores of others who had long been granted such rights, equivalent to the Mughal *jagir* or zamindari (see Chapter 20), and Delhi attached little importance to the 1717 concession. Indeed, it seems important now only because we know what followed and can recognize it as the first step toward English territorial sovereignty in India.

After the death of Aurangzeb, the Mughals as well as local and provincial authorities had ceased to maintain order. In this context, the English East India Company was at least able to keep up a semblance of government in its fortified bases and, with the help of small private armies, in the areas immediately around the bases as well. The embassy to Delhi in 1714 had to fight off large bands of armed robbers even on the imperial road from Agra. Most of the rest of India was in even worse condition. The Company could survive and prosper only if it could create security for trade goods in storage and in transit and could offer its Indian partners similar security. Areas of production could generate trade commodities also only if they could be kept orderly. The main consequence of the fading of Mughal power was thus not that the English rose politically in India but that they were driven increasingly to provide their own defense, policing, revenue collection, and local government. They did this well enough to survive and to attract Indian merchants to deal with them and even become residents of the English bases, where their profits and property could also be secure.

Within a few years Madras, Calcutta, and Bombay were overwhelmingly Indian in population, home to many laborers and servants as well as numerous merchants, artisans, bankers, and agents, all having selected the still tiny English-dominated world of the fortified ports over any Indian alternative. Apart from the Mughals, who counted for little in any case, local states and rulers were often also willing to have the Company manage trade, collect taxes, and keep order. Civil order and healthy conditions for trade, which the English offered, were more than enough to ensure the cooperation of most Indians.

The Company prospered, and Indian cottons became so popular in England that Parliament in 1701, concerned to protect English textiles, prohibited their import. When that ban was ignored, a parliamentary ruling in 1720 prohibited their use or wear, but reexport to the Continent continued and even domestic consumption could not be prevented. Indian cottons were clearly superior to Western products, and the finest of them have never been surpassed. A widely repeated story told how the emperor Aurangzeb had reproved his daughter for appearing naked at court, to which she is said to have replied that she was wearing seven thicknesses of Dacca muslin.

The Company was not alone in its prosperity. From the first factory at Surat to Indian independence in 1947, Indians found employment in the expanding economy of what became the colonial ports and later their inland equivalents, as well as in the colonial bureaucracy. English and Scots who prospered were greatly outnumbered by Indians, but most of the biggest gainers were British. Most Indians remained poor, and most of those who prospered did so as junior partners, especially after 1830, despite British economic and social discrimination against them. For most peasants the gradual spread of Company rule meant at least protection against banditry or Maratha raids and a growing new market within India and abroad for their commercial crops. Commercialization of agriculture proved ruinous to some but profitable to many. In any case, the Company could never have succeeded without extensive Indian collaboration, particularly the connections with domestic trade networks and production provided by Indian merchants, agents, and bankers. All were dependent on the Company's ability to maintain order.

Anglo-French Rivalry and the Conquest of Bengal

The French had also been active contenders for the trade of India since the founding of the French East India Company in 1664 and had established a warehouse of their own at Surat; an east coast base at Pondicherry, south of Madras; and another warehouse just up river from Calcutta. The French bases, in India as in all their other overseas ventures, were government-sponsored and -controlled. They had the advantage of superb leadership under Joseph Dupleix (1697–1764), who favored an expansionist policy. He was supported by able military and naval commanders. Their forces captured Madras in 1746 and went on to defeat the local Indian ruler of the southeast, becoming the dominant power in the whole of South India. Unfortunately for them, they got little support from home, and the Treaty of Aix-la-Chapelle in 1748 restored Madras to the English. Two years later the English Company agent Robert Clive defeated both the French and their southern Indian allies with a small force.

When the Seven Years' War (1756–1763) erupted in Europe, fighting spread to India as well as North America, and the British and French provided troops and ships to supplement the Indian forces who did most of the actual fighting. Now deprived of the leadership of Dupleix, who had been called home for allegedly spending too much of the French company's resources in "unprofitable adventures," the French lost out in this struggle. A major lesson of the conflict was that very small numbers of European troops, operating with somewhat larger numbers of Indian soldiers trained in Western methods, could repeatedly defeat enormously larger Indian armies. Those on the European sides were disciplined to fire regular volleys on command and to plan and coordinate their actions. Their guns and cannon were better, but organization and leadership made them more effective, as did morale enhanced by regular pay and uniforms.

Western military power was, however, tested most severely by a Bengali challenge to the growing English position in and around Calcutta. As their local authority increased, the English became less deferential to the still technically sovereign rulers of Bengal, now independent of the Mughals. No longer humble petitioners who had regularly kissed the feet of the nawab (king) of Bengal, their independent behavior and their addition to the fortifications of Fort William offended the new nawab, Siraj-ud-Dawlah, who came to the throne in 1756. In a last flash of imperial fire, his army and war elephants overwhelmed Calcutta and its small corps of defenders in June 1756. Some escaped in boats and fled to Madras, but about 60 were left behind, to be thrown into the fort's tiny, airless dungeon. Next morning two-thirds of them were dead of suffocation. The incident of the so-called Black Hole of Calcutta became infamous. It seemed the end of the English position in Bengal, but appearances were deceiving. Within four months an expedition sailed from Madras under the same Robert Clive who had earlier ousted the French from the south. In January 1757 he retook Calcutta and then drove the French from their remaining bases in Bengal. With support from Indian groups, in June he defeated the huge army of the nawab at the Battle of Plassey, some 75 miles north of Calcutta.

Although no one seemed fully to realize it at the time, the English were now masters of Bengal. They had no effective rivals, nor were there viable alternatives to British rule. Their military victory was, however, due in large part to Indian collaboration, including, perhaps most important, bankers who had lent money to both sides and who calculated that an English victory was more desirable on practical grounds. The English paid their debts, as the nawab did not, and as a merchant group the English East India Company furthered trade rather than preying on it. The leading Indian banker in fact paid very large sums to troops on the nawab's side to persuade them not to fight; the reserves, which were to have swept the field at Plassey when the battle hung in the balance, never came. But the traditional Indian armies of the day were usually composed of different groups who were often rivals and were rarely effectively led. Contingents often deserted, failed to appear, or decided to throw their lot in with another side.

ROBERT CLIVE AND THE BEGINNINGS OF BRITISH INDIA

Robert Clive (1725–1774) had shipped out to Madras as an East India Company clerk, but he soon developed a reputation as an adventurer. He found his clerk's job so boring that he tried unsuccessfully to blow his brains out with a pistol that misfired. Adventure soon came when the French captured Fort St. George in 1746 and he was taken prisoner. He escaped and took a commission in the Company's small army. His first military expedition, against a powerful southern kingdom allied with the French, was won by brilliant strategy even though his opponents outnumbered his forces 20 to 1. Clive was acclaimed as a hero and repeated his success by driving out the French and their Indian allies in the major Deccan kingdom of Hyderabad. Still only 27 years old, he was praised as a deliverer and granted two years' home leave. Sent out again with the rank of colonel in 1756, he reached Madras just as Calcutta was being overwhelmed by the armies of the nawab of Bengal.

Robert Clive accepting tribute from Mir Jaffar, the puppet whom he had placed on the throne of Bengal after the Battle of Plassey, as depicted in an oil painting by Francis Hayman, c. 1760. [National Portrait Gallery, London]

Already known to Indians by a nickname roughly translatable as "He Who Is Daring in War," Clive sailed north with a small force. He recaptured Calcutta, defeated the greatly superior army that tried to stop him just north of the city, and four months later met the main Bengali contingent at Plassey. By this time he had just over 1,000 British troops and about 2,000 Indians under his command. The Bengali army totaled 18,000 cavalry and 50,000 foot soldiers, with more than 50 field guns managed by French artillerymen. Again Clive's tactical genius won the day, confusing, outmaneuvering, and finally routing the enemy. He then marched to the Bengali capital, where he installed his own Indian client and ally as ruler.

Clive and his English and Indian colleagues helped themselves to the provincial treasury, and the Company too was richly repaid in reparations and new revenues now under its control. After consolidating his conquests with further victories against Indian and French forces, Clive devoted his enormous energy to strengthening the Company's army, refortifying Calcutta, and administering the new domains. Four years of incessant activity broke his health, and he spent five years in England. He was sent back to India in 1765 to check the plundering excesses of his successors and to reorganize what now amounted to the Company's government of Bengal.

Two years later he was back in England to face charges in Parliament that he had defrauded the Company and enriched himself by extortion. The accusations were brought by many of the same people whom he had tried to restrain from similar behavior and who were jealous of his successes. Although in the end he was cleared, he brooded over his grievances, and still suffering from poor health, he shot himself in 1774 at the age of 49. The same mercurial temperament that had made him try suicide as a young man and then carried him to the heights of success proved his undoing. Yet more than any other person, he began the process that was to lead to British rule in India. He was far more than a brilliant field commander and was concerned about the implications of British policy in India. His immediate successors were more interested in personal enrichment.

The Establishment of British Rule

With Bengal now in their hands, many of the English turned to plunder as well as trade, extorting silver and jewels from the rich and also demanding what amounted to protection money. After a few years this brought severe criticism from home, parliamentary inquiries, and finally, in 1784, the India Act, which created a board of control for India in London. Meanwhile, beyond Bengal, the rest of India remained in turmoil. Afghan armies repeatedly laid waste the northwest and looted Delhi again in 1757, slaughtering most of the inhabitants. A huge Maratha army gathered to repel yet another Afghan invasion in 1760 was crushed in a great battle near Delhi early in 1761. The Afghans then withdrew, but they had in effect removed the only Indian power able to contest the English. Three years later outnumbered Company forces soundly defeated a final Indian coalition organized by leading Bengalis, ending the last serious challenge to their power in the north.

From this point on the policy of both the Company and its London supervisors was to acquire no more territory but to achieve their ends through alliances with Indian princes, offering them military protection in exchange for trading rights. In Bengal as in the smaller areas around Madras and Bombay, they continued to collect taxes and run the administration as nominal agents of the local or regional Indian rulers. Administration was expensive and distracted from the Company's main business, trade. The collection of rural taxes was farmed out to Bengali agents, or zamindars. The zamindars, with British encouragement, seized land from defaulting taxpayers, thus allying themselves with the new Company administration. Calcutta was made the capital of all of British India; after 1785 the Company, under parliamentary supervision from London, concentrated on promoting trade but also administered justice and defense. Indian agents were necessarily employed in the lower echelons of government; all higher administrative and military posts were reserved for the British.

The official policy of discouraging further direct conquest yielded in the 1790s to the strategic pressures of the Napoleonic wars. The French still had small footholds in South India and a history, like that of the English, of alliances with various Indian rulers. Successive heads of state in Mysore had had some dealings with the French and had also periodically threatened Madras. In 1799 Mysore was overwhelmed by Company troops. Half of it, including the commercially important coastal strip, was annexed outright, thus linking the Madras area to the west coast. Most of the rest of it was given to a loyal Indian ally, the neighboring state of Hyderabad, which was to remain nominally independent until 1947. The peninsular south was now firmly under Company control, but the Marathas remained a formidable power, and their home base in Maharashtra blocked Bombay's access to inland markets. Taking advantage of internal Maratha division, the Company signed a treaty with one side in 1802 promising military support in exchange for territorial rights. When the Maratha puppet the British had installed tried later to revive his power, the Company defeated his forces and took over all Maratha domains in 1818, soon joining them to Bombay Presidency, the major British territory in western India.

Meanwhile in Bengal, Warren Hastings (1732–1818)

Cultural blending in colonial India: an Indian ruler in Rajasthan in British uniform, by an Indian artist. [Victoria and Albert Museum, London]

ruler of Mysore and dispatched a Company army to defend Madras. All this cost money, and Hastings was driven to extort funds from several of his Indian tributary states to support the pacification of India, which he argued was in everyone's interest. Jealous rivals at home engineered impeachment proceedings against him, and when the new India Act of 1784 was passed, setting up the Board of Control in London, he felt further threatened. He resigned in 1785 and left India for good.

Hastings was succeeded as governor-general by Lord Cornwallis, the same man who had surrendered the British forces to the Americans and French at Yorktown but who had a reputation for honesty. He cracked down still more on extortion and corruption, but in 1793 he confirmed the landowning rights of the Indians, mainly Bengalis, who had been made zamindars; this "permanent settlement" strengthened an exploitative system that became still more so in subsequent years. Cornwallis, anxious not to be responsible for losing another colony, further pursued the campaign against Mysore. He also issued a new administrative code for all the British territories, establishing rules for all services, courts, and revenue systems and empowering British district magistrates to administer justice.

In 1798 Richard Wellesley, whose younger brother would become the duke of Wellington and defeat Napoleon at Waterloo, succeeded to the governor-generalship. He completed the conquest of Mysore in 1799 and subsequently added still more territory in the south to British control. In 1801 he reached up the Ganges valley to force British "protection" on the Indian state of Oudh. Most historians contend that Britain's Indian empire and attendant imperialist attitudes first took coherent shape under Wellesley, who remained as governor-general until 1805.

The central Ganges valley west of Bengal, through which India's major trade route ran, was too important to be left uncontrolled. This is why the ruler of the state of Oudh was forced to accept British protection, although he remained nominally sovereign. The same arrangement was made with the Mughal emperor for his domains in the Delhi-Agra area. Southern Gujarat, including the commercially important port of Surat, was also brought under Company control. Only Rajasthan, the Indus valley and Sind, Kashmir, and Punjab remained outside the British sphere. Much of what the British controlled was, however, nominally ruled by allied Indian princes.

The British, troubled by the French threat and reminded of French naval successes in the Bay of Bengal 50 years earlier, moved on Dutch-held Ceylon after Napoleon's occupation of the Netherlands. Their first concern was to take over the fine natural harbor of Trincomalee on the east coast of Ceylon, where they could base their naval vessels. There were no harbors safe to enter or leave during the northeast monsoon of winter

had been appointed governor of Fort William in 1772 and later confirmed as governor-general of British-run Bengal, Madras, and Bombay. Hastings had by then a long experience of working for the Company and, like so many of the Englishmen who went to India, had become fascinated by its rich tradition; he was a scholar of Persian and Urdu and had many Indian friends. This gave him valuable insight into Indian customs and attitudes but also encouraged him to play the role of absolute ruler, in the Indian tradition. He largely checked the widespread extortion and corruption of Company officers and made sure that the official revenue collections got to his government rather than into private pockets. Hastings reduced the nawab of Bengal even more to a British client and stopped the annual tribute hitherto paid to the Mughal emperor. But he also began the British strategy of intervention in the factional fighting within the Maratha Confederacy, partly to forestall the French, partly to strengthen the overall British position in India and to meet the still serious threat of Maratha power. Hastings also took the first moves against the

anywhere on the Indian east coast, nor were any of them large enough for the fleet, which had to be withdrawn to winter haven in distant Bombay. Trincomalee filled this urgent need, and the British occupied it in 1795, subsequently taking over all of the other Dutch holdings in Ceylon.

As the French threat faded, British attention shifted to the far more productive southwestern lowlands of Ceylon, and the colonial capital was fixed at Colombo. From there roads were built crisscrossing the island and, after the final conquest of the Kandyan kingdom in 1815, into the central highlands, followed by railways after 1858. Coffee plantations spread rapidly with this improved access to export markets, as did coconut production, and by midcentury Ceylon had the plantation economy it retained until after independence. Tea was introduced after a disastrous coffee blight in the 1870s, and rubber was added at the end of the century. Tamil laborers were brought in from overpopulated South India to build roads and railways and to provide labor for the new plantations. Ceylon was designated a crown colony separate from British India and was administered as such despite its long and close Indian connections.

The conquest of India by a relative handful of British settlers, merchants, and troops, at first almost a private venture, could not have happened without native support or without the factional divisions that fatally weakened Indian resistance. Most people accepted Company control either because they benefited from it as merchants, bankers, collaborators, agents, or employees or because they saw it as preferable to control by the Mughals, the Marathas, or any of the local rulers, whose record was not attractive. Most contemporary Indian states were oppressive, taxing merchants and peasants unmercifully and often arbitrarily while at the same time failing to keep order, suppress banditry, maintain roads and basic services, or administer justice acceptably. Revenues went disproportionately to support court extravagances and armies, which spent their energy more in interregional conflict than in genuine defense. This was partly the legacy of the Delhi sultanate and particularly of the Mughals. It became clear to most Indians that, in fact, only the British were both willing and able to protect them from banditry, ensure the security of life and property, and foster conditions under which trade and agriculture could again prosper. That was enough to win their support or at least ensure their acquiescence. At any rate, nearly a century was to pass between the last Bengali resistance in the mid-1760s and the first major uprising against British rule in 1857.

The Indians accommodated themselves to the British as they had to foreign conquerors in the past. Mindful of the early English rapacity in Bengal, the Company generally tried as much as possible to avoid displacing or offending Indians or disrupting local customs except for slavery and *sati*. This maturation of policy was illustrated in a letter from the directors to the Company offices in Bombay in 1784:

> **By the exercise of a mild and good government people from other parts may be induced to come and reside under our protection. Let there be entire justice exercised to all persons without distinction, and open trade allowed to all.**[1]

Such a plan reflected the original exclusive aim of trade profits, more bluntly stated almost a century earlier: "Merchants desire no enemies, and would create none."[2]

The Orientalists and the Bengal Renaissance

As British administration was extended, more and more Company employees were not merchants or clerks but officials and magistrates. British and Indian merchants had obvious common interests, and many even appreciated each other's culture. Some Company traders and officials, such as Sir William Jones (1746–1794), found themselves fascinated by the rich variety of the Indian tradition. Jones, a judge in late-eighteenth-century Bengal, had the usual classical education in England and then had to learn Persian (still used for Mughal law), Sanskrit (the classical language of India and of Hindu texts, which were often cited in law cases), and the modern languages of North India spoken by the people who appeared in court: Bengali, Hindi, and so on. He began to realize after his arrival in 1783 the close connections among them and between them and Greek, Latin, and the languages of modern Europe, including English. In 1786 he published a paper that convincingly made the case for an Indo-European language family, thereby earning himself the nickname "Oriental" Jones. Other Englishmen studied and translated the Indian classics and the great traditions of Indian religion and art and carried out archaeological work of great importance, including the later rediscovery of Harappa, Mohenjo Daro, and the Mauryan empire.

British scholars of Indian culture and history founded the Asiatic Society of Bengal in Calcutta in 1784, whose *Journal* published Jones' paper and many others on a wide variety of Indian topics. Most of the members and contributors were Company employees or officials who pursued their research on the side, but some found their Indian studies so engrossing that they retired to devote all their time to what was now known as Indology. Many took Indian wives, though few brought them home in retirement.

These British Orientalists, as they were called, were

◉ The British Indicted ◉

In 1772 one of the early Orientalists, Alexander Dow, criticized the English.

Posterity will perhaps find fault with the British for not investigating the learning and religious opinions which prevail in those countries in Asia into which either they or their commerce or their arms have penetrated. The Brahmins of the East possessed in ancient times some reputation for knowledge, but we have never had the curiosity to examine whether there was any truth in the reports of antiquity upon that head. . . . Literary inquiries are by no means a capital object to many of our adventurers in Asia.

But William Jones was soon to join Dow and others. This is what he wrote in 1783.

It gave me inexpressible pleasure to find myself . . . almost encircled by the vast regions of Asia, which has ever been esteemed the nurse of science, the inventress of delightful and useful arts, and scene of glorious actions, fertile in the production of human genius, . . . abounding in natural wonders, and infinitely diversified in the forms of religion and government, in the laws, manners, customs, and languages as well as in the features and complexions of men. . . . [Later he wrote:] It was my desire to discharge my public duties with unremitted attention, and to recreate myself at leisure with the literature of this interesting country. . . . I am no Hindu, but I hold the doctrine of the Hindus concerning a future state to be incomparably more rational, more pious, and more likely to deter men from vice than the horrid opinions inculcated by Christians on punishments without end.

Sources: A. Dow, *History of Hindoostan* (1772), p. 107; P. Mudford, *Birds of a Different Plumage* (London: Collins, 1974), pp. 88–90 passim.

---

matched by Indian scholars who learned perfect English, studied Latin and Greek, wrote in the English literary and academic tradition, and also produced what is known as both the Hindu Renaissance and the Bengal Renaissance, begun primarily by the work of the Bengali Ram Mohun Roy (1772–1833). Roy and others who followed him—some Company employees, others private scholars—sought their own cultural identity as well as Western learning and helped restore the pride of educated Indians in their rich religious, philosophical, and literary heritage.

Roy founded a society in Calcutta to pursue these efforts, which made a deep impact on successive generations of Bengalis and Indians everywhere. Members of the society and like-minded Indians studied India's classical texts and led a revival of interest in the power and virtue of the Indian cultural tradition. H. L. Derozio (1809–1831), of mixed Indian and British parentage, became in his short life a brilliant teacher and poet, inspiring young Bengalis to pursue, as he had done, learning in both the Indian and the Western or British traditions. He thus served to promote a true meeting of East and

West, as his British counterparts among the Orientalists also attempted to do.

One prominent member of the society was Dwarkanath Tagore (1794–1846), an outstanding Western-style entrepreneur, banker, merchant, and industrialist who became, like Roy and many others, an Anglicized Indian. These Western and Eastern synthesizers of the two cultures worked together, especially in Calcutta, to promote the similar education of young upper-class Indians, founding schools and libraries and publishing jointly a number of journals and books. Their efforts foreshadowed the full-scale emergence of the westernized Indian middle class of intellectuals and businesspeople later in the nineteenth century, including Tagore's grandson Rabindranath Tagore (1861–1941), India's greatest modern literary figure, who devoted most of his life to bridging East and West. The Hindu Renaissance was also concerned to reform what in the perspective of the nineteenth century had come to seem the less desirable aspects of Hinduism, such as sati and child marriage, and in time to make Hinduism an appropriate vehicle for modern Indian nationalism.

❧ CALCUTTA, COLONIAL CAPITAL

By 1810 Calcutta's population had reached a million, and it was already being labeled "the second city of the British Empire," a title it retained until Indian independence in 1947. It was also known as "the city of palaces," adorned not only with government buildings and the governor's residence but also with the mansions of rich British and Indian merchants, which made an imposing façade along the river. Behind the façade was the reality of mass squalor. Rudyard Kipling was later to call Calcutta "the City of Dreadful Night" for its hot, humid climate and the vast slums and shanty settlements that sat back from the river. From the beginning, it was overwhelmingly Indian in population. British residents found its tropical environment a trial, the more so because fashion required them to wear the woolen outfits expected of a gentleman at home, to overeat, and to consume large quantities of wine and whiskey. Anyone who aspired to a position in society had to keep a carriage, dress in fashion, and entertain lavishly. Westerners also had no immunity to regional diseases, and the death rate among them was high until well into the twentieth century. Malaria, dysentery, typhoid, and cholera were the major killers; it was in Calcutta in 1899 that Sir Ronald Ross first proved the theory that malaria was carried by mosquitoes and began preventive measures. Home leave was not common until after the opening of the Suez Canal in 1869, but the colonial administration, which remained in Calcutta until 1912, retired to the cool foothills of the Himalayas for the hottest summer months. It became the custom for Britons to meet each year in November, when the cool season began, to congratulate each other on having survived another year. Probably fewer than half the Britons who came to Calcutta during the first century of British dominion survived to return home.

Calcutta was picked in 1690 for the site of the Company's trading base in Bengal, in part because the Hooghly River, one of the many mouths of the Ganges, widened a little there and formed a deep pool where the ships of the time could anchor. There was a small trading fair there already where Indian merchants periodically brought their goods, but Calcutta probably took its name from the nearby shrine to the goddess Kali at Kalighat. It prospered from the start and became the predominant trading center first for Bengal and then for all of eastern India. It enjoyed an advantageous position in the Ganges delta with easy access to inland routes and coastal shipping. After 1850 a network of railways was built with Calcutta as the major hub, and textile and metalworking factories rose beside the Hooghly, joined toward the end of the century by a wide range of other industrial enterprises. The biggest industry was the weaving of jute, a coarse fiber from a plant grown along delta streams and made into gunnysacks and twine, of which Calcutta had a near world monopoly. The city became the largest industrial center in India, as well as its biggest city. Kipling wrote a short poem about it in 1905 that caught it well:

> *Me the sea captain loved, the river built,*
> *Wealth sought and kings adventured life to*
> *hold.*
> *Hail England! I am Asia, power on silt;*
> *Death in my hands, but gold!*[3] *

Calcutta was the major base for the English plunder of Bengal after 1760, and many fortunes made in those chaotic years were reflected in the splendid houses along the river. This was the extravagant culture of the people called "nabobs" (a corruption of the Indian title *nawab*), who had "shaken the pagoda tree" in India and displayed their new wealth ostentatiously. As Calcutta grew and industrialized, it became mainly a city of dingy warehouses, factories, and slums. It was also, however, the scene of the Bengal Renaissance, a remarkable flowering of the blend between Western and Indian cultures. The present-day city remains India's most lively literary, intellectual, and cultural center. Western visitors find its grimy slums depressing, like those of any Third World city, but it is still, as for all of its short history, an immensely vigorous and creative place.

The Subjugation of India

Until well into the nineteenth century much of British rule in India was conducted through the formal sovereignty of the so-called Princely States and their Indian rulers and was to a large extent collaborative. Even in recently conquered Maharashtra, as elsewhere, the British attracted support by their suppression of banditry and furthering of production and trade. Most elite Indians who had any dealings with the British were content with their new rulers, and many were enthusiastic. Peasants who had been accustomed to the harsh exactions of Indian states had come to distrust all government. Most, indeed, were only dimly aware at first that a new group of foreigners now dominated politics, especially since local administration was left largely in Indian hands. Indirectly, however, peasant welfare was increasingly affected by the spread of zamindar landlordism encouraged by the British and by the spread of commercial crops and market forces. Freedom from banditry and

---

*Jute was often referred to in India as "gold on silt."

◉ British Life in India ◉

The English who succeeded in trade or in the higher administration of the East India Company lived luxuriously and affected an extravagant style. Here are some sample accounts, the first describing the governor's entourage in Madras about 1710.

The governor seldom goes abroad with less than three or four score peons armed; besides the English guards to attend him he has two union flags carried before him. . . . He is a man of great parts, respected as a prince by the rajahs of the country, and is in every way as great.

The secretary to a high Company official in Calcutta in the mid-1770s voiced complaints.

The cursed examples of parade and extravagance they [the Indian servants] are holding up forever to us. "Master must have this. Master must do that." A councillor never appears in the street with a train of less than twenty fellows, nor walks from one room to another in his house unless preceded by four silver staves. . . . What improvement India may make in my affairs I know not, but it has already ruined my temper.

Another account of Calcutta in the 1770s describes the life of the colonialists.

Most gentlemen and ladies in Bengal live both splendidly and pleasantly, the forenoon being dedicated to business, and after [midday] dinner to rest. . . . On the river sometimes there is the diversion of fishing or fowling or both, and before night they make friendly visits to one another, when pride or contention do not spoil society, which too often they do among the ladies, as discord and faction do among the men.

Things were much the same at Bombay in 1812, according to a visiting English lady, who might have been describing pretentious expatriate society anywhere and at any time, including the present.

With regard to the Europeans in Bombay, the manners of the inhabitants of a foreign colony are in general so well represented by those of a country town at home that it is hopeless to attempt making a description of them very interesting. The ladies are under-bred and over-dressed, ignorant, and vulgar. The civil servants are young men taken up with their own imaginary importance.

Sources: C. Lockyer, *An Account of the Trade of India* (London: Crouch, 1711), p. 24; B. Francis and E. Kean, eds., *Letters of Philip Francis*, vol. 1 (London: Murray, 1901), p. 219; J. T. Wheeler, *Early Records of British India* (Calcutta: Newman, 1879), p. 53; J. Forbes, *Oriental Memoirs*, vol. 1 (London: White, Cochrane, 1813), p. 42.

from arbitrary or excessive taxation was an important gain, but there was a significant rise in tenancy and a decline in net economic well-being for many who lost their land or were exploited by new commercialization, such as the notorious indigo plantation system, which ruined many thousands of Indian peasants.

Just as the British worked largely through native rulers, so, at first, they left the structure of Indian society intact. Except for their suppression of *sati*, banditry, and slavery, the British did not tamper with Indian customs. Even Christian missionaries, whom the Company had excluded as "disruptive" until 1813, were limited for some time to running schools, which attracted many young Indians as a means of rising in the new colonial society and gaining employment in the colonial system. Rooted in commerce, the Indian middle class made money in the expanding trade promoted by the British order, and they too founded or joined as partners in new Western-style banks, corporations, agency houses, and joint-stock companies. In 1833 Parliament abolished the Company's previous monopoly of all trade in and with India in response to the demand for entry into this vast and lucrative market, and India was opened to all kinds of private enterprise.

As the nineteenth century wore on, however, and industrialization and technological progress brought Britain unprecedented wealth and power, British attitudes began to change. The growing conviction that Britain was the appropriate leader of the world in all things replaced the earlier interest in Indian culture with a new ethnocentric arrogance. The domination of the Indian economy and its subjection to British interests at home had similarly harmful effects. Machine-made cloth from the mills of Lancashire ended most of the Indian cotton exports that had for so long been the chief basis of trade. Mass-produced British cloth invaded the Indian market, throwing millions of Indian hand spinners of cotton out of work, although raw cotton continued to be shipped to looms in Britain. Imported machine-spun yarn did help keep traditional Indian weavers viable, as did yarn from mills in Bombay after the 1850s.

At same time, British policymakers for India decided that it was the chief duty of government to "civilize" and "improve" Indians, that is, to bring them into conformity with British cultural norms. Such policymakers included a series of governors-general, beginning with William Bentinck in 1828, who were followers of the new British school of utilitarian liberalism. It was decreed in 1835 that English and Western learning should be the main objects of education, in order, in the words of the Liberal spokesman Thomas Babington Macaulay, "to form a class who may be interpreters between us and the millions whom we govern, a class of persons Indian in blood and color, but English in taste, in opinions, in morals, and in intellect."[4] The views of the Orientalists and their admiration of Indian civilization were set aside; Indians were now to be educated along British lines. A new law code was devised for all of British India, which incorporated many aspects of Indian tradition but created an essentially British system of law and jurisprudence. Although from 1809 all British recruits to the East India Company and later to the Indian civil service were required to learn at least one Indian language and something of the country's history and culture, fewer and fewer bothered to learn Sanskrit or to study the Indian classics.

After midcentury, British control of India was extended and facilitated by improvements in transportation and communication. The first rail lines were begun in 1850, reaching inland from Calcutta and Bombay. By 1855 all of India's major cities had been linked by telegraph and by postal service down to the village level. Railways and telegraph service were soon to be of vital importance to the British in suppressing the mutiny of 1857, but their primary use was to haul raw materials and agricultural goods to the rapidly expanding urban markets. Many Britons had doubted that caste-conscious Hindus would crowd together on trains, but

◉ The Charter Act, 1833 ◉

The rise of humanitarianism and liberalism in Britain led to a new Charter Act for India in 1833 when the Company's monopoly was removed. This was often cited later by Indian nationalists as showing the hypocrisy of British rule, but it stated a principle that many colonial administrators made an effort to follow.

No native [of India], nor any natural-born subject of His Majesty resident therein, shall by reason of his religion, place of birth, descent, color, or any of the above, be disabled from holding any place, office, or employment under the Company. . . . On a large view of the state of Indian legislation, and of the improvements possible in it, it is recognized as an indisputable principle that the interests of the native subjects are to be consulted in preference to those of Europeans whenever the two come in competition, and that therefore the laws ought to be adapted to the feelings and habits of the natives rather than to those of Europeans.

Source: S. Wolpert, *A New History of India* (New York: Oxford University Press, 1982), p. 213.

An East India Company official studying an Indian language with a *munshi* (native language teacher), c. 1813. Especially after 1800, the Company began to require that all of its officials learn at least one Indian language fluently, an obvious necessity for those engaged in dispensing justice, in administration, or in trade. [British Library]

rail travel was popular from the start and indeed typified the flexibility of caste in a changing environment.

At the same time, British ambition faced potential competition. The British watched with growing concern as Russia successively took over the independent kingdoms of central Asia. Soon only Afghanistan stood between the two empires. To block Russian influence there, the British ill-advisedly sent an expedition to Kabul in 1839, assuming control of the lower Indus valley (the province of Sind) along the way. Afghan guerrilla resistance finally forced the British to retreat in 1841 through the wild mountain and gorge country along the route to India, a natural setting for a devastating ambush. Only one British survivor of the nearly 20,000-man Army of the Indus reached safety. Fierce Afghan tribal warriors had humbled yet another proud empire, but Sind was brutally reconquered in 1843 as "strategic territory."

The Sikhs of Punjab had refused passage to the ill-fated expedition to Afghanistan, and now Punjab challenged the British as the only part of India not under their direct or indirect control. Factional conflicts over the political succession there gave the British a chance to intervene in 1845–1846. The Sikhs were defeated and

Punjab and Kashmir were formally annexed, although the British had to mount a second campaign and did not finally prevail until 1849. Having won the war, the British, appreciating the military skills of the Sikhs, offered them a prominent place in their army. This was the beginning of a long partnership that paid an early dividend in Sikh support for the British in the mutiny of 1857.

Images of British Rule

Until the nineteenth century the British had been far from seeing themselves as conquerors, nor had they planned to govern India. By 1800, however, they had achieved dominance, and by 1818 their empire had been largely established. Having acquired an Indian empire, the British then had to decide how to rule it. Part of the debate centered on what sort of educational and legal system would best serve British interests as well as those of the new dominions. The Orientalists, who had learned to admire and study Indian civilization, argued that young Indians should be educated in their own culture and its great tradition, which they regarded as the moral equivalent of Christianity. This included the study of Sanskrit, the Indian counterpart of Latin or Greek, and of the classical Indian texts.

Orientalists saw the study of the Hindu cultural and religious legacy as valuable for its own sake but also as a guide to proper social behavior. One of the British members of the Asiatic Society of Bengal wrote:

> Hinduism little needs the ameliorating hand of Christianity to render its votaries a sufficiently correct and moral people for all the useful purposes of a civilized society. . . . In the vast region of Hindu mythology I discover piety in the garb of allegory, I see morality at every turn blended with every tale. . . . It appears the most complete and ample system of moral allegory that the world has ever produced.[5]

The contrary view, which ultimately became the dominant one, argued that Britain had "a moral duty to perform" in "civilizing" India according to the modern British model. This meant that English would replace Sanskrit and that science, mathematics, and Western history and literature would replace the traditional Indian curriculum for Indians being trained for careers in business and government.

Governor-General William Bentinck chose the young Thomas Babington Macaulay, later famous as a historian, to preside over the education committee that was attempting to resolve the debate between the two sides and to plan British India's education system in 1834. Macaulay asserted that "a single shelf of a good European library is worth the whole native literature of India," and

Governor Bentinck in the end declared that "the great object of the British government ought to be the promotion of European literature and science among the natives of India." The education system that resulted from such official designs was strongly English in character and content, although most upper-class Indians continued to study their own culture and linguistic tradition as well. Macaulay also drafted virtually single-handedly a new penal code for British India that produced legal uniformity for the first time throughout India. Many punishments under the new code were less severe than those under the English law of the time. Indian judges, trained in both Indian and Western-style law, were made part of the system, and by the end of the colonial period they constituted the great majority of the bench.

English-style education and law had a lasting impact on India. Both have been retained with relatively little change in modern India, adapted by Indians to their own uses. Most educated Indians became as familiar with English literature and history as educated Englishmen. Many members of the Indian upper classes went on to British universities, where they competed successfully with British students and often outdistanced them. The Hindu Renaissance, which was partly a reaction to British influence, helped balance it, and as a result most Indians also learned about their own cultural tradition.

Indians had never before been effectively unified politically or culturally. British education accomplished this for the elite, and national integration was greatly facilitated by modern means of transportation. Before the nineteenth century the strength of Indian regionalism resulted in part from the great difficulty of communication among its parts, given India's size and topography and the absence of navigable rivers in most of the country. Even the Ganges and the Indus were usable only by small boats over most of their courses, and the rivers of central and southern India were essentially unnavigable. The rail and road systems built after 1850 tied India together and brought most educated or commercial Indians into contact with each other; and English gave them a single common language for the first time.

Early British officials frankly acknowledged Indian hostility to their presence and argued for fair administration on the grounds of expediency. Charles Metcalfe, the British resident at Delhi, wrote in 1835:

> Our dominion in India is by conquest; it is naturally disgusting to the inhabitants and can only be maintained by military force. It is our positive duty to render them justice, to respect and protect their rights, and to study their happiness. By the performance of this duty, we may allay and keep dormant their innate dissatisfaction.[6]

Some farsighted Britons recognized that these processes must bring about a demand for national independence. Charles Trevelyan, a secretary in the political department of the government in Calcutta, wrote in 1838:

> The existing connection between two such distant countries as England and India cannot in the nature of things be permanent; no effect of policy can prevent the natives from ultimately regaining their independence. But there are two ways of arriving at this point. . . . One must end in the complete alienation of mind and separation of interests between ourselves and the natives; the other in a permanent alliance, founded on mutual benefit and goodwill.[7]

For much of the final century of British rule, particularly after 1857, the first way seemed all too likely an outcome.

The Mutiny of 1857

The arrangement that left Indian princes in formal control of much of India, although under British supervision, was in many ways unsatisfactory to the new im-

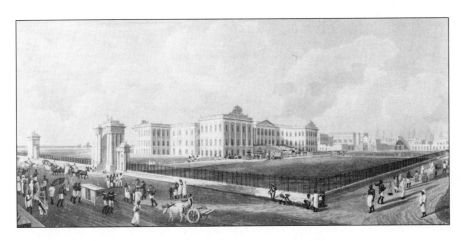

Government House, Calcutta, in 1826: all very Western in style, although the sedan chair (left foreground) was a traditional Asian institution too. [British Library]

perialist policy. Using the pretext that disputes over succession were disruptive of political order (as they often were), the Company assumed direct sovereignty over several central Indian states in the 1850s, and in 1856, despite earlier treaty promises, annexed the rich kingdom of Oudh in the central Ganges. Mounting British arrogance had already provoked discontent among Indian troops, and the new territorial seizures had created potentially powerful enemies among deposed elites, who made common cause with the disgruntled soldiery. The hereditary aristocracy saw not only that they had been displaced as rulers by the British but also that their place in Indian society was being taken by the upstart collaborators of a rising commercial and westernized Indian middle class. Many of the troops were incensed at being required to accept service overseas, which was forbidden to caste Hindus.

Conditions were ripe for an explosion, and a pretext soon arrived. Early in 1857 an improved rifle was introduced. It was rumored that the cartridges were coated in pork lard and other animal fat and had to be bitten off before loading, something deeply offensive to vegetarian Hindus and to Muslims. That had indeed been so originally, but although the process was quickly changed, the rumor persisted. The outcry of protest was met not by concession or explanation but by rigid insistence on fol-

lowing orders. Those who refused were dishonorably discharged, many of them men from Oudh.

Several regiments mutinied and killed their British officers. The mutineers captured Delhi and "restored" the last surviving Mughal emperor, now an old man, who had never been formally removed by the Company. Mutineers on the rampage slaughtered the British population of Delhi and of outlying districts there and in Oudh, massacred those who had surrendered from their encampment in the city of Cawnpore (Kanpur), and besieged the somewhat larger group of men, women, and children, including loyal Indians, who had fortified themselves in the grounds of the British Residency in Lucknow, the capital of Oudh.

During the summer of 1857 the British lost control of major portions of the Ganges heartland in northern India and, temporarily, parts of the Punjab and central India. Panic was widespread within the European communities. But most army units remained loyal, and most Indians took no part in the struggle or stood by the British. Once the British recovered from their initial shock, the outcome of the uprising was not in doubt. By July 1858 the British governor-general, Lord Canning, had proclaimed victory, although resistance continued in small pockets in northern and central India until later in the year.

Repulse of a Sortie, a drawing by C. F. Atkinson, depicts an incident in the mutiny of 1857.
[British Library]

INDIA AND IRAN, 1700–1857

India	Iran
Death of Aurangzeb (1707)	
	End of Savafid rule (1736)
Persians sack Delhi (1739)	Nadir Quli (1736–1747)
Clive's victory at Plassey (1757)	Karim Khan (1757–1779)
India Act (1784)	
	Qajar dynasty (1794–1924)
British invasion of Afghanistan (1839–1841)	
Conquest of Punjab (1845–1849)	
Mutiny (1857)	

The British repaid the atrocities they had suffered in kind. Captured rebel soldiers were strapped to cannon and blown away, and entire villages were put to the torch. Fear and hatred created a permanent gulf between rulers and ruled. The British were henceforth frankly an occupying power, despite their continued reliance on native elites. Intermarriage and fraternization greatly decreased, and the colonial regime became more like a walled community that held itself stiffly apart from what some of its members called the "nigger natives." The feeble Bahadur Shah, last of the Mughal emperors, was exiled to Burma, where he died in 1858, and a British captain named Hodson, taking his cue from the early Mughal dynasts themselves, murdered Bahadur Shah's sons in cold blood. Although most Indians remained collaborators, some of them enthusiastically, and many British continued to pursue more tolerant and more positive attitudes and policies, the dream of an equal Anglo-Indian partnership was largely over.

Iran in Transition: The Eighteenth Century

For the Iranians the eighteenth century was a period of transition. The corrupt vestiges of the Safavid dynasty were swept away, and, after a period of violent internal struggle, a new dynasty emerged and undertook an expansionist foreign policy, mostly at the expense of the Ottomans. The stage was set for these developments by Ottoman aggression. The Shi'ite militancy of the Safavids had increasingly antagonized Sunni Muslims, especially the Ottomans, whose sultans regarded themselves as the protectors of the Sunnis. The Ottomans, moreover, were eager to reverse their fortunes after disastrous territorial losses to European states in the late seventeenth and early eighteenth centuries, and Iran seemed an obvious place to expand in the 1720s. With their Sunni allies in Afghanistan, the Ottomans went to war against the Iranian Shi'ites. The Iranians repulsed

the Afghans and Ottomans and checked a Russian assault under Peter the Great as well. Much of Iran's success was due to an ex–robber baron turned general, Nadir Quli (1688–1747), known to history as "the Napoleon of Iran."

Nadir Quli

When the Safavid shah, Tahmasp II, accepted a humiliating peace with the Ottomans in 1732, Nadir ousted him from the throne and governed as regent for Tahmasp's infant son. Four years later the ambitious Nadir had himself crowned as Nadir Shah Afshar. The same year he concluded a series of military campaigns to recover Iranian provinces from the Ottomans, and, exploiting Russo-Turkish rivalry, he persuaded the Russians to cede Iranian territory in their possession. Unsatisfied with these striking gains, he launched an expansionist war against India, defeating the Mughal emperor, Mohammed Shah, in 1739. Nadir's troops plundered Delhi and Lahore, slaughtering some 20,000 people and seizing even the Peacock Throne. Because India was too large for him to hold, Nadir left all but the provinces on the west bank of the Indus in the hands of a subdued Mohammed Shah and returned to Iran with an enormous booty in 1740. Ties with the defeated Mughals were cemented by the marriage of Nadir's second son to the granddaughter of Aurangzeb.

Like the great Indian ruler Akbar, Nadir Shah was interested in finding the common truth he believed was at the heart of competing religions, though he made no attempt, as Akbar did, to found an ecumenical faith. He did, however, order the Bible and the Koran translated into Persian. In the hope of easing tensions between Sunni and Shi'ite Muslims, he ordered a halt to the persecution of Sunnis in Iran, while demanding that the Shi'ites be given special accommodations at Mecca. His scheme to reunify Islam was based on having his Shi'ite people embrace the newly created Ja'fariyah sect, which he insisted should be officially recognized as a Sunni group. But the Ottoman Sunnis branded the new sect unacceptable and authorized their adherents to kill Iranians. In Iran itself any hope of bridging the Sunni-Shi'ite gulf was doomed by the hostility of the Shi'ite religious leaders, who bitterly resented Nadir's attempts to reduce their power.

The influence of such religious leaders was but one of several effective checks on any shah's pretension to absolute power. In theory the shah continued to govern by divine right, though in reality no post-Safavid shah ever regained the spiritual aura that had once been accorded the early Safavids. By the eighteenth century the shah was no more than a political despot, akin to the Ottoman sultan. The shah's influence was checked as well by regional loyalties and poor communications, both of which encouraged the decentralization of power. Thus the authority of any shah ultimately depended on his personal abilities as well as his relationship with Muslim leaders.

Nadir's military talents had enabled him to extend the Iranian frontiers beyond those of the Safavid era, but like Napoleon, this reckless military adventurer had no sense of when to stop. Instead of turning his attention to economic growth and administrative reform, he squandered human and material resources on ruinous military campaigns. He met his match in the Caucasus against the Lezghian tribe, whom he failed to conquer and whose success against Nadir encouraged subject peoples in Iran to revolt. Although the rebels were savagely repressed, Nadir himself became increasingly vindictive, unstable, and vicious, executing many of his own advisers and military officers. In 1747 he was assassinated, a victim of the atmosphere of terror he had created.

For a decade Iran was plunged into strife as rival claimants fought for the throne, sometimes deposing and blinding each other. As in the Safavid era, fratricide and the execution of one's opponents was commonplace. Nadir's nephew and successor, having learned of his new position in an invitation accompanied by Nadir's severed head, ordered the execution of Nadir's children and the disemboweling of those of his widows and concubines believed to be pregnant. He in turn was eventually murdered by supporters of Nadir's grandson, a luckless fellow who was deposed and restored to the throne twice and blinded in the process.

<hr />

Karim Khan

Order was finally restored in 1757 by the more temperate Karim Khan, who governed not as shah but as *vakil*, or deputy, a title once used for the chief officer of state. He was, he insisted, the shah's steward, a position reminiscent of the Ottoman vizier. This was only in part a charade, for Karim Khan was genuinely interested in social justice. He earned his reputation as the "advocate of the peasants" by terminating Nadir Shah's disastrous

Karim Khan, as depicted by a contemporary artist. [British Library]

policy of inducting large numbers of peasants into the army, thereby forcing those who remained in the fields not only to compensate for the lost labor but also to pay higher taxes to support the growing military. Although the state granaries that Karim Khan constructed in every province were primarily to feed his army, he used the stockpiled grain to relieve the poor when famine struck.

Karim Khan's era was one of peace and relative prosperity, notable in part for his beautification of the capital, Shiraz, with new buildings and gardens and for his construction of a palace and new fortifications at Tehran. The key figures in this building program included artists and craftsmen that Nadir Shah had brought from India. Under both Nadir and Karim Khan the artisans of the royal workshops produced sumptuous tapestries, carpets, miniatures, and artistic calligraphy. But unlike Europe or India, Iran in the eighteenth century could not boast great literary achievements.

Under Karim Khan religious minorities enjoyed substantial toleration, not least because of their economic productivity. As in the Safavid period, representatives of Roman Catholic orders such as the Benedictines and the Jesuits were free to live, worship, and trade as they wished, so long as they did not offend the Shi'ites. Native, or Armenian, Christians were also tolerated and in fact had to be restrained from harassing Latin Christians. Iranian Jews periodically suffered persecution in the eighteenth century, though Karim Khan allowed them to have their own quarter in the capital in return for paying a special tax. After his death, however, the Jews were again persecuted.

Although Nadir's military adventurism and the ensuing period of civil chaos had had an adverse impact on the Iranian economy, conditions improved during the rule of Karim Khan. Trade with Russia periodically thrived, as the Iranians shipped raw silk, madder (for red dye), cotton and silk cloth, rice, and dried fish in return for such goods as iron, steel, mirrors, hides, and sugar. But Russo-Iranian trade again declined when Russia's hostile relations with the Ottomans threatened the overland routes in the 1760s. Iran's other major trading partners were the Ottomans, the Indians, and, increasingly, the Europeans. In the eighteenth century approximately a third of Iran's foreign commerce was with the Ottomans, who traded such items as cashmere shawls, cotton, silk, and tobacco for Syrian textiles, European manufactures, jewels, and dyestuffs.

There was an equivalent trade with India, whose peoples were active in all spheres of Iranian commerce, serving even as bankers, brokers, shipping agents, and sailors. In turn the Iranians and Turks played an important role as middlemen in trade between India and Europe. Some of this trade was conducted through the Persian Gulf; most was in the hands of Asian merchants, though a quarter of it was with Europeans, such as the British Levant and East India companies. Trade relations between the Iranians and the Europeans were often strained, yet throughout the century each was irresistibly drawn to the other—the Iranians by the technological superiority of the westerners, the westerners by the lure of trade profits and imperial gains.

Karim Khan sought to tame the bloody nature of Iranian politics, in part by treating one potential enemy, Agha Muhammad Qajar, more like a guest in his home than the hostage he actually was. When, however, Karim Khan lay dying in 1779, Agha Muhammad escaped to launch his own bid for power. After a renewed period of fratricidal fighting, he crowned himself shah in 1794, inaugurating the long Qajar dynasty, which governed Iran until 1924.

Both India and Iran had enjoyed periods of political vigor under strong rulers, accompanied by cultural brilliance and economic revival. The Mughal dynasty in India, especially under Akbar's long reign, was one of the most splendid periods in Indian and world history, and India in those years was one of the greatest and richest of empires. In Iran, Nadir Shah drove the Ottomans out of the Iranian territories they had occupied and even sacked and looted Delhi, but his ruthlessness and repression led to his own assassination and to civil war. His ultimate successor, Karim Khan, restored peace, but on his death, fighting resumed, and Iran never recovered its former glory. Similar bloody struggles over the succession to the Mughal throne in India deeply marred the century after Akbar, whose successors also plundered and neglected the empire while building their gorgeous palaces. Aurangzeb exhausted the country in his fruitless efforts to conquer the south and to persecute Hindus, leaving India at his death in 1707 torn by civil war and economic devastation.

In this critically deteriorating situation, the English East India Company, which had established small trading positions on both west and east coasts in the seventeenth century, began after 1700 to fortify and develop its bases at Bombay, Madras, and Calcutta, becoming the de facto rulers of small areas around each base. As India sank ever deeper into chaos, the Company's small army of mixed Indian and British forces began to acquire control over more territory, primarily to protect trade routes and the storage of trade goods. Clive's victory at Plassey in Bengal in 1757, in retaliation for the Bengali capture of Calcutta the previous year, opened a new phase in which the Company began to take over larger areas in both the north and the south. By 1800 the foundations of a British Indian empire had been laid, in part as the result of the British defeat of French ambitions and the rivalries of the Napoleonic wars. Imperial aims were accompanied by considerable blending of British and Indian cultures and interests, especially on the part of the Orientalists, as they were called, and of the Indian response in the Bengal Renaissance. But as British power and confidence rose, fed by growing industrialization, wealth, and technological progress at home, British arrogance in India increased, culminating in the mutiny of 1857, exactly a century after Plassey. The mutiny was not yet a national war of independence, but it did express long-standing grievances and foreshadowed the later rise of an Indian nationalist movement that would demand the

country's freedom. The nation's political, economic, legal, and cultural institutions would evolve substantially within the patterns worked out during the colonial period.

Notes

1. From Company records, in S. N. Edwardes, *By-ways of Bombay* (Bombay: Tara Porevala, 1912), pp. 170–171.
2. From Company records, reproduced in C. R. Wilson, ed., *Old Fort William*, vol. 1 (London: Murray, 1906), p. 33.
3. R. Kipling, "Song of the Cities," in *The Five Nations and the Seven Seas* (New York: Doubleday, 1915), p. 183.
4. From T. B. Macaulay's "Minute on Education," in S. Wolpert, *A New History of India* (New York: Oxford University Press, 1982), p. 215.
5. G. Moorhouse, *India Britannica* (New York: Harper & Row, 1983), p. 89.
6. Ibid., p. 84.
7. Ibid., p. 97.

Suggestions for Further Reading

India

Bayly, C. A. *Indian Society and the Making of the British Empire.* Cambridge: Cambridge University Press, 1988.

Bearce, G. D. *British Attitudes Towards India, 1784–1858.* Oxford: Oxford University Press, 1961.

Broehl, W. G. *Crisis of the Raj: 1857 Through British Eyes.* Hanover, N.H.: University Press of New England, 1986.

Chandra, B. *Nationalism and Colonialism in Modern India.* New Delhi: Orient Longman, 1989.

Chaudhuri, K. N. *The Trading World of Asia and the English East India Company, 1600–1760.* Cambridge: Cambridge University Press, 1978.

———, ed. *Calcutta: The Living City.* 2 vols. New York: Oxford University Press, 1990.

Das Gupta, A. *Malabar in Asian Trade, 1740–1800.* Cambridge: Cambridge University Press, 1967.

Farrell, J. G. *The Siege at Krishnapur.* London: Weidenfeld & Nicolson, 1973. (A lively novel of India in 1857.)

Furber, H. *Bombay Presidency in the Mid-Eighteenth Century.* New York: Asia Publishing House, 1965.

Kincaid, D. *British Social Life in India, 1608–1937.* London: Routledge & Kegan Paul, 1973.

Kling, B. *The Blue Mutiny: The Indigo Disturbances in Bengal.* Philadelphia: University of Pennsylvania Press, 1966.

———. *Partner in Empire: Dwarkanath Tagore and the Age of Enterprise in Eastern India.* Berkeley: University of California Press, 1976.

———, and Pearson, M. N., eds. *The Age of Partnership.* Honolulu: University Press of Hawaii, 1979.

Kopf, D. *British Orientalism and the Bengal Renaissance, 1773–1835.* Berkeley: University of California Press, 1969.

Laird, M. A. *Missionaries and Education in Bengal, 1793–1837.* Oxford: Clarendon Press, 1972.

Marshall, P. J. *Bengal, the British Bridgehead.* Cambridge: Cambridge University Press, 1988.

———. *East Indian Fortunes: The British in Bengal in the Eighteenth Century.* Oxford: Clarendon Press, 1976.

———, ed. *Problems of Empire: Britain and India, 1757–1813.* New York: Barnes & Noble Books, 1968.

Moon, P. *The British Conquest and Dominion of India.* London: Duckworth, 1989.

Mudford, P. *Birds of a Different Plumage: A Study of British and Indian Relations from Akbar to Curzon.* London: Collins, 1974.

Mukherjee, S. N. *Sir William Jones: A Study in Eighteenth Century British Attitudes to India.* Cambridge: Cambridge University Press, 1968.

Murphey, R. *The Outsiders: The Western Experience in India and China.* Ann Arbor: University of Michigan Press, 1977.

Rothermund, D. *The Economic History of India.* London: Croom Helm, 1988.

Sinha, D. P. *The Educational Policy of the East India Company in Bengal to 1854.* Calcutta: Punthi Pustaic, 1964.

Spear, P. *Master of Bengal: Clive and His India.* London: Thames & Hudson, 1975.

———. *The Nabobs: A Study of the Social Life of the English in Eighteenth Century India.* London: Oxford University Press, 1963.

———. *Twilight of the Mughals.* Cambridge: Cambridge University Press, 1951.

Stokes, E. *The English Utilitarians and India.* Oxford: Clarendon Press, 1959.

———. *The Peasant Armed: The Indian Rebellion of 1857.* Cambridge: Cambridge University Press, 1986.

Waller, J. H. *Beyond the Khyber Pass: The Road to British Disaster in the First Afghan War.* New York: Random House, 1991.

Watson, F. *A Concise History of India.* London: Thames & Hudson, 1979.

Iran

Armajani, Y. *Iran.* Englewood Cliffs, N.J.: Prentice Hall, 1972.

Perry, J. R. *Karim Khan Zand: A History of Iran, 1747–1779.* Chicago: University of Chicago Press, 1979.

Ramazani, R. K. *The Foreign Policy of Iran: A Developing Nation in World Affairs.* Charlottesville: University of Virginia Press, 1966.

Manchu China and Tokugawa Japan

On the eve of the modern world, China and Japan both emerged, in their separate ways, from periods of decay, rebellion, and civil war to found vigorous new orders. In China this occurred with the beginning of the Ch'ing (Qing) or Manchu dynasty, which took power in 1644 and ruled the empire until 1911. Under Manchu rule, China became once again the greatest power in the world as well as its richest and most sophisticated society. Despite their nomadic origins in northern Manchuria and their role as alien conquerors, the Manchus quickly adopted Chinese culture. This began even before 1644 as they built their power base in southern Manchuria, which had long been part of the Chinese system. They called their new dynasty Ch'ing, meaning "pure," in an effort to give legitimacy to their rule; in fact they governed China completely in the Chinese mode and with widespread Chinese cooperation.

Official court painting of Emperor Kang Hsi (1661–1722) by an unknown artist. Note the imperial dragon robes. [Metropolitan Museum of Art, New York]

Under Ch'ing government, China prospered. The commercialization and urbanization begun under the Sung and the Ming dynasties developed still further, while agriculture became far more productive, with total output at least doubling. But population growth, in itself a result of prosperity, began to exceed production, and in the nineteenth century the Ch'ing regime also slowly lost its effectiveness. Peasant poverty bred rebellion, while China was at the same time unable to resist foreign pressures for trade concessions. In the early 1840s the Chinese were humiliatingly defeated by the British in the so-called Opium War. With the 1850s China entered a steep decline that left it largely at the mercy of Western incursions.

In Japan centuries of conflict among rival clans degenerated into open civil war in the sixteenth century. In 1600 a strong new centralized government, the Tokugawa shogunate, emerged to unify the country for the first time. Under Tokugawa control, Japan enjoyed more than two centuries of order, prosperity, and economic growth. But the regime rested on a revived system of feudal ties, and as the economy matured and a new merchant class became more prominent, pressure for change increased. Foreign demands for trade concessions, as in China, finally broke down Japan's self-imposed isolation in 1853. This Western pressure revealed Japan's weakness while feeding domestic discontent with the Tokugawa rulers. The shogunate was ended in 1868 by what is called the Meiji Restoration; although it ostensibly did restore the emperor, it is more accurately seen as a nonviolent revolution that brought to power a new group of radical reformers who set Japan on a course of rapid modernization, while China continued to flounder.

China Under the Manchus

Manchu rule, established in 1644, was only slowly consolidated. Scattered groups of Ming loyalists and others, including former Manchu allies who had been granted fiefs in the south, fought the new conquerors until the 1680s. Once resistance had been crushed, however, the new dynasty made a genuine effort to win not just Chinese support but actual partnership, a far more successful approach than that of the Mongol dynasty four centuries earlier. With Chinese collaboration, the Ch'ing gave the country order and tranquillity under which it prospered as never before.

Like the Mongols, the Manchus, who totaled only a little over a million people, or some 1 percent of the empire, could not hope to rule without the cooperation of the Chinese, who filled about 90 percent of all official posts throughout the dynasty. Manchu aristocrats dominated the top military positions, but the body of the army, militia, and police were predominantly Chinese, as were many generals. Provincial administration was headed by two-man teams of Chinese and Manchu governors working in tandem—and, of course, checking on each other. The gentry, who provided unofficial leadership and authority at all local levels, remained almost entirely Chinese. The gentry continued to supply nearly all of the officials through the imperial examination system, which the Manchus retained and expanded. At the capital in Peking (Beijing), the Grand Secretariat, the various ministries, and the imperial censorate were staffed equally by Chinese and by Manchus. The Manchu spoken language continued to be used, but all Manchus were by now equally at home in Chinese.

The Manchus succeeded also because they had become, even before 1644, as thoroughly Sinified as their "subjects"—indeed, they had long been an outlying part of the Chinese empire themselves. They came from an area of Manchuria where pastoral nomadism merged with Chinese-style intensive agriculture in the Liao valley and where Chinese cultural dominance dated back at least to the Han dynasty. To protect their homeland and their identity, they discouraged further Chinese emigration to Manchuria until around 1870 and kept northern Manchuria as an imperial hunting preserve.

In their administration of China itself, however, they maintained continuity with the now long established imperial structure and its institutions. The emperor appointed all officials down to the level of the county magistrates and presided over a mobile body of civil and military servants who owed direct loyalty to the throne. These officials were rotated as a rule every three years to emphasize their imperial rather than local or regional roles. The emperor was accessible to all his officials, who could send confidential memoranda (known as "memorials") for the emperor alone and to which he could reply in confidence to the sender only. The emperor personally had to approve all policy matters, to sign all death sentences, and to hear appeals.

The Chinese imperial structure was top-heavy, but on the whole it worked at least as well as the administration of other large empires and better than most. Each official had an extensive unofficial staff to help with the otherwise unmanageable burden of administrative routine and paperwork. But even so, it was a thinly spread system and grew progressively more so as a relatively static number of about 30,000 imperially appointed officials served a growing population. Most of China, still over 90 percent rural, continued to govern itself through the Confucian system of the "self-regulating society." But there was a huge amount of imperial administrative business too. Communication was essential among the widely scattered provinces and districts of this enormous empire, considerably larger than the modern United States and far more populous, and between each

29.1 China Under the Ch'ing

of them and the capital, where most important decisions had to be made or approved. The Ch'ing established some 2,000 postal stations along the main and feeder routes of the imperial road system, much of which was paved. The network extended into Manchuria, Mongolia, Sinkiang, and Tibet. Less urgent communications and shipments traveled by water wherever possible, but for emergency messages or documents mounted couriers using relays of fast horses could cover 250 miles a day or more. This still meant nearly a week of travel from Canton to Peking, but it was almost certainly faster than anything in the West and was rivaled, at least before the end of the eighteenth century, only by the courier system of the Roman Empire at its height.

We know more about Ch'ing China than about any previous imperial period, partly because its recency means that far more of the documentation is still available. But we also have a great many foreign accounts, especially after the late eighteenth century. The Europeans were fascinated by China, and they can give us a perspective, and a comparative dimension, lacking for earlier periods. Their accounts help establish a picture of Manchu China as the largest, richest, best-governed, and most sophisticated country in the world of its time. European thinkers of the Enlightenment, including Leibniz and later Voltaire, were much influenced by what they knew of Ch'ing China. They were struck in particular by its emphasis on ethical precepts as opposed to the commands of revealed religion and on selection for office through competitive examination. China, they thought, avoided the evils they ascribed in Europe to a hereditary officeholding nobility. To them China seemed close to the Platonic ideal never achieved in the West, a state ruled by philosopher-kings.

The Ch'ing compiled a vast new law code, dealing mainly with criminal offenses; most civil disputes continued to be handled locally through family, clan, and gentry networks. Chinese law impressed European philosophers and legal scholars for its grounding in Confucian ethics. Admiration of China led also to a European vogue for Chinese art, architecture, gardens, porcelains, and even furniture and wallpaper (another Chinese innovation), all of which became the height of fashion for the upper classes, especially in France and England. The foreign perspective on China began to change in the nineteenth century as China declined and the West entered its steep modern rise. But traces of the original admiration long remained among people less easily blinded by Victorian imperialist arrogance.

Prosperity and Population Growth

The first 150 years of Ch'ing rule were an especially brilliant period, marked by the long reigns of two able and dedicated emperors, Kang Hsi (Kang Xi, 1661–1722) and Ch'ien Lung (Qian Long, 1735–1796). As a direct consequence of the order and prosperity they established, population began an increase that continued until after 1900, tripling over the course of 250 years. Until late in the eighteenth century production and the growth of commerce more than kept pace. Even by the 1840s and 1850s, when per capita incomes had probably been declining for two generations or more, British observers agreed that most Chinese were materially better off than most Europeans. Robert Fortune, a well-informed traveler and resident in China, writing in 1853, succinctly summarized the prevailing view by saying that "in no country in the world is there less real misery and want than in China."[1] Fortune wrote from the perspective of industrializing England, with its repressed proletariat, but his judgment about China was probably accurate and is corroborated by other Western observers.

The massive growth of population and production is a good measure of the success of Ch'ing rule and the confident spirit of the times. Government officials diligently promoted improvements in agriculture, new irrigation and flood prevention works, roads, and canals. More new land was brought under cultivation to feed the rising population, and more new irrigation projects were constructed than in the whole of previous Chinese history. The Ch'ing period also saw the Chinese agricultural conquest of the cultivable areas of the south and

◉ Adam Smith on China ◉

The founder of classical Western economics and advocate of the free market, Adam Smith, commented on China in his Wealth of Nations, *published in 1776, which was based on the accounts of Europeans who had been there.*

The great extent of the empire of China, the vast multitude of its inhabitants, the variety of climate and consequently of productions in its various provinces, and the easy communication by means of water carriage between the greater part of them, render the home market of that country of so great extent as to be alone sufficient to support very great manufactures, and to admit of very considerable subdivisions of labor. The home market of China is perhaps in extent not much inferior to the market of all the different countries of Europe put together.

Source: A. Smith, *The Wealth of Nations,* vol. 2 (New York: Dutton, 1954), p. 217.

THE VISUAL EXPERIENCE
Art of Asia from the Sixteenth to the Nineteenth Century

A *durbar* (celebratory festival) in Calcutta, featuring a traditional Indian formal procession. Note that Indians are the only ones who are walking (or carrying arms), although some Indian notables and guests are riding on the elephants with the top-hatted British. [British Library]

William Prinseps' watercolor of the Calcutta waterfront in the early nineteenth century graphically illustrates the link between the old and the new. The small sampanlike boats in the foreground were used to ferry goods to and from the oceangoing ships in the background, which usually had to anchor in deeper water. Note the European architecture. [Spinks & Sons Ltd., London]

Landscape in the style of the Sung and Yuan masters by Wu Li (active c. 1660–1718). This is part of an album in homage to the old masters but reflecting the artist's own distinctive style. Like many of the Chinese gentry, Wu Li was a poet and a scholar as well as a painter. [National Palace Museum, Taipei]

Peonies, by Wang Hui, dated 1672, from an album of flower studies painted in the manner of various classical masters. These are Chinese tree peonies, whose great size and ruffled petals made them a favorite subject for painters. [National Palace Museum, Taipei]

Flowers and Butterflies, by Ma Ch'uan (1720–1800), one of the few woman painters of traditional China. This screen reflects the Chinese artists' fascination with details of the natural world and also shows a delicate feminine hand. [The Metropolitan Museum of Art, Fletcher Fund, 1947]

Lotus, *Maple*, and *Wisteria*, three hanging scrolls by the Tokugawa artist Hon'ami Koho (1601–1682). In the Chinese tradition, Koho was primarily interested in decorative flower painting. This trio of scrolls is centered on the lotus, with the wisteria on the left and the maple on the right to frame it. [Fujita Art Museum, Osaka]

A detail from *Birds and Flowers in a Landscape* by Kano Yukinobu (died 1575). As the divisions show, this was designed as a folding screen (shoji). Screens often gave Japanese artists an opportunity for flamboyant use of color, as here. [Fenollosa-Weld Collection. Courtesy of Museum of Fine Arts, Boston]

Irises, by Okata Korin (1658–1716), is a striking example of the flamboyant decorative use of color, especially on screens, typical of the Tokugawa. [Nezu Institute of Fine Arts, Tokyo]

southwest, at the expense of the remaining minority non-Han inhabitants (see Chapters 3 and 12). Much of the new tilled land was in the hilly south, where terracing was often pushed to extremes, driving the indigenous population into still more mountainous areas, especially in the southwestern provinces of Szechuan (Sichuan), Yunnan, and Kweichou (Guizhou). Large new acreage was also brought under the plow in the semiarid margins of northern China. Yields everywhere rose with new irrigation, increased fertilization, better seeds, and more intensive cultivation.

Merchants were also allowed a broader scope under the Ch'ing even than under the Ming. Trade with Southeast Asia grew still further, and permanent settlements of Chinese merchants grew with it. Both domestic commerce, greater than that of the whole of Europe, and urbanization reached new levels and remained far more important than overseas connections. Merchant guilds proliferated in all of the growing Chinese cities and often acquired great social and even political influence. Rich merchants with official connections built up huge fortunes and patronized literature, theater, and the arts. Fleets of junks (Chinese-style boats) plied the coast and the great inland waterways, and urban markets teemed with people and goods. General prosperity helped ensure domestic peace. Silver continued to flow in to pay for China's exports to the West, including tea and silk, leaving a large favorable trade balance. Cloth and handicraft production boomed with the sophisticated division of labor and an increasing market.

Along with silver, other New World goods entered the China market through Manila. These included new and highly productive crops from the Americas, including sweet and white potatoes, maize, peanuts, and tobacco. All had been unknown in Asia before, and in many cases they supplemented the staple agricultural system of rice, wheat, and the other more drought-tolerant cereals, such as millet and sorghum, grown in the drier parts of the north. Potatoes could be raised in sandy soils unsuited to cereals, white potatoes in the colder areas, sweet potatoes in the south. Both produced more food energy per unit of land than any cereal crop. Corn yielded well on slopes too steep for irrigated rice. Peanuts and tobacco filled other gaps and added substantially to total food resources or to the list of cash crops, such as cotton.

Early-ripening rice introduced from Southeast Asia in the Sung and Ming periods was further developed under the Ch'ing, and the period from sowing to harvest was progressively reduced. In the long growing season of the south, this meant that more areas could produce two crops of rice a year and some could manage three. The practice of transplanting rice seedlings in spaced rows set in irrigated paddies became universal in the Ch'ing period. This greatly increased yields and shortened the time to harvest.

As population increased and demand for food rose, agriculture was pushed up onto steeper and steeper slopes, as in this photograph from the southwestern province of Yunnan. Terracing required immense labor but could create only tiny strips of level land, and obtaining water for irrigation was a major problem. Terracing was necessary because by the late Ch'ing period all gentler slopes had been occupied, and the population continued to rise.
[Rhoads Murphey]

Food and nonfood crops were now treated with the kind of care a gardener uses for individual plants, fertilized by hand, weeded at frequent intervals, with irrigation levels precisely adjusted to the height and needs of each crop as the season advanced. The use of human manure now also became universal, and the amounts increased as the population rose, providing both the source and the need for more intensive fertilization. Rice yields were more than doubled by a combination of all these methods, and the total output also rose as the result of double and triple cropping and the addition of newly cleared land. Improvements in rice cultivation, China's major crop since Han times, as well as new irrigation and other techniques, were probably the chief source of food increases. Rising population provided both the incentive and the means for improved crop yields under the management of local magistrates and gentry. The irrigation of rice was finely engineered, permitting the alteration of water levels and the draining of the paddies in the last few weeks before harvest. These improvements required immense amounts of labor and organization, but they paid handsomely in increased yields.

These changes, improvements, and additions to the system help explain how an already large population could triple in 2½ centuries and still maintain or even enhance its food and income levels. Agriculture remained the heart of the economy and the major source of state revenue, but its surpluses created a growing margin for both subsistence and commercial exchange. The population figures the Ch'ing compiled, like those of earlier dynasties, were not designed as total head counts and were based on local reports by village headmen enumerating households and adult males fit for military service. Land ownership and output were also recorded for tax purposes, and for a time, as in previous centuries, there was also a head tax. Since everyone knew that population figures were used for calculating taxes and for conscript labor, there was an understandable tendency for local headmen and households to understate the true numbers.

Early in the dynasty it was announced that the head tax would never be raised, and it was later merged with the land tax and a levy on crops. At the same time, the Ch'ing made it plain that reports of population increase were welcome evidence of the prosperity of their reign. Reports showing little or no gain would reflect on the effectiveness of the local magistrate. For these and other reasons having to do with the imprecision, inconsistency, and incompleteness of the count (which often but not always excluded women, servants, infants, migrants, and non-Han people), Ch'ing population figures must be used cautiously, but the long-term trend is clear. From roughly 150 million in the late seventeenth century, the population had reached 400 or possibly 450 million by 1850 and half a billion by 1900. The official figures, almost certainly an undercount at first and possibly an overcount after 1750 or so, show 142 million in 1741 and 432 million in 1851. The rising population was indeed strong evidence of the success of Ch'ing rule, but in time it became a burden that the system could no longer carry successfully, leading to increasing poverty, disorder, and bureaucratic breakdown.

The Reigns of Kang Hsi and Ch'ien Lung

Emperor Kang Hsi, completely Chinese in culture and even an accomplished poet in that language, encouraged literature, art, printing, scholarship, and artisan production. He revived and enlarged the imperial potteries, which with other centers turned out great quantities of beautiful porcelain for the palace and court, the rich merchant elite, and the export trade. A patron of learning, Kang Hsi studied Latin, mathematics, and Western science with Jesuit tutors at his court and corresponded with European monarchs. Toward the end of his reign he lost patience with the sectarian quarreling of the Catholic missionaries and was incensed that a foreign potentate, the pope, should presume to tell the few Chinese Christian converts what they should and should not believe. He remained interested in a wide variety of things, however, and is described by his Jesuit tutors as insatiably curious.

Kang Hsi was a conscientious and able administrator of boundless energy who tried to ensure honesty in government and a harmonious partnership among Chinese and Manchu officials. He went on six major state tours around the empire and showed a great interest in local affairs. He commissioned an ambitious new encyclopedia of all learning, updated and greatly expanded from Yung-lo's compilation under the Ming dynasty. Running to 5,000 volumes, it was probably the largest such work ever written anywhere. The huge dictionary of the Chinese language that Kang Hsi also commissioned, which still bears his name, remains the most exhaustive and authoritative guide to classical Chinese up to his own time. He also supervised the compilation of a voluminous administrative geography of the empire. He encouraged the further spread of private academies for the sons of the gentry and state-supported schools for worthy but poorer boys, to spread classical learning and to open the way to office for those who mastered it. Older scholars and retired officials were sent around the empire at government expense to lecture to the populace on morality and virtue.

Kang Hsi was equally effective in military affairs. He supervised the reconquest of Taiwan, restored Chinese control over Mongolia and eastern Sinkiang, and in 1720 mounted an expedition to put down civil war in Tibet, where he established firm Chinese authority. His armies had earlier chased the Russians out of the Amur region of northern Manchuria. He then negotiated the Treaty of Nerchinsk in 1689 with the tsar's representatives, confirming Chinese sovereignty in the Amur valley and southward. This was both China's first significant engagement and its first treaty with a Western power. The Ch'ing clearly emerged as victors, successfully defending China's traditionally threatened landward frontiers. The Russian negotiators were kept on the frontier and not received in Peking; Nerchinsk was a minor border post, and relatively minor Chinese officials were sent to deal with them, assisted by Jesuit interpreters.

Far less attention was paid to the westerners already attempting to trade at Canton and to extend their efforts farther northward along the coast. These traders, mostly Portuguese, Dutch, and English, were regarded as a minor nuisance in the same category as bandits or pirates. They were certainly not perceived as representatives of civilized states with whom China should have any dealings. The difference in response to the Russians reflected the perennial Chinese concern about their continental borders, the source of so much trouble in the past, as compared with the maritime frontier, which had never presented any major security problem. Their defenses, their front doors, and their military priorities faced westward toward the great Eurasian landmass whence the Mongols and other invaders had come.

Ch'ien Lung, Kang Hsi's grandson, succeeded him in 1735. He might have reigned officially until his death, but filial piety prompted him to retire in 1796 after 60 years so as not to stay on the throne longer than his grandfather. However, he remained the real power until his death three years later at the age of 89. Less austere and more extroverted than Kang Hsi, Ch'ien Lung, with his grand manner, has often been compared to King Louis XIV of France. Until his last years Ch'ien Lung was a diligent and humane ruler who continued his grandfather's administrative and patronage model in all respects; comparison with Louis XIV does him less than justice. He commissioned the collection and reprinting of an immense library of classical works in over 36,000 volumes. But his support for learning was marred by the destruction of more than 2,300 books that he thought were seditious or unorthodox.

Ch'ien Lung was, of all Chinese emperors, probably the greatest patron of art. He built up in the imperial palace a stupendous collection of paintings and other works of art from all past periods as well as his own. Most of it is still intact. Ch'ien Lung also spent huge sums on refurbishing, embellishing, and adding to the imperial buildings inherited from the Ming.

Militarily, too, he was an aggressive and able leader. Despite Kang Hsi's expeditions, the Mongols had remained troublesome. Ch'ien Lung completely and permanently destroyed their power in a series of campaigns in the 1750s, after which he reincorporated the whole of Sinkiang into the empire. A revolt in Tibet shortly afterward led to a Ch'ing occupation that fixed Chinese control there even more tightly. Punitive expeditions were launched against Nepal, northern Burma, and northern Vietnam to compel tributary acknowledgment of Chinese overlordship.

Until the 1780s Ch'ien Lung, like the men who preceded him on the Dragon Throne, dealt personally with an immense mass of official documents and wrote his own comments on them. One of the Grand Council secretaries remarked in wonder at his diligence: "Ten or more of my comrades would take turns every five or six days on early morning duty, and even so would feel fatigued. How did the Emperor do it day after day?"[2] But as Ch'ien Lung grew older, he became more enamored of luxury and surrounded himself with yes-men. In old age he left matters of state increasingly in the hands of his favorites. His chief favorite, the unscrupulous courtier Ho-shen (Heshen), entered the palace in 1775 as a handsome young bodyguard of 25 and, becoming grand councillor within a year, built up a clique of corrupt henchmen and plundered the empire. At his fall after

Ch'ing glory: the Altar of Heaven, just outside the Forbidden City in Peking, originally a Ming structure but rebuilt by the Ch'ing. Here the emperor conducted annual rites to intercede with Heaven for good harvests. The temple roofs are covered with magnificent colored and glazed tiles. [Marburg/Photo Resource]

Ch'ien Lung's death, the private wealth Ho-shen had extorted was said to be worth the equivalent of $1.5 billion, an almost inconceivable sum for that time and probably a world record for corrupt officials. He concentrated all power in his own hands, holding as many as 20 different positions simultaneously. He betrothed his son to the emperor's daughter and clearly intended to take over the dynasty.

Ho-shen's rise was symptomatic not only of Ch'ien Lung's growing senility but also of the deterioration of the administrative system as a whole. The army, too, was neglected. A major rebellion by the White Lotus sect (see Chapter 21) erupted in 1796. The rebels were finally put down only after Ho-shen's fall, by the new emperor, Chia Ch'ing (Jia Qing). In 1799 he moved quickly against Ho-shen, stripping him of his power and wealth.

Ho-shen's career illustrates the importance of personal connections in imperial China (and to some degree in China now), despite the merit system of examinations. Corruption, connections, and nepotism (favoring one's relatives) were aspects of China, and of Asia generally, that westerners criticized as more widespread than in their own political and economic systems. Westerners were at least embarrassed by it at home; Asians supported it as proper. Family loyalties and the ties of friendship were valued as the highest goods. Anyone with wealth or power who did not use it to help relatives and friends was considered morally deficient. The family was the basic cement of society and with its support system of mutual aid was regarded as a microcosm of the empire as a whole, in which the emperor was seen as the nurturing father of his people as well as his officials. The connections of friendship were also part of the Confucian-sanctified "five relationships" (see Chapter 7) and took precedence over other considerations. In addition, political office was relatively poorly paid, and it was expected that officials would use their position to provide for their families and friends by diverting funds or receiving "presents." People of rank were expected to live well, in keeping with the dignity of their position. Even now one hears repeated the traditional saying, "Become an official and get rich." Ho-shen was only the most extreme example of a normal practice that was grossly abused.

The Later Ch'ing: Symptoms of Decline

By the 1750s the Ch'ing dynasty was already well into its second century. The eighteenth century saw the pinnacle of its glory, prosperity, and harmony, but even before the death of Ch'ien Lung, decline had begun. Prosperity remained widespread, accompanied by a major output of art and literature. This included new popular novels such as *The Dream of the Red Chamber* (also known as *Story of the Stone*), which prophetically dealt with the decline and degeneracy of a once great family and is still widely read.

Part of the government's problem was the failure of its officialdom to keep pace with the growth in population. Despite the rapid increase in overall numbers, there was only a small increase in the number of official posts, perhaps 25 percent versus a 200 to 300 percent boost in the population as a whole. This had an obviously negative effect on both governmental effectiveness and morale. A prestigious career in the bureaucracy, once a reasonable ambition for able scholars, became harder and harder to realize. At the same time, the imperial examinations became still more rigidified exercises in old-fashioned orthodoxy and the memorization of traditional texts. These were to be commented on in the infamous eight-legged essays (see Chapter 21), allowing no scope for imagination or initiative. "Men of talent," as the best of the scholar-gentry had been called since the Han period, were often weeded out by this process. The examination failure rate climbed rapidly, and only students who lacked or suppressed all creativity could hope to pass.

Disappointed examination candidates and others who passed but were not called to office became a larger and larger group of alienated intellectuals. Paradoxically, the problem was only made worse by the earlier Ch'ing efforts to expand education and to open it to larger sections of the population. Learning had always been the key to advancement. Now, however, it was far from necessarily so. The system had hardened just when flexibility was most needed. Instead of preserving the Great Harmony, it bred discontent. One result was new corruption. Degrees, once attainable only by examination, and occasionally even offices, began to be sold. Failed candidates and disappointed office seekers provided the leadership for dissident and ultimately rebellious groups, whose numbers increased rapidly after 1785.

The lack of firm leadership and virtuous example, under Ho-shen and again after the death of Emperor Chia Ch'ing in 1820, aggravated the burdens of overworked officials. A magistrate of the Sung dynasty 500 years earlier had been responsible for an average of about 80,000 people in his county. By the end of the eighteenth century the average county, still administered by a single magistrate and his staff, numbered about 250,000; many were larger, and the average rose to about 300,000 in the nineteenth century. Local gentry, landlords, merchant guilds, and sometimes dissident or even criminal groups began to fill the vacuum. This led to a revival of anti-Manchu sentiment, for the Ch'ing was, after all, an alien dynasty of conquest.

The most basic and intractable problem the dynasty faced was a product of its own earlier success. By the last quarter of the eighteenth century, population growth had probably outrun increases in production. Per capita incomes stabilized and then began slowly to fall. The poorest areas suffered first, and local banditry started to rise. By the end of the century open rebellions were breaking out. The secret society of the White Lotus, revived from a long quiescence, reemerged in a major uprising in 1796. Its reappearance tended to suggest to many Chinese that once again the ruling dynasty was perhaps losing the Mandate of Heaven. The secret and semi-Buddhist rituals of the White Lotus and its promise to overthrow the Ch'ing attracted many followers, including distressed peasants. Until 1804 the rebels defied the imperial army from mountain strongholds in the upper Yangtze valley along the borders of three provinces. The enormous expense of suppressing the White Lotus bled the treasury and fed corruption in the military. The unnecessarily long campaign also revealed the decline in the effectiveness of the army, which ultimately prevailed only with the help of some 300,000 local militiamen.

New Barbarian Pressures: The Westerners

Despite these mounting problems, China was still able to awe westerners, who now appeared in unprecedented numbers and who tried to deal with the Dragon Throne as an equal and to obtain trading privileges. Like all foreigners, they had from the beginning been fitted into the tributary system, the traditional Chinese way of dealing with outsiders. At Canton, the only port where westerners were permitted to trade, they could stay only for the trading season of about six months and were forbidden to bring in firearms and women, to enter the city proper, or to trade elsewhere on the China coast. They were obliged to deal only with the official monopoly that controlled all foreign trade, a restraint that they found galling in view of the huge potential market that China represented. Westerners were seen as potential troublemakers and perverters of Chinese morality. They should, it was felt, be kept on the fringes of the empire and walled off from normal contact with its people.

Various attempts by the British and the Dutch to trade elsewhere or with other merchants were rebuffed. In 1755 the English trader James Flint had sailed into several ports north of Canton, including Shanghai and Tientsin (Tianjin), in an effort to establish trade there. He was jailed and then deported, but the emperor ordered execution for the Chinese who had served as his interpreter and scribe. By the 1790s the restrictions at Canton seemed intolerable, especially to the British, then in their own view the greatest mercantile and naval power in the world and tired of being treated like minor savages.

In 1793 Britain's King George III sent an embassy to Ch'ien Lung led by a British nobleman, Viscount Macartney, to request wider trading rights and to establish relations with China as an equal power. He brought with him samples of British manufactures as presents to convince the Chinese of the benefits of trade with the West; these articles were not yet refined enough to impress the Chinese, though they included samples of the contemporary pottery of Josiah Wedgwood—hardly likely to appeal to the inventors of porcelain. The Chinese could still make most of the things Macartney brought better and cheaper and saw no need for British goods. The mission was a comedy of errors on both sides, since both were still profoundly ignorant of each other and lacked any standard of comparison. The Chinese interpreted the visit and the presents as a standard tribute mission, although from an especially distant and hence backward group of people, too far from China to have picked up any civilization. Chinese politeness obliged them to accept the presents, but with the kind of tolerance a kindly parent might display for the work of children.

The Chinese expected Macartney to perform the *k'e t'ou* (kowtow), or ritual submission, as all tribute missions did, before the Son of Heaven. Macartney, a typical Georgian aristocrat in his satin knee breeches who also suffered from gout, refused. He offered instead to bend one knee slightly, as he would to his own sovereign. Macartney further offended his hosts by pompously saying that he was "sure the Chinese would see that superiority which Englishmen, wherever they go, cannot conceal." One can almost hear him saying it! As a result, he never had a real audience with Ch'ien Lung, although he was kept waiting in Peking for over a month. Instead Ch'ien Lung sent him a letter for George III that was a masterpiece of crushing condescension:

> I have already noted your respectful spirit of submission. . . . I do not forget the lonely remoteness of your island, cut off from the world by intervening wastes of sea. . . . [But] our Celestial Empire possesses all things in abundance. We have no need for barbarian products.[3]

One can imagine the reaction of George III and Macartney.

In 1793 it was still possible for China to get away with such haughty behavior, and it was true that China was happily self-sufficient. A Dutch embassy of 1795 that also asked for better trade conditions was similarly rejected, even though the Dutch, perhaps less concerned with power or dignity than with profits, vigorously performed the kowtow several times as they lined up at court with other representatives from other countries sending tributary missions. A later British embassy under Lord Amherst in 1816 had a similarly humiliating experience. Amherst had the bad luck to turn up just when the British in India were fighting the Gurkhas of Nepal, a Chinese tributary since 1792, and was ordered out of the country by the emperor without an audience.

Nevertheless, the accounts of China given by members of the Macartney and Amherst parties as they traveled south from Peking to Canton, nursing their rage at the way they had been treated, were still strongly positive. They found China prosperous, orderly, and agriculturally productive, with an immense commerce and numerous large cities. Here are a few samples from the diary kept by a member of the Amherst mission in 1816:

Tranquility seemed to prevail, nothing but contentment and good humor. . . . It is remarkable that in so populous a country there should be so little begging. . . . Contentment and the enjoyment of the necessities of life [suggest that] the government cannot be a very bad one. . . . The lower orders of Chinese seem to me more neat and clean than any Europeans of the same class. . . . Even torn, soiled, or threadbare clothing is uncommon. . . . All the military stations are neatly whitewashed and painted and kept in perfect repair, and instead of mud cabins the houses of peasants are built in a neat manner with brick. The temples are also handsome and numerous.[4]

Stagnation and Vulnerability

China may have declined from its eighteenth-century peak, but it was far from collapse. Although the emperors after Ch'ien Lung fell short of his level of brilliance, they were conscientious and honest. The corruption that had marred Ch'ien Lung's last years was greatly reduced, his scheming favorites were disposed of, and a renewed atmosphere of responsibility and service was established. The official salt monopoly, which had become semiparalyzed by corruption, was totally reformed in the 1830s. This was one indication that the imperial bureaucracy still had resilience and the power to correct weaknesses.

At its best Ch'ing art remained magnificent, although much of later Ch'ing painting, decoration, and ceramics lacked originality and toward the end became overly ornate. Like much of the scholarship and philosophy of the time, it was technically accomplished but without the exuberance or imagination of earlier periods. Urban culture continued to thrive as merchant wealth was more widely diffused and city dwellers could read the new vernacular literature, enjoy the art of the time, and attend popular plays. China remained a sophisticated society as well as a prosperous one, still generally confident, even complacent. Imperial slights to barbarian upstarts like the British were in keeping with what most Chinese thought.

Yet the state really had no adequate long-run means to respond to the relentless pressures of increasing population. Decline was slow at first. China was immense, and its society and economy, largely independent of state management except for the official monopolies, took time to decay. Signs of trouble here and there did

not mean that the whole system was rotten—not yet. Nor did governmental or military inefficiency or corruption among some officials mean that the whole administration was in trouble. Most of the Chinese world was only indirectly affected by the political sphere and continued to flourish after political decay was far advanced. Government was a thin layer on top of traditional controls.

Both foreign and Chinese critics were often misled by signs of administrative weakness into concluding that the whole country was falling apart. But the basic problem of growing rural poverty, especially after 1850, remained as population continued to rise faster than production. Traditional agricultural technology had reached its limit of productivity, and all usable land had been pressed into cultivation. Only new technology could break this jam. Chinese agriculture, only a century before the most advanced in the world, was now rapidly falling behind the West's but showed no readiness to adapt. There was little interest in the now superior technology of Europe and especially not in the disruption that would inevitably have accompanied its spread. China continued to protect itself against any ideas or innovations of foreign origin that might disrupt traditional ways. A different sort of response might have come from a new and vigorous dynasty, but the Ch'ing was now old, rigid, and fearful of change. Always sensitive about their alien origins, they feared to depart in any way from their self-appointed role as the guardians of the ancient Chinese way in all things.

The growing wealth of commercial elites did not fuel other kinds of growth or change, as it did in Europe. Individual or family wealth came not so much from increasing production as from acquiring a greater share of what already existed, through official connections or through managing the state monopolies. Merchants and their guilds never became an independent group of entrepreneurs or sought to change the system to their advantage, as their European counterparts did. In the Chinese view, they prospered by working within the existing system and had few incentives to alter it. For long-term investment, land was the preferred option since it was secure and offered social prestige as well. Capital earned in trade went into land, moneylending at usurious rates, or luxurious living but rarely into manufacturing or new technology.

Leisure and gracious living in gentry style were more valued in China than in the modern West, and there was less interest in further accumulation for its own sake. The gentry and the scholar-officials dominated Ch'ing China as they had since at least the Han dynasty, leaving little separate scope for merchants, who were still looked down on as parasites and who depended on their gentry or official connections to succeed. They neither could nor wished to challenge the Confucian bureaucracy but were content to use it for their own ends. All of this

◉ Omens of Crisis ◉

For all his pompousness and the failure of his mission, Viscount Macart-
ney was an astute observer. Though he was impressed by China's pro-
ductivity and its well-ordered society, he accurately saw political trou-
ble ahead.

The empire of China is an old first-rate man of war, which a succession of vigilant officers has continued to keep afloat for these 150 years past, and have overawed their neighbors merely by her bulk and appearance. [Here, of course, he spoke also from his own humiliating experience.] But whenever an insufficient man happens to have command on deck, adieu to the discipline and safety of the ship. She may perhaps not sink outright; she may drift for a time as a wreck, and then be dashed to pieces on the shore; but she can never be rebuilt on the old bottom.

But the economy continued to flourish well into the nineteenth century.
Here is part of the account of a French traveling priest, the Abbé Huc,
written in 1850.

European productions will never have a very extensive market in China. . . . China is a country so vast, so rich, so varied that its internal trade alone would suffice abundantly to occupy that part of the nation which can be devoted to mercantile operations. . . . Foreign commerce cannot offer them any article of primary necessity which they do not already produce themselves, nor even of any real utility, and they would see it stopped altogether . . . with a certain feeling of satisfaction.

Sources: J. L. Cranmer-Byng, ed., *An Embassy to China* (London: Longman, 1962), pp. 212–213; E. R. Huc, *The Chinese Empire* (London: Longman, 1855), p. 365.

discouraged or prevented the rise of private capitalism and the kinds of new enterprise and investment that were basic to the commercial and industrial revolutions in the modern West.

Until the eighteenth century China had been in most respects the world's most technically advanced society. Iron-chain suspension bridges, canal locks, mechanical threshers, water-powered mills, looms, clocks, and the basic technology of the motor—crankshaft, connecting rods, and piston rods for converting rotary to longitudinal motion and back—all originated in China and were still spreading under the Ch'ing. But Chinese accomplishments, like those of earlier periods, were primarily a catalog of cumulative empirical discoveries rather than the result of systematic or sustained scientific inquiry. Confucianism offered little scope for abstract theorizing or empirical investigation. Learning concentrated on the Confucian classics and on records of the past as the proper guide for the present and the future.

The tradition of the learned man as a gentleman also created a deep division between those who "labored with their minds," as Mencius put it, and those who worked with their hands. Chinese artisans were highly skilled and ingenious but rarely engaged in theory or experiments, and most were not even literate. Scholars regarded all manual work, even experimental work, as beneath them, whereas the joining of theory, design, experiment, and practice from the time of Leonardo da Vinci produced the achievements of modern science and technology in the West. No such fusion occurred in China, which rested on its already high level of development.

It seems easier to understand why China did not become capitalistic or move on from its early achievements in science and technology than to understand why Europe did. The abrupt break with its own past that the transformation of the modern West involved and the explosion of modern science are harder to explain. China remained sufficiently successful not to seek or require such fundamental change. To a poorer and less developed Europe, change was more compelling, as the means to "progress." By the nineteenth century, however, China had fallen critically behind the resurgent West and was ruled by a dynasty old in office and suffering from complacency and loss of efficiency. The weakened government faced a population bigger than ever before and now sliding into economic distress, as well as a threat posed by militant westerners. Neither was adequately dealt with.

Corruption is endemic in all systems; its seriousness is only a matter of degree. As the nineteenth century wore on, corruption in China became a growing cancer sapping the vigor of the whole country. Confucian morality began to yield to an attitude of "devil take the hindmost." People and families with connections had their lands and fortunes removed from the tax rolls, as in the last century of all previous dynasties. This put a heavier burden on the decreasing number who had to provide the state's revenue, mainly peasants. The strain on their already marginal position led many of them into banditry and rebellion. In all of these respects, late Ch'ing China was especially unprepared to meet the challenge of an aggressive, industrializing West. It was hard also to readjust Chinese perspectives, which had always seen the landward frontiers as the major area of threat. China was slow to recognize that external danger now came from the sea and along the coast.

The Opium Wars

China's resources, and those of the economy as a whole, were also depleted by a reversal of the earlier flow of silver that accounted for its favorable export balance. Exports of tea, silks, porcelain, and other wares continued, but imports of opium rose dramatically after 1810, mostly from India, where the English East India Company encouraged its cultivation as a cash crop for exchange on the Chinese market. By the 1820s opium imports exceeded China's total exports in value, and a river of silver flowed out, disrupting the economy.

Opium had been imported from Persia and was later grown in China for many centuries. It was widely used medically, but it began to be smoked as a recreational drug on a large scale in the late eighteenth century. Chinese addicts and their merchants and middlemen created the booming market for imported opium, which was thought to be superior to the domestic variety. No foreign pressure was necessary to encourage its use.

Although the imperial government declared opium smoking and traffic a capital offense, the profits of the trade were high, and the ban was ineffective. Westerners, including American as well as European traders, delivered opium to Chinese smugglers on the coast, who distributed it throughout the country through a vast network of dealers. Most of the fortunes won by early American traders to China rested on opium. Its growing use in China was a symptom both of the growing despair of

the disadvantaged and of the degeneracy of a once proud and vigorous system, including many of its now self-indulgent upper classes.

Meanwhile, opium provided the occasion for the first Anglo-Chinese war of 1839–1842, popularly called the Opium War. Nearly 50 years had passed since Ch'ien Lung's rebuff of Macartney and his trade requests. Opium was the immediate issue that sparked the outbreak of hostilities, but much larger matters were involved. British patience was wearing thin; the British wanted freer access to the huge Chinese market as well as diplomatic recognition, as equals, by its government. They saw China as out of step with a modern world where free trade and regular diplomatic relations were the common ground of all "civilized" nations. China's resistance to such demands was taken as proof of its backwardness, and as India had been brought under the blessings of Western civilization, now, they thought, it was China's turn. China's arrogance toward the West was now matched by the West's toward China.

In 1839 the Chinese sent an imperial commissioner, Lin Tse-hsu (Lin Zexu), to Canton to stop the traffic in opium. Lin ordered stocks of the drug destroyed as contraband. The British regarded their lawful property as having been taken and used the incident as a pretext to declare war. A small mobile force sent mainly from India soon destroyed the antiquated Chinese navy, shore batteries, and coastal forces. With the arrival of reinforcements it attacked Canton, occupied Shanghai and other ports northward on the coast, and sailed up the Yangtze River to Nanking (Nanjing) to force the Chinese government to grant what the British wanted. Because of distances, supply problems, and the stubbornness of the Chinese government, the war dragged on fitfully for more than three years. Each encounter ended in a Chinese rout that demonstrated the overwhelming superiority of Western military technology. The Chinese finally capitulated in the Treaty of Nanking (1842). Signed on board a British naval vessel, the agreement was the first in a long series that the Chinese came to call "the unequal treaties." Western imperialism had come to China.

Reunification and the Tokugawa Shogunate in Japan

Late medieval Japan under the Ashikaga shogunate had been marked by the rise of regional feudal lords and their armies, as summarized in Chapter 12. Ashikaga rule from Kyoto became increasingly ineffective in the sixteenth century. Although the shogunate had never

The Opium War: the British steam-powered paddle wheeler *Nemesis* destroying a Chinese fleet in a battle on January 7, 1841, near Canton. The *Nemesis* was one of the first iron-hulled steam vessels. It was designed with a shallow drft so that it could attack inland shipping. Its guns had far greater range and accuracy than those of Chinese ships or shore batteries, and its name as well as its devastatingly easy success made it a symbol of Western naval and military ascendancy. [BBC Hulton/Bettmann Archive]

been in control of more than central Japan, even areas beyond the immediate vicinity of Kyoto became more and more independent under their own daimyo (feudal lords), each with an army of samurai based in impressive fortified castles. Fighting between such armies became chronic, and with the final collapse of the Ashikaga shogunate in 1573, Japan dissolved into civil war.

Japan was still a small, poor, relatively backward country on the edge of the major Asian stage, divided among warring clans. The settled area of the country was only a fraction of the whole, and its total population was about 15 million, the size of a single Chinese province. The refined court and urban culture of Kyoto was luxurious, and technologically Ashikaga Japan had made much progress, even surpassing China in such fields as steelmaking and the production of fine swords.

Trade with the rest of East Asia was extensive, and Japanese shipping by the fifteenth century dominated the East China Sea. Japan's relatively small size and population and its weak central government worked to its advantage in this respect, making it easier to develop a national commercial system and a strong and semi-independent merchant class, unlike China or India. Foreign trade was proportionately more important than in China or India, more nearly on the scale of European countries. Most rural areas, by contrast, were isolated and lagged culturally and economically behind the urban centers. The political chaos of the late sixteenth century tore Japan apart once more, but it was to emerge from its troubles to find a new national unity.

The rising power of the daimyo destroyed the Ashikaga. The continued growth of their feudal domains, each more and more like a state in miniature, needed only common leadership to turn Japan into a national political unit. That was essentially the nature of the Tokugawa regime. The Tokugawa founders started out as

MANCHU CHINA AND TOKUGAWA JAPAN

China	Japan
	Oda Nobunaga (1568–1582)
	Toyotomi Hideyoshi (1582–1598)
	Beginning of Tokugawa shogunate (1600)
	Tokugawa Ieyasu (1600–1616)
	Expulsion of last westerners (1638)
Manchu rule begins (1644)	
Kang Hsi (1661–1722)	
Ch'ien Lung (1735–1796)	Hokusai, artist (1760–1849)
Macartney mission (1793)	
White Lotus rebellion (1796)	
First Opium War (1839–1842)	
	Perry in Tokyo Bay (1853)
	"Unequal Treaties" (1854–1858)
	End of Tokugawa shogunate (1869)

daimyo like any of the others. Over about a generation a series of three exceptionally able leaders progressively conquered all their daimyo rivals and superimposed their dominance on an essentially unchanged feudal order. The subject daimyo were given substantial authority in their areas in return for formal submission to the Tokugawa shogun and periodic attendance at his court. Tokugawa central authority was far stronger and extended over a much larger area than any government in previous Japanese history. Despite its feudal trappings, it was in many respects in a class with the emerging national states of contemporary Europe. Samurai served not only as military officers but also as administrators. The flourishing merchant group provided revenue to add to land or agricultural taxes and also transported troops and supplies.

The Era of the Warlords

The process of unification began even before the formal end of the Ashikaga shogunate when Oda Nobunaga (1534–1582),* a powerful daimyo who ruled the area around Nagoya, seized Kyoto in 1568 and became supreme in central Japan. He later captured the great temple-castle of Osaka, until then the independent seat of the militant Shin Buddhist sect. Nobunaga was murdered by a vassal in 1582, but his place was assumed by

---

*Japanese names, like Chinese names, are customarily given with surname or family name first and personal name second. Somewhat inconsistently, however, Nobunaga, Hideyoshi, and Ieyasu are commonly referred to by their personal names only.

This daimyo castle in Nagoya is a typical example of the fortresses built during the last troubled decades of the Ashikaga dynasty and in the early Tokugawa period by local lords who were then conquered by or swore allegiance to the Tokugawa shogunate. The massive wall was surrounded by a moat. Such castles could usually be taken only after a long siege leading to the surrender of the starving defenders. [Wim Swann]

29.2 Tokugawa Japan

his chief general, Toyotomi Hideyoshi (1536–1598), born a peasant, who rose to the top through his ability and driving ambition. Hideyoshi soon eliminated the remaining faction of Nobunaga's family, subdued its vassals, and rebuilt the castle at Osaka as the base of his military government. In a campaign westward, he crushed the Satsuma clan on the island of Kyushu. In 1590 all of eastern and northern Honshu submitted to him after he had defeated the chief daimyo in the Edo (Tokyo) area. Hideyoshi scorned the title of shogun (the emperor's military adviser) and ruled instead as a dictator, although warlord is probably a more appropriate title.

With a large and unified army of professional fighters, Hideyoshi now looked abroad for more worlds to conquer. China was an obvious target, but to reach it he needed passage through Korea. When this was refused, he invaded Korea in 1592 and made rapid progress until a joint Korean and Chinese army forced him back almost to the coast.

Hideyoshi's death in 1598 ended this wasteful and destructive adventure, and his troops welcomed the chance to return home. His place was soon taken by one of his leading vassals, Tokugawa Ieyasu (1542–1616). Ieyasu had already built a castle-headquarters at Edo, where he had served as Hideyoshi's deputy. In 1600 he won a great victory in the battle of Sekigahara, near Nagoya, over a coalition of rivals. This established his power as Hideyoshi's successor, and he solidified it by capturing Osaka Castle in 1615.

Tokugawa Rule

Ieyasu wanted to build a strong, centrally controlled political system. He and his able Tokugawa successors largely achieved this, creating stability and peace for the next 250 years. They did so by enforcing a set of rigid controls on society as well as on political behavior and by repressing change. Tokugawa feudalism was even more hidebound than that of earlier eras, and the shoguns also tried to control dangerous thought with the help of a fearsomely efficient secret police. They themselves administered the central core of the country, from the Edo area to Kyoto, Osaka, and the peninsula south of Osaka, placing members of their own clan in the key centers of Mito, Nagoya, and Wakayama. This was, then as now, the economic heart of Japan, containing most of its best farmland and most of the commercial towns and cities. Other loyal allies and early supporters of Ieyasu were given fiefs in the rest of this central area. Beyond it, to the north and to the west, the Tokugawa bound other daimyo to them by feudal ties, helping ensure their loyalty by requiring them to leave members of their own families, including wives and sons, in Edo as hostages. Daimyo were required to keep a permanent residence in Edo and to alternate their time between attendance at court and service in their distant fiefs, but armies were not permitted to leave their fiefs. The expenses of this required travel, with their retinues, and of maintaining two residences, which were often luxurious, put the daimyo increasingly in debt to merchants, whose unofficial power thus slowly increased.

A close eye was kept on the construction or repair of daimyo castles to keep them from becoming potential bases for rival military power, as they had been in earlier centuries. The shogunate created a new group of officials who acted as censors, on the Chinese pattern, and the secret police watched for any threats to Tokugawa rule. At Edo a new castle was built as the shogun's headquarters, a vast fortress inside massive walls and moats arranged in a series of concentric rings about 2 miles across. The innermost ring, with its moat and walls, remains as the imperial palace in the center of downtown Tokyo today. The emperor was left in place with his court at Kyoto, and the ancient fiction of imperial divinity

◉ Hideyoshi Writes to His Wife ◉

Hideyoshi wrote to his wife while he was besieging a daimyo castle in the spring of 1590.

Now we have got the enemy like birds in a cage, and there is no danger, so please set your mind at rest. I long for the Young Lord [his son], but I feel that for the sake of the future, and because I want to have the country at peace, I must give up my longing. So please set your mind at rest. I am looking after my health. . . . There is nothing to worry about. . . . Since as I have thus declared it will be a long siege, I wish to send for Yodo [his concubine]. I wish you to tell her and make arrangements for her journey, and tell her that next to you she is the one who pleases me best. . . . I was very glad to get your messages. We have got up to within two or three hundred yards and put a double ditch around the castle and shall not let a single man escape. All the men of the eight eastern provinces are shut up inside. . . . Though I am getting old, I must think of the future and do what is best for the country. So now I mean to do glorious deeds and I am ready for a long siege, with provisions and gold and silver in plenty, so as to return in triumph and leave a great name behind me. I desire you to understand this and to tell it to everybody.

Source: G. B. Sansom, *Japan: A Short Cultural History,* rev. ed. (New York: Appleton-Century-Crofts, 1962), p. 410.

and supremacy was preserved. Technically, the shogun was only the emperor's military chief of staff; in reality, he was the acknowledged ruler of the country.

By the time Ieyasu died in 1616, having prudently transferred power to his son so as to avoid a dispute over the succession, the new feudal order was firmly established. It is called feudal because it preserved many feudal forms, but the new central authority of the Tokugawa makes the label only partly appropriate. A new post of prime minister was created, assisted by a council of state, in part to ensure that the system would not weaken or collapse under a less effective shogun. In time a rela-

The procession of a daimyo and his retainers along their journey from his local domains to take up required residence at Edo. [Marburg/Photo Resource]

tively complex central administration grew up, with posts filled first largely by able members of the Tokugawa clan or from the families of loyal daimyo and later from the expanding gentry class in the central area.

Merchant groups and other commoners had begun to acquire new power and even some independence as Ashikaga rule deteriorated. Large-scale trade centered in the Osaka area. The neighboring commercial center of Sakai, now part of greater Osaka, was actually a self-governing city run by merchants with their own army, like a Renaissance city-state in Italy. The Tokugawa suppressed the rising political power of the middle and lower classes as a threat to their authority. Merchants were restricted and supervised in their activities and were made subservient to the new aristocratic order. Sakai's walls were demolished, its armies were dissolved, and its government was absorbed into the Tokugawa system.

The same order was brought into the countryside. Peasants were made to surrender their swords and other weapons to the government, and the hereditary warrior class of samurai was left in complete charge of military affairs. Swords became the badge of the samurai and came to symbolize their dual role as "gentlemen warriors" and as administrators. Firearms, which the Japanese knew of both from the Chinese and from the Portuguese and Dutch, were also seen as potentially disruptive. They too were successfully outlawed, and Japan remained free of them for the more than two centuries when foreigners were also banned. Swords became even more an exclusive hallmark of the aristocracy, not easily challenged by unarmed peasants. In isolation from the world, Japan prolonged a medieval technology and the social system that went with it.

Peasants and artisans were essential producers, but merchants, despite their obvious accomplishments, literacy, cultivation, and wealth, were regarded as parasites and put into the lowest social order of all. This reflected classic Confucian values, revived by the Tokugawa, which admirably suited their feudal and hierarchical system. Merchants were forbidden to wear the fine clothes or materials of the upper classes, to ride in sedan chairs, or to omit the groveling and subservient bowing also required of peasants and artisans to samurai or other aristocrats whom they encountered. Those who did not bow low enough might have their heads chopped off by samurai guards.

The Expulsion of Foreigners

The Portuguese had reached Japan by 1543, and for nearly a century they and later the Spanish and the Dutch carried on an extensive export and import trade. Catholic missionaries came too and made numerous converts. Japan was more curious about westerners than China was, having long understood the value of learning from others. But the Tokugawa grew irritated by the factional bickering among the different missionary orders and the allegiance converts had to give to a distant and alien pope. The foreigners and their intrigues were disturbing to the smooth order the Tokugawa had worked so hard to establish. In the years after Ieyasu's death in 1616, all missionaries were killed or expelled and converts executed or forced to recant. The persecution culminated in the suppression of a rebellion by impoverished Christian peasants in the area of Nagasaki, which had been the chief trade port for westerners, in 1638. The survivors were slaughtered and thousands were crucified, but a few escaped and kept Christianity

◉ Tokugawa Ieyasu: ◉
Instructions to His Successors

Tokugawa Ieyasu was a careful planner, a good judge of men, and one who understood the virtue of patient waiting until the time was right for action. Here is one of the instructions he left to his successors.

The strong manly ones in life are those who understand the meaning of the word patience. Patience means restraining one's inclinations. There are seven emotions: joy, anger, anxiety, love, grief, fear, and hate, and if a man does not give way to these he can be called patient. I am not as strong as I might be, but I have long known and practiced patience. And if my descendants wish to be as I am, they must study patience.

Source: A. L. Sadler, *The Maker of Modern Japan* (London: Allen & Unwin, 1937), pp. 389–390.

alive on an underground basis until the reappearance of Western missionaries in the 1860s.

All Western merchants were expelled by 1638, and Portuguese envoys who came in 1640 to ask for a re-opening of trade relations were executed. Japanese were forbidden to go abroad, and no ships capable of overseas trade were built. In order not to lose complete touch with what was happening in the rest of the world, one or two Dutch ships a year were permitted to come for trade, on the island of Deshima in Nagasaki harbor, remote from the main centers of Japanese population.

Culture and Nationalism

With such an array of controls over people's lives, the Tokugawa did indeed ensure peace and stability. For about two centuries they also largely succeeded in re-tarding most change, especially in social or political mat-ters. Japan was still a relatively poor country, and there were periodic peasant rebellions and urban revolts as expressions of economic distress, but they were easily put down. Economically, however, Japan continued to develop, now, under the long Tokugawa peace, more rapidly than ever before. Production and internal trade grew, and with it, despite their low status in Tokugawa society, an expanding merchant class. A truly national market developed for many basic commodities, aided by the use of a system of paper credit. None of this fit well with the formally feudal arrangement of the social and political systems, and in the long run it had the same disruptive effects on Japanese feudalism as the revival of trade, towns, and merchants had in late medieval Eu-rope. As rich merchants began to lend money to needy or extravagant noblemen and then to marry their daugh-ters, they could no longer be treated as beneath the no-tice of daimyo and samurai. The cultural life of Toku-gawa Japan was largely urban, and merchants came to dominate it as a new bourgeoisie.

The amusement quarters in the cities, especially Edo, were patronized mainly by merchants and by occasional samurai who sought relaxation from the stiff conven-tions of aristocratic society. This was the great age of the geisha, women carefully trained to cater to a male clientele as entertainers who specialized in singing, dancing, lively conversation for male patrons, and some-times sex. Artists and novelists loved to depict geisha scenes, which became a distinct genre of refined eroticism.

The arts, too, produced relief from a highly conven-tionalized society. These included popular puppet plays and, from the seventeenth century, a new dramatic form, Kabuki, which is still popular in Japan. Kabuki catered to less refined tastes than the classical Noh theater and

emphasized realism, comedy, and melodrama. Classical poetry, based on Chinese models, was reduced to three- or four-line miniatures, the haiku, which at their best were superb snapshots of a moment of thought or feel-ing. Painting became more flamboyant, colorful, and grand, but still in keeping with the remarkable Japanese sense of good taste. Magnificent decorated screens and wall panels were produced for the palaces of the shogun and of noblemen, who wore gorgeous silk brocades and furnished their tables with beautiful lacquer ware and porcelain. In time, much of this splendor could also be found in the houses of rich merchants, but popular art became more important, and commoners' houses were more often decorated with woodblock prints. This is probably still the Japanese art best known abroad; it reached the climax of its development in the work of

Tokugawa splendor: a view of the main audience hall at Nijo Castle, Kyoto. The superb screen paintings, beautifully set off by the plain tatami (rush mat) floor, are fine examples of early Tokugawa decorative art for the elite. [Anne Kirkup]

◎ Japanese Women: An Outsider's View ◎

From the early accounts of the Dutch at Deshima, some American authors in 1841 compiled this account of the state of women in Japan.

The position of women in Japan is apparently unlike that of the sex in all other parts of the East, and approaches more nearly their European condition. The Japanese women are subjected to no jealous seclusion, hold a fair station in society, and share in all the innocent recreations of their fathers and husbands. The minds of the women are cultivated with as much care as those of men; and amongst the most admired Japanese historians, moralists, and poets are found several female names. The Japanese ladies are described as being generally lively and agreeable companions, and the ease and elegance of their manners have been highly extolled. But, though permitted thus to enjoy and adorn society, they are, on the other hand, during their whole lives, kept in a state of tutelage: that is, of complete dependence on their husbands, sons, or other relatives. They have no legal rights, and their evidence is not admitted in a court of justice. Not only may the husband introduce as many unwedded helpmates as he pleases into the mansion over which his wife presides but he also has the power of divorce, which may be considered unlimited, since he is restrained only by considerations of expediency. The Japanese husband, however, is obliged to support his repudiated wife according to his own station, unless he can allege grounds for the divorce satisfactory to the proper tribunal; among which, the misfortune of being without children takes from the unhappy wife all claim to maintenance. Under no circumstances whatever can a wife demand to be separated from her husband. At home, the wife is the mistress of the family; but in other respects she is treated rather as a toy for her husband's amusement, than as the rational, confidential partner of his life. She is expected to please him by her accomplishments, and to cheer him with her lively conversation, but never suffered to share his more serious thoughts, or to relieve by participation his anxieties and cares. She is, indeed, kept in profound ignorance of his business affairs; and so much as a question from her in relation to them would be resented as an act of unpardonable presumption.

Source: P. F. Siebold, *Manners and Customs of the Japanese in the Nineteenth Century* (London: Murray, 1852), pp. 122–124.

Hokusai and Hiroshige in the last decades of the Tokugawa regime early in the nineteenth century.

A good deal of information about the outside world continued to filter in by way of the Dutch at Nagasaki, including Western advances in medicine, shipbuilding, and metalworking. A few Japanese scholars began to study Western science; they compared Dutch texts on anatomy with traditional Chinese medical texts, for example, and through their own dissection of the corpses of executed criminals, demonstrated as early as 1771 that the Dutch version was accurate, whereas the Chinese was not. The Chinese rejected dissection, taboo in light of Confucian respect for the body. The Japanese also acquired a new national consciousness, thanks to the Tokugawa unification. They were able to adopt ideas and techniques from foreign sources, as they had long done from China, without in any way diluting their own cultural and national identity. Japan's separateness as an island nation further reinforced its sense of uniqueness.

Together with a renewed interest in things foreign, the late Tokugawa period saw a nationalist-inspired revival of Shinto, the ancient Japanese worship of natural forces. Shinto legends and myths about the divine origin of the emperor, and through him of the Japanese people, appealed more to the new nationalist attitudes, although Shinto never replaced Buddhism or the Confucianism of the upper classes and intellectuals as the dominant religion. These and other developments were slowly transforming Japan, despite its unchanging surface, toward modernity, including a commercial economy and society that would soon be ready to burst the artificial restraints imposed on them.

❦
EDO AND THE "FLOATING WORLD"

By 1770 it is probable that the population of Edo and its immediate environs had reached a million, rivaled only by Peking and larger than any city in Europe. This urban concentration (the population of Japan by then was about 30 million) resulted from a combination of administrative centralization under the shogunate and the rapid commercialization of the economy. Edo and Osaka were the major centers of a national trade system and the headquarters of large merchant groups. The requirement that all daimyo had to maintain households in Edo, where they left their wives and family members as hostages, further swelled the population, as did their regular formal visits with their large retinues. Daimyo family estates, the large court of the shogun, and rich merchant families employed very large numbers of servants and artisans who provided them with luxurious furnishings and works of art.

Edo was also a major port; much of Japan's coastal trade passed through it, in addition to the trade that came by land. Much of the site had originally been swampy or prone to flooding, and large new tracts were drained and reclaimed as the city grew. Areas were set aside for daimyo and merchant residence and for shops, open-air markets, temples, and amusement quarters around the landward sides of the huge new castle built by Ieyasu. Thousands of soldiers based in Edo added to the numbers, as did the even more numerous laborers whose work supported the huge population.

Merchants dominated the bourgeois culture of Edo. Rich commoners wore forbidden silk under their plain outer clothing. The arts and amusements centered around what was called the Floating World, a pleasure quarter of theaters, restaurants, baths, and geisha houses. The main pleasure quarter was at the northern edge of the city, outside the official limits. Lesser aristocrats and their retainers and even artisans frequented this quarter, mingling with merchant patrons on a temporary basis of equality.

Rapid growth and crowding made for many problems, not the least of which was fire. Except for the shogun's castle and a few daimyo mansions, Edo was built almost entirely of wood, like all Japanese cities of the time, and fires often could not be controlled. The city burned down almost completely several times, but on each occasion it was rebuilt, larger and grander.

This was a new urban age of great cultural vigor, reminiscent in some ways of Sung dynasty Hangchow but increasingly dominated by bourgeois tastes. Culture was not necessarily vulgarized; merchants in fact often insisted on high aesthetic standards.

❦
HOKUSAI, MASTER ARTIST

Probably the best known of Japanese woodblock printmakers under the Tokugawa was the man called Hokusai (1760–1849), whose astonishingly prolific career spanned eight decades. He was born in Edo of unknown parentage and was adopted at age 3 by a craftsman named Nakijima, who made mirrors for the shogunate. The boy seems to have shown a talent for drawing by the time he was 5, and by the age of 13 he had been apprenticed to an engraver of woodblocks. Hokusai was a devout Buddhist and chose the name by which he is known, which means "north studio," to honor a Buddhist saint who was thought to be an incarnation of the North Star. His early work centered on book illustration, and he also made many portraits of contemporary actors. His prints are very Japanese in style but had become enormously popular in the West even before the end of Japan's seclusion policy.

Hokusai emerged at a period when Japan's arts had again begun to penetrate an international market. Japanese artisans had begun to copy the Chinese blue-and-white porcelain ware, so popular with westerners that it became an important Japanese export. It did not occur to the Japanese that westerners would find their art desirable, although the woodblock prints in which their artists specialized were turned out in large numbers, sold very cheaply, and could easily be duplicated from the original block. But the freshness, color, and simple lines of Hokusai's work, like that of many of his contemporaries, appealed strongly to a Europe already impressed and influenced by Chinese art. The European craze for chinoiserie in the late eighteenth and early nineteenth centuries was joined by an enthusiasm for "japonaiserie." Many Japanese prints in fact arrived in Europe as wastepaper, used for wrapping porcelain and other export goods, but they soon became prized and collected. Return trade to Japan brought, among other things, the color and materials for Prussian blue, which Hokusai and others soon used to brighten and enliven their work.

Perhaps the best known of Hokusai's prints in the West is his *Thirty-six Views of Mount Fuji*. His style and that of his contemporaries had a great influence on Western artists, especially in late-nineteenth-century France. Most of the impressionists acknowledged their debt to Hokusai, and many of them painted pictures in an avowedly Japanese style during the craze for things Japanese after 1870, including Vincent van Gogh's careful copy of a print by Hokusai's great contemporary Hiroshige (1797–1858). Thus while Meiji Japan was busily adopting Western ways as fast as it could, Western artists were returning the compliment.

Hokusai, "The Breaking Wave," from *Thirty-six Views of Mount Fuji*, perhaps the best-known woodblock print outside Japan. Note Mount Fuji in the background. [Metropolitan Museum of Art, Henry L. Phillips Collection]

Foreign Pressures and Domestic Unrest

The political system controlled so tightly from Edo ran relatively smoothly through the first half of the nineteenth century, and there were few outward expressions of dissent. In time the pressures building up behind the orderly façade of Tokugawa life would probably have forced basic change. As it happened, an outside force provided the impetus that destroyed the shogun's power and compelled Japan to face the world fully. It is not surprising that, having been so long suppressed, the change that resulted was on a truly revolutionary scale.

Among the outsiders, Americans were most eager to open Japanese ports to foreign trade. First American whalers, then clipper ships plying the China trade, then steamships in need of coal supplies sought permission to obtain provisions in Japan. The Tokugawa response was sharply negative. American and European sailors shipwrecked on Japanese shores were often handled roughly. American, British, and Russian expeditions after 1800 were repelled by the Edo government, and their requests were rejected. Finally, the American government took matters into its own hands. In 1853 it sent a small but powerful naval force under Commodore Matthew Perry with a letter to the shogun demanding trade relations and better treatment of foreign castaways.

Perry's squadron anchored in Tokyo Bay, in full view of Edo. The government was duly impressed by the size and the guns of the Americans' steam-powered "black ships," against which they realized Japan was defenseless. The Japanese tried to stall, and conservative forces, which dominated the Tokugawa, urged that the foreigners be refused and ejected. When Perry renewed the show of force the next year, the government capitulated. It signed a treaty, opening two ports and allowing a limited amount of regulated trade. Similar treaties ensued with European powers, and in 1858 a set of more detailed commercial treaties followed.

Foreigners could now reside in five ports as well as Osaka and Edo and could trade with whom they liked.

The political backlash was severe. Many Japanese still felt strongly that the foreigners must be expelled before they further sullied the sacred soil of Japan. The official who had signed the trade agreements was assassinated by conservative elements in 1860. Other extreme nationalists murdered an Englishman near Yokohama, a former fishing village that had become the main foreign settlement. There were, of course, reprisals, and the Tokugawa government was caught in a dilemma. It was neither able to resist foreign pressures nor to control its own subjects, who increasingly felt that the government had failed them and revealed its impotence. The outer daimyo domains in western Japan had always been restless under Tokugawa domination and now saw their chance to challenge it. They and others began to intrigue at the court in Kyoto and finally confronted Edo's forces militarily.

When the emperor died in 1867, the shogun, bowing to the general pressure, formally handed over power to the new boy emperor, Meiji, and his advisers, among whom samurai from rebellious western Japan had a prominent place. A little over a year later they persuaded the outer daimyo to offer their domains to the emperor, and feudal lords in the rest of Japan followed suit. The emperor moved to the more modern Edo, which thenceforward was known as Tokyo ("eastern capital"). This largely nonviolent revolution of 1868 and 1869 is known as the Meiji Restoration, for technically the emperors of Japan had never surrendered their sovereign powers. But it was a revolution nonetheless, and it brought to power new forces bent on rapid and radical change. The daimyo were compensated for their surrendered lands, and some remained as governors and other officials of the new government. Feudalism in Japan was over; the way was clear for the wholesale remaking of the nation as a modern industrial power.

The growth of cities, trade, and merchants and the rise of a strong centralized government helped make it possible for Japan to modernize itself rapidly along Western lines while Manchu China floundered. Tokugawa rule had been profoundly conservative, even hidebound in its feudal forms, but its often harsh political controls had created the stability that made economic development possible. Antiquated though the feudal forms seemed, late Tokugawa Japan, like late medieval Europe, was a society on the eve of economic revolution.

In China late Ch'ing rule was also conservative, but its central administrative controls weakened after 1800, and Western penetration accelerated its collapse. The economy remained dominated by peasant agriculture, and urban life was never more than a small part of a basically agrarian system. China was too big to be affected by new trends except very slowly. The inherent conservatism of both the peasants and their rulers worked against change. But none of this was clear as of 1860 or even 1870. Most foreign observers still looked to China as the dominant force in the East Asian economy. Within the next century, however, Japan, with a population still less than a tenth of China's, was to outstrip its neighbor in productivity, wealth, and power.

Notes

1. R. Fortune, *Three Years' Wanderings in the Northern Provinces of China* (London: Murray, 1853), p. 196.
2. J. K. Fairbank, E. O. Reischauer, and A. Craig, *East Asia: Tradition and Transformation* (Boston: Houghton Mifflin, 1978), p. 228.
3. J. L. Cranmer-Byng, ed., *An Embassy to China* (London: Longman, 1962), pp. 212–213.
4. G. Stanton, *Notes of Proceedings During the British Embassy to Peking in 1816* (London: Murray, n.d.), pp. 153–225 passim.

Suggestions for Further Reading

China

Fairbank, J. K., ed. *The Cambridge History of China*, Vol. 10: *Late Ch'ing*. Cambridge: Cambridge University Press, 1978.

Fay, P. W. *The Opium War*. Cambridge: Cambridge University Press, 1975.

Kahn, H. L. *Monarchy in the Emperor's Eyes: Image and Reality in the Ch'ien Lung Reign*. Cambridge, Mass.: Harvard University Press, 1971.

Metzger, T. *The Internal Organization of Ch'ing Bureaucracy.* Cambridge, Mass.: Harvard University Press, 1973.

Miyazaki, I. *China's Examination Hell: The Civil Service Examinations in Imperial China,* trans. C. Schirokauer. New York: Weatherhill, 1976.

Naquin, S., and Rawski, E. S. *Chinese Society in the Eighteenth Century.* New Haven, Conn.: Yale University Press, 1988.

Perkins, D. *Agricultural Development in China, 1368–1968.* Chicago: University of Chicago Press, 1969.

Polachek, J. M. *The Inner Opium War.* Cambridge, Mass.: Harvard University Press, 1992.

Rawski, E. S. *Education and Popular Literature in Ch'ing China.* Ann Arbor: University of Michigan Press, 1978.

Rawski, T. G., and Li, L. M., eds. *Chinese History in Economic Perspective.* Berkeley: University of California Press, 1991.

Rozman, G. *Urban Networks in Ch'ing China and Tokugawa Japan.* Princeton, N.J.: Princeton University Press, 1973.

Spence, J. *Ch'ing Sheng-tsu, Emperor of China.* New York: Knopf, 1974.

Van der Sprenkel, S. *Legal Institutions in Manchu China.* London: University of London Press, 1962.

Wakeman, F. *The Great Enterprise: The Manchu Reconstruction of Imperial Order in Seventeenth-Century China.* Berkeley: University of California Press, 1986.

Will, P. E. *Bureaucracy and Famine in Eighteenth-Century China.* Stanford, Calif.: Stanford University Press, 1990.

Wong, R. B., and Will, P. E. *Nourish the People: The State Granary System in China, 1650–1850.* Ann Arbor: University of Michigan Press, 1992.

Japan

Beasley, W. G. *The Rise of Modern Japan.* New York: St. Martin's Press, 1990.

Bix, H. P. *Peasant Protest in Japan, 1590–1884.* New Haven, Conn.: Yale University Press, 1986.

Bolitho, H. *Treasures Among Men: The Feudal Daimyo in Tokugawa Japan.* New Haven, Conn.: Yale University Press, 1974.

Dore, R. P. *Education in Tokugawa Japan.* Berkeley: University of California Press, 1965.

Dunn, C. J. *Everyday Life in Traditional Japan.* London: Batsford, 1969.

Elison, G., and Smith, B. *Warlords, Artists, and Commoners: Japan in the Sixteenth Century.* Honolulu: University Press of Hawaii, 1981.

Gerstle, C. A., ed. *Eighteenth-Century Japan: Culture and Society.* New York: HarperCollins, 1990.

Koschmann, J. V. *The Mito Ideology in Late Tokugawa Japan.* Berkeley: University of California Press, 1987.

Michener, J. A. *The Floating World.* Honolulu: University Press of Hawaii, 1983.

Nakane, C., and Oishi, S. *Tokugawa Japan,* trans. C. Totman. Tokyo: University of Tokyo Press, 1991.

Storry, R. *A History of Modern Japan,* rev. ed. New York: Penguin Books, 1982.

Totman, C. *Tokugawa Ieyasu: Shogun.* San Francisco: Heian, 1983.

Varley, H. P. *Japanese Culture.* Honolulu: University Press of Hawaii, 1984.

Vlastos, S. *Peasant Protests and Uprisings in Tokugawa Japan.* Berkeley: University of California Press, 1986.

I N D E X